T0303914

VARIORUM COLLECTED STUDIES SERIES

Commercial Exchange Across the Mediterranean

David Jacoby

Commercial Exchange Across the Mediterranean

Byzantium, the Crusader Levant, Egypt and Italy

Routledge
Taylor & Francis Group

LONDON AND NEW YORK

First published 2005 by Ashgate Publishing

2 Park Square, Milton Park, Abingdon, Oxfordshire OX14 4RN
711 Third Avenue, New York, NY 10017

Routledge is an imprint of the Taylor & Francis Group, an informa business

First issued in paperback 2018

ISBN 978-0-86078-980-2 (hbk)
ISBN 978-1-138-37572-7 (pbk)

British Library Cataloguing in Publication Data
Jacoby, David
    Commercial exchange across the Mediterranean : Byzantium, the Crusader Levant, Egypt and Italy. – (Variorum collected studies series)
    1. Shipping – Middle East – History – To 1500 2. Shipping – Mediterranean Region – History – To 1500 3. Commercial products – Middle East – History – To 1500 4. Middle East – Commerce – History – To 1500 5. Mediterranean Region – Commerce – History – To 1500 6. Middle East – Commerce – Italy
    7. Italy – Commerce – Middle East
    I. Title
    382'.0956045'0902

US Library of Congress Control Number: 2005927745

VARIORUM COLLECTED STUDIES SERIES CS836

CONTENTS

This volume contains x + 352 pages

PREFACE

The study of eastern Mediterranean commerce from the eleventh to the mid-fifteenth century is largely dominated by a eurocentric and bipolar perspective. Trade and shipping in that area are mostly, if not exclusively viewed in the context of relations between the West on the one hand and, on the other, Byzantium, the Muslim Levant and the crusader states of the twelfth and thirteenth centuries. The focus is on the expansion of Italian and other maritime powers, as well as on the impact of that process, and each of the regions bordering the eastern Mediterranean is treated in isolation. To be sure, the West acquired a dominant role in trans-Mediterranean trade and shipping, yet it is also considered to have been the only dynamic factor in that framework, while the eastern Mediterranean regions are supposed to have fulfilled an essentially passive one. Moreover, in this fragmented view of Mediterranean commerce the emphasis is on long-distance trade in oriental spices, dyestuffs, aromatics, eastern raw materials such as cotton, as well as grain in exchange for Western woollens and other finished products.

This approach reflects the biased historiographical perspective of the age of colonialism antedating World War Two. Indeed, it has been largely shaped by two monumental works that paved the way for modern research on medieval trade in the Mediterranean. The first, by Wilhelm Heyd, initially appeared in German and was later published in a revised French translation under the title *Histoire du commerce du Levant au moyen âge*, Leipzig, 1885–1886; the second work, by Adolf Schaube, *Handelsgeschichte der romanischen Völker des Mittelmeergebiets bis zum Ende der Kreuzzüge*, which appeared in Munich in 1906, deals with a more limited period. The approach of the two authors has been enhanced and seemingly vindicated by the relative abundance of Western sources bearing on trade and shipping, in particular the increasing number of notarial documents from the eleventh century onward, and the paucity of relevant Byzantine and Levantine sources. The works of Heyd and Schaube remain indispensable, yet one should remember that they are based exclusively on sources already published at the time they were written. In addition, language barriers have restricted the access to Byzantine, Arabic, Persian and Hebrew sources untranslated into Western languages and limited the range of evidence consulted by the two scholars and later ones. Since the publication of their work the body of evidence bearing on medieval trade in the medieval Mediterranean has been substantially enriched in two ways: by the edition of numerous documents and, possibly even more so, by the use of unpublished notarial charters and official registers preserved in Italian archives. The thousands of Jewish commercial letters and other documents found in a synagogue of Old Cairo, known as the Geniza documents, deserve special mention among the newly adduced pieces of evidence, since they fill a major gap in our evidence by providing new insights in trade conducted and perceived in the eastern Mediterranean itself. Surprisingly, despite the addition of that large body of new evidence, the approach of Heyd and Schaube is still common nowadays.

The studies reproduced in this volume (the sixth of mine in the *Variorum* series) adopt a different outlook and suggest a more balanced and integrated perspective of maritime trade in the eastern Mediterranean. They underscore the vitality of the regional economies in that area, their agricultural and industrial potential, their production of surpluses for export, as well as the importance of exchanges between them. These factors warrant special attention to short and medium-range trade and shipping within the eastern Mediterranean, so far mentioned in passing only. This type of activity was of considerable importance for the regional economies, whose merchants and carriers operated on their own or in connection with their Western counterparts. The existence of major trading networks within the eastern Mediterranean itself amply demonstrates that the economies of that area were not exclusively geared toward the West, as generally assumed, although they were partly linked to trans-Mediterranean exchanges. From the second half of the eleventh century onward the eastern Mediterranean trade system was in fact structured within a triangular, rather than within a bipolar pattern, since it connected the West both with Byzantium and Egypt, as well as these two regions (articles I, IV, VII, VIII and IX). The privileges and quarters obtained by the Italian maritime powers fulfilled a significant function in that framework (articles I, II, III and V).

The studies in this volume also illustrate the large range of commodities handled in eastern Mediterranean commerce (articles I, IV, V, VII and IX) and emphasize the significant role assumed by some goods to which little attention has been paid so far. Cheese was a staple protein food of Mediterranean populations traded in large quantities (articles I, VII and VIII). Since the eleventh century timber, iron and alum were of major importance in Western exchanges for precious oriental commodities available in Egypt, both with respect to volume and value. The transportation of these bulky and heavy goods required an increase in shipping capacity well before grain became an important factor in that respect in the second half of the thirteenth century (articles I and II). While the role of cotton and woollens in Mediterranean trade has been explored, silk and silk textiles have been overlooked, partly because they are considered to have been luxury products with a restricted market. However, the investigation of silk economics reveals the production of a wide variety of silken fabrics and pieces responding to a broad demand at various levels of the social scale (articles X–XII).

I wish to thank the following editors, publishers and institutions for granting permission to reproduce the studies included in this volume, which originally appeared in periodicals or collective volumes, some of which are often difficult to find: Prof. Chryssa Maltezou, Director, Istituto Ellenico di Studi Bizantini e postbizantini a Venezia (I); the Institute of Asian and African Studies, The Hebrew University, Jerusalem (II); Prof. Alfonso Leone and the editors of the *Archivio Storico del Sannio* (IV); Prof. Evangelos Chrysos, Director of the Institute for Byzantine Research, The National Hellenic Research Foundation (VI); the Istituto Veneto di Scienze, Lettere ed Arti (VII); the University of Illinois Press (VIII); Dr. A.-M. Talbot, Director of Byzantine Studies, Dumbarton Oaks (IX); Prof. Gino Benzoni, Fondazione Cini, Venice (X); Prof. M. Marcenaro, Director, Istituto Internazionale di Studi Liguri, Bordighera (XI); the Politistiko Technologiko Idryma ETBA, Athens (XII); finally, Ashgate for two studies (III and V) published in other collective volumes.

Some mistakes have been corrected in the text and notes of the studies reproduced below, while others as well as omissions and additions are listed in the *Addenda et Corrigenda* preceding two indices at the end of this volume, one of names and the other of important subjects.

DAVID JACOBY

The Hebrew University,
Jerusalem, 2005

PUBLISHER'S NOTE

The articles in this volume, as in all others in the Variorum Collected Studies Series, have not been given a new, continuous pagination. In order to avoid confusion, and to facilitate their use where these same studies have been referred to elsewhere, the original pagination has been maintained wherever possible.

Each article has been given a Roman number in order of appearance, as listed in the Contents. This number is repeated on each page and is quoted in the index entries.

Corrections noted in the Addenda et Corrigenda have been marked by an asterisk in the margin corresponding to the relevant text to be amended.

I

BYZANTINE TRADE WITH EGYPT FROM THE MID-TENTH CENTURY TO THE FOURTH CRUSADE

I. INTRODUCTION

Little attention has been devoted to Byzantine seaborne trade with Egypt after the loss of the Empire's eastern provinces to the Arabs in the seventh century. Several reasons explain this neglect, yet three in particular should be mentioned: first, some general conceptions of modern historians regarding the Empire's foreign commerce; secondly, the common aproach to the structure of the Mediterranean trade and shipping networks since the eleventh century; and, finally, the nature of the source material bearing on Byzantine trade with Egypt from the mid-tenth to the early thirteenth century. The three factors just mentioned deserve to be examined at some length.

It is almost axiomatic among Byzantinists that until the Fourth Crusade the Empire was more or less self-sufficient, its economy was turned inward, and trade was not a primary factor in that framework. According to this line of argument, the imperial government was adverse to Byzantine foreign trade. As a result, there was no state incentive to engage in exchanges beyond the Empire's boundaries. Moreover, the number of Byzantine merchants active in foreign trade was small, all the more so since on the whole the Empire's subjects were reluctant to undertake long commercial voyages. It was expected that foreigners would bring their goods to the Empire and especially to Constantinople.

Significantly, the most comprehensive attempt to analyze the nature and operation of the Byzantine economy from the tenth to the early thirteenth century, published a dozen years ago, deals only marginally with foreign

An extended stay at the Istituto Ellenico di Studi bizantini e postbizantini in Venice has greatly contributed to the preparation of this study. I wish to thank hereby Professor Chryssa Maltezou, Director of the Istituto, for her hospitality and friendship.

trade. It briefly examines the activity of Italian merchants in the Empire in that period, in view of their penetration into the Byzantine domestic market. Some other studies dealing with this development are also concerned with its long-term implications for the Empire's economy and finances. Whatever the case, foreign trade is primarily discussed in the context of exchanges between the Empire and the West. Trade with Egypt is mentioned in passing only, if at all.[1] Despite some rare criticism of the common views noted above,[2] there has yet been no attempt to reconstruct the nature and evolution of Byzantine foreign trade or to assess its role within the Empire's economy since the tenth century.[3]

The neglect of Byzantine foreign trade is also shared by western medieva-

---

1. See A. Harvey, *Economic Expansion in the Byzantine Empire 900-1200*, Cambridge 1989, p. 298, index, s.v. Venetians; for Alexandria and Egypt, not even cited in the index, see pp. 174-175. Similar approach in P. Magdalino, *The Empire of Manuel I Komnenos, 1143-1189*, Cambridge 1993, pp. 142-148; N. Oikonomides, «The Economic Region of Constantinople: from Directed Economy to Free Economy, and the Role of the Italians», in G. Arnaldi e G. Cavallo, eds., *Europa medievale e mondo bizantino. Contatti effettivi e possibilità di studi comparati* (Istituto Storico Italiano per il Medio Evo, Nuovi studi storici - 40) Roma 1997, pp. 221-238; and the recent review article with ample references to earlier studies by M. Angold, «The Road to 1204: The Byzantine Background to the Fourth Crusade», *Journal of Medieval History* 25 (1999), 269-278. R.- J. Lilie, *Handel und Politik zwischen dem byzantinischen Reich und den italienischen Kommunen Venedig, Pisa und Genua in der Epoche der Komnenen und der Angeloi (1081-1204)*, Amsterdam 1984, pp. 285-290, deals briefly with Byzantine foreign trade and shipping, citing only a few wellknown references to Egypt. Several of his arguments are rightly criticized by G. Prinzing, «Zur Intensität der byzantinischen Fern-Handelsschiffahrt des 12. Jahrhunderts im Mittelmeer», in E. Chrysos, D. Letsios, H. A. Richter und R. Stupperich, eds., *Griechenland und das Meer* (Studien zur Archäologie und Geschichte Griechenlands und Zyperns, 4), Mannheim und Möhnesee 1999, pp. 141-150; this study too deals only briefly with Egypt.

2. A. E. Laiou, «Byzantine Traders and Seafarers», in S. Vryonis, Jr., ed., *The Greeks and the Sea*, New Rochelle, N.Y. 1993, pp. 79-96, rightly stresses the importance of Byzantine seaborne trade, yet dwells mainly on domestic commerce and devotes little space to exchanges with Egypt on pp. 81-82.

3. Brief references to Byzantine involvement in foreign trade after the period examined here in A. E. Laiou-Thomadakis, «The Byzantine Economy in the Mediterranean Trade System: Thirteenth-Fifteenth Centuries», *Dumbarton Oaks Papers* 34-35 (1980-1981), 193, 206, and eadem, «The Greek Merchant of the Palaeologan Period: A Collective Portrait», Πρακτικὰ τῆς Ἀκαδημίας Ἀθηνῶν 57(1982), 102; both studies are reproduced in eadem, *Gender, Society and Economic Life in Byzantium*, Aldershot 1992, nos. VII and VIII respectively. N. Oikonomidès, *Hommes d'affaires grecs et latins à Constantinople (XIIIe-XVe siècles)*, Montréal-Paris 1979, pp. 83-92, provides a somewhat more extensive treatment. See also G. Makris, *Studien zur byzantinischen Schiffahrt* (Collana storica di fonti e studi, diretta da G. Pistarino, 52), Genova 1988, pp. 67-101, 261-275. More sources have been published since these studies appeared and the subject is far from being exhausted.

lists, whose study of Mediterranean commerce since the eleventh century has been largely dominated by a eurocentric approach and a bipolar perspective. Trade and shipping in that region have been mostly, if not exclusively viewed in the context of relations between West and East, with a focus on the expansion of the western maritime powers in the eastern Mediterranean, as well as on the impact of that process. The relative abundance of western sources bearing on trade and shipping, in particular of notarial documents since the twelfth century, and the paucity of relevant Byzantine and Egyptian evidence have enhanced and seemingly vindicated that biased approach. By contrast, short, medium and long-distance maritime commerce within the eastern Mediterranean itself have been mentioned in passing only. The existence of a major trade network specific to that region connecting the Empire and Egypt, with the addition of the crusader states of the Levant in the twelfth and thirteenth century, has been largely overlooked.[4] As illustrated by the evidence presented below, this network was tightly interwoven with trans-Mediterranean exchanges between East and West. It follows that, in any event since the second half of the eleventh century, the eastern Mediterranean trade system was structured within a triangular, rather than within a bi-polar pattern.

Numerous studies deal with the political relations and military confrontations between Byzantium and Muslim powers. Some attention has also been paid to ·trade between the Empire and its Muslim neighbors, yet Byzantine-Egyptian commerce has been practically overlooked by students of the Muslim world. Strangely, these scholars have adopted the bipolar approach of western medievalists with respect to Mediterranean trade and shipping. They focus on exchanges between Muslim countries and the West and ignore the existence of the triangular trade pattern just mentioned, within which Byzantium was firmly integrated. Their biased approach to the Empire's role in that context has strongly influenced their interpretation of various sources referring to al-Rūm.

This term originally designated Romans and Byzantines.[5] However, in the period examined here it was often used by Oriental Christians, Muslim geographers and travelers, Egyptian officers and Jews for both Byzantines

---

4. E. Malamut, *Les îles de l'Empire byzantin, VIIe-XIIe siècles* (Byzantina Sorbonen-·sia, 8), Paris 1988, II, esp. pp. 434-455, 536-561, deals with maritime trade within the Byzantine region or Romania and with the waterways linking Constantinople and various islands to Cyprus and Jaffa, the latter with respect to pilgrimage, yet hardly mentions Byzantine-Egyptian trade.

5. The entry 'Rūm' by C. E. Bosworth in *Encyclopaedia of Islam*, [2]VIII, Leiden 1995, pp. 601-606, does not cover the entire range of uses.

and Westeners.[6] Yahyā of Antioch, who records the massacre of Rūm *malā-fita* or Amalfitan Rūm at Old Cairo in 996, considers them a specific group and clearly distinguishes between them and other Rūm.[7] Yet elsewhere he applies Rūm to the members of the Melchite or Chalcedonian community living in Egypt.[8] A different use is found in the letter of a Jewish woman from Jerusalem writing shortly after the fall of the Holy City to the crusaders in 1099, since she calls the latter Rūm.[9] Between 1101 and 1130 an official Fatimid document applies the term Rūm to both an Amalfitan and a Genoese,[10] and a Jewish letter from Alexandria does so with respect to Venetians.[11] The taxation treatise compiled by al-Makhzūmī around 1170, which reflects Egyptian practice of that time, uses Rūm for all the subjects of Christian lands.[12] In his travel account of the 1180s Ibn Jubayr, who hailed from Spanish Granada, distinguishes between the Rūm of Constantinople and the Genoese Rūm, two of whorn served as captains of two ships on which he sailed.[13] It follows that in some instances the precise identity of the Rūm is obvious, while in others it is not. Nevertheless, scholars consider as Westeners the

6. This was common as late as the second half of the twelfth century, contrary to S. D. Goitein, *A Mediterranean Society. The Jewish Communities of the Arab World as Portrayed in the Documents of the Cairo Geniza*, Berkeley and Los Angeles 1967-1993, I, p. 43, who claims that Rum and Ifranj, Byzantines and Westeners respectively, were clearly and regularly distinguished in that period.

7. Yahya-ibn-Sa'id d'Antioche, *Histoire*, ed. and trans. I. Kratchkovsky et A. Vasiliev (Patrologia Orientalis, vol. 23, fasc. 3), Paris 1932, pp. 447-448. On this event, see C. Cahen, «Un texte peu connu relatif au commerce oriental d'Amalfi au Xe siècle», *Archivio storico per le provincie napoletane*, n.s. 34 (1953-1954), 3-8, repr. in idem, *Turcobyzantina et Oriens Christianus*, London 1974, no. A.

8. Yahya-ibn-Sa'id d'Antioche, *Histoire*, p. 465; see F. Micheau, «Les guerres arabo-byzantines vues par Yahyā d'Antioche, chroniqueur arabe melkite du Ve/XIe siècle», in EYΨYXIA. *Mélanges offerts à Hélène Ahrweiler* (Byzantina Sorbonensia, 16), Paris 1998, II, p. 546.

9. Ed. by S. D. Goitein, «Tyre-Tripoli-Arqa. Geniza Documents from the Beginning of the Crusader Period», *The Jewish Quarterly Review*, n.s. 66 (1975-1976), 70 (dating), 80 (Hebrew text), 81 (translation).

10. Ed. by S. M. Stern, «An Original Document from the Fatimid Chancery concerning Italian Merchants», in *Studi orientalistici in onore di Giorgio Levi Della Vida*, Roma 1956, II, 532-533, repr. in idem, *Coins and Documents from the Medieval Middle East*, London 1986, no. V.

11. Goitein, *A Mediterranean Society*, I, pp. 303-304.

12. See C. Cahen, *Douanes et commerce dans les ports méditerranéens de l'Egypte médiévale d'après le Minhādj d'al-Makhzūmī*, Leiden 1964, pp. 223-224. For the dating, see *ibid.*, pp. 218-222, and esp. idem, «Un traité financier inédit d'époque fatimide-ayyubide», *Journal of the Economic and Social History of the Orient* 5 (1962), 139-159.

13. R. J. C. Broadhurst, trans., *The Travels of Ibn Jubayr*, London 1951, pp. 26, 267, 327.

Rūm traders and carriers documented by the Jewish letters from the so-called Genizah or synagogue archive of Fustat or Old Cairo, unless there is explicit evidence pointing to Byzantium.[14] This approach requires a thorough revision.[15] In the absence of direct testimony bearing on the origin of the Rūm, due regard should be paid to the precise context in which they appear as well as to circumstantial evidence, both of which may offer a clue to their identity.

There is only scanty and scattered information regarding the Empire's trade with Egypt from the mid-tenth century to the Fourth Crusade, yet the evidence, whether direct or indirect, proves to be more abundant than generally assumed. Byzantine, Arabic and Persian sources illustrate various aspects of that activity. The Jewish documents from the Cairo Genizah provide invaluable data, especially for the tenth and eleventh century, a period for which rather few other sources on Byzantine-Egyptian exchanges are available. The languages of these documents, Hebrew or Arabic interspersed in some cases with Greek words, the Hebrew script in which they are written, as well as the fact that many of them have neither been published nor translated into western European languages explain why they have been virtually ignored by Byzantinists dealing with topics other than Byzantine Jewry. The western documentation, which becomes gradually more abundant since the mid-eleventh century, also yields some unexpected insights into the evolution of Byzantine-Egyptian trade. One should remember, though, that Byzantine as well as Muslim trade and shipping are markedly underrepresented in that documentation, which projects a western-biased picture.

Before proceeding, two final remarks are in order. This short study is not aimed at an overall reconstruction of Byzantine-Egyptian commerce from the mid-tenth century, shortly before the Fatimid conquest of Egypt in 969, to the Fourth Crusade in the early thirteenth century. Its purpose is more modest, namely to review the evolution of Byzantine trade with Egypt during the two and a half centuries separating these two military events, both of which generated some important changes, whether in the short or the long run, in the pattern of Byzantine-Egyptian commerce.[16] Within that period

---

14. On the Genizah, see Goitein, *A Mediterranean Society*, I, pp. 1-28.

15. In fact, it has created a vicious circle. The assumption that the Empire's merchants and ships were a marginal factor in Egyptian trade has prevented the correct identification of the Empire's subjects called Rūm. In turn, their supposedly limited activity in Egypt has seemingly vindicated the initial assumption.

16. S. W. Reinert, «The Muslim Presence in Constantinople, 9th-15th Centuries: Some Preliminary Observations», in H. Ahrweiler and A. E. Laiou, eds., *Studies on the Internal Diaspora of the Byzantine Empire*, Washington, D.C. 1998, pp. 125-150, deals to some extent

the establishment of the Latin states in the Levant around 1100, in the wake of the First Crusade, signals the beginning of a new phase in these exchanges. This justifies the distinction adopted below between the eleventh and the twelfth century, which at first glance may seem to follow an old-fashioned periodization according to centuries. The second remark concerns a methodological aspect of our investigation. Merchants, ships and goods are generally treated together as components of seaborne trade. The underlying assumption is that their respective movement necessarily coincides and follows a similar course. However, as illustrated by the evidence adduced below, this was definitely not the case with respect to trade between Byzantium and Egypt. Within that framework, therefore, it is essential to consider these three components separately whenever necessary.

II. BYZANTINE TRADE WITH EGYPT FROM THE MID-TENTH TO THE TWELFTH CENTURY

Trade between Byzantium and its former eastern provinces lost in the seventh century continued in the following period, despite occasional disruptions and interruptions caused by armed struggle between the Empire and the Muslims. However, its pattern underwent profound changes as a result of major political and economic developments in the late tenth and the eleventh century. These developments affected the westward flow of a broad range of commodities from the Indian Ocean to the Mediterranean region, namely spices, the most important of which was pepper, in addition to aromatics and dyeing materials.[17] These costly oriental goods, known in the Middle Ages under the generic name of 'spices', were increasingly diverted from the Persian Gulf, plagued by political instability, to the Red Sea and the Nile Valley through which they reached the Mediterranean. The Fatimids, who ruled Egypt since 969, encouraged, protected and controlled this lucrative trade conducted through their territory. As a result Byzantine Trebizond and the cities of Muslim Syria ceased to be the main suppliers of oriental commodities to the Empire and especially to Constantinople. Instead, Alexandria became in the eleventh century the main Mediterranean outlet for these goods,

---

with Egyptian trade in the Byzantine capital, yet a more comprehensive view of that activity in the Empire is still wanting.

17. It is noteworthy that in Constantinople these three types of goods were handled by the μυρεψοί, according to the early tenth-century *Book of the Eparch*: J. Koder, ed. and trans., *Das Eparchenbuch Leons des Weisen. Einführung, Edition, Übersetzung und Indices* (Corpus Fontium Historiae Byzantinae, XXXIII), Wien 1991, p. 110, chap. 10, par. 1.

as well as for frankincense and myrrh produced in the Arabian peninsula.[18]
This shift required a restructuring of the Byzantine supply network in
spices, increased Byzantine dependence upon Egypt in this respect and, more
generally, enhanced trade between the Empire and Egypt. Their exchanges,
however, were not limited to precious wares. The differing and complemen-
tary nature of their economies called for diversified commercial relations,
each partner supplying a large variety of commodities to the other. To the
external trade factor we may add yet another, domestic one furthering an
intensification of Byzantine-Egyptian trade since the eleventh century. Economic growth in the Empire and the increasing prosperity of the Byzantine
social elite and the urban middle stratum, primarily in Constantinople, stimulated changing consumption patterns, the ostentatious display of riches
and an increasing demand for luxury items, whether produced in the Empire
itself such as silk textiles or imported from foreign countries.[19]
Various Arab authors of the second half of the tenth century refer to
trade relations between the Empire and Egypt. 'Umar b. Muhammad al-Kindī

---

18. On Trebizond and its trade routes in the late ninth and in the tenth century, see
R. S. Lopez, «Silk Industry in the Byzantine Empire», 20 (1945), 29 and 30 n. 1, repr. in
idem, *Byzantium and the World around it: Economic and Institutional Relations*, London
1978, no. III; S. Vryonis Jr., *The Decline of Medieval Hellenism in Asia Minor and the Process of Islamization from the Eleventh through the Fifteenth Century*, Berkeley 1971, pp. 15-
20. On the shift in favor of Egypt, see esp. B. Lewis, «The Fatimids and the Route to India»,
Revue de la Faculté des Sciences Économiques de l'Université d'Istanbul 11 (1949-1950), 50-
54; J. Aubin, «La ruine de Sîrâf et les routes du Golfe Persique aux XIe et XIIe siècles»,
Cahiers de Civilisation Médiévale 2 (1959), 295-301; J.- C. Garcin, «Transport des épices et
espace égyptien entre le XIe et le XVe siècle», in *Les transports au moyen âge = Annales
de Bretagne et des pays de l'Ouest* 85 (1978), 305-309; C. Cahen, *Orient et Occident au temps
des croisades*, Paris 1983, pp. 111-113.
19. Economic background: M. F. Hendy, *Studies in the Byzantine Monetary Economy,
c. 300-1450*, Cambridge 1985, pp. 570-582; idem, «'Byzantium, 1081-1204': the Economy
revisited Twenty Years on», in idem, *The Economy, Fiscal Administration and Coinage of
Byzantium*, Northampton 1989, no. III, pp. 21-23; Harvey, *Economic Expansion*, esp. pp.
120-243. Social background: S. Vryonis, Jr., «Byzantine ΔΗΜΟΚΡΑΤΙΑ and the Guilds
in the Eleventh Century», *Dumbarton Oaks Papers* 17 (1963), 287-314, repr. in idem, *Byzantium: its Internal History and Relations with the Muslim World*, London 1971, no. IIIA;
H. Ahrweiler, «Recherches sur la société byzantine au XIe siècle: nouvelles hiérarchies et
nouvelles solidarités», *Travaux et Mémoires* 6 (1976), 99-124, esp. on Constantinople; P. Le-
merle, *Cinq études sur le XIe siècle byzantin*, Paris 1977, pp. 287-293; P. Kazhdan and A. W.
Epstein, *Change in Byzantine Culture in the Eleventh and Twelfth Centuries*, Berkeley 1985,
pp. 74-83. On Byzantine silk production and demand since the eleventh century, see D. Jacoby, «Silk in Western Byzantium before the Fourth Crusade», *Byzantinische Zeitschrift*
84/85 (1991-1992), 452-500, repr. in idem, *Trade, Commodities and Shipping in the Medieval
Mediterranean*, Aldershot 1997, no. VII.

I

32

(d. in 961) composed a work on the merits of Egypt, in which he claimed that the country was the hub of world commerce. He mentions numerous goods and the routes they followed to and from Egypt, insisting on the latter's role in transit trade. In addition to the precious commodities coming from China, the region of the Indian Ocean and the Arabian peninsula, he lists various Mediterranean ports, countries and wares, among them Constantinople, Rhodes, as well as Chios and its mastic. Ibn Zūlāq (d. in 996) follows the same pattern in his work on Egypt, naming Crete and the Empire as destinations of ships leaving Egypt.[20] Arab geographers offer a description of maritime lanes linking Egypt to the Empire and especially to Constantinople, whether of entire routes or sections of them.[21] Ibn Hawqal, who completed a revised version of his *Kitāb ṣūrat al-ard* around 988, deals with the southern coast of Asia Minor, mentioning Attaleia as a port of call and the presence of Byzantine ships at the mouth of the river Lamus, west of Tarsus, where the Empire and Egypt exchanged prisoners. His treatment of Constantinople is more extensive.[22] Byzantine sources also offer scattered and partial evidence on waterways connecting the Empire to Egypt.[23] Though useful, the geographic information found in all these works offers a static picture of seaborne trade and navigation routes between the two regions. It is partly taken from earlier authors and too general for our purposes, since it is devoid of concrete and dated evidence reflecting the nature and evolution of these factors.[24]

20. See S. Y. Labib, *Handelsgeschichte Ägyptens im Spätmittelalter (1171-1517)*, Wiesbaden 1965, pp. 13-14.

21. See T. Lewicki, «Les voies maritimes de la Méditerranée dans le haut moyen âge d'après les sources arabes», in *La navigazione mediterranea nell'alto medioevo* (Settimane di studio del Centro italiano di studi sull'alto meioevo, 25), Spoleto 1978, II, pp. 451-452.

22. Ibn Hauqal, *Kitāb ṣūrat al-ard*, 2 ed. J. H. Kramers (Bibliotheca Geographorum Arabicorum, II), Leiden 1938, pp. 201-202; *Configuration de la terre (Kitab surat al-ard)*, trans. by J. H. Kramers and G. Wiet, Beyrouth-Paris 1964, I, pp. 196-197; see also Lewicki, «Les voies maritimes de la Méditerranée», pp. 451-454, and next note. See also *Oxford Dictionary of Byzantium*, eds. A. P. Kazhdan et al., New York - Oxford 1991, II, p. 973, s.v. Ibn Hawqal, on this author's knowledge of the Empire.

23. See I. Ch. Dimitroukas, *Reisen und Verkehr im Byzantinischen Reich vom Aufang des 6. Jhr. bis zur Mitte des 11. Jhr.*, Athens 1997, II, pp. 474-479.

24. Incidentally, recent studies also offer a rather static view of navigation routes and ascribe to Crete and Cyprus an inflated role in that framework, without properly taking into account commercial and navigational developments during the period discussed here. J. H. Pryor, *Geography, Technology and Wae. Studies in the Maritime History of the Mediterranean, 649-1571*, Cambridge 1988, pp. 7, 70-71, 87-101, heavily relies on evidence related to specific political or military circumstances, which is not always convincing. See also Malamut, *Les îles de l'Empire byzantin*, II, pp. 546-561, with maps on pp. 652-653, 656-663, and S. Bor-

Ibn Hawqal blamed Muslim rulers, eager to reap profit, for allowing the Byzantines to send their ships to Muslim ports for trade and for permitting their agents to travel in Muslim countries, activities that enabled the Empire to secretly gather information about these territories.[25] His criticism implies that Byzantine merchants and their goods were welcome in Egypt, both for commercial and fiscal reasons. They contributed to the provisioning of the country in various commodities, and exported its products as well as precious oriental wares arriving from the region of the Indian Ocean and the Arabian peninsula. The state treasury enjoyed large revenues deriving from this two-way traffic. Cairo was the political, commercial and financial center of Egypt and its largest market.[26] Byzantine merchants were visiting the city shortly before the beginning of the Fatimid period in 969 and the shift in trade routes mentioned earlier. The Arab chronicler al-Mas'ūdī reports that during his stay in Cairo Byzantine ambassadors and merchants arrived by sea from Constantinople and reported the death in exile of Emperor Romanus I Le-

---

sari, *Venezia e Bisanzio nel XII secolo. I rapporti economici* (Deputazione di storia patria per le Venezie, Miscellanea di studi e memorie, 26), Venezia 1988, pp. 19-20, specifically about the two islands. Yet see my strong reservations regarding the latter's functions in D. Jacoby, «Italian Privileges and Trade in Byzantium before the Fourth Crusade: A Reconsideration», *Annuario de estudios nedievales* 24 (1994), 349-356, repr. in idem, *Trade, Commodities and Shipping*, no. II, and idem, «Byzantine Crete in the Navigation and Trade   *
Networks of Venice and Genoa», in L. Balletto, ed., *Oriente e Occidente tra medioevo ed età moderna. Studi in onore di Geo Pistarino*, Acqui Terme 1997, pp. 517-540. On Cyprus, see also below.

25. Ibn Hauqal, *Kitāb ṣūrat al-ard*, p. 198; trans., I, p. 193.

26. On Cairo's functions, see S. D. Goitein, «Cairo: An Islamic City in the Light of the Genizah Documents», in I. M. Lapidus, ed., *Middle Eastern Cities. A Symposium on Ancient, Islamic and Contemporary Middle Eastern Urbanism*, Berkeley and Los Angeles 1969, pp. 80-97, esp. 82; A. L. Udovitch, «A Tale of Two Cities: Commercial Relations between Cairo and Alexandria during the Second Half of the Eleventh Century», in H. A. Miskimin, D. Herlihy, A. L. Udovitch, eds., *The Medieval City*, New Haven and London 1977, pp. 144-148, 158-160; same approach in A. L. Udovitch, «L'énigme d'Alexandrie: sa position au moyen âge d'après les documents de la Geniza du Caire», in *Alexandrie entre deux mondes = La revue de l'Occident musulman et de la Méditerranée* 46 (1987), 71-79. Udovitch in particular seems to have overstated the economic centrality of Cairo. Two of his arguments, *ibid.*, p. 76, are clearly not convincing. Indeed, it is not surprising that in certain instances spices imported through the Red Sea and palm fiber from Yemen or southern Egypt (on the latter, see below, n. 85) should be available in Cairo, where they arrived for local consumption or on their way to the Mediterranean, while the stocks further north in Alexandria had already been exhausted. Nor is it surprising that the price of pepper should have been higher in Alexandria than in Cairo, because of added transportation costs and especially high seasonal demand resulting from the greater concentration of foreign buyers, including Byzantines, within a short period.

34

capenus, which had occured on 15 June 948.[27] In the Middle Ages it was common for merchants to take advantage of the sailing of ambassadors entrusted with special and urgent missions, whose ships were better protected and proceeded with fewer stops than other vessels. Yet the reverse also occured, since ambassadors occasionally boarded ships engaging in mercantile voyages.[28] Whatever the case in the instance just mentioned, we may safely assume that the Byzantine ambassadors and traders traveled on a Byzantine ship as far as Fustat. Vessels sailing in the Mediterranean frequently made their way up the Nile to deliver their cargo directly in that city.[29]

There is good reason to believe that the arrival of Byzantine merchants mentioned by Mas'ūdī was not an isolated case. Indeed, the existence of a 'Market of the Greeks' (shuq ha-Yevanim) in Old Cairo, mentioned in a Hebrew Genizah letter of 959, is highly suggestive in that respect.[30] The specific reference to Greek speakers,[31] and not to Rum, lifts all doubts regarding the identity of the merchants to whom the document alludes.[32] The so-called 'market' was presumably a funduq, in which Byzantine merchants from Constantinople and other cities of the Empire were compelled to reside and trade under the supervision of state-appointed officials.[33] From the assignment

27. Al-Mas'ūdī, Kitâb at-tanbîh wa'l-ischrâf (Bibliotheca Geographorum Arabicorum, VIII), ed. M. J. de Goeje, Leiden 1894, p. 174; Maçoudi, Le livre de l'avertissement et de la revision, trans. by B. Carra de Vaux, Paris 1896, p. 236.

28. Some later examples appear below.

29. See Goitein, A Mediterranean Society, I, pp. 295-296; A. L. Udovitch, «Time, the Sea and Society: Duration of Commercial Voyages on the Southern Shores of the Mediterranean during the High Middle Ages», in La navigazione mediterranea, II, pp. 521-522. It is likely than the Amalfitan traders massacred in 996 in Old Cairo (see above, n. 7) also arrived there on the vessel that had brought them to Egypt.

30. Ed. by S. Assaf, «Ancient Documents from the Genizah [sent from] Erez Israel, Egypt and North Africa» [Hebrew], Tarbiz 9 (1938), 203, line 12; trans. by S. D. Goitein, «Geniza Documents on the Transfer and Inspection of Houses», Revue de l'Occident musulman et de la Méditerranée 13-14 (1973) (= Mélanges Le Tourneau, Aix-en-Provence, 1973), pp. 402-403. The document does not deal directly with the market, but mentions only its location with respect to a piece of property.

31. On 'Yavan' or Greece standing for 'Byzantium', see below, n. 197.

32. However, Goitein, A Mediterranean Society, is ambiguous in this respect: ibid., I, p. 44, he seems to consider the merchants as being European or western, while ibid., IV, p. 27, he hypothesizes that the 'Market of the Greeks' was the one known in the Fatimid period as dār mānak, in which Amalfitan merchants were murdered in 996, and seems to suggest that Byzantine merchants were also housed there. This is excluded, however, since Yahyā of Antioch refers to Amalfitan Rum and thus distinguishes between them and Byzantine Rum: see above, n. 7.

33. See Goitein, A Mediterranean Society, I, pp. 186-192, 349-350; A. L. Udovitch, «Merchants and amirs: Government and Trade in Eleventh Century Egypt», Asian and

of a special *funduq* to the housing of Byzantine merchants we may gather that by 959 these were visiting Old Cairo both regularly and in fairly large numbers. Various agreements concluded by the emperors Leo VI and Romanus I Lecapenus with the rulers of Egypt and Syria since the 880s may have paved the way for that traffic and, conversely, for the presence of Muslim merchants in Constantinople, among them from Egypt.[34] This appears to be confirmed by the *mitaton* for Muslim traveling merchants attested in the city in the late ninth or early tenth century, which more or less fulfilled the same function as the Byzantine *funduq* in Old Cairo.[35]

There is no direct information about the commodities brought by Byzantine merchants to Cairo around the mid-tenth century. However, somewhat later evidence from the early Fatimid period suggests two of them exported from Asia Minor to Egypt, namely storax resin used as incence, in medicine and in perfumery,[36] and timber. The Empire's reconquest of Crete in 961 and its occupation of Cyprus in 965 deprived Egypt of free access to two major sources of raw material for naval construction.[37] Yet both earlier and later evidence points to Southern Asia Minor as another important supplier of timber to Egypt. Arab raids on that region from the seventh to the ninth century were mainly motivated by the need for timber, and occasionally the Arabs occupied areas long enough to build ships on location.[38] In the last quarter of the tenth century Ibn Hawqal mentions Hisn at-Tināt in the Gulf of Alexandretta, close to the large forests of the Amanus Mountains, as a point of embarkation for pine timber sailing to Egypt.[39] Byzantine timber

---

African Studies 22 (1988) (= *The Medieval Levant. Studies in Memory of Eliyahu Asthor [1914-1984]*), pp. 56, 58-59, 65-71; D. Jacoby, «Les Italiens en Egypte aux XIIe et XIIIe siècles: du comptoir à la colonie?», in M. Balard et A. Ducellier, eds., *Coloniser au Moyen Age*, Paris 1995, pp. 76-77, with additional references p. 102 n. 4.

34. See Reinert, «The Muslim Presence in Constantinople», pp. 130-135.

35. On *mitata* in Constantinople, see Lopez, «Silk Industry in the Byzantine Empire», pp. 25-31.

36. Ibn Hauqal, *Kitāb ṣūrat al-ard*, p. 201; trans. I, p. 196.

37. On sources of timber, overview by M. Lombard, «Arsenaux et bois de marine dans la Méditerranée musulmane: VIIe-XIe siècles», and «Le bois dans la Méditerranée musulmane, VIIe-XIe siècles. Un problème cartographié», repr. both in idem, *Espaces et réseaux du haut moyen âge*, Paris - La Haye 1972, pp. 107-151, esp. 129-132 and 153-176 respectively. Yet see the critic of these two studies by C. Cahen in *Journal of the Economic and Social History of the Orient* 2 (1959), 339-342.

38. See Lombard, «Arsenaux», pp. 114-115, 134-137.

39. Ibn Hauqal, *Kitāb ṣūrat al-ard*, p. 182; trans. I, p. 180. Around the mid-twelfth century the Arab geographer al-Idrīsī also mentions such export, yet without referring to Egypt: P.- A. Jaubert, trans., *La géographie d'Edrisi*, Paris 1836-1840, II, p. 132; he seems to quote an earlier source.

was either directly shipped from Asia Minor and neighboring areas, or else was picked up by vessels on their way from Constantinople or other Byzantine ports to Egypt.[40] The caliph's arsenal north of Fustat, in which warships were being built, was obviously one of the main destinations of that timber.[41]

John I Tzimiskes ascended the imperial throne in 969, shortly after the Empire had recovered Crete and Cyprus. The consolidation and expansion of Byzantine rule in the east at the expense of the Muslims required energetic measures to reduce the power of the Egyptian navy. Under the emperor's pressure Doge Pietro Candiano IV of Venice prohibited in July 971 the transfer of timber, oars and arms to Muslim countries.[42] There can be no doubt that a similar ban was issued in the Empire itself, despite the absence of direct evidence to this effect. Ibn Hawqal's reference to the export of timber from Hisn at-Tīnāt is in the past tense, which suggests that it was composed while the Byzantine embargo was still being enforced.[43] Amalfi, subject to imperial authority at that time, may have been compelled to interrupt for some time its deliveries of timber to Egypt.[44] In any event, the ban must have been lifted in 987-988 at the latest following the agreement concluded between Emperor Basil II and the caliph al-'Azīz. One clause of this agreement stipulates freedom of trade for all the Empire's subjects and with respect to all the commodities requested by the Fatimid ruler. Though not explicitly mentioned, timber was clearly among these goods. Another clause of the treaty determines that the caliph's name should be proclaimed in the mosque of Constantinople, which implies the activity of Egyptian merchants there at that time.[45]

The Arab geographer al-Muqaddasī, who completed his 'Best Classi-

---

40. Later evidence in this respect appears below and in D. Jacoby, «The Supply of War Materials to Egypt in the Crusader Period», *Jerusalem Studies in Arabic and Islam* 24 (2000) (in press).

41. On that shipyard, see A. M. Fahmy, *Muslim Sea-Power in the Eastern Mediterranean from the Seventh to the Tenth Century A.D.*, London 1950, pp. 48-50; Cahen, «Un texte peu connu», pp. 3-6; Y. Lev, *Saladin in Egypt*, Leiden 1999, pp. 161-162.

42. G. L. Fr. Tafel and G. M. Thomas, eds, *Urkunden zur älteren Handels- und Staatsgeschichte der Republic Venedig*, Wien 1856-1857, I, pp. 25-30; see also W. Heyd, *Histoire du commerce du Levant au moyen âge*, Leipzig 1885-1886, I, p. 113.

43. See above, n. 39.

44. Its position in Egypt heavily depended on them: see below, n. 97.

45. On the agreement, see G. Schlumberger, *L'épopée byzantine à la fin du dixième siècle*, Paris 1896-1905, I, p. 730; M. Canard, «Les relations politiques et sociales entre Byzance et les Arabes», *Dumbarton Oaks Papers* 18 (1964), 52 n. 83, repr. in idem, *Byzance et les Musulmans du Proche-Orient*, London 1973, no. XIX; and esp. Reinert, «The Muslim Presence in Constantinople», pp. 136-137.

fication for the Knowledge of Regions' in 986 and a revised version in 989, thus shortly after the conclusion of the agreement just mentioned, notes that ships were constantly arriving at Fustat from Arabia and Rum.[46] There can be no doubt that he was referring to maritime trade in the Red Sea and with the Empire. To be sure, Amalfitans traded then in Old Cairo, as mentioned above, and it is likely that those murdered in 996 had arrived there with a cargo of timber. The *funduq* in which they stayed was close to Cairo's port and shipyard.[47] Venetian vessels also reached Egypt in that period and presumably they too sailed up the Nile.[48] Nevertheless, in the last decades of the tenth century Byzantine ships anchoring in Egyptian ports must have definitely been more numerous than the vessels of these western cities, whose maritime trade in the eastern Mediterranean was still fairly limited.[49]

The Persian poet, moralist and theologian Nāṣir-i Khusrau, who visited Jerusalem in 1047, reports in his *Safarnāma* or "Book of Travels", with reference to the late tenth and early eleventh century, that every year many pilgrims from the Empire used to visit the Holy Sepulcher. Among them was supposedly the emperor, who came in disguise, a fact that irritated the caliph al-Hākim to such an extent that it prompted him to destroy the church in 1009.[50] Although apocryphal, the story suggests a large, regular flow of Byzantine pilgrims from various social ranks traveling to Jerusalem. At least some of those coming from cities as distant as Constantinople must have opted for the maritime route to the Holy Land. Since there is no evidence for Byzantine ships specializing in the transportation of pilgrims, they must have boarded vessels engaging in commercial voyages to Cyprus or Egypt. The vessels carrying pilgrims anchored off Jaffa, the coastal city closest to Jerusalem. It is unlikely, however, that this city, devoid of commercial importance and of a proper anchoring for ships, should have been the final destination of vessels carrying merchants from Constantinople. In other words, it is a fair guess that these ships proceeded beyond Jaffa to an Egyptian port, and took the pilgrims again on board on their return journey.[51] Apparently

---

46. Muqaddasī, *Ahsan al-taqāsim fī maʿrifat al-aqālīm*, ed. M. J. de Goeje (Bibliotheca Geographorum Arabicorum, III), Leiden 1906, p. 199; trans. by A. Miquel, «L'Egypte vue par un géographe arabe du IVe/Xe siècle al-Muqaddasi», *Annales islamologiques* 11 (1962), 119.

47. On these merchants, see above, n. 7.

48. See below, n. 121, for a somewhat later case.

49. As we shall see below, this appears to have been the case until the twelfth century.

50. *Nāṣer-e Khosraw's Book of Travels* (Safarnāma), trans. by W. M. Thackston, Jr., [Albany, N.Y.], 1986, pp. 37-38.

51. Such a pattern is indirectly confirmed by the journey of a Byzantine envoy sent by Michael VI to the caliph al-Mustanṣir in 1053, who sailed on a Byzantine ship as far as

the same transportation and navigation pattern still prevailed about a century later, when the Russian abbot Daniel of Chernigov sailed from Constantinople to Jaffa between 1106 and 1108.[52] The abbot does not refer to the identity of the ship he boarded, which carried both pilgrims and merchants, yet it was undoubtedly a Byzantine vessel. This is suggested by its itinerary via the Byzantine province of Cyprus, instead of along the Levantine coast which by then was already largely in Frankish hands.

Nāṣir-i Khusrau's story, reported above, implies regular Byzantine mercantile sailings to Egypt in the late tenth and early eleventh century. A temporary interruption of the Empire's trade with Egypt occured in 1016, when Basil II decreed a ban on commerce with and travel to Muslim countries, except for the territory of Aleppo. One may wonder, however, whether the ban was effectively implemented. In any event, it was lifted in 1027, when Emperor Constantine VIII concluded an agreement with the Fatimid caliph az-Zahīr.[53] A Genizah document of around 1035, adduced below, confirms the resumption of Byzantine trade in Egypt.

Nāṣir-i Khusrau provides somewhat later information about that trade. In 1047 he saw in the Lebanese port of Tripoli, then under Fatimid rule, ships from al-Rum and al-Firank, Byzantium and the Christian West respectively, as well as from Andalusia and the Maghreb. The sultan, or more precisely the Fatimid caliph, kept there commercial vessels sailing to the Empire, Sicily and the Maghreb.[54] It follows that Tripoli was then an important port

---

Cairo. After delivering gifts on behalf of the emperor, he left Egypt on the same ship, accompanied by Fatimid vessels from the Syrian fleet. He went ashore at Jaffa to pray at the Holy Sepulcher in Jerusalem and in all likelihood re-embarked at Jaffa: see M. Hamidulla, «Nouveaux documents sur les rapports de l'Europe avec l'Orient au Moyen Age», *Arabica* 7 (1960), 289; O. Grabar, «The Shared Culture of Objects», in H. Maguire, ed., *Byzantine Court Culture from 829 to 1204*, Washington, D.C. 1997, p. 121. Jaffa was also the destination of Genoese ships transporting western pilgrims later in the eleventh century: see B. Z. Kedar, «Mercanti genovesi in Alessandria d'Egitto negli anni sessanta dei secolo XI», in *Miscellanea di studi storici*, II, Genova 1983 (Collana storica di fonti e studi, diretta da G. Pistarino, 38), pp. 26-28, repr. in idem, *The Franks in the Levant, 11th to 14th Centuries*, Aldershot 1993, no. 1.

52. Account of abbot Daniel, trans. by W. F. Ryan in J. Wilkinson, J. Hill, W. F. Ryan, *Jerusalem Pilgrimage, 1099-1185*, London 1988, pp. 122-126, cap. 2-7. For its dating, see K.- D. Seeman, *Altrussiche Wallfahrtsliteratur. Theorie und Geschichte eines literarischen Genres*, München 1976, p. 175.

53. On the ban, see Schlumberger, *L'épopée byzantine*, II, pp. 452-454, and III, p. 23; W. Felix, *Byzanz und die islamische Welt im früheren 11. Jahrhundert. Geschichte der politischen Beziehungen von 1001 bis 1055*, Wien 1981, pp. 68, 80-81, whose dating is more precise; Reinert, «The Muslim Presence in Constantinople», pp. 138-139.

54. *Nāeṣr-e Khosraw's Book of Travels*, p. 13. On the involvement of Egyptian rulers

of call and transshipment station along the sea lane linking the Empire's capital to Egypt and that it was visited by merchants and ships from both that country and Byzantine territories.[55]

The continuing role of Tripoli in that context is also illustrated by a Genizah letter from the second half of the eleventh century, which records a tumultuous voyage from Alexandria to the Lebanese city on a leaking vessel. The author of the letter reports that some of the linen he had taken along was slightly damaged by the seawater that seeped into the ship. Interestingly, he uses Greek *antliai* for the pumps bailing out the water and notes that each bucket was the size of half a Byzantine barrel.[56] It follows that the merchant was a Byzantine Jew and that his Egyptian linen was intended for the Empire's market, although its precise destination is unknown.[57] It is obvious that the import of Egyptian linen into Byzantium was also carried out by Christian subjects of the Empire. To be sure, flax was cultivated in various Byzantine regions, and in the early tenth century Constantinople imported linen cloth from the Strymon region and the Pontos, as we learn from the *Book of the Eparch*.[58] Egyptian high-quality linen cloth was nevertheless highly valued in the Empire, as we may gather from Nāṣir-i Khusrau's apocryphal story about the Byzantine emperor's interest in the Egyptian city of Tinnīs.

The Persian traveler, who visited Egypt in 1047-1048, was deeply impressed by two types of textiles of high quality woven in Tinnīs. One was multicolored linen used for turbans and women's clothing, the other *buqalamun*, "an irridescent cloth that appears of different hues at different times of the day". *Buqalamun* was a silk textile of Byzantine origin with a peculiar

---

and their officers in maritime trade, see Goitein, *A Mediterranean Society*, I, pp. 309-310; Udovitch, «Merchants and *amirs*», pp. 57-65.

55. Incidentally, in Aleppo, an inland city, he noted the presence of merchants from Byzantine Asia Minor and from Egypt, and mentioned the distance from that city to Constantinople: *Nāṣer-e Khosraw's Book of Travels*, p. 10.

56. Trans. by Goitein, *A Mediterranean Society*, I, p. 321, and see p. 483 n. 55. The undated letter was addressed to Nahray b. Nissīm, a prominent Jewish merchant and banker active in Egypt between 1049 and 1097, on whom see M. R. Cohen, *Jewish Self-Government in Medieval Egypt. The Origins of the Office of Head of the Jews, ca. 1065-1126*, Princeton, N.J. 1980, pp. 102-104.

57. On twenty-six varieties of Egyptian flax, see Goitein, *A Mediterranean Society*, I, pp. 224-228, p. 455 n. 61 to p. 457, and IV, p. 167; on varieties of linen in Egypt, some of which were extremely fine and expensive, and on their uses, see *ibid.*, IV, pp. 164-167, and next note.

58. Koder, *Das Eparchenbuch*, p. 106, chap. 9, par. 1, which also mentions the lining of cotton garments with linen; see also Harvey, *Economic Expansion*, pp. 185-186.

sheen imitated in Egypt.[59] The Persian author adds the following suggestive story: "I heard that the ruler of Byzantium once sent a message to the sultan of Egypt that he would exchange a hundred cities of his realm for Tinnīs alone. The sultan did not accept, of course, knowing that what he wanted with this city was its linen and *buqalamun*". It is noteworthy that Nāṣir-i Khusrau ends his description of Tinnīs by stating that it takes twenty days by ship from there to Constantinople.[60] This is the only Egyptian port for which he provides such information.

While in Cairo Nāṣir-i Khusrau attended the festive opening of the Nile canal at the beginning of the yearly irrigation season. A large pavilion "of Byzantine brocade spun with gold and set with gems" was set up. It was large enough for a hundred of the sultan's horsemen to stand in its shade. When the sultan mounted his own horse, ten thousand horses "with gold saddles and bridles and jewel-studded reins" stood at rest "with saddle-cloths of Byzantine brocade and *buqalamun* woven seamless to order". Interestingly, he adds that "in the borders of the cloth are woven inscriptions bearing the name of the sultan of Egypt". In the caliph's palace he also noted that "all the carpets and pillows (...) of Byzantine brocade and *buqalamun* [were] each woven exactly to the measurements of its place".[61] It follows that these pieces were imitations of Byzantine silks, rather than genuine ones, manufactured according to specifications of the caliph's court in *ṭirāz*, state factories or, by extension, workshops compelled to deliver some of their products or all of them to that court.[62]

Silk textiles, whether or Byzantine origin or imitations, were also found in private Egyptian homes. The Rūmī or Byzantine *mandīl* or kerchief, as well as brocade and cloth used for upholstery appear in many marriage settlements from the tenth to the twelfth century found in the Genizah, yet it is obvious that Jewish brides were not the only ones in Egypt to have them in their trousseau.[63] Richer brides had a Rūmī brocade bedcover which could be worth the money needed by a middle-sized family for five months, or even a more expensive Rūmī brocade couch.[64] It is likely that some high-priced

59. See Jacoby, «Silk in Western Byzantium», p. 458 n. 29.

60. *Nāṣer-e Khosraw's Book of Travels*, pp. 39-40.

61. *Ibid.*, pp. 48, 57.

62. On the *ṭiraz* system, see R. B. Serjeant, *Islamic Textiles. Material for a History up to the Mongol Conquest*, Beirut 1972, pp. 7-15, and for Fatimid Egypt, pp. 157-160.

63. For the latter, see Goitein, *A Mediterranean Society*, I, p. 46; IV, pp. 191, 315, 320, 329-330. Goitein wrongly assumed that Arabic *mandīl* came from a Latin root, like Spanish *mantilla*; he was unaware that it derived from Greek μανδήλιον.

64. *Ibid.*, I, p. 46; IV, pp. 299-300, 302-305, 315, 324.

textile pieces were genuine Byzantine products, while others were imitations manufactured in Egypt or elsewhere. The *tinnīsī rūmī mandīl* or Byzantine kerchief from Tinnīs, made of high-quality linen, was one of several Egyptian imitations of the silken Rūmī or Byzantine kerchiefs.[65] Despite the production of these imitations, we may safely assume that many Byzantine silk textiles were imported into Egypt in the eleventh century, although no direct evidence in this respect has surfaced until now.[66] Some of these fabrics were surely brought by Egyptian merchants, yet the bulk of imports must have been handled by the Empire's traders. These textiles were among the costly goods indispensable for the financing of Byzantine purchases in Egypt, especially those of spices, high-quality linen and other expensive commodities.

In addition to silk textiles, we also find a single Genizah reference to the import of silk as raw material into Egypt. In 1053 a Jew living in Jerusalem asked his correspondent in Fustat to find for him seven *ra*ṭ*l* or between 2 kg. 940 and 3 kg. 080 of "coloured Constantinopolitan silk" of good quality.[67] It is unclear whether that silk was dyed in the Empire's capital or whether the name merely points to a specific variety of coloured silk. In any event, the commodity was clearly of Byzantine origin.[68] Unfortunately, we do not know whether or not the merchant involved in its import into Egypt was a Byzantine subject. The fact that Byzantine silk is mentioned only once in the Genizah documents, while Spanish and Sicilian silk appear frequently, does not necessarily imply that this was an exceptional shipmen.[69] In fact, from

---

65. *Ibid.*, IV, p. 167. On imitations of Byzantine linen and silk textiles in Muslim countries, see *ibid.*, I, p. 50; also Serjeant, *Islamic Textiles*, pp. 43, 117: Tustar in Iran and Damascus manufactured Rūmī brocades.

66. On the shipping of silks to Egypt at a later period, though under different conditions, see below, n. 241.

67. Ed. and Hebrew trans. by M. Gil, *Erets Israel ba-requfa ha-muslemit ha-rishona (634-1099)* [= *Palestine during the first Muslim Period (634-1099)*], Tel Aviv 1983, III, pp. 104-107, no. 460, esp. line 16; mentioned bu Goitein, *A Mediterranean Society*, I, p. 417 n. 21, and IV, p. 402 n. 128, with approximate dates. The *ra*ṭ*l* used for silk must have been the spice weight. Goitein, *ibid.*, I, p. 360, assumes that it was around 450 grams, yet see rather E. Ashtor, «Levantine Weights and Standard Parcels: A Contribution to the Metrology of the Later Middle Ages», *Bulletin of the School of Oriental and African Studies* 45 (1982), 472, repr. in idem, *East-West Trade in the Medieval Mediterranean*, ed. B. Z. Kedar, London 1986, no. II, who on the basis of numerous sources estimates it at between 420 and 440 grams.

68. Since the letter mentions coloured silk together with Spanish crimson, Goitein assumed that it came to Egypt via Sicily: see previous note. This suggestion is unfounded, since the correspondent was requested to find the two commodities wherever he could, which implies that they were not necessarily available at the same shop or warehouse.

69. Various other Byzantine products are also mentioned seldom, although some of

the way it is mentioned we may gather that the commodity was more or less regularly available in Fustat. One may wonder, therefore, whether the restrictions imposed on the export of silk from the Empire, attested by the early ninth-century *Book of the Eparch*, were still in force.[70]

We may now turn to the costly commodities known as spices in the Middle Ages. A Genizah letter from around 1035 reports that the Rūm have acquired odoriferous woods in Old Cairo: "The did not leave a single piece of it when they departed for their country". These Rūm have been identified as Europeans.[71] To be sure, at that time there was a growing demand for luxury products in the Empire and especially in Constantinople, as well as in Italy.[72] It would seem, however, that the purchasing power in the Empire was far greater, judging by the expansion of Byzantine silk manufacture, a process primarily generated by increasing domestic consumption of costly items. There was no contemporary development of a high-grade luxury industry in Italy. In addition, in the eleventh century the volume of Byzantine business in Egypt seems to have exceeded by far that of Italian traders, as suggested by somewhat later evidence that will soon be adduced.[73] Finally, one should take into account that in the 1030s Amalfitan and Venetian traders were supplying goods bought in Egypt exclusively to western markets, and apparently no Italian was yet engaging in trade between Egypt and the Empire.[74] In short, in view of the economic context there is good reason to believe that the massive purchase mentioned in the Genizah letter of 1035 was carried out by Byzantine merchants. Somewhat later Genizah letters sent from Alexandria to Fustat enhance this interpretation.

---

them like cheese were surely imported on a fairly large scale. One should also take into account that the Jews attested in the Genizah conducted maritime trade mainly with Tunisia and Sicily, from where many families originated and where they still had resident relatives.

70. Koder, *Das Eparchenbuch*, p. 100, chap. 6, par. 16. I shall deal extensively with Byzantine silk in a forthcoming book.

71. See Goitein, *A Mediterranean Society*, I, p. 44, whose interpretation of the term 'Rūm' is similar to that of other historians of the Muslim world referring to the Genizah documents: see above, n. 14.

72. See above, n. 19, and D. Jacoby, «Silk crosses the Mediterranean», in G. Airaldi, ed., *Le vie del Mediterraneo. Idee, uomini, oggetti (secoli XI-XVI)* (Università degli studi di Genova, Collana dell'Istituto di storia del medioevo e della espansione europea, n. 1), Genova 1997, pp. 61-63.

73. In the second third of the eleventh century the concentration of Italian traders bying spices in Tunisia, where they were brought from Egypt, was undoubtedly far greater than in the ports of this country. This is also suggested by the fact that they could occasionally impose payments for their purchases in Sicilian and Pisan currencies: see Goitein, *A Mediterranean Society*, I, pp. 44-45.

74. On that involvement, see the detailed discussion below.

We have already noted the Byzantine ship reaching Cairo in 1053 with an imperial embassy on board.[75] In all likelihood the vessel also carried merchants. Genizah documents of the 1060s or early 1070s illustrate the activity of traders and ships from the Empire in Alexandria. One of them refers "to the merchants from Constantinople [who] have already agreed upon prices", while "those from Venice and Crete still hold back".[76] There is no indication about the goods these merchants intended to purchase in Alexandria, yet spices were surely high on their list, if not the exclusive items in which they were interested. Indeed, another letter, written at Alexandria in the summer of 1062, mentions merchants from Constantinople buying various spices, the nature of which is not specified, whereas Cretan and Genoese traders purchased pepper, yet held back with respect to other spices, with the result that the latter's prices fell sharply.[77] The two more or less contemporary letters are noteworthy on several counts. From their specific references to Italian traders we may gather that all the others, whether Cretan or Constantinopolitan, were Byzantine subjects. It follows that by the second half of the eleventh century the conduct of trade between the Empire and Egypt was not the exclusive domain of merchants and ships from the capital. In addition, the letters illustrate for the first time the involvement of Venetian and Genoese traders and vessels in trade between a Byzantine province and Egypt, in these specific cases with respect to Cretan agricultural and pastoral produce. From the phrasing of the two letters we may gather that the appearance of these traders in Alexandria was not exceptional.[78] Since direct sailing from Crete to Egypt was excluded at that time, we must assume that the ships reached their destination via Rhodes and proceeded from there along the Levantine coast or Cyprus.[79]

The shipping of oriental spices from Egypt to Constantinople is further attested by a Genizah letter from Alexandria, dated 1094, which reports that "indigo (...) has gone down in price by one third, this is because the al-Rum

---

75. See above, n. 51.

76. Trans. by Goitein, *A Mediterranean Society*, IV, p. 168.

77. Ed. and Hebrew trans. by M. Gil, *Be-malkhut Yishma'el bi-tequfat ha-geonim* [= *In the Kingdom of Ishmael*], Jerusalem 1997, IV, pp. 445-450, no. 749, lines 1-6; English trans. by S. Simonsohn, *The Jews of Sicily*, I, *383-1300*, Leiden 1997, pp. 314-316, no. 145.

78. On eleventh-century trade between Crete and Egypt, yet without reference to the letter of 1062, see Jacoby, «Byzantine Crete», pp. 521-523. My statement that the Genoese first appeared in Romania at the time of the First Crusade, *ibid.*, p. 530, should be corrected in the light of that letter.

79. *Ibid.*, pp. 537, 540.

have received news that indigo is not selling well in Constantinople".[80] Another letter, from the last years of the eleventh century, states the following: "Please take notice that no pepper, cinnamon or ginger are available in Alexandria. If you have any of these commodities, keep them, for the Rūm are keen solely on them. All the Rūm are about to leave for Old Cairo. They are only waiting for the arrival of two additional ships from Constantinople".[81] The sailing of several vessels from this city to Alexandria in a single season is not surprising. Interestingly, the second letter seems to imply that all the ships would sail up the Nile. As for the identity of the Rūm traders, it is likely that most, if not all of them were subjects of the Empire sailing on Byzantine ships, since the Italian participation in maritime trade between Egypt and Constantinople was still fairly limited in the last decades of the eleventh century.[82] The massive purchase of spices following the arrival of the traders from Constantinople thus points to the substantial purchasing power of Byzantine traders, whose behavior largely determined the strategy of Egyptian merchants and had a direct impact on the fluctuation of market prices.

The eleventh-century Genizah letters mentioned above clearly imply that Egypt was then the Empire's main source of spices. However, occasionally these could also be purchased in ports along the waterway leading to the Empire, to which they had been exported from Egypt. We may safely identify as Byzantines the Rūm traders who around 1075 bought brazilwood, a valuable red dye originating in the East Indies, in an unspecified city of Shām or Syria-Lebanon. It is unlikely that Italians should have bought spices along the Levantine coast rather than in Egypt or Tunisia.[83] Alexandria appears to have been then the only Egyptian port in which they conducted business.[84]

---

80. Ed. and Hebrew trans. by Gil, *Be-malkhut Yishma'el*, III, pp. 441-444, no. 431, lines 20-22; English trans. by Udovitch, «Time, the Sea and Society», p. 528, slightly changed here. Udovitch translates 'al-Rūm' (line 21 of the text) as 'Italians', in accordance with his stand that «in the Geniza terminology, Rūm refers to Italy and the Italians» (in the discussion that followed his lecture, *ibid.*, p. 554), yet see the evidence adduced below.

81. Trans. by Goitein, *A Mediterranean Society*, I, p. 44. For the dating of this document after 1094, see *ibid.*, V, p. 104.

82. See below, p. 47.

83. The case is reported in a letter of 1085, about ten years after the transaction: ed. and Hebrew trans. by Gil, *Be-malkhut Yishma'el*, IV, pp. 63-66, no. 623; mentioned three times, in different ways, by Goitein, *A Mediterranean Society*, I, p. 45 (sale in a Palestinian port with 150 percent profit, which is a slip), 178 (with reference to European buyers), 202 (sale in Syria, with correct figure of profit, namely fifty percent). On Tunisia, see above, n. 73.

84. The earliest evidence about western traders in Damietta appears some thirty-five years later, in a Venetian document of 1119, yet by then their visits in that port had apparently

Therefore, the Rūm expected to proceed from Damietta to Old Cairo some time after the 1070s also appear to have been Byzantine traders. They intended to buy there date palm fiber, used for the manufacture of baskets and ropes.[85]

Some Genizah letters from the eleventh century offer information about Byzantine products marketed in Egypt and about their precise origin, in addition to those already mentioned above. Mastic from Chios, used in the manufacturing of perfumes and in pastries, is attested around 1050 and in the second half of the eleventh century.[86] Although direct evidence is lacking, it would seem that its production and sale were conducted under stringent imperial control. It is likely, therefore, that only Byzantine merchants handled the export of mastic from Chios.[87] Egypt imported cheese from Asia Minor and Crete.[88] Various medicinal plants and drugs were brought from Asia Minor, as attested by a later document.[89] The high-quality Cretan epithymon or dodder of thyme, also a medicinal plant, was partly re-exported from Egypt to the countries of the Indian Ocean, as revealed by a Jewish lawsuit conducted in Cairo in 1097-1098.[90] The same lawsuit also refers to Russian

---

become quite common: R. Morozzo della Rocca - A. Lombardo, eds., *Documenti del commercio veneziano nei secoli XI-XIII*, Torino 1940 (hereafter: *DCV*), I, pp. 43-44, no. 41.

85. See Goitein, *A Mediterranean Society*, I, pp. 44 and 401 n. 17, who hypotesizes that the material was imported from Yemen. However, according to Muqaddasī, *Ahsan al-taqāsim*, p. 203; trans., p. 125, Egypt had excellent palm fiber. The writer of the letter was active between 1060 and 1090: see Goitein, *A Mediterranean Society*, I, pp. 228-229, 379, no. 42; V, pp. 144-145, 545 n. 88.

86. See Goitein, *A Mediterranean Society*, I, pp. 268 and 154, respectively, and for the approximate dating of the latter piece of information, p. 153. Udovitch, «A Tale of Two Cities», pp. 151-153, dates a letter mentioning mastic to the late 1060s.

87. Significantly, in 1302 Andronicus II prohibited Venetian trade in mastic and salt, yet another commodity controlled by the state: G. M. Thomas et R. Predelli, eds., *Diplomatarium veneto-levantinum*, Venetiis 1880-1899, I, p. 14. Two years later he confirmed Genoese freedom of trade in all commodities, except in mastic, salt and grain: L. T. Belgrano, «Prima serie di documenti riguardanti la colonia di Pera», *Atti della Società Ligure di Storia patria* 13 (1877-1884), 105-110. The Genoese lords of Chios from 1304 to 1329 and again after 1348 apparently maintained the existing control system on mastic, yet adapted it to some extent to their own needs. On mastic under Genoese rule, see M. Balard, *La Romanie génoise (XIIe-début du XVe siècle)* (Bibliothèque des Ecoles françaises d'Athènes et de Rome 235), Rome 1978, pp. 119-120, 742-749.

88. See Goitein, *A Mediterranean Society*, I, pp. 46, 124, and above, n. 78.

89. Ed. and Hebrew trans. by S. D. Goitein, «A Letter of Historical Importance from Seleucia (Selefke), Cilicia, dated 21 July 1137» [Hebrew], *Tarbiz* 27 (1958), 528-535; English trans. and commentary by idem, «A Letter from Seleucia (Cilicia), Dated 21 July 1137», *Speculum* 39 (1964), 298-303, and for the information mentioned here, pp. 299, 301.

90. See S. D. Goitein, «From the Mediterranean to India: Documents on the Trade

linen, presumably shipped from Constantinople to Egypt by Byzantine merchants. Russian linen was highly valued in Egypt and also re-exported to India, where it was much appreciated.[91] Incidentally, the document recording the lawsuit reveals an interesting aspect of the function of Constantinople and Egyptian ports as intermediaries in long-distance exchanges between the Black Sea and the Indian Ocean. While oriental spices flowed westward toward the Mediterranean, the two commodities just mentioned point to the movement of specific goods from or via Byzantium in the opposite direction.

It is likely that eleventh-century Byzantine purchases in Egypt were also partly financed by the import of timber from Asia Minor, as in the previous period.[92] Grain appears only once as a trade item in the context of eleventh-century commerce between the Empire and Egypt. Early in 1054, while Egypt was suffering from famine, the Fatimid caliph al-Mustansir requested from Constantine IX Monomachus a large quantity of grain, 400,000 *artabai*, yet after the emperor's death in the following year the empress Theodora refused to deliver it. This was undoubtedly an exceptional case, due to insufficent irrigation by the Nile in the previous two years.[93]

The late tenth and eleventh-century evidence adduced so far suggests regular and intensive maritime trade between the Empire and Egypt, occasionally restricted for short periods by political and military circumstances or by the activity of pirates.[94] Commercial exchanges between the two regions were handled by Byzantine or Muslim merchants and carriers. Yet Italian merchants and vessels began to integrate into the existing trade and shipping patterns around the mid-eleventh century. Their activity was not limited to the waterway linking Crete and Alexandria, already noted earlier. It also extended to sea lanes between other Byzantine provinces and Constantinople, on the one hand, and Egypt on the other. The factors promoting this development as

---

to India, South Arabia, and East Africa from the Eleventh and Twelfth Centuries», *Speculum* 29 (1954), 192, and for the dating, pp. 189 and 191.

91. *Ibid.*, p. 192 and n. 20. Linen brought to Constantinople by Bulgarians and other foreigners is mentioned in the early-tenth century *Book of the Eparch*: Koder, *Das Eparchenbuch*, p. 108, chap. 9, par. 6.

92. See above, nn. 38-40, 44. There is no evidence about timber exports from Cyprus to Egypt.

93. F. Dölger, ed., *Regesten der Kaiserurkunden des Oströmischen Reiches von 565-1433, 2. Teil: Regesten von 1025-1204. Zweite, erweiterte und verbesserte Auflage bearbeitet von P. Wirth*, München 1995, p. 32, no. 912, for the sources, dating and background.

94. On eleventh-century piracy hampering trade with Egypt, see D. Jacoby, «What do we learn about Byzantine Asia Minor from the Documents of the Cairo Genizah?», in Sp. Vryonis, Jr., and N. Oikonomides, eds., ʿΗ Βυζαντινὴ Μικρὰ ᾿Ασία (6ος-12ος αἰ.) [= *Byzantine Asia Minor (6th-12th cent.)*], Athens 1998, pp. 89-92.

I

well as their long-term impact on Byzantine participation in Byzantine-Egyptian trade require a detailed and thorough discussion.

III. THE INTEGRATION OF THE ITALIANS INTO BYZANTINE-EGYPTIAN MARITIME TRADE

The Amalfitans were the first Westerners to intrude into seaborne commerce between the Empire and Egypt. They are attested in Constantinople in 944, yet presumably traded there earlier. Some of them were settled in the Byzantine capital before 1053, and Amalfitan *ergasteria* are mentioned in the charter issued by Alexius I Comnenus in favor of Venice in 1082.[95] The location of the Amalfitan premises is attested for the first time in 1192. They were situated within the Pisan quarter, close to the Golden Horn, and may well go back to the eleventh century. In any event, contrary to common opinion, there was no Amalfitan quarter similar to those held by other Italian maritime powers in Constantinople.[96] Close trade relations with the Fatimids of Tunisia, naval assistance provided to them in 969 for the conquest of Egypt, and continuing supplies of naval lumber and iron ensured the Amalfitans of favorable trading conditions in that country.[97] Between 1101 and 1130 an Amalfitan and a Genoese arrived in Egypt with a cargo of timber, presumably of Italian origin since the Genoese did not yet sail between the Empire and Egypt at that time.[98]

*

The Amalfitans progressively extended the geographic range of their operations both from Constantinople and Egypt along the seaboard of the

---

95. See M. Balard, «Amalfi et Byzance (Xe-XIIe siècles)», *Travaux et Mémoires* 6 (1976), pp. 87-92; Borsari, *Venezia e Bisanzio*, pp. 7-8; V. von Falkenhausen, «Il commercio di Amalfi con Costantinopoli e il Levante nel secolo XII», in O. Banti, ed., *Amalfi, Genova Pisa e Venezia. Il commercio con Costantinopoli e il Vicino Oriente nel secodo XII* (Biblioteca del «Bollettino Storico Pisano», Collana storica, 46), Pisa 1998, pp. 19-24.

96. This is convincingly argued by P. Magdalino, *Constantinople médiévale. Etudes sur l'évolution des structures urbaines*, Paris 1996, pp. 85-88.

97. See Cahen, «Un texte peu connu», pp. 6-7; B. Figliuolo, »Amalfi e il Levante nel medioevo», in G. Airaldi e B. Z. Kedar, eds., *I comuni italiani nel Regno crociato di Gerusalemme* (Collana storica di fonti e studi, diretta da G. Pistarino, 48), Genova 1986, pp. 581-588; Jacoby, «Les Italiens en Egypte», pp. 76-77. Cahen, *Orient et Occident*, pp. 37-38, 259 n. 10, and below, n. 101, insists on favorable taxation and the conjunction of interests between the early Fatimids and the Amalfitans, yet overestimates the latter's contribution to the growth of trade in precious oriental commodities. In addition, in the absence of familiarity with the evidence adduced here he unjustly downplays the role of Byzantine trade in Egypt in the eleventh century.

98. On the timber, see above, n. 10. Genoese trade along that sea route is examined below.

eastern Mediterranean in the first half of the eleventh century. In all likelihood most of not all Christian ships from the West which Nāṣir-i Khusrau noted in the harbor of Tripoli in 1047 were Amalfitan vessels.[99] Indeed, Genizah sources from the second half of the eleventh century reveal that the Amalfitans were routinely sailing between Constantinople and Egypt. This is also confirmed by the letter which an Egyptian Jew, recently settled in Constantinople, entrusted between 1092 and August 1096 to an Amalfitan merchant with whom he was acquainted, on the eve of the latter's departure for Egypt. It follows that cumulatively the Amalfitans established a triangular trading and shipping network connecting their own city, Constantinople and Alexandria, in the framework of which the major ports of Byzantine Asia Minor and the Levant served as transit stations.[100]

Amalfi's advantage over other maritime nations in that context was progressively eroded in the course of the twelfth century. The city's reluctance to join the First Crusade and the subsequent western war effort against the Muslims may be ascribed to its high stakes in Egyptian trade, stimulated by the good relations maintained by the Norman rulers of southern Italy and Sicily with Egypt as late as the 1140s.[101] Amalfi's interests in Egypt explain to a large extent its limited commercial involvement in the crusader states in the first half of the twelfth century.[102] The antagonism between Byzantium and the Norman rulers, commonly blamed for the decline of Amalfitan trade and shipping in the Empire, did apparently not undercut that activity. Indeed, Amalfitans traded in Constantinople throughout the twelfth century, as attested by their premises within the Pisan quarter, mentioned earlier, until they were compelled to leave the city in 1203, at the time of the Fourth Crusade.[103]

Moreover, the Amalfitans also maintained their role as middlemen and carriers in the eastern Mediterranean in the twelfth century. In 1119 some Venetians boarded an Amalfitan vessel leaving the imperial city for Alexan-

---

99. See above, n. 54.

* 100. See Jacoby, «What do we learn about Byzantine Asia Minor», pp. 91, 93-94. For the dating of the letter of the 1090s and the location of its writer, see D. Jacoby, «The Jewish Community of Constantinople from the Komnenan to the Palaiologan Period», *Vizantijskij Vremennik* 55/2 (80) (1998), 32-35.

101. See Cahen, *Orient et Occident*, pp. 70-80, 96-98, 109, 123-125. Von Falkenhausen, «Il commercio di Amalfi», pp. 33-35, overlooks Amalfi's favored treatment in Egypt since the early Fatimid period and underestimates its relations with that country in the first half of the twelfth century.

102. See Cahen, as in previous note.

103. See Cahen, *Orient et Occident*, p. 96; Von Falkenhausen, «Il commercio di Amalfi», pp. 25-38.

dria, presumably because no Venetian vessels were available at the time of their planned departure.[104] Amalfitans appear in 1101, 1149 and 1164 at Antioch, and in the 1160s at Acre and in the Lebanese ports of Tripoli and Laodikeia. From 1163 Amalfi obtained some privileges in the crusader states, the most extensive ones in the Kingdom of Jerusalem in 1190[105]. In addition, Amalfitans also traded in Alexandria in the 1160s, according to the Jewish traveler Benjamin of Tudela.[106] The Amalfitan merchant residing with his family at Phocea around 1172 is noteworthy.[107] All these testimonies should be viewed in the context of an ongoing Amalfitan activity along the waterway linking Constantinople to Egypt, despite the attacks of King Roger II of Sicily on the Nile Delta in 1151 and 1154-1155, which ushered in a period of tension between the Norman kingdom and Egypt.[108]

However, Amalfi's limited resources in men, capital and ships, far inferior to those of its increasingly powerful Italian rivals, Venice, Pisa and Genoa, as well as the absence of naval power account for its lack of leverage to obtain privileges as extensive as theirs, whether in the Empire, the crusader states or Egypt.[109] Amalfi's interest in cabotage along the Levantine coast, explicitly mentioned in the charter it obtained from Guy of Lusignan in 1190, possibly reflects a temporary adaption to the circumstances existing at that time, which prevented regular traffic with Constantinople since the Latins' massacre in 1182, as well as with Egypt since 1187.[110] Yet that interest may have been of a more lasting nature. It suggests the use of comparatively small and at best medium-sized vessels,[111] a partial shift toward short and medium-

---

104. The case was recorded in 1144: L. Lanfranchi, ed., *Famiglia Zusto* (Fonti per la storia di Venezia, Sez. IV: Archivi privati), Venezia 1955, p. 38, no. 16. Another Venetian sailed on an Amalfitan ship from Halmyros to Constantinople in 1111: *DCV*, I, pp. 37-38, no. 35, dated March 1112.

105. See Figliuoli, «Amalfi e il Levante», pp. 609-610, 616-619. On the privileges of 1190, see also D. Jacoby, «Conrad, Marquis of Montferrat, and the Kingdom of Jerusalem (1187-1192)», in L. Balletto, ed., *Atti del Congresso Internazionale «Dai feudi monferrini e dal Piemonte ai nuovi mondi oltre gli Oceani»*, *Alessandria, 2-6 Aprile 1990*, Alessandria 1993, p. 213, in D. Jacoby, *Trade, Commodities and Shipping*, no. IV.

106. M. N. Adler, ed., *The Itinerary of Benjamin of Tudela. Critical text, Translation and Commentary*, London 1907, Hebrew text, pp. 67-68; English trans., p. 76.

107. Von Falkenhausen, «Il commercio di Amalfi», pp. 31, 37.

108. On these attacks, see Cahen, *Orient et Occident*, pp. 125 and 267 n. 22.

109. The loss of Amalfi's archive in the fourteenth century does not explain by itself the lack of Amalfitan privileges.

110. See above, n. 105.

111. On the size of Amalfitan trading ships, see B. M. Kreutz, «Ghost Ships and phantom cargoes: reconstructing early Amalfitan trade», *Journal of Medieval History* 20 (1994), 349-350. On that of other vessels, see below, n. 219.

range traffic in the eastern Mediterranean, and a corresponding reduction of Amalfitan share in exchanges and sailings between Constantinople and Egypt.

Venetian, Pisan and Genoese merchants and ship operators expanded their activity along that same waterway in the wake of the Amalfitans, and in the course of the twelfth century surpassed their predecessors. One of the major factors ensuring their success in this respect was the ability of their respective government to obtain extensive privileges in the Empire,[112] the crusader states,[113] and Egypt.[114] These privileges varied in nature and extent and were not always fully nor continuously implemented,[115] yet on the whole they enhanced the maritime trade of the nations enjoying them in the three regions just mentioned and furthered their exchanges between the latter. The positions acquired by Venice, Pisa and Genoa in the crusader Levant were of particular importance in that framework. Their principal commercial outposts in that region were located at the meeting points of north-south traffic along the Levantine seaboard and trade routes joining the latter to major Muslim emporia inland, primarily Damascus and Aleppo. The crusader ports provided western merchants and ships, yet particularly those of the privileged nations safe maritime havens, logistic support and transshipment services along a major section of the itinerary between the Empire and Egypt.[116] They also served as temporary bases for their naval forces, a factor that enabled these nations to acquire and maintain supremacy over the Egyptian navy and to ensure to a large extent the safety of their own commercial navigation.

Venetian merchants and ships were sailing quite regularly, though se-

---

112. See Lilie, *Handel und Politik*, pp. 8-115; different approach to several issues in Jacoby, «Italian Privileges and Trade in Byzantium», pp. 349-369.

113. See M.- L. Favreau-Lilie, *Die Italiener im Heiligen Land vom ersten Kreuzzug bis zum Tode Heinrichs von Champagne (1098-1197)*, Amsterdam 1989, pp. 327-496, yet see some different interpretation in D. Jacoby, «The Venetian Privileges in the Latin Kingdom of Jerusalem: Twelfth and Thirteenth-Century Interpretations and Implementation», in B. Z. Kedar, J. Riley-Smith and R. Hiestand, eds., *Montjoie. Studies in Crusade History in Honour of Hans Eberhard Mayer*, Aldershot, Hampshire 1997, pp. 155-175; Jacoby, «Conrad, Marquis of Montferrat», pp. 190-219; idem, «Pisa e l'Oriente crociato», in G. Garzella e M. L. Ceccarelli Lemut, eds., «*Pisani viri in insulis et transmarinis regionibus potentes*». *Pisa come modo di comunicazioni nei secoli centrali del medioevo*, Pisa 2000 (in press).

114. See Jacoby, «Les Italiens en Egypte», pp. 76-89; idem, «Pisa e l'Oriente crociato».

115. See Jacoby, «Italian Privileges and Trade in Byzantium», pp. 354-356, 363-364, 367; idem, «The Venetian Privileges in the Latin Kingdom of Jerusalem», pp. 166-170, 172; idem, «Les Italiens en Egypte», pp. 78, 80-81.

116. See D. Jacoby, «The Trade of Crusader Acre in the Levantine Context: an Overview», *Archivio Storico del Sannio*, n.s., 3 (1998), 103-120. On transshipment in crusader ports, see also below, n. 167.

parately, to both Byzantium and Egypt since the ninth century, as illustrated by various pieces of evidence chosen at random. Several coins issued by Emperor Theophilus (829-842) and buried in Venice around the mid-tenth century attest to trade with the Empire in that period.[117] The chrysobull of 992 issued by Basil II and co-emperor Constantine VIII in favor of Venice attests to intensive Venetian commerce in Constantinople.[118] The alleged transfer of the relics of St Mark the Evangelist from Alexandria to Venice in 828 inplies that the Venetians were familiar with the Egyptian port.[119] Shortly after being elected in 991 Doge Pietro II Orseolo sent ambassadors to several Muslim rulers, the Fatimid caliph surely among them.[120] A Venetian ship arrived in Cairo around 1026.[121] We have already noted others sailing to Egypt via Crete in the 1060s or 1070s.[122] In 1071 a Venetian exported alum from Alexandria to Venice via Modon in the southwestern Peloponnese, which supposes an itinerary through the Aegean.[123]

The chrysobull granted by Alexius I Comnenus to Venice in 1082 points to a new development in Venetian trade and shipping. It is noteworthy that the list of cities enumerated in that document follows both in the west and in the east the course of navigation toward Constantinople. It thus reflects the perspective and practical experience of Venetian merchants and sailors, rather than the view of Byzantine officers, and must have been included at the request of Venice. The list mentions Laodikeia as the most southern Byzantine city in the east, followed by Antioch and other ports and islands along the coast of Asia Minor in the direction of the Empire's capital.[124] It suggests

---

117. They were found in 1934: see G. Ortalli, «Il mercante e lo stato: strutture della Venezia altomedievale», in *Mercati e mercanti nell'alto nedieovo: l'area euroasiatica e l'area mediterranea* (Settimane di studio del Centro italiano sull'alto medioevo, 40), Spoleto 1993, p. 126.

118. New ed. by M. Pozza e G. Ravegnani, eds., *I trattati con Bisanzio, 992-1198* (Pacta veneta, 4), Venezia 1993, pp. 21-25, yet see emendations and detailed discussion of the text in my review of that volume, published in *Mediterranean Historical Review* 9 (1994), 140-142.

119. Much has been written about the ecclesiastical and ideological consequences of that transfer, yet only the economic aspect is envisaged here.

120. See Heyd, *Histoire du commerce du Levant*, I, p. 1114; A. Schaube, *Handelsgeschichte der romanischen Völker des Mittelmeergebiets bis zum Ende der Kreuzzüge*, München 1906, pp. 21-22.

121. «Vita S. Symeonis auctore Eberwino abbate S. Martini Treviris», in *Acta Sanctorum*, Iun. I, pp. 86-92.

122. See above.

123. *DCV*, I, pp. 10-11, no. 11: testimony of April 1072.

124. Tafel und Thomas, *Urkunden*, I, pp. 51-54, and new ed. by Pozza e Ravegnani,

I

52

that by then Venetian traders and ships had expanded the geographic range of their operations beyond Constantinople and were sailing from there as far as Antioch and Laodikeia. This is confirmed by a somewhat later document. In 1095 a Venetian merchant traveled from Venice first to Constantinople and from there to Antioch, captured by the Seljuks in 1084. This voyage via the Byzantine capital does not appear to have been exceptional. The familiarity of the Venetians with Antioch and Laodikeia is also illustrated in 1099, when Venetian ships were involved together with Byzantine vessels in the transportation of victuals from these ports to the crusaders besieging Arqa, in the vicinity of Tripoli.[125] In 1100 the Venetians transferred the supposed relics of St Nicholas from Myra to Venice,[126] yet another indication that they were familiar with navigation along the southern coast of Asia Minor. Apparently around that time, if not earlier, Venetian merchants and maritime carriers took advantage of their simultaneous connections with Constantinople and Alexandria to operate between these cities, in addition to their sailings between Crete and Egypt.

It is noteworthy that the commercial and fiscal privileges granted to Venice in the Empire from 1082 also extended to the provinces, while their Italian competitors did not obtain such wide concessions until 1192.[127] The Venetian edge in that respect undoubtedly contributed to the expansion of twelfth-century Venetian trade and shipping between the Byzantine provinces and Egypt, which appear to have been far more diversified, intense and larger in volume than those of Pisa or Genoa. The Venetian participation in Cretan exports to Egypt, already attested in the 1060s or 1070s,[128] must have increased in the course of the twelfth century. Some time before 1161 the Venetian Giacomo Venier passed through Crete on his way from Constantinople to Alexandria and undoubtedly took advantage of the stopover to pick up some of the island's produce, such as cheese and wine.[129] The Venetians were presumably involved on a regular base in the export of Cretan products to Alexandria, mentioned by several Arab authors, among them al-Makhzūmī around

---

I trattati con Bisanzio, pp. 35-45. See also Jacoby, «Italian Privileges and Trade in Byzantium», pp. 349-354.

125. *DCV*, I, pp. 27-28, no. 24; Fulcher of Chartres, *Gesta Francorum Iherusalem Peregrinantium*, ed. H. Hagenmeyer, Heidelberg 1913.

126. See D. M. Nicol, *Byzantium and Venice. A Study in Diplomatic and Cultural Relations*, Cambridge 1988, pp. 71-73.

127. See Jacoby, «Italian Privileges and Trade in Byzantium», pp. 349-368.

128. See above.

129. On twelfth-century exports of Cretan cheese to Egypt, see Jacoby, «Byzantine Crete», pp. 528-530, 536; on Cretan wine, see below, n. 139.

1170.[130] Other Venetians shipped more than 1.200 liters of olive oil from Sparta to Alexandria in 1135.[131] The transfer of agricultural produce from continental Greece to the same destination is also implied by a Venetian contract of 1140 and later twelfth-century Venetian documents.[132] An additional reference appears in the taxation treatise of al-Makhzūmī, who in a registration example mentions Badr the Venetian as an importer of oil, which most likely came from the Peloponnese.[133] In addition, Venetian traders may have exported to Egypt silk textiles from Thebes, a major manufacturing center which they visited continuously since the 1070s.[134] One may wonder, therefore, whether they conveyed to their destinations the Jewish letters exchanged between Egypt and Thebes around 1135.[135]

Venetian trade between Cyprus and Egypt is documented in 1139 and between 1173 and 1176.[136] It is not excluded that Venetian settlers in Cyprus exported the island's wine to Egypt. The Egyptian population mostly drank local wine, yet foreign produce was also available.[137] It is attested in Alexan-

---

130. *DCV*, I, pp. 148 and 156-157, no. 149 and the related no. 159; treatise of al-Makhzūmī: Cahen, *Douanes et commerce*, pp. 235, 286 n. 2, 308-309. See also Jacoby, «Byzantine Crete», pp. 525-530, and above.

131. *DCV*, I, p. 69, no. 65.

132. Lanfranchi, *Famiglia Zusto*, pp. 35-36, no. 14, and see Borsari, *Venezia e Bisanzio*, pp. 96-97, yet for 1140 read there 'Pietro' instead of 'Enrico'.

133. Cahen, *Douanes et commerce*, p. 304. Badr may be safely identified as a member of the Badoer family. Manasse Badoer is attested in Alexandria in 1174: *DCV*, I, pp. 252-253, no. 257.

134. On Venetian silk purchases in, and exports from the Empire, see Jacoby, «Silk in Western Byzantium», pp. 479, 491-492, 494-497.

135. See S. D. Goitein, «The Jewish Communities of Saloniki and Thebes in Ancient Documents from the Cairo Geniza» [Hebrew], *Sefunot* 11 (1967), 23-33, with testimony on a scholar travelling from Egypt to Thebes.

136. *DCV*, I, pp. 77-78 and 444-445, respectively nos. 74 and 454-455. The latter document refers to a Venetian settler in Paphos between 1173 and 1176; correct accordingly the erroneous dating and location in D. Jacoby, «The Rise of a New Emporium in the Eastern Mediterranean: Famagusta in the Late Thirteenth Century», Μελέται καὶ ὑπομνήματα ("Ιδρυμα 'Αρχιεπισκόπου Μακαρίου Γ') 1 (1984), 164-165, repr. in idem, *Studies on the Crusader States and on Venetian Expansion*, Northampton 1989, no. VIII. T. Papacostas, «Secular Landholdings and Venetians in 12th-century Cyprus», *Byzantinische Zeitschrift* 92 (1999), 487-490, convincingly argues that a fairly large number of Venetians held urban and rural property in Cyprus before the island's conquest by Richard the Lionheart in May 1191. It is impossible, however, to date their presence in a precise way by relying on names found in other documents, as attempted by the author (pp. 490-497), in view of the contemporaneous appearance of several hononymous Venetian individuals in Venice and in eastern Mediterranean lands.

137. See Goitein, *A Mediterranean Society*, I, pp. 122-124, and IV, pp. 259-260; on the

dria in 1130-1131, yet the precise identity of the Rūm wine retailers from whom it was purchased is not stated.[138] In any event, it is likely that the foreign wine was of Byzantine origin.[139] Significantly, a number of Venetians established in Cyprus by the second half of the twelfth century owned and exploited vineyards in three villages situated on the southern slopes of the Troodos mountains, in the hinterland of the port of Limassol.[140] Venetian investments in that property may have been partly stimulated by a growing demand for wine in Egypt.[141]

The combination of trading in two or more ports located in different regions of the eastern Mediterranean appears to have been a fairly common Venetian practice. In 1111 a merchant from Venice proceeded beyond Constantinople to Damietta.[142] In 1119 a Venetian vessel sailed from Venice to Bari, from where it was to pursue its journey to Damietta and Constantinople.[143] Another triangular trade operation between Venice, Damietta and Constantinople is attested in 1141.[144] The contract of 1140 mentioned earlier

---

tax on wine, see H. Rabie, *The Financial System of Egypt, A.H. 564-741/A.D. 1169-1341*, London 1972, pp. 119-121.

138. See S. D. Goitein, «The Tribulations of an Overseer of the Sultan's Ships. A Letter from the Cairo Geniza (Written in Alexandria in 1131)», in G. Makdisi, ed., *Arabic and Islamic Studies in Honor of Hamilton A. R. Gibb*, Leiden 1965, pp. 270-284. Imported wine was later sold in the western *funduq*s of Alexandria: see Jacoby, «Les Italiens en Egypte», pp. 79 and 83-86, passim.

139. I. Genov, «Vorbereitung des Weins und Weinsorten in Byzance», *Etudes balkaniques* 25/2 (1989), 119-120, lists Byzantine regions producing wine. For Crete and Cyprus, see also Malamut, *Les îles de l'Empire byzantin*, II, pp. 389-390; D. Tsougarakis, *Byzantine Crete From the 5th Century to the Venetian Conquest*, Athens 1988, p. 287.

140. The Venetians and their vineyards are listed in a Venetian survey carried out in 1243 or 1244: ed. by O. Berggötz, *Der Bericht des Marsilio Zorzi. Codex Querini-Stampalia IV3 (1064)* (Kieler Werkstücke, Reihe C: Beiträge zur europäischen Geschichte des frühen und hohen Mittelalters, herausgegeben von H. E. Mayer, Band 2), Frankfurt am Main 1990, pp. 184-191, esp. p. 191, lines 14-20. Two of the villages have been indentified: see E. Papadopoulou, «Οἱ πρῶτες ἐγκαταστάσεις Βενετῶν στὴν Κύπρο», *Σύμμεικτα* 5 (1983), 320· The third one must have been located in the same region. One Venetian owned *X zarete de vinea*, a reference to its average yearly output of must. G. Boerio, *Dizionario del dialetto veneziano*, Venezia ²1856, p. 807, defines 'zareta' as a small jar. No such Cypriot wine measure in known, yet the larger 'zara' or 'giarra' of the island contained 53.880 liters: see E. Schilbach, *Byzantinische Metrologie* (Handbuch des Altertumswissenschaft, XII/4 = Byzantinishes Handbuch, 4), München 1970, pp. 134-136 and 128 respectively.

141. Papacostas, «Secular Landholdings and Venetians», pp. 498-500, suggests exports to the crusader states and to Constantinople, yet overlooks Egypt.

142. Lanfranchi, *Famiglia Zusto*, pp. 23-24, no. 6; see also Jacoby, «Silk in Western Byzantium», p. 496.

143. *DCV*, I, pp. 43-44, no. 41.

144. *DCV*, I, pp. 80-81, no. 77.

envisaged a complex trading venture extending over two years. The traveling merchant would leave Venice for Constantinople, proceed from there to Corinth or Sparta overland, then to Alexandria and back to the Byzantine capital.[145] In December 1158 a maritime loan granted in Constantinople was to be reimbursed in Venice, the destination being reached either directly or via Alexandria.[146] It is noteworthy that all these operations took place before Venice obtained a *funduq* of its own in Egypt, apparently in 1172.[147] Crusader ports, to which Venetians also sailed from various regions of the Empire,[148] often served as stopovers, transshipment stations or bases of departure. A Venetian contract of 1139 envisaged a journey from Tyre to Venice either via Alexandria or via Constantinople.[149] In the 1160s Romano Mairano conducted trade from Acre both with the Empire and Egypt, partly with his own vessels.[150] Goods traveling from Alexandria to Constantinople were occasionally transshipped in Tyre.[151] The evidence clearly points to the consolidation of Venetian triangular trading and shipping networks joining Venice, the Empire and Egypt in the twelfth century.

Pisa entered the waters of Romania at the time of the First Crusade.[152] Its seaborne trade with the Empire was enhanced by the commercial and fiscal privileges it secured in 1111. However, since these privileges were limited to the sale of goods in Constantinople, it would seem that the range of Pisan trade and shipping in the Empire's provinces remained fairly limited, despite the settlement of some Pisans in Halmyros.[153] The extension of Pisan privileges in 1192 appears to have furthered an expansion of Pisan activity in the provinces, as suggested by the sale of a large quantity of Peloponnesian oil, apparently intended for Constantinople, carried out by a Pisan consortium in Modon shortly before 1201.[154] Pisan exchanges with Egypt were also initiated in the early twelfth century and expanded rapidly, thanks to deli-

145. See above, n. 132.
146. *DCV*, I, pp. 133-134, no. 134.
147. See Jacoby, «Les Italiens en Egypte», p. 79.
148. See also Borsari, *Venezia e Bisanzio*, pp. 94-97.
149. *DCV*, I, p. 78, no. 75.
150. See Borsari, *Venezia e Bisanzio*, pp. 119-122. On transshipment in Acre, see also below, n. 167.
151. As suggested by *DCV*, I, pp. 374-375, 376-381, nos. 381, 383-387.
152. For this whole paragraph, see S. Borsari, «Pisani a Bisanzio nel XII secolo», *Bolletino Storico Pisano* 60 (1991), 59-75; Jacoby, «Italian Privileges and Trade in Byzantium», pp. 357-359, 362-368; idem, «Les Italiens en Egypte», pp. 77-78; idem, «Pisa e l'Oriente crociato».
153. On whom see Borsari, «Pisani a Bisanzio», pp. 65-66.
154. *DCV*, I, pp. 445-446, no. 456.

veries of timber. According to the Arab geographer Zuhrī, who wrote around 1150, Pisan ships were more numerous in Alexandria's harbor than those of any other nation. Pisa obtained a *funduq* of its own in Alexandria at an unknown date before 1153, the first western maritime nation to benefit from such a concession in Egypt, and another one in Cairo in 1154. There is no evidence pointing to Pisan exports from the Empire's provinces to Egypt similar to those carried out by the Venetians and the Genoese, yet this may due to the almost total loss of Pisan notarial charters regarding the eastern Mediterranean. It would seem, though, that the volume of Pisan trade and shipping between the two regions remained inferior to those of its main rivals.

As noted earlier, Genoese merchants and ships were carrying Cretan produce to Alexandria and buying there pepper in 1062.[155] Their activity in the Egyptian port around that time is also attested by another Genizah document mentioning the arrival of ships from Genoa, which seems to imply that these vessels did not stop in Crete on the way.[156] Genoese traders continued to visit Egypt in the following decades. Those present there in the early years of the twelfth century were imprisoned in reprisal for the assistance offered by Genoese forces to the crusader conquests in the Levant.[157] We do not know how long Genoese traders were barred from doing business in Egypt. In any event, by the 1130s they were again routinely active there and even traveled inland to buy local produce. Genoa concluded an agreement with Egypt some time before 1156. Its terms, which are unknown, did apparently not include the concession of a *funduq* in Alexandria, yet Genoa obtained one between 1192 and 1200.[158]

Genoese maritime trade in Romania, beyond Crete, must have expanded after the First Crusade.[159] Yet only since around 1135 do we find Genoese traders reaching Constantinople, whether directly from Genoa or via Alexandria. The two letters illustrating these itineraries, preserved in a stylized

---

155. See above, n. 77.

156. Excerpt trans. by Goitein, *A Mediterranean Society*, I, p. 318; full trans. by Udovitch, «A Tale of Two Cities», pp. 149-151. E. Ashtor, *A Social and Economic History of the Near East in the Middle Ages*, London 1976, p. 353 n. 65, mentions in fact the same document with a mistaken reference, which has led some to assume that there was more evidence about the Genoese around 1065.

157. See Goitein, *A Mediterranean Society*, I, p. 45; Kedar, «Mercanti genovesi in Alessandria d'Egitto», p. 26. Interestingly, al-Malik al-Afdal apparently arrested only the Genoese, although Pisa and Venise too supported the early crusader conquests.

158. See Jacoby, «Les Italiens en Egypte», pp. 78, 81.

159. For this whole paragraph and the following one, see Jacoby, «Italian Privileges and Trade in Byzantium», pp. 359-368; idem, «Byzantine Crete», pp. 530-540. Further evidence regarding Crete appears below.

version, imply that Genoese journeys between Egypt and the imperial capital were no more exceptional by that time.[160] It follows that as early as the 1130s some Genoese traders were engaging in triangular trade ventures between Genoa, Alexandria and Constantinople. This is all the more significant, since they preceded Genoa's first agreements with either Egypt or the Empire. It is noteworthy, though, that the authors of the letters just mentioned sailed to Constantinople on foreign vessels. The one who traveled directly to the imperial capital intended to board a local vessel at Bari. His partner, who visited Egypt, planned to proceed on a ship carrying other Italian merchants as well as Egyptian ambassadors. It was safer to sail along the Levantine coast held by the Franks on an Italian, rather than on an Egyptian vessel, and we may thus assume that the Genoese merchant boarded an Amalfitan, a Venetian or a Pisan boat.

While Genoese ships sailed in Byzantine waters, they apparently did not yet reach Constantinople or rarely did so. Regular Genoese sailings presumably began some two decades later, in the 1150s. This development must have been prompted by the growing number of Genoese merchants interested in trade in Constantinople and provided the background to Genoa's request for privileges in the Empire. Manuel I Comnenus granted some in 1155, more limited than those of Venice. These privileges were curtailed in 1169 and restricted to Constantinople. As a result, the range and volume of Genoese maritime trade in Romania in the second half of the twelfth century appear to have remained more restricted than those of Venice.

Despite the limited extent of their privileges in the Empire, the Genoese took full advantage of their sailings in the waters of Romania to engage in triangular trade and shipping operations. A merchant about to leave Genoa in 1160 was offered the choice either to sail first to Constantinople and from there via Crete to Alexandria or directly from the imperial city to the Egyptian port, or still to travel from Constantinople to Bougie in the Maghreb, Spain, Provence or Genoa, eventually reaching Alexandria, from where he would be free to proceed along the maritime route of his choice.[161] The following year the destination of another merchant leaving Genoa was Constantinople, Alexandria and any other port, which implies that he was also allowed to

---

160. Ed. by W. Wattenbach, «Iter austriacum, 1853», *Archiv für Kunde österreichischer Geschichtsquellen* 24 (1855), 79-80, nos. XIX-XX; see D. Abulafia, *The Two Italies. Economic Relations between the Norman Kingdom of Sicily and the Northern Communes*, Cambridge 1977, pp. 74-76.

161. M. Chiaudano - M. Moresco, eds., *Il cartolare di Giovanni Scriba*, Torino 1935, I, pp. 404-405, no. 752.

travel between the two emporia just mentioned.[162] Around 1170 al-Makh-zūmī cites the name of Guglielmo the Genoese in an example of tax registration recording the arrival of ships from Crete in Alexandria. Crete was then a frequent stopover of Genoese ships.[163] Shortly before December 1174 the Byzantine authorities seized a Genoese vessel carrying a large numbers of oars, beams and large boards, apparently loaded along the coast of Asia Minor and in all likelihood intended for Egypt.[164] A commenda contract concluded in Genoa in 1186 provided for a journey to Constantinople and from there either to Alexandria or Ceuta in the Maghreb.[165]

The function of the crusader ports as stopovers and transshipment stations within triangular Genoese ventures is illustrated by the charter of 1192 wich the ruler of the Kingdom of Jerusalem, Henry of Champagne, issued in favor of Genoa. It mentions both land trade with the Muslim hinterland and maritime trade with Egypt, the Maghreb and territories to the north of Acre as far as Constantinople.[166] The charter reflects Genoa's expectations that regular Genoese trade with Byzantium, interrupted since 1182, and with Egypt, severed in 1187, would soon be resumed.[167] The strong measures taken by Henry of Champagne in the 1190s to stop Pisan piracy in Levantine waters were undoubtedly also motivated by the need to ensure the safety of navigation between Egypt and Constantinople, regardless of the nationality of the merchants and ships involved in that traffic, from which the Levantine ports greatly benefited.[168]

The spice trade undoubtedly continued to play a major role within that framework, as in the eleventh century. We have already encountered the Genoese merchant who around 1135 visited both Egypt and Constantinople, from where he was expected to return home. His wife requested him to bring various items, among them spices and silk textiles.[169] The spices which that merchant was expected to buy in Egypt would have partly financed his pur-

---

162. *Ibid.*, II, p. 44, no. 895.

163. Cahen, *Douanes et commerce*, p. 308, and see Jacoby, «Byzantine Crete», pp. 533-536.

164. See Jacoby, «The Supply of War Materials to Egypt», nn. 46-49.

165. M. Chiaudano, ed., *Oberto Scriba de mercato, 1186*, Torino 1940, p. 8, no. 21.

166. C. Imperiale di Sant'Angelo, ed., *Codice diplomatico della repubblica di Genova dal MCLXIII al MCLXXXX*, Roma 1936-1942, III, pp. 87-89, no. 28; new ed. by D. Puncuh, *I Libri Iurium della Repubblica di Genova*, I/2 (Fonti per la storia della Liguria, IV), Genova 1996, pp. 146-149, no. 335.

167. See Jacoby, «Conrad, Marquis of Montferrat», pp. 218-219, 222-223.

168. On these measures, see M.- L. Favreau, «Die italienische Levante-Piraterie und die Sicherheit der Seewege nach Syrien im 12. und 13. Jahrhundert», *Vierteljahrschrift für Sozial- und Wirtschaftsgeschichte* 65 (1978), 483-492.

169. See above, n. 160.

chases of silk textiles in the Empire. More precise information about the twelfth-century flow of spices to the Empire may be gathered from two other documents. In 1188 a Venetian bought some pepper in Alexandria for export to Constantinople, its weight being expressed in Alexandrian units.[170] Some ten years later a Genoese stated the weight of the pepper he had given to Gafforio in Constantinople in *cantaria* units used at the *catena* or harbor customs of Acre.[171] Egypt appears to have offered cheaper spices than those arriving in Constantinople by other trade routes.[172] We may safely assume, therefore, that in both instances just mentioned the pepper originated in Egypt, yet in the second one it had been transshipped at Acre. Although the evidence is scarce, it would seem that the twelfth-century export of spices from Egypt to the Empire was increasingly handled by Italian merchants. Circumstancial evidence supporting this assumption will be adduced below.

Neither the Empire's merchants and carriers not their Egyptian counterparts enjoyed the favorable trading conditions secured by their Venetian, Pisan and Genoese competitors in the Empire, the crusader states and Egypt. Byzantine subjects were not granted any fiscal concessions in these regions, nor any commercial outposts in foreign lands. Nor did Cyprus, a Byzantine province until 1184 and in fact an independent state from that year until 1191, offer them advantages similar to those provided by the crusader states to the privileged Italian nations. Cyprus was mainly involved in short and medium-range trade with the ports of southern Asia Minor such as Attaleia,[173] the Levantine coast,[174] and Egypt.[175] To be sure, before the First Crusade Christian

170. *DCV*, I, p. 362, no. 368: *de caricaturas de Alexandria*.

171. Imperiale di Sant'Angelo, *Codice diplomatico*, III, p. 198: *ad cantarium catene Accon qui sic est cantaria V ad cantarium Costantinopolim*; at the time of the loss the price of pepper in this city was 20 hyperpers per *cantarium*. The Genoese Gafforio had become a corsair in 1198 and had not paid for the pepper. The case was raised by the Genoese ambassador sent to Constantinople in 1201; for the background, see Heyd, *Histoire du commerce du Levant*, I, pp. 238-242.

172. Even after the opening of the trans-Asian overland route following the Mongol expansion of the thirteenth century spices were cheaper in Alexandria than in other Mediterranean outlets: Marinus Sanutus, *Liber secretorum fidelium crucis super Terrae Sanctae recuperatione et conservatione*, in J. Bongars, ed., *Gesta Dei per Francos, sive orientalium expeditionum et regni Francorum Hierosolomytani historia*, Hanoviae 1611, II, p. 23.

173. See Malamut, *Les îles de l'Empire byzantin*, II, pp. 454-455; Goitein, *A Mediterranean Society*, I, pp. 214 and 453 n. 23.

174. S. D. Goitein, trans., *Letters of Medieval Jewish Traders*, Princeton 1973, pp. 45-47: Cypriot silk in Ramle around 1066, yet the reference to Tripoli in idem, *A Mediterranean Society*, I, p. 453 n. 23, is a slip; *DCV*, I, pp. 85-86, no. 82: trade between Acre and Cyprus before 1143; *DCV*, I, pp. 366-367, no. 373: between Cyprus and Tyre before 1189.

175. See above, n. 136.

and especially Byzantine pilgrims and travelers apparently preferred to board ships passing through Cyprus, a Byzantine province, rather than to sail through Muslim ports, and this was still the case of Byzantine subjects in the twelfth century.[176] There was also commercial traffic between Constantinople and Cyprus and via the island to Egypt.[177] Occasionally vessels anchored in Cyprus on their way from the Levant to Constantinople, as sometime before 1143,[178] and a shipping line connected Cyprus with the Peloponnese via Crete, as illustrated by the geographic treatise of al-Idrīsī, compiled between 1139 and 1154.[179]

However, Cyprus does not seem to have fulfilled in the twelfth and thirteenth century the major function commonly ascribed to it in Mediterranean trade and navigation.[180] Cypriot ports did not serve as indispensable stopovers for vessels engaging in long-distance trade. They lacked most of the elements favoring the variegated commercial and maritime functions assumed by crusader ports, which in addition benefited from proximity to the emporia of their Muslim hinterland. In other words, Cyprus did not offer an alternative to the Levantine seabord, along which the main navigation route connecting the Empire and Egypt proceeded. Genizah documents as well as other sources clearly point to intensive navigation along that waterway in the eleventh and even more so in the twelfth century.[181] The Latin conquest of Cyprus in 1191 did not basically alter conditions in that respect, though it further weakened the standing of Byzantine subjects involved in seaborne trade, including with Egypt.[182] Only after the fall of the crusader states in 1291 did Cyprus become an important destination and maritime transit station in long-distance trade and produce on a large scale export-oriented commodities such as sugar, cotton, precious textiles and salt, in high demand in the West.[183]

---

176. For a list, see C. Galatariotou, *The Making of a Saint. The Life, Times and Sanctification of Neophytos the Recluse*, Cambridge 1991, p. 54, yet for William of Tyre read '1180' instead of '1066', clearly a slip.

177. See above, nn. 51-52.

178. *DCV*, I, pp. 85-86, no. 82.

179. Jaubert, *La géographie d'Edrisi*, II, pp. 126-130; see the maps in Malamut, *Les îles de l'Empire byzantin*, II, pp. 661-662.

180. See above, n. 24.

181. See Goitein, *A Mediterranean Society*, I, pp. 212-214, 318, 323; also Jacoby, «Byzantine Crete», pp. 523-524.

182. Despite the absence of privileges granted by the Lusignan kings in the following decade.

183. See Jacoby, «The Rise of a New Emporium», pp. 145-179; idem, «Τὸ ἐμπόριο καὶ ἡ οἰκονομία τῆς Κύπρου (1191-1489)», in Th. Papadopoullos, ed., Ἱστορία τῆς Κύπρου, Τόμος Δ΄, Μεσαιωνικὸν Βασίλειον, Ἑνετοκρατία, Μέρος Α΄ (Ἵδρυμα Ἀρχιεπισκόπου Μακαρίου Γ΄), Nicosia 1995, pp. 387-454.

The privileges and outposts acquired by the three major maritime nations in eastern Mediterranean lands afforded their merchants and carriers a growing competitive edge over their Byzantine and Egyptian counterparts in that region, as well as over the Amalfitans. It remains to be seen what precise impact this development had on the participation of the Empire's subjects in Byzantine-Egyptian traffic.

IV. THE EVOLUTION OF BYZANTINE TRADE WITH EGYPT
    IN THE TWELFTH CENTURY

The 'market of the Greeks' in Fustat, documented in a Genizah letter of 959, is no more attested after that date. However, by itself this fact does not imply a reduction in Byzantine maritime trade with Egypt since the early Fatimid period, which as noted above appears to have been quite intensive in the eleventh century. The absence of further references to the 'market of the Greeks' may be rather due to the paucity of Genizah evidence regarding institutions with which the Jews of Fustat had little or no contact.[184] It presumably also reflects a shift in the relative importance of Cairo and Alexandria with respect to Mediterranean trade, as well as a change in governmental policy with respect to foreign Christian traders. We have seen that Cairo was the commercial and financial center of Egypt and its largest market, including for exchanges with other Mediterranean countries, although most goods handled in that framework passed through Alexandria.[185] It is not surprising, therefore, that foreign, including Byzantine merchants occasionally sailed up the Nile as far as Cairo, sometimes on their own ships, or reached the city by land.[186] Cairo's functions explain why Pisa requested a *funduq* in that city and obtained it in 1154, in addition to the one it already had in Alexandria.[187] It is noteworthy, however, that after the Frankish invasions if Egypt in the 1160s Saladin refrained from restoring to Pisa the *funduq* it had held in Cairo. Moreover, he limited the activity of western merchants to Mediterranean ports,[188] although he appears to have granted the Pisans

---

184. See above, n. 30.
185. See above, n. 26.
186. See above, nn. 29, 48, 81.
187. See above, p. 394. Note that in 1169 too Pisa requested a *funduq* in Cairo from King Amalric, in anticipation of the Frankish occupation of the city: G. Müller, ed., *Documenti sulle relazioni delle città toscane coll'Oriente cristiano e coi Turchi fino all'anno MD XXXI*, Firenze 1879, p. 15, no. XII.
188. See previous note, and for Saladin's policy, see Labib, *Handelsgeschichte Ägyptens*, p. 29; C. Cahen, «Les marchands étrangers au Caire sous les Fatimides et les Ayyu-

I

62

some freedom of movement inland in 1173.[189] Significantly, the major Italian maritime powers did not obtain and possibly did not even request any *funduqs* in Cairo afterwards. Those of Alexandria appear to have been fulfilled the needs of their nationals engaging in trade in Egypt in the second half of the twelfth century.

Several factory may explain the concentration of western business in Alexandria, even prior to the administrative measures barring Italian merchants from traveling inland. The expansion and intensification of Italian trade and shipping throughout the Mediterranean since the early twelfth century undoubtedly enhanced the function of Alexandria as a commercial center and reduced to some extent the economic centrality of Cairo.[190] Moreover, proceeding beyond Egyptian ports was apparently not indispensable, especially for merchants importing large cargoes of timber and iron. Trade in these commodities was a state monopoly handled by government officials, who took hold of the shipments upon arrival at the Mediterranean ports of Egypt, where the alum used by the state as partial payment for iron and timber was concentrated. Moreover, even sales on the free market were controlled by the authorities. As a result, the diffusion of goods inside Egypt was overwhelmingly in the hands of state officials or local merchants.[191] Alexandria may have indirectly benefited from yet another factor. The growing size of Italian ships in the second half of the twelfth century either prevented them from sailing up the Nile in certain periods of the year or made such journeys less attractive.[192]

The participation of Byzantine merchants and carriers in twelfth-century

bides au Moyen Age», in *Colloque international sur l'histoire du Caire*, 27 mars - 5 avril 1969 (Arab Republic of Egypt, Ministry of Culture, General Egyptian Book Organization), Cairo 1969, pp. 99-100; idem, Cahen, *Orient et Occident*, p. 146; Jacoby, «Les Italiens en Egypte», p. 78.

189. M. Amari, ed., *I diplomi arabi del R. Archivio Fiorentino*, Firenze 1863, p. 260, no. VII: letters confirming the grant of privileges were sent to officials *per totam terram nostram*. See Jacoby, «Les Italiens en Egypte», p. 78. Incidentally, the Genoese author of one of the letters written c. 1135 traveled inland and for three days awaited there Egyptian traders with whom he intended to do business: see above, n. 160. He presumably intended to buy flax in the countryside, as done by local merchants: see Goitein, *A Mediterranean Society*, I, p. 224.

190. The factors accounting for the twelfth-century economic rise of Alexandria adduced here have been overlooked in studies dealing with the economic function of Cairo, on which see above, n. 26.

191. On state control, see Cahen, *Douanes et commerce*, pp. 235-243, 257-262; Rabie, *The Financial System of Egypt*, pp. 82-85, 91-94; Goitein, *A Mediterranean Society*, I, pp. 192-195; Jacoby, «The Supply of War Materials to Egypt», nn. 1-20.

192. On the size of ships, see below, n. 219.

exchanges between the Empire and Egypt is attested both explicitely and indirectly, and appears likely in other cases. It has been suggested above that the ship on which the Russian abbot Daniel sailed from Constantinople to Jaffa between 1106 and 1108 also carried merchants and in all likelihood proceeded to Egypt.[193] The same apparently applies to the numerous Byzantine ships captured by the Fatimid fleet off Jaffa in 1151-1152, according to the Arab chronicler Ibn al-Qalanisi.[194] A Genizah letter dispatched from Old Cairo in January 1133 reports that "business is at a standstill, for no one has come from the West, and only a few Rum have arrived", clearly a reference to Byzantine merchants.[195] Decisive evidence regarding their activity in Egypt appears in a charter issued in 1154 by the Egyptian caliph az-Ẓāfir in favor of Pisan traders. He promised to uphold the existing reduction of taxes which they enjoyed, adding that "you know well that we levy higher dues from Muslims and Greeks".[196] Benjamin of Tudela, who visited Alexandria around 1165, encountered there merchants from many nations, including those from "Yavan, who are called Grigos" or Greeks, thus clearly Byzantines.[197] Byzantines merchants are again attested in Alexandria in 1192.[198] The Arab chronicler Ibn al-Athīr reports that Franks and Rūm, respectively Westeners and Byzantines, traded in Acre before its conquest by Saladin in 1187.[199] It is likely that some of these Byzantine merchants proceeded beyond Acre, which as noted earlier was an important port of call and transshipment station between Constantinople and Egypt.[200] The document of 1133 mentioned above is the latest available testimony about Byzantine merchants reaching Cairo, presumably on a Byzantine vessel sailing up the Nile. One may wonder to what extent the growing concentration of foreign maritime

---

193. See above, n. 52.

194. H. A. R. Gibb, *The Damascus Chronicle of the Crusade, extracted and translated from the Chronicle of Ibn al-Qalanisi*, London 1932, p. 308.

195. Goitein, *A Mediterranean Societu*, I, p. 45. The writer was obviously referring to the Jewish year and, therefore, to the autumn sailings of 1132 from the Empire. A letter of 1141 states that «ships going to Spain, al-Mahdiyya, Tripoli in Lybia, Sicily and Byzantium have departed and have encountered a propitious wind», see *ibid.*, I, pp. 301-302. It is unclear whether the reference is to Egyptian or to Byzantine merchants and boats.

196. Amari, *I diplomi arabi*, p. 247: *et bene scitis quia magis diricturas capimus a Saracenis et a Grecis quam a vobis*. For the correct dating of the letter, see Heyd, *Histoire du commerce du Levant*, I, p. 394 n. 1.

197. Benjamin of Tudela, Hebrew text, pp. 67-69; the English translation is mine.

198. See below, p. 71.

199. Ibn al-Athīr, «Kamel Altevarikh», in *Recueil des Historiens des Croisades, Historiens orientaux*, Paris 1872, I/1, p. 689.

200. See above, n.n 105, 150, 166, 171.

business in Alexandria affected the Empire's traders and vessels. Whatever the case, it is a reasonable guess that the participation of Byzantine forces in the invasion of Egypt by King Amalric of Jerusalem in the autumn of 1169 induced Saladin to extend the ban on inland trading to the Empire's subjects.[201]

There is possibly only one instance in which we may identify a Byzantine merchant reaching Egypt. Niketas Choniates reports that a Constantinopolitan 'money-changer' by the name of Kalomodios, arrested in 1200, had amassed a fortune in arduous long-distance trade operations.[202] To be sure, Benjamin of Tudela notes that Byzantine merchants traded in the 1160s in Barcelona and Montpellier. The Jewish traveler remarks about this city that "all nations are found there doing business through the medium of the Genoese and the Pisans", which is certainly correct with respect to Byzantine traders.[203] Indeed, by the 1160s Genoa and Pisa had acquired a dominant role in mercantile transportation between Provence and the eastern Mediterranean.[204] Yet there is no evidence of Byzantine traders in the West in the late twelfth century. Although Kalomodios may have conducted business in the Black Sea, it is more plausible that the crusader Levant and Egypt were the destinations of his arduous long-distance journeys.

The assertion of the Jewish traveler Benjamin of Tudela that each nation had its own *funduq* in Alexandria is not supported by other sources and may be safely dismissed. Indeed, at the time of Benjamin's visit there in the 1160s only Pisa had been granted such premises, while Venice and Genoa apparently obtained theirs only later, in 1172 and between 1192 and 1200 respectively.[205] The absence of a Byzantine *funduq* in the Egyptian port is all the more surprising in view of the existence of a similar residential and commercial facility for visiting Muslim merchants in Constantinople. Their *mitaton* was located

---

201. On the invasion, see R.- J. Lilie, *Byzantium and the Crusader States, 1096-1204*, Oxford 1993, pp. 198-202; on the ban, see above, n. 188.

202. Niketas Choniates, *Historia*, ed. J. L. van Dieten -Berlin-New York 1975) (Corpus Fontium Historiae Byzantinae, XI), I, pp. 523-524. Oikonomides, «The Economic Region of Constantinople», p. 235, challenges the common interpretation of this passage, claiming that Kalomodios himself did not travel and only invested in commercial ventures carried out by others. The text, however, points to personal involvement: ἀργαλέας καὶ δολιχὰς ἐκδημίας.

203. Benjamin of Tudela, Hebrew text, pp. 1-3; English translation, pp. 2-3.

204. On the struggle between the two powers in this respect, see Schaube, *Handelsgeschichte*, pp. 570-571, 574-575, and esp. H. E. Mayer, *Marseilles Levantehandel und ein akkonensisches Fälscheratelier des 13. Jahrhunderts* (Bibliothek des Deutschen historischen Instituts in Rom, 38), Tübingen 1972, pp. 60-65.

205. See above, nn. 152, 147 and 158 respectively.

between the Golden Horn and the northern city wall, close to the church of St Irene in the Perama area.[206] At the request of Saladin Emperor Isaac II Angelus built in 1188 a mosque within that *mitaton*, and numerous Muslim traders attended its inauguration in the following year. The willingness of the emperor to comply with the sultan's wishes was largely due to political considerations.[207] The location of the mosque close to the Golden Horn implies that Muslims involved in maritime commerce were already trading in that urban area, and it is likely that the *mitaton* went back to the tenth century.[208] Since 1082 at the latest the Empire adopted a liberal policy with respect to the residence of western merchants in Constantinople, reflected by the concession of quarters to the major Italian maritime powers and the lifting of time restrictions on their stay in the Empire.[209] It is unclear whether in the 1160s the same policy was applied to Muslims or, in other words, whether they were still compelled to reside in their *mitaton* or did so by choice, in view of the convenience it afforded them. Benjamin of Tudela, who visited Constantinople in the early 1160s, mentions the presence of merchants from Fatimid territories in the city, yet does not specify where they resided.[210]

The lack of reciprocity in Egyptian-Byzantine relations with respect to residential and commercial premises is striking. It illustrates the relatively weak position of Byzantine traders in Egypt, compared to that of their Italian competitors. Pisa, Venice and Genoa obtained their respective *funduq* in Alexandria and other concessions in Egypt in the course of the twelfth century thanks to the conjunction of two main factors, namely their growing trade, partly linked to large deliveries of timber and iron,[211] and the political backing offered by their respective governments. We may surmise that the number of

---

206. On the location of St Eirene, see D. Jacoby, «The Venetian Quarter of Constantinople from 1082 to 1261: Topographical Considerations», in C. Sode, S. A. Takàcs, eds., *Novum Millenium*, Aldershot 2000, p. 178.

207. For dating and circumstances, see D. Jacoby, «Diplomacy, Trade, Shipping and Espionage between Byzantium and Egypt in the Twelfth Cemtury», in Gordula Scholz und Georgios Makris, eds., ΠΟΛΥΠΛΕΥΡΟΣ ΝΟΥΣ, *Miscellanea für Peter Schreiner zu seinem 60. Geburtstag* (Byzantinisch Archiv. Band 19), München 2000, pp. 95-97.

208. Magdalino, «Constantinople médiévale», p. 88, convincingly argues that the name *mitaton* given to the mosque in popular parlance points to the earlier existence of commercial premises. By contrast, Reinert, «The Muslim Presence in Constantinople», pp. 141-142, postulates that the mosque was built with subsidiary buildings and became the nucleus of a mercantile Muslim neighborhood established shortly afterwards, which gave its name to the mosque. Such a scenario is not plausible.

209. The important change in this respect has been largely overlooked.

210. Benjamin of Tudela, Hebrew text, p. 14; English translation, p. 12.

211. See Jacoby, «The Supply of War Materials to Egypt».

Byzantine merchants visiting Alexandria in any given season was inferior to that of anyone of the major Italian maritime nations, which in the second half of the twelfth century may have reached several hundred.[212] The gap between the strength of the Byzantine and Italian contingents of visiting traders grew constantly, as a result of various developments which will be examined below. In any event, the number of the Empire's subjects was apparently not sufficient to warrant the establishment of a separate *funduq* for them in Alexandria. More importantly perhaps, the Byzantine emperors lacked the necessary leverage to ensure such a measure. While the Empire heavily depended on the supply of spices from Egypt, Byzantine merchants do not seem to have brought there the commodities in which the Egyptian rulers were most interested, namely timber and iron, or imported them is small quantities only. It should be stressed that the activity of Byzantine traders in Egypt in the twelfth century does not necessarily imply that all of them, nor all their goods sailed on Byzantine vessels.

Byzantine mercantile shipping is poorly documented, yet was undoubtedly very intensive in the twelfth century. During the First Crusade a large number of Byzantine boats of small tonnage from the Aegean islands and Cyprus were

---

212. Documents of 1154-1155 refer to some eighty western merchants imprisoned in Egypt as reprisal for the murder of Egyptian subjects who had sailed on a Pisan ship in 1153: Amari, *I diplomi arabi*, pp. 241-242, 248, 250-251. M. Balard, «Notes sur le commerce entre l'Italie et l'Egypte sous les Fatimides», in M. Barrucand, ed., *L'Egypte fatimide, son art et son histoire*, Paris 1999, p. 629, considers that figure as reflecting more or less the strength of the Pisan mercantile community temporarily staying at Alexandria. This is highly doubtful for two reasons. First, around 1150 the number of Pisan ships in Alexandria's harbor was superior to that of any other nation: see above, n. 152. If we suppose, for instance, that in 1153 six of them had arrived, the average number of traders per vessel would have been a dozen only, clearly too low. Secondly, the Pisan ship involved in the incident of 1153 presumably left Alexandria during the autumn sailing season and the news of the incident arrived there in late autumn or in the winter. If so, only the Pisan merchants who had not yet managed to leave or who intended to spend the winter in Alexandria would have been arrested. The figure of eighty would thus apply to them only, yet not to all the visiting Pusan traders. A higher figure is also suggested by later data, although one should take into account that the number of western ships and traders visiting the Egyptians port grew after 1153. In the fall of 1187 thirty-eight western ships anchored in the harbor of Alexandria: M. R. Morgan, ed., *Le continuation de Guillaume de Tyr (1184-1197)* (Documents relatifs à l'histoire des Croisades publiés par l'Académie des Inscriptions et Belles-Lettres, XIV), Paris 1982, pp. 74-75, par. 61. It would seem that even around 1215 only a small number of Pisans spent the winter in Egypt, although the total number of western merchants visiting the country had substantially increased. According to the Arab chronicler al-Maqrīzī the Egyptian authorities of Alexandria arrested in 1215-1216 three thousand of them, quite a plausible figure for that period: see Jacoby, «Les Italiens en Egypte», pp. 82 and 81 respectively.

heavily involved in the provisioning of the crusader forces besieging Antioch, and in the following decade Cypriot crafts supplied victuals to the Franks besieging the Lebanese city of Tripoli.[213] Numerous Byzantine merchants and vessels conducted trade between the Empire's provinces, as well as between the latter and Constantinople. The substantial volume of their activity is implied by various commercial privileges and fiscal exemptions granted by the emperors to some large landowners, monasteries and churches, as well as by other sources[214]. While the Italians clearly expanded their handling of Byzantine goods within Romania, there is no reason to believe that they acquired a dominant role in the region since the late eleventh century.[215] Their approach was selective. They were interested only in medium and long-distance trade in specific goods and their transportation along a number of major sea lanes, while leaving short-distance traffic entirely in Greek hands. Moreover, they could have a not mustered sufficient ships for operation within the complex maritime network of Romania.[216] This brings us to the impact of Italian shipping upon maritime transportation between the Empire and Egypt.

One may wonder whether the tonnage of vessels was a weighty factor in the competition between Italian and Byzantine carriers. The Empire built large warships of the dromon type which had a crew of more than 200 oarsmen and 70 fighting personnel.[217] As for western warships, it is noteworthy that according to Anna Comnena a large three-mast pirate vessel with 200 rowers was hired in 1096 by a Norman prince for the transport of troops from Italy across the Adriatic.[218] These were exceptionally large crafts which, however, did not carry goods. The twelfth century witnessed an increase in the construction of large mercantile vessels in the West, furthered by the transfer of military

---

213. See J. France, *Victory in the East. A Military History of the First Crusade*, Cambridge 1994, pp. 209-210, 236-237; Lilie, *Byzantium and the Crusader States*, pp. 32-33; Galatariotou, *The Making of a Saint*, pp. 47-48.

214. See Harvey, *Economic Expansion*, pp. 236-241. There is yet no comprehensive study of Byzantine commercial shipping. Makris, *Studien zur byzantinischen Schiffahrt*, deals only with some aspects of that topic at a later period and only incidentally refers to the centuries preceding the Fourth Crusade.

215. As argued by Malamut, *Les îles de l'Empire byzantin*, II, p. 438, who speaks of «la mainmise des marchands étrangers». On Crete and Cyprus, see below.

216. On the other hand, manpower was not an obstacle since local sailors could be hired. For later evidence in this respect, see Makris, *Studien zur byzantinischen Schiffahrt*, pp. 118-124.

217. See V. Christides, «Two Parallel Naval Guides of the Tenth Century: Qudama's Documend and Leo VI's Naumachia: A Study on Byzantine and Moslem Naval Preparedness», *Graeca-Arabica* 1 (1982), 84-85.

218. Anne Comnène, *Alexiade*, chap. 10, par. 8, ed. B. Leib, Paris 1937-1945, II, p. 215.

forces, horses and equipment for the crusades, in addition to numerous pilgrims to and from the Holy Land, as well as the conveyance of bulky and heavy commodities such as timber, iron and other metals, as well as alum and grain across the Mediterranean. Western large ships appear to have been more numerous than Muslim or Byzantine ones by the second half of that period.[219] The large three-mast craft owned by the Venetian Romano Mairano was one the largest ships sailing in the Mediterranean in 1171, when it arrived in Constantinople. Although sold to the imperial treasury, it managed to escape after the arrest of the Venetians in the Empire ordered by Manuel I.[220] In 1173 it was scheduled to carry some 450 metric tons of timber from Venice to Egypt, and would have returned with a large cargo of alum and other commodities.[221]

However, it is the nature of the goods moved from one port to another and their destinations that determined the extent to which larger ships offered a possible advantage to Italian traders and carriers over their Byzantine and Muslim counterparts. As noted above, costly commodities such as spices and high-quality textiles were important items in Egyptian-Byzantine trade, yet the volume of these goods was small. Nor did the transportation of agricultural and pastoral commodities require large vessels. Al-Makhzūmī mentions around 1170 convoys or a large number of ships, clearly of small tonnage, arriving from Crete to Alexandria with Cretan commodities on board.[222] Twelfth-century and later sources, some of which have been adduced above, illustrate the continuing importance of small and medium-sized boats, on which the bulk of mercantile traffic in the eastern Mediterranean relied. Though later than the period discussed here, a contract of 1306 offers some indication in this respect. It provided for the transportation of some thirty metric tons of

---

219. On Muslim ships: Goitein, *A Mediterranean Society*, I, pp. 215, 305-207, 315, 331-332, with some reservations about large numbers of passengers quoted in Genizah letters; an early eleventh-century Muslim ship supposedly carried some four hundred of them: idem, *Letters of Medieval Jewish Traders*, pp. 39-42; see also Udovitch, «Time, the Sea and Society», pp. 522-523; Pryor, *Commerce, Shipping and Naval Warfare*, pp. 28-29. On Byzantine vessels: H. Antoniadis-Bibicou, *Etudes d'histoire maritime de Byzance. A propos du «thème des Caravisiens»*, Paris 1966, pp. 129-137, dealing with tonnage. On western vessels, see Pryor (as above), pp. 29-31; U. Tucci, «L'impresa marittima: uomini e mezzi», in G. Cracco - G. Ortalli, eds., *Storia di Venezia*, II, *L'età del Comune*, Roma 1995, pp. 627-639.

220. Ioannes Kinnamos, *Epitome rerum ab Ioanne et Alexio Comnenis gestarum*, ed. A. Meineke (Corpus Scriptorum Historiae Byzantinae), Bonn 1836, p. 238, lines 4-19; see also Borsari, *Venezia e Bisanzio*, p. 124 and n. 87, 126.

221. Jacoby, «The Supply of War Materials to Egypt», nn. 50-55. The projected voyage did not take place.

222. See above, n. 130.

Cretan cheese to Cyprus or Cilician Armenia on a ship with a crew of twelve.[223] Even the vessels carrying timber from southern Asia Minor and Cilician Armenia to Egypt in the 1270s were at best medium-sized.[224] The western ship carrying in 1191 or 1192 some 180 metric tons of cheese, apparently from Crete, was much larger. To be sure, the circumstances in which it sailed were exceptional, since the cargo was apparently intended for the numerous crusader forces besieging Acre.[225] Yet it is not excluded that occasionally such ships brought Byzantine products to Egypt. In short, while the larger capacity of western ships was a decisive asset in trans-Mediterranean voyages along an east-west axis, it played only a limited role in exchanges between north and south. It is nevertheless clear that Italian ships were increasingly involved in the transportation of Byzantine passengers and goods along specific navigation routes. A brief look at contemporary developments in the western Mediterranean may prove useful in this respect.

Already by the mid-eleventh century Muslims from that region were sometimes compelled to travel on board Christian ships. By the twelfth century this had become commonplace, as illustrated in various instances. In 1153 Egyptian merchants embarked with wives and children on a Pisan ship leaving Alexandria for a Muslim port. In the 1160s the Jewish traveler Benjamin of Tudela implies that Muslim merchants reache Montpellier on board Genoese and Pisan vessels.[226] From al-Makhzūmi's taxation treatise, compiled in Egypt around 1170, we may gather that Muslims often boarded Italian mercantile vessels.[227] Ibn Jubayr reports that he was among numerous Muslim pilgrims heading for Mecca who left Ceuta for Alexandria on a Genoese ship in 1183. The following year he departed from Acre to Messina on his return voyage on another Genoese craft. After proceeding on two small vessels and overland from Messina to Trapani, he boarded a third Genoese craft bound westward.[228] In 1190 or somewhat earlier a ship from Salerno transporting

223. Venezia, Archivio di Stato, *Notai di Candia*, b. 186, Angelo de Cartura, fol. 28v. This document will be shortly edited by A. M. Stahl, whom I wish to thank for sending me its text.

224. See Jacoby, «The Supply of War Materials to Egypt».

225. For details, see Jacoby, «Byzantine Crete», p. 536.

226. Amari, *I diplomi arabi*, pp. 241-242; Benjamin of Tudela, as above, n. 203, and on the role of Genoese and Pisan ships in transportation, see above, n. 204.

227. See Cahen, *Douanes et commerce*, pp. 269-270, 299.

228. *The Travels of Ibn Jubayr*, pp. 26-29, 326-340, 343-346, 350, 357, 361-362. Interestingly, in Trapani he met two ships, one of which had carried him from Ceuta to Alexandria. Both were heading westward with Muslim pilgrims and merchants on board: *ibid.*, p. 350. Somewhat later he encountered in the port of Favignana, an island to the southwest of

Christian and Muslim merchants was attacked by Pisans. In 1227 a Muslim merchant from Alexandria traveled from Marseilles to Ceuta on a Marseillais ship.[229] In short, on the basis of these and other testimonies it is generally believed that the Italians dominated maritime traffic between Egypt and the Maghreb. It has even been claimed that in the twelfth century they acquired a virtual monopoly along that axis and, in addition, evicted Muslim ships from the sealanes connecting Egypt and the Maghreb to Sicily.[230]

These views, however, require serious qualifications. First, one should discern between the southern sea route following with some variations the northern coast of Africa, an area ruled by Muslim powers, and the northern waterway proceeding from Egypt toward the European shores and then following these westward.[231] There can be no doubt that traders and carriers from Muslim countries opted whenever possible for the shorter, southern route along friendly shores, as illustrated by various Genizah documents. With respect to tonnage, it should be noted that in the eleventh century a large number of relatively small Muslim ships sailed in any given year between Egypt and the Maghreb along the southern route, and there is no reason to believe that any change occured in that pattern in the twelfth century. Large Muslim vessels carrying merchants and cargo or pilgrims were definitely the exception.[232] As for Italian carriers, they followed the northern route, even when sailing to or from Muslim ports or crossing the entire Mediterranean on an east-west axis. This is illustrated by a Genoese contract of 1160 envisaging a journey from Bougie to Alexandria and by the itineraries of Genoese ships recorded by Ibn Jubayr.[233] In short, in the twelfth century we witness a division of the western Mediterranean, the Muslims continuing to dominate traffic along the southern sea route connecting Egypt, the Maghreb and Muslim Spain, while Italian ships established a virtual monopoly along the northern route.

Trapani, another Genoese ship returning from Alexandria with more than two hundred Muslim pilgrims, his fellow-passengers on his outbound voyage from Ceuta: *ibid.*, 362.

229. Favreau, «Die italienische Levante-Piraterie», pp. 505-506; L. Blancard (ed.), *Documents inédits sur le commerce de Marseille au moyen-âge*, Marseille 1884-1885, pp. 18-19.

230. See Goitein, *A Mediterranean Society*, I, pp. 59, 313, 332. On that evolution, with an extreme statement in that respect, see Cahen, *Orient et Occident*, pp. 109, 137-139.

231. On the southern sea route, see the eleventh-century Genizah evidence in Goitein, *A Mediterranean Society*, I, pp. 211-212, 319-320; Udovitch, «Time, the Sea and Society», pp. 510-511 (Table I), 541-545. On both sea lanes, see R. Gertwagen, «Geniza Letters: Maritime Difficulties along the Alexandria-Palermo route», in S. Menache, ed., *Communications in the Jewish Diaspora. The Pre-Modern World*, Leiden 1996, pp. 75-86.

232. See above, n. 219.

233. See above, nn. 161 and 228.

I

The evolution of twelfth-century mercantile shipping in the eastern Mediterranean was strikingly different. Italian, Byzantine and Muslim vessels followed the same major sea routes between the Empire and Egypt, although Byzantine boats occasionally sailed via Cyprus, especially until its conquest by Richard the Lionheart in 1191.[234] The competition between the various maritime nations was therefore fiercer than between Muslim and western vessels in the western Mediterranean. One should distinguish, however, between the Constantinople-Alexandria axis and other sea lanes connecting the Empire's provinces with Egypt, both with respect to the factors determining the nature and evolution of trade and shipping and the Italian impact on Byzantine activity.

While considerations about tonnage and navigation routes should not be neglected, there were also other factors that furthered the expansion of Italian shipping at the expense of Byzantine vessels in the twelfth century. As elsewhere traffic in the eastern Mediterranean was affected by political factors, as well as by the activity of pirates and corsairs, a parennial disease. In particular Muslim ships sailing along the coast of the crusader Levant were in constant danger of being attacked and captured by Christians, even in periods of truce or peace between the Franks and their neighbours. On the other hand, both Muslim and western attacks hampered Byzantine maritime links with Egypt. These suffered especially in periods of tension or open conflict between the Empire on the one hand, Venice, Genoa or Pisa on the other.[235]

Twelfth-century sources reveal that Byzantine and Egyptian subjects alike increasingly depended and relied upon Italian shipping, especially between Constantinople and Egypt. On the whole, Italian carriers offered safer journeys, although not always devoid of danger.[236] Their role is illustrated at several occasions. The Genoese merchant whose letter of c. 1135 has already been mentioned at several occasions planned to board in Alexandria an Italian ship carrying Italian merchants and the ambassadors of the Egyptian caliph to Constantinople.[237] An Egyptian embassy apparently dispatched to Constantinople in 1174 traveled on board a Genoese vessel.[238] In 1192 Byzantine ambassadors and envoys of Saladin sailed together with Byzantine and western merchants from Alexandria to Constantinople on a Venetian ship, which was

234. See above, nn. 51-52, 176.
235. See Favreau, «Die italienische Levante-Piraterie», pp. 461-510.
236. See Jacoby, «Diplomacy, Trade, Shipping and Espionage», pp. 84-85.
237. See above, n. 160.
238. Jacoby, «Diplomacy, Trade, Shipping and Espionage», pp. 86-94.

attacked by Genoese and Pisan pirates.[239] In all these instances the ambassadors' choice of vessels was clearly determined by safety considerations, although in the last case this did not prevent an attack near Rhodes by a fleet of Genoese and Pisan pirates under the command of the Genoese Guglielmo Grasso. To be sure, the sailings just mentioned took place in special circumstances, yet they suggest that Byzantine merchants were thoroughly acquainted with Italian shipping services. We may surmise, therefore, that it was fairly common for them to use them on strictly mercantile voyages or for the dispatch of goods.

Indeed, by increasing their share in trade and shipping between Romania and Egypt the Italians also enhanced their role as middlemen and carriers handling Byzantine goods on behalf of Byzantine traders and producers. In 1111 the Greek Kalopetros Xanthos, a *vestioprates* or merchant of silk garments in Constantinople, entrusted several pieces of silk cloth to the Venetian Enrico Zusto, who was about to sail to Damietta, in return for a fixed sum which ensured him in advance a good profit.[240] Incidentally, the same Venetian merchant invested in 1119 in business between Constantinople and Alexandria, while another member of his family, Pietro, was involved in 1140 in a triangular trade venture between Venice, Constantinople, central Greece and Alexandria.[241] These cases illustrate the integration of Italian middlemen operating between the Empire and Egypt within the broader context of Mediterranean trade. In July 1167 the Greek Michael Anaxioti, like seven Latin merchants, granted a maritime loan to the Venetian Romano Mairano, who was about to leave Constantinople for Alexandria. Anaxioti was promised a profit of forty percent on his investment of fifty hyperpers, which he obtained upon Mairano's return in March 1168.[242] The documents recording the business ventures of the two Greeks of Constantinople just mentioned imply that such deals were by no means exceptional, although no other such cases have been found.[243] They are of considerable interest, since they reveal that

---

239. Letters of Isaac II to Genoa in November 1192 and October 1193 respectively: F. Miklosich et J. Müller, eds., *Acta et diplomata graeca medii aevi sacra et profana*, Wien 1862-1890, III, pp. 37-46 nos. 6-7 (Greek version), and Imperiale di Sant'Angelo, *Codice diplomatico*, III, pp. 78-80, 101-107 (Latin); to Pisa: Müller, *Documenti*, pp. 61-64, 66-67, nos. 38, 41.

240. Lanfranchi, *Famiglia Zusto*, pp. 23-24, no. 6; see also Jacoby, «Silk in Western Byzantium», p. 496.

241. See above, n. 132.

242. *DCV*, I, pp. 201-202, no. 203; see also Borsari, *Venezia e Bisanzio*, pp. 120-121 and n. 73.

243. It is noteworthy that the two cases are recorded in Venetian documents, which again emphasizes the absence of relevant Byzantine documentation.

the operation of Italian middlemen in Byzantine-Egyptian trade was not necessarily detrimental to the interests of the Byzantine merchants who relied upon them.

One may wonder whether Byzantine traders and carriers managed to take advantage of particular twelfth-century political circumstances to maintain their own links with Egypt or even expand them at the expense of their Italian counterparts, at least temporarily. At first glance it would seem that such favorable conditions existed between 1182 and 1192. The full resumption of Venetian trade in the Empire, after its abrupt interruption in 1171, took place only in 1183, some three and a half years before a new formal Venetian-Byzantine agreement was reached in 1187. In addition, Pisan and Genoese activity in the Empire was sharply reduced after the massacre of the Latins in Constantinople in 1182. It was at best intermittent and remained marginal until 1192.[244] The full interruption of western traffic in Egyptian ports from 1187 to the spring of 1192 seems to have presented yet another opportunity for the strengthening of Byzantine trade with Egypt,[245] all the more so since Isaac II and Saladin maintained fairly close relations from 1188 to the autumn of 1192.[246] It is doubtful, however, that Byzantine trade and shipping could benefit from these circumstances, in view of the hostility of Pisa and Genoa toward the Empire from 1182 until the renewal of their formal relations in 1192 and the activity of Pisan and Genoese pirates, both in Byzantine waters and along the Levantine coast.[247] Moreover, it would seem that both after 1171 and 1182 the Italians pursuing their activity in the Empire largely replaced their evicted Italian competitors and fully exploited their position in maritime trade with Egypt. This is for instance illustrated in 1192, when the envoys dispatched by Isaac II to Saladin sailed on a Venetian vessel before the full resumption if Pisan and Genoese activity in the Empire.

The Italian impact on seaborne trade and shipping between the Empire and Egypt was enhanced in the last decade of the twelfth century by several developments, some specific to Romania and others to Egypt. The Byzantine-Venetian agreement of 1187 enabled the renewal of regular Venetian activity in the Empire. It was followed in 1192 by treaties concluded by Emperor Isaac II Angelus with Pisa and Genoa, which provided the merchants of both these

---

244. See Jacoby, «Conrad, Marquis of Montferrat», pp. 220-223, 237, n. 117.

245. See *ibid.*, pp. 217-219; idem, «Les Italiens en Egypte», p. 90.

246. See Lilie, *Byzantium and the Crusader States*, pp. 230-242; Jacoby, «Diplomacy, Trade, Shipping and Espionage», pp. 94-99.

247. See Favreau, «Die italienische Levante-Piraterie», pp. 476-477, 481-483; Lilie, *Handel und Politik*, pp. 304-308.

powers with more extensive tax exemptions and furthered thereby their trade in the Empire.[248] In that same year western traders returned to Egypt, after about four years of absence due to the war between Saladin and the Latins. Their activity was encouraged by that sultan and his successors, they visited Egypt in growing numbers, and several of them extended their stay there beyond a single sailing season. As a result the *funduq*s held by Pisa, Venice and Genoa in Alexandria evolved into full-fledged colonies with a core of stable population, thus affording a more solid base for continuous economic activity.[249] The Pisan Leonardo Fibonacci provides invaluable evidence to this effect in his *Liber abbaci*, a manual of mathematics composed in 1202 that faithfully reflects the realities of contemporary commercial life. An exercise in his work refers to two business partners, one of whom lived for more than five years in Alexandria, while the other resided in Constantinople.[250] The origin of the two western merchants is not stated, yet they were most likely Pisans. Their temporary settlement for several years in the two Mediterranean emporia was obviously aimed at promoting bilateral trade between Egypt and the Empire. Fibonacci's wording suggests that this was not an isolated case. Partnerships like theirs must have further reduced the share of Byzantine and Egyptian merchants and shipping in exchanges between their respective countries.

The Latin conquest of Constantinople and the establishment of the Latin empire in 1204, followed shortly afterwards by the creation of the Venetian maritime empire abruptly altered the geo-political and geo-economic structure of the eastern Mediterranean. These events deprived the Empire of its capital and of extensive territories, resulted in a severe contraction of its economy, and disrupted Byzantine trade with Egypt for some time. The same events also affected the balance of power between the major maritime nations. They enhanced Venice's standing at the expense of its Italian rivals, Genoa and Pisa, both in Constantinople and in Romania at large and ensured it of a dominant position as an intermediary between this region and Egypt until the Byzantine reconquest of the imperial capital in 1261. These developments require an extensive treatment, which cannot be undertaken here.

---

248. See Jacoby, «Conrad, Marquis of Montferrat», pp. 220-223; Jacoby, «Italian Privileges and Trade in Byzantium», pp. 361-368.

249. See Jacoby, «Les Italiens en Egypte», pp. 80-82.

250. B. Boncompagni, ed., *Scritti di Leonardi Pisani, I, Il liber abbaci di Leonardo Pisano*, Roma 1857, pp. 274-276.

V. CONCLUSIONS

The sources illustrating Byzantine trade and shipping with Egypt from the mid-tenth to the early thirteenth century point to the virtually continuous involvement of Byzantine merchants and carriers in that traffic. The nature, intensity and volume of their participation varied from one region of Romania to another, as well as over time. Byzantine seaborne trade with Egypt was increasingly affected by Italian commerce and transportation services since the later eleventh century. It should be stressed, however, that the twelfth-century Italian impact along the Constantinople-Alexandria waterway differed from that felt along other sea lanes connecting the Empire's provinces with Egypt.

The privileged status of the Italians in the Empire, in Egypt, and especially in the crusader states of the Levant provided them a major advantage over Byzantine subjects. In the Levant they engaged in conjunction with local traders and carriers in short and medium-range traffic, as between Alexandria and Acre and, more generally, between the crusader ports of the Levant. As noted above, these served as transit and transshipment stations in the framework of inter-regional trade. The major role of the Italians along the Levantine seaboard furthered their activity in long-distance traffic between Constantinople and Egypt and was one of the decisive factors that enabled them to acquire a dominant function in that framework in the twelfth century.[251]

Trade with Egypt along other sea lanes proceeded within different parameters. The Venetian and Genoese export and transportation of agricultural and pastoral products from the Empire's provinces to Egypt relied on seasonal transit trade and shipping, whether largely or exclusively according to the region. On the one hand that pattern provided an advantage, yet on the other it necessarily limited the scope of the traffic both in time and volume. By contrast, the Byzantine traders and carriers of the provinces, in any event of Crete about which we are better informed, operated continuously in the framework of bilateral exchanges with Egypt, apparently with a larger number though smaller vessels.[252] The Italian impact on twelfth-century Cretan exports appears to have been at best moderate.[253] This assessment, based on contemporary sources, is strengthened by later evidence from the period following

---

251. Cahen, *Orient et Occident*, p. 210, considers that the crusades did not contribute to the expansion of maritime trade. This radical position is convincingly contradicted by the evidence adduced here.

252. Some of the goods obtained in Egypt were re-exported to other destinations.

253. See Jacoby, «Byzantine Crete», pp. 524-540.

the Fourth Crusade. The participation of local traders and vessels in exchanges with Egypt was then quite substantial, despite Venetian rule on the island and the involvement of Venetian and other western settlers in that activity.[254] Although not directly documented, we may assume that the pattern of Italian and local exchanges between Cyprus and Egypt was more or less similar. In sum, one may wonder whether the Italians ever acquired an edge over Byzantine competitors with respect to Crete and Cyprus in the twelfth century. In any event, if such an edge existed, it must have been definitely more limited than along the Constantinople-Alexandria axis.

Whatever its nature and intensity, twelfth-century Italian activity along the various Byzantine-Egyptian waterways benefited from its integration within the broader Mediterranean trade and shipping patterns. The triangular business ventures in which many Italians engaged enabled them flexibility with respect to itineraries, cargoes, passengers and undoubtedly also freight charges, far more than their Byzantine counterparts. The profits they derived could be reinvested in trade and transportation between the Empire and Egypt. Direct Byzantine commercial and maritime activity with Egypt was gradually reduced, possibly in absolute terms, in any event proportionally.[255] The Empire's subjects increasingly sailed on Italian vessels and resorted to Italian middlemen and ship operators, investing in their trade ventures or sending their goods with them. This development was especially pronounced between Constantinople and Egypt.

The impact of the growing Italian involvement in twelfth-century exchanges between the Empire and Egypt was complex. On the microeconomic level, it deprived some Byzantine merchants and carriers of income or reduced their profits. On the other hand, it did not prevent others from pursuing their activity in a profitable way, whether on their own or by integrating within Italian trade and shipping patterns. The Byzantines had become thoroughly familiar with Italian credit, trade and partnership operations.[256] To be sure, on the macro-economic level the Italians diverted toward the West a substantial share of profits deriving from trade and shipping between the Empire and Egypt. However, the increasing volume of economic activity conducted between these two regions, regardless of whether it was in Byzantine,

---

254. See D. Jacoby, «Creta e Venezia nel contesto economico del Mediterraneo orientale sino alla metà del Quattrocento», in G. Ortalli ed., *Venezia e Creta* (Atti del Convegno internazionale di studi, Iraklion-Chanià, 30 settembre - 5 ottobre 1997), Venezia 1998, pp. 95-102.

255. The surviving data is too casual to allow any quantified assessment.

256. See A. E. Laiou, «Byzantium and the Commercial Revolution», in Arnaldi e Cavallo, *Europa medievale e mondo bizantino*, pp. 239-246, 252-253.

Muslim or Italian hands, must have had a rather positive impact on the Empire. Like exchanges between the West and Byzantium, Italian activity contributed to the growth of domestic business and services and enhanced the flow of capital, in any event in specific regions. These developments should be taken into account in any assessment of the economic evolution of twelfth-century Byzantium. They are also essential for an evaluation of the Empire's function within the broader context of the eastern Mediterranean economy.

The is yet one more conclusion of a general nature worthy of particular consideration. The evidence produced above dispels once and for all a stereotype common among modern historians: that of a Byzantine mercantile group devoid of daring and initiative, apprehensive of long voyages, and passively awaiting at home the arrival of merchandise carried by foreigners.[257] In the period examined here Byzantine merchants and ships definitely operated beyond the waters of Romania, in any event in the eastern Mediterranean as far as Egypt.

---

257. The same remark is implied with respect to other regions and shorter journeys by Hendy, «'Byzantium, 1081-1204': the Economy revisited», p. 22.

II

THE SUPPLY OF WAR MATERIALS TO EGYPT
IN THE CRUSADER PERIOD

It is well known that twelfth and thirteenth century Egypt was short
of war materials. By the twelfth century continuous deforestation had
severely reduced its timber resources, and this process was continuing at
a rapid pace as reported by Ibn Mammātī in the 1190s and al-Nābulsī
in the 1240s.[1] Genizah documents from the eleventh century reveal that
Egypt imported precious wood such as teak and ebony from the regions
bordering the Indian Ocean, yet this timber was either too expensive
or inadequate for use in naval and other construction on a large scale.[2]
The country also lacked iron and pitch. Despite some mining in and
around Egypt,[3] iron and steel were imported from India via Aden. These
were quite expensive and considered so precious that in 1139 a Jewish
merchant employed divers from Aden to retrieve a cargo of iron from
a ship foundered at Bāb al-Mandab.[4] Other shipments are mentioned
in two letters written between 1132 and 1149.[5] However, Egypt's main
sources of timber, iron and pitch were located around the Mediterranean.
Its provisioning in these commodities became ever more complex, first
because of the loss of Fāṭimid domination over Ifrīqiya and Sicily and the
establishment of the Frankish states in the Levant and, secondly, because
Egypt's military confrontation with the Christians in the period of the
crusades required growing quantities of these same items.[6] By contrast,

---

[1] Both quoted by Fahmy, *Muslim Sea-Power*, pp. 76–79, 143–147, esp. 145–146.
For a general, though incomplete, background on timber, see M. Lombard, "Arsenaux
et bois de marine dans la Méditerranée musulmane: VIIe-XIe siècles," and "Le bois
dans la Méditerranée musulmane, VIIe-XIe siècles. Un problème cartographié," in
idem, *Espaces et réseaux du haut moyen Age* (Paris-La Haye, 1972), pp. 107–151,
esp. 129–132, and 153–176. Teak was utilized only for some parts of the vessels built
at the shipyard of Fustat: see Lombard, "Arsenaux", pp. 133 and 149, n. 170.

[2] Goitein, *Mediterranean Society*, 4:114, 131: teak; ibid., 4:113, 137, 379: ebony.

[3] A general, yet incomplete background is provided in M. Lombard, *Les métaux
dans l'ancien monde du Ve au XIe siècle* (Paris-La Haye, 1974), pp. 162–165.

[4] S. D. Goitein, "From the Mediterranean to India: Documents on the Trade to
India, South Arabia, and East Africa from the Eleventh and Twelfth Centuries,"
Speculum 29 (1954), pp. 193–194, on the 1090s; Goitein, *Letters*, pp. 187–189: letter
of 1139.

[5] Edited and translated by S. D. Goitein, "From Aden to India. Specimens of the
Correspondence of India Traders of the Twelfth Century," *JESHO* 23(1980): 43–66.

[6] The Frankish states included wooded areas, yet some of these had already been
severely depleted in previous centuries, and there was some iron mining in the vicinity
of Beirut: M.-L. Favreau-Lilie, *Die Italiener im Heiligen Land vom ersten Kreuzzug*

western merchants and carriers enjoyed fairly easy access to them, and in the course of that period acquired supremacy in Mediterranean maritime trade. As a result, Egypt became increasingly dependent upon their services for the delivery of war materials.

This traffic has drawn some attention, though only in passing, within the broader context of Egypt's fiscal system and of its military, political and commercial relations with Christian powers. The relevant evidence is sparse and fragmentary. Nevertheless, with the help of previously overlooked and unpublished sources it seems possible to determine to some extent the sources of timber and iron supplied to Egypt, the means of transportation and navigation networks by which these commodities reached their destination, as well as some of the quantities involved. Various factors affected the flow of these articles, namely diplomatic tensions or wars between Egypt and Christian powers, papal or governmental interferences, and large-scale shipbuilding on the eve of the crusades in the West. Limitations of space prevent any comprehensive treatment of these factors, although they will be mentioned occasionally. The present paper aims at presenting an overview of the supply of war materials to Egypt in the crusader period.

The *diwān al-Khums* was the goverment office dealing with foreign Christian traders arriving in Egyptian ports. After the goods were unloaded they were brought to a state warehouse in the harbor, where they awaited the decision of the authorities regarding their sale.[7] State monopolies on the purchase and sale of various commodities, among them raw materials and foodstuffs, were enforced in Egypt since 1052/1053.[8] Their existence is confirmed indirectly by a Genizah letter sent from Fustat to Alexandria, presumably in the late 1060s, which refers to iron without stating its origin. Interestingly, the letter uses the Hebrew *barzel* instead of the Arabic term. It also refers to an incident involving its transportation and conveys the secrecy surrounding its handling, all of which suggest some illegal practice infringing a state regulation.[9] The state monopolies were administered by the *Matjar* or Trade Office which had branches in Alexandria, Damietta, as well as in Tinnīs, until this city was abandoned and ceased to function as a commercial port in 1192/1193. The *Matjar* purchased incoming cargoes of timber, iron and pitch, commodities that could not be re-exported, and determined the prices it paid for them according to the ratio of supply and demand.[10]

---

bis zum Tode Heinrichs von Champagne (1098–1197) (Amsterdam, 1989), pp. 2–18.

[7] Cahen, *Douanes*, pp. 235–237, 239–240, 242–243, 284; however, in Alexandria the state warehouse was not called *Dār-Malik*, but *Dār Manak*: see correction in Goitein, *Mediterranean Society*, vol. 4, p. 355, n. 134.

[8] Rabie, *Financial System*, p. 92.

[9] Translation and dating by Udovitch, "A Tale of Two Cities," pp. 151–153. See also Goitein, *Letters*, p. 18.

[10] Rabie, *Financial System*, pp. 91–93; Cahen, *Douanes*, pp. 241, 257–262, esp. 259,

II

These sales to the *Matjar* were liable to the payment of duties reaching slightly more than 12.5 percent, much lower than on goods sold for private consumption.[11] There is no evidence concerning the handling of imported arms by the *Matjar*, although these were important articles among those purchased by the state. Occasionally the *Matjar* resold timber and iron at a profit on the open market after ensuring the priority of state needs, especially for naval and military purposes.[12] Generally, however, goods channelled toward private consumption were offered at a *ḥalqa*, a public wholesale auction called *calega* or *galega* in western languages. The *ḥalqa* was conducted by local officials serving at the harbor's *dīwān*, referred to as *doana* or *duganna* in western documents, and entailed the payment of taxes amounting to more than thirty percent.[13] The auctioned goods also included certain varieties and amounts of timber and iron directly offered for private consumption, apparently without passing through the *Matjar*.[14] It is impossible to determine whether such was also the case with the pitch which, according to a Genizah letter, was available in Alexandria in the 1070s or 1080s.[15]

It is clear, that, although imposed, the fluctuating prices paid by the *Matjar* for timber, iron and pitch, combined with low taxes, were sufficiently attractive to encourage importers to pursue their activity. The high level of private demand also ensured good profits, despite higher taxes for sales at the *ḥalqa*. In 1177 Saladin remarked to the Pisans that these commodities were inexpensive in their own city and fetched high prices in Egypt. He added that their sale provided substantial gains to the merchants handling them and at the same time was most helpful to his own country.[16] Some specific commodities available in Egypt provided western merchants with an even more powerful incentive to import war materials. By the eleventh century the main westward flow of spices, aromatics and colorants originating in countries bordering the Indian Ocean had definitively shifted from the Persian Gulf to the Red Sea, and Egypt had established itself as the main supplier of these goods to the Mediterranean region. It also offered frankincense and myrrh coming from the south of the Arabian peninsula. Moreover, Egypt itself produced substantial quantities of alum, a mineral used on

---

n. 1, and translation ibid., 282, 301–303, 310–311. Fluctuating prices are mentioned in the Pisan-Egyptian treaty of 1154: see below, n. 27. Ibn Mammātī hints at them in the late twelfth century: Cahen, "L'alun," p. 435. On Tinnīs, see Lev, *Saladin in Egypt*, pp. 165–166.

[11] In any event, such was the rule since 1173: see below, n. 30.
[12] Rabie, *Financial System*, pp. 92–94.
[13] Cahen, *Douanes*, pp. 240–243, 260–261; Goitein, *Mediterranean Society*, 1:192–195.
[14] Cahen, *Douanes*, pp. 258–259.
[15] Translation and dating by Udovitch, "A Tale of Two Cities," pp. 155–158.
[16] Letter in Amari, *Diplomi*, p. 264.

a large scale in the expanding textile industries of the West and to lesser extent in the preparation of skins and leather in medicine. All the alum produced in Egypt was compulsorily delivered to the *Matjar*, which had a monopoly on its sale. This monopoly yielded both fiscal and financial revenues. According to Ibn Mammātī, writing in the late twelfth century, the *Matjar* used alum to pay two thirds of the amount owed for purchases from western merchants after deducting the taxes to which they were liable.[17] Such payments, however, may have been restricted to Alexandria, where alum was being concentrated for export since the Ayyubid period. Moreover, they may have ceased to be the rule in the first half of the thirteenth century. Indeed, the Venetian-Egyptian treaty of 1208 states that Venetian traders are free to buy the goods they wish and should not be compelled to buy or receive against their will.[18] The Pisan-Egyptian treaty of 1215 explicitly mentions alum in a similar context.[19] One should also take into account that Egypt's ability to impose payments in alum was severely weakened since the 1230s, when the mineral began to be exported from Asia Minor to the West.[20]

Western merchants and carriers used their imports of timber and iron to finance their purchases of oriental goods and alum and to obtain improvements in trading conditions. On the other hand, on various occasions Egypt made their operations and the granting of privileges in its ports conditional upon the supply of these commodities, vital for the strengthening of its naval and land forces and, more generally, of its economy. This pattern of exchanges was based on a subtle interplay between the interests of both sides. The favored treatment enjoyed in Egypt by the merchants and ships from Amalfi since the early Fatimid period until the mid-twelfth century was partly, if not largely, linked to the supply of naval lumber.[21] A document from the reign of the caliph al-Āmir (1101–1130) reports the arrival of timber brought by five Christian merchants, one of them Amalfitan and another Genoese.[22] Its

---

[17] Cahen, "L'alun," pp. 434–440, and for the concentration of alum, esp. p. 435 and n. 16; Rabie, *Financial System*, pp. 82–85. A Venetian document of 1184 mentioning alum *de tercia doane*, "from the third of the customs", seems to refer to that type of payment: *DCV*, no. 345. In 1252 a Pisan refers to a payment in alum by the *dugana* of Alexandria: C. Froux Otten, "Les Pisans en Egypte et à Acre dans la seconde moitié du XIIIe siècle: documents nouveaux", *Bollettino Storico Pisano*, 52 (1983), p. 174, no. II. In the second half of the eleventh century alum was also sold privately to foreign merchants: Goitein, *Mediterranean Society*, 1:45, 153–54.

[18] Confirmation in 1238; the *doana* or *diwān* is explicitly mentioned in 1254: TTh, 2:188, 341, 485. Correct dating of the first document by Heyd, *Histoire*, 1:401–404.

[19] Amari, *Diplomi*, p. 285 par. 7, and p. 288 par. 7.

[20] On these alternative sources, see Cahen, "L'alun," pp. 440–447.

[21] Cahen, *Orient et Occident*, pp. 79–80, 96, 97–98, 109.

[22] S. M. Stern, "An Original Document from the Fatimid Chancery concerning Italian Merchants," in *Studi orientalistici in onore di Giorgio Levi Della Vida* (Roma, 1956), 2:532–534, reprinted in idem, *Coins and Documents from the Medieval Middle*

106

origin is not stated, yet the joint venture of these merchants points to Italy.

Pisa enjoyed a double advantage over Amalfi, which enabled it to become the major western trading partner of Egypt in the first half of the twelfth century and to obtain commercial privileges, as well as a *funduq* in Alexandria prior to 1153.[23] Pisa was closer than its rival to dense and extensive forests located in its hinterland, to which it had easy access, and to centers of iron production both in the region surrounding it and in the island of Elba. Moreover, metalwork and the manufacture of arms were highly developed in Pisa.[24] Western iron metallurgy had made much progress since Antiquity and surpassed that of Muslim countries, "Frankish" swords being particularly appreciated and expensive there.[25] Around 1150 the Arab geographer Zuhrī referred to the large consignments of timber exported from Pisa and to the manufacture of excellent swords in that city. He also remarked that Pisan ships were more numerous in the harbor of Alexandria than those of any other nation.[26] The Pisan-Egyptian treaty of 1154 confirms that Pisans were bringing timber, iron and pitch to Alexandria.[27] Two years later King Baldwin III of Jerusalem granted various privileges to the Pisans active in his kingdom, except to those who were found shipping these commodities, as well as arms, to Egypt.[28] Pisa did not promise to suppress that traffic, and there is good reason to believe that it was pursued with the connivance of the Pisan authorities. Occasionally, though, Egyptian rulers had to offer some additional incentives or exert some pressure to that effect.

This policy is well illustrated by the Egyptian-Pisan treaty of 1154, which distinguishes between Pisans settled in the Frankish states or supporting them in periods of war and others who would continue to enjoy their customary privileges in Egypt.[29] In 1173 Saladin lowered the duties

East (London, 1986), no. V.

[23] Jacoby, "Italiens en Egypte," p. 78.

[24] Wood: Schaube, *Handelsgeschichte*, pp. 628–629, and Herlihy, *Pisa*, pp. 22–25, 31; iron and metalworking: ibid., pp. 26, 128–134, 143–144, 166–167; Sprandel, *Eisengewerbe*, pp. 76–77, 88, 101–102, 105–106. There were numerous metal workers in Pisa: E. Salvatori, *La popolazione pisana nel Duecento. Il patto di alleanza di Pisa con Siena, Pistoia e Poggibonsi del 1228* (Pisa, 1994), pp. 162–167.

[25] They were still very expensive in thirteenth century Egypt: Cahen, *Orient et Occident*, pp. 62–63.

[26] M. Hadj-Sadok, ed., "Kitāb al-Dja'rāfiyya. Mappemonde du calife al-Ma'mūn, reproduite par Fazārī (IIIe/IXe s.), rééditée et commentée par Zuhrī (VIe/XIIe s.)," *Bulletin d'études orientales*, 21(1968), p. 229 par. 202, and for the dating, ibid., p. 25.

[27] Amari, *Diplomi*, pp. 241–249, esp. 243, nos. II-III; correct dating by Heyd, *Histoire*, 1:394, n. 1. The price was fixed *sicuti valet in illa hora*, "as it is worth at that time."

[28] G. Müller, ed., *Documenti sulle relazioni delle città toscane coll'Oriente cristiano e coi Turchi fino all'anno MDXXXI* (Firenze, 1879), pp. 6–7, no. V.

[29] Amari, *Diplomi*, pp. 253, 285 par. 4.

on Pisan imports of timber, iron and pitch or else restored the customary
rate, and the Pisans undertook to deliver these commodities in addition
to arms, as they had done in the past.[30] We have noted that in 1177
Saladin reminded the Pisans of the substantial profits yielded by this
activity.[31] To be sure, in 1207 the Pisan ambassador to Sultan al-Malik
al-ʿĀdil was instructed not to promise deliveries of timber, iron, pitch or
arms to Egypt. Pisa was apparently reluctant to undertake any formal
obligation in that respect. Yet the growth of Pisan activity in Egypt after 1192, and the privileges it obtained later from Egyptian rulers, imply
the continuation of that traffic.[32]

Venice and Genoa were also involved in the shipping of war materials
to Egypt. The Alps to the north, as far as Istria to the east and the
Appenines around Modena, supplied Venice with large quantities of timber which floated down the rivers and reached the head of the Adriatic.
Iron came to Venice from the area of Brescia in northern Italy and from
Carinthia.[33] Venetian deliveries of war materials to Egypt, including
timber, are suggested by a Venetian ban of 971.[34] The forceful Byzantine
intervention aimed at stopping them, recorded in the Venetian decree,
implies that they were already quite substantial by that time. Venetian
timber exports to Egypt appear to have become a matter of routine by
the twelfth century. They presumably increased after the eviction of the
Venetians from Byzantium in 1171, which led to a growth in Venetian
trade with Egypt. These deliveries may have been among the factors
that prompted Saladin to grant Venice a *funduq* in Alexandria at the
request of Doge Sebastiano Ziani, apparently in 1172.[35] Somewhat later
the doge seems to have engaged in more negotiations with Saladin; his
two envoys spent the winter of 1174–1175 in Alexandria.[36]

---

[30] Ibid., 258, 260; see also Cahen, *Douanes*, p. 261, n. 3.

[31] See above, n. 16.

[32] Amari, *Diplomi*, p. 281; Jacoby, "Italiens en Egypte," pp. 78, 81–82, 84–86. Note
that according to the agreement of 1215, the Pisans would not be compelled to sell
their arms to a Muslim: Amari, *Diplomi*, p. 286 par. 29. The reference is clearly to
arms carried on ships for their own protection.

[33] Timber: Rösch, *Venedig*, pp. 87, 93–94, 103–104, 106, 109, 117–118, and map at
the end of the volume; F. C. Lane, *Venetian Ships and Shipbuilders of the Renaissance* (Baltimore, 1934), pp. 217–219; Schaube, *Handelsgeschichte*, p. 671: timber
from Recanati, south of Ancona. Iron: Sprandel, *Eisengewerbe*, pp. 88, 110–113;
Rösch, *Venedig*, pp. 83, 128.

[34] TTh, 1:26–27. Egypt is not explicitly mentioned in the decree, yet Venetians
traded there around this time: Schaube, *Handelsgeschichte*, pp. 21–22. G. Ortalli,
"Il mercant e lo stato: strutture della Venezia altomedievale", in *Mercati e mercanti
nell'alto medioevo: l'area euroasiatica e l'area mediterranea* (Settimane di studio del
centro italiano sull'alto medioevo, 40), Spoleto, 1993, pp. 105–106.

[35] On trade: Borsari, *Venezia e Bisanzio*, pp. 22, 97–98, 111–112, 119–120, 124–127;
on the *funduq*: Jacoby, "Italiens en Egypte," pp. 78–79. On large deliveries planned
in 1173, see below, n. 50.

[36] On these envoys: Th. F. Madden, "Venice's Hostage Crisis: Diplomatic Ef-

Liguria supplied an abundant amount of timber used in shipbuilding to Genoa and to the seaboard under its domination. In the twelfth century Genoa was dependent upon Pisa for its iron supply, yet later obtained it from northern Italy. It also had a well-developed weapons industry.[37] A Genoese ship was sold at Alexandria in 1146, in all likelihood to the local authorities.[38] Such sales are mentioned in the *Minhāj* of al-Makhzūmī, a fiscal treatise compiled around 1170. The ships were used for sailing or were dismantled for their timber.[39] In 1151 Genoa imposed a ban upon the territories under its domination on the export of arms, oars, as well as boards and timber for naval construction to Muslim countries. The ban was lifted only in those cases where official authorization was granted.[40] The decree implies that this traffic had become quite substantial by that time, and that the shipping of timber not included in the categories just mentioned was permitted. It is unclear to what extent the embargo was effective or how long it remained in force. In any event, by the 1170s it had definitely been lifted. At that time, Saladin and Genoa were on excellent terms. In 1173 a Genoese ship sailing from Alexandria carried alum belonging to Saladin's brother al-ʿĀdil,[41] and apparently in the following year another Genoese craft took an Egyptian envoy to Constantinople.[42]

In a letter of 1174–1175 to the Abbasid Caliph of Baghdad, Saladin rightfully boasted that Venetians, Genoese and Pisans were delivering their arms and riches to him; this clearly included war materials and

---

forts to secure Peace with Byzantium between 1171 and 1184," in E. E. Kittel and Th. F. Madden eds., *Medieval and Renaissance Venice* (Urbana and Chicago, 1999), pp. 98–99. However, the author's hypothesis that they sailed to Alexandria to meet King William II of Sicily, who was known to have planned an attack on that city, is neither backed by the sources nor plausible. Since the envoys left Venice in July or August 1174, they would have learned along the way about the failure of the Sicilian siege of Alexandria, which was lifted on the 1st of August 1174: dating by F. Chalandon, *Histoire de la domination normande en Italie et en Sicile* (Paris, 1907), 2:396–397. If they nevertheless continued their journey to Egypt, the purpose of their mission must have been to meet Saladin and not William II. Besides, one of the envoys was supposed to receive a sum of money in Alexandria in December 1174, which proves that he planned to be there at that time: *DCV*, no. 256.

[37] Schaube, *Handelsgeschichte*, p. 628; Sprandel, *Eisengewerbe*, pp. 87, 88; G. Jehel, *Les Génois en Méditerranée occidentale (fin XIᵉ - début XIVᵉ siècle). Ebauche d'une stratégie pour un empire* (Centre d'Histoire des Sociétés. Université de Picardie) (Amiens–Paris, 1993), pp. 256–262, 351.

[38] This sale was recorded in a verdict of January 1147: Schaube, *Handelsgeschichte*, p. 148.

[39] Cahen, *Douanes*, pp. 263, 284.

[40] *CDG*, 1:274, no. 224; new ed. by A. Rovere, *I Libri Iurium della Repubblica di Genova*, I/1 (Fonti per la storia della Liguria, II) (Genova, 1992), p. 223, no. 151.

[41] Amari, *Diplomi*, pp. 262–263, nos. VIII and IX; Cahen, *Orient et Occident*, p. 146.

[42] Jacoby, "Diplomacy," pp. 91–92.

occasionally ships.[43] Saladin's claim is confirmed in various ways. Ibn al-Ṭuwayr, who served as a high official in Egypt at the end of the Fatimid period, reports the existence of stocks of Frankish arms in the caliph's palace, and large shields apparently of western origin are attested in Saladin's armies.[44] At a church council held at Montpellier in 1162, Pope Alexander III apparently prohibited the delivery of arms, naval lumber and iron to the Muslims, and in 1179 he imposed a similar general ban at the Third Lateran Council. These papal decrees clearly imply a substantial traffic in war materials. In 1179 the pope also threatened those serving as pilots on Muslim vessels with severe punishments.[45]

An incident involving a Genoese ship in Byzantine waters some time before 1174 reveals a new aspect of timber supplies to Egypt. Byzantine officials confiscated the vessel and its cargo, which consisted of 1,332 oars, 120 beams and an unspecified number of large boards and small wooden columns.[46] The origin of these articles is not stated, yet we may safely assume that they were purchased along the coast of Asia Minor, possibly in Attaleia or Anṭālyā, a port of call with a hinterland rich in timber situated along the waterway leading to the Frankish Levant and Egypt. Genoese trading in Anṭālyā is attested since 1156.[47] Egypt was the likely destination of the sequestered Genoese ship. The number of oars, more or less sufficient for equipping ten galleys, rules out the Frankish states, where shipwrights seem to have limited their activity to the maintenance and repair of large and medium-sized vessels and built only small crafts.[48] The incident of c. 1174 suggests that by that time some western merchants and vessels were taking advantage of their sailing expeditions along the coast of Asia Minor, whether from Genoa or from Constantinople, to extend the geographic range of their supply network of war materials to Egypt. Incidentally, one may wonder whether in that framework Italian merchants were also bringing

---

[43] Abou Chamah, "Deux Jardins," 4:178.

[44] Cahen, *Orient et Occident*, p. 133.

[45] The decisions of the church council held in 1195 at Montpellier refer to a ban issued there at a similar gathering in 1162, under Pope Alexander III. However, the extant text of the latter council does not contain it: Mansi, *Sacrorum Conciliorum nova et amplissima collectio*, 21:1160, 22:668; for 1179, see ibid., 22:230–231, par. 24.

[46] *CDG*, 2:219, note, col. 1. For the dating of the incident, see Jacoby, "Diplomacy," pp. 93–94. The wooden columns were clearly not intended for military or naval use.

[47] See R.-J. Lilie, *Handel und Politik zwischen dem byzantinischen Reich und den italienischen Kommunen Venedig, Pisa und Genua in der Epoche der Komnenen und der Angeloi (1081–1204)* (Amsterdam, 1984), pp. 150–153. On later timber exports from that region, see below.

[48] Oars already appeared in the Genoese decree of 1151: see above, n. 40. Twelfth-century galleys had around 100 to 120 and occasionally up to 140 oarsmen on board: H. C. Krueger, *Navi e proprietà navale a Genova. Seconda metà del sec. XII* (Genova, 1985), p. 163; Pryor, *Geography*, pp. 62, 77. I shall deal elsewhere with shipbuilding in the Frankish states.

iron from Asia Minor and pitch originating in the Black Sea region from Constantinople.[49]

The moving of bulky and heavy items over long maritime distances was most profitable when performed in large quantities. This is well illustrated in March 1173, when Romano Mairano agreed to carry 1,400 trunks "from Verona," presumably fir or larch, and 600 planks of fir wood from Venice to Alexandria.[50] The assignment appears to have been routine, judging by the language of the contract, yet the weight of the cargo was by all means exceptional, since it may have reached around 450 metric tons.[51] In all likelihood it was to be transported on Mairano's three-masted ship, one of the largest vessels sailing in the Mediterranean at that time.[52] Mairano was also entrusted with various sums of money, with which he was supposed to purchase pepper in Alexandria. He carried out these assignments in the following year on board another of his ships. In 1175 he returned once more from Alexandria, this time with alum.[53] Since the evidence regarding his activities is fragmentary, we do not know if during these two years he carried timber to Egypt. In any event, his business operations point to the link existing between the import of war materials to Egypt and the export of spices and alum. Unfortunately it is impossible to assess the number of western

---

[49] Cahen, *Orient et Occident*, p. 111. For more on the origins and exportation of this iron, see below.

[50] *DCV*, no. 248. The contract was cancelled in June 1173, apparently because the timber had not been delivered in May as planned. As a result Mairano used his ship to assist Venice's siege of Ancona, which was already underway: see below, n. 52. Fir and larch from Valsugana floating down the Adige passed along Verona: G. Monticolo e E. Besta, *I capitolari delle arti veneziane sottoposte alla Giustizia Vecchia dalle origini al MCCCXXX* (Roma, 1896–1914), 2:4–6. On fir, see also below, n. 59. Strangely, in 1155 Mairano had carried timber from Venice to Constantinople, although this city enjoyed ample supplies of it:*DCV*, no. 118.

[51] According to the Venetian regulations of 1262, standard planks for naval construction measured between 5.56 m. and 11.13 m. in length and around 0.34 m. in width, depending on the type of wood and its origin: Monticolo e Besta, *I capitolari*, 2:4–7. For other measurements, see below, n. 115. According to my own calculations it appears that the planks must have been fairly small, about 6 m. long, 0.20 m. wide and 0.05 m. deep, thus reaching a volume of 0.06 m³. At the rate of some 850 kg. per cubic meter for fir, among the lightest woods, the plank weighed 51 kg., hence 600 planks amounted to 30.6 metric tons. A trunk of the same length and a diameter of 50 cm. weighed at least six times as much as a plank or 306 kg., hence 1,400 trunks reached 428.4 metric tons. Therefore, the total cargo must have been around 459 tons. On a later shipment of fir, see below, n. 59. One cubic meter of oak, widely utilized in medieval shipbuilding, is heavier since it weighs around one metric ton.

[52] This vessel escaped from Constantinople in March 1171, yet was lost at the siege of Ancona in June 1173: Borsari, *Venezia e Bisanzio*, p. 124 and n. 87. Borsari, however, does not make the connection with the shipping of timber to Egypt. See also above, n. 50.

[53] *DCV*, nos. 261–262, 266. Another cargo of alum exported that same year from Alexandria was at Tyre in January 1176, on its way to Venice:*DCV*, nos. 454–455; the latter document provides the date.

ships carrying timber to Egypt during a single year. Thirty-eight Italian vessels were anchoring in Alexandria in the autumn of 1187, after having been prevented from sailing by Saladin, who was waging war against the Franks.[54] We may safely assume that the number of western ships which visited the Egyptian port in that year was far greater. Even if only some of them carried cargoes of timber smaller than the one mentioned above, the total volume must have been quite substantial.

The activity of western merchants in Egypt expanded after 1192 and throughout the thirteenth century.[55] A Genizah letter from Alexandria dated 1208 reports the arrival of two Venetian ships carrying timber, adding that the news had not yet been confirmed. Whatever the case, it is noteworthy that Venetian shipments of timber were expected precisely in the same year in which a new Egyptian-Venetian agreement was signed.[56] The interest displayed by Jewish merchants in these cargoes implies that at least a part of their contents would be available for private consumption. In 1224, however, Venice prohibited the shipment of war materials to Egypt.[57] The decree was addressed to Venetian citizens and the residents of the Adriatic regions under Venetian domination or control. This included Chioggia to the south-west of Venice, as well as Zara and Ragusa or Dubrovnik on the Dalmatian coast, two cities benefiting from ample supplies of timber and iron from their respective hinterland.[58] Venice enjoined merchants and ship operators to make deposits guaranteeing compliance with the embargo, and vessels smuggling prohibited commodities or suspected of doing so were seized and their cargoes confiscated. Timber is explicitly mentioned in several instances in this context, and fir wood is mentioned in one case.[59] The authorities also sequestered goods, mainly pepper and alum, brought by merchants known to ship, or suspected of shipping, contraband war materials. These merchants sometimes returned from Alexandria on foreign ships, possibly in the hope of evading detection. The type of vessel most frequently recorded in connection with this illegal trade is the *banzonus*, a two-decked, two-masted lateener merchantman with a carrying capacity of 200 to 300 *milliaria* or 94 to 141 metric tons, which was

---

[54] Jacoby, "Conrad," pp. 217–218.

[55] Jacoby, "Italiens en Egypte," pp. 80–82.

[56] Document edited and dated by N. Zeldes, M. Frankel, "Trade with Cicily–Jewish Merchants in Mediterranean Trade in the 12th and 13th Centuries" (Hebrew), *Michael*, 14 (1997), pp. 118–122, no. 4; English translation in S. Simonsohn, *The Jews of Sicily, I, 383–1300*, Leiden, 1997, pp. 442–43, no. 205; see also Goitein, *Mediterranean Society*, 1:301–302. On the treaty of 1208, see above, n. 18.

[57] For what follows: Schaube, *Handelsgeschichte*, pp. 183–185; the relevant evidence appears now in *DMC*, 1:10–169, passim.

[58] Ragusa's trade with Egypt is attested in 1232, 1236 and 1252: TTh, 2:311, 332, 468.

[59] On trunks and fir wood, which was apparently sawed: *DMC*, 1:82 par. 134.

large enough to transport a sizeable cargo of timber.[60] Surprisingly, in one case a *plata* participated in that traffic, although this small two-masted vessel apparently carrying less than 40 metric tons was mainly involved in cabotage and short-distance transportation in the Adriatic and only rarely sailed beyond that region.[61] The embargo does not seem to have covered the shipping of wooden chests or crates used as containers; these materials were inadequate for shipbuilding. The Venetian-Egyptian treaty of 1254 refers to the import duties on such timber.[62]

The evidence regarding the Venetian embargo reveals that its enforcement encountered serious difficulties, and that illegal shipments to Egypt were continuing on a fairly large scale. It is against this background that in July 1226 Venice empowered a Venetian shipowner to police the Adriatic on its behalf and to act decisively against transgressors. The problem, however, was not limited to this region. A few months earlier, in March 1226, Venice had ordered its officials serving in several locations around the eastern Mediterranean to seize and destroy ships carrying timber, iron, pitch or other war materials to Egypt, and to confiscate goods bought there with the proceeds from the latter's sale. Middlemen involved in these practices were to be punished.[63]

These instructions point to a previously unrecorded aspect of Venetian supplies of war materials to Egypt. Not surprisingly, the officials administering the colonies of Coron and Modon in the south-western Peloponnese and Crete or the Venetian outposts in the Frankish Levant were ordered to act, since they were stationed along the navigation routes leading from the Adriatic to Egypt. On the other hand, the dispatch of these instructions to the officials serving in the Venetian outposts of Negroponte or Euboea, Constantinople and elsewhere in the eastern Mediterranean, implies that Venetian merchants were also acquiring war materials for Egypt outside the Adriatic. This was clearly not a recent development connected with attempts to circumvent the embargo, but had been a common practice for some time. Indeed, in February 1221,

---

[60] *SMV*, p. 54 par. 8–9; 121 par. XLVII, figures of between 200 and 300 *milliaria*. See U. Tucci, "La navigazione veneziana nel duecento e nel primo trecento e la sua evoluzione tecnica," in A. Pertusi, ed., *Venezia e il Levante fino al secolo XV (Atti del Convegno internazionale di storia della civiltà veneziana (Venezia, 1968)* (Firenze, 1973), I/ 2:824; Tucci, "L'imprese marittima," pp. 636–637.

[61] For a *plata* with two anchors: Jacoby, "Venetian Anchors," pp. 5–6. I have assessed the approximate deadweight tonnage by taking into account that a Venetian round ship carrying 200 *milliaria* or 94 metric tons had to be fitted with six anchors, while one of 300 *milliaria* was fitted with ten anchors: *SMV*, p. 54 pars. 8–9.

[62] TTh, 2:488. In view of its high cost, wood was used in Egypt only for the packing of a very limited number of goods: Goitein, *Mediterranean Society*, 1:334.

[63] TTh, 2:260–264, and new ed. M. Pozza, *Gli atti originali della cancelleria veneziana, II (1205–1227)* (Ricerche. Collana della Facoltà di Lettere e Filosofia dell'Università di Venezia) (Venezia, 1996), pp. 78–80, no. 21, for March 1226; *DMC*, 1:106–107 par. 195, and 1:186 par. 62, for July 1226.

Pope Honorius III granted the newly elected patriarch of Constantinople, Matthaeus, the right to absolve those who had been selling timber and other prohibited commodities to the Muslims.[64] It is unclear whether the pope was referring to the delivery of war materials to Egypt at that time, i.e., during the Fifth Crusade, which began in May 1218 with the landing of Christian forces near Damietta. In any event, it is likely that even earlier some Venetians based in Constantinople had been loading timber from Asia Minor when sailing to Egypt. This practice recalls the case of the Genoese vessel carrying timber, which was confiscated by the Byzantine authorities c. 1174.[65]

The Venetians' access to timber and iron along the southern coast of Asia Minor was undoubtedly promoted by several agreements concluded by Venice with the Christian Kingdom of Cilician Armenia from 1201,[66] as well as by its treaties with the Seljuk sultans of Rūm. The first of these was presumably signed shortly after Kaikhusraw I (c. 1205–1211) captured Anṭālyā in 1207.[67] At this time the city was the Mediterranean outlet of caravan routes arriving from inner Asia and was visited by Egyptian merchants as well as by Venetian traders and ships. Venice's maritime statutes of 1229 and 1255 mention sailing expeditions between Alexandria and Anṭālyā.[68] This is precisely the period to which the geographer Ibn Saʿīd, who wrote around the mid-thirteenth century, is referring. He reports that timber from the Gulf of Fethiye, west of Anṭālyā and opposite Rhodes, was being exported to Egypt and other regions.[69]

It is noteworthy that the Venetian instructions of 1226 concerning the embargo do not mention the Venetian consul in Alexandria. The reason for this omission is obvious. At that time the consul had no effective way of preventing or even detecting the import of war materials. To be sure, since 1208 Venetian merchants were allowed to sell their goods wherever they chose in Alexandria, if they had not already been sold in

---

[64] A. L. Tautu, ed., *Acta Honorii III (1216–1227) et Gregorii IX (1227–1241) e registris Vaticanis aliisque fontibus* (Pontificia commissio ad redigendum codicem iuris canonici orientalis, 3rd. ser., III) (Vatican City, 1950), pp. 102–103, no. 74.

[65] See above, n. 46.

[66] TTh, 1:381–385 (1201); 2:426–429 (1245); *L'Armeno-veneto. Compendio storico e documenti delle relazioni degli Armeni coi Veneziani. Primo periodo, secoli XIII–IV* (Venezia, 1893), 2:7–10 (1261); TTh, 3:115–118 (1271); correct dating of the second charter by Heyd, *Histoire*, 1:371.

[67] The treaty of 1220, which has been preserved, alludes to earlier treaties: TTh, 2:221–225. See also next note.

[68] C. Cahen, "Le commerce anatolien au début du XIIIe siècle," *Mélanges Louis Halphen* (Paris, 1953), pp. 92–93, 96, repr. in idem, *Turcobyzantina*, no. XII; *SMV*, 60–61 par. 27; 134–135 par. LXX.

[69] Cited by C. Cahen, "Ibn Saʿīd sur l'Asie Mineure seldjuquide," p. 42, repr. in idem, *Turcobyzantina*, no. XI.

the harbor area, as implied by the treaties of 1238 and 1254.[70] However, in order to conceal their activity, those involved in the illegal trade of war materials could finalize the latter's sale with the officials of the *Matjar*, or those in charge of organizing a *ḥalqa*, as soon as they disembarked. As a result the prohibited goods never reached one of the two *funduqs* granted to Venice, in which the merchants were compelled to stay in accordance with the policy of residential segregation imposed by the Egyptian authorities. Nor would the hired guard, who kept watch over stored goods, be in a position to discover contraband goods.[71]

The charter of Baldwin III issued in 1156 to Pisa mentioned above, implies that war materials on the way to Egypt were occasionally discovered on board ships calling at Frankish ports.[72] The instructions of 1226 concerning the embargo addressed to the bailo or official Venetian representative at Acre underscore the function of these ports as transit and trans-shipment stations and the involvement of local middlemen in the transfer of war materials to Egypt. The latter's role is also suggested by a specific case worthy of mention. In August 1228 Venice enjoined the co-owner of a ship to abstain from selling his share of the vessel in a Frankish port, unless authorized by Venetian officials.[73] It was presumably feared that the ship would later be brought to Egypt. Incidentally, the same could have happened with unworked iron and other metals shipped to the Levant. The Venetian maritime statutes of 1233 and 1255, stating that these metals should serve as ballast to enhance the safety of navigation on the eastward journey, suggest that such cargoes were both large and frequent.[74] Thus, paradoxically, the provisioning of the Frankish kingdom of Jerusalem in timber, iron and weapons, aimed at strengthening its military capability against the Muslims, enabled and even furthered the shipping of these same commodities to Egypt.

At the first Church council of Lyons, held in 1245, Pope Innocent IV issued once more the customary ban on the sale of war materials, adding a prohibition against delivering ships to the Muslims or assisting them in the construction of war engines.[75] It is clear that the ban had no effect. However, Baybars' conquests since 1265 heightened western and Frankish concerns about the survival of the crusader states. When Prince Edward, the future King Edward I of England, arrived at Acre in May 1271 he was appalled by the activity of Latin merchants delivering weapons and victuals to Egypt. A Venetian ship was about to leave for

---

[70] TTh, 2:188, 338, 485.
[71] On the *funduqs* and the guard: Jacoby, "Italiens en Egypte," pp. 77, 79–80, 82–83.
[72] See above, p. 106.
[73] *DMC*, 1:157–158 par. 93.
[74] *SMV*, 82 par. VI; 160 par. CIII.
[75] Mansi, *Sacrorum Conciliorum nova et amplissima collectio*, 23:631.

that destination. According to an English chronicler, the prince punished the merchants involved in these operations. More convincingly, the fourteenth century doge Andrea Dandolo reports that the Venetian bailo at Acre, Filippo Belegno, produced charters with which he appeased the prince.[76] The charters issued by the rulers of the kingdom of Jerusalem granted the Venetians complete freedom of trade and did not place any restrictions on their exports to Muslim countries.[77] In addition, Belegno may have relied on a charter of privileges issued by Sultan Baybars I to Venice sometime after he came to power in 1260.[78] This document, which has not survived, must have largely reproduced the clauses of the Egyptian-Venetian treaty of 1254, in which there is no reference to Venetian imports of war materials to Egypt.[79] We do not know whether Venice maintained the embargo attested from 1224 to 1228 or if it was renewed later.[80] In any event, it was not implemented, or at least not effectively, with respect to foreign merchants in 1273.

Indeed, in that year four merchants from Messina bought in Venice iron and timber, which they transferred on a Pisan ship to Alexandria. Oliver of Termes, a commander in the French regiment stationed at Acre, was informed of this operation and sent a letter naming the four merchants to the commander of the port of Messina. The latter, however, failed in his attempt to arrest them upon their return to Sicilian waters in the spring of 1274.[81] The letter suggests that Charles I of Anjou, king of Sicily since 1265, had imposed an embargo on the sale of war materials to Egypt and, therefore, was expected to punish his subjects involved in such operations. Merchants from the Kingdom of Sicily circumvented the embargo in two ways. They purchased war materials elsewhere and conveyed them to Egypt on board foreign vessels, as in the case just adduced, or else pretended that their shipments from the kingdom of Sicily were intended for Acre. In 1272 Pope Gregory X induced Charles I to ensure the delivery of the goods in that port by requesting from returning ships bills of unloading issued by the patriarch of Jerusalem

---

[76] Matthew of Westminster, *Flores Historiarum*, ed. H. R. Luard (Rolls Series, 95) (London, 1890), 3:21; Andrea Dandolo, "Chronica per extensum descripta," ed. E. Pastorello, in *Rerum Italicarum Scriptores*, XII/1 (Bologna, 1938), p. 318.

[77] D. Jacoby, "The Venetian Privileges in the Latin Kingdom of Jerusalem: Twelfth and Thirteenth Century Interpretations and Implementation," in B. Z. Kedar, J. Riley-Smith and R. Hiestand, eds., *Montjoie. Studies in Crusade History in Honour of Hans Eberhard Mayer* (Aldershot, 1997), pp. 155–175.

[78] The charter has not been preserved, yet its delivery is revealed by the Venetian version of a letter sent by Sultan Jaqmāq to Venice in 1442: *DVL*, 2:357, no. 189.

[79] TTh, 2:483–489.

[80] The extant registers of the *Liber Plegiorum* offer daily evidence regarding legal actions taken against the transgressors of official decrees in the years 1224–1229. There are, however, no similar Venetian sources for the remaining thirteenth century.

[81] Filangieri, *I registri*, 11:203–204, no. 79. On Oliver of Termes, see C. Marshall, *Warfare in the Latin East, 1192–1291* (Cambridge, 1992), pp. 80–81.

and the grand-masters of the Hospitallers and the Templars.[82] In August 1274 Charles I extended the embargo to Provence, also under his rule. It would seem, however, that he lifted it there after some time.[83]

We have noted that in 1271 Venetian merchants were continuing to deliver war materials to Egypt via Frankish ports. Middlemen fulfilled important functions in this context. Yet only beginning on 10 July 1281 did the Venetian government take renewed action against these shipments. The Great Council of Venice instructed Venetian citizens and those enjoying Venetian status, including the citizens of Zara and Ragusa, to unload timber and iron shipped to the Levant exclusively at Acre or Tyre. The Venetian officials stationed in these ports were ordered to inspect the goods and determine whether they included any prohibited articles, to inquire about their final destination should re-export be envisaged, and to deliver the appropriate licences. Merchants violating the rules were to be severely punished, whether overseas or in Venice proper, by the confiscation of the goods or fines equal to their value if they had already been sold. It was decided to add these provisions to the set of instructions delivered to officials departing for their posts in Acre, Tyre or Alexandria.[84] Merely nine days later the Great Council of Venice adopted a second decree, which permitted the shipping of wooden chests and boards up to six Venetian feet or around 2.10 m. long to Egypt. The pressure exerted by the exporters of these items had led to a partial relaxation of the embargo.[85] Only the first decree appears in a yet unpublished formulary dated 1284, which contains all the instructions intended for the Venetian consul serving in Alexandria.[86] Once more in June 1285 the Great Council ordered the Venetian officials stationed at Acre to inquire about the illegal export of timber and iron to Egypt and to implement the appropriate measures against those involved in that traffic.[87]

Venetians were also shipping arms to Egypt during these years, as re-

---

[82] See P. V. Claverie, "Un aspect méconnu du pontificat de Grégoire X: les débuts de sa politique orientale (1271–1273)," *Byzantion*, 68 (1998), p. 307, who relies on a MS. of the Bibliothèque Nationale in Paris containing the *Dictamina* of Bérard of Naples (personal communication).

[83] The entry in Filangieri, *I registri*, 11:315, no. 223, is based on A. de Boüard, *Actes et lettres de Charles 1ᵉr roi de Sicile concernant la France (1257–1284)* (Paris, 1926), p. 220, no. 775, which in addition contains the following statement: *Deregistrata quia fracta*, or "scrapped from the register because abolished."

[84] *DMC*, 2:355 par. XV.

[85] *DMC*, 2:72, par. CXVI. This had already been the case in Venice in 971, when the sale of beams, boards and wooden containers up to five feet, or around 1.75m long, was permitted, despite a general embargo on the export of war materials to the Muslims: TTh, 1:26–27.

[86] I am preparing an edition of this document, which has been preserved at the Archivio di Stato in Venice.

[87] *DMC*, 3:111 par. 87.

vealed by the unpublished formulary of 1284 mentioned earlier. Venice's consul in Alexandria was instructed to confiscate any weapons arriving in Egypt on a Venetian vessel, whether shipped by a Venetian or a foreigner, and to question the ships' owners or operators or any other individual he thought adequate under oath in order to discover the identity of the merchants dealing in these articles. He was also ordered to confiscate weapons brought for sale by Venetians arriving on foreign vessels and to act against those who had already sold them in Egypt. Finally, after returning to Venice, he would report who among those violating the embargo had refused to hand over the weapons or to pay the fines. The instructions of 1281 regarding timber and iron and those of 1285 concerning weapons imply that, contrary to the situation in 1226, the Venetian consul was now in a position to exercise some measure of control over incoming Venetian merchants and ships. Indeed, since 1238 a scribe representing the consul was attached to the customs office at the harbor in order to ensure the rights and privileges of Venetian merchants, as well as the possession of their merchandise.[88] This scribe would thus be present at the unloading of the goods, when they were stored in the state's warehouse, and at their sale to the *Matjar* or at a ḥalqa. The Venetian embargo apparently did not affect the relations between Venice and Egypt. Trade between the two countries was intensive in the 1270s and the 1280s,[89] and Venice obtained new privileges from Qalawun in 1288.[90] It would seem that the volume of Venetian contraband in war materials was so large that it induced the first Mamlūk rulers to overlook the official ban.

The policy of the other maritime powers regarding these articles varied. An undated Pisan decree reproduced in the *Breve Pisani Comunis* of 1287 banned the delivery of weapons, unworked or cast iron, sawed or unsawed timber, pitch, hemp or oakum to the Muslims. However, Pisan merchants used Sardinia as a transit station to circumvent the embargo on iron.[91] Another undated decree permitted the sale of "wooden" arms to the Muslims. These were presumably small pieces of wood used in the construction of crossbows, shafts and similar items.[92] There were apparently no official impediments in Marseilles. Two contracts con-

---

[88] TTh, 2:340, 488.

[89] Ashtor, *Levant Trade*, pp. 9–10; Jacoby, "La Venezia d'oltremare," pp. 276–277.

[90] L. de Mas Latrie, *Traités de paix et de commerce et documents divers concernant les relations des Chrétiens et des Arabes de l'Afrique septentrionale au moyen-âge, Suppléments* (Paris, 1872), pp. 81–82, no 6. A reference to Qalawun's charter appeared in 1442: see above, n. 78.

[91] Bonaini, *Statuti*, 1:412–414; new ed. and dating by A. Ghignoli, *I Brevi del Comune e del Popolo di Pisa dell'anno 1287* (Istituto Storico Italiano per il Medioevo, Fonti per la Storia dell'Italia Medievale) (Roma, 1998).

[92] Bonaini, *Statuti*, 1:353. This decree also mentions "false" arms, the nature of which is unclear.

cluded there in 1288 openly deal with shipments of iron to Acre and Alexandria. The latter shipment was possibly delivered via the Frankish port.[93] Such operations must have been customary within the continuous traffic between Marseilles and Egypt.[94] The same may be safely assumed about timber with respect to the Genoese, who were on excellent terms with Baybars, since they regularly brought from the Crimea slaves reinforcing the Mamlūk contingents of the Egyptian army. Genoa apparently concluded an agreement with Baybars in 1275.[95] The treaty of May 1290 with Sultan Qalawun, which has survived, explicitly mentions timber imports liable to the low duty of ten percent.[96] King Jaime I of Aragon and Catalonia encouraged and supported trade between his territories and Egypt since 1258.[97] Montpellier and Narbonne, ruled by Aragon, exported weapons, iron, timber for naval construction and ships to the Muslims. In his letters to these cities Pope Gregory X, on 25 and 26 August 1272, respectively, accused some of their citizens of serving as pilots on the vessels of Muslim pirates or assisting the Muslims in the construction of war engines.[98] It is unclear whether these last activities were indeed taking place or whether the pope was merely repeating a formula used by some of his predecessors. In 1274, under papal pressure, King Jaime I imposed an embargo on the shipping of war materials, horses, wheat and barley to Mamlūk territories. In 1281 his successor Pedro III rejected a request submitted by the town council of Barcelona to relax that embargo.[99] However, the extension of Aragon's rule over Sicily in 1282 resulted in a change in the eastern Mediterranean policy of the kingdom. In 1290 Alfonso III of Aragon promised Qalawun

---

[93] Blancard, *Documents*, 2:436, nos. 51–52 (summaries).

[94] See Heyd, *Histoire*, 1:420–421. Marseilles sent an embassy to Baybars in 1265: Thorau, *Lion of Egypt*, p. 163; its trade with Egypt is also attested in 1278: Blancard, *Documents*, 2:415, no. 14.

[95] Thorau, *Lion of Egypt*, pp. 121–122, 125, 163; Ashtor, *Levant Trade*, pp. 10–12.

[96] S. de Sacy, ed., "Pièces diplomatiques tirées des archives de la république de Gênes," *Notices et extraits des manuscrits de la Bibliothèque du Roi*, 11 (1827), p. 36. On this treaty, see also Holt, *Early Mamlūk Diplomacy*, pp. 141–151. On the origin of the timber, see below.

[97] For more on the years 1258–1268: E. Marco Hierro, *Die byzantinisch-katalanischen Beziehungen im 12. und 13. Jahrhundert unter besonderer Berücksichtigung der Chronik Jakobs I. von Katalonien-Aragon*(Miscellanea Byzantina Monacensia 37) (München, 1996), pp. 222–225, 229–232, 248–251, 371–374.

[98] A. Germain, *Histoire du commerce de Montpellier, antérieurement à l'ouverture du port de Cette* (Montpellier, 1861), 1:266–270, no. LVI, and Claverie, "Un aspect méconnu: 304 (where the first date is erroneous) and n. 95. On the sale of ships, see above, pp. 108, 114, and on assistance to the Muslims, above, p. 114.

[99] A. de Capmany y de Monpalau, *Memorias históricas sobre la marina, comercio y artes de la antigua ciudad de Barcelona*, reedición anotada (Barcelona, 1962), 2/1:41–42, 45–46, nos. 26, 30. Ashtor, *Levant Trade*, pp. 13–14, contends that the embargo was not enforced; more correctly, it was not effectively implemented.

not to hamper the delivery of timber and iron to Egypt, whether carried out by his own subjects or by those of other rulers.[100] The sources examined so far deal mainly with the delivery of war materials from the West within the framework of trans-Mediterranean trade and shipping. Only occasionally do they hint at supplies reaching Egypt from eastern Mediterranean lands. However, Genoese notarial documents drafted at Ayas or Laiazzo during the early Mamlūk period, in 1274, 1277 and 1279, suggest that such supplies were both substantial, continuous, and far more important than it would seem at first glance. Ayas had become the main port of Cilician Armenia and the main Mediterranean outlet of the Asian overland route since around the mid-thirteenth century, in the wake of the Mongol expansion in Asia.[101] The Genoese charters provide invaluable information regarding the origin and nature of the timber and iron sent to Egypt, as well as about the contracts, means of transportation and sale procedures concerning them. They also imply that this traffic had been customary in the preceding period.

In 1266 Baybars demanded that King Hethoum I of Cilician Armenia submit to him and allow his own subjects to trade freely in the king's territory. In return he promised freedom of trade for the latter's subjects in Syria. The Syriac version of the chronicle of Bar Hebraeus refers to foodstuffs, while the Arabic version mentions horses, mules, wheat, barley and iron.[102] It has been argued that the king had prohibited all trade with the Mamlūk territories in order to exert political pressure on the sultan.[103] This hypothesis may be safely discarded, considering Hethoum's fear of an attack by Baybars in these years.[104] Moreover, the Cilician kingdom, its subjects and foreigners trading there would have been adversely affected by such a ban. And, finally, Baybar's request

---

[100] Holt, *Early Mamlūk Diplomacy*, pp. 129–140, esp. 136 par. 13. According to a biography of Qalawun, the ambassadors of the king of Aragon relied on a treaty concluded between Emperor Frederick II and al-Malik al-Kāmil: ibid., 131. The reference is obviously to commercial clauses, yet we do not know whether the treaty also dealt with the export of timber, iron and arms to Egypt, as suggested by Heyd, *Histoire*, 1:407–408.

[101] On Ayas: Heyd, *Histoire*, 2:73–92; Jacoby, "La Venezia d'oltremare," pp. 274–275.

[102] E. A. W. Budge, English trans., *The Chronography of Gregory Abul Faraj* (London, 1932), 1:445. This translation is garbled, since it implies that Baybars was willing to submit to Hethoum. See Ibn al-ʿIbrī, *Taʾrīkh Mukhtaṣar al-duwal*, second edition. Beirut, 1958, p. 285.

[103] R Grousset, *Histoire des croisades et du royaume franc de Jérusalem*, Paris, 1934–1936, 3:632, 634, and, less emphatically, M. Canard, "Le royaume d'Arménie-Cilicie et les Mamelouks jusqu'au traité de 1285," *Revue des Études Arméniennes*, N. S. 4 (1967): 228, n. 49, reprinted in idem, *Byzance et les Musulmans du Proche-Orient*, London, 1973, no. IV.

[104] See R. Amitai-Preiss, *Mongols and Mamlūks. The Mamlūk-Ilkhanid War, 1260–1281* (Cambridge, 1995), pp. 110–111, 116–117.

was apparently not related to particular circumstances, since clauses dealing with freedom of trade were routinely included in all the treaties concluded by the sultan and his successors with the Christian powers of the eastern Mediterranean.[105]

In any event, the Genoese notarial documents clearly prove that in the 1270s there were no impediments preventing the export of war materials from Ayas to Egypt. One of the contracts concerns a ship headed for Damietta or Alexandria, which was to load as much timber as possible either at Caramella or Canamella, a place held by the Templars some 20km north of present-day Iskenderun or Alexandretta, or else at any location along the gulf of Caramella chosen by the merchants involved in the transaction.[106] Another contract deals with the consignment of 25 beams from a variety of oak (*Quercus Robur*), 6 to 7.5m long and around 25cm wide and deep, which was to be delivered at the Templars' wharf at Ayas.[107] A third cargo consisted of 400 beams from another variety of wood, around 5.90m long and around 20cm wide and deep, a cargo weighing at least 80 metric tons.[108] Timber from the Isaurian forests was floated down the river Göksu past Salefo or Seleukeia, modern Silifke, and reached the coast opposite Cyprus. A cargo of 300 planks from that city was to be carried to Damietta on board a ship partly

---

[105] See e.g., the treaties of Baybars with the Hospitallers in 1267 and with Lady Isabel of Beirut in 1269, and the one between Qalawun and King Leo III of Cilician Armenia: Holt, *Early Mamlūk Diplomacy*, p. 40, pars. 27–28; 46, pars. 5–8; 99, par. 5.

[106] Balletto, *Notai*, FdP, no. 60. C. Cahen, *La Syrie du Nord à l'époque des croisades et la principauté franque d'Antioche*, Paris, 1940, pp. 149–50 and 208 n. 8; identifies Canamella with Ḥisn at-Tīnāt, which is more plausible than with Payas as suggested by Hild - Hellenkemper, *Kilikien*, p. 223, s.v. Canamella. I also rely in this respect on a personal communication from Prof. Scott Redford, Georgetown University, who has conducted archeological excatvations in the area. Ḥisn at-Tīnāt is mentioned as a port of embarkation of pine timber for Egypt by the tenth-century Ibn Hauqal, *Kitāb ṣūrat al-arḍ*, second edition, J.H. Kramers (Bibliotheca Geographorum Arabicorum, II), Leiden, 1938, p. 182; *Configuration de la terre (Kitāb ṣūrat al-arḍ)*, translation by J.H. Kramers and G. Wiet (Beyrouth-Paris, 1964), 1:180. Around the mid-twelfth century the Arab geographer Idrīsī also mentions the export of timber from Ḥisn at-Tīnāt, yet without referring to Egypt: P.-A. Jaubert, translation, *La géographie d'Edrisi*, Paris, 1836–1840, 2:132; he seems to quote an earlier source.

[107] Balletto, *Notai*, PdB, no. 64: the beams were between 8 and 10 cubits long and one palm of a *canna* wide and deep. Since the notary was Genoese, the length units were presumably also Genoese. The Genoese cubit used in naval architecture measured three palms or 0.747 m. In 1277 a Genoese notary calls these pieces *barzena*, while in 1274 another one uses the term *barcinarii*: Balletto, *Notai*, PdB, nos. 35, 36, 39, 64, and FdP, nos. 27, 49, 50, 60, 61, 91, 97, 106. Both terms are western renderings of Armenian *barzounag*. This term has not been explained convincingly until now; apparently it referred to a particular type of beam. The Armenian term appears in the Genoese-Armenian treaty of 1288, with its equivalent *barzana* in the official Latin translation: Langlois, *Trésor des chartes*, pp. 155, 159.

[108] Balletto, *Notai*, PdB, no. 39. I have used the weight of fir as basis for my calculations, as above, n. 51.

belonging to a local resident.[109] The largest consignments recorded on a single ship sailing from Ayas to Egypt in the 1270s consisted of 600 beams and 300 planks respectively.[110] The freight rate was always calculated on the basis of one hundred units, while that of iron was determined by weight.[111] In the first decade of the fourteenth century the Venetian Marino Sanudo, who relied on information collected from merchants, pointed to the region west of Silifke, especially Candeloro or modern Alanya and Anṭālyā, as a major source of timber for Egypt.[112] An anonymous Florentine commercial manual, which may be ascribed to the 1320s, reports that large quantities of timber were being carried from Alanya to Damietta and Alexandria.[113] There is good reason to believe that this was already the case in the 1270s.

The notarial documents from Ayas do not refer to masts and yards, yet it is likely that the timber cargoes they record were at least partly intended for shipbuilding. Such was surely the case of two cargoes, the origin and destination of which are not stated. One of the owners of the first cargo was a Pisan shipwright established at Ayas, where shipbuilding is attested at that time.[114] The Genoese charters mention beams whose measurements were shorter than those used in the construction of contemporary large vessels in the West, which suggests that they were either intended for smaller ships or for other purposes.[115] This assump-

---

[109] Balletto, *Notai*, FdP, nos. 32, 86. See also Hild - Hellenkemper, *Kilikien*, p. 284, s.v. Kalykadnos, and pp. 402–405, s.v. Seleukeia.

[110] Balletto, *Notai*, FdP, nos. 61 and 32.

[111] See e.g., Balletto, *Notai*, PdB, no. 35.

[112] Marinus Sanutus, *Liber secretorum fidelium crucis super Terrae Sanctae recuperatione et conservatione*, in J. Bongars, ed., *Gesta Dei per Francos, sive orientalium expeditionum et regni Francorum hierosolomitani historia...* (Hanoviae, 1611), p. 29 (1:4:4).

[113] R.-H. Bautier, "Les relations économiques des Occidentaux avec les pays d'Orient au Moyen Age. Points de vue et documents," in M. Mollat, ed., *Sociétés et compagnies de commerce en Orient et dans l'Océan indien*(= Actes du 8e Congrès international d'histoire maritime, Beyrouth, 1966) (Paris, 1970), p. 317, reprinted in R.-H. Bautier, *Commerce méditerranéen et banquiers italiens au Moyen Age* (Aldershot, 1992), no. IV.

[114] Balletto, *Notai*, FdP, nos. 3 and 37, each refers to a number of *iauroni* of wood, a term hitherto unexplained. The Latin version of the Genoese-Armenian treaty of 1288 mentions a tax of 18 *dirhams* on a *barzana* of timber and 4 *dirhams* on a *janconus*: ed. Langlois, *Trésor des chartes*, p. 159. This last term is explained as a measure of one cubit and is considered equivalent to a quarter of the *barzounag* (ibid., p. 98, 159, n. 9). This is excluded, however, in view of the length of some beams which by far exceed four cubits: see above, n. 107. From a paleographic point of view, *ianconus* and *iavronus* are quite similar, and one could be mistaken for the other. One may wonder whether *iavronus* is not identical with *çavrono*, a particular type of beam recorded in a Venetian trade manual of the 1320s: Stussi, *Zibaldone da Canal*, p. 40, fol. 25v, lines 19–20, and see glossary ibid., p. 141. On shipbuilding at Ayas in the 1270s: S. Velle, "I Genovesi a Laiazzo sulla fine del Duecento," *Saggi e documenti*, III (Civico Istituto Colombiano, Studi e testi, 4) (Genova, 1983), pp. 112–113.

[115] In 1226 the Venetian government ordered sawed oak 18 paces or 31.32 m long for

II

122

tion is enhanced by the sale procedure envisaged, which points to private consumers.[116] In any event, it is obvious that the fragmentary evidence from Ayas examined here reflects neither the entire geographic range, nor the variety or volume of timber exports from southern Asia Minor and Cilician Armenia to Egypt in the 1270s.[117]

Iron was also shipped from Ayas to Egypt in that period, as had presumably been the case earlier. Ore of good quality was extracted in the Taurus mountains of Cilicia and Cappadocia and around Diyarbakır in eastern Turkey.[118] Metalworking appears to have been well developed in Cilician Armenia. In 1274 a Pisan merchant sent 420 cases of iron weighing a total of 38 *cantars* of Acre from Ayas to Damietta. He promised to reimburse the loan he had received within twenty days after the arrival of the ship at destination.[119] The total consignment weighed 8.5 metric tons and, therefore, each case weighed around 20 1/4 kg.[120] A cargo shipped from Ayas to Cyprus in 1277 hints at the nature of the iron sent to Egypt. It contained between 35 and 40 *cantars* or between 7.829 and 8.950 metric tons of unworked or cast iron in large or small chunks. The latter presumably included scrap iron, which recalls the iron, nails and broken nails bought by the *Matjar* around 1170, as reported by al-

the construction of two sailing ships:*DMC*, 1:98 par. 171, and 1:101 par. 178. In 1227 it ordered 25 masts of 13.92m and 25 of 14.79m, in addition to 25 yards of 24.36m and 25 others of 22.62m, all with the proper diameter, which is not stated: *DMC*, 1:181 par. 45. Measurements of beams, masts and yards according to thirteenth century contracts in Genoa and Venice are mentioned by Pryor, "Transportation," p. 107, 118; idem, "The Naval Architecture of Crusader Transport Ships: a Reconstruction of some Archetypes for Round-hulled Sailing Ships, *The Mariner's Mirror* 70 (1984): 181–191, 200–212, 219, 284–290, 375–378. Both studies are reproduced in Pryor, *Commerce*, nos. V and VII, respectively.

[116] See below, p. 123.

[117] The surviving registers cover only a limited period of the two notaries' stay at Ayas, and other notaries were also active there.

[118] C. Cahen, *La Syrie du Nord à l'époque des croisades et la principauté franque d'Antioche* (Paris, 1940), p. 475; Hild-Hellenkemper, pp. 116–117, 188–189; F. Taeschner, ed., *Al-'Umarī's Bericht über Anatolien in seinem Werke Masālik al-abṣār fī mamālik al-amṣār* (Leipzig, 1929), pp. 23–24, for an important mine in the vicinity of Ermenek, inland between Silifke and Alanya, documented in the first half of the fourteenth century and presumably also exploited earlier.

[119] Balletto, *Notai*, FdP, no. 33.

[120] According to Francesco Balducci Pegolotti, *La pratica della mercatura*, ed. A. Evans (Cambridge, Mass., 1936), p. 68, before 1291 the grossweight *cantar* of the *catena* or harbor customs of Acre used for iron was the same as that of Cyprus, and the latter was equivalent to 469 grossweight pounds of Venice: Stussi, *Zibaldone*, p. 55, fol. 34r, lines 18–19; similar rate ibid., p. 56, fol. 34v, lines 12–13. Since this Venetian pound weighed 0.477 kg., the Cypriot *cantar* reached 223.713 kg., and 38 *cantars* equalled c. 8.500 kg. As a result, each case of iron weighed 8,500 kg: 420 = c. 20 1/4 kg. E. Ashtor, "Levantine Weights and Standard Parcels: A Contribution to the Metrology of the Later Middle Ages," *BSOAS* 45 (1982): 479, arrives at a *cantar* of 225.9 or 227 kg.; repr. in idem, *East-West Trade in the Medieval Mediterranean*, ed. B. Z. Kedar (London, 1986), no. II.

Makhzūmī.[121] The same cargo also included ten cases or some 225kg of horse shoes.[122] These apparently came with the nails needed to affix them. It is noteworthy that the ten-year treaty of 1285 concluded between Qalawun and King Leon III of Cilician Armenia stipulated the latter's obligation to deliver 10,000 horse shoes with their nails annually. The first shipment would take place immediately, which implies the existence of large stocks in the Armenian kingdom.[123] Another contract drafted in 1277 mentions the shipment of 40 or more *cantars* or at least 8.950 metric tons of iron from Ayas to the Levantine coast extending from Tortosa (Tarṭūs) to Acre.[124] In 1279 the recipient of a loan invested in iron undertook to sell the merchandise "wherever I shall go" (*quo iturus sum*). This expression implies cabotage along the Levantine coast, presumably as far as Egypt.[125] One cannot exclude the possibility that these two documents, like several others, failed to mention any specific destination in order to conceal direct shipments to Egypt or indirect ones via Frankish ports. Only one of the Genoese charters of the 1270s from Ayas contains direct evidence regarding iron sent to Egypt. We may safely assume, though, that this traffic was conducted on a fairly large scale.

The shipping contracts of the 1270s from Ayas mentioning Egyptian destinations refer to Egypt in general, Damietta or Alexandria, mostly to the former.[126] Those regarding timber stipulate payments in Egyptian currency within a specific period after the *ḥalqa* at Damietta.[127] It is noteworthy that the proceeds from the sale of timber belonging to a Genoese merchant who had died at Damietta were kept at the local *duganna* or harbor customs, in charge of organizing that wholesale.[128] The reference to the *ḥalqa* implies that the timber recorded in our contracts was to be purchased by private consumers. On the other hand,

---

[121] Cahen, *Douanes*, p. 282. I assume that the weight units were those of Acre and Cyprus: see previous note.

[122] Balletto, *Notai*, PdB, no. 46: *ferri grossi et subtilis; capsias* (...) *claponorum de equis*. For the *capsia* or *cassa* of iron as a standard weight and tax unit at Ayas: Stussi, *Zibaldone*, p. 63, fol. 38r, lines 24–25. For its weight, see above, n. 120.

[123] Description by Ibn 'Abd al-Ẓāhir and text of the treaty translated by Holt, *Early Mamlūk Diplomacy*, pp. 94, 99–100. Holt follows E. M. Quatremère, *Histoire des sultans mamlouks de l'Egypte* (Paris, 1837–1845), 2/1:202, n. 1, who defines *taṭābīq* as an iron or a copper plate with a nail used for harnessing or for horse shoes. The contract of 1277 mentioned above removes all doubt regarding the meaning of that term. Incidentally, one and a half case of horse shoes (*de ferris de cavallis*) appears in an inventory compiled in 1307 at the royal chancery of Cilician Armenia:*DVL*, 1:66, no 37.

[124] Balletto, *Notai*, PdB, no. 35.

[125] Ibid., no. 70.

[126] Balletto, *Notai*, FdP, respectively nos. 27, 94; 60; 32, 49, 50, 59, 87, 91, 97, 106, and PdB, no. 88.

[127] Balletto, *Notai*, FdP, nos. 27, 50, 59, 87, 106.

[128] Ibid., no. 97.

there is no reference to *ḥalqa* with respect to the cargo of iron sent to Damietta, as noted earlier; in all likelihood this is because it would be sold to the *Matjar*. Incidentally, the Ayas documents confirm the continuity of some administrative practices recorded by al-Makhzūmī around the 1170s.

Pisans were involved in most shipments to Egypt recorded in the Ayas documents of the 1270s, whether as merchants or as shipowners.[129] They enjoyed especially favorable marketing conditions at Damietta, where they had their own *funduq*.[130] Since most contracts openly state Egypt as a destination, it is unlikely that the Pisan embargo on the sale of war materials to Egypt, recorded in 1287, was operative in the 1270s when Pisa's viscount at Ayas and its consul at Damietta were in a position to monitor the movement of goods and to enforce the ban.[131] The Genoese were also involved in the export of timber and iron from or via Cilician Armenia to Egypt, undoubtedly on a far larger scale than hinted by some of our documents, since that traffic is explicitly mentioned in the Genoese-Armenian treaty of 1288.[132] From the evidence adduced above it is clear that at least some, if not most, of the timber to which the Genoese-Egyptian agreement of 1290 alludes was imported to Egypt around that time from eastern Mediterranean lands.[133]

The important function of Frankish ports and Frankish settlers as intermediaries in the supply of timber, iron and weapons to Egypt is again illustrated in the last years of the Latin Kingdom. Following the fall of Tripoli to Qalawun in April 1289, Pope Nicholas IV proclaimed a total embargo on trade with Egypt in December of that year.[134] This measure met with determined resistance on the part of Frankish middlemen and carriers, whose livelihood largely depended on exchanges with Egypt. They invoked a recent truce with the sultan, that of 1283, which furthered such trade.[135] In the absence of the king, the patriarch of Jerusalem, Nicholas of Hanapes, in office at Acre, acted as virtual head of state in charge of temporal affairs. As such he had a more realistic

---

[129] Balletto, *Notai*, FdP, nos. 27, 32, 33, 50, 60, 61, 86, 87, 91, 94, 106; PdB, nos. 35, 36. Note the Pisan notary leaving on business for Damietta in 1274: Balletto, *Notai*, FdP, nos. 94, 97.

[130] Mentioned after 1215 and attested in 1287: Jacoby, "Italiens en Egypte," p. 82.

[131] For evidence on the Pisan viscount at Ayas and on trade between that port and Egypt in 1264, see Herlihy, *Pisa*, p. 162, n. 3; on the consul attested at Damietta after 1215 and in 1287: Jacoby, "Italiens en Egypte," pp. 80, 84–85, and see also Bonaini, *Statuti*, 1:191. On the embargo, see above, p. 117.

[132] Langlois, *Trésor des chartes*, pp. 155–156 (Armenian), 159–160 (Latin version). Individuals considered Genoese are recorded in Balletto, *Notai*, FdP, nos. 60, 94 and 97.

[133] On the treaty of 1290, see above, p. 117.

[134] Langlois, *Nicholas IV*, pp. 901–902, no. 6789.

[135] Truce in Holt, *Early Mamlūk Diplomacy*, pp. 83–84 pars. 13–15, and pp. 85–86 par. 20.

approach than the pope to the issue of trade with Egypt, and allowed its resumption, except with respect to war materials and horses. There is good reason to believe that the official representatives of Venice and Pisa in the kingdom, who served as members of the council of war assisting the patriarch, decisively contributed to that decision. Pope Nicholas IV was compelled to follow suit. In October 1290 he eased the embargo and permitted the shipment of victuals and other goods to Egypt, barring war materials, in periods of truce.[136] The control of cargoes leaving Acre for Egyptian ports was clearly not effective enough to prevent merchants and ship operators from handling war materials. Viviano de Ginnebaldo was apparently engaged in such trade, as suggested by various notarial charters drafted several years after he had fled from Acre, presumably in 1291, to the Cypriot port of Famagusta. Within the following decade he exported war materials to Egypt, possibly even weapons, despite papal prohibitions. This activity and his fluency in Arabic suggest that he had already engaged in the same lucrative trade prior to 1291.[137]

At first glance it would seem that the treaties concluded by Qalawun with the Templars in 1282, the Latin Kingdom in the following year and Cilician Armenia in 1285, contradict the sultan's efforts to obtain arms. These treaties renewed previous prohibitions against purchasing weapons and military equipment on either side.[138] The purpose of these clauses, however, was to prevent illegal sales from Mamlūk territory to Christians, which occured in the 1280s when an Egyptian vizier sold arms taken from the sultan's stores to the Franks. In addition, both Baybars and Qalawun wanted to prevent the Franks and Cilician Armenians from supplying weapons to disaffected and dissident elements among the population of Muslim Syria.[139]

It is noteworthy that Muslims are not recorded as participants in the import of timber, iron and pitch from Mediterranean ports to Egypt. This may be partly explained by the nature of our documentation, which is overwhelmingly of western origin and, therefore, does not adequately reflect their activities. Yet there were also some decisive factors that severely reduced the share of Muslim traders and ship operators in the handling of war materials or even induced them to abstain from that

---

[136] Langlois, *Nicholas IV*, pp. 641–642, nos. 4402–4403. See also S. Schein, "The Patriarchs of Jerusalem in the Late Thirteenth Century -*Seignors espiritueles et temporeles?*" in B. Z. Kedar, H. E. Mayer, R. C. Smail, eds., *Outremer. Studies in the History of the Crusading Kingdom of Jerusalem, Presented to Joshua Prawer* (Jerusalem, 1982), pp. 301–303.

[137] D. Jacoby, "The Rise of a New Emporium in the Eastern Mediterranean: Famagusta in the Late Thirteenth Century," *Meletai kai hypomnemata, Hidryma archiepiskopou Makariou III*, 1 (Nicosia, 1984), pp. 174–176, repr. in idem, *Studies on the Crusader States and on Venetian Expansion* (Northampton, 1989), no. VIII.

[138] Holt, *Early Mamlūk Diplomacy*, p. 68 par. 6; 82 par. 10; 101, par. 14.

[139] Irwin, "Supply," pp. 80–82.

traffic. These Muslim traders had no access to the latter's sources in the West and faced fierce competition in the eastern Mediterranean from their western and Frankish counterparts, whose carrying capacity was far greater than theirs. Moreover, contrary to the Christians, the Muslims did not enjoy fiscal and commercial privileges in ports of call along the way to Egypt or within that country's borders. And, finally, they were far more vulnerable than their competitors to attacks by Christian ships.

Our survey of the evidence regarding the supply of so-called war materials to Egypt in the period of the crusades calls for some remarks regarding naval activity and the uses of these materials. The Fatimid naval operations of the 1150s along the Levantine coast held by the Franks were carried out by a large number of ships.[140] The successors of the Fatimids had no permanent navy,[141] yet Saladin and Baybars nevertheless initiated intense naval activity. Saladin set out to rebuild the Egyptian navy, which had been partly destroyed in November 1168 when the vizier Shāwar set fire to Fusṭāṭ in order to prevent the city's fall to King Amalric of Jerusalem.[142] He raised the pay of his sailors in 1172.[143] Beginning in 1176 the Egyptian navy engaged in raids against Christian ships on the high seas. The following year Saladin ordered the construction of a fleet, and in 1179–1180 he attacked Acre from the sea. In 1182 thirty galleys participated in a combined sea and land attack against Beirut. His naval operations intensified in the years 1187–1191, when the provisioning of Acre became a priority in his struggle against the Christian forces. He also launched some raids, yet his efforts ultimately ended in failure.[144] However, regardless of the performance of Saladin's navy, the most noteworthy factor for the present discussion is the ongoing construction of ships for the Egyptian navy. The occasional capture of Christian vessels in Levantine waters and others, thanks to the extension of Saladin's rule over North Africa, were not sufficient to offset the losses suffered by the Egyptian naval forces and merchant fleet. Nor was the seizure of planks and shipwrights on board a Christian *batsha* on its way to Acre in 1182–1183, although the planks were utilized and the craftsmen presumably put to work in Egyptian shipyards.[145] The large-scale shipbuilding in Saladin's reign implies the existence of substantial

---

[140] Lev, *State and Society*, pp. 113–114; Pryor, *Geography*, pp. 124–125.

[141] Ayalon, "Mamlūks and Naval Power," pp. 4–7. Yet this was also the case of the major western maritime powers, as rightly noted by Pryor: see previous note.

[142] Ehrenkreutz, "Place of Saladin," p. 103. Lev, *State and Society*, p. 114, speaks of the total destruction of the navy. Yet in the spring of 1169 Saladin sent a naval squadron of six ships on patrol, two of which were captured by a Byzantine fleet: Niketas Choniates, *Historia*, ed. J. A. Van Dieten (Corpus Fontium Historiae Byzantinae, XI/ 1) (Berlin-New York, 1975) 1:161 (V. 4).

[143] Ehrenkreutz, "Place of Saladin," p. 105.

[144] Lev, *Saladin in Egypt*, pp. 168–175. A thorough assessment may be found in Pryor, *Geography*, pp. 125–130.

[145] Abou Chamah, "Deux Jardins," 4:235. Arabic sources use *batsha* as a generic

stocks of lumber and other materials, accumulated in the framework of a deliberate naval policy implemented by the sultan.[146] This is especially obvious in the years 1187–1192, during which western deliveries ceased entirely.[147]

The derisive and derogatory statements of Baybars I about maritime warfare and his contempt for naval crews clearly reflected the mentality of a military society of horsemen, yet they also were derived partly from the realization that he could not challenge the superiority of western navys.[148] Nevertheless, the sultan did not neglect his own navy as an effective weapon in diversionary tactics and in defensive strategy. The arrival of Prince Edward of England and his troops at Acre in May 1271 induced him to order the building of galleys, as well as bridges of boats to cross the Nile from Fusṭāṭ to al-Jīza. A month later his fleet was ready to sail to Cyprus, a move intended to compel King Hugh III to leave Acre and return to his island. When Baybars learned of the failure of that naval expedition, he wrote to Egypt ordering the construction of twenty more galleys. Late in 1271 or early in 1272 the Sultan, "according to his custom," went to the arsenal to see how the work was proceeding. He sat among the beams and timbers, while the *amīrs* carried loads and the galleys were being assembled. The importance Baybars attached to the operation of his navy is also illustrated by his successful efforts to free the Egyptian pilots captured by the Franks off Limassol, who had been transferred to Acre. In 1273 the accumulating information about an impending western attack on Egypt prompted the sultan to pay particular attention to his galleys and to the erection of a large number of mangonels on the walls of Alexandria.[149]

The focus of both medieval sources and modern historians dealing with timber, iron and pitch in Egypt has been on maritime quality lumber and pitch required for its navy and on iron for the manufacture of arms. Yet timber had additional military uses, such as in siege engines, mangonels, crossbows and shafts, while pitch also entered into the preparation of the so-called Greek fire.[150] Moreover, large volumes

---

term for a two-masted sailing ship, and occasionally distinguish between large and ordinary vessels of that type: Lev, *Saladin in Egypt*, pp. 169–170, 180–181. It is impossible, therefore, to draw any conclusion about the volume of the captured cargo. The term *batsha* may stand for western *buzus* or *bucius*, a round-hulled sailing ship: see Tucci, "L'imprese marittima," p. 637.

[146] On other aspects of this policy: Lev, *Saladin in Egypt*, pp. 166–168.

[147] Regular sailing expeditions from western and Frankish ports to Egypt were resumed in the spring of 1192: Jacoby, "Italiens en Egypte," pp. 80–81, and idem, "Conrad," pp. 217–219.

[148] Ayalon, "Mamlūks and Naval Power," pp. 5–6, yet cf. Pryor, *Geography*, pp. 130–134.

[149] Ibn al-Furāt, 1:177, 193–196, 198, 202–203; translation, 2:140, 152–154, 156, 159–160. See also Thorau, *The Lion of Egypt*, pp. 206–208, 221–222.

[150] Some of these uses are outlined in C. Cahen, ed., "Un traité d'armurerie com-

of timber were also needed for non-military purposes. Throughout the period of the crusades we find Egyptian commercial vessels sailing in the Mediterranean, including the early Mamlūk period, despite western supremacy in maritime trade.[151] The memorandum sent by King Henry II of Cyprus to Pope Clement V in 1310–1311 rightly insists on the role of timber in the construction of barks and barges for the Nile traffic, a vital factor in the Egyptian economy.[152] In addition, wooden beams were utilized in the construction of houses, mainly in urban centers. Timber was required especially for building the ceilings of these houses, as well as furnishing them with cupboards, chests, doors, shutters and panelling.[153] Irrigation channels were lined with planks,[154] and timber entered in the construction of hydraulic equipment as well as oil and sugar presses. According to the late-twelfth century Ibn Mammātī, local timber for presses had been rare and very expensive even before his time.[155] It is likely, though, that local wood was used for firing in the extraction of minerals and the production of ceramics, glass and sugar, as well as in heating. Iron was also required for numerous non-military purposes in the form of nails, always in short supply in Egypt, tools for craftsmen, agricultural implements and common objects for daily life.[156] In short, it would be mistaken to assess the importance of timber, iron and pitch for Egypt solely or even mainly in military terms. In fact, in view of their multiple and extensive uses the operation of the entire Egyptian economy heavily depended on their import. It is within this broad context that one should consider the consistent and successful policy of the Egyptian rulers aimed at securing an adequate and continuous flow of these commodities. They implemented this policy with the help of incentives offered to both individual suppliers and Christian powers and of pressure applied upon them.

---

posé pour Saladin," *Bulletin d'Etudes Orientales* 12 (1947–1948), pp. 108–121, 123 (Arabic), 129–144, 146 (French trans.).

[151] Irwin, "Supply," pp. 82–83; Holt, *Early Mamlūk Diplomacy*, pp. 42–43; Thorau, *Lion of Egypt*, p. 221; Heyd, 1:415–416. Various treaties of Baybars and Qalawun with Christian powers refer to merchant vessels from Mamlūk territories: Holt, *Early Mamlūk Diplomacy*, p. 68 par. 7; pp. 83–84 par. 13; p. 101 par. 12; p. 114 pars. 11–12; p. 135 par. 8.

[152] Ed. L. de Mas Latrie, *Histoire de l'île de Chypre sous le règne de la maison de Lusignan* (Paris, 1852–1861), 2:121 par. 5.

[153] Goitein, *Mediterranean Society*, 1:46, 109; 4:105–149, passim. Genizah records from around 1040 mention that sycamore, pine and acacia wood were used in the construction and repair of houses: ibid., 2:435–436 par. 178; in 1243 the Jewish community of Fusṭāṭ was planning to use timber in its possession for the rebuilding of a house: ibid., 2:431 par. 155. Origins are not stated. See also above, p. 102.

[154] See reference cited above, n. 152.

[155] Cited by Fahmy, *Muslim Sea-Power*, p. 145.

[156] On the chronic shortage of nails, see sources in Fahmy, *Muslim Sea-Power*, pp. 81–82, and above, p. 122. Goitein, *Mediterranean Society*, 1:109, deals with blacksmiths who manufactured objects for daily use.

The conjunction of large-scale official and private demand for so-called war materials in Egypt and the shipment of precious oriental goods and alum to the West yielded substantial profits. Christian merchants and ship operators were not willing to forgo this lucrative trade, even at the risk of having their goods occasionally seized or paying heavy fines when the traffic was banned by western or Frankish authorities. These same factors explain the differing and changing attitudes of Christian powers regarding war materials and their apparent lack of determination to enforce effectively the embargoes they themselves decreed. The extension of the Christian supply network of timber and iron to Egypt, especially since the early thirteenth century, may have been partly prompted by attempts to evade such bans. Yet it was also enhanced by growing western awareness of the resources of Asia Minor and Cilician Armenia and the easier access to them, promoted by local rulers. The opening of the overland route from inner Asia to Ayas in the wake of the Mongol conquests added a powerful incentive for the intensification of western trade and shipping along the seaboard extending from Asia Minor to Egypt. Frankish settlers in the region made a decisive contribution to that process, as illustrated especially by the Genoese documents from Ayas examined above.

BIBLIOGRAPHY and ABBREVIATIONS

(Only sources and studies cited more than once are listed below)

Abou Chamah. "Le Livre des Deux Jardins," in *Recueil des historiens des croisades, Historiens orientaux*, IV–V, Paris, 1898–1906.

Amari, M., ed., *I diplomi arabi del R. Archivio Fiorentino*. Firenze, 1863.

Ashtor, E. *Levant Trade in the Later Middle Ages*. Princeton, N.J., 1983.

Ayalon, D. "The Mamlūks and Naval Power - A phase in the Struggle between Islam and Christian Europe." *Proceedings of the Israel Academy of Sciences and Humanities* 1 (1965): 1–12, reprinted in idem, *Studies on the Mamlūks of Egypt*, London, 1977, no. VI.

Balletto, L., ed., *Notai genovesi in Oltremare. Atti rogati a Laiazzo da Federico di Piazzalunga (1274) e Pietro di Bargone (1277, 1279)* (Collana storica di fonti e studi, diretta da G. Pistarino, 53). Genova, 1989 (notary Federico di Piazzalunga = FdP; notary Pietro di Bargone = PdB).

Blancard, L., ed., *Documents inédits sur le commerce de Marseille au moyen-âge*. Marseille, 1884–1885.

Bonaini, F., ed., *Statuti inediti della città di Pisa dal XII al XIV secolo*. Firenze, 1854–1870.

II

130

Borsari, S. *Venezia e Bisanzio nel XII secolo. I rapporti economici.* Venezia 1988.

Cahen, C. *Douanes et commerce dans les ports méditerranéens de l'Egypte médiévale d'après le* Minhādj *d'al-Makhzūmī.* Leiden, 1964.

_____. "L'alun avant Phocée. Un chapitre d'histoire économique islamo-chrétienne au temps des Croisades." *Revue d'histoire économique et sociale* 41 (1963): 433–447, reprinted in idem, *Turcobyzantina*, no. i.

_____. *Orient et Occident au temps des croisades.* Paris 1983.

_____. *Turcobyzantina et Oriens Christianus.* London, 1974.

CDG–
Imperiale di Sant'Angelo, C., ed., *Codice diplomatico della repubblica di Genova dal MCLXIII al MCLXXXX.* Roma, 1936–1942.

Cracco, G. - Ortalli, G., eds., *Storia di Venezia*, II, *L'età del Comune.* Roma, 1995.

DCV–
Morozzo della Rocca, R. - Lombardo, A., eds., *Documenti del commercio veneziano nei secoli XI-XIII.* Torino, 1940.

DMC–
Cessi, R., ed., *Deliberazioni del Maggior Consiglio di Venezia.* Bologna, 1931–1950.

DVL–
Thomas, G. M. et Predelli, R., eds., *Diplomatarium veneto-levantinum.* Venetiis, 1880–1899.

Ehrenkreutz, A. S. "The Place of Saladin in the Naval History of the Mediterranean Sea in the Middle Ages." *Journal of the American Oriental Society* 75 (1955): 100–116.

Fahmy, A. M. *Muslim Sea-Power in the Eastern Mediterranean from the Seventh to the Tenth Century A. D. (Studies in Naval Organisation).* London, 1950.

Filangieri, R. et al., eds., *I registri della cancelleria angioina*, XI. Napoli, 1958.

Goitein, S. D. *A Mediterranean Society. The Jewish Communities of the Arab World as Portrayed in the Documents of the Cairo Geniza.* Berkeley and Los Angeles, 1967–1988.

Goitein, S. D. *Letters of Medieval Jewish Traders.* Princeton, 1973.

Herlihy, D. *Pisa in the Early Renaissance. A Study of Urban Growth.* New Haven, 1958.

Heyd, W. *Histoire du commerce du Levant au moyen âge.* Leipzig, 1885–1886.

Hild, F. und Hellenkemper, H. *Kilikien und Isaurien* (Österreichische Akademie der Wissenschaften, Philosophisch-historische Klasse, Denkschriften, 215 =*Tabula Imperii Byzantini*, 5). Wien, 1990.

Holt, P. M. *Early Mamlūk Diplomacy (1260–1290). Treaties of Baybars and Qalāwūn with Christian Rulers.* Leiden, 1995.

Ibn al-Furāt–
Lyons, U. and Lyons, M. C., eds. and trans., *Ayyubids, Mamlūkes and Crusaders. Selections from the* Tārīkh al-Duwal wa'l-Mulūk *of Ibn al-Furāt. Historical introduction and notes by J. S. C. Riley-Smith.* Cambridge, 1971.

Irwin, R. "The Supply of Money and the Direction of Trade in Thirteenth-Century Syria," in Edbury P. W. and Metcalf D.M., eds., *Coinage in the Latin East. The Fourth Symposium on Coinage and Monetary History* (B.A.R., British Archaeological Reports, International Series, LXXVII). Oxford, 1980, 73–104.

Jacoby, D. "La Venezia d'oltremare nel secondo Duecento," in Cracco - Ortalli, *Storia*, 2:263–299.

_____. "Conrad, Marquis of Montferrat, and the Kingdom of Jerusalem (1187–1192)," in L. Balletto, ed., *Atti del Congresso Internazionale "Dai feudi monferrini e dal Piemonte ai nuovi mondi oltre gli Oceani," Alessandria, 2–6 Aprile1990.* Alessandria, 1993, 187–238, reprinted in idem, *Trade*, no. IV.

_____. "Diplomacy, Trade, Shipping and Espionage between Byzantium and Egypt in the Twelfth Century." in C. Scholz and G. Makris, eds., ΠΟΛΥΠΛΕΥΡΟΣ ΝΟΥΣ *Miscellanea für Peter Schreiner zu seinem 60. Geburtstag.* (Byzantinisch Archiv, Band 19) (München, 2000), pp. 83–102.

_____. "Les Italiens en Egypte aux XIIᵉ et XIIIᵉ siècles: du comptoir à la colonie?" in M. Balard et A. Ducellier, eds., *Coloniser au Moyen Age.* Paris, 1995, 76–89, 102–107 (notes).

_____. *Trade, Commodities and Shipping in the Medieval Mediterranean.* Aldershot, 1997.

_____. "Venetian Anchors for Crusader Acre." *The Mariner's Mirror* 71 (1985): 5–12, reprinted in idem, *Trade*, no. XII.

Langlois, E., ed., *Les registres de Nicholas IV. Recueil des bulles de ce pape.* Paris, 1886–1893.

_____. ed., *Le trésor des chartes d'Arménie ou cartulaire de la chancellerie royale des Roupéniens.* Venise, 1863.

Lev, Y. *Saladin in Egypt.* Leiden, 1999.

_____. *State and Society in Fatimid Egypt.* Leiden, 1991.

Mansi, G. D., ed., *Sacrorum Conciliorum nova et amplissima collectio*, revised ed. by J. P. Martin and L. Petit. Paris-Arnheim-Leipzig, 1901–1927.

Pryor, J. H. *Commerce, Shipping and Naval Warfare in the Medieval Mediterranean.* London, 1987.

_____. *Geography, Technology and War. Studies in the Maritime History of the Mediterranean, 649–1571.* Cambridge, 1988.

——————. "The Transportation of Horses by Sea during the Era of the Crusades: Eight Century to 1285 A.D." *The Mariner's Mirror* 68 (1982): 9–27, 103–125, reprinted in idem, *Commerce*, no. V.

Rabie, H. *The Financial System of Egypt, A.H. 564–741/A.D. 1169–1341*. London, 1972.

Rösch, G. *Venedig und das Reich. Handels- und verkehrspolitische Beziehungen in der deutschen Kaiserzeit*(Bibliothek des Deutschen Historischen Instituts in Rom, 53). Tübingen, 1982.

Schaube, A. *Handelsgeschichte der romanischen Völker des Mittelmeergebiets bis zum Ende der Kreuzzüge.* München, 1906.

SMV –
Predelli, R. - Sacerdoti, A., eds., *Gli statuti marittimi veneziani fino al 1255*. Venezia, 1903.

Sprandel, R. *Das Eisengewerbe im Mittelalter*. Stuttgart 1968.

Stussi, A., ed., *Zibaldone da Canal. Manoscritto mercantile del sec. XIV* (Fonti per la storia di Venezia, Sez. V - Fondi vari). Venezia, 1967.

Thorau, P. *The Lion of Egypt. Sultan Baybars I and the Near East in the Thirteenth Century*. London-New York, 1992.

TTh –
Tafel, G. L. Fr. und Thomas, G. M., eds., *Urkunden zur älteren Handels- und Staatsgeschichte der Republik Venedig*. Wien, 1856–1857.

Tucci, U. "L'impresa marittima: uomini e mezzi," in Cracco - Ortalli, *Storia*, 2:627–659.

Udovitch, A. L. "A Tale of Two Cities: Commercial Relations between Cairo and Alexandria during the Second Half of the Eleventh Century," in Miskimin, H. A., Herlihy, D., Udovitch, A. L. eds., *The Medieval City*. New Haven and London, 1977, 143–162.

III

The Venetian Quarter of Constantinople
from 1082 to 1261[*]

TOPOGRAPHICAL CONSIDERATIONS

Constantinople's topography has been the subject of numerous publications, some of them quite recent. Its reconstruction faces a series of major obstacles, namely the fragmentary nature of the written documentation, erroneous identifications of sites in medieval sources, especially in hagiographic works, faulty Latin transcriptions of Greek place names, the absence of comprehensive archeological surveys of the urban territory, and the lack of systematic excavations. All these factors often prevent the siting of structures mentioned in the sources or the identification of material remains. Paradoxically, the western documentation is sometimes more helpful than Byzantine sources with respect to specific sections of the urban territory. This is especially the case of both official and private charters bearing on the Venetian quarter of Constantinople between 1082 and 1261. Many of them deal with pieces of land and buildings and yield detailed, precise and reliable topographical information on their location and boundaries, some of which can be fairly accurately placed on the ground. To the published or cited documents, not always fully exploited, one should add unedited and overlooked charters. A few dozen of these, drafted during the Latin occupation of Constantinople from 1204 to 1261, deserve particular attention[1]. Since Venice's territory in the city expanded substantially soon after the Latin conquest of 1204, these sources also reveal some hitherto unknown features of the urban texture existing before the Fourth Crusade[2].

* * *

---

[*] Paul Speck has always displayed a vivid interest in the history of Constantinople. It is therefore appropriate to offer him a study devoted to a particular aspect of this topic.

[1] Unpublished documents are cited below according to their location: ASV = Archivio di Stato, Venice, and MP = Mensa Patriarcale, a section of the latter; ASP = Archivio di Stato, Padua. Maltezou, Quartiere, quotes topographical data from a number of unpublished charters; for the sake of convenience, I refer to their respective number in that study, yet base my arguments on their full text. The documents published by TTh contain many faulty versions of place names, corrected in more recent editions also mentioned below.

[2] On the topography of the Venetian quarter, see Brown, Quarter, pp. 74–80; Janin, Constantinople, pp. 247–249, 291f.; Borsari, Venezia, pp. 31–39; Magdalino, Constantinople, pp. 80f. However, none of these studies locates in a satisfactory way the boundaries of the Venetian quarter either before or after the Fourth Crusade. E. Concina, Fondaci. Architettura, arte e mercatura tra Levante, Venezia e Alemagna, Venice 1997, pp. 66–75, relies exclusively on published sources to analyze the quarter's functions, without referring to its boundaries.

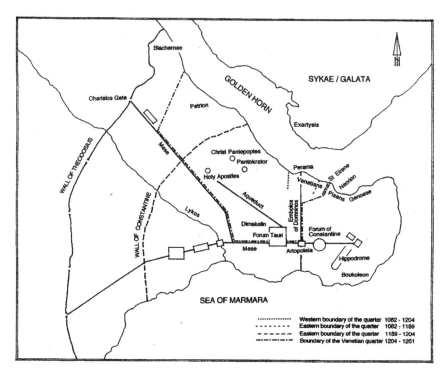

The Venetian quarter of Constantinople was established in 1082 by Emperor Alexios I Komnenos[3]. It was located on the southern shore of the Golden Horn and consisted of two sections, one behind and the other outside the northern city wall, a distinction that should be borne in mind in view of later developments. The first section behind the sea wall included all the houses and *ergasteria* or shops and workshops along the *embolum* or portico street extending from the Ebraïka or former Jewish quarter in the east to Vigla in the west[4]. More precisely, the western boundary of the quarter followed the watercourse descending from the heights of Vigla into the Golden Horn, as illustrated by a charter of 1090[5]. Greek ἔμβολος

---

[3] TTh, I, p. 52; new ed. Pozza-Ravegnani, Trattati, p. 39, § 5. Only Latin translations of the original Greek text have survived.

[4] This is the only possible interpretation of the text, taking into account that Latin has no definite articles, whereas they exist in Greek. There is no basis for the reading of M. E. Martin, The Chrysobull of Alexius I Comnenus to the Venetians and the Early Venetian Quarter in Constantinople, ByzSlav. 39 (1978) 22f., who argues that Alexios I granted separate pieces of property and that the quarter came into being only in 1148. By 1082 the Ebraïka was no more inhabited by the Jewish community, which by imperial order had previously been resettled beyond the Golden Horn in the quarter of Galata-Pera. On the Ebraïka and the Jewish gate, see Jacoby, Quartiers juifs, pp. 168–183.

[5] TTh, I, pp. 55–63, esp. p. 56; new ed. Lanfranchi, S. Giorgio Maggiore, II, no. 69, and Pozza, Atti, pp. 31–36, no. 1, esp. p. 32: *a compreenso saro da Vigla qui percurrit ad Portam Peramae usque ad Iudeca.*

and Latin *embolum* later acquired a wider meaning, both in local popular and in western use, and became synonymous with this section of the Venetian quarter and even with the quarter itself[6]. In 1082 the initial Venetian territory within the city included the church of St Akindynos, already previously in Venetian hands. The will of Giovanni Badoer, drafted in Constantinople in 1148, mentions three more churches, namely S. Marco, S. Nicolò and S. Maria, apparently built by the Venetians themselves. Their names generally appear with the addition of *nostri Embuli* or *de nostro Embulo*[7].

The second section of the Venetian quarter was located beyond the city wall. It included three *scalae*, Greek σκάλαι, a term originally used for jetties or landing stages, which had also acquired a broader meaning. In the context of 1082 the *scalae* were in fact narrow strips of land between the city wall and the shore of the Golden Horn, which for lack of an adequate term are called wharves in this paper[8]. It is likely that at that time they were already partly covered by dwellings, shops, workshops, warehouses, taverns and the offices or tables of merchants, money-changers and notaries, yet it is unclear to what extent[9]. These wharves were obviously contiguous to the territory which Venice held behind the sea wall, yet did not entirely cover its northern flank[10]. The inconsistent use of names for the wharves along the Golden Horn raises serious problems regarding their identification, location and extent. It is clear, though, that the *scala de Drongario*, which faced the Droungarios gate, modern Odun kapı, was the most western wharf among the three obtained by Venice in 1082[11]. Further east and adjacent to it came the Perama wharf, situated close to the *Porta Peramae* located *within* the Venetian quarter[12]. In

---

On the meaning of *sarum*, from Greek σάρρα, a heap of stones in the bed of a torrent, see Maltezou, Quartiere, p. 37f. By extension the Venetians used the term for the torrent itself: see the text just cited and below, n. 23. See also Brown, Quarter, p. 76f.

[6] The popular use is recorded by Ioannes Kinnamos, Epitome, 6, 10; p. 281 (Bonn); on the Venetian use, see below.

[7] Ed. M. Pozza, I Badoer. Una famiglia veneziana dal X al XIII secolo, Padova 1982, pp. 118f. The first two are also mentioned in the chrysobull issued by Manuel I in 1148: see below, n. 18. On these churches, see Borsari, Venezia, pp. 31–33, 36–39.

[8] The narrow meaning appears for instance in Michael Attaleiates, Historia, pp. 277f. (Bonn), who explicitly mentions wooden jetties. A Venetian document of February 1207, wrongly dated in TTh, II, p. 4, distinguishes between *scalae* and *scalaticae*, the latter jetties proper. Version E in Pozza-Ravegnani, Trattati, p. 39, § 5, is more precise in its wording than D, since it clearly distinguishes between the two sections of the quarter.

[9] Around 1100 a Byzantine notary was practicing at the church of St. Eirene of Perama, on the shore of the Golden Horn: see Magdalino, Constantinople, pp. 34f.; on the location of this church, see p. 159. Buildings and economic activity on Venetian wharves are attested for instance in 1148, between 1156 and 1171, in 1169, and in a cadaster compiled in 1240 or 1241: see below, respectively nn. 20, 30, 25 and 16.

[10] See below.

[11] ASV, MP, b. 9, c. 18 = Maltezou, Quartiere, no. 29; also TTh, II, pp. 4f. For the location of the gate, see Brown, Quarter, pp. 76f., and Janin, Constantinople, p. 291, yet with wrong siting on map no. 1.

[12] See text cited above, n. 5. Its mistaken reading has led to the erroneous identification of the *Porta Peramae* with the Jewish gate and to its siting in the eastern part or at the eastern edge of the Venetian quarter: see Brown, Quarter, pp. 78f., and map, p. 74; Janin, Constantinople, pp. 291f., 406. Correct also my own statement about the location in Jacoby, Quartiers juifs, p. 171

1090 Doge Vitale Falier transferred the two wharves and most of the Venetian quarter to the Venetian monastery of S. Giorgio Maggiore[13]. The third and largest wharf obtained by Venice in 1082, the *scala maior*, is also attested under that name in 1184, 1206 and 1208[14]. In 1090 it remained under the state's direct authority, which explains its alternative name, *scala comunis*. A lease of 1242 describes without name a wharf extending from a marble column on the territory of S. Giorgio Maggiore to the *scala comunis*[15]. We may safely identify the former with the Perama wharf, situated to the west of the latter and contiguous to it. The cadaster compiled in 1240 or 1241 for the patriarchate of Grado lists the Droungarios wharf, the Perama wharf and the *scala comunis* in that order, which seems to confirm their siting from west to east[16]. It should be noted in this context that the name Perama was applied both to a large section of the southern shore of the Golden Horn which included the three wharves just mentioned and, in a more restricted sense, to an area close to the narrowest point of it from which barks crossed over to Sykae-Galata. The *Makros Embolos* of Domninos and Maurianos, the main *decumanus* and thoroughfare of the Constantinian city, connected Perama with the commercial center of Constantinople[17].

Manuel I Komnenos enlarged the Venetian quarter in 1148. The outline of the new southern border can neither be reconstructed nor accurately placed on the ground, despite numerous topographic details provided by his chrysobull[18]. There was no change in the original western boundary. Two depositions made more than fifty years later, in February 1201, confirm that it still followed the watercourse descending from the heights of Vigla to the Golden Horn[19]. To the east the section of the Venetian quar-

---

[13] See document cited above, n. 5. Maltezou, Quartiere, p. 34, assumes the existence of a *scala S. Nicolai* in 1090 after mistakenly identifying the monastery of S. Nicolò mentioned in that year as a Venetian monastery in Constantinople, whereas in fact it was S. Nicolò di Lido, to which a small portion of the Venetian quarter had been transferred somewhat earlier. The Venetian church of S. Nicolò in Constantinople was constructed after 1090: see above, p. 155.

[14] ASV, MP, b. 9, cc. 9, 13, 20, and TTh, II, pp. 43f. = Maltezou, Quartiere, respectively nos. 6, 23, 31 and 22.

[15] ASV, MP, b. 9, c. 32: *scalam positam secus mare prope ripam de Perma secundum quod extenditur a sellis comunis usque ad columpnam marmoream que est de iure Gradensis patriarchatus* = Maltezou, Quartiere, no. 46. The words *a sellis* or 'from saddles' are devoid of sense in this topographical context and must be a slip presumably due to the notary Giacomo Viviano, who copied the document from his own register. The original reading was presumably *a scalla* or *a scallis*; it is supported by the cadaster mentioned in the next note.

[16] Property on the first two wharves is listed in the first three sections of the cadaster compiled for the Patriarchate of Grado in 1240 or 1241, the second with the heading *Aput Drongarium*. Faulty and incomplete edition in TTh, II, pp. 8–11; on p. 11, after *scala de Drongario*, add *scala de Perama, prope scalam comunis*. Analysis and new dating of the cadaster in Jacoby, Settlers, pp. 189–195.

[17] The first use of Perama is illustrated in the documents cited above, n. 14, for instance in ASV, MP, b. 9, c. 9: *ad ripam de Perma in scala maiore*. The names of the Perama gate and wharf reflect the second use. Lack of distinction between the two has led to erroneous identifications and locations. On the *decumanus*, see C. Mango, Le développement urbain de Constantinople (IVe–VIIe siècles), (Travaux et mémoires du centre de recherche d'histoire et civilisation de Byzance, Collège de France. Monographie, 2), Paris 1985, p. 31, and Berger, Untersuchungen, pp. 442–447.

[18] TTh, I, pp. 109–113; new ed. Pozza-Ravegnani, Trattati, pp. 70–75. See also Borsari, Venezia, pp. 33f.

[19] ASV, Procuratori di S. Marco de Supra, b. 135. See the excerpt cited by Maltezou, Quartiere, p. 38.

ter behind the city wall bordered on the former Jewish quarter, as it had since 1082. Yet between the wall and the Golden Horn Manuel I added the *scala Sancti Marciani*, located near the hospital bearing that name. This wharf, the fourth to be transferred to Venice, was clearly situated to the east of the three contiguous ones granted by Alexios I in 1082. No other wharf is explicitly mentioned in the emperor's chrysobull of 1148[20], yet according to a document issued in 1156 his grant included *four* wharves. In 1151 or 1152 the Commune leased them to a consortium of seven Venetian *boni homines* for a period of four years. Interestingly, the four wharves were situated between others remaining under the Commune's direct administration and, therefore, were not contiguous[21]. One of them was known by the names Cacegalla, Cuzugaia or Cuzugala. A note added to a document issued in 1184 mentions it as the fifth Venetian wharf[22]. This charter refers to a piece of land on the *scala Cuzugaia* bounded on one side by *Perma* or Perama, a section of the shore of the Golden Horn, and on the other by a watercourse, which cannot have been identical with the one along the quarter's western boundary, adjacent to the Droungarios wharf. Indeed, two documents drafted respectively in 1188 and 1195 mention another torrent, which reached the Jewish wharf[23]. The Cuzugala wharf mentioned in 1184 was thus situated at the eastern edge of the Venetian quarter and contiguous with the former Jewish quarter. Apparently it was already in Venetian hands by 1152[24]. We may safely assume, therefore, that it too was granted by Manuel I in 1148. Somewhat later, in any event before 1169, the Commune transferred the Cuzugala wharf to the Patriarchate of Grado, which leased then its entire waterfront to Romano Mairano for six years[25]. It is unclear how many other wharves were included, if at all. The Patriarchate's ownership of the Cuzugala wharf, abolished by the Byzantine seizure of the Venetian quarter in 1171, was renewed when

---

[20] TTh, I, pp. 191, 194; new ed. Pozza-Ravegnani, Trattati, pp. 72, 74: *scala Sancti Marciani (...) cum universa eius comprehensione et continentia et que in ea sunt, domibus et ergasteriis.* On the *hospitalis Sancti Marciani* and its location, see G. Dagron, Constantinople. Les sanctuaires et l'organisation de la vie religieuse, in: Actes du XIe Congrès international d'archéologie chrétienne, Rome 1989, pp. 1076f.; also Magdalino, Constantinople, pp. 30, 80, 83, who p. 30, n. 78, locates the hospital at the northern end of the main *decumanus* of the Constantinian city. Yet the topographical indications provided by the chrysobull of 1148 clearly point to a site further east.

[21] L. Lanfranchi (ed.), Famiglia Zusto (Fonti per la storia di Venezia, Sez. II: Archivi privati), Venice 1955, no. 24. The consortium obtained *toto eo quod Manuel serenissimus Constantinopolitanus imperator noviter nostro comuni dederat (...) de scalis que adiacent inter nostras scalas*; see also ibid., no. 23. The four wharves had previously been leased to other individuals.

[22] All the names are attested in 1184: DCV, no. 344; ASV, MP, b. 9, cc. 7 and 10 = Maltezou, Quartiere, nos. 5 and 7. The note, which appears on the last document, is cited by Maltezou, ibid., p. 38, n. 48; see also ibid., pp. 37–39.

[23] Lanfranchi, S. Giorgio Maggiore, III, no. 500: *supra sarum qui discurrit in scala que dicitur Ebreaky*; see also no. 581, with similar formulation.

[24] As suggested by an unpublished document of that year referring to the *scala Cacegalla*: see Maltezou, Quartiere, p. 37, n. 41.

[25] DCV, no. 245: *de tota nostra ripa de Constantinopolis et domibus et tabernis.* The only known twelfth-century grant of Venetian state property in Constantinople to the Patriarchate, in 1107, does not include wharves, although one may wonder whether the taverns appearing in that context allude to them: TTh, I, pp. 67–74.

III

the Venetians returned to it twelve years later[26]. It is attested shortly afterwards in 1184[27].

The uncertainty about the number of wharves granted by Manuel I in 1148 and their location is enhanced by a transfer of property to the church of S. Nicolò *de Embulo* made by Doge Vitale Michiel II between his election in 1156 and the events of 1171[28]. A piece of land adjacent to the *scala petrinea Sancti Nicolai*, the stone wharf of S. Nicolò, is documented in December 1183[29], shortly after the Venetians returned to their quarter. At that time, before Byzantium and Venice signed a new treaty in 1187, there was some disagreement between them about the number and extent of the Venetian wharves, clearly those owned by Venice since 1148. Therefore, in 1185 the three ambassadors sent by Doge Orio Malipiero to Constantinople were willing to confirm the grant made to S. Nicolò *de Embulo* before 1171, yet firmly refused to include the wharf, on which twelve houses stood[30]. Whatever the number of wharves transferred by Manuel I, it is only after 1148 that Venice held the entire waterfront covering the northern flank of its territory behind the sea wall. Anna Komnene's definition of the Venetian quarter, ἀπὸ τῆς παλαιᾶς Ἑβραϊκῆς σκάλας μέχρι τῆς καλουμένης Βίγλας, reflects this new situation, rather than the chrysobull of 1082 issued by her father Alexios I[31]. It should be borne in mind that she wrote the *Alexiad* after 1148.

German and French quarters existed in Constantinople before 1189. They consisted of territory behind the sea wall and wharves in their vicinity and must have been contiguous[32]. It was undoubtedly Manuel I who granted premises to the Germans in response to King Conrad III of Germany, either after the emperor's marriage to the king's sister-in-law Bertha of Sulzbach in 1146 or, more likely, during Conrad's sojourn in Constantinople in 1148, which enabled a strengthening of the alliance between them[33]. The French

---

[26] On this dating, see D. Jacoby, Conrad, Marquis of Montferrat, and the Kingdom of Jerusalem (1187–1192), in: L. Balletto (ed.), Atti del Congresso Internazionale "Dai feudi monferrini e dal Piemonte ai nuovi mondi oltre gli Oceani", Alessandria, 2–6 Aprile 1990, Alessandria 1993, p. 221 (rpt. in: D. Jacoby, Trade, Commodities and Shipping in the Medieval Mediterranean, Aldershot 1997, no. IV).

[27] See above, n. 22.

[28] NDCV, no. 35. The recipient of the grant, abbot Domenico Contarini of S. Nicolò di Lido, is attested in 1161: DCV, no. 150. This confirms the identity of the doge and prevents any confusion with a predecessor and namesake.

[29] Lanfranchi, S. Giorgio Maggiore, III, no. 455, of May 1185, with reference to the earlier date.

[30] NDCV, no. 35: *in contentione inter nos et Grecos.*

[31] Anne Comnène, Alexiade, 6, 5, ed. B. Leib, Paris 1937–1945, II, p. 54. In Jacoby, Quartiers juifs, p. 170, I wrongly suggested that this definition was based on the chrysobull of 1082, which is impossible in view of the arguments adduced here. Note that Anna also errs in claiming that Alexios I allotted an annual payment in gold to *all* the churches of Venice.

[32] TTh, I, pp. 208f.; new ed. Pozza-Ravegnani, Trattati, pp. 107f.: *embolos Alemanorum et Francigenarum et maritimas eorum scalas.* While the French could sail on the Mediterranean, the German merchants reached Constantinople by land and, therefore, it is unclear why they needed a wharf.

[33] On their relations, see Magdalino, Manuel I, pp. 38, 42f., 52f. The dating of the grant to the Germans is supported by Conrad's letter of 1142 requesting a piece of land in Constantinople, on which a German church would be constructed; it implies that the premises had not yet been offered at that time: see Otto of Freising, continued by Rahewin, Gesta Frederici seu rectius Cronica, 1, 25; ed. F.-J. Schmale, Darmstadt 1965, pp. 174–176. The church is not mentioned later and was apparently never built.

premises were presumably conceded at the request of Louis VII, who also passed through Constantinople in 1147 in the course of the Second Crusade, possibly because Manuel I sought to ease the strained relations between them[34]. In June 1189 Emperor Isaac II Angelos transferred the little used commercial premises and wharves of the Germans and the French to Venice, in response to the latter's pressure. The yearly fiscal revenue they would yield was estimated at some fifty gold pounds[35]. Since the western boundary of the Venetian quarter remained unchanged from 1082 to 1204, as noted above, the German and French quarters with their respective wharves must have been situated to the east of Venice's territory. Their location is revealed by a charter of February 1207, according to which the German wharf, the most eastern one, bordered on the church of St. Eirene of Perama[36]. This church thus stood outside the city wall on the shore, at the edge of the Pisan quarter, as we learn from a reference to a religious disputation which took place in its vicinity in 1136 and from a Venetian charter of 1212[37]. It was presumably sited close to modern Bahçe kapı[38]. In other words, the German and the French quarters were situated within the former Jewish area separating the Venetian quarter from the Pisan one. It follows that their respective wharves, whose names are not mentioned, covered sections of the Jewish wharf, known both from Anna Komnene and from two Venetian private documents drafted respectively in 1188 and 1195[39]. In any event, the recently suggested location of the German and French quarters to the west of the Venetian quarter is definitely excluded[40].

[34] On these relations, see Magdalino, Manuel I, pp. 47–52.

[35] See above, n. 32.

[36] TTh, II, pp. 4–8, esp. p. 6: *proprietates terrarum cum duabus voltis circa curtem S. Herinis foris muri usque in dictam ecclesiam S. Herinis versus proprietates que quondam fuerunt Alemanorum*; note also Henricus Allemannus, who in 1206 and 1207 resided close to St Eirene: ASV, MP, b. 9, c. 11 = Maltezou, Quartiere, no. 19; TTh, II, pp. 52–54.

[37] Anselm of Havelberg, Dialogi, in PL 188, col. 1163: *in vico qui dicitur Pisanorum juxta ecclesiam Agie Irene*, in the Pisan street or quarter at a place *close* to St. Eirene. Janin, Les églises, p. 107, considers that the passage places St. Eirene *within* the Pisan quarter. His reading, commonly accepted, is clearly excluded for two reasons. First, since the Pisan quarter enjoyed ecclesiastical autonomy, St. Eirene should have been a Pisan church, yet is never mentioned as such; more importantly, if it had been inside the Pisan quarter, the Venetian podestà could not have granted property contiguous to it in 1207, as illustrated in the previous note. For the charter of 1212, see below, n. 56.

[38] On the church, see Janin, Les églises, pp. 106f., and Berger, Untersuchungen, pp. 447–449. Berger's location is imprecise. According to the Vita of Markianos, St. Eirene was so close to the shore that the nearby wharf had to be strengthened to enable its construction: see Berger, Intersuchungen, p. 499. The evidence adduced here, nn. 36 and 56, proves that the church survived the fire of 1203: contra Berger, Untersuchungen, p. 449. On the other hand, both the nearby mosque apparently built in 1188 and the *mitaton* of the Muslim merchants in which it stood were destroyed: see D. Jacoby, Diplomacy, Trade, Shipping and Espionage between Byzantium and Egypt in the Twelfth Century, n. 75, in: G. Makris — C. Scholz (eds.), Festschrift für Peter Schreiner (in press).

[39] See above, p. 158 and p. 157, n. 23.

[40] Suggestion made by Magdalino, Constantinople, p. 80, n. 180, and p. 89, whose siting of St Eirene to the west of the Venetian quarter, ibid., p. 106 (map), is also mistaken. The area requested by Genoa from Manuel I in 1171 may also have been to the east, rather than to the west of the Venetian quarter as hypothesized by Magdalino, ibid., p. 80, n. 181, and p. 89.

The Fourth Crusade and the Latin conquest of Constantinople, completed by 13 April 1204, enabled Venice to enlarge substantially its quarter. About a month before the conquest, in March 1204, Doge Enrico Dandolo on behalf of Venice and the leaders of the crusader armies concluded a treaty, which also dealt with the territorial partition of Constantinople. The future emperor was allotted one quarter of the city, including the Blachernae and Boukoleon palaces situated respectively in its northern and southeastern sections, while the Franks and Venice obtained three eighths each of the urban territory[41]. In fact, after the conquest Venice exercised political authority over its share and the emperor over the other portion of the city. The boundary between the two does not appear in the treaty of March 1204, yet there is good reason to believe that it had already been sketched, if not determined, before the latter's signing. According to Niketas Choniates, within the first five days following the conquest some Venetians residing outside Venice's quarter abandoned their house since it was situated in an area allotted to the Franks[42]. It was thus already known by then how the city would be divided, and the implementation of the partition must have followed promptly[43]. Moreover, from Choniates we may gather that while some Venetians lived outside the quarter before 1204[44], after the conquest the Venetians established themselves exclusively in the enlarged Venetian quarter. This rule applied both to former residents of Constantinople, some of whom were compelled to resettle, as noted earlier, as well as to new immigrants. It follows that transactions in real estate involving the Commune, Venetian ecclesiastical institutions or Venetian individuals in the years following the Latin conquest may offer conclusive evidence regarding the boundary and extent of the enlarged Venetian quarter from 1204 to 1261.

Venice's eastern boundary along the Pisan quarter, established in 1189, remained unchanged from 1204 to 1261. This quarter continued to exist as an autonomous entity, despite the heavy damage it had suffered from the fire of August 1203[45]. Presumably Baldwin I, more likely Henry of Flanders in 1207 renewed Pisa's privileges, which must have included the preservation of the latter's quarter. The privileges were confirmed by Robert of Courtenay, who reigned from March 1221 to January 1228, and in the following month by his sister Mary, who acted as regent of the Empire after his death. Throughout these years successive Pisan *vicecomites* were in charge of their city's interests in Constantinople[46]. To the two churches in the Pisan quarter, S. Nicola and S. Pietro, Pope Innocent III added the Greek monastery of the Holy Saviour τῶν 'Απολογοθετῶν, located outside the Neorion gate and contiguous to a

---

[41] TTh, I, pp. 447, 450.

[42] Nicetas Choniates, Historia, ed. J. A. van Dieten (CFHB XI), Berlin — New York 1975, I, pp. 587–589. Choniates left the city five days after its fall.

[43] It is unlikely that it took place as late as the summer of 1204, during the absence of Emperor Baldwin from Constantinople, as suggested by A. Carile, Partitio terrarum imperii Romanie, Studi Veneziani 7 (1965) 153, who for this dating relies on Robert de Clari, La conquête de Constantinople, ed. Ph. Lauer, Paris 1956, p. 102, § CVII.

[44] As recorded also by Ioannes Kinnamos, Epitome, 6, 10; pp. 280–282 (Bonn).

[45] On the Pisans and their quarter in the twelfth century, see Borsari, Pisani, pp. 59–75; Madden, Fires, pp. 74–76, 93 (map).

[46] Müller, Documenti, pp. 86f., nos. 55–56; Borsari, Rapporti, pp. 479–481.

Pisan wharf[47]. The prior of the Pisan church of S. Pietro, Benenatus, already attested in 1197, before the Fourth Crusade, was still in office in 1223. In 1230 Pope Gregorius IX sent a letter to Caitanus, *prior ecclesiae campi Pisanorum*[48]. These priors managed to uphold the autonomy and rights of the Pisan church within the confines of Pisa's quarter against the attempts of the Latin patriarchs of Constantinople to quash them[49]. Pisa's hold over its quarter was also ensured by its good relations with Venice, illustrated by the treaties the two powers signed in 1206 and 1214[50].

Despite the partition effected soon after the conquest, the issue of the border between the Venetian and imperial sections of the city was not entirely settled. It was raised anew in 1205 with respect to the strip of land between the city wall and the shore of the Golden Horn, which included the *via de Longario*. The existence of this street, apparently beginning at the Droungarios gate, was the outcome of building activity over more than a whole century. Venice claimed property rights over the section of the *via de Longario* and the territory on both its sides within an area extending along the entire northern flank of its pre-1204 quarter[51]. The Venetian position was contested by the imperial side, apparently because it was only partly backed by documents[52]. Venice took advantage of the accession of Emperor Henry of Flanders to the position of *moderator* or regent of the Latin Empire in August 1205 to exert pressure on him. Henry ordered the marshal of the Empire, Geoffroy of Villehardouin, to reach an agreement with the podestà Marino Zeno, as reported by the latter[53]. The Venetian claim was recognized in October 1205[54], as confirmed both directly and indirectly by later evidence. Indeed, land and buildings in the area between the city wall and the Golden Horn were included among the pieces of property which the podestà Marino Zeno transferred to the Patriarchate of Grado in February 1207[55]. In 1212 Doge Pietro Ziani granted to the

---

[47] Müller, Documenti, pp. 48 (Greek), 57 (Latin), no. 34; pp. 84–86, no. 54: *prope campum Pisanorum*; pp. 93f., no. 62. *Campus* appears here in the sense of quarter, as below, n. 59. By 1182 Pisa had several wharves: see Borsari, Pisani, pp. 62–64. See also Janin, Les églises, pp. 573f.

[48] Müller, Documenti, p. 78, no. 47; p. 84, no. 54; p. 93, no. 62; p. 98, no. 67.

[49] See previous note and Borsari, Rapporti, pp. 483–486.

[50] W. Heyd, Histoire du commerce du Levant au moyen âge, Leipzig 1885–1886, I, pp. 289f.; Müller, Documenti, pp. 88–90, no. 57.

[51] *Longario* was apparently a popular western derivation from Greek *Droungarios*. Venice's claim to the street and the latter's location are mentioned in 1231: see below, n. 58. The first three sections of the cadaster compiled in 1240 or 1241 list property on both sides of the street: see above, n. 16.

[52] See below, n. 54.

[53] TTh, II, p. 5: *tam ea omnia que dicta sunt foris muri civitatis (...) nos et Jufredus mariscalcus Imperii, quidem voluntate et ex precepto dom. Henrici imperatoris insimul determinavimus.* Since Henry was crowned emperor on 20 August 1206, he was mentioned as such in this and some later documents dealing with the agreement: see below. However, see the confirmation of Peter of Courtenay in 1217, below, n. 57.

[54] Dating provided by Henry's proclamation of October 1205 that the two sides had reached an agreement, including about Venice's claims to various possessions before 1204 *tam cum scripto quam sine scripto*: TTh, I, pp. 571–574, esp. p. 573; new ed. J. Longnon, Recherches sur la vie de Geoffroy de Villehardouin, suivies du catalogue des actes des Villehardouin, Paris 1939, pp. 191–194, no. 74.

[55] See text cited above, n. 53.

monastery of S. Tommaso dei Borgognoni di Torcello land situated close to St. Eirene of Perama and extending as far as the Pisan quarter, thus within the area annexed in 1189[56]. The agreement of 1205 regarding the *via de Longario* was confirmed by Emperor Peter of Courtenay in 1217, as we may gather from the latter's reference to the understanding reached by Henry of Flanders as *moderator* with the podestà Marino Zeno[57]. Emperor John of Brienne explicitly confirmed it once more in 1231, obviously under Venetian pressure[58].

The imperial and Venetian parties also strongly disagreed for several years about other areas annexed by Venice after the conquest. In 1223 Emperor Robert of Courtenay and the podestà Marino Storlato decided to set up a joint imperial-Venetian commission, which within two years would reach a decision about the respective rights of the two parties regarding the commercial premises held by Latin nations before 1204. During the two year-period Vitale Ferro, a prominent Venetian resident of the city, would be entrusted with all the revenues accruing from the disputed territories and their inhabitants, whether deriving from Venetian or imperial regulations[59]. In fact, several issues were easily solved, as we may gather from the absence of any reference to them in Robert's declaration of February 1224[60]. The emperor recognized Venice's ownership of its quarter within the boundaries existing in 1204, including the German and French premises situated in the former Jewish quarter. This is implied by the preservation of Venice's eastern border of 1189 with the Pisan quarter throughout the Latin period and confirmed by two transactions. In 1258 the monastery of S. Tommaso dei Borgognoni di Torcello leased two pieces of land in the *ruga Alemanorum* to Andrea Scotto, and in 1259 another one adjacent to St Eirene to the widow of Biagio Sirano[61]. Moreover, for obvious reasons there was no dispute with respect to the autonomous Pisan quarter. Finally, Venice acknowledged

---

[56] F. Cornelius [Corner] (ed)., Ecclesiae Torcellanae, Venice 1749, I, pp. 220f: *petium de terra nostri comunis Venetiarum in Constantinopoli positam juxta ecclesiam Sancte Hereni in latere in Constantinopoli, in parte austri, (...), versus orientem usque ad divisionem que est inter nos et gentes Tuscanorum,* a clear reference to the Pisan quarter. In February 1207 some property transferred to the patriarchate of Grado is described as being adjacent to those of St. Eirene and to the Lombards (*firmat in Lombardis*), an obvious slip for Tuscans since there is no evidence regarding a Lombard quarter in Constantinople: TTh, II, p. 6. On the annexation of 1189, see above, p. 159.

[57] TTh, II, pp. 194f.

[58] TTh, II, pp. 282–284, 291f.: *loca et viam que vocatur de Longario extra murum civitatis Constantinopolitane usque ad aquam que currit a veteri possessione Venetorum eiusdem civitatis usque ad novam.* Since the old and the new territory of Venice were contiguous, the topographical definition regarding Longario refers to a continuous stretch of land.

[59] TTh, II, pp. 253f.: *de facto omnium camporum gentium latinarum Constantinopolis et eorum iurisdictionum, quos campos ipse latine gentes habebant in tempore Grecorum.* Vitale Ferro served as counsellor to the Venetian podestà in 1220: F. Cornelius [Corner] (ed.), Ecclesiae Venetae Antiquis Monumentis nunc etiam Illustratae, Venice 1749–1753, III, p. 99.

[60] TTh, II, p. 255.

[61] ASV, S. Tommaso dei Borgognoni di Torcello, in Madonna dell'Orto, b. 1 Perg., Rialto, 25 July 1258, notary Andrea Moro, and ibid., 16 December 1259, notary Giovanni Beltrami. On the location of St Eirene of Perama at the eastern edge of the former Jewish quarter, see above, p. 159.

the inclusion of the former Genoese quarter in the imperial portion of the city. Genoa was not officially represented in Constantinople, nor did it exercise any authority over its former quarter during the Latin period[62], despite the four agreements it concluded with Venice from 1218 to 1251[63]. Territorial continuity was a guiding principle in Venice's expansion in Constantinople, and since the former Genoese quarter was located to the east of the Pisan one[64], there was no Venetian motivation to claim it.

Eventually, the dispute between the imperial and Venetian parties was restricted to two issues. One of these was the fate of the quarter granted at an unknown date in the twelfth-century to Provençal and Spanish merchants. The absence of any reference to wharves in this context implies that their quarter did not reach the shore of the Golden Horn, contrary to the German and French premises. We have seen that Venice's quarter was contiguous to the Pisan one since 1189 and remained so after 1204. Therefore, the joint Provençal-Spanish premises appear to have stood to the south of the French and German quarters and like them within the former Jewish area. In 1224 Robert of Courtenay agreed that these premises should be divided according to the partition treaty of March 1204 and that, consequently, Venice should retain three eighths of them, which it had already obtained shortly after the conquest[65].

Apparently at that time Venice also took hold of a shipyard, the possession of which similarly became a matter of dispute between the Latin emperors and Venice in the following years. With respect to this installation Venice had to forgo the principle of territorial continuity implemented in annexations. There was no arsenal on the shore of the Golden Horn along which Venice expanded west of its existing quarter[66]. Three shipyards are known to have existed in the Golden Horn at the time of the Latin conquest, two of them on its southern and one on its northern coast[67]. It is quite unlikely that Venice should have used the arsenal in the port of Kosmidion to the northwest of the Blachernae, an area under imperial authority, since it was far removed from its quarter. Another shipyard, also on the southern shore, functioned in the port of the Neorion, yet its precise location there is unknown. The Pisan quarter, placed between this port and Venice's quarter since 1189, blocked Venetian access to it by land. We have already

---

[62] See M. Balard, Les Génois en Romanie entre 1204 et 1261. Recherches sur les minutiers notariaux génois, in: Mélanges d'archéologie et d'histoire, publiés par l'Ecole Française de Rome 78 (1966) 475–477, 480, 483f., 486 (rpt. in: id., La mer Noire et la Romanie génoise [XIIIe–XVe siècles], London 1989, no. I). Genoese merchants were nevertheless active there: see also Jacoby, Settlers, pp. 198f.

[63] Giordano-Pozza, Trattati, pp. 53–221; S. Origone, Die Verträge der ersten Hälfte des 13. Jahrhunderts zwischen Genua und Venedig, Mitteilungen des Bulgarischen Forschungsinstituts in Österreich 8 (1986) 89–95, esp. 92, rightly stresses that all the clauses referring to a Genoese official presence in Constantinople were formulated in the future tense and that their repetition implies that they were never implemented.

[64] See M. Balard, La Romanie génoise (XIIe–début du XVe siècle) (Bibliothèque des Ecoles françaises d'Athènes et de Rome 235), Rome 1978, pp. 108–112, 179–182.

[65] TTh, II, p. 255.

[66] On this annexed area, see below.

[67] See H. Ahrweiler, Byzance et la mer. La marine de guerre, la politique et les institutions maritimes de Byzance aux VIIe–XVe siècles, Paris 1966, pp. 430–435.

III

The Venetian Quarter of Constantinople from 1082 to 1261

noted that the Pisan quarter suffered severe damage from the fire of August 1203[68]. Since it was adjacent to the Neorion gate, one may wonder whether this had also been the fate of the neighboring shipyard. This would explain the importance acquired by the third arsenal, the Exartysis, situated to the west of Sykae opposite the territory annexed by Venice in 1204. George Pachymeres reports that the Latins took advantage of this arsenal throughout the Latin period[69]. Although he does not explicitly mention Venice in this context, there is good reason to believe that when John of Brienne confirmed Venice's right over the arsenal in 1231, he referred to the Exartysis[70].

Venice's quarter expanded substantially to the northwest along the Golden Horn as far as the Blachernae region, allotted to the emperor by the treaty of March 1204[71]. The sea wall extending along the Golden Horn from the last tower in the vicinity of the monastery of Christ Evergetes to the Blachernae tower, especially in the area of Petrion situated between the Constantinian and the Theodosian walls, had severely suffered from the Latin attacks of 17 July 1203 and April 1204[72]. Between June 1205 and March 1207 the podestà Marino Zeno rebuilt this section of the sea wall, which now belonged to Venice. In February 1208 Doge Pietro Ziani granted fishing rights along the same section to the Venetian monastery of S. Giorgio Maggiore[73]. The residential area of Petrion, which lay behind the sea wall[74], was extensively damaged by the fire of 17–18 July 1203, yet apparently not all its buildings were destroyed[75]. Some of them were either preserved or else restored, as suggested by later evidence on Venetian settlement in this area. In 1234 Pope Gregory IX ordered an inquiry regarding the ecclesiastical rights of St. Akindynos over the Venetians residing in Constantinople. According to one witness, Marino Bon resided in the vicinity of S. Euphemia, undoubtedly the church bearing that

---

[68] See above, p. 160.

[69] Georges Pachymérès, Relations historiques, 5, 10, ed. A. Failler, Paris 1984, II, p. 469; wrong interpretation and location in the commentary, which does not take into account Ahrweiler's arguments, on which see above, n. 67.

[70] TTh, II, pp. 284, 293.

[71] See above, p. 160.

[72] On 17 July 1203, attack along the shore of Petrion (on which see below): Nicetas Choniates, Historia, I, p. 545 (van Dieten), and a letter of Hugh of St. Pol in: Chronica regia Coloniensis, ed. G. Waitz, Monumenta Germaniae Historica, Scriptores rerum Germanicarum, XVIII, pp. 206f. (TTh I, p. 309); on 9 and 12 April 1204, attacks along the entire section, especially on Petrion: Nicetas Choniates, Historia, I, p. 568 (van Dieten). On 9 April Alexios V oversaw the action from the monastery of Christ Pantepoptes (on which see below, p. 165). Location of Petrion in Janin, Constantinople, pp. 407f.

[73] TTh, II, pp. 47–49, and III, pp. 23f.; new ed. and correct dating of the first document by Pozza, Atti, pp. 39–41, no. 7: *ab ultima turri Virgioti versus Wlachernam ... usque ad turrim Wlachernam*. On the monastery of Christ Evergetes, see Magdalino, Constantinople, p. 70. On the Blachernae tower built by Isaac II Angelos, yet without reference to this document, see Janin, Constantinople, p. 126. The rebuilding of the wall is mentioned in both charters. On Zeno's term of office, see R. L. Wolff, A New Document from the Period of the Latin Empire of Constantinople. The Oath of the Venetian Podestà, Annuaire de l'Institut de philologie et d'histoire orientales et slaves 12 (1952) (= Mélanges Henri Grégoire, IV), p. 559 (rpt. in: id., Studies in the Latin Empire of Constantinople, London 1976, no. VI).

[74] See Magdalino, Constantinople, p. 89.

[75] See Madden, Fires, pp. 73f., 90, 93 (map).

name in the area of Petrion[76]. Marco Venier was established in that area sometime before August 1250, as well as his brother Stefano[77]. Marco may have already been settled there in 1233, when he conducted business on behalf of his father[78].

The absence of adequate documentation prevents us from determining the depth of the territory annexed by Venice to the south of Petrion. We are more fortunate, though, with respect to the area enclosed by the Constantinian wall and the aqueduct of Valens which lay to the west of the Venetian quarter existing on the eve of the Fourth Crusade. This area included the monastery of Christ Pantokrator, which consisted in fact of a building complex, namely the monastery proper, three churches, a hospital and a hospice for old people[79]. The Pantokrator, which offered ample space for gatherings, offices and storage, became the new center of Venice's administration in Constantinople since shortly after the conquest, as implied by an incident involving the first Venetian podestà, Marino Zeno. In 1206 he forcefully removed the sacred icon of the "Virgin who points the way," the Hodegetria, thought to have been painted by St Luke, from the church of St. Sophia to the Pantokrator[80]. In 1238 a Venetian resident of the city, Nicolò Querini, provided 13,134 hyperpers for the consolidation of a number of loans previously advanced by other merchants to the leading barons governing the Latin Empire. As surety he received the Crown of Thorns supposedly worn by Christ, which was to be kept by Pangrazio Gaversono, in charge of the Commune's treasury located at the Pantokrator[81]. On 20 February 1251 the podestà Marco Gausoni summoned Marco Venier to appear before him *infra Pantogratorem*, where his council convened to deal with judicial matters[82]. The monastery of Christ Pantepoptes, the church of which is identified with Eski Imaret mesciti, was situated to the northwest of the Pantokrator. It was taken over some time after 1204 by the Venetian monastery of S. Giorgio Maggiore, which in 1244 leased it to the bishop of Heraclea, Benedict, in return for an annual payment[83]. Shortly after the conquest Venetian settlers established themselves in the vicinity of the church of the Holy Apostles, at some distance west of the Pantokrator[84]. In 1209 Pietro Marconi sold his land and

---

[76] ASV, Cancelleria inferiore, Notai, b. 153, no. 8. On the church and the adjoining monastery, yet without reference to the Latin period, see Janin, Les églises, pp. 127–129, § 6, and Magdalino, Constantinople, pp. 65, 75.

[77] Injunction of Doge Marino Morosini issued on 29 August 1250 regarding Marco Venier, resident *in Constantinopoli in loco Petriis*, included in a document issued by the podestà Marco Gausoni: ASP, Archivio Diplomatico, no. 1924. Stefano Venier is mentioned as *olim habitator Constantinopoli in loco Petrum* in 1266, thus after the Byzantine reconquest of the city: ASP, Archivio Diplomatico, nos. 2234–2235.

[78] NDCV, no. 86.

[79] See Janin, Les églises, pp. 515–523, § 18, and for specific buildings, pp. 175f., § 31; p. 344, § 16; p. 556, § 21; pp. 46f. The churches are known today as Zeyrek Kilise Camii.

[80] See R. L. Wolff, Footnote to an Incident of the Latin Occupation of Constantinople: the Church and the Icon of the Hodegetria, Traditio 6 (1948) 319–328.

[81] TTh, II, pp. 346–349; better ed. in A. Teulet, Layettes du Trésor des Chartes, II, Paris 1866, pp. 391f., no. 2744. On Querini and the loans, see Jacoby, Settlers, p. 193.

[82] See first document cited above, n. 77.

[83] Janin, Les églises, pp. 513–515, § 17; TTh, II, pp. 422f.

[84] On the church, see Janin, Les églises, pp. 41–50.

house located close to the church to Matteo Acotanto. The following year Pietro Bernardo sold to the Holy Apostles two thirds of several houses and some land in its vicinity, which he had acquired from Viviano the physician[85]. The pieces of property sold in these two transactions were obviously situated within the territory annexed by Venice shortly after the Latin conquest. Since they did not previously belong to Venetian ecclesiastical institutions, it is clear that their owners had obtained them from the Commune itself.

Two unpublished documents drafted in Constantinople provide more precise information about the southern boundary of the enlarged Venetian quarter. According to a deposition made in April 1234 the Venetian Marco Beaqua resided *in loco qui vocatur Diomakelli*[86]. More details about this area appear in the contract drafted on 28 March 1252, by which Pietro Querini sold to his brother Nicolò three pieces of property, the nature and location of which are of particular interest for our purposes[87]. One of them was a *palacium*, a term equivalent to Italian palazzo, which in thirteenth century parlance as nowadays points to a large building several stories high. The other pieces of property, a plot of land and a field, were adjacent to this structure, called Lanissa and Alanissa in the sale contract. All of them were included in the area of *Diumachelli*. To the north the building abutted upon the *pons de Agogo* which, in fact, was not a bridge but an aqueduct, Greek ἀγωγός. The name Agogos was applied to the main aqueduct bringing water into Constantinople, largely completed by 373 under Emperor Valens and called after him. The aqueduct proceeded from the northwestern section of the Theodosian wall enclosing the city in a southeastern direction and ended at a *castellum divisorium* placed at the Forum Tauri or Forum of Theodosius, modern Beyazit square[88]. It is precisely in that area that we may site the building Lanissa or Alanissa, since a section of the Forum Tauri was called Alonitzion (᾽Αλωνίτζιον)[89]. As noted above, the building was contiguous to the Valens aqueduct. It follows that the latter's last section reaching the Forum Tauri was still standing in the mid-thirteenth century. This is further confirmed by the location of Diumachelli, mentioned in the contract of 1252. It is commonly assumed that Dimakelin (Διμάκελιν) was identical with Leomakellon or Leomakellion, either identified as the meat market τὸ Μάκελλον situated behind the Forum of Constantine[90], or else placed to the north of the aqueduct in the vicinity of the Pantokrator[91]. However, the contract clearly locates the building Alanissa and the area

---

[85] ASV, S. Zaccaria, b. 36 Perg., notary Nicolò Tinto; DCV, no. 527.

[86] ASV, Cancelleria inferiore, Notai, b. 153, no. 8.

[87] ASV, Cancelleria inferiore, Notai, b. 8, no. 19.

[88] Janin, Constantinople, pp. 198–200, 306, yet see now C. Mango, The Water Supply of Constantinople, in: C. Mango — G. Dagron, Constantinople and its Hinterland. Papers from the Twenty-Seventh Spring Symposium of Byzantine Studies, Oxford, April 1993, Aldershot 1995, pp. 12–15.

[89] Janin, Constantinople, p. 68.

[90] Ibid., pp. 379f., 383.

[91] See Berger, Untersuchungen, pp. 513–516, and map, no. 139.

of Dimakelin south of the aqueduct at the Forum Tauri[92]. Dimakelin thus appears to have been distinct from both Leomakellon or Leomakellion and τὸ Μάκελλον. The document of 1252 also mentions a church of St Makarios, not attested otherwise, standing along a colonnaded street in Dimakelin to the west of Alanissa[93].

Constantin I built several palaces at Alonitzion to house dignitaries coming from Rome. Leo I (454–474) constructed at the Forum Tauri a large and beautiful palace, which had disappeared by the mid-fourteenth century, and Justinian I added one for his sister Vigilantia in the vicinity[94]. One of these structures, presumably among those of Constantine I, apparently still survived in the thirteenth century. Indeed, the charter of 1252 applies the names Lanissa and Alanissa to a specific building, which must have been repaired and restored at several occasions over the centuries. Before becoming the property of Pietro Querini, Alanissa had belonged to his father Giberto and had apparently served as the latter's residence since shortly after his arrival in Constantinople in 1209 or somewhat earlier[95]. In addition to the property transferred to his son Pietro, Giberto had also granted other, contiguous pieces of real estate to his younger son Nicolò. It is noteworthy that Pietro also leased some adjacent land from the Commune. Among their neighbors we find several Venetians. The region around the Forum Tauri, which included Dimakelin, did not suffer from the fires of 1203–1204[96], which may explain both Venice's interest in its annexation and Venetian settlement in that area.

* * *

The evidence about Venetian property in Constantinople from 1082 to 1261 is more abundant than commonly believed. Although fragmentary, it enables some tentative conclusions regarding the territorial development of the Venetian quarter in that period. In the first phase of its existence, which extended to the Fourth Crusade, the quarter's western boundary along the watercourse descending from the Vigla heights remained stable, while its eastern and southern borders underwent substantial changes. The quarter expanded eastward in two stages, first between the city wall and the Golden Horn in 1148, and later, along its entire eastern flank in 1189. It covered then a section of the former Jewish quarter, reaching St. Eirene of Perama and becoming contiguous with the Pisan quarter. The most vexing questions, which remain unsolved, are the depth of the quarter southward of the sea wall and the outline of its southern boundary, both before as well as after 1148. In any event, although it was the

---

[92] Since generally western documents of the thirteenth century refer only to the four cardinal points, north in the charter of 1252 may also stand for northwest or northeast with respect to the location of Alanissa.

[93] Three other churches stood in the vicinity of the Forum Tauri: see Janin, Constantinople, p. 68.

[94] See Janin, Constantinople, pp. 68, 134f.; G. Dragon, Naissance d'une capitale. Constantinople et ses institutions de 330 à 451, Paris 1974, pp. 520f.

[95] On Giberto, see D. Jacoby, The Venetian Presence in the Latin Empire of Constantinople (1204–1261): the Challenge of Feudalism and the Byzantine Inheritance, Jahrb. Österr. Byz. 43 (1993) 167–173, 184–187, and id., Settlers, pp. 184–186.

[96] See Madden, Fires, pp. 79, 92 and 93 (map).

largest among the quarters of the Italian maritime cities, it covered a fairly limited territory, the extent of which cannot be properly determined for lack of secure topographical clues[97].

The second phase of the quarter's existence began soon after the Latin conquest of Constantinople in 1204 and lasted until the Byzantine recovery of the city on 15 August 1261. The new border remained unchanged throughout this period and can be roughly sketched. To the east it followed the Pisan quarter from the Golden Horn southward. At some distance south of the sea wall it presumably turned westward toward the *Makros Embolos* of Domninos and Maurianos and followed it from north to south as far as the Artopoleia, placed between the Forum of Constantine and the Forum Tauri[98]. The fire of August 1203 inflicted heavy damage to the east of that line and, therefore, Venice was not inclined to expand in that area[99]. From the Artopoleia the Venetian border apparently proceeded westward to the Forum Tauri. In this area we are on safer ground, since Dimakelin to the west of the Forum and to the south of the Valens aqueduct was in Venetian hands. It is likely that from the Forum Tauri the Venetian boundary followed the Mese leading to the Charisios or modern Adrianople gate. This road passed slightly to the west of Dimakelin and of the church of the Holy Apostles, both in Venetian hands[100]. However, beyond the Constantinian wall the Venetian border appears to have left the Mese in a northeast direction until it reached the foot of the Blachernae hill, under imperial authority. It then turned right as far as the Golden Horn, which it joined to the northwest of Petrion. Once the boundary suggested here is transcribed on a map, the full extent of the Venetian quarter in the Latin period becomes obvious. It appears to have covered approximately three eights of Constantinople, in conformity with the partition treaty of March 1204. Yet the Byzantine recovery of the city in 1261 put an abrupt end to the enlarged quarter and resulted in Venice's return to a limited territorial framework.

Bibliography

Berger, Untersuchungen
  A. Berger, Untersuchungen zu den Patria Konstantinupoleos (Ποικίλα Βυζαντινά 8), Bonn 1988.

Borsari, Pisani
  S. Borsari, Pisani a Bisanzio nel XII secolo, Bollettino Storico Pisano 60 (1991) 59–75.

---

[97] P. Schreiner, Untersuchungen zu den Niederlassungen westlicher Kaufleute im byzantinischen Reich des 11. und 12. Jahrhunderts, Byz. Forsch. 7 (1979) 179–181, 184, is therefore understandably cautious in this respect.

[98] On their location, see Janin, Constantinople, pp. 91, 95f.; on the Artopoleia, see also Berger, Untersuchungen, pp. 312–316.

[99] See Madden, Fires, pp. 79–83, 93 (map).

[100] See Janin, Constantinople, pp. 37f., 281f.

Borsari, Rapporti
S. Borsari, I rapporti tra Pisa e gli stati di Romania nel Duecento, Rivista Storica Italiana 67 (1955) 477–492.

Borsari, Venezia
S. Borsari, Venezia e Bisanzio nel XII secolo. I rapporti economici, Venice 1988.

Brown, Quarter
H. F. Brown, The Venetians and the Venetian Quarter in Constantinople to the close of the Twelfth Century, Journ. Hell. Stud. 40 (1920) 68–88.

DCV
R. Morozzo della Rocca — A. Lombardo (eds.), Documenti del commercio veneziano nei secoli XI-XIII, Turin 1940.

Giordano-Pozza, Trattati
M. Giordano–M. Pozza (eds.), I trattati con Genova, 1136–1251 (Pacta veneta 7), Venice 2000.

Jacoby, Quartiers juifs
D. Jacoby, Les quartiers juifs de Constantinople à l'époque byzantine, Byzantion 37 (1967) 167–227 (rpt. in: id., Société et démographie à Byzance et en Romanie latine, London 1975, no. II).

Jacoby, Settlers
D. Jacoby, Venetian Settlers in Latin Constantinople (1204–1261): Rich or Poor?, in: Ch. Maltezou (ed.), Πλούσιοι καὶ φτωχοὶ στὴν κοινωνία τῆς ἑλληνολατι‐ νικῆς Ἀνατολῆς (= Ricchi e poveri nella società dell'Oriente grecolatino) (Biblioteca dell'Istituto ellenico di Studi bizantini e postbizantini di Venezia, no 19), Venice 1998, pp. 181–204. *

Janin, Constantinople
R. Janin, Constantinople byzantine, Paris ²1964.

Janin, Les églises
R. Janin, La géographie ecclésiastique de l'Empire byzantin. Première partie: Le siège de Constantinople et le patriarcat oecuménique, tome III: Les églises et les monastères, Paris ²1969.

Lanfranchi, S. Giorgio Maggiore
L. Lanfranchi (ed.), S. Giorgio Maggiore (Fonti per la Storia di Venezia, Sez. II: Archivi ecclesiastici), Venice 1967–1974.

Madden, Fires
T. F. Madden, The Fires of the Fourth Crusade in Constantinople, 1203–1204: À Damage Assessment, Byz. Zeitschr. 84–85 (1991–1992) 72–93.

Magdalino, Constantinople
P. Magdalino, Constantinople médiévale. Etudes sur l'évolution des structures urbaines (Travaux et mémoires du Centre de recherche d'histoire et civilisation de Byzance, Collège de France. Monographies 9), Paris 1996.

Magdalino, Manuel I
P. Magdalino, The Empire of Manuel I Komnenos, 1143–1180, Cambridge 1993.

Maltezou, Quartiere

Ch. Maltezou, Il quartiere veneziano di Costantinopoli (Scali marittimi), Thesaurismata 15 (1978) 30–61.

Müller, Documenti

G. Müller (ed.), Documenti sulle relazioni delle città toscane coll'Oriente cristiano e coi Turchi fino all'anno MDXXXI, Florence 1879.

NDCV

A. Lombardo — R. Morozzo della Rocca (eds.), Nuovi documenti del commercio veneto dei sec. XI-XIII, Venice 1953.

Pozza, Atti

M. Pozza (ed.), Gli atti originali della cancelleria veneziana, I, 1090–1198, Venice 1994; II, 1205–1227, Venice 1996.

Pozza-Ravegnani, Trattati

M. Pozza — G. Ravegnani (eds.), I trattati con Bisanzio, 992–1198 (Pacta veneta 4), Venice 1993.

TTh

G. L. Fr. Tafel — G. M. Thomas (eds.), Urkunden zur älteren Handels- und Staatsgeschichte der Republik Venedig, Vienna 1856–1857.

IV

THE TRADE OF CRUSADER ACRE IN THE LEVANTINE CONTEXT: AN OVERVIEW*

Two monumental works have paved the way for modern research on medieval trade in the Mediterranean. The first, by Wilhelm Heyd, appeared more than one hundred years ago, in 1885-1886, and was later published in a revised French translation under the title *Histoire du commerce du Levant au moyen âge*, Leipzig, 1885-1886; the second work, by Adolf Schaube, *Handelsgeschichte der romanischen völker des Mittelmeergebiets bis zum Ende der Kreuzzüge*, appeared in Munich in 1906. These two works remain indispensable, despite the discovery of numerous sources unknown to their authors and the publication of hundreds, if not thousands of studies bearing on Mediterranean trade and shipping in the Middle Ages. With few exceptions, though, even recent studies dealing with these subjects and especially with the regional economy of the Levant in the twelfth and thirteenth century are still dominated by the basic approach shaped by the works of Heyd and Schaube. Their perspective is fundamentally eurocentric, with an emphasis on the expansion of the western maritime powers and its implications. Moreover, they treat separately each of the regions bordering the Eastern Mediterranean, without sufficiently taking into account the strong economic interaction between them. As a result, each of these regions is generally examined in isolation and viewed as part of a bi-polar trans-Mediterranean trade system operating according to a colonial pattern, in which the West had a dominant and dynamic role and the Eastern Mediterranean regions, including the Levant an essentially passive one. According to

* Relazione presentata al Convegno «Economia e territorio nel Medioevo», tenutosi a Barcellona nei giorni 23-26 ottobre 1996, promosso dall'Istituto Italiano di Cultura di Barcellona.

this line of argument, these regions merely reacted to western stimulus. They mainly supplied the raw materials they produced and served as intermediaries for goods originating in inner Asia, all of which were exchanged for the finished products of the West.

This approach is flawed in many ways, and a change in perspective is badly needed. Without going into details at this stage, I already wish to draw attention to some important considerations that should be taken into account. First, the twelfth and thirtheenth century Levant not only engaged in bi-lateral exchanges with the West, but was also integrated within other complex and wide-ranging trade systems. One of these connected Byzantium and Egypt between themselves as well as with the West, thus creating a triangular pattern of Eastern Mediterranean shipping and trade. Significantly, numerous Italian merchants and shipmasters did not restrict their activity to the Byzantine region, the Crusader Levant or Egypt, but combined visits to two or more of the major emporia of these regions, such as Constantinople, Acre and Alexandria. At the same time the Levant was also oriented toward the East and inserted within a continental Asian trade system extending as far as China, different in nature from the Mediterranean trade system. The assesment of the regional economy of the Levant itself also requires a fundamentally new approach. There has been much emphasis on trade and shipping in this framework, and too little attention to the agricultural and especially the industrial sector. As a result, these two sectors have been largely underrated and their major contribution to the operation and dynamics of the Levantine economy has been overlooked[1]. With these general considerations in mind, we may now turn to Acre.

The establishment of four Latin states in the Levant around the year 1100, in the wake of the First Crusade, generated a major change in geo-political conditions in the Eastern Mediterranean. These new conditions were decisive for the rise of Acre and for its major economic role in the twelfth and thirteenth century. The city, situated along the coast of present-day Israel, north of the bay of Haifa, was captured by Christian forces in 1104 and incorporated into the so-called Latin Kingdom of Jerusalem. It remained under Latin rule until 1187, when it was conquered by the Muslims, and was recaptured four years later, in 1191, by the Christian forces participating in the Third Crusade. The second period of Latin rule in Acre lasted

---

[1] For the general framework and some of my arguments, see D. JACOBY, *Nuovi e mutevoli orizzonti: verso ed oltre l'Oriente mediterraneo*, in *Storia d'Europa*, III, *Il Medioevo*, a cura di G. Ortalli, Torino, 1994, pp. 1143-1192.

exactly one hundred years, from 1191 to 1291. It is in this century that the city reached the peak of its urban, demographic and economic development in the Middle Ages. This is also the best known period in its long history.

The rise of Acre was launched within the first twenty years of Latin rule. In this period Tyre, which had been the major Levantine port and emporium before the First Crusade, remained under the rule of the Fatimids of Egypt. By 1124, when Tyre was finally conquered by Christian forces, Acre had already become the main landing point along the Levantine seabord for western military forces, immigrants, merchants and goods. In addition, it was also the most convenient place for the disembarkation of pilgrims eager to visit Jerusalem, Bethlehem and Nazareth. Finally, Acre catered to the needs of those reaching it from the West, served as a friendly and secure port-of-call for ships and merchants in transit, and offered them logistical support for short, medium and long-distance maritime trade. It is also within the first twenty years of Latin rule that Genoa and Venice obtained wide-ranging privileges in return for their naval support in the establishment and consolidation of Latin rule in the Levant. These privileges included for each of the cities a quarter of its own, as well as extensive commercial, fiscal and judicial concessions. Pisa obtained similar privileges in 1168. The multiple economic functions fulfilled by Acre fostered its demographic growth in the course of the twelfth century. Acre's capitulation to the Christians in 1104 had been followed by the exodus of most of its inhabitants. All the Muslims left and only few Oriental Christians and Jews remained. As a result of immigration, however, the Latins soon became the dominant group withing the city's population.

Paradoxically, Acre greatly benefited from the crushing defeat suffered by the Latins in 1187, inflicted at the battle of Hattin by Egypt's sultan Saladin. After its reconquest by the Christians four years later, in 1191, it replaced Jerusalem as the political and ecclesiastical capital of the Latin Kingdom and became the seat of its social elite. Many other Latins who had abandoned inland cities conquered by the Muslims in 1187 also resettled in Acre. A similar movement was generated since 1265 by the progressive Muslim conquest of the coastal strip held by the Latins. On the other hand, the surging economic activity in Acre attracted immigrants from the West. These two factors contributed to a constant growt in population in the course of the thirteenth century, and Acre became the most populated city of the crusader Levant. Despite the proximity of the Christian-Muslim border and at times unstable political relations with the Muslim neighbors, the city continued to be a major emporium and enjoyed an increasing prosperity, closely linked to the intensification and expansion of Mediterranean shipping and trade[2].

Acre's trade during the crusader period was inserted within three geographic and economic settings, which were closely interlocked and partly overlapped: the city's rural hinterland; the larger land and maritime networks linking the city with major urban markets in the Levant; and, finally, beyond these networks, the frameworks of trans-Asian and trans-Mediterranean commerce. A separate inquiry into each of these settings is essential in order to determine the nature of Acre's role within its own regional context. The complexity of this role derived from the multiple functions which the city fulfilled in the provisioning of its own population and the supply of logistical support for maritime and land trade, military expeditions, and pilgrimage, each of which required different types of exchange along particular itineraries. The examination of the three settings may also enable us to assess the impact of Latin presence in the Levant on the evolution of Acre's trade in the twelfth and thirteenth century.

Before engaging into an investigation along these lines, however, a word of caution may be in order. Many commercial transactions between Acre and its rural hinterland, within the first setting, were either paid in cash or based on barter and did generally not involve any formal written agreements. Besides, most notarial documents of the twelfth and thirteenth century drafted in the Levant itself have perished. The few extant ones owe their survival to the fact that they involved maritime trade and were brought to the West. On the other hand, as we shall see below, contracts registered in the West often conceal the true nature and destinations of commercial and maritime enterprises. Finally, the total absence of Arabic and Byzantine notarial documents recording

---

[2] For a general view about Acre, see D. JACOBY, *L'évolution urbaine et la fonction méditerranéenne d'Acre à l'époque des croisades*, in *Città portuali del Mediterraneo, storia e archeologia, Atti del Convegno Internazionale di Genova 1985*, a cura di E. Poleggi, Genova, 1989, pp. 95-109, repr. in IDEM, *Trade, Commodities and Shipping in the Medieval Mediterraneo*, Aldershot, 1997, n. V; IDEM, *Acre à l'époque des croisades (XIIe et XIIIe siècles): conjoncture et modalités du développement urbain*, «Villes, histoire et culture», 2 (1997); IDEM, *Crusader Acre in the Thirteenth Century: Urban Layout and Topography*, «Studi medievali», 3a serie, 20 (1979), pp. 1-45, repr. in *Studies on the Crusader States and on Venetian Expansion*, Northampton, 1989, n. V; on pilgrimage in particular: D. JACOBY, *Pèlerinage médiéval et sanctuaires de Terre Sainte: la perspective vénitienne*, «Ateneo veneto», 173 (N.S. 24), 1986, pp. 27-31, repr. in IDEM, *Studies*, n. IV.

trade and shipping in, or related to Acre constitutes yet another obstacle, to any investigation, while the Jewish sources of the Cairo Genizah or synagogue archive offer only very limited evidence in this respect. Nevertheless, a partial reconstruction of Acre's trade within the Levantine context can be achieved with the help of these and other written sources, archeological finds and surveys, two medieval maps of Acre, as well as ancient drawings and aerial photographs[3].

Research on the economy of crusader Acre has been focused on maritime commerce, hardly, if any attention being paid to the city's relations with its rural hinterland or its function in land trade. This unbalanced view calls for correction. As in the Muslim period before 1104, crusader Acre depended for its basic provisioning in food and industrial raw materials upon its immediate and more remote rural hinterland. The geographic range of this supply system depended on the specific commodities in demand. Agricultural and pastoral surpluses produced by peasants on their own land or on the lords' domain were brought into town and marketed either directly by producers or by middlemen. On the other hand, Acre exported to the rural hinterland its own finished products as well as imported goods.

This two-way traffic is hardly documented, for reasons already noted above. Fortunately, however, a unique source provides some information in this respect. Goods entering or leaving Acre by land had to pass through the royal *fonde*, which served as a customs station[4]. It was located near one of the land gates along the eastern city wall. A tariff providing the rates of taxation levied at this toll station has survived[5]. It mentions a large number of commodities, among them victuals or products from Acre's immediate rural hinterland, like grain, carobs, apples, grapes, garlic, onions, sesame, olives, sesame and olive oil, butter, hens, turkeys, honey, sugar, containers such as jars and other ceramic ware, raw materials like flax, wool, silk, straw for baskets, leather, in addition to wood for burning. Other products came from more distant regions, like wine from the area of Nazareth in Lower Galilee, and dates from the area of Tiberias or further south in the Jordan Valley. In the late

---

[3] On these sources, see D. JACOBY, *L'évolution urbaine*, cit., p. 95, and IDEM, *Crusader Acre in the Thirteenth Century*, cit., pp. 1-7.

[4] The french term is identical to Italian *fondaco*.

[5] *Livre des Assises de la Cour des Bourgeois*, in A.A. BEUGNOT, *Recueil des historiens des croisades. Lois*, Paris, 1841-1849, II, pp. 173-181, chap. 242-243. I will return to the location of the *fonde* in a forthcoming study.

IV

years of crusader rule in Acre some Venetian merchants travelled as far as Tiberias, then under Muslim rule, to buy cotton directly from local growers[6]. The use of donkeys and camels for transportation was so common, that for many items trade taxes at the *fonde* were calculated according to donkey or camel-load. Finished products exported from the city to its hinterland were intended for daily use. They included leather straps and saddles, shoes bought by the Muslims coming to town, glassware, as well as ceramics.

The tariff does obviously not cover all the commodities traded in Acre or flowing between the city and its hinterland through the *fonde*. It appears to be composed of clauses updating and adjusting earlier rates of taxation, which were presumably inherited from the Fatimid pre-crusader period, and reflects to some extent the chronological sequence in which the new rates were enacted[7]. Thus, for instance, several clauses in its second part clearly reflect the political conditions existing after 1191 and particularly in the first half of the thirteenth century, when the Christian-Muslim border was fairly close to Acre. One of these clauses mentions peasants from villages under Muslim rule buying salt in Acre, and another refers to cheese brought from such villages, *c'on aporte des kasaus des Sarasins*[8].

The second setting in which Acre's trade was conducted in the crusader period extended to cities under Latin rule, both along the coast from Egypt to Asia Minor and inland, as well as to the Muslim cities of Syria. As noted above, in the Fatimid period Tyre had been the main port and maritime emporium of the Levant and had also served as a transit station between Damascus and the Nile delta, whether by sea or by land. Acre, on the other hand, had been no more than a port-of-call for ships sailing along the coast or a stopover on the land route linking Tyre to Egypt. The major role assumed by Acre in the first twenty years of Latin rule and the growth in its economic activity and population generated a partial shift in trade routes at the expense of Tyre. Although the land route between Damascus and Tyre was shorter and more convenient than the one connecting Damascus and Acre, this last route witnessed growing

[6] *Zibaldone da Canal. Manoscritto mercantile del sec. XIV*, a cura di A. Stussi (Fonti per la storia di Venezia, sez. V – Fondi vari), Venezia, 1967, p. 63: *all te[n]po ch'Acre iera in pie*, or at the time Acre was standing, thus before its destruction by the Muslims in 1291.

[7] For this interpretation, see the study mentioned above, n. 5.

[8] *Livre des Assises de la Cour des Bourgeois*, cit., chap. 243, paras. 5 and 39, pp. 179 and 181, respectively.

commercial activity. In 1184 the Arab traveller Ibn Jubayr made the journey from Damascus to Acre with a caravan in what appears to have been a regular traffic. It is significant that he believed that his chances to find room on board a ship sailing westward were better in Acre rather than in Tyre, which proved to be correct[9]. A clause in the Acre tariff that clearly belongs to the twelfth century provides another illustration of Acre's trade with Damascus. It mentions Egyptian flax in transit from Cairo to the Syrian city, *c'on aporte de Babiloine à Doumas*[10]. However, Acre's role as intermediary between the two Muslim areas presumably diminished after Saladin's conquests in 1187, which established territorial continuity between Egypt and Syria and enabled the unhindered passage of caravans on land routes within his territories. Transit between Egypt and Damascus via Acre obviously ceased entirely in times of political tension and warfare between Latins and Muslims.

Ibn Jubayr's account of his journey to Acre in 1184 seems to imply that in the second half of the twelfth century trade between this city and Damascus was in the hands of merchants based in Syria or more distant lands under Muslim rule. To be sure, merchants from these territories must have dominated trade with the crusader ports in the twelfth century, and apparently still did so in the first half of the thirteenth. Acre was the visited by merchants from Damascus, whose precise group identity is unknown, as well as by Nestorian Christians from Mosul or other localities in northern Iraq, called Mosserins in French, who travelled via the Syrian city. However, after the Mongol sack of Damascus and Mosul in 1260-1261 some of the Mosserins became exiles permanently living in Acre. They were then numerous enough to enable the formation of a confraternity of their own[11].

Trade with Damascus, however, was not exclusively conducted by Syrian and Iraqi merchants. Shortly after the recapture of Acre in 1191, if not earlier, western merchants extended and diversified their activity and no more restricted themselves to maritime trade. They increasingly travelled to the major inland cities under Muslim domination. In 1192 the ruler of the Kingdom of Jerusalem, Henry of Champagne, mentio-

[9] *The Travels of Ibn Jubayr*, trans. R.J.C. Broadhurst, London, 1952, pp. 313-321.

[10] *Livre des Assises de la Cour des Bourgeois*, chap. 242, para. 20, p. 175.

[11] See D. JACOBY, *A venetian Manual of Commercial Practice from Crusader Acre*, in *I comuni italiani nel Regno crociato di Gerusalemme*, a cura di G. Airaldi e B.Z. Kedar (Collana storica di fonti e studi, diretta da Geo Pistarino, 48), Genova, 1986, p. 407, n. 17, and p. 428, Addendum, repr. in IDEM, *Studies* no. VII.

ned land trade with the Muslim hinterland in the charter he issued in Acre in favor of Genoa[12]. In the first half of the thirteenth century it became customary for Venetians either based in Acre or arriving there from overseas to proceed inland, as we may infer from a similar activity attested for Beirut in 1222[13]. Between 1242 and 1244 the Venetian representative in the Levant, Marsilio Zorzi, bitterly complained that royal officials in Acre imposed dues on Venetian merchants engaged in overland trade, despite the full fiscal exemption to which these merchants were entitled. They exported goods originating in Venice to Damascus and other inland cities under Muslim rule, and returned with merchandise they intended to sell either in Acre or in Venice. Evasion from payment, whether full or partial, was possible only if the merchants bribed the officials[14]. The commodities handled are not specified, yet it is likely that the Venetians returned from Damascus with goods such as precious silk and cotton textiles produced in Muslim industrial centers, for which there was a high demand both in Acre and in the West.

Other western merchants proceeding to Damascus were involved in the purchase of military equipment. In 1240 some of them acquired arms, and in 1251 an envoy of Louis IX of France, who stayed then at Acre, purchased in Damascus raw materials for the manufacturing of crossbows[15]. We may safely assume that these were of high quality. The manufacture of military equipment in Acre must have been substantial and an important branch of the city's economy, in particular in the thirteenth century. It supplied not only local military needs, but was also geared to export. In 1239 Emperor Frederick II ordered the purchase of large crossbows in Acre, which in all likelood had been manufactured there[16]. There is good reason to believe that this was not the first or only such purchase.

---

[12] *Codice diplomatico della repubblica di Genova dal MCLXIII al MCLXXX*, a cura di C. Imperiale di Sant'Angelo, Roma, 1936-1942, III, pp. 87-89.

[13] G.L. FR. TAFEL und G.M. THOMAS (eds.), *Urkunden zur älteren Handels-und Staatsgeschichte der Republik Venedig*, Wien, 1856-1857, II, pp. 232-234.

[14] See D. JACOBY, *The Venetian Privileges in the Latin Kingdom of Jerusalem: Twelfth and Thirteenth-Century Interpretations and Implementation*, in B.Z. Kedar and J. Riley-Smith (eds.), *Montjoie. Studies in Crusade history in Honour of Hans Eberhard Mayer*, 1997, n. 168-169.

[15] See above, n. 11.

[16] J.L.A. de Huillard-Bréholles (ed.), *Historia diplomatica Frederici secundi*, Parisiis, 1852-1861, V. p. 587.

Trade between Acre and Tyre in the crusader period was conducted both by sea and by land, as it had been earlier. It must have largely been carried out by land, as it had been earlier. It must have largely been carried out by merchants based in these two cities, yet apparently in the thirteenth century travelling merchants also participated in it. The concentration of military forces in Acre required the supply of horses and other riding and pack animals. Specially built and equipped ships were needed for their transportation from western ports to the Levant. Sea transportation was costly and involved a high mortality rate among the animals. It is not surprising, therefore, that horses were raised in the crusader states or acquired in neighboring Muslim territories and brought to Acre overland. In 1229 Frederick II rewarded the Pisans for their political support during his presence in the Kingdom of Jerusalem by exempting them from the tax on the import or export of horses and other riding animals, whether by sea or by land. Venetian merchants were also involved in this type of trade[17].

Goods arriving or leaving Acre by sea had to pass through the *chaine* or *catena*, the toll station of the harbor. Its location is marked on two sets of maps of Acre drafted around 1320[18]. No tariff of the *chaine* similar to the one of the *fonde* has survived, yet within the latter there are several significant references to trade between Acre and other Levantine ports. Our focus on long-distance navigation has deflected attention from tramping, the picking up and unloading of cargo and passengers in various ports along waterways. It has obscured the fact that this traditional type of activity constituted an integral part of the Mediterranean shipping pattern, also common to small and middle-sized ships based in Levantine ports and sailing between them, yet poorly documented. Tramping often involved relatively short jouneys between ports and, therefore, agreements between carriers and merchants or between the latter may have often entailed payment in cash or been limited to oral understandings. In any event, only few commercial and shipping contracts or other documents drafted in the Levant have survived, as already noted above. Fortunately, however, some other sources provide information about tramping along the Levantine coast. A twelfth century clause in the tariff of the *fonde* of Acre mentions goods brought by La-

---

17 *Documenti sulle relazioni delle città toscane coll'Oriente cristiano e coi Turchi fino all'anno MDXXXI*, a cura di G. Müller, Firenze, 1879, p. 97, doc. 66; D. JACOBY, *The Venetian Privileges in the Latin Kingdom of Jerusalem*, cit., p.168.
18 See D. JACOBY, *Crusader Acre in the Thirtheenth Century*, cit., pp. 16-18.

tins, Oriental Christians and Muslims to Acre *par mer de la riviere*, 'by the sea along the coast'[19], and others refer to maritime imports from Egypt as well as from Antioch and Lattakia[20]. A charter delivered in 1190 by the King of Jerusalem, Guy of Lusignan, refers to small ships of Marseilles involved on a regular basis in transportation along the Levantine coast, *cum (…) lignis parvis de riberia*[21]. In the thirteenth century this shipping pattern was substantially fostered by the growing concentration of Levantine goods in Acre, examined below.

Acre served as a major destination or port of call for trade between the Levantine coastal cities. This trade appears to have intensified since the mid-thirteenth century, in the wake of Mongol expansion in Asia. It is in this period that Ayas or Laiazzo expanded its activity and became the most important port of the Christian kingdom of Lesser Armenia. Its role was further enhanced after the Mongol sack of Baghdad and Damascus, which generated a northward shift of the inner Asian trade route about 1260. Laiazzo served as the main Mediterranean outlet for goods originating in inner Asia and had direct access to the neighboring Mamluk territories. It handled cotton, raw silk, Anatolian alum, precious stones, pearls, as well as luxury textiles. Its traffic with Acre and Egypt is coumented since the 1260s. About 1263 a company engaging in trade along the Levantine seaboard included six residents of Laiazzo, five of Antioch, two of Tyre and six others of Acre, among them one belonging to the group of Mosserins mentioned above[22]. Expressions such as *per riperiam Armenie, Syrie et Egipti* referring to tramping appear in contracts drafted by Genoese notaries based in Laiazzo, Lattakia and Beirut. They record eleven separate sailings along the Levantine coast within four months of 1274 and thirteen more within eleven months of 1279, several with Acre as stopover or destination. About that same time and somewhat later Pisan and other Latin merchants based in the Egyptian port of Damietta, and probably others in Alexandria, were engaging

---

[19] *Livre des Assises de la Cour des Bourgeois*, cit., chap. 242, para. 12, p. 174.

[20] *Ibid.*, chap. 242, paras. 15, 19, 60, pp. 174-175, 177.

[21] H.E. MAYER (ed.), *Marseilles Levantehandel und ein akkonensisches Fälscheratelier des 13. Jahrhunderts* (Bibliothek des deutschen historischen Instituts in Rom 38), Tübingen, 1972, p. 185.

[22] See J. RILEY-SMITH, *The Feudal Nobility and the Kingdom of Jerusalem, 1174-1277*, London, 1973, pp. 78-79, yet the suggestion that trade ventures were organized from Mosul at that time is excluded, as the city had been sacked by the Mongols only a few years earlier. See above. See also next note.

in middle-range trade with Acre and Laiazzo and in tramping along the Levantine coast in small and middle-sized vessels. Oriental spices were among the priced items they carried from Alexandria to Acre, as illustrated by a commercial manual compiled in this city about 1270[23]. These few surviving pieces of evidence provide some insight into a regional trade that appears to have been very intensive in these years.

Only little attention has been paid to the function of Acre in long-distance seaborne trade within the eastern Mediterranean itself. Acre and other ports under Latin rule were conveniently positioned along the waterway linking Egypt with the Byzantine Empire. In the course of the twelfth century these ports, as well as the commercial outposts of the privileged nations established in them afforded the merchants and carriers of these nations a growing advantage over foreign competitiors. The share of Byzantine and Egyptian merchants in commercial operations between Alexandria and Constantinople was sharply reduced, and these merchants became increasingly dependent upon Italian shipping. Thus, for instance, in 1111 a Byzantine trader in silk textiles entrusted a piece of cloth to a Venetian merchant who was about to leave Constantinople for Egypt[24], and in 1192 Byzantine merchants and ambassadors as well as the envoys of Saladin sailed on a Venetian ship on their way from Alexandria to Constantinople[25].

The heavy involvement of Italian carriers and merchants along this maritime route is also attested later. In 1192 Henry of Champagne mentioned seaborne trade with Egypt and with territories to the north of Acre as far as Constantinople in the charter he issued to Genoa. This charter clearly reflects Genoese expectations of a resumption of regular traffic with Byzantium, interrupted since 1182, and the re-establishment

[23] For this whole paragraph, see D. JACOBY, *La Venezia d'oltremare nel secondo Duecento*, in *Storia di Venezia, II, L'età del Comune*, a cura di G. Cracco - G. Ortalli, Roma, 1995, pp. 275-278; IDEM, *Les Italiens en Egypte aux XIIe et XIIIe siècles: du comptoir à la colonie?* in M. Balard et A. Ducellier (eds.), *Coloniser au Moyen Age*, Paris, 1995, p. 84; on spices, see D. JACOBY, *A Venetian Manual of Commercial Practice*, cit., pp. 419-420. For the Laiazzo documents, see now *Notai genovesi in Oltramare: Atti rogati a Laiazzo da Federico di Piazzalunga (1274) e Pietro di Bargone (1277, 1279)*, a cura di L. Balletto (Collana storica di fonti e studi, diretta da G. Pistarino, 53), Genova, 1989.

[24] *Famiglia Zusto*, a cura di L. Lanfranchi (Fonti per la storia di Venezia, Sez. II: Archivi privati), Venezia, 1955, doc. 6.

[25] *Codice diplomatico della repubblica di Genova*, cit., III, pp. 79-81, 102-103; *Documenti sulle relazioni delle città toscane*, cit., p. 66, doc. 41.

IV

114

of relations with Egypt, severed in 1187[26]. Both indeed took place somewhat later. The transit of commodities along the route lingking these two countries via Acre is well illustrated in 1197, when a Genoese who had arrived in Constantinople stated the weight of a shipment of pepper, obviously exported from Alexandria, in units used at the *chaine* or toll station of Acre's harbor[27].

The slave trade in the thirteenth century offers yet another illustration of Acre's function as transit station between Constantinople and Alexandria. This trade expanded substantially after the consolidation of Mongol presence north of the Black Sea. Between 1242 and 1244 the Venetian bailo in Acre, Marsilio Zorzi, complained that Venetians importing slaves for sale in Acre were taxed[28]. A few years later, in 1246, Pope Innocent IV accused Genoese, Venetian and Pisan merchants of trading in Greek, Bulgarian and Ruthenian slaves, many of whom undoubtedly originated in the Black Sea region[29]. These slaves were transported from Constantinople to Acre in order to be sold to the Muslims. Their final destination was apparently Egypt, in constant need of slaves for its military contingents. This type of trade and transportation was considerably enhanced and virtually monopolized by the Genoese after the Byzantine recovery of Constantinople in 1261.

The regional trade system of the Levant, of which Acre was an important component, interacted and partly overlapped with trans-Mediterranean and trans-Asian traffic, the largest settings within which the city was inserted. The business strategies of various merchant families contributed to the connection between regional and wider trade networks. Thus, for instance, in the early thirteenth century members of the Venetian Morosini family residing in Acre and Tripoli joned in trade ventures linked to these networks[30]. This was also the case before 1282,

[26] See above, n. 10, and D. JACOBY, *Conrad, Marquis of Montferrat, and the Kingdom of Jerusalem (1187-1192)*, in *Atti del Congresso Internazionale «Dai feudi monferrini e dal Piemonte ai nuovi mondi oltre gli Oceani»*. *Alessandria. 2-6 Aprile 1990*, a cura di Laura Balletto, Alessandria, 1993, pp. 218-219, 222-223, repr. in IDEM, *Trade, Commodities and Shipping*, cit., no. IV.

[27] *Codice diplomatico della repubblica di Genova*, cit., III, p. 198: *ad cantarium catene Accon qui sic est cantaria V ad cantarium Costantinopolim*.

[28] See D. JACOBY, *The Venetian Privileges in the Latin Kingdom of Jerusalem*, cit., pp. 168-169.

[29] E. BERGER (ed.), *Les registres d'Innocent IV*, Paris, 1884-1921, I, p. 316, doc. 2122.

[30] According to unpublished documents, which will be analysed elsewhere.

when Marino da Canal, active at Laiazzo, had an agent in Acre and a contract involving trade with Montpellier[31].

The connection between the Levantine network and the Asian continental one and its relation to Acre is well illustrated in the framework of western penetration into inner Asia. In the 1260s Latin merchants began to proceed from Laiazzo to Tebriz in northern Persia, the under Mongol rule. In 1264 Pietro Vioni provided in his will, drafted in Tebriz, that after his death his goods should be transferred to the Venetian bailo or state representative in Acre. The itineraries followed by members of the well-know Venetian Polo family offer yet another example of the Levantine-Asian link. When Marco Polo's father and uncle returned from China in 1269, the last stage of their continental trip led them from Tebriz to Laiazzo, where they boarded a ship leaving for Acre in order to find there transportation to Venice. Two years later, in 1271, the Polo brothers, this time accompanied by the young Marco, began their second voyage to China by sailing from Venice to Acre. After going on pilgrimage to Jerusalm, then in Muslim hands, they proceeded to Laiazzo, from where they began their overland trip[32]. The interaction of regional Levantine and trans-Mediterranean trade is best illustrated by the range of Acre's traffic, as registered in the commercial manual compiled in this city about 1270[33]. Venetian merchants travelling between their mother city and Damascus via Acre have already been mentioned[34]. Tramping along the Levantine coast provides yet another facet of the linkage between the two networks. This type of activity was not restricted to vassels sailing between Levantine ports, but appears to have also been commonly practiced by middle-sized and large vessels engaged in trans-Mediterranean journeys. However, it is largely concealed by our documentation. Indeed, numerous Genoese and Venetian shipping and commercial contracts rerfer to the Levant in general terms only, as *Syria o Ultramare*, without specifying destinations or ports of call on the way. Some of them state that trade should be conducted *per riperiam*, along the Levantine seabord, a flexible formula enabling the travelling partner to decide o which port to sail and where it would be profitable to load

[31] D. JACOBY, *A Venetian Manual of Commercial Practice*, cit., pp. 422-423, and IDEM, *La dimensione demografica e sociale*, in *Storia di Venezia, II, L'età del Comune*, cit., p. 703.
[32] D. JACOBY, *La Venezia d'oltremare nel secondo Duecento*, cit., p. 274.
[33] D. JACOBY, *A Venentian Manual of Commercial Practice*, cit., pp. 403-428.
[34] See above.

or unload merchandise[35]. It was customary that the majority of merchants on board a ship should decide to which port to sail. Thus, for instance, in 1200 Tommaso Viaro received in Venice 100 pounds in Venetian currency from Marco Correr for trade up to Alexandria or *ubicumque maior pars eiusdem navis se concordaverint*[36]. Although these contracts rarely mention Acre as destination, we may be sure that many merchants and carriers included this city in their itineraries. Between 1242 and 1244 the Venetian bailo in Acre, Marsilio Zorzi, complained about a shipping taw imposed in Acre upon Venetian vessels in transit[37].

The link between the Levantine and Mediterranean networks is also illustrated by an activity which, for obvius reasons, is poorly documented. Time and again popes, princes and city governments prohibited western exports of war materials to Egypt, especially timber and pitch for naval construction and iron for the manufacturing of arms. Venetian regulations enacted in 1282 specified that this export was permitted to Acre and Tyre, yet not beyond these cities. It is obvious, though, that a large-scale illegal trade in these materials was conducted along the Levantine seabord and headed toward Alexandria and Damietta. It was encouraged by the Egyptian authorities, which offered high prices fot these commodities[38].

While serving as transit port, Acre also fulgilled the role of warehouse and transshipment station within the Levantine context. We have already encoutered some instance illustrating these two functions, which were firmly linked to the operation of the trans-Mediterranean and trans-Asian trade systems. Their major contribution to Acre's economy and trade requires a short explanation. Acre's resident population in the twelfth and especially in the thirteenth century was undoubtedly much larger than in the Fatmid period. Moreover, twice a year, especially in the spring, yet also in the autumn, when maritime convoys arrived from

---

[35] Genoese example of 1253 in A. FERRETTO, *Documenti intorno alle relazioni fra Alba e Genova (1141-1270)* (Corpus chartarum Italiae, XIV), Pinerolo, 1906, I, pp. 183-184, no. 211.

[36] Unpublished contract in the Archivio di Stato of Venice, to which I will return in the near future.

[37] D. JACOBY, *The Venetian Privileges in the Latin Kingdom of Jerusalem*, cit., p. 170.

[38] D. JACOBY, *L'expansion occidentale dans le Levant: les Vénitiens à Acre dans la seconde moitié du treizième siècle*, «Journal of Medieval History», 3 (1977), p. 237, repr. in Id., *Recherches sur la Méditerranée orientale du XIIe au XVe siècle. Peuples, sociétés, économies*, London, 1979, no. VII; D. JACOBY, *The Rise of a New Emporium in the Eastern Mediterranean: Famagusta in the Late Thireenth Century*, «Meletai kai hypomnemata, Hidryma archiepiskopou Makariou III», 1 (1984), pp. 175-176, repr. in IDEM, *Studies*, no. VIII.

the West, this population was enlarged by the arrival of thousands of pilgrims, military personnel, merchants and sailors. While pilgrims stayed in Acre for a few days only and travelling merchants and sailors somewhat longer, military contingents were sometimes stationed there for longer periods in order to strengthen the city's defence or in expectation of field action. In addition, a growing number of ships engaged in various types of sailings called in Acre to pick up or unload cargo and provisions. This concentration of visitors and activity within short spans of time generated a considerable surge in demand and in purchasing power which, though temporary, had some significant implications on trade in the city.

The range of basic commodities coming from the rural hinterland to Acre must have remained unchanged after the Latin conquest. On the other hand, there is good reason to believe that their volume increased. Nevertheless, it would seem that Acre's hinterland could not supply all the needs of the city or the variety of products in demand at certain periods of the year, a situation that called for imports from other Levantine areas. The tariff of the *fonde* lists wine from Antioch and Lattakia, besides wine from Galilee and Muslim territories, as well as sugar, presumably from Tyre, in addition to the produce of Acre's own rural area, while salted fish was brought from Egypt[39].

Acre also relied on imports at a higher level of demand. Both written sources and archeological finds reveal that the Latins residing in the Levant were receptive to various material aspects of eastern daily life. Indeed, they apparently adopted the domestic architecture, which was suited to the Levantine climate[40], and used ceramics, glassware, textiles, carpets and other artifacts bearing Muslim or Byzantin designs that were produced by local and foreign artisans[41]. Moreover, the growing acquaintance of pilgrims, crusaders, merchants and sailors with Oriental commodities generated an increasing demand for them,

---

[39] *Livre des Assises de la Cour des Bourgeois*, cit., chap. 242, paras. 15-17, 19, 60, and chap. 243, para. 15, pp. 174-175, 177, 179.

[40] See D. JACOBY, *Crusader Acre in the Thirteenth Century*, cit., pp. 43-44.

[41] On ceramics *de Païenime*, from Muslim countries, *Livre des Assises de la Cour des Bourgeois*, cit., chap. 243, pares. 7 and 16, p. 179; on archeological material and a more general view, see B. Porëe, «Le royaume latin de Jérusalem aux XIIe et XIIIe siècles: les céramiques croisées, témoins des échanges culturels», in *Pélerinages et croisades (Actes du 118e congrès national annuel des sociétés historiques et scientifiques, Pau, octobre 1993, Section Archéologie et histoire de l'art)*, Paris, 1995, pp. 333-350.

which in turn was stimulated by their diffusion in the West. Many of those returning home were surely eager to take along small quantities of spices, textiles and artifacts either for their own use, to sell them in the West in order to cover their travel expenses, or else to present them to relatives, friends, lords, vassals or ecclesiastical institutions. For instance, when Earl William II de Mandeville returne from Acre to Englan in 1178, he offered silks he had brought from the Holy Land to the churches of his fief[42]. In 1239 an agent of Frederick II bought in Acre pieces of silk cloth, the provenance of which is not stated, for the emperor[43]. This type of demand, concentrated within short periods, increased the need for the storage of imported wares, already required in anticipation of the large volume of commercial demand and shipping. Indeed, in addition to spices brought from Alexandria, Acre imported costly silk textiles from Antioch and from other center of production[44]. In the thirteenth century these textiles constituted in terms of value an increasingly important factor in both commercial and non-commercial exports, as well as in Acre's balance of trade.

Another aspect of the city's function as warehouse and transshipment station is connected with the rise of the cotton and silk industries in Italy since the twelfth, and especially their expansion in the thirteenth century. These industries strove to enlarge their market by catering to the tastes and financial capability of a diverse clientele. The growth in output, as well as the refinement and diversification of their products depended on a steady, yet variegated flow of raw materials, attested by the Venetian maritime regulations of 1233 and 1255, as well as by four trade manuals, one of them compiled in Acre about 1270[45]. These sources reveal that in the thirteenth century bales of cotton produced in various regions, among them Acre's own rural hinterland, as well as around Aleppo in Syria, were brought to Acre in order to be shipped in large quantities to western ports located fairly close to the centers of the

---

[42] RALPH of DICETO, *Opera historica*, ed W. Stubbs (Rolls Series, 68), London, 1876, I, p. 428.

[43] HUILLARD-BRÉHOLLES, *Historia diplomatica Frederici secundi*, cit., V, p. 587.

[44] See above, n. 23, and *Livre des Assises de la Cour des Bourgeois*, cit., chap. 243 para. 8.

[45] R. PREDELLI e A. SACERDOTI (eds.), *Gli statuti marittimi veneziani fino al 1255*, Venezia, 1903, p. 73, para. 2, and pp. 161-162, paras. CV and CVIIII. On the manuals, see above, n. 33, and D. JACOBY, *La Venezia d'oltremare nel secondo Duecento*, cit., pp. 265-266.

cotton industry[46]. The grouping of silk bales from different areas in Acre followed a similar pattern. This razionalization of transportation, which lowered freight costs, involved an intensification of Levantine coastal shipping and its close coordination with trans-Mediterranean sailings.

The pivotal position of Acre within the regional Levantine system and its ramifications is illustrated in yet some other ways. After the recovery of Acre in 1191, Venice, Genoa and Pisa, the main maritime powers in the period under consideration, established in Acre permanent and centralized administrations of their own in order to exercise control over their respective commercial outposts in the Levant and neighboring regions[47]. When the citizen of one of these powers died overseas, his property was brought by fellow merchants to the officer in charge of the nearest outpost of their mother-city. In turn this officer took steps to ensure that the belongings were delivered to the heirs of the deceased merchant. In the absence of an official in the Venetian colony of Alexandria it was the rule since 1254 that the property of a Venetian would be entrusted either to the doge in Venice or to the Venetian bailo in Acre[48]. Similarly, this bailo took charge of the belongings of Venetian merchants dying in Cyprus, since there was no resident Venetian representative in the island until after the fall of Acre in 1291. The will of Pietro Vioni, drafted in Tebriz in 1264, also included a clause to this effect[49].

The geo-political conditions resulting from the First Crusade were of paramount importance for Acre's economic development in the twelfth and thirteenth century. They enabled the city to become a major intersection of land and maritime trade, a bustling market, an major warehouse and a transshipment station. These conditions also promoted the settlement of merchants monitoring the movement of commodities, monies, people, and means of transportation, as well as the establishment of other immigrants. Furthermore, they enhanced the flow of goods, the lucrative pilgrim traffic, exclusively directed toward Acre, and the influx of cash deriving from the stationing of military contingents, the payment for services, financial support for military purposes, assistance to various institutions, and pious donations. Services accounted

---

[46] See above, n. 6, and D. JACOBY, *A Venetian Manual of Commercial Practice*, cit., pp. 415-416, 420-421, 425.

[47] D. JACOBY, *Conrad, Marquis of Montferrat*, cit., p. 224.

[48] TAFEL und THOMAS, *Urkunden*, cit., II, 486.

[49] See above, n. 32.

for a substantial segment of economic activity and fiscal revenue in Acre. The frailty of the conditions upon which this *conjoncture* rested was strikingly demonstrated at the time of the Fifth Crusade. The prolonged presence of the Christian armies in northern Egypt since 1218 increasingly diverted military reinforcements and pilgrims toward this region. This was also the case with maritime traffic and goods, since merchants considered it more profitable to take advantage of the war economy and supply the Latins present in Egypt than to continue their activity according to previous trade patterns. This diversion was so substantial that in 1220 it drastically reduced the volume of economic activity in Acre and Tyre, to the extent that shipping and commercial taxes hardly yielded any fiscal revenue in these cities. To be sure, the economy of both cities recovered from this temporary decline shortly after the crusade had ended in failure. In 1291, however, a more profound and lasting change occured. The Muslim conquest of Acre and of the other remaining Latin strongholds along the Levantine seabord decisively altered the geo-political balance in the region. As a result, the growth that Acre had enjoyed for almost two centuries came to an abrupt end.

The Venetian Privileges in the Latin Kingdom of Jerusalem: Twelfth and Thirteenth-Century Interpretations and Implementation

Venice obtained extensive privileges in the Kingdom of Jerusalem in the first quarter of the twelfth century in return for naval assistance to military operations. In June 1100 Godfrey of Bouillon bestowed upon it various grants, yet only ten years later did it gain hold of a section of Acre. Several years of negotiations, from 1119 to 1123, ensured Venice of much larger concessions, recorded in the charter issued in 1123 by the patriarch of Jerusalem, Gormond of Picquigny, in the name of Baldwin II who was then in Muslim captivity. A few months later Venice decisively contributed to the crusader conquest of Tyre. After his release by the Muslims the king issued in early May 1125 another charter, based on the previous one. Modern historians generally believe that the two documents do not differ markedly, except with respect to Venetian military obligations. As a result they have focused their attention on the first charter, commonly known as *Pactum Warmundi*, considered the foundation of Venice's property and privileges in the kingdom until its fall in 1291. Moreover, they have basically relied on this charter to assess both the policy of the kings of Jerusalem toward Venice and the latter's reaction to what it considered encroachments upon its rights and interests by the crown's officials. The long and detailed memorandum compiled between 1242 and 1244 by the Venetian *bailo* in Acre, Marsilio Zorzi, is particularly eloquent in this respect.

These issues are reconsidered here in the light of a new reading of Venice's privileges in the Kingdom of Jerusalem. The twelfth and thirteenth-century interpretations and implementation of these privileges are examined in their respective contemporary context, in relation both with developments in the crusader states of the Levant and Venice's Eastern Mediterranean expansion. Such an approach is of particular importance in the first stage of our investigation, devoted to a close scrutiny of the charters issued in 1123 and 1125, respectively. While reflecting similar conditions prevailing at the time of their drafting, these two charters differ substantially one from another. Moreover, like other legal documents, under changing circumstances their clauses were subjected in the following period to an ongoing and dynamic re-evaluation and were open to new and at times conflicting interpretations by the parties concerned. Consequently, it is essential to refrain from explaining the charters of 1123 and 1125 in the light

V

of later developments, nor should their implementation and long-term impact on the Kingdom of Jerusalem be solely measured by their original formulation.[1]

A Venetian hagiographic work is the only source offering some evidence about the terms of the agreement concluded between Godfrey of Bouillon and Venice in the spring of 1100. In return for naval assistance during a limited period, from 24 June to 15 August, Venice was to receive a church and a marketplace in each coastal and inland city held by the crusaders or still to be captured. In all cities conquered jointly Venice was entitled to one third of the booty and in Tripoli, to half of it. In addition, the Venetians were to enjoy full and indefinite immunity from commercial taxes and freedom from the customary shipwreck rights exercised by Frankish lords.[2] It should be noted that Godfrey's concessions included neither urban quarters nor jurisdiction and were thus far less important than generally assumed. Venice's emphasis was clearly on adequate conditions for the conduct of maritime trade with Levantine cities, as well as on cash and goods. Settlement was apparently not yet contemplated. In short, there appears to be no reason to doubt the reliability of the information provided by the Venetian source, despite its nature and the fact that it was compiled after 1116.[3] It appears, however, that the agreement of 1100 was not implemented. After the conquest of Haifa, Venice supposedly ceded to the crusaders its share of the booty collected in Haifa, conquered shortly afterwards.[4] Neither in this city nor in Acre, captured in 1104, did it receive the property it had been promised. It may have refrained from requesting a church and a marketplace in Haifa, because the city lacked any potential for commercial expansion. Significantly, Venice never referred to it in later negotiations with the kings of Jerusalem. However, a similar explanation for the absence of Venetian property in Acre in the first years following its conquest is excluded, in view of the city's new role in maritime traffic.

Venice's contribution to the conquest of Sidon in 1110 was considered important enough to bring about an agreement with King Baldwin I, the terms of which are unknown. In any event, this agreement was not merely a confirmation of the one signed in 1100, since it was followed by the transfer of a small section of Acre into Venetian hands. It is noteworthy that a later charter issued in 1123 records this first territorial acquisition of Venice in the kingdom, without

---

[1] My reading of the evidence widely differs here from that found in previous studies, including some of my own. In order to shorten the notes, references to these studies appear below only when absolutely necessary.

[2] Monachus Littorensis, *Historia de translatione sanctorum Magni Nicolai (...) eiusdem avunculi (...)*, cap. 33, RHC Occ 5/1:272.

[3] Background in Marie-Luise Favreau-Lilie, *Die Italiener im Heiligen Land vom ersten Kreuzzug bis zum Tode Heinrichs von Champagne (1098–1197)* (Amsterdam, 1989), pp. 68–79, who, however, erroneously claims that the Venetians obtained one-third of the cities (p. 71), whereas this division concerns the booty alone.

[4] Monachus Littorensis, *Historia*, cap. 43, RHC Occ 5/1:278.

referring to the agreement of 1100. [5] By 1110 Acre had already replaced Jaffa as the main destination of western crusaders, pilgrims and supplies and as the maritime gateway to the holy places. [6] The nature of Venice's authority over its quarter in Acre is unknown. Yet a charter of 1123 suggests that it included the right to appoint officials, impose taxes on Venetians living within the limits of the quarter, and apply Venetian law in commercial cases involving Venetians among themselves, provided they voluntary submitted to the Venetian court. [7] These developments imply that Venice was envisaging Venetian settlement in Acre, a projection presumably based on contemporary experience in Byzantium. Indeed, in addition to merchants, some Venetian women were already established in Constantinople by 1110. [8]

The promise of naval support for the conquest of either Tyre or Ascalon, the last Muslim strongholds along the Levantine coast, yielded far more extensive privileges. [9] The *Pactum Warmundi* of 1123 lists various territorial, legal and fiscal concessions to Venice, while others are implied by the wording of its text. The first clause stipulates that Venice would receive in each royal and baronial city a whole quarter (*ruga*), the size of which is not specified, with a church, a marketplace (*plathea*), a bathhouse and an oven. Not content with this general disposition, Venice requested the right to establish these facilities and a mill in its quarter of Acre (§3), where they apparently did not exist. The Venetian quarters would be held free of charge as hereditary and perpetual property, like the king's own possessions, 'iure hereditario imperpetuum possidenda, ab omni exactione libera, sicut sunt regia propria' (§1).[10] Venice obtained a similar definition with respect to one third of the cities and rural land of the lordships of Tyre and Ascalon, if it participated in their capture. Its portion there would be held 'libere

---

[5] Background in Favreau-Lilie, *Italiener*, pp. 130–133.

[6] David Jacoby, 'Pèlerinage médiéval et sanctuaires de Terre Sainte: la perspective vénitienne,' *Ateneo veneto* 173 [n. s. 24] (1986), 27–29 = idem, *Studies on the Crusader States and on Venetian Expansion* (Northampton, 1989), no. 4.

[7] For details see below, p. 158.

[8] David Jacoby , 'La dimensione demografica e sociale,' in Giorgio Cracco, Gherardo Ortalli (eds.), *Storia di Venezia* (Rome, 1995), 2:691.

[9] The charters of 1123 and 1125, discussed below, have been edited in TTh 1:84–89, 90–94, respectively; Marco Pozza, 'Venezia e il Regno di Gerusalemme dagli Svevi agli Angioini,' in Gabriella Airaldi and Benjamin Z. Kedar (eds.), *I Comuni italiani nel regno crociato di Gerusalemme*, Collana storica di fonti e studi 48 (Genoa, 1986), pp. 373–379, 379–385; and Oliver Berggötz, *Der Bericht des Marsilio Zorzi. Codex Querini-Stampalia IV3 (1064)*, Kieler Werkstücke, Reihe C: Beiträge zur europäischen Geschichte des frühen und hohen Mittelalters 2 (Frankfurt a/M, 1990) [hereafter cited as Zorzi], pp. 108–112, 112–116. I use the latter's edition and its numbering of the clauses of the two charters, with references to the more easily available, yet at times faulty texts in TTh. Page numbers in these editions are cited only when indispensable. For the circumstances, Favreau-Lilie, *Italiener*, pp. 138–149.

[10] For the meaning of *ruga*, see David Jacoby, 'Crusader Acre in the Thirteenth Century: Urban Layout and Topography,' *Studi medievali*, 3a ser. 20 (1979), 14–15 = idem, *Studies*, no. 5. 'Plathea sive balneum,' a somewhat ambiguous formulation, was apparently used in a cumulative sense, as in the charter of 1125 where *sive* is replaced by *que*: Zorzi, pp. 109 and 113 = TTh 1:85 and 91.

et regaliter,' like the two thirds remaining in royal hands (§15). In other words, the property allotted to Venice would be neither a fief nor a burgage tenure, but a collective allodium in which Venice would exercise the same rights as the king in his own domain. Compared with the grant of 1110, Venice was promised substantial territorial gains and a consolidation of its legal rights over the property it acquired.

Indeed, the legal formulations of the *Pactum Warmundi* had wide-ranging implications, which in turn generated important developments in the following period.[11] It has been suggested above that Venice was entitled since 1110 to appoint its own officials and courts and that these could exercise a limited authority over Venetians in fiscal and judicial matters. This authority was considerably expanded in 1123, both territorially, to all of Venice's urban and rural property, and in substance. The Commune was now empowered to exercise full rights in jurisdiction and taxation over the Venetians, and it was mandatory to submit cases between them to Venice's courts. While not explicitly stated, these dispositions are indirectly confirmed by two clauses extending Venice's judicial competence beyond the limits just mentioned. One of them stipulates that Venetian courts were also entitled to judge commercial cases ('placitum vel negocii litigationem') brought by foreigners against Venetians; however, crown officials retained their authority in similar suits involving Venetians as plaintiffs (§11).[12] To this extension *ratione materiae* was added yet another one, *ratione soli*. Venetian officials would also exercise rights of jurisdiction and taxation over foreign burgesses residing in Venetian quarters and houses, 'in vico et domibus Veneticorum habitantes,' regardless of their origin, like the king over the burgesses living on territory subject to his own authority (§14). The specific reference to houses implies that these were located outside the quarters. However, the extension of Venice's judicial authority, based on the Venetian ownership of these houses, was limited to their temporary or permanent residents, while the king retained full rights over the territory on which they were built.[13] There was yet another important restriction. Since these residents were *burgenses*, the Venetian courts were entitled to judge citizens of other maritime powers and subjects of the king and feudal lords, provided they were not knights.[14] In 1123 the whole issue had immediate practical implications in Acre, since the *Pactum Warmundi* granted Venice a section of the city inhabited by foreigners. It would also be of major importance in the portion of the lordship of Tyre that Venice received after the city's conquest the following year.[15]

---

[11] Joshua Prawer, *Crusader Institutions* (Oxford, 1980), pp. 218–226, has underlined their importance, yet his backward projection of later evidence blurs the subsequent evolution.

[12] The wording clearly points to commercial matters only.

[13] For a somewhat similar issue, see below, n. 41.

[14] Similar restrictions *ratione personae* appeared later with respect to Pisan jurisdiction: Prawer, *Crusader Institutions*, pp. 241–246.

[15] See below.

The *Pactum Warmundi* fails to define the precise nature of Venice's jurisdiction over the residents of Venetian quarters and houses. It is generally believed that criminal justice entailing corporal or capital punishment was included, an assumption based on later Venetian complaints about the infringement of the Commune's privileges in the kingdom.[16] This is hardly plausible. The barons and knights of the kingdom hailed from areas in the West in which High Justice was viewed as one of the foremost expressions of seignorial and especially royal authority, never granted to urban communes or rural settlements. Considering the political conditions, as well as the prevailing conceptions about jurisdiction and the mentality shared by the high feudal lords of the kingdom in the 1120s, it was inconceivable that the king should waive his prerogative in criminal cases. Later sources clearly illustrate this attitude as a permanent feature of royal policy. We may safely assume, therefore, that while agreeing in 1123 to important territorial, fiscal and legal concessions to Venice, the royal party never envisaged the grant of High Justice. The absence of any elaboration as to the nature of Venetian jurisdiction may be ascribed to an understanding between both parties that the competence of Venetian courts would be restricted to civil cases. We will soon encounter similar tacit understandings with respect to the nature of fiscal exemptions.

Despite the general provision concerning urban quarters, Venice requested additional dispositions regarding four specific cities. Venice was primarily interested in ports favouring its seaborne commerce, yet nevertheless requested a quarter in Jerusalem, an inland city, in which it was promised as much property as owned by the king (§2).[17] It is noteworthy that in Byzantium Venetian citizens were also active in inland cities such as Thebes, an important industrial centre producing silk fabrics, where their presence is attested since about 1070. Adrianople was another inland city to which they had access.[18] In 1123 Venice apparently believed that the pilgrim traffic, in which it was already involved,[19] would generate substantial profits in Jerusalem. Eventually, however, it never took advantage of its privileges there because its citizens failed to display any

---

[16] Jonathan Riley-Smith, *The Feudal Nobility and the Kingdom of Jerusalem, 1174–1277* (London, 1973), pp. 67–68; Prawer, *Crusader Institutions*, p. 222; Favreau-Lilie, *Italiener*, p. 438. The opposite view is upheld by Jean Richard, *Le Royaume latin de Jérusalem* (Paris, 1953), p. 220; idem, *The Latin Kingdom of Jerusalem*, trans. Janet Shirley (Amsterdam, 1979), pp. 272–273.

[17] The quarter was defined as *plathea* in 1123 and *ruga* in 1125, these terms being thus interchangeable: *Zorzi*, pp. 109 and 113 = TTh, 1:85 and 91. The formulation 'tantum ad proprium habeant, quantum rex habere solitus est' surely refers to immovables, as with respect to grants elsewhere in the kingdom mentioned in the charter. This interpretation seems more plausible than the one appearing in the French version of William of Tyre's chronicle, which refers to revenue: 'autant de rante en leur proprieté,' RHC Occ 1/1:551.

[18] David Jacoby, 'Silk in Western Byzantium before the Fourth Crusade,' *Byzantinische Zeitschrift* 84/85 (1991–92), 494–496; idem, 'Italian Privileges and Trade in Byzantium before the Fourth Crusade: a Reconsideration,' *Anuario de estudios medievales* 25 (1995), 352.

[19] See below p. 162.

interest in retail trade and settlement in the city.[20] In Tyre and Ascalon Venice was to receive one third of the urban territory, a much larger section than in other cities, in addition to one third of their respective rural hinterland (§15). In this region Venice held after 1124 numerous villages and benefited from one third of the income deriving from those it shared with other lords.[21] The royal concession of a section of the countryside was clearly made at the insistence of Venice, which apparently wanted to ensure not only the provisioning of its citizens and ships in agricultural and pastoral produce, but also gain direct access to the production and export of expensive commodities such as sugar.[22] One should remember that when Tyre was captured in 1124, the rural area around it had already been occupied for several years by Christian forces and the Venetians were thus fully acquainted with its resources.[23]

The *Pactum Warmundi* devotes no less than seven of its seventeen clauses to Acre (§§3–9).[24] Venice's request for an extension of the urban section it had obtained in 1110, which was granted (§8), reflected its awareness of Acre's potential for economic development. The city's fast expanding economy was clearly attracting settlers, several of whom are mentioned by name as house owners (§§8–9). One of them was Guibert of Jaffa, presumably not a Venetian since his house was located in an urban section remaining in royal hands until 1123. Apparently motivated by economic factors, his move from Jaffa to Acre points to internal migration, a factor that has hitherto been overlooked for the early years of the Kingdom of Jerusalem. Incidentally, the charter's testimony about this individual supports the contemporary claim of the chronicler Fulcher of Chartres that Latin settlers in the Levant had 'become Orientals' and 'had forgotten the places of [their] birth,' which were 'not mentioned anymore.'[25] In practical terms this meant that they had begun to shed their western surnames and, instead, adopted eastern toponymic surnames. The paucity of Venetian documentation bearing on Acre and, more generally, on the crusader Levant in the first half of the twelfth century may partly explain the absence of direct evidence about Venetian settlement. One should also take into account the possible return of settlers to Venice, either in old age after a long and busy commercial career overseas, or earlier for some other reasons. From later sources we know that Venetian settlement in the crusader Levant and in Byzantium did not necessarily

---

[20] Prawer, *Crusader Institutions*, pp. 85–101, on the nature of Latin settlement in Jerusalem.

[21] Ibid., pp. 145–156.

[22] On which W. Heyd, *Histoire du commerce du Levant au moyen âge*, 2 vols. (Leipzig, 1885–1886), 2:685–686.

[23] WT 13.13, lines 42–63, pp. 601–602.

[24] §§3 and 4 are linked, and so are 8 and 9; they all refer to Acre. This is also the case of §5, which largely covers the same issues as the general disposition in §10, and of §6, connected to §5. Hence §7, inserted between other dispositions regarding Acre, also bears on this city. For a detailed justification of this reading, see below. The failure to perceive that the seven clauses deal exclusively with Acre has generated in the past some misunderstanding about these and other dispositions of the charter.

[25] FC 3.37. 2–3, pp. 747–748. This passage of the chronicle is dated to 1124–1127: ibid., pp. 47–48.

entail life-long residence in these regions and was in many cases temporary, though in any event longer than between two sailing seasons.[26] The economic advantages deriving from a continuous long-term presence overseas were already obvious in Byzantium, as noted above, and must have been similarly perceived by the 1120s with respect to the crusader Levant. It is hard to believe, therefore, that the Venetians waited until the second half of the twelfth century before settling in some coastal cities of this region.[27] In any event, Venetian settlement in Acre between 1110 and 1123 is suggested by building activity in the first section of the city granted to Venice, in which some huts made of clay-plastered canes were replaced by two stone houses (§8).[28] More convincingly, it is implied by Pietro Zanni's ownership of a house in the same urban area, although his identification as a member of the powerful Venetian Ziani family has been called into question.[29]

Venice obtained in 1123 some substantial fiscal privileges, namely a general exemption from entrance, departure and sojourn taxes in the entire kingdom, including baronial lands, as in Venice (§10). An explicit exemption from commercial dues was added for Acre, since this was the only city of the kingdom in which the Venetians conducted trade at that time (§5).[30] These clauses appear to be a repetition of the fiscal disposition obtained in 1100, yet it is not clear whether the latter had been duly implemented since then. There was an important addition, however, since it was agreed that the royal treasury would not compensate itself for the resulting loss of revenue by raising the taxes imposed upon foreigners trading with Venetians (§7). The inclusion of this clause was clearly prompted by Venice's experience in the Byzantine Empire, where the introduction of this device by the imperial authorities, sometime between 1082 and 1118, must have seriously curtailed Venetian commercial profits. Only in 1126, thus three years after the delivery of the *Pactum Warmundi*, did Venice obtain from Emperor John II Comnenus that his officials desist from this practice.[31] On

---

[26] Jacoby, 'La dimensione demografica e sociale,' pp. 698, 703.

[27] Favreau-Lilie, *Italiener*, pp. 498–508, rightly criticizes Prawer, *Crusader Institutions*, pp. 226–229, for mistaking commercial transactions as proof of Venetian settlement in the Levant since shortly after the *Pactum Warmundi*. She favours a much later date, yet fails to take into account temporary settlement and the fact that some settlers retained surnames referring to the Venetian parish from which they originated, thus making it difficult to identify them as settlers: see above, n. 26.

[28] *Zorzi*, p. 110: 'duas lapideas mansiones (...), que quondam casule de cannis esse solebant.' TTh, 1:86, have mistakenly assumed that 'cannis' was a proper name.

[29] Irmgard Fees, *Reichtum und Macht im mittelalterlichen Venedig. Die Familie Ziani*, Bibliothek des historischen Instituts in Rom 68 (Tübingen, 1988), pp. 51, 84, and next note. One argument against the identification is that the spelling of his surname does not conform with the one generally found, which may have been due to the royal chancellor Payen who drafted the charter of 1123. The other is that later in the twelfth century some members of the Ziani family were involved in commercial dealings with Acre, yet none are attested there as settlers: ibid., pp. 51, 60–61, 88–91, and Favreau-Lilie, *Italiener*, pp. 503–504. On temporary residence see n. 26 above.

[30] *Zorzi*, pp. 109–110. Note that the words *vendendo, comparando* appear in the second instance only.

[31] Jacoby, 'Italian Privileges and Trade,' pp. 354–355.

the other hand, the king's right to the collection of the *terciaria* from incoming and departing Venetian ships was maintained. Venice would be compensated by a yearly payment of three hundred Saracen besants from the king's portion in the revenue accruing from the royal market at Tyre, shared with Venice (§6).[32] Since the charter uses the term *peregrini* in this context, it is generally assumed that the *terciaria* was a pilgrims' tax.[33] In fact, however, it was a due collected from shipmasters that amounted to one third of the fare paid by a vessel's passengers for themselves and their belongings, merchants sailing with their goods being exempted as implied by the term *peregrini*.[34] The royal treasury was unwilling to forgo its share of the substantial benefits expected from the expanding movement of pilgrims and crusaders, in which the Venetians were attempting to increase their own share. The inclusion of this clause among the dispositions regarding Acre is not surprising, in view of the city's major role in maritime traffic.[35]

The *Pactum Warmundi* included some further fiscal concessions entailing losses to the royal treasury. In Acre the king's right to impose the exclusive use of his oven, mill and bathhouse was relinquished and Venice obtained the right to build and operate such facilities, the residents of the Venetian quarter being free to utilize them. The royal party also renounced the king's monopoly on markets, balances and standards, namely for the sale of wine, olive oil and honey, all of which were local products. Following Venice's request, Venetians would be compelled to use the Commune's scales and measures when trading among themselves or when selling to foreigners.[36] On the other hand, when they purchased goods from foreigners the parties were allowed to utilize royal weights and measures, in return for the customary taxes paid for their use, 'dato precio,' these transactions being then carried out in royal markets (§§3–4). While not amounting to a total transfer of monopolies from the king to Venice, these dispositions were likely to contribute to the strengthening of the Commune's authority over its own quarter in Acre and to enlarge the revenue deriving from it. Incidentally, such a development was largely precluded in twelfth-century

---

[32] The king was entitled to two thirds of this revenue, according to §15.

[33] Eg., Favreau-Lilie, *Italiener*, pp. 123, 329, 464, 469, 471–472, 483, 485, 496, 539–540.

[34] The term applied to both pilgrims and crusaders and, more generally, to passengers in a maritime context, yet there was a clear distinction between merchants and other passengers: Benjamin Z. Kedar, 'The Passenger List of a Crusader Ship, 1250: Towards the History of the Popular Element on the Seventh Crusade,' *Studi medievali*, 3a ser. 13 (1972), 268–269 = idem, *The Franks in the Levant, 11th to 14th Centuries* (Aldershot, 1993), no. 16. The general meaning is confirmed by the charter delivered in 1190 by King Guy of Lusignan to Marseilles, which stipulated that the *terciaria* would also be levied from small ships involved in cabotage along the Levantine coast ('lignis parvis de riberia'); these vessels transported passengers, yet definitely not pilgrims, as suggested by their itinerary: ed. by Hans E. Mayer, *Marseilles Levantehandel und ein akkonensisches Fälscheratelier des 13. Jahrhunderts*, Bibliothek des deutschen historischen Instituts in Rom 38 (Tübingen, 1972), p. 185. For another, similar instance, see below, n. 67.

[35] The clause does not refer to ports other than Acre, contrary to Favreau-Lilie, *Italiener*, p. 464.

[36] The emphasis was on their own facilities, and not on their own goods, as in the translation of Riley-Smith, *Feudal Nobility*, p. 71.

Egypt, where the use of the state's facilities was mandatory. In 1172 the Pisans were allowed to use their own weights within their *funduq* of Alexandria, thus exclusively for transactions among themselves, yet this privilege was not renewed in 1207 or 1208.[37] In the Byzantine Empire the utilization of Venetian weights and measures was similarly restricted to dealings among Venetians. In both countries it was voluntary and could not be enforced.[38]

The *Pactum Warmundi* includes two legal concessions directly related to the exercise of trade. The crown renounced its right to property left by a Venetian, regardless of whether he died testate or intestate (§12). A similar rule would apply to goods washed ashore or belonging to an owner who had drowned (§13), apparently a repetition of the relevant disposition of 1100. All these cases were in respect of movable property, which from now on would be delivered to its legal heirs or, should none of them be available in the kingdom, to other Venetians who would transfer them to destination. These provisions imply that at that time Venetians, both travelling merchants and settlers, were in the Levant mostly on their own, without any relatives nearby. The reference to Venetians in general, and not to a specific official of the Commune, reveals the absence of any Venetian governmental structure or permanent representation in the Levant. This feature, also common to other Venetian communities existing around the Eastern Mediterranean, was to last until after the Third Crusade, when Venice finally stationed in Acre a senior official in charge of its interests in the Levant.[39]

From a comparison between the charters of 1123 and 1125 it is clear that tough bargaining between the two parties preceded the drafting of the *Privilegium Balduini*. To be sure, the formulation of some dispositions was slightly changed without altering their meaning.[40] Yet, contrary to common belief, this document was not largely a confirmation of the *Pactum Warmundi*, since the two widely differ in wording, in the disposition of their clauses, and in content. While Venice basically safeguarded its main achievements of 1123, Baldwin II reduced them both in matters of principle and in practical terms. The undertaking of Patriarch Gormond to compel Baldwin II, once released from captivity, or any successor to the throne to confirm the agreement he had reached with Venice (§16) was omitted, since by issuing his document the king was fulfilling Gormond's pledge. One of the king's main concerns was to preserve his full royal authority, despite the concessions made to Venice. He presumably considered the reference to the obligation of the king's successors to abide by the original agreement too stringent

[37] David Jacoby, 'Les Italiens en Egypte aux XIIe et XIIIe siècles: du comptoir à la colonie?,' in Alain Ducellier and Michel Balard (eds.), *Coloniser au Moyen Age* (Paris, 1995), pp. 80, 84.

[38] Silvano Borsari, *Venezia e Bisanzio nel XII secolo. I rapporti economici*, Deputazione di storia patria per le Venezie, Miscellanea di studi e memorie 26 (Venice, 1988), pp. 54–55, fails to stress this last aspect.

[39] David Jacoby, 'Conrad, Marquis of Montferrat, and the Kingdom of Jerusalem (1187–1192),' in Laura Balletto, (ed.), *Atti del Congresso Internazionale 'Dai feudi monferrini e dal Piemonte ai nuovi mondi oltre gli Oceani'* (Alessandria, 1993), pp. 216, 224.

[40] Eg., above, n. 17.

(§1), and deleted it. While maintaining Venice's rights to its urban quarters and rural territories around Tyre and Ascalon, the king opposed the notion that their grant was perpetual, which might have implied that the territories held by Venice were no more included in the kingdom. In order to reassert royal authority over them the word *imperpetuum*, used twice in 1123 (§§1, 15), was scrapped from the corresponding clauses of 1125 (§§1, 12). This purposeful omission entailed both legal and practical implications. It was closely linked to the obligation of military service by a number of cavalrymen, which the king imposed in 1125 upon Venice in return for its portion of the lordship of Tyre (§13). As a result, this portion lost its allodial status and became a fief held from the king.

While gaining the upper hand in these legal issues, Baldwin II was compelled to yield in others. Venice obtained some seemingly minor changes in the formulation of two judicial dispositions. As noted earlier, the *Pactum Warmundi* conferred judicial authority to Venetian courts over commoners residing in Venetian houses situated outside the Commune's quarters, 'in (...) domibus Veneticorum' (§14). The replacement of the preposition *in* by *super* in 1125 entailed a further extension of this authority to the houses themselves, 'super domos eorum' (§11), which amounted to an expansion of Venice's territorial rights beyond the boundaries of its quarters.[41] In view of the king's stand regarding royal prerogatives, noted earlier, the change in wording is rather surprising, yet Baldwin II may have been willing to pay the price for concessions wrung from Venice that he considered of greater significance. In addition, the king omitted the explicit reference to commercial litigation from the other clause dealing with Venetian jurisdiction (1123, §11, and 1125, §8: 'placitum vel litigationem'). It is difficult to believe that Baldwin II would have concurred with Venice's request in this respect, unless there was an understanding between the two parties that the Venetian courts would continue to deal exclusively with commercial suits along the lines determined in 1123. In both cases the king and his councillors failed to foresee the far-reaching implications which the new wording would acquire in the long run. It opened the way for a much broader interpretation of Venetian judicial prerogatives at the expense of royal authority and carried a potential for serious strife between the two parties.

Baldwin II also achieved some successes in fiscal matters. The mandatory use of Venice's scales and measures, previously imposed in specific cases upon the Venetians in Acre (1123, §4), was abolished and the latter were thus free to use royal facilities. There is good reason to believe that Venice collected lower dues than the king in order to induce both Venetians and their foreign business partners to conclude deals within the boundaries of the Venetian quarter of the city and ensure thereby a revenue for its own treasury. Royal pressure upon Venice also resulted in the lifting of the disposition prohibiting the levy of heavier royal dues from those trading with Venetians (1123, §7). The king apparently resented

---

[41] In 1187 Pisa failed in its attempt to extend its authority over houses owned by Pisans outside its quarter of Tyre: Jacoby, 'Conrad, Marquis of Montferrat,' p. 198.

this clause because it appeared to limit royal authority in fiscal matters, yet at the same time he must have promised Venice that he would not take advantage of its omission. Significantly, there was no reference to the original disposition of 1123 in the following period. In addition, the clause of 1123 granting total fiscal exemption in Acre (§5) was scrapped, since it appeared to be covered by the general disposition of the same nature (§10), taken over in 1125 (§6). Three of the clauses dealing with Acre in 1123 (§§3, 8 and 9) were repeated and grouped in 1125 (§§3, 4 and 5), while the one dealing with pilgrimage (§6) was inserted among the general dispositions of Baldwin's charter (§7). In short, in 1125 there was more emphasis on general dispositions, presumably at Venice's request, in order to ensure a broader territorial interpretation and implementation of its privileges.

Venice obtained a further concession with respect to passenger traffic. The levy of the *terciaria*, imposed in 1123 in Acre on both incoming and departing vessels carrying pilgrims and warriors, was henceforth limited to outbound ships (1123 and 1125, §2). The new disposition was clearly advantageous to Venetian ship operators, since it ensured them of the full fare paid by passengers for the journey to the Holy Land (§7). Moreover, from experience these operators already knew that not all passengers travelling eastwards returned home, some of them dying on the way or in the Levant and others remaining in this region. Pilgrims must have generally paid in advance for the round trip,[42] while the *terciaria* collected from ship-masters was presumably proportionate to the total amount of transportation fees paid by actual passengers, thus leaving further profits in the hands of the operators. In 1123 the *terciaria* appeared in the section of the charter devoted to Acre, while in 1125 it was included among the general dispositions. This change in location, however, did not entail any practical implications, since Acre retained its function as the main port of call for Venetian passenger traffic. Venice raised yet another fiscal issue in 1125. It would seem that its right to collect fees in return for the utilization of its own scales, measures, bathhouse, oven and mill in Acre was disputed by residents of its quarter, possibly on the ground that the charter of 1123 stipulated that they were free to use them. In 1125, therefore, Venice insisted upon the addition of an explicit reference to payment for the use of these facilities. The king readily agreed to this request, since it did not entail any concession on his part.[43]

At this juncture it may prove useful to draw attention to some basic features of the agreements of 1123 and 1125, which had a major impact upon later relations of Venice with the kings of Jerusalem and some barons. First, under the circumstances prevailing in the 1120s in the Eastern Mediterranean and in the Kingdom of Jerusalem, in particular, both parties considered their agreements as essentially bearing on Venetian merchants engaging in maritime and local trade

---

[42] This practice is duly attested since the thirteenth century.

[43] 1123, §3: 'quicumque voluerit coquere (...), libere liceat;' 1125, §3: 'libere liceat, quicumque voluerit, (...) precio suo coquere...'

in the kingdom's ports and residing temporarily there in order to further their business. In 1164 Doge Vitale Michiel still referred to these original features with respect to the Venetian quarter of Tyre, 'que data et concessa fuit nostro comuni pro hospitatione Venetorum, quando illuc irent.'[44] Secondly, it should be borne in mind that the *Pactum Warmundi* of 1123 was superseded in 1125 by the *Privilegium Balduini* and, consequently, the latter was the only legally binding document since then. In 1164 Vitale Michiel explicitly mentioned Baldwin II when dealing with the annual sum of 300 bezants from the royal revenue in Tyre, although it had also been mentioned in the charter of 1123.[45] In the early 1240s Marsilio Zorzi similarly referred to the charter of 1125 as authoritative.[46] This basic Venetian approach is not contradicted by the opportunistic submission of a copy of the *Pactum Warmundi* to Conrad of Montferrat in the spring of 1191, when Venice requested a confirmation of its privileges in the Kingdom of Jerusalem. At that time, shortly before the reconquest of Acre from the Muslims, the immediate concern of Venice's representatives in Tyre was the recovery of lost Venetian property in this city and especially its countryside, as confirmed by the first clause in Conrad's charter of 7 May 1191.[47] From a Venetian point of view the *Pactum Warmundi* was then more advantageous than the charter of 1125, since it lacked the military obligations imposed by Baldwin II in return for the holding of property in the lordship of Tyre.

The combination of allodial rights with the exercise of jurisdiction and taxation in specific cases, as defined in 1125, provided Venice's quarters and rural possessions with a quasi extra-territorial status. This status, however, could not be fully achieved as long as the exercise of criminal justice remained in royal hands. Despite this important limitation, Venice's achievement in the realm of jurisdiction was substantial and in principle enhanced the Commune's authority over its possessions, though not necessarily in practical terms. This is convincingly illustrated by the progressive erosion of Venice's privileges and property, which began shortly after 1125. King Fulk, who ruled from 1131 to 1143, unilaterally suspended the yearly payment of three hundred bezants to which the Commune was entitled. Venice had not yet recovered it by 1164.[48] In addition, it suffered from growing usurpation of its property and revenue in the countryside and city of Tyre from about that period, a process that continued until 1242.[49] In the spring of that year the Venetian government instructed Marsilio Zorzi, appointed bailo in Acre, to seek redress for these and other infringements of Venetian privileges and interests in the Levant. During his stay in the region, which lasted from 1242 to 1244, Zorzi compiled an extensive memorandum that

---

[44] TTh 1:140.
[45] TTh 1:141.
[46] See below, n. 81.
[47] TTh 1:212–215, with wrong dating. On the circumstances: Jacoby, 'Conrad, Marquis of Montferrat,' pp. 216–217.
[48] TTh 1:141.
[49] Jacoby, 'Conrad, Marquis of Montferrat,' pp. 196–197, 200, 216–217.

was to provide legal arguments for the maintenance and recovery of Venice's privileges and property.[50] At first glance this document comprises what appears to be a curious mixture of sources, which nevertheless are closely linked one to another.[51] Zorzi chose two long excerpts from a French version of the chronicle of William of Tyre, the great twelfth-century historian of the Latin Kingdom, which offer the historical background for the granting of the *Pactum Warmundi* and the *Privilegium Balduini*.[52] Between the two narrative texts he inserted the original Latin version of these two documents.[53] Later on he added the charter of December 1221 in favour of Venice issued by the lord of Beirut, John of Ibelin.[54] Furthermore, he included inventories of Venice's property in the lordship of Tyre and in Acre, and enumerated the assets confiscated in Cyprus from the Commune and Venetian individuals.[55] He also listed Venice's grievances against the royal administration, which he accused of encroaching upon Venice's privileges and, finally, reviewed his own action to obtain redress.

The inclusion of several chapters from William of Tyre's chronicle is a highly original feature of Zorzi's memorandum. His choice of a Levantine, rather than a Venetian chronicle, and of a French version, rather than the original Latin one, illustrates his historical awareness and political acumen. William of Tyre not only provided the most elaborate account of the events leading to the granting of the charters of 1123 and 1125. In the Kingdom of Jerusalem his chronicle was also considered an authoritative source, with which Venetian legal argumentation could be enhanced. In the thirteenth century the members of the nobility displayed a poor knowledge of Latin, and their preference for French is duly illustrated by the books that circulated in their milieu, whether fictional prose, poetry or historical and legal works.[56] At the time of Zorzi's sojourn in Acre the French version of William of Tyre's chronicle was undoubtedly more readily available there and would anyhow have been better understood than the Latin one. By contrast, Zorzi preferred the original and authoritative Latin texts of the charters

[50] An incomplete version of this memorandum is edited in TTh 2:351–398, and its full text in *Zorzi*, pp. 101–191. Its purpose is stated in two preambles: *Zorzi*, p. 101, lines 4–12, and p. 135, lines 1–5 = TTh 2:354, for the second section.

[51] For the order in which they appear: *Zorzi*, pp. 1–2.

[52] *Zorzi*, pp. 102–108, 116–134. The first excerpt is preceded by the following: 'Incipit ystoria et privilegium.' The introductory 'incipit ystoria' intended for the second excerpt was misplaced by a copyist and, instead, appears before Zorzi's report on his activity in the Levant, p. 135, line 1.

[53] *Zorzi*, p. 108, line 8 to p. 116, line 11.

[54] *Zorzi*, pp. 182–183 = TTh 2:230–232.

[55] For Cyprus: David Jacoby, 'The Rise of a New Emporium in the Eastern Mediterranean: Famagusta in the Late Thirteenth Century,' *Meletai kai hypomnemata, Hidryma archiepiskopou Makariou* III 1 (1984), 164–166 = idem, *Studies*, no. 8.

[56] David Jacoby, 'La littérature française dans les états latins de la Méditerranée orientale à l'époque des croisades: diffusion et création', in *Essor et fortune de la chanson de geste dans l'Europe et l'Orient latin. Actes du IXe Congrès international de la Société Rencesvals pour l'étude des épopées romanes (Padoue-Venise, 1982)* (Modena, 1984), pp. 617–646, and idem, 'Knightly Values and Class Consciousness in the Crusader States of the Eastern Mediterranean,' *Mediterranean Historical Review* 1 (1986), 158–186 = idem, *Studies*, nos. 2 and 1, respectively.

of 1123 and 1125, rather than their much abridged version incorporated in the French text from which he drew the narrative sections of William of Tyre.[57] Though aware that only the second document was binding, he included both of them in his memorandum, presumably because he considered that they could be used selectively to further Venetian interests. We have already noted that the Venetians produced the text of the *Pactum Warmundi* when it suited them, as in Tyre in 1191.[58] At first glance it is rather puzzling, therefore, that Zorzi omitted the charter of June 1222 issued by the lord of Beirut, John of Ibelin, in various ways more favourable for Venice than the previous one of December 1221.[59]

Marsilio Zorzi bitterly complained that in various circumstances the royal administration imposed dues on Venetian merchants, despite the full fiscal exemption to which they were entitled. Thus taxes were levied in Acre on the sale of merchandise imported from Damascus and other inland cities under Muslim rule, half their amount being imposed if the goods were in transit on their way to Venice. Evasion from the tax, whether full or partial, was possible only if the merchant had reached an agreement with the royal customs official collecting the dues or, in other words, if he bribed him before his own departure.[60] Venetian exports from Acre to Damascus and other Muslim inland cities, the overland transfer of goods originating in Venice from crusader ports to Acre, and the import of slaves and horses for sale in Acre were all taxed.[61] Zorzi referred to these practices as 'iniusticia' and contended that in all these cases the royal officials were violating Venetian privileges. Modern historians have concurred with this partisan view. Yet Zorzi's memorandum also reveals that the dues he mentioned were customary and had been collected from Venetians for so many years that no one even remembered since when. In the past repeated Venetian protests had failed to yield any results.[62] One may wonder, therefore, whether after all the royal administration did not have some strong legal arguments justifying the enforcement of its fiscal practices.

We have already noted that in the 1120s, when the *Privilegium Balduini* was drafted, Venetian activity in the Levant was limited to seaborne commerce and local trade in the ports of the region. However, the diversification and geographic expansion of Venetian trade in the course of the twelfth century generated new and unforeseen problems in the interpretation and implementation of the

---

[57] RHC Occ 1/1:550–553.

[58] See above, n. 47.

[59] The former in TTh 2:230–232. An explanation for the omission is suggested below pp. 170–171.

[60] *Zorzi*, p. 180, lines 1–6 = TTh 2:397–398. The first amount was obviously 8 bezants (not 9, as in the manuscript) and 8 carats, and the second 4 bezants and 4 carats, thus half that sum *pro centenario*. Zorzi's claim that the taxes were sometimes collected and sometimes not, 'et quandocumque evenit, quod recipiunt, et quandocumque non,' also hints at the bribing of crown officials.

[61] *Zorzi*, p. 180, lines 7–17 = TTh 2:398.

[62] See esp. *Zorzi*, p. 180, lines 17–19 = TTh 2:398: 'Et de istis supradictis longo tempore nos molestaverunt et acceperunt nobis ita, quod fere non exstat memoriam, sed tamen semper est eis contradictum, quod iniuste faciunt et recipiunt.'

dispositions upon which Venice and Baldwin II had agreed. When the Venetians began to engage in overland trade, they were taxed like other, non-privileged merchants. The royal officials presumably argued that this new type of trade was covered neither by the spirit of the agreement reached in 1125, nor by precedents. By contrast, Venice relied on the wording of the charter to claim that the tax exemptions were valid, regardless of the circumstances. These conflicting interpretations are indirectly confirmed by the two charters in favour of Venice issued by John of Ibelin some twenty years before Zorzi's arrival in the Levant. The one of December 1221 restricted Venetian tax exemptions in Beirut to imports through the *cathena* or maritime toll station of the city and to local purchases in its *funda* or seignorial market, in conformity with the spirit of the *Privilegium Balduini*.[63] However, strong Venetian pressure compelled the lord of Beirut to issue a new charter only seven months later, which explicitly extended tax exemptions to overland commerce, 'etiam de omnibus mercibus que veniunt per mare et per terram.'[64] Venice failed to obtain a similar success in the royal domain, where the king's officials were merely applying the rules in good faith, in accordance with precedents and to the best of royal interests.

This was also the case with the tax of one bezant levied on the slaves and horses the Venetians imported for sale in Acre.[65] It had been imposed for many years, both upon Venetians and upon the merchants of other maritime nations supposedly exempt from all commercial dues. In 1229, though, Frederick II rewarded the Pisans for their political support during his presence in the kingdom by exempting them from the tax on the import or export of horses and other riding animals, whether by land or by sea.[66] Zorzi also raised the issue of the *terciaria*. The charter of Baldwin II had stipulated that this tax would be imposed exclusively upon outbound ships carrying passengers who were not merchants. Yet contrary to this charter, 'contra formam nostri privilegii et pacta,' royal officials were also levying it from incoming ships and vessels in transit, which implies that the Venetians had also extended and diversified their activity in shipping and in the transportation of passengers.[67] Zorzi obtained the strict implementation of the clause regarding the *terciaria*. However, he failed to gain total exemption from this tax, a request of his conceived as compensation for the suspension of the yearly payment of 300 bezants promised to the Commune in 1125.[68]

One of Zorzi's main concerns was the recovery of Venetian property and rights in Tyre, a city held since July 1242 by Balian of Ibelin in his capacity as royal

---

[63] See above, n. 54.

[64] See above, n. 59.

[65] *Zorzi*, p. 180, lines 1–17 = TTh 2:397–398.

[66] Giuseppe Müller, ed., *Documenti sulle relazioni delle città toscane coll'Oriente cristiano e coi Turchi fino all'anno MDXXXI* (Florence, 1879), p. 97, no. 66.

[67] *Zorzi*, p. 179, lines 19–23: 'ab omnibus nostris Venetis, qui aliquos homines in suis navibus et vasscellis portant per dictum regnum vel alibi.' Note the absence of the term *peregrini* in this context.

[68] *Zorzi*, p. 179, lines 24–28 = TTh 2:397. See also above, n. 48.

custodian of the lordship of Tyre.[69] Zorzi restored the Commune's authority over its quarter and some of its property in the countryside, yet not over all Venetian possessions in the city. In addition, he obtained the cancellation of abusive royal taxation on the sale of various commodities in the Venetian quarter and managed to restore the Commune's exclusive authority in this field. He also recovered the Venetian portion of the revenues shared with the king, which had been usurped by the representative of Emperor Frederick II, Riccardo Filangieri.[70] In line with the charter of 1125, he re-established Venetian jurisdiction and taxation over the Syrian and Jewish residents of the quarter, denied to Venice since the reign of King John of Brienne or even earlier. He forcefully asserted that this quarter constituted a separate territorial and legal entity, distinct from the royal portion of the city, and that the Commune enjoyed in it full jurisdiction, like the king in his own section. The wording was clearly a reflection of the formulation found in the charter of 1125 (§§1 and 11).[71] Yet, since neither this document nor the ancient oath of the Venetian judges in Tyre defined the precise nature of Venetian jurisdiction, conflicts between royal and foreign jurisdictions were bound to arise.[72] When Zorzi contended that the Commune's judicial competence included criminal justice and that the latter had been denied to Venice for many years, he encountered the fierce opposition of the royal officials and was rebuffed.[73]

In their charters in favour of Pisa both King Baldwin III in 1156 and, even more explicitly, King Amalric I in 1168 had stated that High Justice was an exclusive royal prerogative.[74] The kings of Jerusalem, their officials and the barons of the kingdom staunchly maintained this policy in their dealings with the maritime powers throughout the twelfth and thirteenth centuries. This is further illustrated by a comparison of the charters issued in favour of Venice by the lord of Beirut, John of Ibelin, in December 1221 and June 1222 respectively. Both documents grant the Commune the right to establish its own court in Beirut and to exercise justice except in three cases, namely homicide, rape and theft. While enlarging Venice's fiscal privileges, the second charter contains a significant addition bearing on jurisdiction. It was obviously introduced at John of Ibelin's insistence in order to put an end once and for all to Venetian claims to High Justice. The three types of criminal offences just mentioned, it maintains, should be handled as in Acre, which confirms that High Justice indeed remained there outside the reach of the Venetian court.[75] This explicit restriction of Venice's jurisdiction to civil matters explains why Zorzi refrained from including in his memorandum the charter delivered by John of Ibelin in June 1222: it could not

---

[69] On the circumstances: David Jacoby, 'The Kingdom of Jerusalem and the Collapse of Hohenstaufen Power in the Levant,' *DOP* 40 (1986), 83–94 = idem, *Studies*, no. 3.

[70] *Zorzi*, p. 135, lines 6–10 and p. 140, line 13 to p. 141, line 7 = TTh 2:354, 359–360.

[71] *Zorzi*, p. 139, lines 4–9, 21 to p. 140, line 12 = TTh 2:358–359.

[72] Zorzi found the oath 'in consuetudine antiqua:' *Zorzi*, p. 141, lines 8–17 = TTh 2:360.

[73] *Zorzi*, p. 139, lines 10–11 = TTh 2:358.

[74] Müller, *Documenti*, pp. 7 and 14, nos. 5 and 11, respectively.

[75] TTh 2:233: 'Et ista tria, sicuti habent in Anco' [*sic* for 'Accon'].

be submitted to the royal administration to sustain Venice's claims to criminal justice. Zorzi's attempt to enlarge the Commune's authority in this field was based on the widest possible literal interpretation of the judicial privileges granted to Venice in 1125. By contrast, the royal party relied on the spirit of this charter and precedents, as in various fiscal matters examined above. In sum, despite Zorzi's contention Venice had not suffered any curtailment of its jurisdiction.

Zorzi's efforts to gain authority in criminal cases were eventually rewarded. At first, shortly after his return from Tyre to Acre in July 1242, the royal viscount of that city refused to extradite a Venetian accused of theft, as he had requested, on the ground that the Venetian court lacked authority in *ius sanguinis*. The viscount nevertheless handed the culprit over to the master of the Templars, who in turn transferred him to Zorzi. Additional cases were handled in a similar way. It appears, then, that the two sides had reached a compromise. While maintaining his stand in principle, the royal official enabled the Venetian *bailo* to exercise High Justice.[76] A somewhat different arrangement along the same lines was implemented in Tyre with the agreement of the royal castellan Ugo Amiratus or Amirallus and Gerardo Pisani, apparently his successor, who transferred to Zorzi a Venetian accused of having stolen sugar canes, as well as several others for unspecified reasons. The viscount Salvaçu acted similarly. In addition, the lord of Beirut, Balian of Ibelin, delivered to Zorzi a Venetian from Cyprus who had stolen money from one of his own knights. Zorzi stresses that he conducted the trials in public in order to establish precedents and consolidate thereby Venice's right to High Justice.[77] Yet the restrictions imposed upon him contradict his claim that he freely exercised justice in cases of theft and murder. He was compelled to accept the presence of royal officials at the trials of Venetians for theft and, since he fails to mention specific cases of homicide, we may be sure that none were brought to his court.

Venice's position in Acre was decisively strengthened by its victory in the War of St. Sabas, which ended in 1258. In the following period the Commune pursued in the city an expansion policy sustained by the annexation and purchase of property located outside its own quarter and surrounded both its old and new territory by a wall. It consolidated its hold on that territory by extending over it its own jurisdiction in conformity with the *Privilegium Balduini* (§11), yet at the expense of royal rights. In addition, Venice managed to gain recognition of the ecclesiastical authority of the church of San Marco over its own enlarged quarter, at the expense of Acre's bishop.[78] Marsilio Zorzi's successors continued to exercise High Justice, although we lack information about the procedure

---

[76] *Zorzi*, p. 138, lines 10–17 = TTh 2:357.

[77] *Zorzi*, p. 139, lines 10–20: 'et his fecimus ut curie nostre fuit visum faciendi.' Ugo Amiratus was still in office in April 1243: Peter Jackson, 'The End of Hohenstaufen Rule in Syria,' *Bulletin of the Institute of Historical Research* 59 (1986), 25–26, and *Zorzi*, p. 200.

[78] David Jacoby, 'L'évolution urbaine et la fonction méditerranéenne d'Acre à l'époque des croisades,' in Ennio Poleggi, ed., *Città portuali del Mediterraneo, storia e archeologia. Atti del Convegno Internazionale di Genova 1985* (Genoa, 1989), p. 103.

followed. Neither the royal administration, which mostly represented absentee kings, nor King Hugh III of Lusignan, the barons or the high ecclesiastical dignitaries were able or willing to prevent these developments.[79] Conditions appeared to have changed in the summer of 1277 after the arrival of Ruggero di San Severino, the representative of the new king of Jerusalem, Charles I of Anjou.[80] He initiated a forceful policy aimed at the recovery of the crown's lost rights and property, which not only endangered Venice's achievements of the last twenty years in Acre, but also some of those it had obtained as far back as 1125. Ruggero di San Severino contested both Venice's right to High Justice and its judicial authority over the residents of its own quarter. Never before had the latter been called into question. Moreover, he refused to exempt Venetian land trade from taxation, also denied during Zorzi's term of office. Finally, he requested the payment of the *terciaria* from incoming ships carrying passengers, a flagrant infringement of the relevant disposition of 1125. These issues were listed in the detailed letter of instructions given to the ambassadors dispatched by Venice to King Charles I. These ambassadors also carried with them a copy of the *Privilegium Balduini*. As in the past, differences in the interpretation of this charter were at the root of the frictions between Venice and the royal officials.[81] The outcome of the negotiations with Charles I is unknown, yet it would seem that the status quo existing at the time of Ruggero di San Severino's arrival in Acre was restored.[82] In any event, Venice did not raise the same issues in the following years, although this did not prevent it from pursuing its expansionist policy in Acre.[83]

By contrast to Acre, Marsilio Zorzi's achievements in Tyre were lost when the city's lord, Philip of Montfort, expelled the Venetians from his city in 1256 or 1257, in the course of the War of St. Sabas.[84] In 1277 the fear of an attack by the joint forces of Ruggero di San Severino and Venice induced Philip's successor, John of Montfort, to reach an agreement with Venice's *bailo* in Acre, Albertino Morosini, to whom he made far-reaching concessions.[85] According to the agreement of the 1 July 1277 the Commune recovered its property, rights

---

[79] This is also implied by the Venetian document mentioned below, n. 81.

[80] For his course of action: Marco Pozza, 'Acri e Negroponte: un capitolo delle relazioni fra Venezia e Carlo d'Angiò (1277–1282),' *Archivio Storico per le Provincie Napoletane*, 3a ser. 21 (1982), 29–33, 36–37, 42–45.

[81] The relevant instructions are edited ibid., pp. 67–72. Note p. 69: 'formam pacti nostri de quo portatis exemplum,' the nature of this copy being revealed by the reference to the *terciaria* as defined in 1125. See also p. 70, with respect to Charles I: 'dicendo (...) quod aliter intelligit verba pacti quam nos intelligamus.'

[82] Ibid., pp. 52–54.

[83] David Jacoby, 'L'expansion occidentale dans le Levant: les Vénitiens à Acre dans la seconde moitié du treizième siècle,' *Journal of Medieval History* 3 (1977), 230–231 = idem, *Recherches sur la Méditerranée orientale du XIIe au XVe siècle. Peuples, sociétés, économies* (London, 1979), no. 7.

[84] The exact date is unknown: Georg Caro, *Genua und die Mächte am Mittelmeer, 1257–1311. Ein Beitrag zur Geschichte des XIII. Jahrhunderts*, 2 vols. (Halle, 1895), 1:36–37.

[85] TTh 3:150–158. On the circumstances: Pozza, 'Acri e Negroponte,' pp. 37–43.

and jurisdiction in the lordship of Tyre, both in the city and its rural hinterland, and individual Venetians regained possession of their assets. As explicitly stated, there would be a return to the situation existing during Zorzi's tenure of office. This specific reference was clearly requested by Venice, which relied on the precedents he had established to achieve further gains, particularly obvious in the legal field. Venice would hold its portion of the lordship 'libere et regaliter,' as defined in 1125 (§15). Henceforth the two parties, the lord of Tyre and Venice, would be in this respect on an equal footing as 'consortes et veri domini,' each of them enjoying the same authority in its respective portion. The foremost expression of this equality was Venice's right to exercise both civil and criminal justice over Venetians, as well as over the permanent and temporary residents of its portion. Philip of Montfort had already concluded a similar agreement with Genoa in 1264. It is likely that the verdicts of the Venetian court in criminal cases were to be carried out by the lord of Tyre, as stipulated in that agreement.[86] With respect to Venice, the shift from its tolerated exercise of High Justice, as in Zorzi's days, to the recognition of its full authority in this field was a highly significant achievement. It was explicitly stated, however, that the lord of Tyre retained judicial authority over his liegemen and burgesses residing in the Venetian quarter. A similar rule had been imposed in the past with respect to Pisans holding fiefs or burgage tenures from the king.[87] In 1277 this restriction must have also been prompted by John of Montfort's fear that some of his subjects, whether or not living in Venice's quarter, might invoke the Venetian nationality they had acquired to evade trials in his courts. Venice's occasional grant of this privilege to foreigners, including royal vassals and burgesses, is attested in Acre in 1257 and may have already been practiced earlier.[88] The whole formulation of 1277 was supposedly in accordance with the terms of the *Privilegium Balduini*, 'secundum terminos definitos ab antiquo.' In fact, however, the extent of Venetian jurisdiction conformed with Venice's widest interpretation of the charter of 1125, while the restriction *ratione personae* flatly contradicted it. At Venice's explicit request John of Montfort added that the use of his title 'lord of Tyre' would not impinge upon the rights of the parties to the treaty.[89]

The charter of 1277 also settled several other issues. Individuals visiting Tyre would be tried by the court of the city's portion in which they committed an offence. The principle that Venetian defendants would be judged in the bailo's court in cases in which they were opposed to the lord's subjects followed the rule of 1125. Full exemption from taxation was promised for both seaborne and land trade, an improvement on the privilege of 1125. The ownership of a plot of land in the city, on which a tower had been built, would be determined. John of Montfort promised to repair the public buildings of the Commune or compensate it for

---

[86] Cornelio Desimoni (ed.), 'Quatre titres des Génois à Acre et à Tyr,' *AOL* 2/2 (1884), 225–226.
[87] Prawer, *Crusader Institutions*, pp. 244–245.
[88] Jacoby, 'L'expansion occidentale,' pp. 245–246.
[89] TTh 3:152, 157–158.

V

their destruction. He would also transfer to Venice's representatives the revenue yielded by the property belonging to the Commune and Venetian individuals, which he and his father had collected in the city and its rural hinterland since 1256 or 1257. An arbitration committee composed of the patriarch of Jerusalem and the masters of the Templars and the Hospitallers would determine the sums owed by the lord of Tyre and the respective rights of the parties, if any disagreement between them arose. In each such case John of Montfort was to obtain the king's approval to the procedure of arbitration. The respective rights of the parties or the king would not be prejudiced, should the latter delay his answer up to one month.[90] To be sure, as royal vassal the lord of Tyre was careful to avoid any alienation of crown rights.[91] One may wonder, however, whether he was not also seeking a way to evade some of his own obligations toward Venice, a course of action facilitated by the policy pursued by Ruggero di San Severino since his arrival in Acre.

This appears to be confirmed by John of Montfort's numerous infringements of his agreement with Venice. In August 1283 Venice's *Maggior Consiglio* adopted the advice of a committee which included Albertino Morosini, the signatory of the treaty of 1277. The Venetian *bailo* serving in Tyre was instructed to conduct negotiations with the lord of the city and demand the full implementation of the charters of 1125 and 1277. The Commune should enjoy its share of the land and fiscal revenues of the city and countryside of Tyre, in conformity with the original partition. It should also exercise full sovereignty, as well as civil and criminal justice in its portion of the lordship, 'cum tertia parte pleni et liberi dominii et signorie.' In addition, the Venetians should benefit from total tax exemption in all types of trade. In sum, all the major issues supposedly settled in 1277 had to be reconfirmed. Finally, Venice would contribute one third of the expenses incurred in matters useful to its own interests, provided a prior agreement between the two parties had been reached.[92] Work in the harbour was presumably envisaged. There is no evidence regarding the outcome of the talks with John of Montfort.

Contrary to widespread belief, the concessions granted to Venice in the *Pactum Warmundi* did not amount to the 'creation of a state within the kingdom' of Jerusalem since 1123.[93] During the entire crusader period the Venetian privileges, as defined in the authoritative *Privilegium Balduini* of 1125, were the subject of conflicting interpretations by Venice on the one hand, the crown and some barons on the other. Their preservation and implementation required constant vigilance and efforts on the part of Venice. Two factors in particular prompted the Commune to seek an extension of its privileges and authority: important changes

[90] TTh 3:154–155.

[91] Riley-Smith, *Feudal Nobility*, pp. 224–225.

[92] Roberto Cessi, ed., *Deliberazioni del Maggior Consiglio di Venezia*, 3 vols. (Bologna, 1931–1950), 3:43–44, §129.

[93] As stated by Prawer, *Crusader Institutions*, p. 222.

in the nature of Venetian trade and presence in the kingdom since the twelfth century, and the acquisition of wide-ranging jurisdiction in its portion of the Latin Empire of Constantinople and its own colonies after the Fourth Crusade. Venice attempted to exploit vague formulations and loopholes in the charters it had obtained, yet encountered the strong opposition of royal and baronial officials, who at times even limited arbitrarily the implementation of privileges the interpretation of which was not disputed. High Justice was undoubtedly the most sensitive issue between the parties. In this field Marsilio Zorzi was the first to achieve some significant success for Venice, between 1242 and 1244, since he created a precedent on which the Commune was able to build in the following period. In practice Venice's quarter in Acre and its portion of the lordship of Tyre became truly extra-territorial enclaves in the Kingdom of Jerusalem, despite some apparent restrictions on the Commune's exercise of criminal justice. Not until 1277, though, did Venice obtain recognition of its right to this type of jurisdiction in the lordship of Tyre. It is not clear to what extent it managed to maintain effectively its achievements in this field in the last years of crusader rule.

VI

Migration, Trade and Banking in Crusader Acre

Acre was a city of minor importance in the Arab period preceding the First Crusade. It merely served as an agricultural market, as well as a port of call and a land station on the route between Egypt and Tyre. At that time Tyre, located to the north of Acre, was the main industrial, commercial and maritime centre along the Levantine coast[1]. The crusader conquest of 1104 opened a new era in Acre's history, in which it attained the peak of its economic, demographic and urban development since the Hellenistic period[2]. During the Latin period, which lasted almost two centuries (1104-1187, 1191-1291), Acre became the main emporium of the crusader states of the Levant and one of the major commercial centres of the Eastern Mediterranean. It also experienced a growth of population and an extension of territory[3]. These various processes were largely prompted by the new functions Acre assumed after 1104 and by the Latin migration these functions generated. Indeed, there was a close interaction between migration on the one hand, trade and banking, on the other.

The rise of Acre began shortly after the crusader conquest. It primarily derived from the new geo-political context created by the First Crusade, with its focus on the liberation of Jerusalem and the preservation of Latin presence in the Holy Land. Latin rule in this region was still fragile in the first decades after the conquest, and its consolidation required a constant flow of western military reinforcements and provisions, as well as the establishment of Latin immigrants in the conquered territories. Along the Levantine coast Acre offered the best access to the newly-founded Kingdom of Jerusalem for these purposes, all the

---

1. On Tyre, see S. D. Goitein, *A Mediterranean Society. The Jewish Communities of the Arab World as Portrayed in the Documents of the Cairo Geniza*, Berkeley and Los Angeles 1967-1988, vol. I, pp. 81, 109-110, 190, 212-214, 293. On a load of peaches, presumably dried, sent from Acre to Cairo: *ibid.*, vol. I, p. 278.

2. For the general background, see the standard histories of the crusades and of the Kingdom of Jerusalem.

3. For what follows, see D. Jacoby, L'évolution urbaine et la fonction méditerranéenne d'Acre à l'époque des croisades, in E. Poleggi (ed.), *Città portuali del Mediterraneo, storia e archeologia, Atti del Convegno Internazionale di Genova 1985*, Genova 1989, pp. 95-109.

more so because Tyre remained in Muslim hands up to 1124. By then Acre had already largely established its dominant role among the ports of the Levant. Moreover, even after 1124 it retained the advantage of being closer than Tyre to Jerusalem, Bethlehem and Nazareth, the main destinations of pilgrims and, therefore, was a more convenient place than Tyre for their disembarkation. It follows that the Latin presence generated two closely related developments which decisively enhanced the economic function of Acre: first, a shift from purely economic to a combination of economic, ideological and military priorities and, secondly, a concomitant geographical shift from the axis linking Tyre to Damascus to more southern axes connecting Acre both to this city and to Jerusalem[4]. The primary functions of Acre since its conquest by the Latins was to serve as the main landing port for Western crusaders, pilgrims, immigrants and supplies and, in addition, to furnish the necessary services to those reaching it from the West. These functions, which remained of vital importance throughout the Latin period, created the favourable context for the city's swift and impressive economic rise and provided the main impetus to this process.

In the twelfth and thirteenth century Acre thus assumed an economic role it had never fulfilled before. In addition to the services it offered to passing ships, it supplied housing, food, administrative and religious assistance, guides and to some extent land transport to military forces, pilgrims and other visitors alike. The operation of this logistical infrastructure promoted the expansion of the local market, which diversified its functions. Thanks to the concentration of capital in Acre, to which we shall soon return, the city developed into a transit station, entrepot and distribution centre for wares shipped from the West, collected in Egypt and along the Levantine coast, and those arriving from the Muslim hinterland. As a result, Acre became a major port of call for ships engaged in long-distance sailing. The city's convenient maritime link with Alexandria, the main source of spices in the Mediterranean, and its role in transit trade are attested some time before 1201, for instance, when a load of pepper arriving in Constantinople was assessed according to the standard

---

4. On trade between Damascus and Acre in 1184: *The Travels of Ibn Jubayr,* trans. R. J. C. Broadhurst, London 1952, pp. 301, 313-318; for the thirteenth century: D. Jacoby, A Venetian Manual of Commercial Practice from Crusader Acre, in G. Airaldi e B. Z. Kedar (eds.), *I comuni italiani nel Regno crociato di Gerusalemme* (Collana storica di fonti e studi, diretta da Geo Pistarino, 48), Genova 1986, p. 407, n. 17, repr. in Idem, *Studies on the Crusader States and on Venetian Expansion,* Northampton 1989, no. VII.

weight of Acre[5]. In short, the city became firmly integrated within the complex triangular trade and maritime networks connecting Egypt with the Byzantine Empire and the West.

The financing of services and trade in Acre was made possible by the movement of men of arms, pilgrims, immigrants and ships. This movement generated a large influx of liquid capital, amplified by funds sent for the defence of the Kingdom of Jerusalem, pious donations made to ecclesiastical institutions, and commercial capital invested in coins and bullion[6]. The outlay involved in the temporary sojourn of a crusader lord is illustrated by the account established in Acre in 1266 after the death of Eudes, Count of Nevers. It lists the wages of men of arms and servants, rent paid for lodging, expenses incurred for the exchange of foreign money into local currency, the purchase of provisions, including poultry, as well as other items[7]. The contribution of pilgrimage to the flow of cash to Acre was all the more important, because this was practically the only Levantine port benefiting from this factor. It is noteworthy that in the first half of the thirteenth century some ships sailing from Marseille to Acre took more than 1,000 pilgrims on board. Although the pilgrimage season was brief, the large numbers of visitors it brought to Acre resulted in a substantial enhancement of economic activity[8]. The similarity with present-day tourism is striking.

The increase in services and trade, however, ultimately depended on the growth of Acre's population. When Acre surrendered to the crusader armies in 1104, the Muslim inhabitants were allowed to leave[9]. Later on, Muslims occasionally visited the city and stayed in it for short periods of time, whether

---

5. C. Imperiale di Sant'Angelo (ed.), *Codice diplomatico della repubblica di Genova*, Roma 1936-1942, vol. III, p. 198: *cantaria .XXII. piperis ad cantarium catene Accon*. See also below, n. 35.

6. On the non-commercial influx: F. A. Cazel, Jr., Financing the Crusades, in K. M. Setton (ed.), *A History of the Crusades*, Madison, Wisconsin 1969-1989, vol. VI, pp. 116-149; H. E. Mayer, Henry II of England and the Holy Land, *English Historical Review* 97 (1982), pp. 721-739, repr. in Idem, *Kings and Lords in the Latin Kingdom of Jerusalem*, Aldershot 1994, no. X; D. Jacoby, Three Notes on Crusader Acre, *Zeitschrift des Deutschen Palästina-Vereins* 109 (1993), pp. 91-96, and bibliography p. 91, n. 50. On trade and banking, see below.

7. A. M. Chazaud, Inventaire et comptes de la succession d'Eudes, comte de Nevers (Acre 1266), *Mémoires de la société nationale des antiquaires de France* 32 (1870), pp. 176-206, with introduction pp. 164-176.

8. On these aspects, see D. Jacoby, Pélerinage médiéval et sanctuaires de Terre Sainte: la perspective vénitienne, *Ateneo Veneto* 173 (n. s. 24) (1986), pp. 27-31, repr. in Idem, *Studies on the Crusader States and on Venetian Expansion*, Northampton 1989, no. IV.

9. See S. Runciman, *A History of the Crusades*, Cambridge 1953-1954, vol. II, p. 88.

VI

to sell their agricultural produce, engage in trade or board a ship, like the traveller Ibn Jubayr in 1184. A small oratory in the former main mosque of the city, transformed into a Latin cathedral, was set aside for their worship, yet no Muslims resided permanently in Acre[10]. On the other hand, Arabic-speaking Oriental Christians, including those who belonged to the Byzantine Church, remained in the city after the crusader conquest and their ranks were later reinforced by immigration[11]. The continuity of Jewish residence is implied by a letter sent from Acre by a Jew shortly after the city's siege in 1104, as well as by later sources up to the Muslim conquest[12]. The Latins, however, rapidly became the dominant element in Acre's population. Participants in the First Crusade were the first to settle, and immigrants arriving from the West soon joined them. In 1123 we find the earliest evidence of internal Latin migration within the Kingdom of Jerusalem itself. A former resident of Jaffa was settled by then in Acre[13], a clear sign of the increasing economic activity and attraction of this city. The growing Latin population established in the Kingdom constituted an important market for agricultural produce, spices, aromatics, industrial raw materials and finished products[14]. In short, there was a clear interaction between demographic growth and economic factors, the latter substantially furthering an increase in size of Acre's Latin population up to 1187.

---

10. *The Travels of Ibn Jubayr*, pp. 318-319. General background: B. Z. Kedar, The Subjected Muslims of the Frankish Levant, in J. M. Powell (ed.), *Muslims under Latin Rule, 1100-1300*, Princeton, New Jersey 1990, pp. 135-174.

11. General background on the Christian communities: J. Prawer, Social Classes in the Crusader States: the 'Minorities', in Setton, *A History of the Crusades*, vol. VI, pp. 65-82; B. Hamilton, *The Latin Church in the Crusader States. The Secular Church*, London 1980, pp. 163-164, 312-313, 316-317, 333, 347-349, 355; on some of their churches and monasteries, see Jacoby, *Three Notes on Crusader Acre*, pp. 83-88.

12. Letter translated by Goitein, *A Mediterranean Society*, vol. I, p. 132. J. Prawer, *The History of the Jews of the Latin Kingdom of Jerusalem*, Oxford 1988, pp. 42 and 51, seems to suggest that no Jews were left in Acre, yet adopts a different stance on pp. 60-61; for the following period, see *ibid.*, p. 295, index, s. v. Acre.

13. G. L. Fr. Tafel und G. M. Thomas (eds.), *Urkunden zur älteren Handels- und Staatsgeschichte der Republik Venedig*, Wien 1856-1857 [hereafter: *TTh*], vol. I, p. 87: in 1123 an area in Acre extending *usque ad domum Guiberti de Jopen*; see also p. 91, in 1125.

14. Oriental and Levantine commodities, including silk fabrics manufactured in Antioch, appear in a thirteenth century customs list: Comte Beugnot (ed.), *Livre des Assises de la Cour des Bourgeois*, chap. 242-243, in *Recueil des historiens des croisades, Lois*, vol. II, Paris 1843, pp. 173-181; on Aleppo cotton and wheat from the West and the Black Sea, see Jacoby, *A Venetian Manual*, p. 425.

From that year, however, military and political developments contributed their share to demographic growth in Acre. The loss of Jerusalem and other inland cities to the Muslims in 1187 brought a large flow of Latin settlers withdrawing from the interior of the Kingdom of Jerusalem to the coastal strip. Many of them settled in Acre after the Latin recovery of the city in 1191, following four years of Muslim occupation. A new suburb enclosed by a double rampart was added to the north of Acre before 1212. In the thirteenth century the city also became the main destination for the Latin settlers retreating before the advancing Muslim armies. In addition, Acre role's as political and ecclesiastical centre of the Latin Kingdom, instead of Jerusalem, also stimulated economic growth, which in turn furthered immigration from the West[15]. And, finally, one should not forget the importance of religious motivation as an incentive to western settlement in the Holy Land. Numerous monasteries, churches and hospices were built in thirteenth century Acre by religious orders, for instance the Carmelites, as well as by national groups of immigrants, such as the English and the Bretons, in order to attend to the needs of the sick, the poor and the pilgrims[16].

Within the general migratory movement affecting Acre, mercantile migration deserves particular attention because of its direct link to trade and banking, the particular features it acquired as a result of this link, and the considerable impact it had on the city's economy. Except for the provisioning of the local population, regional and inter-regional trade in crusader Acre essentially followed a seasonal rhythm, dictated by weather conditions, winds and sea currents. The diffusion of navigational instruments and advances in ship design lengthened the yearly period of sailing in the late thirteenth century, yet did not alter this basic pattern. Trade in Acre reached its peak when convoys of western ships arrived in the spring and in the autumn. Some of these ships stayed in Acre's waters for a short period only, up to a fortnight, before returning to the West, while others spent the winter there and awaited the resumption of sailing in the spring. A strong correlation existed between the

15. D. Jacoby, Montmusard, Suburb of Crusader Acre: the First Stage of its Development, in B. Z. Kedar, H. E. Mayer, R. C. Smail (eds.), *Outremer. Studies in the History of the Kingdom of Jerusalem, presented to Joshua Prawer*, Jerusalem 1972, pp. 205-217, repr. in Jacoby, *Studies*, no. VI.

16. See D. Jacoby, Some Unpublished Seals from the Latin East, *Israel Numismatic Journal* 5 (1981), pp. 85-88. On the English in particular, see also A. Forey, The Military Order of St Thomas of Acre, *English Historical Review* 92 (1977), pp. 481-503, repr. in Idem, *Military Orders and Crusades,* Aldershot 1994, no. XII.

VI

dynamics of shipping and those of mercantile migration. As a rule merchants returned to their base of departure in the West and thus followed a cyclic, circular and largely seasonal migration pattern[17]. This pattern was also reflected in the nature of services offered to merchants visiting Acre. In the Venetian quarter the Commune rented out dwellings, warehouses and shops in two ways: to visiting merchants and pilgrims on a monthly basis, and to residents of the city for the year. Not surprisingly, the monthly rates for these facilities were proportionally much higher than the yearly ones, as nowadays housing and food are for the seasonal tourists[18].

The twelfth century also witnessed the emergence and gradual strengthening of another type of mercantile migration, which took place along the same routes as the one just described. It entailed a shift from circular to linear migration and led to settlement in Acre. The growing combination of trade, banking and transport, the diversification of investments in business ventures and goods, the growing volume of maritime commerce and, finally, the increasing regularity of its rhythm, all these provided a strong incentive to long-distance emigration from the West to Acre. Indeed, the economic activities of merchants and bankers could be enhanced by their all-year-round, continuous presence in Acre, where they could conveniently observe the movement of goods, people, transport facilities, moneys and credit. Their sojourn in Acre during the 'dead' seasons extending between the arrivals of the spring and autumn convoys also enabled them to do profitable business, since prices were then low and credit cheap[19]. Mercantile settlement in Acre was furthered by the grant of fiscal exemptions, judicial privileges and quarters to the leading maritime powers, namely Genoa in 1104, Venice in 1110, with an extension in 1123, and Pisa in 1168. Their quarters included market places, churches, ovens and baths, or some of these facilities. The privileges bestowed upon them were confirmed or extended at the time of the Third Crusade (1189-1191). Thereafter

---

17. General background: D. Jacoby, The Migration of Merchants and Craftsmen: a Mediterranean Perspective (12th-15th Centuries), in *Le migrazioni in Europa, secc. XIII-XVIII*, a cura di Simonetta Cavaciocchi (Istituto Internazionale di Storia Economica "F. Datini", Prato, Serie II - Atti delle "Settimane di Studi" e altri Convegni, 25), Florence 1994, pp. 538-541.

18. Report of 1243: O. Berggötz, *Der Bericht des Marsilio Zorzi. Codex Querini-Stampalia IV3 (1064)* (Kieler Werckstücke, Reihe C: Beiträge zur europäischen Geschichte des frühen und hohen Mittelalters, herausgegeben von Hans Eberhard Mayer, Band 2), Frankfurt am Main 1990, pp. 172-179; previous edition in *TTh*, vol. II, pp. 389-397.

19. On this type of migration and settlement: Jacoby, *The Migration of Merchants and Craftsmen*, pp. 541-544.

these quarters enjoyed internal autonomy, those of Venice and Pisa even an extraterritorial status[20].

The advantages deriving from settlement in Acre for the gathering of information are clearly illustrated by an unpublished Venetian commercial manual. It was apparently compiled by a Venetian merchant or notary established in Acre about 1270. The geographical range it covers extends from Alexandria to Acre and Constantinople in the east, and from there to Venice, the Maghreb and Montpellier in the west. It lists numerous commodities and reveals the complexity of trade and shipping networks both within the Eastern Mediterranean and between this region and the West. The manual enumerates an impressive number of spices, aromatics and dye materials imported from Alexandria to Acre, and is familiar with weights, measures and the operation of the mint in both these cities. In addition, it illustrates the collection of various grades of cotton, brought to Acre from both Northern Syria and the city's own rural hinterland in order to be shipped to the centres of the Italian cotton industry. While the Acre manual appears to be the earliest western work of that type, it is obvious that merchants and notaries established in the city had begun much earlier to gather useful information about actual trade practices and trade opportunities[21].

Mercantile settlement was not necessarily permanent. It could also be temporary, lasting a few years only, yet in any event beyond a single shipping season as required by wintering in Acre. The distinction between the two variants of settlement is essential for an understanding of this phenomenon, and the failure to do so has led in the past to some erroneous conclusions. The repeated presence of a merchant in Acre does not necessarily imply settlement in the city, nor does the reference to the parish of his mother-city from which he

20. On the quarters: D. Jacoby, Crusader Acre in the Thirteenth Century: Urban Layout and Topography, *Studi medievali*, 3a serie, 20 (1979), pp. 19-39, repr. in Idem, *Studies*, no. V. On the privileges: M.-L. Favreau-Lilie, *Die Italiener im Heiligen Land vom ersten Kreuzzug bis zum Tode Heinrichs von Champagne (1098-1197)*, Amsterdam 1989, pp. 438-454, 462-483, passim, yet some different interpretations are required in connection with grants bestowed in Tyre: see D. Jacoby, Conrad, Marquis of Montferrat, and the Kingdom of Jerusalem (1187-1192), in G. Pistarino (ed.), *Atti del Congresso Internazionale "Dai feudi monferrini e dal Piemonte ai nuovi mondi oltre gli Oceani"*, Alessandria 1993, pp. 197-202, 207, 211, 213-214, 235, n. 90. See also D. Jacoby, L'expansion occidentale dans le Levant: les Vénitiens à Acre dans la seconde moitié du treizième siècle, *Journal of Medieval History* 3 (1977), pp. 225-264, repr. in Idem, *Recherches sur la Méditerranée orientale du XIIe au XVe siècle. Peuples, sociétés, économies*, London 1979, no. VII.
21. Jacoby, *A Venetian Manual*, pp. 403-428.

originated disprove it[22]. Indeed, some Venetians who resided in Constantinople after the Fourth Crusade for long periods of time continuously recorded the name of their parish in Venice while living abroad[23]. There is good reason to believe that some Venetians in Acre behaved similarly, and one cannot therefore take it for granted that they were not temporary or permanent residents in the city.

Solid evidence for settlement is conveyed by the terms *habitator* and *burgensis* which, at Acre as in other cities of the Eastern Mediterranean, were loosely used with respect to residence and were devoid in this context of the legal connotations common in the West[24]. Yet the testimony they offer does not always reveal the precise nature of settlement and is valid only for the time at which it appears. Indeed, the individual identifying himself as *habitator* was either a recent settler, one who had not yet made up his mind to stay on permanently, or else one who upheld his self-perception as temporary resident. In this respect, the number of years was irrelevant. By 1162 the Venetian Pietro Morosini was already established in the city for some time, since he appears then as *de Acris*. Nevertheless, four years later, in 1166, he still registered with a notary as *habitator* of Acre[25]. Eventually, the *habitator* could decide to settle permanently in this city, considering himself and being considered by the authorities a *burgensis*. Thus, for instance, before his death in 1275 or 1276 Burgus Mallactor had been a *burgensis* of Acre established in the Pisan quarter of this city[26]. Yet even the *burgensis* sometimes returned to his mother-city and

22. This is the line of argument adopted by Favreau-Lilie, *Die Italiener im Heiligen Land,* pp. 498-508, in her criticism of J. Prawer, *Crusader Institutions,* Oxford 1980, pp. 226-229. Yet her view is untenable in the face of clear evidence to the contrary, adduced below.

23. See the case of Zaccaria Staniario: D. Jacoby, La dimensione demografica e sociale, in G. Cracco - G. Ortalli (eds.), *Storia di Venezia. L'età del Comune,* Rome 1995, pp. 698, 703.

24. Examples for Acre: Jacoby, *L'expansion occidentale dans le Levant,* p. 232 and p. 256, nn. 30 and 31. In the Kingdom of Jerusalem there were two more uses, one as a socio-legal definition of the status of the free commoner, distinct from that of the knight, and the other to convey subjection to a specific lord or commune. For this last meaning, see Prawer, *Crusader Institutions,* pp. 244-247.

25. A. Lombardo e R. Morozzo della Rocca (eds.), *Nuovi documenti del commercio veneto dei sec. XI-XIII,* Venice 1953, no. 17 (1162); R. Morozzo della Rocca - A. Lombardo (eds.), *Documenti del commercio veneziano nei secoli XI-XIII,* Torino 1940, (hereafter: *DCV*), vol. I, no. 171 (1166).

26. C. Froux Otten, Les Pisans en Egypte et à Acre dans la seconde moitié du XIIIe siècle: documents nouveaux, *Bollettino Storico Pisano* 52 (1983), pp. 179-180, no. 6: *olim Burgi Mallactoris burgensis de Accon olim de ruga pisana de Accon.* The second *olim* would seem to

resettled there after a number of years abroad. Finally, one should remember that permanent settlers travelled on business and were occasionally recorded in notarial documents drafted elsewhere, which does not imply that they had left Acre for good.

Evidence on linear mercantile migration and settlement in Acre possibly appears as early as 1123. The charter of privilege the Patriarch of Jerusalem, Warmundus, granted to Venice in that year contains a reference to the house of Pietro Zanni. In all likelihood this individual belonged to a prestigious and wealthy Venetian family, the Ziani, which would also account for the location of his house within the original Venetian quarter established in 1110[27]. One Pietro Ziani appears a few years earlier, in 1112, at Halmyros in the Byzantine Empire, yet it is impossible to ascertain whether this was the same individual as the one recorded in Acre or a namesake[28]. In any event, there is no additional information on real estate owned in Acre by members of this family, although some of them based in Venice invested in trade with the city in the 1160s and the 1170s[29]. It is not precluded, then, that after residing a few years in Acre, Pietro Ziani returned to Venice. This appears to have been a common pattern in Venetian merchant families, whose members established abroad maintained close relations with kinsmen living in Venice and elsewhere, often conducted business jointly with them, and retained their family property in their mother-city. Once they had reached an advanced age and wished to retire from active business life, they could easily resettle in Venice[30].

---

imply that this Pisan had left Acre to return to Pisa. However, he still resided at Acre at the time of his death since his will was drafted in the Levant and his bequest was expressed in the local currency.

27. *TTh*, vol. I, pp. 86 and 91, in 1123 and 1125, respectively. New edition by Berggötz, *Der Bericht des Marsilio Zorzi*, p. 110.

28. *DCV*, I, no. 35. Trade between Acre and the Byzantine Empire is attested in these years, namely in 1120: see *ibid.*, vol. I, no. 45. The name Pietro was quite common among the Ziani: see I. Fees, *Reichtum und Macht im mittelalterlichen Venedig. Die Familie Ziani* (Bibliothek des deutschen historischen Instituts Rom, Band 68), Tübingen 1988, p. 525, index, s. v. Ziani, Petrus.

29. *DCV*, I, nos. 167 (1165), 289-290, 292, 298 (1178), 300, 301 (1179).

30. See above, n. 23; D. Jacoby, The Venetian Presence in the Latin Empire of Constantinople (1204-1261): the Challenge of Feudalism and the Byzantine Inheritance, *Jahrbuch der Österreichischen Byzantinistik* 43 (1993), pp. 183-187; for Acre: Idem, *L'expansion occidentale dans le Levant*, pp. 244-245. Hugo *de Acri*, who appears as witness in Genoa in 1190, may similarly have returned home: M. Chiaudano - R. Morozzo della Rocca (eds.), *Oberto Scriba de Mercato (1190)*, Torino 1938, no. 270.

Acre was not only an important trading centre. It also acted as a financial and monetary market. Throughout the whole period of Latin rule there was a constant influx of Western moneys to the Levant for the financing of crusader expeditions and the upkeep of the Military Orders, which provided a standing army for the defence of the crusader states, for other military contingents, and for ecclesiastical institutions. In addition, large amounts of coins were imported by merchants, pilgrims and immigrants[31]. Acre enjoyed a large share in this flow, which grew even further after 1191, when the city's functions were enhanced[32]. Gold and silver bullion shipped to Acre were either directly used in trade, for the repayment of loans[33], or else brought to the royal mint operating in the city[34]. Various sources, including the Acre commercial manual compiled about 1270, refer to the delivery of gold to the local mint[35].

Up to the mid-thirteenth century the Order of the Temple was the major institution in Acre engaging in large-scale transfers of funds from the West, the exchange of moneys, and the grant of credit to rulers and feudal lords, pending reimbursement abroad[36]. It would seem that its activity in these fields largely accounts for the surprising absence of the Italian banking-trading companies from Acre until then. While the widespread business of these companies in the West has been repeatedly examined, hardly any attention has been paid to their expansion into the Eastern Mediterranean, let alone to their presence in Acre in the last decades of Latin rule[37]. The operation of these companies required

---

31. Foreign coins: J. Porteous, Crusader Coinage with Greek or Latin Inscriptions, in Setton, *A History of the Crusades*, vol. VI, pp. 355-359, 372, 385; J. Prawer, *The Latin Kingdom of Jerusalem. European Colonialism in the Middle Ages*, London 1972, p. 383, on a find at the edge of the Templar's compound in Jerusalem; see also below, n. 42.

32. On these functions, see above, pp. 105-106, 109-110.

33. For the latter: Beugnot, *Livre des Assises de la Cour des Bourgeois*, chap. 50, *Lois*, vol. II, pp. 48-49.

34. Striking of coins in Acre: Porteous, *Crusader Coinage*, pp. 381, 385, 387, 399, 400; M. L. Bates and D. M. Metcalf, Crusader Coinage with Arabic Inscriptions, in Setton, *A History of the Crusades*, vol. VI, pp. 429-430, 441-449, 452, 456, 458, 468-469, 473. Prawer, *The Latin Kingdom of Jerusalem*, p. 390, n. 76, reports the find of a silver coin with oriental design issued by Henry of Champagne; it was certainly minted at Acre.

35. See Jacoby, *A Venetian Manual*, p. 426. In this period crusader coinage was also transferred from Acre to Constantinople: *ibid.*, p. 427.

36. General background: L. Delisle, *Mémoire sur les opérations financières des Templiers* (Mémoires de l'Académie des Inscriptions et Belles-Lettres, 33/2), Paris 1889. For examples, see below, n. 42.

37. S. Borsari, L'espansione economica fiorentina nell'Oriente cristiano sino alla metà del Trecento, *Rivista Storica Italiana* 70 (1958), pp. 477-507, is the only study on the Eastern

the establishment of permanent agencies, manned by partners or factors, outside their respective home-city. The company was conducted by a sedentary merchant from his headquarters and relied heavily on correspondence with the agencies. There was a close connection between its pattern of activity and mercantile migration. Indeed, the stationing and moving of business personnel abroad entailed not only a definite shift from circular to linear migration and settlement, but also the introduction of a new type of rotating migration. Some of the partners and factors of these firms settled permanently at one place or resided there for a number of years only before moving to another agency, thus in a sense rotating around their centre, or returning at one point to the latter[38]. This was the pattern followed by Guido Filippi dell'Antella. In his *ricordanze* or private diary he noted that he became *compagno* or partner of the Florentine company (*societas*) of the Scali in 1278 and remained with it for twelve years. During this period he served in Florence, the Kingdom of France, Provence, where he was the chief representative of the company, then at Pisa, Rome, Naples and, finally, at Acre. He left this city in 1290, presumably after residing there less than two years, and in 1291 joined another company in France, to which he was affiliated for three years. He spent a rather short time at each location[39].

Merchants from the Italian inland cities were active in Acre in the first half of the thirteenth century. Some testimonies of 1245 reveal that the Tuscans, except for the Luccans, operated there under Pisan diplomatic protection[40]. It

Mediterranean, yet is restricted to Florence and refers in passing only to the crusader Levant.

38. See Jacoby, *The Migration of Merchants and Craftsmen*, pp. 544-545. The career of Francesco Balducci Pegolotti, the author of the well-known fourteenth century trade manual, fully illustrates this type of mobility.

39. F. Polidori (ed.), Ricordi di cose familiari scritti da varie persone (1298-1425), *Archivio Storico Italiano* 4 (1843), pp. 5-6; repr. in A. Castellani (ed.), *Nuovi testi fiorentini*, Florence 1952, vol. II, pp. 804-805, lines 20-26: *andai a dimorare cho la conpangnia de li Scali (...) per loro stetti (...) in Acri, e fui loro conpangno*. He had previously stayed for 18 months only with the company of a relative in Genoa. With the Scali he served in seven places during twelve years and his stay in Acre, therefore, cannot have exceeded two of them. Polidori, *ibid.*, p. 6, wrongly identified *Acri* with a locality close to Naples, since he was not aware that Italian banking-trading companies had agencies in Acre.

40. For the crusader Levant, see D. Abulafia, Crocuses and Crusaders: San Gimignano, Pisa and the Kingdom of Jerusalem, in B. Z. Kedar, H. E. Mayer, R. C. Smail (eds.), *Outremer. Studies in the History of the Crusading Kingdom of Jerusalem, Presented to Joshua Prawer*, Jerusalem 1982, pp. 227-243, repr. in Idem, *Italy, Sicily and the Mediterranean, 1100-1400*, London 1987, no. XIV; Idem, The Levant Trade of the Minor Cities in the Thirteenth and Fourteenth Centuries:

would seem, though, that the involvement of the Italian banking-trading companies in Acre's economic life and the establishment of their permanent agencies in the city was not primarily related to trade. Rather, it was prompted by the financing of military expeditions launched by western rulers and feudal lords and the prolonged presence of the latter's armies in the Kingdom of Jerusalem. The banking-trading companies offered not only loans, but also specialised in foreign exchange operations with built-in interest charges and in the transfer of sums of money without moving currency in specie; in addition, they engaged in trade[41]. The Templar house in Acre pursued its traditional financial activity in the second half of the thirteenth century[42]. However, it lacked sufficient liquid resources of its own to meet the growing demand for loans. The appearance of the Italian banking-trading companies in Acre was clearly related to the extensive credit operations required by the preparations for the crusade of Louis IX in 1247-1248, the pressing needs for cash of the king and other crusader lords during their sojourn in Cyprus and Egypt in 1248-1249 and, finally, their prolonged stay in the Holy Land from 1250 to 1254. The large-scale fortification work carried out by Louis IX at Acre, Jaffa, Caesarea and Sidon in these years further added to the financial burden resting on him, and in 1253 he was compelled to borrow massively from the Italians[43].

Strengths and Weaknesses, *Asian and African Studies* 22 (1988), pp. 183-202 [= B. Z. Kedar and A. L. Udovitch (eds.), *The Medieval Levant. Studies in Memory of Eliyahu Ashtor (1914-1984)*], pp. 187-191, 197-198, repr. in Idem, *Commerce and Conquest in the Mediterranean, 1100-1400*, Aldershot 1993, no. XI. Further research on the subject is required. On Pisan protection in Egypt, see D. Jacoby, Les Italiens en Égypte aux XIIe et XIIIe siècles: du comptoir à la colonie?, in M. Balard et A. Ducellier (eds.), *Coloniser au Moyen Age*, Paris 1995, p. 87.

41. There is a vast number of studies on these companies. On their operations in the West, see recently T. W. Blomquist, Some Observations on Early Foreign Exchange Banking based upon New Evidence from Thirteenth-Century Lucca, *The Journal of European Economic History* 19 (1990), pp. 353-375. I will deal more extensively with their activity in Acre in a forthcoming study.

42. During the crusade of Louis IX the Templars kept deposits and, acting on behalf of the king, disbursed sums that were to be repaid later in Paris: see A.-E. Sayous, Les mandats de Saint Louis sur son trésor et le mouvement international des capitaux pendant la septième croisade (1248-1254), *Revue Historique* 167 (1931), pp. 262-266, 270-271, 278-288. A shipment of coins sent by the Duke of Burgundy to his son Eudes, Count of Nevers, arrived at Acre in August 1265 and was deposited with the Templars: Chazaud, Inventaire et comptes de la succession d'Eudes, p. 185; on the exchange of foreign money and loans extended by them, see *ibid.*, pp. 183 and 181, respectively.

43. W. C. Jordan, *Louis IX and the Challenge of the Crusade. A Study in Rulership*, Princeton, N. J. 1979, pp. 104-105, 116-123, points to internal French problems as a major factor accounting for the king's shortage in money in 1253.

But let us first return to 1247. After reaching an agreement with the envoys of Louis IX, fifty-seven bankers from Piacenza established at Genoa, members of families belonging to the elite of their native city, undertook to finance the construction and outfit of the ships, as well as the transport of men and horses to the East. They also offered to transfer funds required by the crusaders while on the crusade[44]. We are particularly well informed about the loans offered by the Genoese in the following years, yet it would seem that their money came primarily from the sale of merchandise in the Levant. They did not specialise in credit operations like the banking-trading companies of Italian inland cities[45]. The Scotti company of Siena was one of these. It extended credit in Cyprus in 1248-1249 and in Egypt in August-September 1249, when it was represented by two of its partners, Boscolo Albertini and Rosso Consilii; in 1251 the latter also appeared at the king's camp next to Caesarea[46]. It is not precluded, then, that the company had created a permanent agency at Acre before 1248, and that its members active in Cyprus, Egypt and the Kingdom of Jerusalem were based in this city[47]. Yet as the earlier activity of the Sienese in Acre was apparently limited to trade[48], it is equally possible that the new conditions arising from the crusade of Louis IX constituted the decisive factor which induced the Scotti to establish an agency in Acre. One of the first Florentine banking companies, the Scali, also appeared at Damietta in 1249. They later founded an agency at Acre, which they apparently maintained, as implied by the testimony of Guido Filippi dell'Antella bearing on the years 1288-1290[49].

There are indeed good reasons to believe that the Italian banking-trading companies already established at Acre about 1250 continued to operate in the

---

44. Sources in L. T. Belgrano (ed.), *Documenti riguardanti le due crociate di S. Ludovico IX, re di Francia*, Genova 1859. On these bankers and the reimbursement of the loans in Paris, see above, n. 42.

45. See Sayous, *Les mandats de Saint Louis*, pp. 268-269, 271-272, 274-278, 282.

46. See *ibid.*, 266-267, 269-270, 273.

47. The company had previously had some trade connections with Acre. In 1248 one of its partners in Marseilles sent saffron to Acre with a Provençal factor: L. Blancard (ed.), *Documents inédits sur le commerce de Marseille au moyen âge*, Marseille 1884-1885, I, Cartulaire d'Amalric, no. 230.

48. See above, p. 115. In 1268 Siena obtained some privileges from Conradin of Hohenstaufen: G. Müller (ed.), *Documenti sulle relazioni delle città toscane coll'Oriente cristiano e coi Turchi fino all'anno MDXXXI*, Florence 1879, pp. 100-101, no. 70. The charter was devoid of practical value because Conradin lacked effective authority in Acre, yet nevertheless it reveals that the Sienese continued to trade in this city.

49. Sayous, *Les mandats de Saint Louis*, pp. 269-270, and above, n. 39.

city and that others joined them in the period which followed. The need for extensive credit in Acre did not cease with the departure of Louis IX for France in 1254. In order to strengthen the defence of the Kingdom of Jerusalem, the king left behind one of his captains, Geoffroy of Sargines, with a contingent of one hundred knights, the French crown taking charge of its upkeep[50]. After 1261, however, Geoffrey ran out of money at several occasions[51]. The expenditure involved in the maintenance of his and other contingents, in military expeditions launched from Acre, and the need to face mounting Muslim pressure required considerable resources and offered ample opportunity for the activity of the Italian banking-trading companies. In 1265 three representatives of one of them based in Piacenza, which included members of the Burrini and Speroni families, provided in Acre 1,000 livres tournois to Geoffroy of Sargines. The Latin Patriarch of Jerusalem and the Grand Masters of the military Orders served as guarantors for the reimbursement of the loan[52]. This was common practice in the dealings of the Italian bankers with the local authorities in Acre and is also attested by later documents. In 1267 two representatives of the Sienese firm Buonsignori, which acted at that time as papal bankers, delivered a large sum[53]. In August 1290 two Pisans received in Bologna a loan of 54 florins, which they promised to repay within four months in Acre to a member of the Ammannati company, the most ancient and by that time the largest and richest banking firm of Pistoia[54].

The financing of the war effort during the final siege of Acre by the Muslims in 1290-1291 involved considerable expenses. In April 1291, about one month before the fall of Acre, the two local representatives of a Sienese company allied with the Buonsignori yielded to the combined pressure of the Patriarch of Jerusalem and the Grand Masters of the three Military Orders of

---

50. On the contingent and its successive commanders, see Ch. Marshall, *Warfare in the Latin East, 1192-1291*, Cambridge 1992, pp. 77-83.

51. G. Servois, Emprunts de Saint Louis en Palestine et en Afrique, *Bibliothèque de l'École des Chartes* 19 (4e série, 4) (1858), pp. 114-116.

52. *Ibid.*, pp. 123-126, nos. 1-2, and commentary pp. 113-117.

53. *Ibid.*, pp. 128-131, no. 4-6, and commentary pp. 117-118. On the Buonsignori at a later period, see below.

54. G. Zaccagnini (ed.), I banchieri pistoiesi a Bologna e altrove nel sec. XIII. Contributo alla storia del commercio nel medio-evo, *Bullettino Storico Pistoiese* 21 (1919), p. 121, no. 13. On the Ammannati in the thirteenth century, see *ibid.*, *Bullettino Storico Pistoiese* 20 (1918), pp. 37-48. The *besants sarrasinois* was the local currency of the Kingdom of Jerusalem, and not that of Constantinople as asserted by the author, p. 46, n. 1.

the Hospitallers, the Templars and the Teutonic Knights, and granted a loan of 50,000 deniers tournois for the defence of the city. From the papal registers of the first half of the fourteenth century we learn that the loan had not been repaid by the Papacy, held responsible for the debts incurred by the Patriarch and the Orders[55].

The fall of Acre to the Muslims in May 1291 destroyed the geo-political foundation which had made possible the city's economic expansion and prosperity. Acre lost its Latin population and was largely in ruins as a result of the conquest. It could no more fulfil its function as a secure logistic base for the provisioning of Latin military forces, pilgrims, settlers, merchants and ships. Nor was there room for western linear migration, settlement, large-scale trade or banking. The economic activity of Acre, resumed shortly after the conquest, was sharply reduced and limited to the visits of a small number of Latin travelling merchants[56]. The events of 1291 dealt a severe blow to the city, from which it never recovered.

---

55. Dott. Mario Borracelli, Siena, kindly sent me the relevant excerpt of this text, which he will publish. I wish to thank him here for his kindness. The two representatives were Giacomo Franchi and Maso Bosi. The former had already served in the Levant in 1285-1286, together with a relative of the latter, Senso Bosi: see E. D. English, *Enterprise and Liability in Sienese Banking, 1230-1350*, Cambridge 1988, pp. 37-38 and n. 101.

56. See D. Jacoby, La Venezia d'oltremare nel secolo Duecento, in Cracco - Ortalli, *Storia di Venezia*, vol. II, p. 285.

VII

CRETA E VENEZIA NEL CONTESTO ECONOMICO
DEL MEDITERRANEO ORIENTALE
SINO ALLA METÀ DEL QUATTROCENTO

Per più di quattro secoli e mezzo, dall'inizio del Duecento sino al 1669, il destino di Creta è rimasto intrinsecamente associato a quello di Venezia. Studi anche recenti hanno messo a fuoco il ruolo giocato dall'isola nell'ambito dell'espansione politica, navale, commerciale e marittima di Venezia nel Mediterraneo orientale, così come il suo posto nel sistema coloniale veneziano. Si è trattato, però, in larga misura, di studi che si sono arrestati ad una lettura statica delle diverse funzioni esercitate da Creta. Al contrario, il presente contributo, pur non pretendendo di essere esauriente, si propone di ricostruire la loro dinamica, con l'individuazione dei fattori che nel tempo hanno agito, spiegando le fluttuazioni accadute nella loro evoluzione. Per valutare l'essenziale del ruolo economico-politico di Creta è anche necessario inquadrarlo nel contesto dei modelli commerciali e marittimi mediterranei ed analizzarlo in una prospettiva di lunga durata: dall'epoca bizantina sino alla metà del Quattrocento.

È quasi assiomatico che nel Medioevo Creta sia sempre stata un incrocio naturale delle rotte marittime nel bacino orientale del Mediterraneo. L'esame delle fonti dimostra, tuttavia, che ciò è vero soltanto per alcuni periodi, in relazione a porti specifici, e secondo modalità di volta in volta differenti. Queste riserve si confermano già a proposito dei rapporti intercorsi fra Venezia e Creta prima della quarta Crociata. Risultando scarse le testimonianze dirette circa tali rapporti, alcuni studiosi hanno pensato di utilizzare e leggere retrospettivamente le fonti veneziane posteriori, più abbondanti e quindi in grado di colmare i vuoti riscontrati nella documentazione[1]; un ap-

1) Così ha proceduto D. TSOUGARAKIS, *Byzantine Crete From the 5th Century to the Venetian Conquest*, Athens 1988, per la sua ricostruzione dell'economia cretese.

proccio metodologico alle fonti estremamente pericoloso, che alla luce degli sviluppi successivi, di cui si tratterà più avanti, sembra anzi prudente evitare.

I Veneziani commerciavano con Creta bizantina già nel secolo XI. Nel 1022 Leone da Molino portava a Costantinopoli un carico di almeno 2.860 kg di formaggio, con tutta probabilità di produzione cretese[2]. Una testimonianza più sicura ricaviamo da una lettera ebraica scritta tra il 1060 e il 1070, conservatasi presso la Geniza del Vecchio Cairo (un archivio rinvenuto nel Novecento in una sinagoga della capitale egiziana). La lettera rivela che alcuni mercanti di Venezia e di Creta operavano allora fianco a fianco ad Alessandria. Sembra che questi Veneziani e Cretesi fossero giunti assieme da Creta ad Alessandria, entrambi coinvolti almeno parzialmente nell'esportazione dei prodotti della pastorizia e dell'agricoltura cretesi[3]. L'interesse dei mercanti veneziani per siffatte mercanzie fu stimolato sin dal secolo XI dalla convergenza di due fattori rilevanti; da un lato la crescente richiesta dei centri urbani bizantini, in specie Costantinopoli, di derrate agricole per l'approvvigionamento cittadino, importate anche da mercati lontani, una richiesta sostenuta dall'innalzamento del tenore di vita e dall'accresciuto potere d'acquisto delle popolazioni in oggetto; dall'altro la progressiva integrazione dei Veneziani nelle reti del commercio e del trasporto marittimo dell'impero bizantino[4].

Pare che il volume del commercio veneziano con Creta fosse ancora decisamente esiguo nel 1082. L'isola non figura nella lista delle città e delle regioni inclusa nella crisobolla dell'imperatore Alessio I Comneno, che concedeva ampi privilegi commerciali a Venezia; non

---

*

2) *Documenti del commercio veneziano nei secoli XI-XII*, a cura di R. MOROZZO DELLA ROCCA-A. LOMBARDO, Torino 1940 [= *DCV*], n. 2; D. JACOBY, *Byzantine Crete in the Navigation and Trade Networks of Venice and Genoa*, in *Oriente e Occidente tra medioevo ed età moderna. Studi in onore di Geo Pistarino*, a cura di L. BALLETTO, Genova 1997, pp. 521-522.

3) S. D. GOITEIN, *A Mediterranean Society. The Jewish Communities of the Arab World as Portrayed in the Documents of the Cairo Geniza*, Berkeley-Los Angeles 1967-88, IV, p. 168; JACOBY, *Byzantine Crete* cit., pp. 522, 528. È attestata anche la presenza di mercanti di Costantinopoli, impegnati però nel commercio di altri generi.

4) D. JACOBY, *Silk in Western Byzantium before the Fourth Crusade*, «Byzantinische Zeitschrift», 84-85 (1991-92), pp. 472-473, 494, rist. in ID., *Trade, Commodities and Shipping in the Medieval Mediterranean*, Aldershot (Hampshire) 1997, n. VII.

figura nemmeno nella conferma sottoscritta dall'imperatore Giovanni II nel 1126[5]. Tuttavia la penetrazione commerciale veneziana nell'isola godeva di un rapido incremento, sfociato, già prima del 1136, nell'intervento delle autorità veneziane presso l'imperatore per sollecitare l'applicazione a Creta di quei trattamenti preferenziali che i privilegi ottenuti assicuravano ai mercanti lagunari[6]. Come conseguenza, già nella prima metà del XII secolo si poteva comprare formaggio cretese di alta qualità nel quartiere veneziano di Costantinopoli; non è neppure escluso che i Veneziani importassero anche vino cretese nella capitale dell'impero[7].

Inizialmente l'organizzazione di un viaggio commerciale con scalo a Creta appariva proficuo solo se inserito nelle linee di traffico della navigazione transmediterranea, quindi nelle rotte tra Venezia e Costantinopoli o tra Venezia e il Levante, come rilevano fonti relative agli anni 1129 e 1130. Tuttavia, a partire dal 1161 ci sono attestati viaggi di Veneziani da Costantinopoli ad Alessandria, con scalo nell'isola, mentre nel 1165 abbiamo notizia di una nave veneziana in rotta da Acri a Creta con ritorno ad Acri, Antiochia o Alessandria, ma anche di collegamenti diretti di queste regioni fra di loro[8]. Queste testimonianze confermano l'ampliamento progressivo del volume del commercio veneziano con Creta e l'inserimento dell'isola nelle reti commerciali e marittime colleganti non solo Venezia con Costantinopoli, gli stati crociati del Medio Oriente e l'Egitto. Soprattutto evidenziano la mutata posizione dell'isola all'interno di questi traffici, non più utilizzata come semplice stazione di transito, ma ora anche punto d'approdo dotato di una propria rilevanza commerciale. Indubbiamente Creta rimane, e così sarà almeno sino alla quarta Crociata, una base commerciale secondaria per Venezia, mancante tra

---

5) *Urkunden zur älteren Handels- und Staatsgeschichte der Republik Venedig*, a cura di G. L. TAFEL-G. M. THOMAS, Wien 1856-57, I, pp. 51-54, 95-98 [= *TTh*]; per una più recente edizione dei documenti vedi *I trattati con Bisanzio, 992-1198*, a cura di M. POZZA-G. RAVEGNANI, Venezia 1993 (Pacta Veneta, 4), pp. 35-45, 51-56. L'omissione di Creta non sembra doversi attribuire ad una precisa politica bizantina mirante ad impedire il commercio veneziano nell'isola, come la storiografia ha spesso evidenziato: cfr. D. JACOBY, *Italian Privileges and Trade in Byzantium before the Fourth Crusade: A Reconsideration*, «Anuario de estudios medievales», 24 (1994), pp. 349-356, rist. in ID., *Trade, commodities and Shipping* cit., n. II.

6) *TTh*, I, p. 214; *I trattati con Bisanzio* cit., pp. 63-64; JACOBY, *Italian Privileges and Trade* cit., pp. 355-356; ID., *Byzantine Crete* cit., p. 526.

7) *Ibid.*, pp. 525-528.

8) *DCV*, nn. 56-57, 149, 167.

76

l'altro di un insediamento stabile – ma anche solo temporaneo – di coloni veneziani; colonie veneziane sono invece presenti a Costantinopoli e in alcune altre città dell'impero[9]. Inoltre, e per tutto l'XI secolo, le forze navali veneziane e il grosso delle navi mercantili in viaggio tra Venezia e i porti del Mediterraneo orientale continueranno a preferire il tragitto lungo le coste del Peloponneso e ad evitare Creta: malgrado ciò le rotte che facevano di Creta la base intermedia dei viaggi tra Venezia e il Levante diventavano di giorno in giorno sempre più frequentati[10].

Non sorprende che per molto tempo Venezia non abbia manifestato alcun interesse particolare per la posizione strategica di Creta nel cuore del Mediterraneo orientale. La decisa inversione di tendenza si sarebbe registrata solo a partire dalla seconda metà del Duecento, in concomitanza con il verificarsi di almeno tre circostanze: l'incremento della produzione agricola cretese e conseguentemente del volume delle sue esportazioni[11], la rivalità crescente tra Venezia e Genova, e certi mutamenti nei percorsi di navigazione delle navi delle due potenze. Dagli anni Cinquanta del XII secolo Creta accentuava il suo ruolo di scalo e la sua funzione di base logistica per i mercanti e i bastimenti genovesi in navigazione tra Genova ed i porti del Mediterraneo orientale, risultando il percorso via Creta decisamente più breve rispetto a quello lungo le coste della Grecia continentale. L'ancoraggio nel porto di Chandax, Candia per i Latini, permetteva inoltre ai Genovesi di rifornirsi dei prodotti cretesi da smerciare nelle città bizantine e mediorientali[12]. D'altra parte, proprio in questo periodo sembra che fossero introdotti certi miglioramenti nelle tecniche di costruzione navale; c'era un aumento del tonnellaggio e quindi la possibilità di portare a bordo maggiori riserve di acqua potabile; furono inoltre adottati strumenti di navigazione più perfezionati. I mutamenti intervenuti permisero di fatto a particolari vascelli di navigare tra l'Italia e il Levante in mare aperto, e di accorciare il tragitto costeggiando Creta anziché il Peloponneso, anche senza dovere per forza attraccare nei porti dell'isola. I nuovi percorsi fecero accrescere l'importanza di Creta quale stazione di tran-

9) JACOBY, *Italian Privileges and Trade* cit., pp. 365-366; ID., *Byzantine Crete* cit., pp. 539-540.

10) *Ibid.*, pp. 523-525.

* 11) D. JACOBY, *Changing Economic Patterns in Latin Romania: the Impact of the West*, in *The Crusades from the Perspective of Byzantium and the Muslim World*, a cura di A. E. LAIOU-R. P. MOTTAHEDEH, Washington (D. C.) 1998 pp. 218-220.

12) JACOBY, *Byzantine Crete* cit., pp. 533-536.

sito, e nello stesso tempo la investirono di funzioni di controllo e protezione delle linee di traffico del bacino orientale del Mediterraneo[13].
All'acquisizione di Creta da parte di Venezia, avvenuta nel 1204,
non fece seguito l'immediata occupazione militare dell'isola. Del
vuoto di potere approfittava il genovese Enrico Pescatore, che tenta-
va tra il 1206 e il 1211 di stabilire il suo dominio personale su Creta.
Venezia interveniva militarmente nel 1207 conquistando Chandax, o
Candia, la città principale dell'isola; Genova rispondeva appoggian-
do sia militarmente che finanziariamente l'impresa privata del Pescatore[14]. È comunque sbagliata l'opinione ampiamente condivisa
che l'aspra lotta tra Venezia e Genova per il dominio su Creta fosse
motivata esclusivamente, o comunque principalmente, da ragioni di
carattere strategico. Non si debbono tralasciare altre considerazioni,
per la verità spesso trascurate. È significativo che le flotte e le forze
militari delle due potenze in navigazione verso l'isola fossero ac-
compagnate da mercanti. Per esempio, il mercante Tommaso Viadro,
prima di intraprendere il viaggio con la flotta veneziana, aveva ricevuto nel febbraio del 1209 grandi somme di denaro sotto forma di
prestiti marittimi, tra cui ben 120 lire veneziane da Maria, moglie del
doge di Venezia Pietro Ziani[15]. Il commercio veneziano che legava
Creta a Costantinopoli, Alessandria e Venezia non si arrestò durante
gli anni incerti della conquista veneziana dell'isola, tra il 1205 e il
1211, e nemmeno era rallentata l'attività dei mercanti genovesi nei

13) *Ibid.*, p. 540; JACOBY, *Changing Economic Patterns* cit.

14) S. BORSARI, *Il dominio veneziano a Creta nel XIII secolo*, Napoli 1963, pp. 12-
13, 21-25; D. ABULAFIA, *Henry Count of Malta and his Mediterranean Activities: 1203-1230*, in *Medieval Malta: Studies on Malta before the Knights*, a
cura di A. T. LUTTRELL, London 1975 (Supplementary Monographs of the British School at Rome), pp. 114-118, rist. in D. ABULAFIA, *Italy, Sicily and the
Mediterranean, 1100-1400*, London 1987, n. III; CH. A. MALTEZOU, *Creta fra
la Serenissima e la Superba*, in *Oriente e Occidente* cit., pp. 763-767, che si
propone quale nuovo esame delle fonti. Per la conquista di Candia, cfr. anche
D. JACOBY, *La colonisation militaire vénitienne de la Crète au XIIIe siècle:
une nouvelle approche*, in *Le partage du monde. De la présence coloniale au* *
dessein politique dans le monde méditerranéen du moyen âge aux temps mo-
dernes*, a cura di M. BALARD-A. DUCELLIER, Paris 1998 (in corso di stampa).

15) Il contratto con la dogaressa prevedeva il viaggio *in presenti venturo stolo*: vedi *Nuovi documenti del commercio veneto dei sec. XI-XIII*, a cura di A. LOM-
BARDO-R. MOROZZO DELLA ROCCA, Venezia 1953, n. 73. La destinazione ci è
rivelata da un altro documento dello stesso mese, nel quale un investitore precisa al Viadro che *ire debebas in exercitu Veneciarum: ibid.*, n. 74. La flotta lasciava Venezia sotto il comando di Giacomo Longo: BORSARI, *Il dominio veneziano* cit., p. 23.

porti cretesi[16]. Paradigmatica in questo senso risulta la lettera ducale emanata da Pietro Ziani nel 1211, che oltre ad enumerare i diritti e le obbligazioni del primo contingente di coloni militari inviati a stabilirsi nell'isola, conteneva diversi provvedimenti in materia di commercio dei prodotti isolani. Una clausola prevedeva il controllo dello stato sull'esportazione dei cereali[17]. La ducale dimostra la profonda conoscenza del potenziale economico e fiscale di Creta da parte del governo veneziano, consapevolezza condivisa negli stessi anni da Genova[18]. Altrettanto significativa rimane la presenza, nel primo gruppo di coloni veneziani, di diversi mercanti dotati di una solida esperienza del commercio nell'Adriatico e nel Mediterraneo orientale, Creta inclusa, tra cui il sunnominato Tommaso Viadro. Questi coloni-mercanti, nel momento in cui si imbarcavano per Creta, non avevano alcuna intenzione di rinunciare al commercio marittimo; anzi, sfruttando le risorse dell'isola e la sua posizione geografica, continuavano ad esercitarlo con investimenti e partecipazione personale[19]. In definitiva, la convergenza delle considerazioni strategiche, economiche e fiscali dei governi veneziano e genovese, sommate agli interessi e alle pressioni esercitate dai privati, spiegano la rivalità tra i due contendenti per il possesso di Creta all'inizio del Duecento.

La struttura di fondo e i meccanismi di funzionamento dell'economia cretese non subirono sostanziali modificazioni subito dopo l'imposizione del potere veneziano su Creta, appoggiato dall'insediamento dei coloni militari latini voluto da Venezia per saldare e potenziare il suo dominio[20]. Tuttavia, l'abolizione dei controlli restrittivi sull'economia cretese esercitati nel passato dallo stato bizantino, la dominazione diretta di Venezia, il trasferimento del grosso delle risorse agrarie nelle mani dei coloni militari, così che la loro presenza e quella di altri Latini nell'isola produsse alcuni mutamenti importanti negli assetti economico-commerciali di Creta. Innanzitutto favorirono l'accesso diretto dei Latini alle fonti di produzione locali e, più generalmente, determinarono un rapido e sostanziale ampliamento dell'ingerenza latina nell'economia cretese. La crescente richiesta di

16) *DCV*, nn. 469, 516, 518. Relativamente ai mercanti genovesi cfr. sopra, alla nota 14, il saggio di D. Abulafia.

17) Questo sembra essere il significato del termine *victualia*: *TTh*, II, p. 132. Cfr. anche JACOBY, *La colonisation militaire vénitienne* cit., pp. 300, 303-306.

18) JACOBY, *Changing Economic Patterns* cit.

19) JACOBY, *La colonisation militaire vénitienne* cit., pp. 299-300, 305-306.

20) Sui coloni: *ibid.*, pp. 298-313.

merci cretesi all'estero, in special modo proveniente da Venezia, stimolava i mercanti e i coloni militari veneziani ad impegnare grossi investimenti di denaro e di lavoro nel settore rurale dell'isola. Il flusso di contante promuoveva la monetizzazione a la commercializzazione dell'economia rurale e ne orientava decisamente la produzione verso l'esportazione. Si assistette così ad un ricorso sempre più ampio ed articolato dell'attività creditizia, soprattutto dei pagamenti anticipati, per incentivare la produzione di derrate alimentari quali il frumento, l'orzo, il vino e il formaggio, e di materie semilavorate o lavorate come la lana e il pellame. Inoltre, i diversi tipi di contratti di locazione prestarono maggiore attenzione all'individuazione del profitto, sollecitando l'estensione delle superfici coltivate, specialmente a vigneto o ad alberi da frutto, ed utilizzando ampiamente la soccida per l'allevamento del bestiame[21]. Nel 1300 circa questi prodotti dell'agricoltura e dell'allevamento risultavano essere le principali voci di esportazione cretesi, alle quali un po' più tardi si aggiungerà il cotone[22]. La prima sicura testimonianza relativa all'esportazione del cotone è del 1307[23]. La sua coltivazione ebbe un notevole incremento a partire dai decenni iniziali del Trecento[24]. Sebbene ci sia attestata

21) D. JACOBY, *La Venezia d'oltremare nel secondo Duecento*, in *Storia di Venezia*, II: *L'età del Comune*, a cura di G. CRACCO-G. ORTALLI, Roma 1995, pp. 271-272; A. E. LAIOU, *Quelques observations sur l'économie et la société de Crète vénitienne (ca. 1270-ca. 1305)*, in *Bisanzio e l'Italia. Raccolta di studi in memoria di Agostino Pertusi*, Milano 1982, pp. 183-187; M. GALLINA, *Finanza, credito e commercio a Candia fra la fine del XIII secolo e l'inizio del XIV*, «Memorie della Accademia delle Scienze di Torino, Classe di Scienze morali, Storiche e Filologiche», s. V, 7-8 (1986), pp. 34-40, 50-54; ID., *Una società coloniale del Trecento. Creta fra Venezia e Bisanzio*, Venezia 1989 (Deputazione di storia patria per le Venezie, Miscellanea di studi e memorie, XXVIII), specialmente pp. 95-139; D. JACOBY, *Cretan Cheese – a Neglected Aspect of Venetian Medieval Trade*, in *Venice: Society and Crusade. Studies in Honor of Donald E. Queller*, a cura di E. E. KITTEL-TH. F. MADDEN, Champaign (Illinois) 1999 (in corso di stampa); JACOBY, *Changing Economic Patterns* cit. Massicce esportazioni di lana sono già attestate nel 1225, con un carico del peso di oltre 3,5 tonnellate: *Deliberazioni del Maggior Consiglio di Venezia*, a cura di R. CESSI, Bologna 1931-1950, II, pp. 36-38, §§ 140, 142, 145-148.

22) Il documento relativo ai canoni di tassazione nell'*ordo porte ripe maris* di Candia è edito in E. GERLAND, *Das Archiv des Herzogs von Kandia*, Strassburg 1899, pp. 108-109; per la datazione del documento al 1298-1299 vedi *ibid.*, p. 107, nota 1 e p. 135.

23) In *Le deliberazioni del Consiglio dei Rogati (Senato). Serie mixtorum*, I, a cura di R. CESSI-P. SAMBIN, Venezia 1960, p. 122, § 240, si parla espressamente di *bambatium natum in Creta*.

24) F. THIRIET, *La Romanie vénitienne au Moyen Age. Le développement et l'exploitation du domaine colonial vénitien (XIIe-XVe siècles)*, Paris 1959 (Bibliothèque

un'esportazione di sale cretese attorno al 1300, non possiamo dire
che continuasse per molto tempo; la produzione del sale rimase, invero, decisamente minore[25]. Sin dall'inizio del Trecento la richiesta
esterna aveva stimolato una prorompente espansione della produzione vinicola, in particolare della malvasia, vino pregiato e prodotto di
lusso[26]. Spesso i grandi proprietari terrieri latini e greci, e gli stessi
mercanti all'ingrosso latini e greci (questi ultimi in misura minore),
riuscivano a concentrare nelle proprie mani considerevoli scorte dei
prodotti isolani destinati all'esportazione[27]. Tali processi di incentivazione della produzione agricola nell'isola e delle sue esportazioni furono allo stesso tempo incoraggiati dall'incremento del volume complessivo dei mezzi di trasporto marittimo e dal più fermo inserimento
di Creta nel sistema veneziano di navigazione transmediterranea.

Sino ad oggi il commercio marittimo di Creta nel periodo seguito alla conquista veneziana è stato esaminato soprattutto in rapporto
al contributo che ha fornito all'economia della metropoli. Nei fatti,
risulta essere un commercio molto più sfaccettato, con traffici, reti
ed orientamenti diversificati, pur manifestando continuità rispetto al-
l'età bizantina. Gli scambi dell'isola nel contesto mediterraneo si
sviluppavano essenzialmente secondo quattro raggi d'azione. Il primo era rivolto all'approvvigionamento dei centri urbani posti lungo
le coste cretesi, che fungevano, allo stesso tempo, da luoghi di concentrazione dei prodotti destinati all'esportazione e di distribuzione e
smistamento delle merci importate. Il secondo, convergente sulle
isole dell'Egeo e sul Peloponneso, aveva il respiro più ampio del

des Écoles françaises d'Athènes et de Rome, 193), pp. 321-322. Per la prima
metà del Quattrocento si vedano C. N. SATHAS, *Documents inédits relatifs à l'histoire de la Grèce au Moyen Age*, Athènes-Paris 1880-90, II, pp. 119, 126, 154;
H. NOIRET, *Documents inédits pour servir à l'histoire de la domination vénitienne en Crète de 1380 a 1485*, Paris 1892, pp. 165-166, 355. Il cotone era già colti-
vato a Creta in epoca bizantina: GALLINA, *Una società coloniale* cit., pp. 19-20.

25) Cfr. qui sopra GERLAND, *Das Archiv des Herzogs von Kandia* cit., come alla nota
22; un'indicazione indiretta circa spedizioni di sale a Venezia attorno al 1310 è re-
cuperabile in *Zibaldone da Canal. Manoscritto mercantile del sec. XIV*, a cura di
A. STUSSI, Venezia 1967 (Fonti per la storia di Venezia, sez. V – Fondi vari), p. 60
[= *Zibaldone da Canal*]; attorno al 1330 Creta non appare già più tra i fornitori di
sale di Venezia: FRANCESCO BALDUCCI PEGOLOTTI, *La pratica della mercatura*,
a cura di A. EVANS, Cambridge (Mass.) 1936, pp. 153-154. Più tardi la produzione di Creta non sempre coprirà la richiesta interna, tanto da dover ricorrere ad importazioni di sale: J.-CL. HOCQUET, *Le sel et la fortune de Venise*, I: *Production et
monopole*, Lille 1978, pp. 94, 125, 254-255, 279, ma soprattutto pp. 293-296.

26) GALLINA, *Una società coloniale* cit., pp. 42-43, 52-54, 92-93. 98-99, 133-138.

27) JACOBY, *Cretan Cheese* cit.

commercio intraregionale, e coinvolgeva porti di transito inseriti nel quadro della navigazione a lunga distanza, quali Negroponte nell'Eubea e Corone, Modone e Chiarenza nel Peloponneso sotto dominio latino e Monemvasia, principale porto del cosiddetto Despotato bizantino della Morea. Il terzo raggio d'azione del traffico marittimo cretese copriva le regioni dall'Asia Minore all'Egitto incluso [28], mentre il quarto portava alle destinazioni più lontane: a Costantinopoli, ai territori bizantini vicini al Mar Nero e, dall'altra parte, a Venezia. Le correnti di traffico a media e lunga gittata impegnavano Creta su livelli di commercio e di trasporto differenziati: un commercio basato esclusivamente sugli scambi bilaterali, ed un commercio che inseriva l'isola nelle maglie più ampie del traffico transmediterraneo, che trasformava i porti cretesi in basi di transito ma anche di raccolta di merci di importazione e di smistamento verso altre destinazioni. Lo stesso transito poteva inoltre avvenire semplicemente per ragioni tecniche, ossia in quanto condizionato dalla convergenza delle linee di navigazione sull'isola, o, altrimenti, perché i mercanti e vettori cretesi adempivano a un ruolo di intermediari attivi, con propri interessi. Se il commercio cretese a breve e medio raggio si svolgeva praticamente durante tutto l'anno, il traffico transmediterraneo a lunga gittata era invece esclusivamente stagionale.

Nonostante la continuità nelle strutture e negli orientamenti del commercio cretese, già nella prima metà del Duecento sono evidenziabili mutamenti progressivi in diversi settori. Nell'isola l'insediamento dei coloni militari e delle loro famiglie e soprattutto la continua immigrazione latina e l'inurbamento della popolazione greca determinarono fenomeni importanti di concentrazione urbana, con la conseguente amplificazione della domanda nei principali centri cretesi. A loro volta questi processi favorirono una maggiorazione del volume dei prodotti trattati, sia locali che importati, contribuendo ad una più decisa espansione ed accelerazione dell'attività economica. Soprattutto Candia, già capitale amministrativa dell'isola in epoca bizantina, seppe sfruttare sotto il dominio veneziano l'ampliamento delle sue funzioni, legato sostanzialmente all'inserimento del porto nel più ampio contesto dei traffici mediterranei[29].

L'impatto degli sconvolgimenti geopolitici non poteva non ripercuotersi nei rapporti bilaterali di Creta con altri paesi, provocando sostanziali variazioni nell'importanza relativa dei terminali commerciali delle esportazioni cretesi e nel volume degli scambi con loro.

---

28) BORSARI, *Il dominio veneziano* cit., pp. 67-71.

29) Sulla comunità latina, cfr. JACOBY, *La colonisation militaire vénitienne* cit.; su Candia vedi GALLINA, *Finanza, credito e commercio a Candia* cit., pp. 5-12.

Soprattutto ne fece le spese il commercio con Costantinopoli. La conquista latina della capitale bizantina nel 1204, nel corso della quarta Crociata, aveva generato una contrazione sostanziale della sua economia urbana, protrattasi per tutto il periodo dell'occupazione latina, quindi sino al 1261, e superata parzialmente soltanto negli anni Quaranta e Cinquanta del Duecento[30]. Per questa ragione Creta non poté sfruttare il primato commerciale acquisito dai Veneziani a Costantinopoli durante gli anni del dominio latino. L'indebolimento del grande mercato della metropoli, verso il quale era diretto il grosso delle esportazioni cretesi in epoca bizantina, esigeva una modifica parziale ma immediata negli orientamenti dei propri flussi commerciali. Questo portò ad una riconversione degli scambi cretesi e ad un loro inserimento nei quadri del commercio marittimo vertente su Venezia e sugli interessi mercantili della città lagunare. Tale mutamento, su cui torneremo più avanti, era già irreversibile nel 1261, l'anno della riconquista bizantina di Costantinopoli.

La congiuntura sfavorevole in questa città non aveva comunque avuto come esito la cessazione dei rapporti bilaterali fra Creta ed i mercati rimasti sotto il dominio bizantino. La restaurazione del dominio greco a Costantinopoli fu seguita immediatamente dal ripopolamento della capitale, dalla ripresa su grande scala della sua attività economica, ma anche dal ritorno dei Veneziani e dalla restituzione del loro quartiere residenziale. Nel 1268 e soprattutto nel 1277 Venezia otteneva da Bisanzio privilegi commerciali addirittura più ampi di quelli goduti precedentemente al 1204. L'apertura del Mar Nero ai mercanti e alle navi di Genova e di Venezia comportò, sin dal 1261, l'integrazione della regione nel sistema commerciale e marittimo mediterraneo, coordinamento mantenuto nei due secoli successivi, cioè sino alla conquista ottomana di Costantinopoli avvenuta nel 1453. Questo processo rinforzò il ruolo della capitale bizantina come stazione di transito e di trasbordo[31]. Di più, aprì nuovi mercati ai prodotti cretesi. Il commercio bilaterale dell'isola con Costantinopoli e col Mar Nero fu avviato subito dopo il trattato del 1268 tra Venezia e l'impero[32]. Nel 1271 sono attestati viaggi da Creta alla capitale bizantina ed a Tana, il porto del mare di Azov destinato a divenire la base commerciale veneziana più impor-

---

30) Sull'attività economica della città in quest'epoca vedi D. JACOBY, *Venetian Settlers in Latin Constantinople (1204-1261): Rich or Poor?*, in *Rich and Poor in the Society of the Greco-Latin East*, a cura di CH. MALTEZOU, Athens 1998 (in corso di stampa). In un saggio in preparazione offrirò una panoramica più ampia relativamente agli ultimi due decenni.

31) JACOBY, *La Venezia d'oltremare* cit., pp. 266-270.

32) Cfr. anche infra, p. 89.

tante del Mar Nero[33]. Un secolo più tardi, nel 1371, troviamo un mercante di Candia a Trebisonda, sulla costa nord dell'Asia Minore, sbocco importante delle rotte commerciali provenienti dall'entroterra asiatico[34]. È interessante sottolineare che la linea di navigazione che collegava Venezia a Costantinopoli e al Mar Nero, battuta sia dalle navi private che dalle galere *da mercato*, un servizio istituito dallo stato nei primi anni del Trecento, toccava i porti di Modone, Corone e Negroponte ma non quelli di Creta[35].

Dopo la riconquista bizantina di Costantinopoli il volume del traffico veneziano con la città e col Mar Nero crebbe presto sino ad attestarsi su livelli di una certa rilevanza. Il suo ampliamento fu promosso dall'attività congiunta di mercanti cretesi, latini (sia veneziani che di altre provenienze), greci ed ebrei, alcuni di passaggio, altri insediati nella capitale bizantina[36]. Nella prima metà del Quattrocen-

33) *Imbreviature di Pietro Scardon (1271)*, a cura di A. LOMBARDO, Torino 1942 (Documenti della colonia veneziana di Creta, I), nn. 132, 233 [= *Scardon*].

34) M. I. MANOUSSAKAS, *O poietes Leonardos Ntellaportas diermeneas tou Benetou Baïlou sten Trapezounta (1371-1372)*, «Thesaurismata», 21 (1991), pp. 19-20, doc. IV. Sul commercio tra Creta e Trebisonda nel 1404: *Moretto Bon, notaio in Venezia, Trebisonda e Tana, 1403-1408*, a cura di S. DE' COLLI, Venezia 1963 (Fonti per la storia di Venezia, Sez. III - Archivi notarili), nn. 3, 10, 11.

35) D. STÖCKLY, *Le système de l'incanto des galées du marché à Venise (fin XIIIe—milieu XVe siècle)*, Leiden 1995, pp. 101-119. Una sosta a Creta fu prevista solo nei primi anni: *ibid.*, pp. 103, 105.

36) A. E. LAIOU, *Un notaire vénitien à Constantinople: Antonio Bresciano et le commerce international en 1350*, in M. BALARD-A. E. LAIOU-C. OTTEN-FROUX, *Les Italiens à Byzance*, Paris 1987 (Byzantina Sorboniensia, 6), pp. 79-91, 99-101, 107, elenco n. III, con riferimenti agli atti e ai regesti editi alle pp. 109-146. Per i Greci vedi *ibid.*, p. 89, anche se la loro presenza si fa più consistente solo più avanti. Due mercanti cretesi insediati a Costantinopoli nel 1375 ci sono attestati da J. CHRYSOSTOMIDES, *Venetian Commercial Privileges under the Palaeologi*, «Studi Veneziani», 12 (1970), p. 288, nota 42 e p. 345, doc. n. 13. Costanzo Peramanda o Paramanda da Creta appare in documenti del 1439 e del 1450: *Il libro dei conti di Giacomo Badoer*, a cura di U. DORINI-T. BERTELÈ, Roma 1956 [= *Badoer*], pp. 698-699, e CH. MALTEZOU, *Ho thesmos tou en Konstantinoupolei Benetou baïlou (1268-1453)* [= L'istituzione del bailo veneziano a Costantinopoli (1268-1453)], En Athenais 1970, p. 219, n. 64. Per altri mercanti greci vedi *Badoer*, pp. 72, 204, 217, 338, 358, 411, 752, anche se non è sempre possibile accertare se si tratti di mercanti di passaggio o residenti in città. Per i mercanti ebrei: D. JACOBY, *Les quartiers juifs de Constantinople à l'époque byzantine*, «Byzantion», 37 (1967), pp. 209, 213, 223-227 [ed. di documento], rist. in ID., *Société et démographie à Byzance et en Romanie latine*, London 1975, n. II; ID., *Les Juifs vénitiens de Constantinople et leur communauté du XIIIe au milieu du XVe siècle*, «Revue des études juives», 131 (1972), pp. 406-407, rist. in ID., *Recherches sur la Méditerranée orientale du XIIe au XVe siècle. Peuples, sociétés, économies*, London 1979, n. XII. Cfr. anche la nota seguente.

84

to vi troviamo operante un mercante greco di Creta, che sembra essere l'agente residente di una azienda commerciale famigliare con sede nell'isola, impegnata come intermediaria del traffico tra Costantinopoli, Alessandria e Venezia[37]. Probabilmente non si trattava nemmeno di un caso isolato, visto che i Cretesi, come gli altri cittadini e sudditi veneziani, godevano nella capitale bizantina della protezione diplomatica di Venezia e delle esenzioni fiscali da essa stessa ottenute[38]. A partire dal Trecento, ma soprattutto nel secolo e mezzo successivo, la partecipazione di vascelli cretesi al traffico con Costantinopoli non si limitò più ai soli scambi bilaterali[39]. Li troviamo altresì impegnati nei traffici che collegavano Costantinopoli con Cipro, Beirut, Salonicco, Modone, Messina e forse perfino Barcellona in Catalogna[40]. Nel 1436 una nave cretese giungeva fino a Caffa in Crimea[41]. Qualche anno dopo, nel 1453, anche capitani greci di Creta partecipavano alla difesa di Costantinopoli[42]. La caduta della capitale bizantina in mano ottomana ridusse fortemente il traffico con Creta per qualche tempo, ma poi il commercio si sviluppò nuova-

37) KL.-P. MATSCHKE, *Griechische Kaufleute am Übergang von der byzantinischen Epoche zur Türkenzeit*, in *Die Kultur Griechenlands in Mittelalter und Neuzeit*, a cura di R. LAUER-P. SCHREINER, Göttingen 1996 (Abhandlungen der Akademie der Wissenschaften in Göttingen, Philologisch-historische Klasse, Dritte Folge, 212), pp. 77-78.

38) D. JACOBY, *Les Vénitiens naturalisés dans l'Empire byzantin: un aspect de l'expansion de Venise en Romanie du XIIIe au milieu du XVe siècle*, «Travaux et mémoires», 8 (1981), pp. 217-235, rist. in ID., *Studies on the Crusader States and on Venetian Expansion*, Northampton 1989, n. IX.

39) Nel 1302 una piccola nave comprata a Costantinopli veniva venduta a Candia: *Benvenuto de Brixano, notaio in Candia, 1301-1302*, a cura di R. MOROZZO DELLA ROCCA, Venezia 1950 (Fonti per la storia di Venezia, Sez. III – Archivi notarili), n. 554 [= *Benvenuto de Brixano*]. Intorno al 1350 un cretese comprava a Costantinopoli biscotti per l'approvvigionamento della sua nave: LAIOU, *Un notaire vénitien à Constantinople* cit., pp. 109-110, 130, nn. 2, 35.

40) T. BERTELÈ, *Il giro d'affari di Giacomo Badoer. Precisazioni e deduzioni*, in *Akten des XI. Internationalen Byzantinisten Kongresses*, München 1960, pp. 56-57. Un mercante cretese viaggiò nel 1436 da Costantinopoli a Saragozza nella Spagna, ovviamente tramite Barcellona, ma non è chiaro se raggiungeva questo porto a bordo di una nave cretese: *Badoer*, p. 78, righe 25-27; p. 80, righe 2-5; p. 81, righe 2-5.

41) *Ibid.*, p. 93. BERTELÈ, *Il giro d'affari di Giacomo Badoer* cit., pp. 56-57, riporta erroneamente Tana.

42) M. MANOUSSAKAS, *Les derniers défenseurs crétois de Constantinople d'après les documents vénitiens*, in *Akten des XI. Internationalen Byzantinisten Kongresses* cit., pp. 331-340.

mente, anche se i rapporti marittimi diretti dei mercanti e delle navi veneziani e cretesi con il Mar Nero saranno da quella data sospesi[43].

Le principali esportazioni cretesi verso Costantinopoli e il Mar Nero, attestate dai documenti ufficiali e dai contratti notarili veneziani del tempo, erano il vino e il formaggio[44]. Il libro di mercatura di Francesco Balducci Pegolotti, compilato tra il 1330 e il 1340, accenna ad esportazioni di vino cretese a Costantinopoli ed a Tana, porto nel quale operava una colonia veneziana e su cui convergevano le galere *da mercato* di Romania sin dagli anni Venti del Trecento[45]. Il frammento di un libro di conti greco, presumibilmente compilato a Costantinopoli verso il 1360, fa riferimento a parecchi carichi di formaggio cretese[46]. Nel Trecento i vini cretesi di buona qualità erano venduti anche nelle taverne veneziane della città ubicate fuori dal quartiere veneziano, come confermato da un *pamphlet* greco della prima metà del Quattrocento; gli imperatori tentarono di limitarne il numero[47]. Nel 1375 l'imperatore Giovanni V, che si era lamentato con Venezia per l'aspra concorrenza dei vini stranieri, giunse a vietarne l'importazione, misura peraltro già abolita l'anno successivo[48]. Nel suo libro di conti il mercante veneziano Giacomo Badoer, residente a Costantinopoli negli anni tra il 1436 e il 1440, menziona importazioni di formaggio, senz'altro cretese, e di vino isolano[49]. Nel

43) Ci fu anche una riduzione nelle pubbliche entrate in Creta, poiché il commercio cretese *erasi conglutinado con el trafego de Costantinopoli*, stando a una lettera da Candia del 1454, cit. in THIRIET, *La Romanie vénitienne* cit., p. 433, nota 5. Per i traffici posteriori al 1453: NOIRET, *Documents inédits* cit., pp. 448-449, § 8; JACOBY, *Les Vénitiens naturalisés* cit., p. 230.

44) Per il vino vedi CHRYSOSTOMIDES, *Venetian Commercial Privileges* cit., pp. 298-311; LAIOU, *Un notaire vénitien à Constantinople* cit., pp. 85-86; JACOBY, *Les Vénitiens naturalisés* cit., pp. 225-226. Per il formaggio vedi JACOBY, *Cretan Cheese* cit., p. 58.

45) PEGOLOTTI, *La pratica della mercatura* cit., pp. 40 e 24 rispettivamente; B. DOUMERC, *La Tana au XVe siècle: comptoir ou colonie?*, in *Etat et colonisation au Moyen age et à la Renaissance*, a cura di M. BALARD, Lyon 1989, pp. 251-266; STÖCKLY, *Le système de l'incanto* cit., pp. 101-119.

46) *Texte zur spätbyzantinischen Finanz- und Wirtschaftsgeschichte in Handschriften der Biblioteca Vaticana*, a cura di P. SCHREINER, Città del Vaticano 1991, (Studi e Testi, 344), pp. 33-65; ma circa l'origine dei conti vedi JACOBY, *Cretan Cheese* cit., p. 58.

47) JACOBY, *Les Vénitiens naturalisés* cit., pp. 225-226; N. OIKONOMIDÈS, *Hommes d'affaires grecs et latins à Constantinople (XIIIᵉ – XVᵉ siècles)*, Montréal-Paris 1979, p. 95, nota 170.

48) CHRYSOSTOMIDES, *Venetian Commercial Privileges* cit., pp. 304-307.

49) THIRIET, *La Romanie vénitienne* cit., p. 425; *Badoer*, pp. 256, 486, 698, 706.

novembre del 1452 otto navi cretesi cariche di vino arrivarono a Costantinopoli; nel febbraio del 1453 riuscirono a fuggire dalla capitale nonostante l'assedio turco[50]. Creta produceva anche vino destinato al consumo delle comunità ebraiche, preparato secondo le prescrizioni rabbiniche. Ebrei cretesi esportavano tale vino a Costantinopoli, dove era venduto nel quartiere veneziano, nella genovese Pera, ma anche nella parte bizantina della città[51]. Pare che verso il 1450 l'importazione del prodotto fosse divenuta tanto importante da indurre l'impero a stabilire, per la sua tassazione, un ufficio speciale chiamato *scribania vegetum Judeorum venetorum*, come appare da un documento redatto nello stesso anno[52]. Anche i Genovesi esportavano vino cretese a Costantinopoli a bordo delle loro navi, per rivenderlo nel loro quartiere di Pera[53].

Dalla capitale bizantina arrivavano a Creta merci diverse provenienti dal Mar Nero e dai territori dell'impero orientale. Le merci importate erano in parte destinate al consumo locale e in parte convogliate verso gli scambi dell'isola con altri paesi. Sin dall'inizio del Trecento un importante traffico di schiavi originari dei paesi confinanti con il Mar Nero transitava a Creta dopo aver fatto scalo a Costantinopoli; Creta ne assorbiva una parte, quindi fungeva da mercato per la distribuzione degli altri[54]. Nel 1387, anno di carestia, alcuni mercanti veneziani furono inviati da Creta a Costantinopoli con denaro della *respublica* per comprare cereali e, nel 1394, per acquistare grasso e canapa[55]. Nel 1405 un mercante catalano spediva a Creta

50) K. M. SETTON, *The Papacy and the Levant (1204-1571)*, II: *The Fifteenth Century*, Philadelphia 1978, p. 111, nota 9.

51) Su queste tre comunità si veda JACOBY, *Les quartiers juifs de Constantinople* cit., pp. 189-216.

52) JACOBY, *Les Juifs vénitiens de Constantinople* cit., pp. 409-410.

53) Carichi nel 1339 e nel 1399: LAIOU, *Un notaire vénitien à Constantinople* cit., pp. 85-86; G. G. MUSSO, *Navigazione e commercio genovese con il Levante nei documenti dell'Archivio di Stato di Genova*, Roma 1975, pp. 251-252; G. PISTARINO-G. OLGIATI, *Tra Creta veneziana e Chio genovese nei secoli XIV e XV*, «Cretan Studies», 2 (1990), pp. 200, 204.

54) CH. VERLINDEN, *L'esclavage dans l'Europe médiévale*, II: *Italie-Colonies italiennes du Levant-Levant latin-Empire byzantin*, Gent 1977, pp. 613-614, 622-623, 642-644, 802-884 *passim*, 888, 908-910, 963, 995-996, 1018; LAIOU, *Un notaire vénitien à Constantinople* cit., pp. 91-93, 101. In *Régestes des arrêts civils et des mémoriaux (1363-1399) des archives du duc de Crète*, a cura di E. SANTSCHI, Venise 1976 (Bibliothèque de l'Institut hellénique d'études byzantines et post-byzantines de Venise, 9), *Memoriali*, n. 1326, si ha notizia di uno schiavo russo giunto a Creta da Costantinopoli nel 1390.

55) *Ibid.*, nn. 1192, 1549.

parecchie botti di pesci salati a bordo di una nave cretese[56]. Nel 1437 furono spediti carichi di cera da Costantinopoli, via Candia, a Venezia e di rame ad Alessandria, mentre pannilana di Venezia furono stranamente riesportati dalla capitale bizantina verso Candia[57]. Ai Cretesi, ai Veneziani e agli altri Latini coinvolti negli scambi tra Bisanzio e Creta s'aggiungevano i sudditi dell'impero. Nel 1313 merci stimate 150 iperperi di un *homo imperatoris* che aveva fatto sosta a Creta, nel viaggio di ritorno da Alessandria, furono confiscate dagli ufficiali veneziani dell'isola[58]. Il fatto che costui venisse dall'Egitto passando per Creta fa supporre che si trattasse di un mercante residente a Monemvasia, il porto principale del Despotato bizantino di Morea, come d'altronde la maggioranza dei mercanti bizantini impegnati negli scambi con Creta. Tra di essi troviamo negli anni 1328-1333 un piccolo armatore della famiglia Notaras, membro quindi di una casata bizantina che negli ultimi anni del secolo diventò ricca e potente[59]. Monemvasioti sono anche attestati a Creta negli anni 1336-1337[60]. Nonostante le istruzioni a riguardo impartite nel 1324 dal governo agli ufficiali veneziani in servizio oltremare, la reciprocità nelle esenzioni doganali non era da questi osservata, come si evince dalle rimostranze presentate in più occasioni, dal 1350 al 1414, da sudditi bizantini penalizzati dalla mancata applicazione della disposizione. È verosimile che gli interventi degli imperatori in questo campo fossero particolarmente rivolti a favorire il commercio dei Monemvasioti[61].

56) *Duca di Candia. Ducali e lettere ricevute (1358-1360; 1401-1405)*, a cura di F. THIRIET, Venezia 1978 (Fonti per la storia di Venezia, Sez. I – Archivi pubblici), n. 180.

57) *Badoer*, p. 42, righe 1-5, 46-49; p. 111, righe 16-18; p. 294, righe 16-18 e p. 295, righe 29-31.

58) *Diplomatarium Veneto-levantinum*, a cura di G.M. THOMAS-R. PREDELLI, I, Venetiis 1880-1889, p. 126 [= *DVL*].

59) CH. GASPARES, *He nautiliake kinese apo ten Krete pros ten Peloponneso kata ton 14° aiona*, «Ta Istorika», 9 (1988), pp. 287-318, passim. Sui Notaras vedi *ibid.*, pp. 294, 296, e KL.-P. MATSCHKE, *Personengeschichte, Familiengeschichte, Sozialgeschichte: die Notaras im späten Byzanz*, in *Oriente e Occidente tra medioevo ed età moderna* cit., pp. 787-812, ma specialmente pp. 791-792.

60) *Lettere di mercanti a Pignol Zucchello (1336-1350)*, a cura di R. MOROZZO DELLA ROCCA, Venezia 1957 (Fonti per la storia di Venezia, Sez. IV – Archivi privati), pp. 7-8, 10, 14-15.

61) *Le deliberazioni del Consiglio dei Rogati* cit., p. 286, § 46; riferimenti ai documenti in oggetto in JACOBY, *Les Vénitiens naturalisés* cit., p. 229, nota 106, e relativamente al 1406 in KL.-P. MATSCHKE, *Bemerkungen zu den sozialen Trägern des spätbyzantinischen Seehandels*, «Byzantino-Bulgarica», 7 (1981), p. 256.

La decisa riconversione dei traffici cretesi verso i mercati occidentali, seguita alla conquista veneziana dell'isola, fu in larga misura determinata da due fattori. Il primo fu la crescita prepotente della domanda spontanea di prodotti isolani da parte di Venezia, di cui si è detto in precedenza. A tal proposito va ricordato che sin dal secolo XII la città lagunare serviva anche da centro per la ridistribuzione dei prodotti importati nell'entroterra padano[62], e che già dal principio del Trecento abbiamo notizia di riesportazioni di vino cretese di alta qualità, quindi di un prodotto di lusso, verso i mercati di Fiandra[63]. Il secondo potente fattore di promozione delle esportazioni cretesi verso Venezia fu la politica interventista e il dirigismo crescente dello stato nelle scelte e negli indirizzi dell'economia veneziana. La politica protezionistica di Venezia favoriva il commercio marittimo dei suoi cittadini mediante l'applicazione di tariffe doganali preferenziali. Inoltre i 'patroni' di navi veneziane godevano di sicuri vantaggi rispetto ai loro concorrenti, per effetto dell'obbligo imposto da Venezia ai suoi mercanti di trasportare merci veneziane esclusivamente a bordo di navi veneziane, a meno che non fosse esplicitamente consentito fare altrimenti[64]. La stessa imposizione riguardava diversi prodotti trasportati a bordo delle galere *da mercato*, le cui linee, come detto, furono istituite dal governo sin dagli albori del Trecento.

L'intervento statale veneziano, fin dal momento della conquista dell'isola, ebbe dirette ripercussioni anche sulla stessa economia cretese, attraverso l'applicazione di un rigido controllo sul commercio del frumento destinato sia al fabbisogno interno che all'esportazione. Il governo impose ai coloni militari ed ai grandi proprietari terrieri greci, gli arconti, quote annuali di cereali da consegnare allo stato a fronte di un prezzo fissato di anno in anno[65]. Non si trattò, in realtà,

---

62) G. RÖSCH, *Venedig und das Reich. Handels- und verkehrspolitische Beziehungen in der deutschen Kaiserzeit*, Tübingen 1982 (Bibliothek des Deutschen Historischen Instituts in Rom, 53), pp. 164-179.

63) *Le deliberazioni del Consiglio dei Rogati* cit., p. 164, § 209 e p. 171, § 289 (anni 1316 e 1317); *Apophaseis Meizonos Symbouliou Benetias, 1255-1669*, a cura di SP. M. THEOTOKES, Athenai 1933 (Akademia Athenon, Mnemeia tes Ellenikes Istorias, tomos A/2), pp. 87-88 (con riferimenti del 1317 a decreti anteriori). Cfr. anche H. ZUG TUCCI, *Un aspetto trascurato del commercio medievale del vino*, in *Studi in memoria di Federigo Melis*, Napoli 1978, III, pp. 318-319.

64) Indicazioni in tal senso sono rintracciabili in diversi documenti veneziani: si veda anche PEGOLOTTI, *La pratica della mercatura* cit., pp. 140-142.

65) GALLINA, *Finanza, credito e commercio a Candia* cit., pp. 36-38.

di una politica cerealicola pienamente monopolistica, come è stato spesso sostenuto; esisteva, infatti, un commercio libero dei cereali cretesi svincolato dalle quote dovute allo stato, seppure anch'esso sotto stretto controllo pubblico. L'esportazione era permessa soltanto verso Venezia, verso porti veneziani quali Modone e Corone (secondo le priorità espresse dal Comune), o verso altre destinazioni in risposta a specifiche richieste[66]. Un vero monopolio era invece stato imposto dalla *respublica*, sin dal 1281, sull'importazione e sul commercio del sale a Venezia. A partire da tale data tutte le navi veneziane di ritorno in città erano costrette ad avere carichi di sale a bordo ed i loro 'patroni' erano tenuti a venderlo allo stato[67]. Anche a Creta esisteva un monopolio statale sull'acquisto e sulla vendita del sale, instaurato già nel 1279. Veniva soltanto autorizzato, per i fabbisogni domestici e per la produzione dei formaggi, l'uso del sale stoccato nei magazzini pubblici e messo poi in vendita dal Comune[68].

Il dominio veneziano su Creta migliorò, per ovvie ragioni, l'approvvigionamento di Venezia in prodotti cretesi. Tuttavia il ruolo dell'isola in materia di rifornimenti della città lagunare può essere correttamente valutato solo se confrontato con i contributi forniti in tal senso dalle altre regioni del Mediterraneo. Subito dopo la ripresa del commercio veneziano con Bisanzio, negli anni Sessanta del Duecento, si registrano importazioni veneziane di cereali dalla Tracia, dalla Macedonia, dalla Tessaglia e dai paesi del Mar Nero, confermate indirettamente dalle richieste di indennizzo inoltrate da mercanti veneziani, vittime di misfatti commessi da ufficiali e pirati bizantini[69]. L'importanza agricolo-commerciale delle sunnominate regioni spiega perché nei suoi trattati con Bisanzio del 1268 e del 1277 Venezia abbia preteso clausole circa il libero commercio del frumento, con restrizioni permesse soltanto in caso di carestia a Costantino-

---

66) *Deliberazioni del Maggior Consiglio* cit., III, pp. 41-42, § 111; GALLINA, *Finanza, credito e commercio a Candia* cit., pp. 63-64, 127-132; D. TSOUGARAKES, *He sitike politike tes Benetias sten Krete ton 13°-14° aiona*, «Mesaionika kai nea ellenika», 3 (1990), pp. 333-385; per l'esportazione verso Modone e Corone vedi *ibid.*, pp. 366-367, e GASPARES, *He nautiliake kinese* cit., pp. 309-310.

67) J.-CL. HOCQUET, *Le sel et la fortune de Venise*, II: *Voiliers et commerce en Méditerranée*, Lille 1979, pp. 199-208, 249-255.

68) Vedi la documentazione edita in J. JEGERLEHNER, *Beiträge zur Verwaltungsgeschichte Kandias im XIV. Jahrhunderts*, «Byzantinische Zeitschrift», 13 (1904), p. 454, § 24 e pp. 469-470, § 16. Cfr. anche *supra*, nota 25.

69) G. MORGAN, *The Venetian Claims Commission of 1278*, «Byzantinische Zeitschrift», 69 (1976), pp. 411-438, soprattutto p. 434 e l'indice a p. 436.

poli, e spiega altresì le frizioni tra le due potenze in materia[70]. Nel Duecento la Tunisia e particolarmente il regno di Sicilia rimanevano serbatoi importanti di tale derrata alimentare per Venezia[71]. Nel 1284 il Comune veneziano pagava meno per il frumento importato da Creta che per quello acquistato da altri paesi[72]. La conclusione nel 1374 della pace coi Mongoli vicini alla base veneziana di Tana procurava un ribasso del 17% del prezzo del frumento proveniente dalla cosiddetta Romania, la regione compresa nell'impero bizantino prima della quarta Crociata. La trasmissione della notizia a Venezia effettuata da un mercante residente a Candia ribadisce l'importanza del Mar Nero quale fonte di rifornimento[73].

Venendo al commercio del formaggio, anche in quest'ambito il ruolo esercitato da Creta nell'approvvigionamento del mercato veneziano va comparato con le importazioni provenienti a Venezia da altre regioni. Alcuni mercanti spedivano grossi carichi di formaggio da Creta; sappiamo, per esempio, di un carico del peso di più di 13 tonnellate giunto a Venezia nel 1337[74]. Sfortunatamente, non è possibile stimare il volume complessivo annuale di tali importazioni. Possiamo farci un'idea delle importazioni dalle altre regioni considerando che nel 1329 la compagnia fiorentina dei Bardi da sola importava a Venezia più di 190 tonnellate di formaggio pugliese[75]. Soltanto per i

70) CHRYSOSTOMIDES, *Venetian Commercial Privileges* cit., pp. 312-327; A. E. LAIOU-THOMADAKIS, *The Byzantine Economy in the Mediterranean Trade System: Thirteenth-Fifteenth Centuries*, «Dumbarton Oaks Papers», 34-35 (1980-81), pp. 183-185, 213-215; JACOBY, *La Venezia d'oltremare* cit., pp. 268-270. PEGOLOTTI, *La pratica della mercatura* cit., p. 150, menziona importazioni da Tana a Venezia.

71) JACOBY, *La Venezia d'oltremare* cit., pp. 288-289. Per un'analisi d'insieme delle fonti di rifornimento di Venezia vedi G. LUZZATO, *Storia economica di Venezia dall'XI al XVI secolo*, Venezia 1961, pp. 51-54; R. ROMANO, *A propos du commerce du blé dans la Méditerranée des XIVe et XVe siècles*, in *Hommage à Lucien Fèbvre. Eventail de l'histoire vivante*, Paris 1953, II, pp. 149-161, soprattutto p. 152.

72) *Deliberazioni del Maggior Consiglio* cit., III, p. 65, § 23. Il prezzo garantito era di 18 grossi a staio (non 80 come riportato da BORSARI, *Il dominio veneziano* cit., p. 73, nota 35), ma soltanto di 16 grossi per il frumento cretese.

73) *Lettere di mercanti* cit., p. 73; egli trasmise anche i prezzi vigenti nella stessa Creta e a Palatia nell'Asia Minore.

74) *Pietro Pizolo, notaio in Candia (1300, 1304-1305)*, a cura di S. CARBONE, Venezia 1978-85 (Fonti per la storia di Venezia, Sez. III – Archivi notarili), n. 2 [= *Pietro Pizolo*].

75) R. DAVIDSOHN, *Forschungen zur Geschichte von Florenz*, III, Berlin 1901, p. 93, n. 974.

vini di alta qualità, in particolare la malvasia, l'apporto di Creta al mercato di Venezia, in ritmi costanti di crescita dagli inizi del Trecento, diviene maggiore[76]. Va rilevato che non si trovano prodotti finiti tra le esportazioni cretesi a Venezia, e questo ovviamente in ragione della loro modesta qualità che non permetteva a tali manufatti di sostenere la concorrenza dei prodotti veneziani o di quelli importati da altri paesi. Unica eccezione in questo panorama rimangono i fazzoletti di Candia, inclusi in un inventario redatto a Venezia nel 1404, anche se questi non pesavano certamente molto nel bilancio commerciale tra Creta e la Serenissima[77].

In cambio dei suoi prodotti e di altri in transito per il suo porto, Candia importava da Venezia merci diverse. Tra queste troviamo legname da costruzione, sapone[78], vetro e ferro, quest'ultimi parzialmente riesportati[79]. Sin dalla prima metà del Trecento i mercanti di vino insediati a Creta dipendevano per le loro necessità dalle botti, dai cerchi e dai vinchi spediti da Venezia[80]. Già nel Duecento i pannilana occidentali, tra cui quelli fiamminghi, risultavano pesare notevolmente sulla bilancia commerciale cretese[81]. In parte erano destinati all'autoconsumo, mentre il grosso serviva da merce di scambio nel quadro dei rapporti bilaterali di Creta con molteplici empori mediterranei. Il governo veneziano lucrava con decisione sulla richiesta locale di pannilana, imponendo sull'importazione dei tessuti un canone di tassazione più pesante che su tutte le altre merci[82]. L'accre-

76) Cfr. *supra* p. 80.

77) L'edizione del documento in P. G. MOLMENTI, *La storia di Venezia nella vita privata*, Venezia 1927-28[7], I, p. 513, n. VIII. Vedi anche riferimenti in un documento del 1390: B. CECCHETTI, *La vita dei Veneziani nel 1300. Le vesti*, Venezia 1886, p. 88, nota 2.

78) Per il legname vedi BORSARI, *Il dominio veneziano* cit., p. 71; per il sapone, LAIOU, *Quelques observations* cit., p. 182, e *Lettere di mercanti* cit., pp. 22, 34, 37-38, 41-43, 45.

79) Per il vetro vedi *ibid.*, p. 38; per il ferro, *Zibaldone da Canal*, p. 58, e PEGOLOTTI, *La pratica della mercatura* cit., p. 105; carichi di ferro sino a 100 *milliaria* (ossia 47 tonnellate) verso Nauplia, porto del Peloponneso, tra il 1326 e il 1356, e sei aratri di ferro commerciati nel 1326 ci sono attestati da GASPARES, *He nautiliake kinese* cit., p. 310. È possibile che gli aratri provenissero da Venezia, come nel 1381: E. SANTSCHI, *Régestes. Memoriali* cit., n. 1033. Esisteva una piccola produzione di ferro nell'isola, ma non sufficiente per l'esportazione: TSOUGARAKIS, *Byzantine Crete* cit., pp. 272-274.

80) ZUG TUCCI, *Un aspetto trascurato del commercio medievale del vino* cit., p. 340.

81) Un peso maggiore di quanto suggerito da LAIOU, *Quelques observations* cit., p. 182.

82) PEGOLOTTI, *La pratica della mercatura* cit., p. 106.

sciuto tenore di vita di diversi esponenti delle comunità latina, greca ed ebraica nell'isola favoriva fenomeni di ostentazione sociale del lusso, che il governo cretese si premurò di combattere: nel giugno del 1339 pubblicò una serie di provvedimenti suntuari che limitavano l'uso di indumenti confezionati con seta di alta qualità importata da Venezia, ed impreziositi con ornamenti costosi d'oro e di perle[83]. Nondimeno, l'importazione cretese di panni carissimi continuava: i documenti notarili degli anni 1373-1375 ci informano, infatti, di tessuti di lana fiamminghi giunti prima a Venezia con le galere delle Fiandre, di pannilana italiani e di tessuti serici, tra i quali vi erano velluti, verosimilmente prodotti a Venezia[84].

Un intenso traffico impegnava Creta con le isole dell'Egeo, fra cui Nasso, Santorini, Serifo e Negroponte, e con i porti del Peloponneso Corone (la destinazione principale), Modone, Nauplia, Chiarenza e Monemvasia[85], un commercio illustrato da molti atti notarili e da una lista di danni subiti da sudditi veneziani, compilata nel 1278. Le principali esportazioni cretesi erano il formaggio, il vino e il frumento, quest'ultimo spedito sia da Candia che da Canea[86]. Il ferro riesportato, il catrame e il bitume partivano esclusivamente da Candia con destinazione Corone e Modone, scali delle navi impegnate nei viaggi transmediterranei. Le merci viaggiavano su piccole navi e barche sia cretesi che straniere[87].

Il ruolo economico di Creta nell'Egeo era intrinsecamente connesso con le sue funzioni militare e navale, delle quali si dirà più

83) JEGERLEHNER, *Beiträge zur Verwaltungsgeschichte Kandias* cit., pp. 464-465, §§ 14-22. Da rimarcare la circostanza che il manuale del Pegolotti, seppur compilato pochi anni prima, non faccia menzione di importazione di tessuti di seta.

84) S. BORSARI, *Il mercato dei tessuti a Candia (1373-1375)*, «Archivio Veneto», s. V, 143 (1994). pp. 5-30; L. MOLÀ, *La comunità dei Lucchesi a Venezia. Immigrazione e industria della seta nel tardo medioevo*, Venezia 1994 (Istituto Veneto di Scienze, Lettere ed Arti, Memorie, Classe di Scienze morali, 53), pp. 252, 258. Sull'industria serica di Venezia dopo il 1314, si veda l'*op. cit.*

85) Su Monemvasia cfr. *supra* pp. 80-81, 87.

86) BORSARI, *Il dominio veneziano* cit., pp. 68-70; MORGAN, *The Venetian Claims Commission* cit., pp. 411-438, ma soprattutto pp. 427-432; *TTh*, III, pp. 236, 254-255, ma nel 1274 un carico di frumento e orzo risulta essere stato inviato da Negroponte a Creta: *ibid.*, p. 225. Per il Trecento si veda GASPARES, *He nautiliake kinese* cit., pp. 287-318.

87) *Ibid.*, pp. 310-311. Canea funzionava da stazione di smistamento del frumento anche verso Famagosta e Venezia: PEGOLOTTI, *La pratica della mercatura* cit., pp. 93, 149; cfr. anche p. 113.

avanti. Nel Trecento, considerando queste funzioni dell'isola e la sua posizione geografica, il governo veneziano decise di affidare ai duchi, responsabili del governo cretese, la condotta delle trattative diplomatiche con gli emirati turchi dell'Asia Minore occidentale, con le quali Venezia procurava di regolamentare i commerci reciproci, di assicurare gli approvvigionamenti di Creta in certi prodotti, di garantire la protezione dei propri sudditi e di impedire l'attività di corsari e pirati turchi rivolta contro navi e territori veneziani[88]. I trattati con gli emirati di Menteshe e di Aydin, rispettivamente del 1331 e del 1353[89], ci rivelano, tra le altre cose, i traffici all'epoca attivi tra Creta e i paesi turchi. I Cretesi e gli altri sudditi veneziani vi esportavano non soltanto i prodotti dell'isola, come il formaggio o il vino[90], ma anche i tessuti, il sapone e il ferro provenienti da Venezia[91] e vi compravano allume, cera, pellame, tappeti, cavalli e altro bestiame. L'acquisto dei cavalli necessari a rifornire le guarnigioni cretesi, attestato sin dall'inizio del Trecento, era incoraggiato e finanziato con il denaro del Comune[92]. Ancora, l'isola importava dai territori turchi numerosi schiavi[93] e, in periodo di carestia (come nel 1354-1355), anche cereali[94].

A Rodi, dal 1309 sotto il dominio degli Ospedalieri, Creta spediva frumento e vino, ma anche prodotti importati da Venezia quali il vetro veneziano e i pannilana[95]. Le relazioni commerciali tra Creta e

---

88) THIRIET, *La Romanie vénitienne* cit., pp. 246-247, 335; E. A. ZACHARIADOU, *Trade and Crusade. Venetian Crete and the Emirates of Menteshe and Aydin (1300-1415)*, Venice 1983 (Library of the Hellenic Institute of Byzantine Studies, 11), pp. 3-104.

89) *Ibid.*, pp. 18-20, 54-60.

90) Per il vino vedi *ibid.*, pp. 171-172. Per il formaggio: *ibid.*, p. 192, § 11; p. 198, § 22; p. 222, § 22. Le clausole elencano tutte le merci commerciate, ma è chiaro che vino e formaggio vengono da Creta.

91) *Ibid.*, pp. 4-5, 169-170, 172-173; LAIOU, *Quelques observations* cit., p. 181.

92) ZACHARIADOU, *Trade and Crusade* cit., pp. 4-5, 159, 165-169; THIRIET, *La Romanie vénitienne* cit., p. 335.

93) LAIOU, *Quelques observations* cit., pp. 181-182; ZACHARIADOU, *Trade and Crusade* cit., pp. 4-5, 160-163; THIRIET, *La Romanie vénitienne* cit., p. 335.

94) *Ibid.*, p. 336; ZACHARIADOU, *Trade and Crusade* cit., pp. 163-165.

95) A. LUTRELL, *Crete and Rhodes: 1340-1360*, in *Pepragmena tou G' diethnous kretelogikou synedriou* (= Atti del terzo Congresso internazionale di studi cretologici), II, Athenai 1974, pp. 168-175, rist. in ID., *The Hospitallers in Cyprus, Rhodes, Greece and the West, 1291-1440*, London 1978, n. VI.

VII

Chio, testimoniate già durante il dominio bizantino, continuarono anche dopo la conquista genovese dell'isola avvenuta nel 1346 e furono interrotte soltanto in tempo di guerra e nei momenti di maggiore attrito tra Venezia e Genova[96]. I mercanti e le navi genovesi di Chio impegnati nel commercio dell'Egeo esportavano da Creta vino e granaglie[97]. Nel Quattrocento i bastimenti genovesi in navigazione da Chio verso le Fiandre ancoravano di tanto in tanto a Candia, dove caricavano vino[98]. In altri casi il vino cretese veniva prima trasportato a Chio, quindi inviato nelle Fiandre, come fu, per esempio, con le più di 3.000 botti spedite nel 1452. Si trattava di un traffico estremamente dannoso per gli interessi dei mercanti e delle navi veneziane e cretesi[99]. Nonostante l'aumentato tonnellaggio (dal 1300 circa) delle navi veneziane impegnate nel traffico del vino[100], nel trasporto a lunga distanza della mercanzia i Genovesi godevano di indubbi vantaggi, determinati dall'utilizzazione delle cocche, superiori alle navi e alle galere veneziane in quanto capaci di trasportare un numero maggiore di botti a costi inferiori. Nel 1441 e nel 1451 Venezia vietava il trasporto di vino cretese a bordo di vascelli stranieri, potendo ora contare su di un numero sufficiente di bastimenti di grande tonnellaggio[101].

Il dominio veneziano su Creta consolidò la funzione dell'isola quale base di transito del commercio tra Venezia e il Levante. Dal Duecento l'ancoraggio di navi veneziane nei porti cretesi o la navigazione lungo le sue coste erano diventate la regola, come ci confer-

96) *Benvenuto de Brixano*, n. 284; LAIOU, *Quelques observations* cit., pp. 180-181.

97) PISTARINO-OLGIATI, *Tra Creta veneziana e Chio genovese* cit., pp. 199-200, 202, 204; si ha notizia di una schiava in viaggio nel 1451 da Chio a Candia in VERLINDEN, *L'esclavage dans l'Europe médiévale* cit., II, p. 880.

98) Per esempio nell'inverno del 1428-1429: *Les relations commerciales entre Gênes, la Belgique et l'Outremont d'après les archives notariales génoises, 1400-1440*, a cura di R. DOEHARD-CH. KERREMANS, Bruxelles-Rome 1952 (Institut historique belge de Rome, Etudes d'histoire économique et sociale), pp. 460-461, n. 593; la stessa destinazione ci è attestata per una nave genovese salpata da Genova nel 1414: *ibid.*, pp. 200-201, n. 193.

99) NOIRET, *Documents inédits* cit., pp. 437, 441; cfr. anche L. BALLETTO, *Tra l'isola di Creta e la "Communitas" genovese nel XV secolo*, «Atti della Società Ligure di Storia Patria», s. V, 50 (1993), pp. 463-475.

100) U. TUCCI, *Le commerce vénitien du vin de Crète*, in *Maritime Food Transport*, a cura di K. FRIEDLAND, Köln-Weimar-Wien 1994, pp. 199-202.

101) ZUG TUCCI, *Un aspetto trascurato del commercio medievale del vino* cit., pp. 321-323.

mano le istruzioni impartite al duca di Creta nel 1226 in materia di viaggi di ritorno dei bastimenti veneziani dal Levante e di trasporto di legname, ferro, catrame ed altri materiali 'bellici' verso l'Egitto[102]. Un documento del 1271 ci informa di un viaggio da Candia ad Acri con ritorno nel porto cretese e prosecuzione verso Venezia[103]. Eppure Candia non era.una stazione di transito indispensabile per il traffico tra la città lagunare e il Levante. Il frammento di un portolano redatto verso il 1270 descrive un percorso da Alessandria ed Acri a Venezia costeggiando Cipro, passando tra le isole di Gozzo e Creta a sud di quest'ultima e continuando verso Capo Spatha, nel nordovest di Creta, e verso Modone, senza alcuna sosta nei porti cretesi[104].

Il consolidamento del dominio mongolo nell'Asia verso la metà del Duecento introduceva nuovi elementi nel quadro dei commerci con il Levante. Dal 1260 circa il porto di Laiazzo, nella piccola Armenia, era diventato (posizione poi mantenuta per i settanta anni successivi) il principale sbocco mediterraneo della strada transcontinentale che giungeva dalla Cina e dall'India. D'altra parte, il ruolo commerciale di Cipro era andato aumentando di pari passo con la progressiva caduta dei porti crociati nelle mani dei Musulmani dagli anni Sessanta del Duecento. La conquista nel 1291 delle ultime roccaforti latine lungo la costa del Levante innescava una serie di mutamenti profondi nelle condizioni geopolitiche della regione, tali da rendere necessaria una ristrutturazione sostanziale delle reti del commercio con i paesi levantini. L'embargo papale che vietava il commercio di materiale bellico tra Cristiani e Musulmani e i rifornimenti di derrate alimentari fu ribadito nello stesso 1291 da Niccolò IV, che anzi dispose forme di controllo navale, sanzioni ecclesiastiche e multe pecuniarie in caso di violazione. Comunemente si crede che l'embargo sia stato rigidamente applicato fino al 1344. Certo, il divieto papale impediva, almeno parzialmente, il traffico diretto delle navi occidentali con l'Egitto e con la Si-

102) *TTh*, II, pp. 260-264.

103) *Scardon*, n. 367.

104) Del portolano esiste una prima edizione del 1909 peraltro incompleta e scorretta: K. KRETSCHMER, *Die italienischen Portolane des Mittelalters. Ein Beitrag zur Geschichte der Kartographie und Nautik*, Berlin 1909, pp. 235-236; l'edizione più recente in P. GAUTIER DALCHÉ, *Carte marine et portulan au XIIe siècle. Le* Liber de existencia Riveriarum et forma maris nostri Mediterranei *(Pise, circa 1200)*, Rome 1995 (Collection de l'Ecole française de Rome, 203), pp. 181-182. Sulla sua probabile datazione cfr. D. JACOBY, *A Venetian Manual of Commercial Practice from Crusader Acre*, in *I comuni italiani nel regno crociato di Gerusalemme*, a cura di G. AIRALDI-B. Z. KEDAR, Genova 1986 (Collana storica di fonti e studi, 48), pp. 406-409, 411-415, 422, rist. in JACOBY, *Studies* cit., n. VII.

ria, ma allo stesso tempo incoraggiava il commercio illecito, praticato con imbarcazioni di medio e piccolo tonnellaggio, tra i territori mamelucchi da una parte e la Piccola Armenia e Cipro dall'altra. Per circa cinquant'anni questi due paesi, e i loro porti di Laiazzo e di Famagosta, godettero della posizione privilegiata di avamposti cristiani verso il Levante musulmano e servirono da stazioni di transito e trasbordo dei traffici con la regione[105].

Gli sviluppi prodotti dalla caduta degli stati latini del 1291 ampliarono il ruolo di Creta nel rifornimento di Cipro e della Piccola Armenia. I mercanti cretesi vi commerciavano olio, vino, formaggio, frumento e altre derrate alimentari, in parte consumate in loco, in parte destinate alla riesportazione[106]. Indicativo, in tal senso, rimane un contratto del 1306 relativo al trasporto di più di 30 tonnellate di formaggio cretese su una *platida* di proprietà di un Veneziano di Costantinopoli; il contratto prevedeva che la piccola imbarcazione, con a bordo un equipaggio di 12 marinai, caricasse la merce a Candia, sostasse due giorni in ciascuno dei tre porti ciprioti di Paphos, Limassol e Famagosta, e, se necessario, proseguisse il suo viaggio fino a Laiazzo[107]. Una forma di cabotaggio che, tra l'altro, rappresentava solo uno dei molteplici aspetti del commercio cretese con Cipro e con il Levante dopo il 1291. Diverse lettere inviate tra il 1346 e il 1349 e diversi documenti notarili illustrano i tempi e i modi del traffico tra Creta e Cipro, sia che l'isola cipriota fungesse da scalo di destinazione, sia che servisse da stazione di transito verso i territori mamelucchi[108]. Alla navigazione privata dobbiamo aggiungere le galere dello stato che collegavano Venezia con Cipro e Laiazzo, con soste programmate nella stessa Candia[109].

---

105) JACOBY, *La Venezia d'oltremare* cit., pp. 273-275, 280-286.

106) D. JACOBY, *The rise of a New Emporium in the Eastern Mediterranean: Famagusta in the Late Thirteenth Century*, «Meletai kai hypomnemata, Hidryma archiepiskopou Makariou III», 1 (1984), p. 168, rist. in ID., *Studies* cit., n. VIII; LAIOU, *Quelques observations* cit., p. 179; *Benvenuto de Brixano*, nn. 306, 307, 352, 354; *Pietro Pizolo*, nn. 11, 25, 70, 73, 101, 321, 473, 574, 594, 633, 975; *Zibaldone da Canal*, p. 60; PEGOLOTTI, *La pratica della mercatura* cit., p. 93.

107) ASV, *Notai di Candia*, b. 186, notaio *Angelo de Cartura*, c. 28v. Il documento sarà edito prossimamente a cura di A. M. Stahl, che ringrazio per avermene trasmesso il testo.

108) *Lettere di mercanti* cit., pp. 55, 87-88, 104-106, 122-123; *Nicola de Boateriis, notaio in Famagosta e Venezia (1355-1365)*, a cura di A. LOMBARDO, Venezia 1973 (Fonti per la storia di Venezia, Sez. III – Archivi notarili), pp. 385, 389, *ad indicem*, s. v. *Candida, Creta*.

109) STÖCKLY, *Le système de l'incanto* cit., pp. 119-124.

Gli scambi di Creta con il Levante musulmano meritano una trattazione ampia sia per la loro complessa evoluzione sia perché, nel corso del tempo, il loro volume e valore aumentarono a tal punto da diventare inferiori, per importanza, ai soli rapporti commerciali dell'isola con Venezia. Nel Duecento il commercio cretese con l'Egitto e gli stati crociati, principalmente quello con Acri, partecipò della crescita generale degli scambi veneziani con le due regioni[110]. Eppure Creta rimase in secondo piano nel quadro del commercio levantino almeno fino al 1291. Negli anni seguenti sviluppò soprattutto funzioni di transito delle merci tra il Levante e l'Occidente, peraltro senza sostituirsi a Cipro, che godeva di un ruolo maggiore. Così nella prima decade del Trecento mercanti veneziani, genovesi, catalani e anconitani, sia in transito che residenti nel capoluogo cretese, viaggiavano da Candia ad Alessandria riportandone spezie[111].

Molto più importante fu il ruolo giocato dai Cretesi nel contesto degli scambi bilaterali con i porti mamelucchi. Un manuale di mercatura veneziano compilato verso il 1310, il cosiddetto *Zibaldone da Canal*, attesta l'esportazione di derrate cretesi ad Alessandria e l'importazione di pepe, zenzero e altre merci a Creta[112], prodotti parzialmente o del tutto riesportati a Venezia come confermato da diverse testimonianze. Le ceneri che nel 1300 giungevano a Creta dalla Siria e dall'Egitto erano certamente destinate alle industrie veneziane del vetro e del sapone[113]. Ancora, nel 1317 fu spedito da Creta a Venezia un carico di seta, incenso, zenzero ed allume, tutte mercanzie di indubbia provenienza dai paesi del Levante musulmano[114]. I mercanti e i vettori cretesi seppero sfruttare a fondo le stesse possibilità offerte dal commercio illecito con i territori mamelucchi. Di fronte alle insi-

---

110) D. JACOBY, *L'expansion occidentale dans le Levant: les Vénitiens à Acre dans la seconde moitié du treizième siècle*, «Journal of Medieval History», 3 (1977), pp. 246-247, 249, rist. in ID., *Recherches* cit., n. VII; D. JACOBY, *Venice, the Inquisition and the Jewish Communities of Crete in the Early 14*th *Century*, «Studi Veneziani», 12 (1970), pp. 140-141, rist. in ID., *Recherches* cit., n. IX.

111) JACOBY, *The rise of a New Emporium* cit., p. 173; E. ASHTOR, *Levant Trade in the Later Middle Ages*, Princeton (N. J.) 1983, pp. 38-39. Nel 1304 una galea veneziana partita da Candia il 21 luglio faceva ritorno nel porto cretese prima del 20 novembre dello stesso anno: *Pietro Pizolo*, nn. 804, 1026. Cfr. anche *supra*, nota 105.

112) *Zibaldone da Canal*, p. 60.

113) *Pietro Pizolo*, n. 321.

114) *Apophaseis* cit., pp. 94-96, nn. 45-46. Creta aveva in questo periodo una produzione limitata di seta, tale da non risultare esportabile.

stenti pressioni esercitate da papa Giovanni XXII Venezia arrivò a vietare ai propri sudditi, nel gennaio del 1323, ogni traffico con l'Egitto e con la Siria[115]. Non riuscì pero ad impedire che tale attività fosse praticata da Creta, dove gli Ebrei e gli stranieri residenti nell'isola, pur dovendosi accollare i pesanti dazi doganali imposti a chi non risultava essere suddito veneziano, rivendicarono la loro posizione di estraneità nei confronti di tale proibizione. Nel luglio del 1324 il doge Giovanni Soranzo estese il divieto a tutti gli abitanti di Creta; permise soltanto, qualche tempo dopo, ai mercanti veneziani, di recuperare le proprie merci ancora ferme ad Alessandria utilizzando esclusivamente navi straniere[116]. Nello stesso periodo il geografo musulmano Abu'l-Fida elencava i prodotti cretesi esportati ad Alessandria[117].

La continuazione dei traffici veneziani con i territori mamelucchi negli anni successivi è illustrata dal manuale di mercatura di Francesco Balducci Pegolotti, compilato negli anni Trenta del Trecento. Sebbene manuali di questo tipo includano spesso informazioni obsolete, le notizie fornite dal Pegolotti sul commercio levantino sono affidabili, e questo in ragione del fatto che il mercante fiorentino risiedeva allora a Cipro, punto di osservazione ottimale per la sua posizione strategica. Pegolotti ci svela così che Venezia incoraggiava con tariffe doganali preferenziali il traffico di Creta con l'Egitto e con la Siria. La vendita nell'isola delle merci importate dalle regioni che da Cipro si estendevano fino al Magreb incluso era gravata di un'imposta del 2 %, così come l'esportazione ad Alessandria di merci acquistate a Creta; di contro, le merci destinate ad altri scali o provenienti dai paesi occidentali erano tassate al 4 %, mentre sui pannilana e sulle mercanzie comperate reinvestendo il denaro ottenuto dalla loro vendita nell'isola pesava un canone pari all'8 %[118]. Un'altra conferma della prosecuzione del commercio di Creta con l'Egitto, nonostante i divieti, la ricaviamo da alcune lettere mercantili spedite da Candia negli anni tra il 1336 e il 1344; queste lettere, che descrivono i rapporti commerciali bilaterali tra Creta e i paesi musulmani, testi-

115) G. ORTALLI, *Venice and Papal Bans on Trade with the Levant: the Role of the Jurist*, «Mediterranean Historical Review», 10 (1995) (= *Intercultural Contacts in the Medieval Mediterranean. Studies in Honour of David Jacoby*, a cura di B. ARBEL, London 1996), pp. 242-258, ma specialmente 244-248.

116) *Duca di Candia. Bandi*, a cura di P. RATTI VIDULICH, Venezia 1965 (Fonti per la storia di Venezia, sez. I – Archivi pubblici), nn. 342, 371, 382, 383.

117) *Géographie d'Aboulféda*, trad. a cura di M. REINAUD, Paris 1848-1883, II/1, p. 276.

118) PEGOLOTTI, *La pratica della mercatura* cit., p. 106.

moniano l'accresciuto ruolo dell'isola negli scambi tra il Levante e Venezia e, più in generale, all'interno dei traffici del Mediterraneo orientale[119]. Insomma, quando il sultano egiziano scriveva nel 1345 al doge Andrea Dandolo che i mercanti veneziani non avevano *za vintitré anni navegado a le nostre parte*[120], è ovvio che si riferiva soltanto alle galere dello stato, visto che le altre navi continuavano ad intrattenere traffici regolari anche in questo periodo.

La contrazione drastica del flusso delle spezie lungo la strada continentale transasiatica, sin dagli anni Trenta del Trecento, condusse nel 1344 all'attenuazione dell'embargo papale e, l'anno successivo, alla conclusione di un nuovo accordo tra Venezia e l'Egitto[121]. Il ristabilimento del traffico diretto tra le due potenze fu reso evidente dalla ripresa del servizio delle galere dello stato sull'asse Venezia-Alessandria, un servizio destinato a rimanere attivo per oltre due secoli, con brevi interruzioni durante la crociata cipriota del 1365 contro Alessandria e nei momenti di particolare tensione tra la Serenissima e l'Egitto[122]. Anche le cocche veneziane frequentavano i porti musulmani del Levante. La rapida espansione dei rapporti commerciali diretti fra Venezia e questi porti, associata ai tempi di navigazione e ai costi di trasporto ora ridotti, significarono per Creta, malgrado Venezia appoggiasse le sue linee di transito proprio sull'isola, una riduzione del volume degli scambi bilaterali con i porti mamelucchi e, più generalmente, del suo ruolo di intermediaria nel commercio levantino per circa tre decenni.

Le condizioni mutarono radicalmente, questa volta a tutto vantaggio di Creta, con l'occupazione genovese di Famagosta avvenuta nel 1374[123] (occupazione protrattasi poi fino al 1464). Da allora la maggioranza delle navi veneziane impegnate nei commerci con il Levante non transitò per il porto cipriota e privilegiò Candia quale stazione di transito sostitutiva, rinvigorendone le funzioni e il ruolo commerciale. Nel 1374 il governo prese misure per garantire il trasporto a Venezia delle spezie e delle altre mercanzie levantine immagazzi-

---

119) *Lettere di mercanti* cit., pp. 15, 30.

120) *DVL*, I, p. 291.

121) ASHTOR, *Levant Trade* cit., pp. 64-70.

122) STÖCKLY, *Le système de l'incanto* cit., pp. 130-143; P. EDBURY, *The Kingdom of Cyprus and the Crusades, 1191-1374*, Cambridge 1991, pp. 166-171; ASHTOR, *Levant Trade* cit., pp. 88-99.

123) EDBURY, *The Kingdom of Cyprus* cit., pp. 202-209.

nate a Candia[124]. La linea Venezia-Cipro delle galere *da mercato* fu sospesa dal 1373 al 1445; nell'inverno del 1373-1374 fu attivata in sua sostituzione una linea da Candia a Beirut, che vedeva impegnate due galere per tre viaggi all'anno, e, più tardi, un'altra linea che collegava direttamente la città lagunare al porto libanese. Questo servizio fu coordinato, a partire dagli anni Venti del Quattrocento, con i movimenti della carovana diretta ad Alessandria; entrambi i convogli furono regolarmente fatti sostare a Candia[125]. Pur registrando delle fluttuazioni annuali, dovute in parte alle modificazioni della congiuntura politico-economica, l'ammontare degli appalti delle galere di stato su queste linee si mantenne particolarmente alto, e questo ad attestazione dell'importanza dei traffici commerciali con i porti levantini in confronto con le altre linee delle galere *da mercato*[126].

Dobbiamo ricordare, inoltre, che esisteva una intensa attività mercantile parallela fondata sulla navigazione libera privata. In questo contesto Creta aveva una funzione distinta, di intermediario e di stazione di deposito. Le cocche in navigazione tra l'isola e i mercati mamelucchi sbarcavano le merci orientali nei porti cretesi. Una grossa porzione del commercio libero tra Creta e i paesi islamici era gestita da mercanti cretesi, alcuni dei quali residenti per lunghi periodi nei porti egiziani[127]. Emanuele Piloti, stabilitosi in Egitto tra il 1396 e il 1438 e ivi resdiente per ben 22 anni, ci ha lasciato informazioni preziose circa il commercio tra Alessandria, Creta ed altri paesi. Da lui veniamo a sapere che le principali derrate esportate dall'isola in Egitto erano il vino, il formaggio, il miele e la cera[128], e che il trasporto si faceva utilizzando piccoli vascelli cretesi. Latini, Greci ed Ebrei cretesi conducevano ad Alessandria questi prodotti isolani ed il pellame, ma anche tessuti di manifattura occidentale concentrati a Creta per essere riesportati[129]. Molti mercanti e vettori cretesi riportavano in patria piccole quantità di pepe, altre spezie e merci diverse, che vendevano nell'isola o esporta-

124) *Thespismata tes Benetikes Gerousias, 1281-1385*, a cura di SP. M. THEOTOKES, Athenai 1936-37 (Akademia Athenon, Mnemeia tes Ellenikes Istorias, tomos B, 1-2), II, pp. 182-184, n. 35, *Ordo specierum Candide*.

125) THIRIET, *La Romanie vénitienne* cit., pp. 333-334; STÖCKLY, *Le système de l'incanto* cit., pp. 138-140, 143-152.

126) *Ibid.*, pp. 225-243.

127) JACOBY, *Cretan Cheese* cit., p. 58.

128) *Traité d'Emmanuel Piloti sur le Passage en Terre Sainte (1420)*, a cura di P.-H. DOPP, Louvain-Paris 1958, § 105. Per la datazione del libro al 1438 circa, cfr. *ibid.*, pp. V-VI, XVIII-XXVI.

129) Per esempio nel 1374, come si evince da BORSARI, *Il mercato dei tessuti* cit., p. 8 e nota 6.

vano, spesso segretamente. Quando nell'isola si accumulavano consistenti quantità di merci, il governo veneziano mandava navi, talvolta anche straniere, per trasportare a Venezia tali mercanzie[130]. La coordinazione dei flussi commerciali tra Creta e il Levante con quelli tra l'isola e Venezia permetteva di aumentare il volume e la rapidità del traffico levantino[131].

Il governo veneziano continuò a stimolare e a valorizzare la funzione dell'isola quale intermediaria principale tra Venezia e il Levante; nello stesso tempo perseguiva una politica di stretto controllo sul commercio di transito, soprattutto al fine di impedire il contrabbando su grande scala delle spezie verso Venezia o altri mercati. Già prima del 1374 aveva disposto l'esenzione dai dazi doganali per le merci provenienti dalla Siria e dall'Egitto, spezie incluse, trasportate a Creta su navi veneziane e destinate ad essere reimbarcate verso Venezia, a condizione che tali preziose mercanzie rimanessero sotto chiave nei magazzini del Comune fino al momento della loro partenza. Nello stesso 1374 i pedaggi di entrata e uscita dei carichi trasportati da mercanti stranieri in transito per l'isola furono ribassati all'1%[132]. È significativo che l'adozione di queste misure fiscali, il cui obiettivo era chiaramente quello di incentivare la navigazione con scalo a Creta, coincida con il calo dei traffici veneziani diretti a Famagosta seguìto alla conquista genovese della città[133]. La politica del governo tesa a favorire Creta nella sua funzione di stazione di transito fu mantenuta anche dopo il 1421, anno in cui si determinò una profonda crisi tra l'Egitto e le potenze occidentali, destinata a durare per circa tre decenni[134]. Il governo veneziano reagì limitando e controllando più strettamente il commercio dei suoi sudditi con i paesi mamelucchi; pur tuttavia, nel 1430, il Senato veneziano autorizzava i mercanti cretesi ad esportare i prodotti dell'isola verso la Siria e l'Egitto, e questo nonostante l'interruzione in atto (seppur temporanea) del commercio veneziano con questi paesi[135].

La prosecuzione dei commerci con il Levante andava di pari

130) THIRIET, Candie cit., pp. 346-347.

131) M. ABRATE, Creta – colonia veneziana nei secoli XIII-XV, «Economia e storia», 4 (1957), pp. 257-258.

132) Thespismata cit., II, pp. 167-168, n. 21.

133) Cfr. supra pp. 99-100.

134) Vedi ASHTOR, Levant Trade cit., pp. 283-331.

135) NOIRET, Documents inédits cit., p. 343, riporta l'edizione parziale dell'autorizzazione.

passo con l'attività di contrabbando delle spezie praticata anche sfruttando il commercio di esportazione dei vini cretesi. Una grande quota dei vini cretesi era trasportata direttamente dall'isola verso le destinazioni finali, senza transitare per Venezia. Nel 1440 il governo prese alcune misure per impedire il traffico illecito di spezie nascoste nelle botti di vino destinate ai mercati di Fiandra e dell'Inghilterra[136]. Alcuni anni prima, e precisamente nel 1429, aveva stabilito che le spezie giunte a Creta da Beirut dopo la partenza delle galere statali veneziane dovessero attendere per il loro trasporto a Venezia l'arrivo del convoglio successivo destinato a tale servizio[137]. Contro tale imposizione si levò alta la protesta dei mercanti e dei marinai cretesi coinvolti nel commercio delle spezie, che nel 1462 (e sembra non sia stata la prima volta) si lamentarono per i danni provocati ai loro interessi da misure del genere. Per loro, infatti, risultava di fondamentale importanza poter smerciare al più presto le spezie importate (secondo quanto asserito dalla protesta tali spezie venivano in larga misura consumate nella stessa Creta), per poter rimborsare i prestiti ricevuti per l'acquisto dei prodotti destinati ai mercati levantini. Inoltre, il trasporto delle spezie a bordo delle galere *da mercato* li obbligava a ricorrere in Venezia ai costosi servizi di intermediari per la vendita della mercanzia, minacciando così, sempre secondo i contestatori, la loro sussistenza e la stessa sopravvivenza dell'attività marinara di Creta. Pur coscienti di dover sostanzialmente mitigare affermazioni così perentorie, i toni della contesa testimoniano l'ampiezza raggiunta dal commercio illecito delle spezie tra i mercanti e i marinai cretesi. Tuttavia, nonostante le proteste, il governo proseguì nella rigida politica di vigilanza già impostata[138].

Il commercio di Venezia con il Magreb portò nel 1231 alla negoziazione di un primo trattato con i signori di Tunisi[139]. L'espansione dei traffici fra Venezia e questa regione nella prima metà del Quattrocento indusse il governo veneziano a stabilire un nuovo servizio di galere di stato: la linea di Barberia[140]. Pare che il traffico dei Cretesi con i porti magrebini crescesse molto dagli anni Quaranta[141]. Nel

---

136) *Ibid.*, pp. 390-391; THIRIET, *Candie* cit., pp. 350-351.

137) NOIRET, *Documents inédits* cit., p. 335 (regesto della disposizione).

138) *Ibid.*, p. 483, § 21.

139) JACOBY, *La Venezia d'oltremare* cit., pp. 286-289.

140) STÖCKLY, *Le système de l'incanto* cit., pp. 169-173.

141) THIRIET, *Candie* cit., pp. 349.

1462 Venezia istituì la linea *del Trafego*, l'ultima ad essere attivata tra le carovane gestite dallo stato; Candia vi fu inserita quale scalo alternativo nel quadro di un servizio che collegava i porti del Levante con quelli del Magreb[142]. L'intreccio dei fattori commerciali e navali era particolarmente forte nell'Egeo. Dall'esame fin qui condotto risulta evidente il ruolo vitale esercitato dalle infrastrutture cretesi in appoggio alle navi di passaggio e per le merci depositate nei magazzini in attesa di riprendere il viaggio verso i mercati di destinazione[143]. L'isola rappresentava, inoltre, una delle chiavi del sistema di difesa veneziano nel Mediterraneo orientale[144]. Candia fungeva da base permanente di una squadra navale dotata di varie funzioni: combattere i pirati e i corsari bizantini e genovesi e, dall'inizio del Trecento, anche turchi; proteggere le linee di navigazione veneziane e le galere dello stato; vigilare sulle coste cretesi e ogni tanto partecipare alle spedizioni navali[145]. L'arsenale di Candia, costruito intorno al 1282 e restaurato dopo il terremoto del 1303, serviva anche da deposito per il materiale navale, le armi e il legname spediti dall'arsenale di Venezia per rinforzare il sistema di difesa dell'isola e consentire il suo contributo allo sforzo navale e militare[146]. La sistemazione del porto, soggetto a fenomeni continui di insabbiamento, venne attuata a scopi sia commerciali che militari nel 1333, su progetto di un ingegnere in-

---

142) STÖCKLY, *Le système de l'incanto* cit., p. 175.

143) Cfr. anche THIRIET, *Candie* cit., pp. 346-347.

144) Per una panoramica d'insieme vedi THIRIET, *La Romanie vénitienne* cit., p. 243-251.

145) Sui pirati turchi: D. JACOBY, *Catalans, Turcs et Vénitiens en Romanie (1305-1332): un nouveau témoignage de Marino Sanudo Torsello*, «Studi Medievali», s. III, 15 (1974), pp. 246-247, 251-253, 257-261, rist. in ID., *Recherches* cit., n. V; E. ZACHARIADOU, *Holy War in the Aegean during the Fourteenth Century*, «Mediterranean Historical Review», 4 (1989), pp. 212-218, rist. in *Latins and Greeks in the Eastern Mediterranean after 1204*, a cura di B. ARBEL-B. HAMILTON-D. JACOBY, London 1989. Su altri pirati cfr., per esempio, il documento del 1402 edito in NOIRET, *Documents inédits* cit., pp. 127-128.

146) D. JACOBY, *Les gens de mer dans la marine de guerre vénitienne de la mer Égée aux XIVe et XVe siècles*, in *Le genti del mare Mediterraneo (XVII Colloquio internazionale di storia marittima, Napoli, 1980)*, a cura di R. RAGOSTA, Napoli 1981, I, pp. 172-174, rist. in ID., *Studies* cit., n. XI. Riferimenti ad attrezzature spedite da Venezia nel 1403 per la galea di Candia in *Duca di Candia. Ducali* cit., n. 99; cfr. inoltre la nota seguente.

viato da Venezia[147]; tuttavia, non si arrivò ad una soluzione del problema e lavori di riparazione furono necessari a più riprese durante tutto il Trecento[148]. La difesa di Creta e la protezione della sua navigazione comportavano per la popolazione isolana carichi finanziari onerosi. Ma, d'altra parte, le funzioni militare e navale di Candia producevano l'afflusso di denaro pubblico, che volta contribuì a stimolare e ad incentivare l'economia isolana. Candia rappresentava un centro importante di reclutamento di manodopera artigianale specializzata nella costruzione e nella riparazione delle navi e di assoldamento di equipaggi, di arcieri e di balestrieri, questi ultimi particolarmente ricercati[149]. Più generalmente Creta forniva derrate alimentari per l'approvvigionamento delle flotte veneziane; nel 1402, per esempio, una spedizione in rotta verso Costantinopoli imbarcava nell'isola da 300 a 500 *staria* di biscotti e 2 tonnellate e mezzo di formaggio, pari a circa 60.000 razioni quotidiane[150]. Da ultimo era anche una base di pirati e di corsari, attività che attirava consistenti quantità di capitale liquido investito nel finanziamento delle loro spedizioni. Nel 1319 l'imperatore Andronico II Paleologo giunse a lamentarsi per i danni causati dalla pirateria cretese ai propri sudditi. I pirati e i corsari, sia cretesi che stranieri, spesso vendevano nella stessa Candia i prigionieri e il bottino conquistati durante le loro razzie[151]. Così fecero nel 1352 anche i Catalani dopo la battaglia navale

147) R. GERTWAGEN, *The Venetian port of Candia, Crete (1299-1363): Construction and Maintenance*, «Mediterranean Historical Review», 3 (1988), pp. 141-158. I lavori sono contemporanei alla costruzione dell'Arsenale nuovo a Venezia: E. CONCINA, *L'Arsenale della Repubblica di Venezia*, Milano 1984, pp. 25-40, ma soprattutto pp. 34, 36, 40.

148) Riferimenti negli anni 1336, 1341, 1356, 1357, 1371, 1372, 1375 e oltre in *Thespismata* cit., I, pp. 166-167, 203; II, pp. 24-25, 51, 143, 146-147, 160, 186-189.

149) JACOBY, *Les gens de mer* cit., pp. 174-188, 195-201. Nel 1400 Venezia ordinava al governo di Creta di fornire quindici balestrieri per ognuna delle galere di stato in navigazione verso Tana e di pagarne gli stipendi, e ancora nel 1407 chiedeva una galea di Candia e una di Venezia per proteggere le galere *da mercato* in navigazione verso Tana; cfr. NOIRET, *Documents inédits* cit., pp. 105, 183 (regesti dei documenti).

150) *Duca di Candia. Ducali* cit., n. 5; JACOBY, *Cretan Cheese* cit., p. 55.

151) BORSARI, *Il dominio veneziano* cit., pp. 65-66, 101-102; GALLINA, *Finanza, credito e commercio a Candia* cit., p. 59; *DVL*, I, pp. 125-127; A. E. LAIOU, *Constantinople and the Latins. The Foreign Policy of Andronicus II, 1282-1328*, Cambridge (Mass.) 1972, p. 273.

del Bosforo a fianco dei Veneziani, durante la sosta delle loro galere nel porto isolano sulla via del ritorno in patria[152].

Possiamo ora concludere. L'imposizione del dominio veneziano avviò cambiamenti fondamentali nell'evoluzione e negli orientamenti dell'economia cretese, inserendo Creta, molto più che in epoca bizantina, nei circuiti commerciali e marittimi del Mediterraneo orientale, particolarmente nelle linee di traffico veneziane. Questo stimolò una dialettica sempre più vivace tra gli sviluppi economici interni dell'isola e le sue funzioni commerciali esterne, sia quale partner negli scambi bilaterali con i diversi paesi del Mediterraneo, sia quale stazione di transito, con variazioni notevoli dell'apporto cretese, sino alla metà del Quattrocento, in rapporto ai mutamenti geopolitici ed economici in atto nelle regioni poste attorno al Mediterraneo orientale. L'isola assunse di fatto, dalla fine del Duecento, un ruolo piuttosto importante, destinato a divenire maggiore dopo il 1374, come stazione di raccolta, di trasbordo e di distribuzione delle proprie merci, di quelle dei propri partner commerciali e di quelle in transito tra Venezia e il Levante. Non vanno d'altronde dimenticati i contributi diretti apportati da Creta a questi traffici e, complessivamente, al sistema commerciale del Mediterraneo orientale, confermati dalla crescente produzione locale di diversi prodotti destinati all'esportazione, dall'ampio spettro delle sue relazioni commerciali bilaterali e dalla potenzialità delle sue infrastrutture e dei servizi offerti alle navi e ai mercanti in transito per l'isola. Tali funzioni furono tutte decisamente incrementate durante il dominio veneziano, di pari passo con lo sviluppo di un servizio invero nuovo rispetto all'epoca bizantina, ossia l'incentivazione del ruolo di mediazione commerciale ora direttamente esercitato dai mercanti e dalle navi cretesi. L'esame fin qui condotto riflette il fatto che sia le attività di intermediazione, sia i capitali in esse investiti raggiungevano volumi abbastanza importanti, finora del tutto sottovalutati. Le diverse funzioni economiche, coniugate assieme, procurarono grossi mezzi finanziari, parzialmente reinvestiti nei diversi settori dell'economia isolana, nel commercio mediterraneo e nella costruzione di navi; più in generale, contribuirono ad incrementare in modo notevole il volume dei traffici e ad accelerare il ritmo degli scambi fra Creta e altri paesi, e quindi ad accrescere la prosperità dell'isola.

Il governo veneziano appoggiò lo sviluppo dell'economia crete-

---

152) A. RUBIÒ I LLUCH, *Diplomatari de l'Orient català*, Barcelona 1947, pp. 270-272, 283-284, n. 209. A Canea fecero riparazioni e presero rifornimenti a bordo: *ibid.*, p. 263, n. 205.

se in diversi modi, ma allo stesso tempo ne controllò e ne limitò la portata, nell'ottica dell'evoluzione complessiva del commercio veneziano nel Mediterraneo e di una politica sempre attenta a perseguire e difendere il primato dello stato e dei cittadini residenti a Venezia. In tale contesto, il ruolo assegnato ai mercanti e ai vettori cretesi era volutamente secondario, specialmente nei confronti del commercio con il Levante musulmano. Insomma, per Venezia Creta rimase soprattutto una fonte di approvvigionamento e di raccolta di proventi fiscali, sfruttata al massimo, ed una base di importanza capitale nel gioco politico, militare ed economico del Mediterraneo orientale.

VIII

Cretan Cheese: A Neglected Aspect of
Venetian Medieval Trade

Venetian trade in the eastern Mediterranean in the Middle Ages, especially since the eleventh century, was more varied than commonly assumed. Historians have generally focused on the expensive commodities handled by Venetian merchants, such as spices imported from Egypt, silk fabrics from Byzantium, and western woolens transiting through Venice to the East. In recent years there has been growing interest in trade in industrial raw materials required by the Italian cotton, silk, and glass industries. Yet foodstuffs other than grain have failed to draw the attention they deserve, although they played an important role in local, regional, and long-distance trade, as illustrated by their place in commercial manuals.

Cheese was widely produced around the Mediterranean in the Middle Ages. It was the staple protein food of the poor, who could afford meat only rarely, if at all, and an important component of the diet of Byzantine monks, from which meat was excluded.[1] It often served as trimmings, known as *prosphagion* in Byzantium, eaten together with bread as a full meal.[2] Cheese also was among the essential foodstuffs taken along by travelers, whether on land or by sea, light troops shadowing the enemy, and seamen engaged in medium and long-distance voyages.[3] Yet, in addition, it was in high demand in the middle and higher ranks of society. In a humorous letter written after 1143 the Byzantine author Michael Italikos praised cheese over pork as the basic human nourishment.[4] To be sure, some regions around the Mediterranean lacked sufficient locally made cheese, yet imports from distant countries were primarily related to the lifestyle and taste of customers who could afford to purchase more expensive foreign cheese. High-quality cheese was considered a delicacy worthy to be offered as a present.[5] Ever larger quantities of cheese were being traded over long distances in the Mediterranean since the eleventh century, as attested by Byzantine, Arabic, Jewish, and western sources. Cheese produced in Crete frequently appears within this framework, and Venetians were involved in its marketing.[6] To date this trade has attracted only marginal attention and at best has been mentioned within the general context of Venetian commerce. Yet it warrants a thorough examination in view of its ramifications within the eastern Mediterranean and its impact on the economy of Venetian Crete.

By the early thirteenth century Crete was rich in livestock, sheep being raised far more extensively than other domesticated animals. A letter written by some Greeks of the island to Doge Pietro Ziani in 1224 or 1225 refers to the period preceding the Venetian conquest. According to this letter, there were then large numbers of sheep in the area of Candia, the district of Milopotamo to the west of this city, Kato Sivrito to the south of Rethymno, and Kalamona in the southwest of the island, while cattle herds, mentioned for the district of Candia, were much smaller.[7] Later sources of the thirteenth and fourteenth century point to livestock practically all over Crete, in the areas of Sitia, Mirabello, Candia, and Canea in its northern part, as well as Castelnuovo and Belvedere in its southern part.[8] The kind of milk used for the production of Cretan cheese is rarely stated and, therefore, it is not always possible to determine it. For instance, a contract of 1300 mentions cheese from *pecudes,* without specifying whether these were goats or sheep.[9] However, the latter's milk must have been far more common in view of the large number of sheep in the island, and its use is implied whenever contracts combine deliveries of cheese and wool.[10] On the other hand, the area of Castelnuovo, in the southern part of central Crete, was renowned for its goat cheese.[11]

Three basic types of cheese were traditionally produced in Crete in the Middle Ages, as in many other areas around the Mediterranean.[12] Soft fresh cheeses such as *apotyron* and *anthotyro* were surely available, although they are not explicitly attested in Crete. Since they had to be consumed within a few days after production, they apparently were not the subjects of commercial contracts.[13] The second type of cheese, known as *myzethra* (pronounced *myzithra*) in the Greek-speaking lands,[14] was called ricotta ('recooked') in Italian dialects. It was a dry or moist cheese made from the whey or watery portion of the milk obtained in the production of other cheeses and cooked a second time at a temperature of 70 centigrade or more. This cheese is mentioned by the fourteenth-century Greek poet Stephanos Sachlikes, who lived in Crete, while the Italian term is well attested by Venetian official and notarial sources.[15] Finally, the other cheeses, which contained more fat, were made from the curd of soured milk pressed together to form a solid mass and were allowed to ripen and harden. An eleventh- or twelfth-century Jewish letter written in Alexandria apparently deals with the production of Cretan *makhlut* or 'mixed' cheese, flavored with seeds or herbs.[16] The cheeses belonging to this group were rubbed with dry salt to extract the remaining acidity, or else were soaked in brine for some time, both methods improving conservation. Finally, the cheese was left on a hurdle to dry in a shady place.[17] Pietro Casola who, on his way to the Holy Land in 1494, visited the capital of Venetian Crete, Candia, offers a vivid description that deserves to be quoted: "They make a large quantity of cheeses, but it is a pity they are so salted. I saw large warehouses full of them, and some in which the 'salmoria' [brine], as we say, was a *braccio* [about 68 cm.] deep, and the large cheeses were floating within. Those in charge of this [operation] told me that the cheeses could not be preserved otherwise, because they are so rich. They do not know how to extract the butter."[18] This last type of cheese was the only one fit for export. For this reason it was often ordered well in advance of the shipping season.[19] A Venetian commercial manual compiled in the 1320s at the latest points to the diminishing weight of this cheese as a result of dehydration, with a loss of some 7 percent during the journey from Crete to Venice.[20] A late sixteenth-century Jewish source refers to this type of hard Cretan cheese as *grana*.[21]

Two late thirteenth-century lists of customs levied in Candia record the second and third type of cheese just mentioned as *recocta* and *caseus*, respectively.[22] Ricotta was apparently very common in Crete at that time and was expected to be "good and ripened,"[23] while hard cheese was to be "good, well prepared and ripened, [and] marketable," as described in several notarial contracts.[24] The quality of the cheese differed according to its distinctive features, yet it was also affected by the amount of salt and foreign bodies mixed with the curd.[25] The best grade was called 'pure' or 'clean', *katharon* in Greek, as noted in the fragment of a Greek account book compiled about 1360.[26] Cretan cheese was generally traded in molds, some of which may have been baskets like those still used nowadays for various types of cheese produced in the island.[27] In 1223 a mold of Cretan cheese was robbed from a merchant on his way to Venice.[28] The size and weight of the molds widely varied. Pieces of sixteen pounds of Candia or 8.20 kilograms and others of eight pounds or more are mentioned in 1224 and 1280, respectively.[29] A letter sent from Candia in 1337 refers to others weighing about 8.9 pounds each.[30] Four or five pieces were sometimes tied together in bundles. Cheese was also packed in baskets or wrapped in sacks to facilitate its transportation.[31]

The fairly rich documentation of the Venetian period bearing on Cretan cheese provides a good insight into the latter's trade patterns. In Venetian Crete the purchase of agricultural and pastoral products, including cheese, was often tied to advance payments for the delivery of an agreed quantity of the produce at a specific date or within a specific period. This sale credit system, with its concealed loans, is illustrated by numerous contracts, the exact terms of which widely varied.[32] Those drafted in Candia in 1271 by the notary Pietro Scardon practically offer their entire range. Cheese was often ordered directly from the producer. Thus Niccolò Lombardo expected grain at his home in Candia, in addition to cheese valued at one hyperper and thus weighing between 36 and 43 kilograms. The Greek producer assumed the transportation costs from his village, while the customer paid the due levied at the city gate.[33] A Jew was to receive from a Greek peasant and a Greek resident of Candia deliveries of 100 pounds in April and 200 in May 1272, or earlier, the total weight amounting to about 45 kilograms.[34] The small quantities of cheese involved in these deals were either intended for private consumption or for local retail trade. Yet other transactions point to wholesalers who in fact acted as entrepreneurs commissioning the production of cheese, handling it in bulk, and selling it either to local retailers or to other merchants who exported it. Two contracts were concluded in April and August 1271, respectively, between a Latin peasant and a Jew of Candia for two consignments of one-half of a *milliarium* each at seven hyperpers, one in February and the second in April 1272.[35] Another Jew of Candia, Moses the dyer, was promised by a Greek of the city one-half of a *milliarium* at six hyperpers till May 1272 and by a Latin resident one *milliarium* at fourteen hyperpers until April 1272, this time delivered at the weighing station located at the marketplace.[36] Deals between residents of Candia for cheese valued at 100 hyperpers, or between 1,090 and 1,272 kilograms, to be delivered until 8 July 1271, and another between a Candiote and a Venetian traveling merchant for fifty hyperpers of wool and cheese, to be delivered in June 1271, were clearly intended for export.[37] The three villages mentioned in these contracts, Çucara, Mathe or Mafu, and Finike, were all located in the *eparchia* of Temenos, less than twenty kilometers to the south of Candia. Yet in other instances the distance was far greater, as from Canea or Belvedere to Candia in 1300 and 1304, respectively.[38]

Venetians and other Latin settlers holding fiefs in Crete often sold the cheese they bought from their Greek villeins, in addition to the produce of their own flocks. In 1279 and 1280 Pietro de la Caliva of Candia made advance payments for the exclusive right to purchase the entire yield of sheep cheese and wool from some fiefholders and their villeins holding land in the area of Sitia, in eastern Crete, with delivery in this city until 29 June 1281. In 1306 Angelo de Rizo, a resident of Candia acting as wholesaler, made a similar deal for the cheese of a fiefholder, storing it in the warehouse he owned on the shore of Sitia, a convenient site for its shipping. According to a contract of 1280 a fiefholder promised storage for the cheese he was to deliver, presumably until it would be transferred elsewhere in Crete or be exported by sea. The price was to be similar to that paid by other fiefholders of the area to their villeins. It is unclear what profit the fiefholders derived from their role as middlemen in such cases. In 1300 Pietro de la Caliva concluded similar deals with two relatives of the Molino family residing in Candia, one of them in return for a payment of 300 hyperpers, transportation by land or by sea being assumed by the landowners.[39] It is likely that throughout the years Pietro had conducted similar ventures, specializing in the advance purchase of large quantities of produce for export. In addition, he extensively engaged in other types of business.[40]

The Candiote Tommaso da Porto also operated on a fairly large scale from 1279 to 1281, making advance payments, whether on his own or together with partners, for the purchase of cheese and wool. The deal he concluded on 4 April 1279 with another Candiote provided for the delivery of seven hundred pounds of cheese and three hundred pounds of wool within the same month.[41] Further transactions in January, February, and March of 1281 were to be completed by April or May of the same year. The concentration of deliveries within two months of the navigation season was clearly aimed at export. No fixed price was stated; instead, the volume of the merchandise was to be determined by the market price at the time of delivery.[42] It was thus not always possible for the creditor to circumvent the regular marketing network and purchase the merchandise at a lower price. Letters written in Candia in March 1344 and October 1345 inform us that cheese cost then 35 and 36 hyperpers per *milliarium,* respectively, because "there was little [of it]."[43] Yet even if we take into account a temporary shortage of exportable cheese, it is clear that these prices were much higher than those paid by creditors relying on advance purchases from producers.

The contract known as *soccida* was an association between the owner of a herd and a peasant offering his labor to raise animals entrusted to him for a specific period, in return for a payment in kind or in cash. A Venetian living in Cordakia (Karidhaki), in the district of Candia, hired 200 sheep for one year in return for 2,200 pounds or 1,228 kilograms of cheese, half in April and half in July 1272, to be delivered at the marketplace of

Candia.[44] In 1300 two villeins hired an unspecified number of young milking sheep for a period of three years from a Greek priest living in Candia. They promised three deliveries per year of specific quantities of hard cheese and ricotta, one contract fixing the quota at 400 pounds of the former and 50 pounds of the latter.[45] In 1301 Greeks from Candia provided peasants with money to buy milking sheep, which they were to keep for a number of years in return for an annual payment in cash and an annual delivery of ricotta.[46] On the other hand, we find flock owners and herdsmen leasing pasture land to graze their own animals and those entrusted to them.[47] Incidentally, the contracts of 1300 and 1301 reveal that Greeks too fulfilled an active role in the local cheese trade.

The producer was not always capable of delivering on time the product he had promised, nor of reimbursing the sum he had received in advance because he had already spent it. Indebtedness was widespread in Crete at all levels of society, yet it particularly affected those of modest means. In order to escape legal actions taken by their creditors, peasants sometimes abandoned their land or even fled abroad. These cases must have been widespread and in 1393 the loss of manpower was important enough to induce the Venetian Senate to prohibit advance payments in return for cheese. The decree, adopted on 11 March, was to be proclaimed everywhere in Crete, yet about six months later, on 26 September, it had to be reconsidered in the light of a letter sent by the governor of Canea. The decree had generated the protest of numerous flock owners, who depended on the loans they had received to buy animals. Once the decree had been published the creditors had reclaimed their money or had taken legal steps to recover it, compelling the herdsmen either to sell their flocks and lose their livelihood or else to flee. The Senate decided that Venetian officials serving in Crete would mediate between creditors and debtors.[48]

Contracts between producers and customers or between merchants were freely determined by the parties concerned. On the other hand, the delivery and marketing of agricultural and pastoral products were strictly controlled by the authorities. These products were channeled toward urban markets in order to enable the state to tax them. Two late thirteenth-century customs lists from Candia, already mentioned above, deal with taxes levied at the land gate (*ordo porte civitatis*) and those paid in the harbor of Candia (*ordo porte ripe maris*), respectively. The taxation unit in land trade was the *somerium* or load carried by a beast of burden bringing the commodities to the city, whereas the unit for export by sea was the Candiote *milliarium*.[49] Once the cheese entered the city it had to be weighed on the Commune's scales at the official weighing station,[50] regardless of whether it would be sold on the market or be delivered to a customer at this station, a private home, or a private warehouse.[51] The weighing was carried out by state-appointed officials (*pesatores*) in the presence of state assessors (*extimatores*), who determined the amount of salt and foreign bodies in the cheese or adhering to its crust and prevented fraud in quality or weight at the expense of the buyer.[52] It is noteworthy that the assessors also acted as official brokers (*messete*) on behalf of the state, and that several of them were Greek.[53] As in all commercial transactions in Venice and her territories overseas, they were responsible for the collection of a brokerage tax called *missetaria*.[54] The official weighing is referred to as late as 1473, when the Senate deplored that some time earlier merchants had begun to buy and store local products in the countryside, depriving thereby the state of revenue and Candia of its economic activity.[55] The state monopoly on the sale of salt in Crete, established in 1279, was yet another source of revenue which the authorities sought to preserve. Since Cretan cheese makers were buying cheaper salt from private sources, it was decreed in 1370 that they were to use exclusively salt purchased from the Commune.[56]

The concentration of a large number of cheese warehouses in Candia was not only related to trade but also to the supply of passing ships. Cheese was one of the five basic components of the diet of seamen, next to ship biscuits, wine, salt pork, and beans. About 1310 Marino Sanudo the Elder listed the daily rations to be distributed to them, presumably on the basis of information collected from the operators of Venetian galleys. Each seaman was supposed to receive some forty grams of cheese per day.[57] As an advanced base overseas Crete fulfilled important functions in the Venetian naval defense system, one of which was the provisoning of the Commune's fleets.[58] In 1402 the duke of Crete, Marco Falier, was ordered to dispatch as fast as possible three to five hundred *staria* of ship biscuits and five *milliaria* or 2,562 kilograms of Cretan cheese, corresponding to 64,062 daily rations, to Bertuccio Diedo, vice-captain of the fleet sailing in Romania toward Constantinople.[59] If, for instance, we assume a crew of some 180 men per ship and a fleet of six ships, this quantity would have been sufficient for about two months.[60] In 1494 Pietro Casola noted that the Cretans "sell a large quantity [of cheese] to the ships that call there. It was astonishing to see the number of cheeses taken by our galley," which carried pilgrims to the Holy Land.[61] Part of it may have been sold to the passengers on board, a practice we have come across earlier,[62] and the rest in Levantine ports.

The medium and long-distance export of Cretan cheese was tied to a seasonal pattern, since it depended on the movement of ships in specific periods of the year. We have already noted above some instances in which deliveries of fairly large consignments to wholesalers were clearly linked to this pattern. Some other cases are worth mentioning. In 1224 two Venetians acknowledged having received from another Venetian in Candia three *milliaria* or 1,538 kilograms of high-quality Cretan cheese. The transaction had taken place before Easter in Candia, yet since all those involved in it were residents of Venice the cheese must have been intended for this city. In 1271 the two operators of a *tareta* and four merchants, all from Venice, agreed about the shipment of a specific quantity of merchandise from Candia to Venice in the autumn, cheese being mentioned in this context.[63] In March of that same year two Venetian fiefholders, Pietro Venier and Giovanni Corner, leased for six years some sections of two villages located south-southeast of Candia to the powerful Greek *archon* Alexius Kalergis, a great landowner, in return for the annual delivery in mid-March of 667 *milliaria* or about 342 metric tons of cheese. Only a small part of this huge consignment, the largest recorded in a single Cretan document, could have been produced in the two villages mentioned in this context.[64] In any event, this cheese was clearly intended for export. Andrea Corner, a prominent fiefholder residing at Candia, exported cheese on a lesser scale. On 7 March 1300 a resident of Canea, Lorenzo Cristiano, who judging by his surname was a Jew converted to Christianity, promised to deliver within three weeks, at his own expense, five *milliaria* or 2,563 kilograms of high-quality ripe cheese at the cost of seventeen hyperpers per *milliarium*. The cheese was to be brought to the Commune's weighing station, where the market price would be known; a possible higher price was taken into account.[65] On 31 March 1300 Francesco Gradenigo promised Pietro de la Caliva ten *milliaria* or 5,127 kilograms of cheese in April, fifteen *milliaria* or 7,691 kilograms in May, and about eight *milliaria* or 4,359 kilograms in June at the same price.[66] The total weight was about 17,177 kilograms, and the delivery clearly planned so as to enable the export of the cheese during the shipping season. A contract of 13 May 1300 mentions the sailing of a vessel loaded with pepper, wine, and cheese to Venice. While the first commodity was clearly in transit, the two others were local products.[67] In 1301 cheese from Canea was first shipped on barks to Candia, where it was loaded on board larger vessels bound for Venice.[68] The following year the captain of a galley was heavily fined in Venice for having unloaded there an unspecified quantity of Cretan cheese without obtaining the customary permit and for selling it without the intervention of official brokers and weighers.[69] In 1337 a single merchant shipped 27,077 *milliaria* or 13,883 kilograms of cheese from Crete to Venice.[70] Exports to Venice, both from Candia and Canea, are further attested in 1356 and 1363. If sent to another destination the cheese was taxed at the rate of one hyperper per *milliarium*.[71] Cheese was among the commodities which six galleys dispatched by the Venetian Senate to Crete in June 1432 were ordered to bring to Venice, the freight being fixed at three ducats per *milliarium*.[72]

It would be tedious to register all the instances in which Cretan cheese was conveyed to Venice. Unfortunately, the extant sources offer only a fragmentary picture of this extensive trade, the volume of which at any given moment cannot be gauged. In any event, it was important enough to be recorded in the *Zibaldone da Canal* about 1320 and in a later Venetian commercial manual, the *Tarifa,* compiled in the second half of the fourteenth or in the early fifteenth century.[73] One should remember, though, that for Venice Crete was just one of several sources of cheese supply, Apulia being another important one.[74] While noteworthy, even the large individual consignments known to have left Crete for Venice were rather small compared with those shipped by the Bardi from Apulia in 1329. This Florentine mercantile and banking company imported then Apulian cheese to Venice on an impressive scale, namely 360,000 Venetian pounds in October and a further 40,000 pounds in December. The following year two partners of the company complained that these two shipments, the total of which amounted to no less than 190.8 metric tons, had been unjustly confiscated by the authorities.[75] It should be stressed that the massive Venetian imports of cheese were not only intended for the city's own consumption. Large quantities of it were reexported to the cities of the Terraferma or Italian mainland.[76] A Florentine commercial manual of the mid-fifteenth century and a late sixteenth-century Jewish source attest to continuity in the import of Cretan cheese to Venice.[77]

Cretan cheese was also exported to various destinations within the eastern Mediterranean itself. In 1269 and 1270 a bark loaded with wine and cheese and another exclusively with cheese were seized by Byzantine pirates on their way to the southern Peloponnesian ports of Coron and Modon, respectively.[78] The treaties concluded between the dukes of Crete and the Turkish emirs of Aydin and Menteshe in 1337 and with the latter in 1358 reveal that Cretan and other Venetian subjects were regularly shipping Cretan cheese to these territories.[79] In 1367 a Cretan nobleman, Marco Salamone, concluded a freight agreement with the Greek Costa Vlissima for the loading of thirty *milliaria* or 15,382 kilograms of good Cretan cheese on his *griparia* at Sitia. The Greek shipowner was to carry the cheese to Cyprus and sell it there, together with his own ten *milliaria* or 5,127 kilograms, the total quantity weighing more than twenty metric tons.[80] The export of Cretan cheese to Famagusta in this period or somewhat later is confirmed by the Venetian *Tarifa*.[81] Its shipping to various destinations in Romania by Venetians and numerous foreigners is further attested in December 1416.[82] More specifically, in 1414 a *griparia* loaded with cheese and wine was seized by a ship from Mytilene while sailing from Crete to Rhodes.[83] The fragment of a Greek account book dated to about 1360 mentions Cretan and Venetian cheese on several occasions. The editor of this text tentatively locates its author in the Crimea and, therefore, assumes that the names of the cheeses do not refer to the latter's origin but rather to the type after which they were locally made.[84] Constantinople, however, appears to be a more plausible site for the compilation of the account.[85] The arrival of Cretan cheese in that city would not be surprising. The Venetians already sold it in their quarter of the Byzantine capital in the twelfth century, and this was still the case in the 1430s, as illustrated by the account book of the Venetian merchant Giacomo Badoer.[86] In addition, about 1360 Cretan cheese may have also been available in the Genoese quarter of Constantinople.[87] In times of peace between Venice and their city Genoese merchants occasionally stopped in Crete on the way between Genoa and Constantinople.[88]

The export of Cretan cheese to Egypt, already attested in the twelfth century,[89] appears to have substantially increased in volume in the course of the fourteenth century, possibly early in that century. It is generally believed that the papal embargo on trade with the Mamluk territories, proclaimed in 1291, was to a large extent and effectively implemented and that it prevented or, at any rate, severely hampered commercial relations between the West and Egypt. Contemporary sources contradict this assumption. The Venetian presence in Alexandria is duly attested and several Venetian, Genoese, and Catalan ships are known to have sailed via Crete to the Egyptian port in the years 1300-1304.[90] We have no information about their cargo, yet cheese was presumably included in it. In January 1323 the Venetian Senate prohibited all Venetian subjects to trade with Mamluk lands,[91] yet this activity was pursued from Crete. About that time the Arab historian and geographer Abu'l-Fida reported that Crete exported cheese to Alexandria.[92] Letters written in 1336 and 1344 by foreign merchants residing in Candia bear witness to the continuation of traffic between Crete and Egypt.[93] Trade along this route intensified after the easing of the papal ban in 1344 and the conclusion of new agreements between Venice and Egypt early in 1345.[94] In 1347 a ship sailing from Candia loaded cheese at Sitia before proceeding to Alexandria.[95]

This traffic continued in the first half of the fifteenth century. Cretan merchants, whether Latins, Greeks, or Jews, were regularly sailing to Alexandria, some of them even residing there temporarily. One of them was Emmanuel Piloti, a Latin who between roughly 1396 and 1438 spent some twenty-two years in Egypt. He reports that wine, cheese, honey, and wax were the major Cretan exports to Alexandria.[96] By 1414 some Cretan merchants exported cheese and wine as far as Cairo, where they bought jewels.[97] Notarial charters drafted in Alexandria confirming the arrival of Cretan cheese are of particular interest, because they offer an unusual view of the foreign receiving end of this traffic. In 1421 several residents of Candia concluded a deal in the Egyptian port involving the future delivery there of seventy-five *milliaria* or about 38.5 metric tons of cheese from Sitia at fifteen ducats the unit, including transportation costs.[98] Since the price of cheese bought directly from the producer was generally less than eighteen hyperpers per *milliarium,* as noted above, the sale at fifteen ducats equivalent to forty-five hyperpers or more ensured a substantial margin of profit, despite freight charges.[99] The troubled relations of Venice with Egypt since 1426 induced Venice to limit, regulate, and even stop the trade of its subjects with the Mamluk territories.[100] Nevertheless, in June 1427 the Venetian Senate ordered two small cogs to pick up at Candia cheese and other commodities awaiting to be exported to the sultan's lands.[101] About three years later, in 1430, the Senate allowed Cretan ships to sail to Syria or Egypt with local products, although the Venetian traffic to these countries had been temporarily suspended.[102] The shipping of cheese from Sitia to Alexandria is also documented in 1450.[103] In 1462 the inhabitants of Crete stressed once more that wine, honey, fruit, hides, and cheese constituted the main sources of income of their island and that these commodities were to a large extent exported to the East on board small vessels.[104]

∽

The Venetian conquest of Crete in the early thirteenth century and the subsequent Latin settlement in the island generated some important long-term developments in the Cretan economy, including in cheese production and marketing. Despite their small numbers, the Latin settlers and their families established in Crete constituted an additional clientele for local produce. More importantly, the expanding demand in Venice for Cretan victuals, primarily grain, wine, and cheese, prompted large-scale

60

investments of money and labor in land cultivation and in the raising of animals.[105] The Venetians and other Latins handled more liquid capital than the Greeks and had easier access than before 1204 to producers, at times without local middlemen. Often acting as entrepreneurs, they ousted the *archontes* from the dominant position they had held in the Cretan commercial network in the Byzantine period, without entirely eliminating them.[106] Advance payments for cheese lowered purchase prices, offered larger profit margins for middlemen, and facilitated the concentration of large quantities of produce in time for the main sailing seasons. The commercialization of Cretan cheese was also furthered by the acquaintance of the Venetians and other Latins with marketing opportunities and networks in Crete itself and especially abroad, the insertion of Crete within the pattern of Venetian long-distance seaborne trade, and the intensification of Cretan shipping in the framework of a regional trade pattern. Cretan merchants and carriers of modest means, the latter often Greeks, operated small crafts conveying the products of their island, including cheese, to Cyprus, Rhodes, Lesser Armenia, Syria, and Egypt,[107] and returned with spices among other commodities.[108] The Venetian government furthered this trade for the sake of its Cretan subjects, yet strictly supervised it in order to ensure the commercial interests of the city of Venice and enhance the revenue of the state treasury.

NOTES

The following abbreviations are used below: BdB = Raimondo Morozzo della Rocca, ed., *Benvenuto de Brixano, notaio in Candia, 1301-1302* (Venice, 1950); *DCV* = Raimondo Morozzo della Rocca and Antonino Lombardo, eds., *Documenti del commercio veneziano nei secoli XI–XIII* (Turin, 1940); *DMC* = Roberto Cessi, ed., *Deliberazioni del Maggior Consiglio di Venezia* (Bologna, 1931–50); LM = Mario Chiaudano and Antonino Lombardo, eds., *Leonardo Marcello, notaio in Candia, 1278-1281* (Venice, 1960); NdB = Antonino Lombardo, ed., *Nicola de Boateriis, notaio in Famagosta e Venezia (1355-1365)* (Venice, 1973); Pegolotti = Francesco Balducci Pegolotti, *La pratica della mercatura,* ed. Allan Evans (Cambridge, Mass., 1936); PP = Salvatore Carbone, ed., *Pietro Pizolo, notaio in Candia (1300, 1304-1305)* (Venice, 1978–85); PS = Antonino Lombardo, ed., *Imbreviature di Pietro Scardon (1271),* Documenti della colonia veneziana di Creta 1 (Turin, 1942); PZ = Raimondo Morozzo della Rocca, ed., *Lettere di mercanti a Pignol Zucchello (1336-1350)* (Venice, 1957); ZF = Antonino Lombardo, ed., *Zaccaria de Fredo, notaio in Candia (1352 -1357)* (Venice, 1968); *Zibaldone* = Alfredo Stussi, ed., *Zibaldone da Canal. Manoscritto mercantile del sec. XIV* (Venice, 1967). BdB, LM, NdB, PP, and ZF have been edited by the Comitato per la pubblicazione delle Fonti relative alla Storia di Venezia, in the series Fonti per la storia di Venezia, Sez. III: Archivi notarili; PZ in Sez. IV: Archivi privati; and *Zibaldone* in Sez. V: Fondi vari.

1. See Shlomo D. Goitein, *A Mediterranean Society: The Jewish Communities of the Arab World as Portrayed in the Documents of the Cairo Geniza*, 6 vols. (Berkeley and Los Angeles, 1967–93), 1:46, 124; Maria Dembínska, "Diet: A Comparison of Food Consumption between Some Eastern and Western Monasteries in the 4th–12th Centuries," *Byzantion* 55 (1985–86): 431–62; Michel Kaplan, *Les hommes et la terre à Byzance du VIe au XIe siècle* (Paris, 1992), pp. 41–42.

2. Nikos A. Bees, "Zu *prosphagion* ('Käse') in einem Brief des Metropoliten Michael Choniatis von Athen," *Annuaire de l'Institut de philologie et d'histoire orientales et slaves* 5 (1937): 31–35.

3. On travelers, see Goitein, *Mediterranean Society*, 4:252; on cheese sold to passengers on board a Genoese ship in 1184, see Ronald J. C. Broadhurst, trans., *The Travels of Ibn Jubayr* (London, 1951), p. 329; a Byzantine military treatise of the second half of the tenth century recommends food for one day consisting "only [of] bread, cheese, or some dried meat" (George T. Dennis, ed. and trans., *Three Military Treatises*, Corpus Fontium Historiae Byzantinae 25 [Washington, D.C., 1985], p. 164, chap. 8, lines 12–14). Ugo Tucci, "L'alimentazione a bordo delle navi veneziane," *Studi veneziani* n.s. 13 (1987): 103–45, deals with the period beginning in the late fifteenth century, yet provides some important general methodological considerations. On ships and seamen, see also below.

4. Paul Gautier, ed., *Michel Italikos: Lettres et discours*, Archives de l'Orient chrétien 14 (Paris, 1972), pp. 237–38, letter 42.

5. Nicholas I, Patriarch of Constantinople, *Letters*, ed. Romilly J. H. Jenkins and Leendert G. Westerink, Corpus Fontium Historiae Byzantinae 6 (Washington, D.C., 1973), p. 422, letter 127: cheese or butter from Paphlagonia.

6. For the period preceding the Fourth Crusade, see David Jacoby, "Byzantine Crete in the Navigation and Trade Networks of Venice and Genoa," in *Oriente e Occidente tra medioevo ed età moderna. Studi in onore di Geo Pistarino*, ed. Laura Balletto (Genoa, 1997), pp. 519–22, 525–30, 535–36. *

7. Giovanni Battista Cervellini, ed., *Documento inedito veneto-cretese del Dugento* (Padua, 1906), pp. 13–18, esp. pp. 14–16. For the dating, see Silvano Borsari, *Il dominio veneziano a Creta nel XIII secolo* (Naples, 1963), pp. 32–33 and esp. n. 17.

8. One should take into account an expansion of breeding in the Venetian period. On pasture and livestock in the island, see Freddy Thiriet, *La Romanie vénitienne au Moyen Age. Le développement et l'exploitation du domaine colonial vénitien (XIIe–XVe siècles)*, Bibliothèque des Ecoles françaises d'Athènes et de Rome 193 (Paris, 1959), pp. 107–8, 322–24.

9. PP, no. 700.

10. As in PP, nos. 170, 327.

11. Freddy Thiriet, *Délibérations des assemblées vénitiennes concernant la Romanie* (Paris, 1966–71), 2:187, no. 1440 (a. 1450).

12. Continuity in this respect may be taken for granted and, therefore, the use of later evidence is warranted.

13. The form *apotyron* appears in a twelfth-century Byzantine poem; see Hans Eideneier, ed. and trans., *Ptochoprodromos*, Neograeca medii aevi 5 (Cologne, 1991), p. 150, IV, verse 211, translated pp. 204 and 238, index, s.v. *apotyron*, as "weichen Quark" or "Molkekäse."

14. Charles du Fresne du Cange, *Glossarium ad scriptores mediae et infimae graecitatis* (Lyons, 1688), s.v. *Mezethra*.

VIII

62

15. Sinodii Dmitrievich Papadimitriu, ed., *Stefanye Sachlikesye i ego stichotvorenie "Aphegesis paraxenos"* (Odessa, 1896), p. 20, fol. 3, verse 136, and see Antonios Jeannaraki [Giannares], ed., *Asmata kretika meta distichon kai paroimion. Kretas Volkslieder nebst Distichen und Sprichwörter. In der Ursprache mit Glossar* (Leipzig, 1876), pp. 374–75. *Myzithra* is mentioned in two Greek commercial accounts, one compiled in eastern Greece and the other presumably in Rhodes, respectively in the first half and the late fourteenth century; see Peter Schreiner, ed., *Texte zur spätbyzantinischen Finanz- und Wirtschaftsgeschichte in Handschriften der Biblioteca Vaticana*, Studi e Testi 344 (Vatican City, 1991), p. 145, no. 8, line 4, and for dating, location, and commentary, pp. 144–45, 148; the second one: p. 70, no. 2, line 46, and see also pp. 66–67, 73, 78. On ricotta, see below.

16. As suggested by Goitein, *Mediterranean Society*, 1:429, n. 66. I wish to thank Dr. Stefan C. Reif, who has kindly informed me that the letter, which probably belonged to the Cairo Genizah or synagogue archive, is now at the Cambridge University Library and listed there as Or. 2116.10. Sesame and pine seeds, thyme, other herbs, and pepper were already used in antiquity; see Ernst Herdi, "Die Herstellung und Verwertung von Käse im griechisch-römischen Altertum," *Programm der Thurgauischen Kantonsschule* (Schuljahr 1917-18), pp. 42–43; also Jacques André, *L'alimentation et la cuisine à Rome* (Paris, 1961), pp. 154–56.

17. For these operations in antiquity see Herdi, "Herstellung und Verwertung von Käse," pp. 38–39. The fourteenth-century Pegolotti refers to them in a section of his manual devoted to "facitura di formaggio" in Apulia; he mentions the crushing of the salt, the water used for the salting, and the expert in charge of this operation, "lo maestro che lo 'nsala" (p. 164).

18. Giulio Porro, ed., *Viaggio di Pietro Casola a Gerusalemme* (Milan, 1855), p. 43; I have slightly altered the translation of M. Margaret Newett, *Canon Pietro Casola's Pilgrimage to Jerusalem in the Year 1494* (Manchester, 1907), p. 203.

19. For examples, see below. For weight calculations it should be noted that the ratio between the gross *milliarium* (1,000 *libre* or pounds) of Venice and that of Candia differs from one source to another; see Erich Schilbach, *Byzantinische Metrologie* (Munich, 1970), pp. 212-13. Yet this author has not taken into account the specific ratio for the weighing of cheese quoted in *Zibaldone*, pp. 59-60, fol. 36v, lines 2-3 and 29-30, which was 1,000:1,075 for the *milliarium* and 100:107 for a unit of 100 pounds, thus somewhat lower. Since the Venetian *milliarium* of cheese was equivalent to 477 kg., that of Candia based on the first ratio was 512.75 kg. Schilbach (*Byzantinische Metrologie*, p. 213) claims that the Candiote *libra* derived from the Genoese one, yet the Genoese partial occupation of Crete lasted a few years only, from 1206 to 1211: see Borsari, *Dominio veneziano*, pp. 21-25. The preservation of a local Byzantine weight system by Venice seems far more plausible. See also below, n. 20.

20. *Zibaldone*, p. 60, fol. 37r, lines 1-2, on shrinkage from one Candiote *milliarium* or 512.75 kg. of cheese to one Venetian *milliarium* or 477 kg., or a loss of 6.83 percent; for another reference to the same process during the journey from Apulia to Venice see p. 20, fol. 9v, lines 12-18. See also John E. Dotson, trans., *Merchant Culture in Fourteenth Century Venice: The Zibaldone da Canal*, Medieval and Renaissance Texts and Studies 98 (Binghamton, N.Y., 1994), pp. 45, n. 41, and 109, n. 189; also below, n. 73.

21. See the rabbinical responsum translated by Robert Bonfil in *Rabbis and Jewish Communities in Renaissance Italy* (Oxford, 1990), pp. 113-14. *Grana* is used nowadays for hard Parmesan cheese.

22. Ernst Gerland, ed., *Das Archiv des Herzogs von Kandia* (Strassburg, 1899), p. 108, lines 15, 20, 29; p. 109, line 1. For the dating of these lists, see pp. 107, n. 1, and 135, in the chronological table under 1298-99. In 1363 the Venetian Senate decided to impose a tax on the retail trade of both types of cheese (Spyridon M. Theotokes, ed., *Thespismata tes Benetikes Gerousias, 1281-1385* [Athens, 1937], 2:106, par. 15). The document of 1307 in Venetian dialect published by Borsari (*Dominio veneziano*, pp. 81-82, n. 76) does not refer to cheese but to grain; instead of *formaco*, read *formento*.

23. BdB, no. 320: "libras recote bone et saxionate .XL." (a. 1301).

24. PP, no. 170: "bonus caseus cretensis bene condictus et sasionatus mercatorius" (a. 1300).

25. On this issue, see below, n. 52.

26. Schreiner, *Texte zur spätbyzantinischen Finanz- und Wirtschaftsgeschichte*, p. 42, no. 1, line 131, and for the dating, pp. 33-36. For its origin, however, see below, n. 85.

27. See Jeannaraki, *Asmata kretika*, pp. 374-75. Baskets made of various materials were already used in the Roman period, see Herdi, "Herstellung und Verwertung von Käse," pp. 35-37.

28. *DMC*, 1:117: "formam I de caseo de Crete"; for other cheeses, without indication of provenance, see pp. 114 (135 *libre*), 116, 121 ("milliarium unum et medium casei valentem libras XXXVIIII÷").

29. *DCV*, vol. 2, no. 617: "de bono et optimo caseo de suprascripta insula a libris sedecim et supra pro unaquaque pecia"; LM, nos. 213, 277.

30. PZ, p. 14, no. 2: a total of 3,048 pieces weighing 27,077 pounds of Candia.

31. PZ, p. 54, no. 24 (*leghate in fasci*), and p. 99, no. 51 (*leghacci*), for maritime transportation in the 1340s. On molds of Sicilian cheese, see Goitein, *Mediterranean Society*, 4:251-52, and Shlomo D. Goitein, trans., *Letters of Medieval Jewish Traders* (Princeton, 1973), p. 196. In the mid-fourteenth century "Muslim" dry cheese was sold in sacks in Constantinople (Schreiner, *Texte zur spätbyzantinischen Finanz- und Wirtschaftsgeschichte*, p. 43, no. 1, line 134).

32. Mario Gallina, "Finanza, credito e commercio a Candia fra la fine del XIII secolo e l'inizio del XIV," *Memorie della Accademia delle Scienze di Torino, Classe di Scienze morali, Storiche e Filologiche*, series 5, vols. 7-8 (1983-84) (Turin, 1986), pp. 34-40.

33. PS, no. 174: "datium porte." The weight is assessed here on the basis of prices of the same period fluctuating between twelve and fourteen hyperpers per *milliarium*. See also BdB, no. 420: 180 pounds of cheese in return for 2.5 hyperpers in 1301, the price per *milliarium* being thus less than thirteen hyperpers. See also below, n. 34.

34. PS, nos. 438 and 280; the sums were twenty-nine *sterlini* and three hyperpers and 8½ *sterlini*, respectively. At twenty-four *sterlini* per hyperper the price of the cheese was 12 and 16.77 hyperpers per *milliarium*, respectively.

35. PS, nos. 218, 436.

36. PS, nos. 421 and 448: "in dicta Candida apud stateram."

37. PS, nos. 354 and 74.

38. PP, nos. 170, 850.

39. LM, nos. 125, 213; PP, nos. 251, 327. On exports directly from Sitia, see below, nn. 40, 80, 95, 98, 103.

40. Pietro de la Caliva was involved in all these contracts except one; see LM, no. 274, and PP, index, s.v. Chaliva (de la), Petrus; on his largest recorded deal of 1300, see below, n. 66. For Angelo de Rizo, see Archivio di Stato, Notai di Candia, B. 186, Angelo di Cartura, fol. 31v-32, nos. 408 and 410. I wish to thank Alan M. Stahl for generously offering me the text of several documents dealing with cheese, to be included in his forthcoming edition of this notary's cartulary.

41. LM, no. 93.

42. LM, no. 390, a purchase from a resident of the Mirabello district "secundum quod vendetur ad stateram Communis"; also nos. 521, 564 (cheese for 17 hyperpers); for the same formula in a deal of one of his partners, see no. 384. On the extensive business operations of Tommaso da Porto, see Gallina, "Finanza, credito e commercio a Candia," pp. 52-54. Note a sale of one hundred sheep at Mirabello in 1300 (PP, no. 498).

43. PZ, p. 23, no. 8, and p. 47, no. 19.

44. PS, no. 440: "in dicta Candida apud stateram."

45. PP, no. 708. One of the contracts was established by a Greek notary. For the hiring of fifty sheep in return for a payment in cash, see no. 705.

46. BdB, no. 247.

47. BdB, no. 396.

48. Hippolyte Noiret, *Documents inédits pour servir à l'histoire de la domination vénitienne en Crète de 1380 à 1485* (Paris, 1892), pp. 55, 59-60. On indebtedness and official mediation in Crete, see David Jacoby, "Les gens de mer dans la marine de guerre vénitienne de la mer Egée aux XIVe et XVe siècles," in *Le genti del Mare Mediterraneo*, XVII Colloquio Internazionale di Storia marittima, Napoli, 1980, ed. Rosalba Ragosta (Naples, 1981), 1:186-87, reprinted in David Jacoby, *Studies on the Crusader States and on Venetian Expansion* (Northampton, 1989), no. 11.

49. Gerland, *Archiv des Herzogs von Kandia*, p. 108, lines 15, 20, 29; p. 109, line 1. In Crete the tax at the land gate was levied each time the merchandise entered a city or a *castrum*: see Elisabeth Santschi, *Régestes des arrêts civils et des mémoriaux (1363-1399) des archives du duc de Crète* (Venice, 1976), p. 45, no. 192. See also above, n. 33.

50. Paola Ratti Vidulich, ed., *Duca di Candia. Bandi,* Fonti per la storia di Venezia, Sez. I: Archivi pubblici (Venice, 1965), no. 34: "camera pesarie comunis ubi sunt statere comunis."

51. For references to specific places of delivery, among them the weighing station, see above, nn. 36, 42, 43, and below, n. 65. In Venice cheese directly delivered to the consumer was also taxed according to weight: *DMC*, 2:285, no. 6; see also Giorgio Zordan, *I Visdomini dei Venezia nel sec. XIII (Ricerche su un'antica magistratura finanziaria)* (Padua, 1971), pp. 213-16.

52. See also above, p. 51. The same practice is attested in Ancona about 1350. State assessors estimated the weight of *immunditia* sticking to the crust, which was deducted from the total weight in wholesale transactions, while below a specific quantity in retail trading cheese was to be sold without its crust (C. Ciavarini, ed.,

Statuti anconitani del mare, del terzenale e dalla dogana, e patti con diverse nazioni [Ancona, 1896], pp. 178-79, par. CVIIII. *De tara casei).*

53. Ratti Vidulich, *Duca di Candia,* no. 32, for cheese; similarly, there were assessors for wool (ibid., no. 33). In 1329 an assessor was beaten by two Greek peasants who apparently did not appreciate his intervention (ibid., no. 485).

54. See David Jacoby, "Venice, the Inquisition and the Jewish Communities of Crete in the Early 14th Century," *Studi veneziani* 12 (1970): 127-44, esp. pp. 130-31, reprinted in idem, *Recherches sur la Méditerranée orientale du XIIe au XVe siècle. Peuples, sociétés, économies* (London, 1979), no. 9. Occasionally Jews too were appointed official middlemen. On the brokerage tax in Venice, see below, n. 69.

55. Noiret, *Documents inédits,* pp. 526-27: "conducebantur sub pondere Candide per rusticos ad mercatum casei" and other products. This practice had been beneficial: "Que res ornabat illam nostram civitatem ex confluentia hominum et abundantia rerum, et Dominium nostrum exigebat debita datia, et mercatura exercebatur, et populares navigabant, faciebant bonam terram illam."

56. Johannes Jegerlehner, ed., "Beiträge zur Verwaltungsgeschichte Kandias im XIV. Jahrhunderts," *Byzantinische Zeitschrift* 13 (1904): 435-79, esp. pp. 469-70. Salt production in Crete did not cover all the island's needs and, therefore, imports were indispensable; see Jean-Claude Hocquet, *Le sel et la fortune de Venise,* vol. 1: *Production et monopole* (Lille, 1978), pp. 94, 125, 254-55, 279, and esp. pp. 293-96. According to Hocquet, Crete produced only sea salt, yet the reference of 1411 to salt from the district of Candia "in parte multo foreste e luntane dalle terre nostre" seems to allude to rock salt from the inland. This salt was preferable for cheese making.

57. Marinus Sanutus, *Liber secretorum fidelium crucis super Terrae Sanctae recuperatione et conservatione,* in Jacques Bongars, ed., *Gesta Dei per Francos, sive orientalium expeditionum et regni Francorum Hierosiolomitani historia . . .* (Hanau, 1611), 2:60-64. For the conversion into grams and the nutritional value, see Frederic C. Lane, "Diet and Wages of Seamen in the Early Fourtenth Century," in Frederic C. Lane, *Venice and History: The Collected Papers of Frederic C. Lane* (Baltimore, 1966), pp. 263-66. According to Lane, the yearly quantity of biscuits per man would have been 261 kg., yet another calculation on the basis of evidence for 1341 and 1343, to which no precise reference is given, yields only 112 kg: see Heinrich Kretschmayr, *Geschichte von Venedig* (Gotha-Stuttgart, 1905-34), 2:620.

58. On these functions, see Jacoby, "Gens de mer," pp. 169-201, esp. pp. 171-75.

59. Freddy Thiriet, ed., *Duca di Candia. Ducali e lettere ricevute (1358-1360; 1401-1405),* Fonti per la storia di venezia, Sez. I: Archivi pubblici, (Venice, 1978), pp. 8-9, no. 5. On Diedo, see also other orders issued in 1402 (Noiret, *Documents inédits,* pp. 130-31, 138-39).

60. For the size of crews, see Frederic C. Lane, "From Biremes to Triremes," in Lane, *Venice and History,* pp. 189-92.

61. See above, n. 18.

62. See above, n. 3.

63. *DCV,* no. 617; PS, no. 367.

64. PS, no. 134. This quantity was worth more than five million ducats and the payment, therefore, excessive. The figure is so large as to be suspect. I wonder whether the editors of this text have not misread the figure. On Alexius Kalergis, see Borsari, *Dominio veneziano,* pp. 48-66.

66

65. PP, no. 170: "conducta ad statera comunis." On Andrea Corner, see Borsari, *Dominio veneziano*, pp. 81–82; PP, index, s.v. Cornario.

66. PP, no. 332: total of 17,177 kg. of cheese for 570 hyperpers at seventeen per *milliarium*. In July of the same year cheese was bought at nineteen hyperpers per *milliarium* (ibid., no. 617). In 1304 prices of 18 and 15 hyperpers per *milliarium* are mentioned on the same day, either reflecting different qualities of cheese or different rates of interest for the same period (ibid., nos. 849 and 850).

67. PP, no. 477.

68. BdB, no. 380.

69. Elena Favaro, ed., *Cassiere della Bolla Ducale-Grazie-Novus Liber (1299–1305)*, Fonti per la storia di Venezia, Sez. I: Archivi pubblici (Venice, 1962), no. 346. On the other hand, he had paid the freight as required.

70. PZ, p. 14, no. 2.

71. Theotokes, *Thespismata tes Benetikes Gerousias*, 2:25, lines 55–57; p. 38, par. 2; p. 105, par. 7; p. 106, par. 15.

72. Summary in Noiret, *Documents inédits*, p. 355. A rate of 3 to 4 Cretan hyperpers per ducat is attested for this period; see Thiriet, *Romanie vénitienne*, p. 307, and idem, *Régestes des délibérations du Sénat concernant la Romanie* (Paris, 1958–61), 1: 227. It follows that the freight per *milliarium* reached between 9 and 12 hyperpers and thus accounted for a sharp increase in the price of the cheese upon arrival in Venice.

73. For *Zibaldone*, see above, n. 19. The *Tarifa* also mentions dehydration, yet notes that if the cheese was still "frescho," i.e., young, the loss of weight was half the usual one ([V. Orlandini, ed.], *Tarifa zoè noticia dy pexi e mexure di luogi e tere che s'adovra marcadantia per el mondo* [Venice, 1925], p. 59, lines 21–23; see also p. 32, lines 7–8, and for the dating, pp. 4–5).

74. Adolf Schaube, *Handelsgeschichte der romanischen Völker des Mittelmeergebiets bis zum Ende der Kreuzzüge* (Munich, 1906), pp. 511–13; Gerhard Rösch, *Venedig und das Reich. Handels- und verkehrspolitische Beziehungen in der deutschen Kaiserzeit*, Bibliothek des Deutschen Historischen Instituts in Rom, 53 (Tübingen, 1982), pp. 108, 110, 134; *DMC*, 2:284, no. 1 (a. 1261); *Zibaldone*, p. 18, fol. 8r, lines 19–22; p. 20, fol. 9v, lines 12–18; Pegolotti, p. 171.

75. Robert Davidsohn, *Forschungen zur Geschichte von Florenz*, part 3 (Berlin, 1901), p. 93, no. 974.

76. See, e.g., Schaube, *Handelsgeschichte der romanischen Völker des Mittelmeergebiets*, pp. 698, 707–8, and Rösch, *Venedig und das Reich*, pp. 158–59, 170–71, to Verona, Brescia, Legnago, Mantova, and Cremona; *Zibaldone*, p. 72, fol. 43r, lines 19–24, and fol. 43v, lines 10–12, to Milan and Cremona.

77. Giorgio di Lorenzo Chiarini, *El libro di mercatantie et usanze de' paesi*, ed. Franco Borlandi (Turin, 1936), p. 66, and above, n. 21.

78. Gottlieb Lucas Friedrich Tafel and Georg Martin Thomas, eds., *Urkunden zur älteren Handels- und Staatsgeschichte der Republik Venedig*, 3 vols. (Vienna, 1856–57), 3:254, no. XII; p. 236, no. VI. The value of the cheese is unknown, since the sums of reparations requested included both the vessels and their cargo. For the dating of these cases, see Gareth Morgan, "The Venetian Claims Commission of 1278," *Byzantinische Zeitschrift* 69 (1976): 411–38, esp. pp. 427–28.

79. Texts in Elizabeth A. Zachariadou, *Trade and Crusade. Venetian Crete and the*

Emirates of Menteshe and Aydin (1300–1415) (Venice 1983), p. 192, par. 11; p. 198, par. 22; p. 222, par. 22. The relevant clauses list various commodities either imported to or exported from the Turkish territories. Cheese, like wine, was clearly imported, since there is no trace of Turkish cheese in Crete or Venice.

80. On this and numerous other transactions of Marco Salomone, see Mario Gallina, *Una società coloniale del Trecento. Creta fra Venezia e Bisanzio*, Deputazione di storia patria per le Venezie, Miscellanea di studi e memorie, 28 (Venice, 1989), pp. 99–100, 119. The Greek shipowner may have already been involved in similar deals at an earlier date, since he was in Famagusta in 1361 (NdB, no. 69). It is not excluded that Cretan cheese reaching Cyprus was sometimes reexported to Egypt (NdB, no. 143 [a. 1362]).

81. *Tarifa,* p. 56, lines 4–5.

82. Venezia, Archivio di Stato, Senato Misti, reg. 51, fol. 173r–v; incomplete summary by Thiriet, *Régestes des délibérations du Sénat*, 2:149, no. 1633.

83. Noiret, *Documents inédits*, p. 230.

84. Schreiner, *Texte zur spätbyzantinischen Finanz- und Wirtschaftgeschichte*, pp. 33–65, no. 1, and see the commentary on cheese, pp. 371–72; *turin benetikon* appears on lines 100, 102, 140, and *turin kritikon* or *kretikon* on lines 109, 130, 131, 133. The editor reads on lines 106, 110, and 117, *apo Benet(ias)*, 'from Venice'. This is clearly impossible in the third instance, where the reference is to caviar. A more plausible reading, therefore, is *apo Benet(ou)*, 'from [the] Venetian', like *apo Moulsouman(ou)*, 'from [the] Muslim' on p. 37, line 2; p. 38, line 40; and p. 43, line 134. Incidentally, the distance separating the Crimea from Crete is not a valid argument against the provenance of "Cretan" cheese from the island, since Cretan wine reached Tana, a port on the Sea of Azov; see Pegolotti, p. 24.

85. A compilation in Crimea, as suggested by Schreiner (*Texte zur spätbyzantinischen Finanz- und Wirtschaftsgeschichte*, pp. 33–37), appears highly questionable in view of the reference to "wheat from the city" (p. 44, line 166), i.e., Constantinople, since wheat was exported *from* the Black Sea area to the Byzantine capital and not in the opposite direction. This would also fit the references to a "Venetian scale" (p. 41, line 111), used in the Venetian quarter, to Byzantine and Venetian coinage, yet not to others, and to hazelnuts and chestnuts, exported in large quantities from southern Italy and especially from Apulia to various localities, including Constantinople; see Pegolotti, pp. 38, 51. These nuts, however, are not cited in commercial manuals with respect to the Black Sea region. Caviar, often mentioned in this account, was sold by the *phouska* (Greek) or *fusco* (Italian), a measure known both in the Crimea and Constantinople, where caviar was extensively traded; see references in the Venetian-Byzantine treaty of 1332 in Franz Miklosich and Josephus Müller, eds., *Acta et diplomata graeca medii aevi sacra et profana* (Vienna, 1860–90), 3:107, and Georg Martin Thomas and Riccardo Predelli, eds., *Diplomatarium veneto-levantinum*, 2 vols. (Venice, 1880–99), 1:231. Pegolotti specifies that the *fusco* was the tail half of the fish's skin full of fish's roe (p. 24).

86. See Jacoby, "Byzantine Crete," p. 527, and Thiriet, *Romanie vénitienne*, p. 425.

87. Schreiner (*Texte zur spätbyzantinischen Finanz- und Wirtschaftsgeschichte*, p. 34) reads *apo t(es) Perati(as)* and considers this a place name, possibly for the Crimea. In view of the arguments adduced here in favor of Constantinople (above, n. 85), the reading should presumably be *apo tou Peratikou* 'from the one living on the

other side', which in the Byzantine capital would mean a resident of Pera, the site of the Genoese quarter in the fourteenth century. The name Peratikos is indeed attested by another Greek account (ibid., p. 243, no. 48, line 31).

88. E.g., Gian Giacomo Musso, *Navigazione e commercio genovese con il Levante nei documenti dell'Archivio di Stato di Genova (Secc. XIV–XV)* (Rome, 1975), pp. 251-52, no. 12 (a. 1399). Although this document refers to a voyage in the opposite direction, the implication is clear.

89. See Jacoby, "Byzantine Crete," pp. 528-30.

90. See David Jacoby, "La Venezia d'oltremare nel secondo Duecento," in Giorgio Cracco and Gherardo Ortalli, eds., *Storia di Venezia, II, L'età del Comune* (Rome, 1995), pp. 263-99, esp. pp. 281-86, and David Jacoby, "La dimensione demografica e sociale," in the same volume, pp. 681-711, esp. p. 691. On shipping, see in particular BdB, nos. 306, 307, 352, 354; PP, nos. 25, 70, 73, 101, 321, 473, 574, 594, 633, 975. In 1304 a Venetian galley about to leave for Alexandria on 21 July 1304 was apparently back in Candia by 20 November of the same year (PP, nos. 804 and 1026).

91. Ratti Vidulich, *Duca di Candia*, no. 342.

92. Joseph Toussaint Reinaud, trans., *Géographie d'Aboulféda* (Paris, 1848), vol. 2, part 1, p. 276. This work was completed in 1321.

93. PZ, p. 15, no. 2; p. 30, no. 12.

94. On which see E. Ashtor, *Levant Trade in the Later Middle Ages* (Princeton, 1983), pp. 64-70.

95. PZ, pp. 85-86, nos. 43-44, letters of Vannino Fecini from Sitia on 1 August and from Alexandria on 11 August.

96. Pierre-Herman Dopp, ed., *Traité d'Emmanuel Piloti sur le Passage en Terre Sainte (1420)* (Louvain, 1958), p. 158, par. 105. For the dating of his work about 1438, see ibid., pp. v–vi, xviii–xxvi.

97. Summary in Noiret, *Documents inédits*, p. 225.

98. Charles Verlinden, "Marchands chrétiens et juifs dans l'Etat mamlouk au début du XVe siècle d'après un notaire vénitien," *Bulletin de l'Institut historique belge de Rome* 51 (1981): 55-56, partial edition of the document: "casei neti, boni, sani et merchandabilis." Verlinden has misunderstood the expressions *de firmo* and *de respectu*, which were used for standard freight charges and others determined by special agreements, respectively; see Federigo Melis, "Werner Sombart e i problemi della navigazione nel medio evo," in *Werner Sombart nel centenario della sua nascità* (Milan, 1964), pp. 131-32.

99. These must have been lower than for shipments to Venice; see above, n. 72, for the exchange rates between the Cretan hyperper and the ducat.

100. See Ashtor, *Levant Trade in the Later Middle Ages*, pp. 283-331.

101. Summary in Noiret, *Documents inédits*, p. 317.

102. Noiret, *Documents inédits*, p. 343, partial edition.

103. Thiriet, *Délibérations des assemblées vénitiennes*, 2:188, no. 1444.

104. Noiret, *Documents inédits*, p. 483.

105. Gallina dwells at length on grain and wine, yet hardly pays attention to livestock and cheese, despite their importance (*Società coloniale*, pp. 95-139).

106. On the *archontes* before 1204, see Jacoby, "Byzantine Crete," pp. 520-21.

107. ZF, nos. 71-72; NdB, no. 125; other examples above.

108. See above, n. 104.

IX

Changing Economic Patterns in Latin Romania:
The Impact of the West

The dramatic fall of Constantinople in 1204 and the Latin conquest of the empire's provinces in the following decade resulted in the dismemberment of Romania. The Latins established a fairly large number of new political entities in the region, most of which remained under their rule for more than two centuries. These long-term political and territorial developments also generated profound economic changes.[1] The present survey is not aimed at providing an overall picture of the complex economic evolution of Latin Romania until around the mid-fifteenth century. Rather, it attempts to determine, as far as possible, the nature, extent, and pace of the Western impact on some of its aspects and trends. To this effect, it will be necessary time and again to look back at conditions and patterns existing before the Fourth Crusade.

It would be tedious to review the complex history of the political entities created by the Latins on Byzantine soil after 1204. However, two of them warrant our attention, since they were of particular importance for the economic evolution of Latin Romania and happen to be fairly well documented: the Venetian maritime empire and the Frankish principality of the Morea in the Peloponnesos. Venice laid the foundations of its centralized maritime empire in 1207, when it began the conquest of Crete and occupied Coron and Modon, two ports of southern Messenia. In 1211 it obtained a quarter in the main city of Euboea, Euripos, called Negroponte by the Latins, a name also used for the island itself. The second stage of Venetian expansion in Romania took place in the 1380s and 1390s, when Venice extended its domination over the island of Corfu, the whole of Euboea, and several cities and lordships in the Peloponnesos and the Aegean.[2] The principality of the Morea was the largest among the lordships created in non-

---

[1] I shall not deal here with the short-lived Kingdom of Thessalonica and Latin Empire of Constantinople, nor with the few islands of the Aegean occupied by the Genoese in the 14th century. They differed markedly from most territories of Latin Romania in their economic evolution.

[2] General historical background and detailed treatment of various issues by S. Borsari, *Il dominio veneziano a Creta nel XIII secolo* (Naples, 1963); idem, *Studi sulle colonie veneziane in Romania nel XIII secolo* (Naples, 1966); F. Thiriet, *La Romanie vénitienne au Moyen Age: Le développement et l'exploitation du domaine colonial vénitien (XIIe–XVe siècles)*, Bibliothèque des Ecoles françaises d'Athènes et de Rome 193, 2d ed. (Paris, 1975); D. Jacoby, *La féodalité en Grèce médiévale: Les "Assises de Romanie." Sources, application et diffusion* (Paris–The Hague, 1971), 185–308; J. Koder, *Negroponte: Untersuchungen zur Topographie und Siedlungsgeschichte der Insel Euboia während der Zeit der Venezianerherrschaft*, Österreichische Akademie der Wissenschaften, Philosophisch-historische Klasse, Denkschriften 112 (Vienna, 1973); short survey by P. Lock, *The Franks in the Aegean, 1204–1500* (London–

IX

198 *Changing Economic Patterns in Latin Romania*

Venetian territories, most of which adopted a Western-type feudal regime. The return of Byzantium to the Peloponnesos in 1262 compelled Prince William II of Villehardouin to seek the support of King Charles I of Sicily, who extended his rule over Frankish Morea after the prince's death in 1278. The direct and indirect domination of the king's successors over the principality continued for more than a whole century.[3] Among other topics, it will be useful to investigate whether differences in political conditions between the Venetian colonies and feudalized areas, primarily Frankish Morea, had any impact on their respective economic evolution.

Two intertwined processes promptly following the conquest had a marked impact on the economy of Latin Romania: the confiscation and redistribution of urban and especially rural resources, the most important components of which were land, the peasantry, and public rights of taxation; and Latin settlement in the conquered territories. The extent to which resources were confiscated varied from one area to another. It was largely determined by the circumstances leading to the submission of the local population, either based on agreements with the Latin leaders or imposed by force, by the size of lordless property, and by the amount of assets required for the needs of the conquerors. Large estates belonging to the Byzantine crown, to members and relatives of the imperial family, as well as to magnates, dignitaries, and ecclesiastical institutions closely associated with the imperial court and based in Constantinople were clearly among the first to be seized by the Latins. Such was the fate, for instance, of estates in the western Peloponnesos held before 1204 by Irene, daughter of Emperor Alexios III Angelos, members of the Kantakouzenos and Branas families, and Constantinopolitan monasteries.[4] There were also estates belonging to the crown and to Constantinopolitan landlords in Crete and in other territories occupied by the Latins.[5] In addition, the conquerors took hold

---

New York, 1995), 142–60; also D. Jacoby, "Byzantium after the Fourth Crusade: The Latin Empire of Constantinople and the Frankish States in Greece," in *The New Cambridge Medieval History*, vol. 5, *c. 1198–c. 1300*, ed. D. Abulafia (Cambridge, 1999), 525–42.

[3] See J. Longnon, *L'Empire latin de Constantinople et la principauté de Morée* (Paris, 1949); A. Bon, *La Morée franque: Recherches historiques, topographiques et archéologiques sur la principauté d'Achaïe (1205–1430)* (Paris, 1969); Jacoby, *Féodalité*, 17–91, 179–83; idem, "The Encounter of Two Societies: Western Conquerors and Byzantines in the Peloponnesus after the Fourth Crusade," *AHR* 78 (1973): 873–906, repr. in idem, *Recherches sur la Méditerranée orientale du XIIe au XVe siècle: Peuples, sociétés, économies* (London, 1979), no. II; K. M. Setton, *The Papacy and the Levant (1204–1571)*, vol. 1, *The Thirteenth and Fourteenth Centuries* (Philadelphia, 1976), 1–162, 405–73; Lock, *Franks*, 1–134, 193–239, 266–309; D. A. Zakythinos, *Le Despotat grec de Morée*, 2d ed. (London, 1975). On Latin Romania in general, see D. Jacoby, "Les états latins en Romanie: Phénomènes sociaux et économiques (1204–1350 environ)," in *XVe Congrès international d'études byzantines (Athènes, 1976), Rapports et co-rapports*, vol. 1.3 (Athens, 1976), 1–51, repr. in idem, *Recherches*, no. I; idem, "Social Evolution in Latin Greece," in *A History of the Crusades*, ed. K. M. Setton, 2d ed. (Madison, Wisc., 1969–89), 6:175–221.

[4] See D. Jacoby, "Les archontes grecs et la féodalité en Morée franque," *TM* 2 (1967): 422–27, repr. in idem, *Société et démographie à Byzance et en Romanie latine* (London, 1975), no. VI. The church of the Theotokos at the Blachernae in Constantinople presumably also had land in the western Peloponnesos prior to 1204. This is suggested by the monastery bearing its name, recorded in the 15th century and later, which stood to the east of Chiarenza; its construction goes back to the Byzantine period: Bon, *Morée*, 325, 561–74.

[5] For a general view of Constantinopolitan estates throughout the empire, see J.-C. Cheynet, *Pouvoir et contestations à Byzance (963–1210)* (Paris, 1990), 237–45; P. Magdalino, *The Empire of Manuel I Komnenos, 1143–1180* (Cambridge, 1993), 160–71.

of assets previously owned or held as *pronoiai* by local landlords who had fled or had opposed the Latin armies. Finally, whenever convenient they curtailed the property of Greek lay landlords, churches, and monasteries remaining under their rule.[6] While varying in density, the number and especially the distribution of knightly fiefs in the Peloponnesos suggest large-scale confiscations.[7] In Crete the state's seizure of property belonging to various archontes who had submitted to Venetian rule triggered a Greek rebellion in 1212.[8]

Confiscated lands and peasants were partitioned and partly allotted, both in feudalized and Venetian territories, in return for specific military and fiscal obligations that do not concern us here. In Crete, however, Venice retained under its direct authority the city and district of Candia, as well as the latter's rural workforce, and appears to have acted similarly in the territories of Coron and Modon.[9] As for the rights of the Byzantine crown, they were privatized in feudalized areas and taken over by the state in Venetian territories. Some Greek archontes, though, benefited from the collapse of Byzantine authority, since they retained in their hands usurped imperial land and rights. The judicial and fiscal prerogatives exercised by Alexios Kallergis in Crete in the late thirteenth century, the most conspicuous and best documented such case, suggest that his ancestors too had enjoyed them since 1204, if not earlier.[10] It has recently been argued that a free peasantry directly accountable to the state still existed in the empire in the early thirteenth century.[11] If this indeed was the case in the territories occupied by the Latins, free peasants too would have been affected by the processes just described.

These processes did not alter the nature of the predominantly agrarian economy of the conquered territories, although they had a definite impact on various phases of its operation that will be examined below. In the short term, however, the remaining Greek and the new Latin landlords as well as the peasantry had a common interest, regardless of the political regime and the changes in lordship imposed by the conquerors in their respective territories. They were eager to ensure the preservation of the Byzantine economic infrastructure in the countryside and the continuity of the latter's exploitation.

---

[6] See Jacoby, "Archontes," 441–42.

[7] R. Hiestand, "Nova Francia—nova Graecia: Morea zwischen Franken, Venezianern und Griechen," in R. Lauer and P. Schreiner, eds., *Die Kultur Griechenlands in Mittelalter und Neuzeit,* Abhandlungen der Akademie der Wissenschaften in Göttingen, Philologisch-historische Klasse, Dritte Folge 212 (Göttingen, 1996), 59, argues that the Greeks of the Peloponnesos who cooperated with the conquerors did not suffer any losses. If this had indeed been the case, no land would have been available for distribution in large areas.

[8] See Borsari, *Dominio,* 32–33, and for an overview of Greek rebellions in the 13th century, ibid., 27–66.

[9] For Crete, see Borsari, *Dominio,* 27–28; for Coron and Modon, Jacoby, *Féodalité,* 225–26.

[10] See Jacoby, "Etats," 11, 26–28; idem, "Evolution," 184–85, 201; C. Maltezou, "Byzantine 'consuetudines' in Venetian Crete," *DOP* 49 (1995): 270–71; further evidence on the standing of Alexios Kallergis in eadem, "Creta fra la Serenissima e la Superba," in *Oriente e Occidente tra medioevo ed età moderna: Studi in onore di Geo Pistarino,* ed. L. Balletto (Genoa, 1997), 768–69.

[11] See J. Lefort, "Rural Economy and Social Relations in the Countryside," *DOP* 47 (1993): 101–13, esp. 111 ff. Archaeological evidence suggests a dwindling free peasantry in southwestern Boeotia already earlier, in the 11th–12th century: see J. Bintliff, "The Frankish Countryside in Central Greece: The Evidence from Archaeological Field Survey," in *The Archaeology of Medieval Greece,* ed. P. Lock and G. Sanders (Oxford, 1996), 4–5; for a more general view, see A. Harvey, "Peasant Categories in the Tenth and Eleventh Centuries," *BMGS* 14 (1990): 250–56. For Crete, see M. Gallina, *Una società coloniale del Trecento: Creta fra Venezia e Bisanzio,* Deputazione di storia patria per le Venezie, Miscellanea di studi e memorie 28 (Venice, 1989), 85–88.

IX

Indeed, there was continuity in the patterns of land and water uses, crops and types of cultivation, animal breeding and pastoral activity, as well as in the production of wine, cheese, hides, wool, and silk, to name the most important products of the rural economy.[12] Continuity also prevailed in the forms of exploitation, either by the peasants themselves in their small household holdings or on domain land held by the landlords, who for that purpose relied on a variety of means. These included corvée or compulsory labor services owed by the peasants, the ἀγγαρεία of the Byzantine period,[13] hired labor,[14] and various contracts associating peasant and landlord and entailing a division of produce between the two parties or the payment of rents by the peasant. Continuity in these fields is well illustrated by the survival of Byzantine institutions and practices, whether administrative, fiscal, or legal, by the structure of the large estates in Frankish Morea, reflected in fourteenth-century surveys, as well as by numerous agricultural and pastoral contracts drafted in Crete, which make abundant use of Greek terms.[15]

It remains to determine the extent of continuity on the ground. The Latin conquest was largely conducted in swift campaigns that do not seem to have affected the operation of the rural economy. Later, however, intermittent warfare in the 1270s between Frankish and Byzantine forces in Euboea must have inflicted some damage upon the countryside.[16] More severe disruptions in the exploitation of rural resources took place in Crete. The first instance occurred in the years 1207–11, during the struggle between Venetian forces and those of the Genoese Enrico Pescatore, who for several years ruled large sections of the island.[17] A letter written by some Cretan Greeks to the Venetian doge Pietro Ziani in 1224 or 1225 offers convincing evidence to this effect.[18] The same

[12] For details, see below.

[13] Originally, the Byzantine ἀγγαρεία constituted a public labor service owed to the state, which occasionally transferred it to landlords and was then used for the cultivation of their domain land: see A. Stauridou-Zaphraka, "Ἡ ἀγγαρεία στὸ Βυζάντιο," *Byzantina* 11 (1982): 23–54. Its public nature was preserved under Venetian rule in the districts of Coron and Modon: see D. Jacoby, "Un aspect de la fiscalité vénitienne dans le Péloponnèse aux XIVe et XVe siècles: Le 'zovaticum,'" *TM* 1 (1965): 408, repr. in idem, *Société*, no. IV. About 1270 labor services existed on a moderate-sized Byzantine estate with about a dozen peasant households: see J. Lefort, "Une exploitation de taille moyenne au XIIIe siècle en Chalcidique," in Ἀφιέρωμα στὸν Νῖκο Σβορόνο, vol. 1 (Rethymno, 1986), 362–72, esp. 366. For Crete, see Gallina, *Società*, 79–80, 86.

[14] For Crete, see Gallina, *Società*, 49–50, 88–89; C. Gaspares, Η γη και οι ἀγρότες στη μεσαιωνική Κρήτη, 13ος–14ος αι., National Hellenic Research Foundation, Institute for Byzantine Research, Monographs 4 (Athens, 1997), 175–78.

[15] See Jacoby, "Evolution," 216–18; idem, review of A. Carile, *La rendita feudale nella Morea latina del XIV secolo* (Bologna, 1974), in *BZ* 73 (1980): 359–61; idem, "From Byzantium to Latin Romania: Continuity and Change," *Mediterranean Historical Review* 4 (1989): 10–23, repr. in *Latins and Greeks in the Eastern Mediterranean after 1204*, ed. B. Arbel, B. Hamilton, and D. Jacoby (London, 1989); Maltezou, "Byzantine 'consuetudines,'" 270–74; eadem, "Ὁ ὅρος 'metacherissi' στὶς ἀγροτικὲς μισθώσεις τῆς βενετοκρατουμένης Κρήτης," *Byzantina* 13 (1985): 1142–46; Gallina, *Società*, 31–58, 71–72, 78–79; Gaspares, Η γη, 143–75; P. Topping, "Viticulture in Venetian Crete (XIII C.)," in Πεπραγμένα τοῦ Δ´ Διεθνοῦς Κρητολογικοῦ Συνεδρίου, vol. 2 (Athens, 1981), 509–20.

[16] On the military operations, see D. J. Geanakoplos, *Emperor Michael Palaeologus and the West, 1258–1282: A Study in Byzantine-Latin Relations* (Cambridge, Mass., 1959), 235–37, 296–99.

[17] On this struggle, see below, pp. 207–8.

[18] Ed. G. B. Cervellini, *Documento inedito veneto-cretese del Dugento* (Padua, 1906), 13–18, esp. 14–16. For its dating, see Borsari, *Dominio*, 32–33, esp. n. 17.

letter refers to the harsh measures implemented during the Greek rebellion of 1222–24 by the duke of Crete, Paolo Querini, which led to the death or flight of numerous peasants.[19] During the Greek rebellions of the thirteenth century, Venetian military operations and forays by the insurgents caused at times severe destruction.[20] In addition, the Venetian government prohibited on several occasions cultivation and grazing in areas likely to provide supplies to the insurgents. Though not continuous, the most serious interruptions in land use resulting from such cases occurred between 1287 and 1299, the year in which the rebellion led by Alexios Kallergis came to an end.[21] In 1307 Andrea Corner requested the Venetian government to compensate him for revenue losses incurred in that period in Lombaro, a village located in the Lassithi area that belonged to the *militia* or fief he had obtained from the Commune.[22] He referred to the period in which the village had been partly deserted, "quando e lomefo deshabitadho," indicating that of the thirty-three villein households settled earlier, only seven remained. He also mentioned damage caused by fire and the neglect of vineyards cultivated by peasants under lease.[23] Incidentally, the detailed document he submitted is of particular interest, since it offers a unique insight into the components and sources of income of a Cretan fief. Several feudatories other than Andrea Corner had suffered similar losses.[24]

It should be noted that in all these instances the disturbances were circumscribed to specific localities or areas of Crete, peasants either fleeing or being moved to new locations in which they contributed to the extension of cultivation.[25] For instance, Gabriele Querini was allowed between 1234 and 1236 to transfer his villeins to the new military tenement the Commune had granted him, since he could not exploit the one he held in the Lassithi plain.[26] Land appears to have been only temporarily abandoned by peasants and herdsmen, generally for less than five years, considering the cases adduced earlier.

---

[19] For the dating of Querini's action, see Borsari, *Dominio*, 32, 39–40, 128.

[20] On Greek rebellions in the first half of the 14th century, see Thiriet, *Romanie*, 164. The one of 1332–33 was short-lived and localized; the one begun in 1342 appears to have inflicted more damage: see F. Thiriet, "La condition paysanne et les problèmes de l'exploitation rurale en Romanie gréco-vénitienne," *StVen* 9 (1967): 59, repr. in idem, *Etudes sur la Romanie gréco-vénitienne (Xe–XVe s.)* (London, 1977), no. XIII.

[21] Borsari, *Dominio*, 82–83; particular instances are recorded in documents drafted in 1307: S. M. Theotokes, ed., Θεσπίσματα τῆς Βενετικῆς Γερουσίας, 1281–1385, Ἀκαδημία Ἀθηνῶν, Μνημεῖα τῆς Ἑλληνικῆς Ἱστορίας, τόμος Β, vol. 1 (Athens, 1936–37), 41–47, 48–56, esp. 43, nos. 9–11, 13–16.

[22] Partial edition by Borsari, *Dominio*, 81–82 n. 76, and full one by Theotokes, Θεσπίσματα, 1:47–48, no. 12, yet both are marred by several mistakes. The legal nature of the Cretan *militie* and *serventaria*, respectively, in feudalized territories: see Jacoby, "Evolution," 192–93.

[23] Note the important share of newly planted vines in the damage estimate: Theotokes, Θεσπίσματα, 1:48, lines 1–3. A contract for the planting and cultivation of a vineyard precisely at Lombaro, dated 1279, appears in M. Chiaudano and A. Lombardo, eds., *Leonardo Marcello, notaio in Candia, 1278–1281*, Fonti per la storia di Venezia, Sez. 3, Archivi notarili (Venice, 1960), no. 102 (hereafter *Marcello*).

[24] See above, note 21, and esp. Theotokes, Θεσπίσματα, 1:53, lines 91–106; Gaspares, Η γη, 201–8 and 299–330, nos. 1–6.

[25] On the status and transfer of villeins, see Jacoby, "Etats," 35–39; M. Gallina, *Vicende demografiche a Creta nel corso del XIII secolo*, Quaderni della Rivista di studi bizantini e slavi, Studi bizantini e slavi 2 (Rome, 1984), 12–21.

[26] C. Maltezou, ed., *Venetiae quasi alterum Byzantium*. Ὄψεις τῆς Ἱστορίας τοῦ Βενετοκρατουμένου Ἑλληνισμοῦ, Ἀρχειακὰ Τεκμήρια (Athens, 1993), 152, no. 9. Similar moves of peasants from the Lassithi area occurred during the rebellion of Alexios Kallergis: see above, note 24.

In 1222 and 1252 the Venetian government expected the military settlers sent to Crete to ensure the resumption of land cultivation in the area granted to them within two years after their arrival, state subsidies ensuring their livelihood in that period.[27] Exceptionally, though, land exploitation was discontinued for some eight years.[28]

In addition to general circumstances, spontaneous peasant mobility also determined the degree of continuity in land use.[29] In Crete peasants mainly moved within the island itself, although some of them attempted to flee. The authorities sought to prevent their escape and to attract immigrants.[30] Peasant mobility appears to have been greater in the Peloponnesos. The unclear definition of boundaries between Frankish Morea and the Venetian enclaves of Coron and Modon, on the one hand, the existence of a Byzantine province in the Peloponnesos since 1262 and its subsequent expansion, on the other, prompted peasants to cross the common borders of these territories, whether in one direction or the other.[31] However, in the late thirteenth and in the first half of the four-teenth century this movement may have been somewhat restricted by the peaceful coex-istence of Latin and Greek lords in specific areas along the Frankish-Byzantine borders. These lords jointly exploited several villages of Frankish Morea and shared their revenues and, therefore, had a vested interest in the stability of the local peasantry.[32] While gener-ating individual mobility, agreed exchanges of peasants between landlords did not disrupt rural work. In Crete the state occasionally granted villeins to military settlers or author-ized these to settle a number of them on their tenements.[33] On the whole, then, it would seem that the thirteenth-century mobility of the rural workforce in Latin Romania was neither general nor continuous, but rather a local or regional phenomenon, limited in both extent and time. Recent research points to demographic growth in eleventh- and twelfth-century Byzantium.[34] This trend appears to have been sustained in the territories occupied by the Latins for another century, as suggested by evidence regarding the peas-antry, the demand for land, and rising yields.[35]

Conditions changed for the worse in several coastal areas and islands of the Aegean from the early fourteenth century, once the Turks of Asia Minor began their forays,

---

[27] D. Jacoby, "La colonisation militaire vénitienne de la Crète au XIIIe siècle: Une nouvelle approche," in *Le partage du monde: Echanges et colonisation dans la Méditerranée médiévale*, ed. M. Balard and A. Ducellier (Paris, 1998), 304, 309, 311. The land granted in 1222 had been hit by the rebellion of 1217–19.

[28] Theotokes, Θεσπίσματα, 1:52, lines 36–37.

[29] For an overview of peasant mobility in Latin Romania, see D. Jacoby, "Une classe fiscale à Byzance et en Romanie latine: Les inconnus du fisc, éleuthères ou étrangers," in *Actes du XIVe Congrès international des études byzantines (Bucarest, 1971)*, vol. 2 (Bucharest, 1975), 139–52, repr. in idem, *Recherches*, no. III; idem, "Etats," 36–39.

[30] See previous note; Gallina, *Vicende*, 12–14; and below, p. 230.

[31] On Frankish-Venetian boundaries, see Jacoby, *Féodalité*, 223–25, 229–30; C. Hodgetts and P. Lock, "Some Village Fortifications in the Venetian Peloponnese," in Lock and Sanders, *Medieval Greece* (as in note 11), 77–80.

[32] See D. Jacoby, "Un régime de coseigneurie gréco-franque en Morée: Les 'casaux de parçon,'" *MélRome* 75 (1963): 111–25; repr. in idem, *Société*, no. VIII.

[33] See above, note 29; for Crete, see also Gallina, *Vicende*, 28–47.

[34] See A. Harvey, *Economic Expansion in the Byzantine Empire, 900–1200* (Cambridge, 1989), 47–67, 245–48, 250–55.

[35] These last two aspects are discussed below. For Crete, see Gallina, *Vicende*, 9–47, an essentially positive as-sessment. I no longer maintain the view to the contrary, expressed in Jacoby, "Classe fiscale," 142.

which occasionally resulted in severe damage and depopulation.[36] On the other hand, territories shielded from their activity, such as Crete, benefited from an influx of refugees.[37] The Black Death appears to have inflicted serious demographic losses, aggravated by subsequent bouts of plague, upon the peasantry of Latin Romania as a whole.[38] The comparison of two surveys of the same villages in Frankish Morea, one carried out in 1338 and the other in 1354, thus before and after the Black Death, respectively, enhances this assessment.[39] It has been argued that in Crete demographic losses were partly offset by the import of slaves. To be sure, slaves were occasionally put to work in the countryside, yet compared with villeins they surely remained a marginal factor in its exploitation, since most of them, whether male or female, lived in urban households.[40] Losses of rural labor resulting from the plague were compounded in the Peloponnesos by unstable political conditions in the following period and the Turkish, Byzantine, and Albanian incursions related to them. In 1396 the prince of Morea requested the return of peasants who had moved from the principality to the Venetian territories of Coron and Modon. Three years later Venice took measures to induce the villeins of Argos to return to their land, while in 1407 Latin landlords of Coron requested manpower from the Commune in order to bring their abandoned land under cultivation.[41] Although many Albanians

---

[36] On their activity, see D. Jacoby, "Catalans, Turcs et Vénitiens en Romanie (1305–32): Un nouveau témoignage de Marino Sanudo Torsello," StMed, 3d ser., 15 (1974): 246–47, 251–53, 257–61, repr. in idem, Recherches, no. v; E. A. Zachariadou, "The Catalans of Athens and the Beginning of the Turkish Expansion in the Aegean Area," StMed, 3d ser., 21 (1980): 821–38, repr. in eadem, Romania and the Turks (c. 1300–c. 1500) (London, 1985), no. v; eadem, "Holy War in the Aegean during the Fourteenth Century," Mediterranean Historical Review 4 (1989): 212–18, repr. in Arbel, Hamilton, and Jacoby, Latins (as in note 15); documents in R.-J. Loenertz, ed., Les Ghisi, dynastes dans l'Archipel, 1207–1390 (Florence, 1975), 236 (lines 63–68), 241 (no. 72), 251 (no. 76): attacks on the area of Corinth and other regions of the Peloponnesos in the 1340s and movement of villeins between Aegean islands and Crete in the 1350s and 1360s.

[37] See Jacoby, "Classe fiscale," 140 n. 6, 149 n. 52; also above, note 35.

[38] M.-H. Congourdeau, "Pour une étude de la Peste Noire à Byzance," in Εὐψυχία: Mélanges offerts à Hélène Ahrweiler, Byzantina Sorbonensia 16 (Paris, 1998), 149–63, also includes information about the plague in Latin Romania until the 1460s. More specifically, for Crete, see Thiriet, "Condition," 59–60, 62–63; Jacoby, "Classe fiscale," 151; Gaspares, Η γῆ, 75, 77, 80; Gallina, Società, 37, refers to heavy losses, yet on 89–90 relies on the high numbers of villeins residing in 1356 in three Cretan fiefs to suggest that they were lower than commonly believed. One may wonder, though, whether these pieces of evidence do not reflect a concentration of villeins in specific tenements, also attested in other periods (see below, note 47), rather than the general picture.

[39] The two surveys appear in J. Longnon and P. Topping, eds., Documents sur le régime des terres dans la principauté de Morée au XIVe siècle (Paris–The Hague, 1969), 55–115, nos. III and IV. These and other surveys drafted from 1336 to 1379 record peasant households in feudal estates of Frankish Morea or offer indirect evidence on demographic trends. They still await a thorough and balanced examination in this respect. Their analysis by Carile, Rendita, 80–183, is unsatisfactory: see my review (cited above, note 15), 358–59.

[40] See Thiriet, Romanie, 314–15, 335, 413, on slaves in agriculture; C. Verlinden, L'esclavage dans l'Europe médiévale, vol. 2, Italie-Colonies italiennes du Levant-Levant latin-Empire byzantin (Ghent, 1977), 876–78, is less emphatic. Thiriet relies on rather slim evidence and remains unconvincing. Inter alia he refers to the loan of 3,000 hyperpers offered in 1393 by the Venetian authorities to encourage the import of male slaves for settlement in villages: document ed. by Verlinden, ibid., 877 n. 553. However, given their average price in Crete around that time, on which see ibid., 875–76, the sum would have sufficed for only about eighty slaves. For the sake of calculation, I assume that sale prices in Crete were double the original purchase prices elsewhere. S. McKee, "Households in Fourteenth-Century Venetian Crete," Speculum 70 (1995): 58–65, has found only two references to slaves settled in the countryside in 785 wills of the 14th century.

[41] For evidence, see above, notes 29, 36, and 39; also D. Jacoby, "Italian Migration and Settlement in Latin Greece: The Impact on the Economy," in H. E. Mayer, ed., Die Kreuzfahrerstaaten als multikulturelle Gesellschaft: *

raised cattle and horses, a number of them tilled the land. Their settlement in continental Greece in the late fourteenth and the early fifteenth century clearly points to partial depopulation.[42] On balance, despite the Greek rebellions of the thirteenth and fourteenth centuries, Crete appears to have enjoyed a greater stability of rural labor than the Aegean islands or the Peloponnesos.

It is in the nature of written sources bearing on populations to emphasize mobility and disruption, rather than to record or reflect stability and continuity.[43] One should remember, though, that unless on a massive scale in a given area peasant mobility did not necessarily result in overall interruption of land exploitation. It is impossible to arrive at quantitative estimates of demographic trends for Latin Romania, except for some villages of the Peloponnesos in a limited period.[44] We have to rely, therefore, on evaluations partly based on circumstantial evidence, as for instance the recent surface prospection of southwestern Boeotia. The pottery, structures, and settlement pattern discovered in this region point to stable conditions, high population and demographic rise, as well as to prosperity and economic expansion throughout the Frankish period up to the Turkish conquest.[45] To be sure, this region willfully submitted to the Frankish conquerors in 1204 and to the Catalan Company in 1311. In addition, it was less exposed than the Aegean islands and coastal areas to foreign incursions. Future field research in other regions of the Greek mainland may well yield similar results.

The general impression, then, is one of a fairly high degree of continuity in rural exploitation in many areas of Latin Romania in the thirteenth and fourteenth centuries. These trends are confirmed by the eagerness of Latins, including merchants and bankers, and indigenous Greeks to obtain landed estates, from feudal lords in feudalized areas and either from the Commune or from the holders of tenements in Crete.[46] The value of Cretan fiefs varied substantially according to their nature, the type and quality of their land, and the number of households they contained, which differed widely.[47] The circumstances of their transfer and the purchasers' expectations were also relevant in this

---

Einwanderer und Minderheiten im 12. und 13. Jahrhundert, Schriften des Historischen Kollegs, Kolloquien 37 (Munich, 1997), 123–24; J. Chrysostomides, ed., *Monumenta Peloponnesiaca: Documents for the History of the Peloponnese in the 14th and 15th Centuries* (Camberley, 1995), 373, 406–7, 506, 571–72, 583–85, 589.

[42] See P. Topping, "Albanian Settlements in Medieval Greece: Some Venetian Testimonies," in *Charanis Studies: Essays in Honor of Peter Charanis,* ed. A. E. Laiou-Thomadakis (New Brunswick, N.J., 1980), 261–71; A. Ducellier, "Les Albanais dans les colonies vénitiennes au XVe siècle," *StVen* 10 (1968): 405–20, reprinted in idem, *L'Albanie entre Byzance et Venise, Xe–XVe siècles* (London, 1987), no. IX. The settlement of some 2,000 Armenians in Crete in 1363 and some 4,000 Greeks from Tenedos in Crete and Euboea in the 1380s also points to rural depopulation, yet it is impossible to evaluate the contribution of these immigrants to rural production. See Thiriet, *Romanie,* 264–65, and further studies cited by Gaspares, H γη, 80.

[43] Thiriet, "Condition," 35–69, and Carile, *Rendita,* 80–183, have failed to take this into consideration and paint excessively bleak pictures of the state of the rural workforce and land exploitation in Latin Romania.

[44] See above, p. 203.

[45] See Bintliff, "Frankish Countryside," 1–18, esp. 4–7. For other regions, see A. Harvey, "The Middle Byzantine Economy: Growth or Stagnation?" *BMGS* 19 (1995): 254–55.

[46] On the bankers, see below, p. 211. On the Moreot archontes, see Jacoby, "Encounter," 891–96; on those of Crete, Borsari, *Dominio,* 35–66, passim.

[47] On the number of villein households per *militia* or fief in Crete, from six to twenty-five, see Gallina, *Vicende,* 12–40, esp. 21–22, yet higher figures appear in 1356, on which see above, note 38. Lombaro had thirty-three villein households before it was hit by the rebellion of Alexios Kallergis: see above, note 22. On higher figures of households in 1414, including free ones, see Gaspares, H γη, 282–84 and 288–90, tables 31 and 37.

respect. On the whole, though, prices appear to have been on the rise,[48] except in areas hit by rebellions.[49] The acquisition of these tenements, whether by residents or by newcomers to the island, was considered a good investment.[50] In Crete some fiefs provided in the late thirteenth century yearly revenues of more than 1,000 or even 1,500 hyperpers.[51] In the Morea and other feudalized territories, the knight's fief was supposed to yield a yearly income of 1,000 hyperpers.[52] The four known figures of the fourteenth century reflecting the actual revenue of entire knightly fiefs differ widely, two being substantially lower.[53] Both in feudalized areas and in Venetian Crete, military tenements remained for several generations within the same families. In the island, though, they changed hands more often as a result of greater mobility among military settlers, some of whom in the thirteenth century returned to Venice or other localities in Italy after residing in Crete for a number of years.[54]

The redistribution of resources in the conquered lands, examined above, was coupled with Latin settlement proceeding on a scale and along patterns unknown earlier in Romania. The geographic distribution of the Latin settlers also differed substantially from what it had been before 1204. These features were bound to have a strong impact on the economic development of Latin Romania. To begin with, there was a swift and significant growth in Latin settlement, encouraged by the new lords, including the Venetian government. To be sure, these lords were eager to strengthen the small Latin nuclei in their respective territories in order to increase their military power and enhance their rule, yet economic considerations were also of major importance in this respect. The collapse of centralized imperial control over specific branches of trade and manufacture, among them silk,[55] brought about a striking departure from traditional Byzan-

[48] Borsari, *Dominio*, 83–84, and table facing 84; Gallina, *Società*, 106–11. In 1216 Giovanni Longo bought two *militie* for 300 Venetian pounds or around 250 hyperpers: R. Morozzo della Rocca and A. Lombardo, eds., *Documenti del commercio veneziano nei secoli XI–XIII* (Turin, 1940) (hereafter *DCV*), no. 574; see Jacoby, "Colonisation," 307 n. 46, for the calculation of this exceptionally low price in Cretan currency, and 304–5. Prices failed to rise around the mid-14th century, presumably in connection with the sequels of the Black Death.

[49] In 1307 the value of a specific sergeantry in the region of Canea was estimated at 300 hyperpers and its annual revenue at 18 hyperpers, in addition to 4 hyperpers paid by each of the ten villein households it contained, thus a total of 58 hyperpers: S. M. Theotokes, ed., Ἀποφάσεις Μείζονος Συμβουλίου Βενετίας, 1255–1669, Ἀκαδημία Ἀθηνῶν, Μνημεῖα τῆς Ἑλληνικῆς Ἱστορίας, τόμος A.2 (Athens, 1933), 49, no. 39. Thiriet, *Romanie*, 273, has mistakenly multiplied by ten the first two figures appearing in the document. Since the sergeantry was equivalent to one-sixth of a fief, the latter would have yielded around 350 hyperpers. Both its low value and low revenue may be explained by severe damage inflicted during the rebellion of Alexios Kallergis, as in the case of Lombaro documented for the same year, on which see above, note 22.

[50] The evidence in this respect contradicts the assumptions of Thiriet, *Romanie*, 137, and Gallina, *Società*, 10, that in the 13th century "normal" economic exploitation in Crete was excluded, and that rather than being concerned with it, the military settlers focused on the establishment and strengthening of military and institutional structures. Incidentally, this was the task of the Venetian authorities.

[51] Theotokes, Θεσπίσματα, 1:53, lines 91–106. On revenues, see also Gaspares, Η γη, 264–65, table 13.

[52] See Jacoby, "Archontes," 449 and n. 156.

[53] See Carile, *Rendita*, 118, 126–27, 140–41, 172: revenues of 768 hyperpers in return for full yearly military service, 1,150 for nine months only, 1,165 for three months only, around 743 hyperpers for a whole year. The reduction of military service in the second and third cases was clearly granted as a favor on a personal basis.

[54] On the fate of some Cretan fiefs, see Gallina, *Vicende*, 28 and 55–57, appendix, tables I–III. On non-Venetians and the return to Italy, see Jacoby, "Colonisation," 307, 313.

[55] On which see D. Jacoby, "Silk in Western Byzantium before the Fourth Crusade," *BZ* 84–85 (1991–92): 452–500; repr. in idem, *Trade, Commodities and Shipping in the Medieval Mediterranean* (Aldershot, 1997), no. VII.

tine attitudes, policies, and practices. The political and territorial fragmentation of Latin Romania created a climate of competition between Latin lords, which induced the latter to attract settlers, merchants, and ship operators, ensure them of safe conditions in their respective territories and ports, enable direct access to local producers, markets, and fairs, and enhance foreign purchases of local goods. In addition, these lords sought ways to stimulate investments, as well as transit trade and shipping through their ports. Their primary purpose was to increase thereby their own financial gains and fiscal revenue.

However, there were some marked differences between the initial settlement patterns affecting non-Venetian and Venetian territories, respectively. Among the latter this was especially true with respect to Crete, due to the particular background and circumstances of its conquest. It is commonly believed that in the early thirteenth century Venice's interest in Crete was exclusively or primarily stimulated by strategic considerations, namely, the island's location at the crossing of important sea lanes, as well as the havens and logistic support it could offer for their control. However, there were also other weighty factors, largely overlooked until now, that prompted Venice to invest considerable means in the purchase of Crete from Boniface of Montferrat in 1204 and in the island's conquest in the following years. Venice displayed substantial interest in the economic and fiscal exploitation of the island. This interest had been especially stimulated from the second half of the twelfth century by the acquaintance of Venetian merchants with the agricultural and pastoral resources of Crete, its growing production and exports, its trade networks, and its increasing role in trans-Mediterranean navigation between Italy and the Levant.[56]

The interplay between private and governmental factors with respect to Crete is further illustrated around the time of the island's conquest. Venetian trade with Crete appears to have continued unabated, regardless of the political vacuum in the island resulting from the collapse of imperial power, partial Genoese occupation from 1206 to 1211, and Venice's efforts to enlarge its rule beyond Candia, captured in 1207.[57] Giovanni Corner was about to leave Venice for Crete in March 1205, after receiving 100 Venetian pounds in *collegantia*.[58] Merchants accompanied the military expedition of 1209 to Crete, as suggested by two *collegantia* contracts concluded in Venice. According to one of them, Maria, wife of Doge Pietro Ziani, entrusted 120 Venetian pounds to Tommaso Viadro, an experienced merchant about to sail for Candia.[59] At that time Venetian merchants must have traded in the territory already held by Venice and were presumably also involved in the provisioning of the military forces stationed in Crete. In the autumn of the same year, Venetians were engaging in trade between Candia and Alexandria, and

[56] On Crete in Venetian trade and shipping in that period, see D. Jacoby, "Italian Privileges and Trade in Byzantium before the Fourth Crusade: A Reconsideration," *Anuario de estudios medievales* 24 (1994): 349–56, repr. in idem, *Trade,* no. II; idem, "Byzantine Crete in the Navigation and Trade Networks of Venice and Genoa," in Balletto, *Oriente* (as in note 10), 517–30, 537–40.

[57] See below, p. 207.

[58] *DCV,* no. 469.

[59] A. Lombardo and R. Morozzo della Rocca, eds., *Nuovi documenti del commercio veneto dei sec. XI–XIII* (Venice, 1953) (hereafter *NDCV*), no. 73: *in presenti venturo stolo;* no. 74: *ire debebas in exercitu Venecianum.*

in the following spring Giovanni Corner, already encountered five years earlier, invested in Constantinople in a business venture with Crete and Venice.[60] Not surprisingly, therefore, the first wave of military settlers leaving Venice for Crete in the autumn of 1211 included merchants such as Tommaso Viadro, who had previously traded in Crete, and others who had surely obtained information about the economic potential of the island. In addition, merchants arriving on their own in Crete also settled on the island in that period.[61] It is noteworthy that the charter delivered by Doge Pietro Ziani to the military contingent of 1211 contains several detailed provisions regarding the future settlers' trade in the island's products. One of them deals with state control over wheat exports, a sensitive issue connected with Venice's food supply.[62] Military settlers became involved in internal trade and in the export of local commodities shortly after their arrival in the island. Some of them also invested in maritime ventures and from 1218, or 1222 at the latest, even directly undertook trade journeys overseas.[63]

A similar conjunction of commercial, fiscal, and strategic factors and interplay between private and state initiatives provided the background for the invasion of Crete by Enrico Pescatore in 1206 and for his efforts to secure his rule over the island, which eventually collapsed in 1211. Although Pescatore's expedition was a private enterprise, Genoa displayed vivid interest in it and provided large-scale naval, military, and financial assistance to ensure its success. In 1208 the Commune responded to Pescatore's request by sending him ships, men-at-arms, and supplies, as well as money for the purchase of horses, obviously in Crete itself. In 1210 he requested further financial assistance and, in return, promised Genoa a quarter with its facilities in each Cretan city, jurisdiction in the whole island, as well as full exemption from taxes to Genoese merchants. The charter he delivered was obviously modeled after those obtained by Genoa in the Crusader Levant. Pescatore further promised the reimbursement in three yearly installments of the financial assistance provided by the Commune, to the amount of 18,000 Genoese pounds, beginning two years after the total subjection of the island to his rule. Finally, he stated that the Commune would inherit Crete should he die without legitimate heirs.[64]

Genoa's interest in the economic and fiscal exploitation of the island was clearly con-

---

[60] *DCV,* nos. 516, 518.

[61] See Jacoby, "Colonisation," 299–300, 303–8.

[62] G. L. F. Tafel and G. M. Thomas, eds., *Urkunden zur älteren Handels- und Staatsgeschichte der Republik Venedig* (Vienna, 1856–57) (hereafter TTh), 2:132 (*victualia,* here clearly wheat), 140.

[63] See Jacoby, "Colonisation," 305–6, 308; M. Gallina, "Finanza, credito e commercio a Candia fra la fine del XIII secolo e l'inizio del XIV," *Memorie della Accademia delle Scienze di Torino, II. Classe di Scienze Morali, Storiche e Filologiche,* 5th ser., 7–8 (1986): 13–21, 23–31, 41–68, passim. Borsari, *Dominio,* 85–87, suggests that those who settled in Crete opted for security with less income, rather than for the high risk involved in maritime trade. This assumption is not convincing, nor is it plausible that the prestige of armed service acted as an additional inducement to settlement in Crete, considering the attitudes, values, and interests of the mercantile milieu. The case of Doge Ranieri Zeno to which Borsari refers cannot be considered typical.

[64] See G. Gerola, "La dominazione genovese in Creta," *Atti dell'I. R. Accademia di Scienze e Lettere ed Arti degli Agiati in Roverete,* 3d ser., 8.2 (1902): 134–75; Borsari, *Dominio,* 21–25, 27; D. Abulafia, "Henry Count of Malta and His Mediterranean Activities, 1203–1230," in A. T. Luttrell, ed., *Medieval Malta: Studies on Malta before the Knights,* Supplementary Monographs of the British School at Rome (London, 1975), 113–19, repr. in D. Abulafia, *Italy, Sicily and the Mediterranean, 1100–1140* (London, 1987), no. III; Maltezou, "Creta," 763–67.

nected with the expectations of Genoese merchants. They had traded there since around the mid-twelfth century.[65] Pescatore's occupation of Crete in 1206 and his power over large sections of it in the following five years prompted private Genoese interest and investments in his Cretan venture, as in 1210.[66] It presumably also stimulated an increase in trade with the island, some merchants personally sailing that same year to Crete on three vessels leaving with reinforcements and provisions for Pescatore, one of them the *Glauca*.[67] Pescatore's eviction from Crete in 1211 was followed by a sharp reduction in the volume of Genoese trade with the island, which remained minimal until the Genoese began to export Cretan wine in the fifteenth century.[68]

The territorial extent and the large population of Crete, presumably also the fierce struggle of 1206–11 with Genoa for the possession of the island, induced Venice to implement an original and unique, highly structured and institutionalized immigration and settlement policy. Combined with strict control over land and peasantry, it was aimed at promoting the state's political and economic interests in the island. The settlement of Venetians liable to serve in a military capacity in return for land granted by the state, initiated in 1211, was partly based on somewhat earlier precedents in Venice's portion of the Latin Empire of Constantinople.[69] The novelty in Crete, in which no Venetian settlers had resided prior to 1204,[70] was that both the immigration and settlement of these individuals were state-sponsored, state-organized, and supported by state subsidies. From 1211 to 1252 Venice established several small military contingents numbering a total of 189 men granted fiefs, who were accompanied by one or two horsemen, and 60 foot soldiers offered sergeantries. In this framework the repopulation and reconstruction of Canea after 1252 was part of Venice's endeavor to consolidate its rule over the western section of the island. Originally the fiefs or sergeantries were to be granted exclusively to Venetian citizens, each of them to a single settler. However, already a few years after the beginning of the military colonization process, we find some Venetians holding several military tenements simultaneously, as well as non-Venetians originating from northern and central Italy among the holders of such tenements.[71] Venice resorted

[65] See Jacoby, "Byzantine Crete," 530–40.
[66] A contract to this effect in Gerola, "Dominazione," 158; Abulafia, "Henry Count of Malta," 116–17. There is reason to believe that there were additional ones. M. Balard, "Les Génois en Romanie entre 1204 et 1261: Recherches dans les minutiers notariaux génois," *MélRome* 78 (1966): 474–75, repr. in idem, *La Mer Noire et la Romanie génoise, XIIIe–XVe siècles* (London, 1989), no. 1, suggests that in 1210 Guglielmo Porco, admiral of the kingdom of Sicily and a close associate of Pescatore, obtained a loan to help him in Crete.
[67] H. C. Krueger and R. L. Reynolds, eds., *Notai liguri del sec. XII e del sec. XIII*, vol. 6, *Lanfranco (1202–1226)* (Genoa, 1953), 1: no. 638: a young man from Rapallo leaving for the island, whether to fight or trade, leases a piece of land until his return; no. 652: *accommendatio* of 12 Genoese pounds for trade *in Creti in nave Glauca et inde quo iero causa negotiandi*; Balard, "Génois en Romanie," 474.
[68] On which see D. Jacoby, "Creta e Venezia nel contesto economico del Mediterraneo orientale fin alla metà del Quattrocento," in *Venezia e Creta*, ed. G. Ortalli (Venice, 1998), 86, 93–94.
[69] See D. Jacoby, "The Venetian Presence in the Latin Empire of Constantinople (1204–1261): The Challenge of Feudalism and the Byzantine Inheritance," *JÖB* 43 (1993): 144–45, 154–61.
[70] See Jacoby, "Italian Privileges," 365–66.
[71] See Jacoby, "Colonisation," 306–11, 313. The figures of military settlers are based on name lists. F. Thiriet, "Recherches sur le nombre des 'Latins' immigrés en Romanie gréco-vénitienne aux XIIIe–XIVe siècles," in *Byzance et les Slaves: Etudes de civilisation, Mélanges Ivan Dujčev* (Paris, 1979), 427, suggests higher figures which, however, are based on the numbers of *expected* settlers, far larger than those of the actual ones. In 1294

again to state intervention from 1301 to 1324 by settling in its colonies of Coron and Modon 124 men-at-arms and craftsmen, among them woodworkers, metalworkers, and stonemasons, whose activities would support specific aspects of local defense or the servicing of naval forces. All these settlers received an annual salary that ensured their service in the local militias, yet were allowed to work for a daily wage. With their respective families, their total number reached around four hundred people.[72] In the fourteenth century Venice sought to encourage foreign Latins to settle in its colonies and outposts of Latin Romania by granting those who undertook to reside there for at least ten years the privileges of Venetian nationality in Romania, the status enjoyed by the subjects of Venice's colonies. In addition to diplomatic protection, this status ensured them the same fiscal privileges as Venetian citizens in Romania, yet not in Venice itself; nor did it confer upon them the commercial advantages enjoyed by citizens. After the Black Death, Venice offered Latins settling in its colonies full Venetian citizenship. These measures had only very limited success.[73] It should be stressed that in Venetian territories the ongoing process of spontaneous nonmilitary immigration of Venetians and other Latins, primarily motivated by private economic considerations, contributed far more than state-sponsored immigration to Latin demographic growth and resulted in a more diversified population.[74] This is clearly attested for Coron and Modon.[75]

Latins settling in Crete displayed an obvious preference for urban residence. Their heaviest concentration occurred in Candia, while others resided in Canea, Rethymno, Sitia, and some inland cities. The overwhelming majority of military settlers lived in a house in Candia or Canea that was included in their tenement. Many of them were involved in trade.[76] Nevertheless, some settlers, like Baldovino Lombardo, apparently

---

and 1299 military equipment for a total of some 500 men was sent to Crete: R. Cessi, ed., *Deliberazioni del Maggior Consiglio di Venezia* (Bologna, 1931–50), 3:354, no. 136, and 447, no. 45. Since it was to be distributed among Cretan fiefholders as well as *burgenses*, it does not provide any indication about the number of the former, contrary to Thiriet, ibid., 430. For the decades following the Black Death, Thiriet, ibid., 430, postulates that each member in the feudatories' council had an average of five family dependents, without taking into account that several members of the same household served on that council. On the territorial aspects of military settlement, see C. Maltezou, "*Concessio Crete.* Παρατηρήσεις στὰ ἔγγραφα διανομῆς φεούδων στοὺς πρώτους Βενετοὺς ἀποίκους τῆς Κρήτης," in Λοιβὴ εἰς μνήμην Ἀνδρέα Γ. Καλοκαιρίνου (Irakleion, 1994), 107–31.

[72] See A. C. Hodgetts, "The Colonies of Coron and Modon under Venetian Administration, 1204–1400" (Ph.D. diss., University of London, 1974), 151–52, 156, 355.

[73] Jacoby, "Etats," 20. On the distinction between Venetian citizenship and nationality in Romania, see D. Jacoby, "Les Vénitiens naturalisés dans l'Empire byzantin: Un aspect de l'expansion de Venise en Romanie du XIIIe au milieu du XVe siècle," *TM* 8 (1981): 217–35, esp. 219–20, repr. in idem, *Studies on the Crusader States and on Venetian Expansion* (Northampton, 1989), no. IX. On the practical implications, see Thiriet, *Romanie,* 279–82.

[74] Both the demographic and military importance of state-sponsored settlement in Crete has been grossly overrated: see Jacoby, "Colonisation," 312–13. The estimates of Latin population in Romania suggested by Thiriet, "Nombres," 428, are purely hypothetical. They are based on the cumulative number of merchants attested over a long period, which does obviously not reflect the number of Latins at any given moment. On variety of origin among the settlers, see above, p. 208.

[75] See below, p. 222.

[76] Jacoby, "Etats," 19. Note that in 1299 the Commune ordered that 110 crossbows out of a total of 430 should be sent to Canea, which clearly points to a much smaller number of Latin settlers in this city: Cessi, *Deliberazioni,* 3:447, no. 45. According to the rule, two Venetian brothers should have resided in the city of Canea

IX

resided or at least spent a few months a year on their estates. In 1285, during a Greek rebellion, Lombardo requested state funding for the building of a defensive tower to enhance his security, implying that his residence in the countryside would strengthen Venice's military position in the area.[77] In the autumn of 1363, shortly after the great rebellion of St. Tito had begun, a number of military settlers were staying in villages included in their respective tenements, presumably in order to inspect them or to collect taxes and payments, yet not as permanent residents.[78] Latins who were not military settlers seem to have been established in larger numbers in the countryside in order to engage in land cultivation and the raising of animals or to practice crafts using local raw materials, such as the dressing of hides and tanning.[79] However, at times Latin surnames in rural areas do not necessarily point to Latin identity, since it was customary for the illegitimate offspring of Latin fathers and Greek mothers to adopt the former's surname, which did not prevent them from remaining in the latter's community.[80] In any event, the number of Latins residing in the Cretan countryside may have increased in the fourteenth century, during which security conditions improved on the whole. On the other hand, it is unlikely that Latins would have settled outside Coron or Modon in the small Venetian enclaves of southern Messenia.

Surprisingly, before 1204 Latin temporary or permanent settlement in the territories later ruled by feudal lords was limited to Thebes and Corinth, with the possible addition of Sparta. Venetians apparently resided in Thebes almost continuously from the 1150s at the latest until the Fourth Crusade and had two churches there. They also had one church in Corinth and another in Sparta.[81] Latin settlement after the Fourth Crusade in the same non-Venetian territories became substantially larger, far more varied in nature, and more dispersed. Fairly small Latin nuclei of Western knights and sergeants owing military service established themselves in castles and fortified mansions in the countryside or in the acropolis of the main cities of major lordships, as in Thebes and Acrocorinth. Shortly after the conquest, some of these nuclei counted less than twelve individuals, yet must have subsequently grown with the arrival from the West of the latter's relatives and additional immigrants.[82] Other knights permanently resided in the major

---

after having inherited sergeantries in this city's district in 1334. In 1339, however, they were allowed to remain in Candia, where for a long time they had been conducting trade: Theotokes, Θεσπίσματα, 1:185, no. 14.

[77] Excerpt from his request ed. by Borsari, *Dominio*, 83.

[78] Lorenzo de Monacis, *Chronicon de rebus venetis*, ed. F. Cornelius (Corner) (Venice, 1758), 179: "omnes nobiles qui extra civitatem diffusi erant per sua casalia." They were there on their own since they, yet not their family members, were murdered by the insurgents who intended to kill all Latins.

[79] A. Lombardo, ed., *Imbreviature di Pietro Scardon (1271)*, Documenti della colonia veneziana di Creta 1 (Turin, 1942), nos. 24, 33, 164, 266, 294, 440; *Marcello*, nos. 256–57, in 1280; E. Santschi, "Contrats de travail et d'apprentissage en Crète vénitienne au XIVe siècle d'après quelques notaires," *Revue suisse d'histoire* 19 (1969): 65, for the 14th century.

[80] See Jacoby, "Etats," 29–30; S. McKee, "Greek Women in Latin Households of Fourteenth-Century Crete," *JMedHist* 19 (1993): 229–30.

[81] *DCV*, no. 166: a Venetian having served for two years as commercial agent in Thebes prior to May 1165; see also Jacoby, "Silk in Western Byzantium," 494–96. On the churches, see also S. Borsari, *Venezia e Bisanzio nel XII secolo: I rapporti economici*, Deputazione di storia patria per le Venezie, Miscellanea di studi e memorie 26 (Venice, 1988), 41; R.-J. Lilie, "Die lateinische Kirche in der Romania vor dem vierten Kreuzzug: Versuch einer Bestandaufnahme," *BZ* 82 (1989): 202–6, 209–11.

[82] The figure twelve is implied by a letter of Pope Innocent III, Epist., XIII.16, PL 216:216. See Jacoby, "Etats," 19.

city located in the vicinity of their fiefs, such as Negroponte, Naxos, or Patras. Some had a secondary residence in Andravida, Chiarenza, Modon, or Coron.[83] The Sienese and Florentine merchants and bankers operating in Chiarenza who obtained fiefs from the princes of the Morea in the second half of the thirteenth and in the fourteenth century maintained their residence in that city.[84] In the principality there may have been 170 knight-fiefs around 1225, with a total of some 450 horsemen. In the 1320s or 1330s the Venetian Marino Sanudo estimated their number at between seven hundred and one thousand. In 1338 or somewhat later the number of fiefs held by the vassals and rear-vassals of the prince of the Morea was calculated at more than one thousand.[85] It is unclear whether these numbers included horsemen endowed with money-fiefs instead of estates, once the land available for distribution had been exhausted. The number of these horsemen at any given time is unknown.[86]

The initial settlement pattern of the knights in non-Venetian territories, concurrent with the territorial fragmentation typical of feudal landholding, as well as military pressure in some regions, led to the repair of existing castles and the construction of new ones. Castles served as secure bases from which neighboring areas could be controlled, defended, or attacked, yet also functioned as administrative and consumption centers. In addition, numerous mansions and towers were erected in the countryside. The distribution, location, and architectural variation of the eighty or so massive towers in Attica and Boeotia and the other fifty in Euboea suggest that most of them were not planned to fulfill a strategic purpose, but rather meant to be status symbols or to serve as administrative bases and provide storage for resources.[87] By contrast, a new phase of construction began in several areas in the late fourteenth century. It was carried out or sponsored by Venice for military purposes in response to the Turkish threat.[88] Some of these buildings contributed indirectly to a growth in rural output and improved marketing by providing protection and enabling a more efficient collection and storage of products. On the other hand, their construction and maintenance diverted substantial means in labor and cash from investments in the expansion of the rural infrastructure. Seignorial and state con-

---

[83] Ibid.; also Jacoby, "Encounter," 901 n. 134; idem, "Migration," 105–6.

[84] See below, p. 224.

[85] See Jacoby, "Etats," 20–21; A. Ilieva, *Frankish Morea (1205–1262): Socio-Cultural Interaction between the Franks and the Local Population* (Athens, 1991), 165–68; Marino Sanudo Torsello, *Istoria del Regno di Romania*, ed. C. Hopf, *Chroniques gréco-romanes inédites ou peu connues* (Berlin, 1873), 102–3, obtained information from Marco II Sanudo, duke of Naxos.

[86] On money-fiefs, see Jacoby, *Féodalité*, 135; idem, "Encounter," 887.

[87] *Livre de la conqueste de la princée de l'Amorée, Chronique de Morée (1204–1305)*, ed. J. Longnon (Paris, 1911), para. 218: "li baron dou pays et li autre gentil homme si commencerent a faire fortresses et habitacions, quy chastel, quy maisons sur sa terre." The passage refers to the period after the capture of Monemvasia by Prince William II in 1248, a dating contested by H. A. Kalligas, *Byzantine Monemvasia: The Sources* (Monemvasia, 1990), 86–94. In any event, construction began much earlier: see A. Bon, "Forteresses médiévales de la Grèce centrale," *BCH* 61 (1937): 136–208; Bon, *Morée*, 601–84; P. Lock, "The Frankish Towers of Central Greece," *BSA* 81 (1986): 101–23; idem, "The Medieval Towers of Greece: A Problem in Chronology and Function," *Mediterranean Historical Review* 4 (1989): 129–45, repr. in Arbel, Hamilton, and Jacoby, *Latins* (as in note 15); P. Lock, "The Towers of Euboea: Lombard or Venetian; Agrarian or Strategic," in Lock and Sanders, *Medieval Greece* (as in note 11), 107–26; Lock, *Franks in the Aegean*, 75–80, 82. See also P. Lock, "The Military Orders in Mainland Greece," in *The Military Orders: Fighting for the Faith and Caring for the Sick*, ed. M. Barber (Aldershot, 1994), 333–39.

[88] See Lock's studies in previous note, and Hodgetts and Lock, "Fortifications," 77–90.

IX

struction, the latter in Venetian territories, was largely achieved by compulsory peasant labor, although it occasionally also relied on salaried work.[89]

Latin commoners spontaneously immigrated to non-Venetian territories in Latin Romania in numbers exceeding by far those of the knights. They established themselves exclusively in cities, some of which the early settlers had visited or inhabited before 1204. These immigrants displayed a marked preference for ports such as Negroponte and Corinth, which, like Candia, Coron, and Modon, had already previously functioned as collection and distribution centers, as outlets for their respective hinterland and neighboring islands, or as regular stopovers for vessels sailing between Italy and eastern Mediterranean ports. Chiarenza, a new port founded on the western coast of the Peloponnesos after the Latin conquest, prospered thanks to favorable geopolitical and economic conditions, attracted settlers, and became the main emporium of Frankish Morea by the second half of the thirteenth century. Latin commoners also settled in cities manufacturing silk textiles, such as Thebes and Negroponte, as well as in old and new political and administrative centers, namely, Andravida, Thebes, Athens, Corinth, and Naxos.[90] These cities also attracted Greek immigrants from the countryside wishing to take advantage of new opportunities in the exercise of crafts and in the service sector, especially in trade and transportation.[91] The most spectacular population growth occurred in Candia and resulted in the development of a new suburb beginning in the second half of the thirteenth century.[92] Generally speaking, Latin immigration and related demographic and economic developments in Latin Romania generated important shifts in the relative importance of cities, as well as in the geographic distribution and the hierarchy of consumption, industrial, and trade centers.

Despite various manifestations of continuity in the countryside of Latin Romania, noted above, a partial restructuring at the basic level of management and exploitation was unavoidable after the Latin conquest. This appears to have been especially the case in confiscated crown and other extensive estates of Constantinopolitan landlords. Their fragmentation into smaller units and the division of their workforce among new landlords must have often prevented the upholding of large-scale compulsory labor services. Yet there also was a tendency to replace services and so-called gifts owed by the peasants with cash payments, in particular in Crete where the state-granted military tenements were rather small and at best moderate-sized. At times commutation was applied even when a fairly large labor force was available, as in the late thirteenth century at Lombaro,

[89] On the economic implications of the latter, see below, p. 229.

[90] See Jacoby, "Migration," 103–8, 112–13; idem, "Etats," 19–22.

[91] For Crete, see Santschi, "Contrats," 34–74, esp. 59, 65; C. Maltezou, "Métiers et salaires en Crète vénitienne (XVe siècle)," *ByzF* 12 (1987): 322–23, 326, 330.

[92] Gallina, "Finanza," 8, 10. Candia's expansion is illustrated by the inclusion of rural churches apparently constructed in the Byzantine period within the newly built urban territory. See M. Georgopoulou, "The Topography of Chandax, Capital of Crete in the Second Byzantine Period," *Cretan Studies* 4 (1994): 91–136, esp. 116–23. Incidentally, the author (ibid., 102 and n. 41) cites a 13th-century Venetian text that she wrongly interprets as ascribing the building of Candia's fortifications to Enrico Pescatore, whose activity in Crete extended from 1206 to 1211. See above, pp. 200, 207. However, the text refers to Candia as being *nondum* (instead of *nundum* [sic]) *muribus circumdata*, "*not yet* surrounded by walls" at that time. This seems to contradict the archaeological evidence, on which see ibid., 102–3.

the village held by Andrea Corner, which included thirty-three peasant households before it was hit by the rebellion of Alexios Kallergis.[93] In other cases commutation was implemented only when the peasants could not carry out their labor service, evaluated in 1281 at 4 hyperpers per year in the village of Apano Trifora.[94] In Frankish Morea villeins were required to perform their *servicium personale*. The latter's evaluation at 5 hyperpers per peasant unit appears only in official documents computing the income of fiefs and, therefore, does not necessarily imply that it was replaced by cash payments.[95] Commutation was a convenient device saving the cost of supervision and the need to coerce peasants to fulfill their obligations. Landlords applying it relied more heavily upon the lease of domain land to peasants and upon profit-sharing ventures with them in land cultivation and animal husbandry.[96]

Far more important and wide ranging, at both the local and regional levels, were changes in the channeling and destinations of agricultural and pastoral surpluses produced by the confiscated estates of large absentee landlords. Before 1204 these surpluses were partly, if not entirely, intended for self-supply, mainly in the capital, or else for gifts to ecclesiastical institutions. Thus, for instance, until 1171 the monastery of St. John of Patmos and other institutions benefited from yearly allowances of wheat from crown lands (βασιλικαὶ ἐπισκέψεις) in Crete. These surpluses remained outside the commercial circuit and were conveyed to their destinations within noncommercial networks. On the other hand, it may sometimes have been more convenient and profitable for absentee landlords residing in Constantinople to sell them at rural markets and fairs or in urban centers located in the vicinity of their estates, and save thereby the cost and nuisance involved in their transportation to the capital.[97] They could then use the proceeds of sales for the purchase of supplies and consumption elsewhere. The Latin conquest and the fragmentation of their extensive estates after 1204 severed the link between the latter and Constantinople. A portion of the surpluses had to be redirected toward the new Latin landlords and the retinues established on their land or in nearby cities, while the rest was transferred to markets and fairs in the region. The volume of produce affected by these changes cannot be assessed, yet may have been quite substantial in areas in which there had been a heavy concentration of Constantinopolitan estates.

---

[93] See above, note 22. For a contemporary case, see above, note 49. Although situated outside the region upon which this study focuses, the case of Lampsakos in western Asia Minor may prove instructive. In 1219 cash equivalents were established for labor services and gifts owed by seventy-two peasant households, commutation being possibly adopted afterwards: see Jacoby, "Presence," 175–77.

[94] Partial edition by Borsari, *Dominio*, 90 n. 105, who reads fourteen days per year, and full edition by Z. N. Tsirpanles, "Κατάστιχο ἐκκλησιῶν καὶ μοναστηριῶν τοῦ Κοινοῦ" (1248–1548). Συμβολὴ στὴ μελέτη τῶν σχέσεων Πολιτείας καὶ Ἐκκλησίας στὴ βενετοκρατούμενη Κρήτη (Ioannina, 1985), 261, no. 187, who reads forty-five days. Both figures are problematic, since the number should either be one day per week or else one or several days per month and thus twelve or a multiple of twelve: see Jacoby, "Presence," 176–77.

[95] See Carile, *Rendita*, 95–98; my review of the latter (cited above, note 15), 359; Longnon and Topping, *Documents*, 271–72; Jacoby, "Migration," 123.

[96] On which see above, note 15.

[97] D. Tsougarakis, ed., *The Life of Leontios, Patriarch of Jerusalem: Text, Translation, Commentary* (Leiden, 1993), 102, chap. 61, and 190–91, commentary. See also P. Magdalino, "The Grain Supply of Constantinople, Ninth-Twelfth Centuries," in *Constantinople and Its Hinterland*, ed. C. Mango and G. Dagron (Aldershot, 1995), 37–39, 45–46, who, however, does not deal with sales by lay landlords.

IX

On a more general level, the patterns of Latin settlement and economic activity generated some significant changes in the siting and relative importance of markets and fairs.
As a result, existing commercial routes were partly deflected to new courses and destinations. Numerous markets were presumably held in the territories included in Latin Romania both before and after the conquest, yet only few are documented, namely, in
Corinth, Cosmina, Vasilicata, and Androusa in the Peloponnesos.[98] The term ἐμπόριον,
used for several places in that region, indicated the existence of a market or a settlement
serving as marketplace.[99] As elsewhere in the empire, fairs too must have been quite
common before the Fourth Crusade in the territories conquered by the Latins. However,
only three of them are documented in the Peloponnesos in the thirteenth and fourteenth
centuries, none of them being attested either earlier or later.[100] The small village fair at
Macona in southern Messenia, recorded in 1338, yielded an annual revenue of only 8
hyperpers. It is not clear whether it was an annual event or was held several times a year,
in connection with the rural calendar.[101] The annual fair at Vervena, attested in 1296,
was undoubtedly far more important. It took place in the Frankish part of the Skorta
region some 10 to 15 km south of Andritsaina, in the vicinity of the Frankish-Byzantine
border newly delineated in the late 1270s, in the wake of the empire's northward expansion in the central Peloponnesos.[102] If this fair perpetuated a Byzantine institution, it
certainly gained in importance after the 1270s, in view of its location. Yet it may also
have been established around that time in order to attract subjects of both the Frankish

[98] Longnon and Topping, *Documents*, 139, line 36; 146, line 20; 162, line 8 (*lo comerchio del merchato*); 168,
line 2; see also 275–76. Silk cocoons were traded at the market of Androusa in 1328: C. Hodgetts, "Venetian
Officials and Greek Peasantry in the Fourteenth Century," in ΚΑΘΗΓΗΤΡΙΑ: *Essays Presented to Joan Hussey for
Her 80th Birthday*, ed. J. Chrysostomides (Camberley, 1988), 493, doc. II, para. 1.
[99] See *ODB* 1:694, s.v. "Emporion" and references in A. Ilieva, "Images of Towns in Frankish Morea: The
Evidence of the 'Chronicles' of the Morea and of the Tocco," *BMGS* 19 (1995): 106–7.
[100] On Byzantine fairs, see S. Vryonis Jr., "The Panegyris of the Byzantine Saint: A Study in the Nature of a
Medieval Institution, Its Origins and Fate," in S. Hackel, ed., *The Byzantine Saint*, Studies supplementary to *So-
bornost* 5 (1981), 196–226; A. E. Laiou, "Händler und Kaufleute auf dem Jahrmarkt," in *Fest und Alltag in Byzanz*, ed. G. Prinzing and D. Simon (Munich, 1990), 53–70, 189–94 (notes), repr. in eadem, *Gender, Society
and Economic Life in Byzantium* (Aldershot, 1992), no. XI; M. Živojinović, "The Trade of Mount Athos Monasteries," *ZRVI* 29–30 (1991): 112–14; K.-P. Matschke, "Die spätbyzantinische Öffentlichkeit," in *Mentalität und
Gesellschaft im Mittelalter: Gedenkschrift für Ernst Werner*, ed. S. Tanz (Frankfurt am Main, 1993), 159–64. On fairs
in the 14th-century Greek Despotate of the Morea and the 17th-century Peloponnesos, see Zakythinos, *Despotat grec*, 2:253–54.
[101] Longnon and Topping, *Documents*, 64, line 12: "Panegerii de Amachonu reddunt in porcione yperpera
quatuor." Note the plural, also used in the following case which clearly refers to annual fairs. The sum mentioned represented half of the total revenue, the fief and its revenue being divided in equal shares between two
lords: ibid., 165, lines 22–23, and 166, lines 8–26. For the location, see ibid., 250. On contemporary village
fairs in the empire on the land of monasteries, also yielding small annual revenues, see Laiou, "Händler,"
62–63; Živojinović, "Mount Athos Monasteries," 112 n. 49.
[102] *Livre de la conqueste*, para. 802–3: "les foires que on claime panejours, lesquelles se font au jour de huy au
demie juyn." The sale of silk is explicitly mentioned: see D. Jacoby, "Silk Production in the Frankish Peloponnese: The Evidence of Fourteenth-Century Surveys and Reports," in *Travellers and Officials in the Peloponnese: De-
scriptions-Reports-Statistics, in Honour of Sir Steven Runciman*, ed. H. A. Kalligas (Monemvasia, 1994), 45, 59–60,
repr. in idem, *Trade*, no. VIII. I correct here the location of Vervena mentioned in that study by relying on Bon,
Morée, 169–70, 380–89, esp. 387–88, 512–15, who presents convincing geographic and archaeological arguments against a proposed siting of Vervena in Arkadia. On the Byzantine advance, which went beyond Kala-
vryta, see Bon, *Morée*, 144–46. It excluded the holding of a Frankish fair in 1296 in Arkadia, which by then had
already been in Byzantine hands for some twenty years.

principality and the Greek despotate and thereby promote exchanges between these territories.[103] It should be noted that the region of Vervena was fairly close to the border-land further west in which later, in 1322, Frankish and Greek lords shared the revenue of several villages of the principality.[104]

The annual fair of St. Demetrius, attested in 1338, was presumably the most important of the three fairs of the Peloponnesos documented in the Latin period. It was held inland at some distance from Chiarenza. Venetian merchants attending it were supposed to return with their goods to that city within eight days after its conclusion.[105] The timing of this fair in late October coincided with the marketing of agricultural and pastoral produce for export and the passing of Venetian state galleys and other ships returning from the eastern Mediterranean to the Adriatic.[106] In view of the Byzantine connotation of its name, one would assume that this fair was inherited from the Byzantine period, yet this is far from certain, in the same way as the use of the Greek term πανηγύρις in its Latin, French, or Italian versions does not offer any clues with respect to continuity or the creation of new fairs in the Latin period.[107] The St. Demetrius fair mentioned here may have developed from a local or regional event into a more important gathering after the foundation of Chiarenza, yet it is not excluded that it was established by a Frankish lord in order to take advantage of that port. As in the Byzantine period, changing circumstances induced landholders to transfer existing fairs to new locations or to establish new fairs on their estates.[108]

In the Venetian territories, developments regarding markets and fairs appear to have been quite different from those occurring in the Peloponnesos. Fiscal expediency prompted the state to impose the channeling of all commercialized rural products to urban markets by land and by sea, regardless of their ultimate destination, in order to supervise and tax their sale. In Crete the maritime transportation of these products was directed toward the main ports of the island, namely, Candia, Canea, Rethymno, and Sitia.[109] Two late thirteenth-century customs lists record taxes levied at the land gate and in the harbor of Candia.[110] Goods brought for sale to the city had to be weighed or measured at the Commune's official station located at the marketplace. This rule applied

[103] The proximity of the border is further illustrated by the events that followed the fair: *Livre de la conqueste*, para. 804–25. Note the chronicler's remark that "*nowadays* [the fairs] are held in mid-June": see text in previous note. It is impossible to determine whether this remark already appeared in the original version of the chronicle, in which case it may reflect a change in timing related to the events of the 1270s, or in the abridged version of 1320–24. On the French versions of the chronicle, see D. Jacoby, "Quelques considérations sur les versions de la 'Chronique de Morée,'" *JSav* (1968): 133–50, 181–89, repr. in idem, *Société*, no. VII.

[104] See Jacoby, "Coseigneurie," 114–15.

[105] Baron Blanc, ed., *Le flotte mercantili dei Veneziani* (Venice, 1896), 59. See also Jacoby, "Silk Production," 60.

[106] On state galleys and timing, see below, pp. 222, 228.

[107] For Latin and French, see above, notes 101 and 102. The 14th-century Francesco Balducci Pegolotti, *La pratica della mercatura*, ed. A. Evans (Cambridge, Mass., 1936), 17, lists several equivalents of Tuscan *mercato* and *fiera*, among them *panichiero in grechesco*.

[108] See Laiou, "Händler," 54–57.

[109] Note the provisions of 1316–17 prohibiting the loading or unloading of goods in the bay of Dermata, to the west of Candia's harbor, only fishing boats being allowed to anchor there: P. Ratti Vidulich, ed., *Duca di Candia: Bandi*, Fonti per la storia di Venezia, Sez. I, Archivi pubblici (Venice, 1965) (hereafter *Bandi*), nos. 144, 174.

[110] Ed. E. Gerland, *Das Archiv des Herzogs von Kandia* (Strasbourg, 1899), 108–9, and for their dating to 1298–99, see 107 n. 1 and 135.

regardless of whether they would be sold or delivered there to a specific customer, according to an earlier agreement, or be transported afterwards to a private home, a private warehouse, or to the harbor for export. The weighing or measuring was carried out by state-appointed officials in the presence of state assessors, who also acted as official brokers on behalf of the Commune. We may safely assume that similar practices existed in the other ports and inland cities of Crete. In any event, they appear in Coron and Modon.[111] In these circumstances, it is rather unlikely that rural fairs should have survived in Crete or that any subsisted outside the cities of Coron and Modon in the exiguous territories of Venetian Messenia.[112]

As before 1204,[113] rural surpluses in Latin Romania were partly conveyed to nearby rural or urban markets and fairs by producers, whether peasants, herdsmen, or craftsmen, who sold their own products or else delivered them to a specific customer, in conformity with a contract between them.[114] Some producers also acted as middlemen between their peers and markets. According to a Venetian document of 1328, a number of Greek peasants from Venetian Messenia sold in Coron their own silk cocoons, as well as others bought in neighboring Frankish Morea.[115] Individuals wishing to avoid the costly and time-consuming transportation and marketing of small amounts of products relied on professional merchants and carriers, such as the traveling Venetian merchants visiting the fair of St. Demetrius in the area of Chiarenza in 1338.[116] Professional merchants settled in Latin Romania took advantage of their greater ability to offer transportation services. In Crete a number of them combined trade with the holding of military tenements.[117]

Large landholders also served occasionally as middlemen between rural producers on the one hand and urban markets and exporters on the other, concentrating large amounts of goods in their hands. Unless delivering their surpluses to a specific customer, many peasants were left with fairly small amounts of them after paying rents and taxes in kind. They may have found it convenient, therefore, to sell them to large landholders rather than to market them on their own. Some Cretan documents refer to such deals.[118] A similar pattern may be assumed for the produce of small estates. From 1341 to 1344 the *serventaria* of Castri in the region of Milopotamo produced for its holder 791 *misure* of wheat or an annual average of about 264 *misure*, around 3.380 metric tons, from which a certain amount had to be deducted for personal consumption.[119] At times, however,

[111] See D. Jacoby, "Cretan Cheese: A Neglected Aspect of Venetian Medieval Trade," in *Medieval and Renaissance Venice*, ed. E. E. Kittel and T. F. Madden (Urbana-Chicago, 1999), 54–55; Hodgetts, "Colonies," 448–53.

[112] In 1473 the Venetian Senate deplored that for some time Cretan merchants were buying and storing local products in the countryside, thereby depriving the state of revenue and Candia of its economic activity: H. Noiret, ed., *Documents inédits pour servir à l'histoire de la domination vénitienne en Crète de 1380 à 1485* (Paris, 1892), 526–27.

[113] For the Byzantine period, see Laiou, as above, note 100.

[114] On the latter, see below, p. 218 and note 129.

[115] Hodgetts, "Officials," 493, para. 1; see also Jacoby, "Silk Production," 44–45, 60–61.

[116] See above, p. 215.

[117] See above, pp. 207, 209 and note 76.

[118] See Jacoby, "Cretan Cheese," 52–53.

[119] E. Santschi, ed., *Régestes des arrêts civils et des mémoriaux (1363–1399) des archives du duc de Crète*, Bibliothèque de l'Institut hellénique d'études byzantines et post-byzantines de Venise 9 (Venice, 1976), Memoriali, no. 735; for the location, see ibid., no. 1100. The wheat *misura* of Crete is estimated at 12.8 kg: see E. Schilbach, *Byzantinische Metrologie* (Munich, 1970), 94–96, 149–50.

large landholders must have applied pressure to acquire from their own as well as from other villeins the products they wished to market. Such a practice may have been fairly common when they had agreed to deliver specific amounts of products to a private customer or a merchant and had to meet a deadline.[120] A similar pattern was even more imperative in Crete with respect to wheat. From the late thirteenth century, Latin military settlers and the powerful Cretan archontes of the Kallergis clan undertook to deliver each year specific amounts of wheat to the Commune, an obligation they had to fulfill at all cost.[121] In these circumstances, pressure on peasants appears all the more likely on the hereditary estates owned by the Kallergis, in which they had preserved and even reinforced their traditional standing and authority.[122]

The function of large landowners as middlemen in the marketing of rural produce is also documented for Frankish Greece. Large landowners did not directly engage in silk growing, which was exclusively carried out by peasants. Moreover, they apparently obtained only small amounts of silk as payment in kind for the use of their processing facilities by the peasants, less than 15 light pounds per village as illustrated by some cases in the 1370s which, admittedly, do not necessarily reflect an average.[123] In any event, we may safely assume that the Greek archon of Frankish Morea who in 1296 came to the fair of Vervena would not have bothered to attend it, had he not assembled a sizable quantity of silk for sale.[124] In addition to the small amounts he had collected as payment from silk growers, he must have purchased silk from his and other villeins willing to sell it or compelled them to do so under pressure. It is not excluded, though, that the archon also acted as middleman between other landholders of his area, who would have collected silk in a similar way, and merchants attending the fair. The same functions of middleman may be assumed with respect to John Laskaris Kalopheros, a Byzantine adventurer who had wedded the daughter of Erard III Le Maure, one of the most powerful barons of Frankish Morea, and had himself become a fiefholder in the principality. In 1381 Kalopheros sold in Modon 2,773 light pounds or around 950 kg of raw silk, quite a sizable amount.[125] A document of 1328 regarding Munista in Venetian Messenia reveals that individual peasant households produced fairly small amounts of cocoons, between 10 and 25 light pounds, which in turn yielded between ca. 2 and ca. 5 light pounds of raw silk.[126] Judging by these figures, the silk sold by Kalopheros would have represented the production of more than 550 peasant households. Only a few landlords of Frankish

---

[120] See Jacoby, "Cretan Cheese," 52–53; *Marcello*, no. 125, a contract of 1279 specifying that the price of cheese and wool would be determined "ad eam videlicet racionem quam villani de Sythea vendiderint eorum dominis." The use of pressure is hinted by the following: "ita tamen quod ipsi villani vendidere non debeant dictum caseum neque lanam," the reference being to free marketing by the peasants themselves. See also ibid., no. 213, drafted in 1280: a feudatory promises to deliver his own cheese and wool as well as those of his villeins.

[121] On which see below, p. 223.

[122] See above, p. 199.

[123] On such payments in Frankish Morea, in all likelihood perpetuating a Byzantine practice, see Jacoby, "Silk Production," 51–53; on amounts, see ibid., 57.

[124] See below, note 214.

[125] Jacoby, "Silk Production," 55, 60. The light pound of Modon weighed 343 g: see ibid., 55 n. 52.

[126] For these and other production figures from Frankish Morea, see ibid., 57. The ratio between the weight of cocoons and silk, respectively, is around 5:1.

Morea would ever have had so many households on their estates.[127] It follows that Kalopheros was not only selling silk produced by his own villeins.

Despite the evidence regarding the archon attending the fair of Vervena, adduced above, most Greek archontes of Latin Romania must have been weakened in their capacity to act as middlemen. Their resources or those they inherited had been reduced after the conquest, and they had lost the high social status and official functions they or their ancestors had enjoyed in the Byzantine period. In addition, they had to face competition from Latin landlords and from Latin merchants in particular. There were nevertheless some individual archontes who were in a better position than their peers, such as the Kallergis in Crete and the few archontes who in Frankish Morea had attained prominent positions within the knightly class or were serving as high-ranking officials in the baronial or princely administrations.[128] As for Kalopheros, a latecomer to the principality, although a Greek he had rapidly integrated into the Frankish feudal elite, which was quite exceptional.

The number of Latin settlers engaging in trade in western Romania appears to have been constantly growing since the early thirteenth century and, in any event, was far larger than before the Fourth Crusade. The continuous presence of these merchants in the region enabled them to monitor trade and shipping and prospect the area around their city of residence. They thereby enhanced trade, banking, credit, and entrepreneurship ventures, whether their own or those of other settlers and traveling merchants. Especially merchants involved in wholesale and export operated with more liquid capital than their peers or than landlords. Their contacts with producers and landlords on the one hand and with customers and other merchants, on the other, was easier and far more extensive than before 1204. The bulk of evidence regarding these practices comes from Crete. Direct transactions regarding agricultural and pastoral products between producers and customers or merchants concentrated in ports enabled both sides to dispense with middlemen. These transactions were often based on sale credit, in the form of anticipated payment for the delivery of an agreed amount of produce at a specific date or within a specific period. There is good reason to believe that sale credit was far more common after the conquest than in the preceding Byzantine period, although the absence of quantitative data prevents any solid assessment. The use of sale credit was greatly furthered by the increasing external demand for the products of Crete, to which I shall soon return, by the infusion of capital it promoted, as well as by the growing monetization of the economy. On the whole this system, with its concealed loan, favored the creditor who was in a position to exert pressure on the producer in need of cash and obtain favorable prices from him.[129] It also eliminated any possibility of collective bargaining by producers. In this respect, after 1204 Latin landlords fared no better than the Greeks. In short, these developments generated a shift from a sellers' market to a buyers' market.

[127] See the small numbers of households in villages surveyed in the 14th century, compiled by Carile, *Rendita*, 117–74, passim.

[128] See Jacoby, "Encounter," 894–95.

[129] See Jacoby, "Cretan Cheese," 51–54; Gallina, "Finanza," 34–40; idem, *Società*, 133. However, in some contracts the parties agreed that payment would be made according to the market price at the time of delivery.

In addition to sale credit, there were also loans and leases based on other types of contract, which stimulated market and export-oriented investments of money and labor in land cultivation and the raising of animals.[130] In Crete the extension of cash crops is illustrated by contracts stipulating the expansion of vineyards, especially the planting of high-quality Malvasia and Athiri vinestocks from the fourteenth century on, in response to a growing external demand for high-grade Cretan wines. Wine became a major item in Cretan exports.[131] Irrigation was already practiced in the Byzantine period. It is attested in 1118 for cotton and vegetable cultivation in Crete and by a letter of Pope Innocent III written in 1209, thus shortly after the conquest, referring to gardens and orchards in the bishoprics of Athens and Negroponte.[132] Cistern and well water was occasionally used for small pieces of land, the latter case attested by a Cretan contract of 1280,[133] yet irrigation was mostly based on the diversion of streams. Irrigation appears to have been substantially extended after the Latin conquest. It was promoted from around the turn of the thirteenth century on the mainland, in Crete and in some Aegean islands, especially by great landholders and investors, who more easily than peasants could muster the large resources needed for the construction and maintenance of expensive watering systems.[134] Cotton growing expanded in Crete, and by 1307 the island was exporting its fiber to Venice. By the second half of the fourteenth century, cotton was also being grown in the countryside of Coron and Modon, as well as in Negroponte, Santorini, and Corfu, obviously in response to the increasing demand of the Venetian cotton industry. In Frankish Morea, cotton was cultivated in the area south of Corinth and presumably also in other areas, since it was partly exported from Chiarenza by Ragusan and Anconitan ships.[135] Irrigation may have occasionally been used for luxury crops fetching a high price on the market, such as cherries, marasca or sour cherries, pomegranates, peaches, and pears.[136] It was indispensable for the growing of citrus, known in

[130] See above, p. 200.

[131] See Topping, "Viticulture," 509–20; Gallina, *Società*, 41–44, 57, 133. See also above, note 23. On external demand and destinations, see Jacoby, "Creta," 80, 85–86, 88, 90–94, 96, 100–102.

[132] See Harvey, *Economic Expansion*, 127–33; Gallina, *Società*, 19–20; Innocent III, Epist., XI.256, PL 215:1560: "flumina unde rigantur horti."

[133] *Marcello*, no. 251.

[134] See Jacoby, "Migration," 124–25; Gallina, *Società*, 19–21, 53–54; Gaspares, Η γη, 105–10. In 1352 the authorities in Crete intervened in a dispute between Venetian landholders over the use of water for irrigation: see Thiriet, *Romanie*, 310–11. The construction of an adequate irrigation system was among the heavy investments envisaged by Marco de Zanono, who in 1428 had obtained a monopoly for the growing of sugar cane in Crete: see D. Jacoby, "La production du sucre en Crète vénitienne: L'échec d'une entreprise économique," in ΡΟΔΩΝΙΑ: Τιμὴ στὸν Μ. Ι. Μανούσακα, ed. C. Maltezou, T. Detorakes, and C. Charalampakes (Rethymno, 1994), 1:172, 175–77, repr. in Jacoby, *Trade*, no. XI.

[135] For Venetian territories, see Jacoby, "Creta," 79; above, note 22, on cotton and flax grown under irrigation at Lombaro before 1307; Thiriet, *Romanie*, 321–22; C. N. Sathas, *Documents inédits relatifs à l'histoire de la Grèce au Moyen Age* (Athens-Paris, 1880–90), 2:119, no. 336; 126, no. 347; 154, no. 385 (respectively in 1404, 1405, 1406). For the Morea, see *bambaso* in Longnon and Topping, *Documents*, 176–78, 188–92, and M. F. Mazzaoui, *The Italian Cotton Industry in the Later Middle Ages, 1100–1600* (Cambridge, 1981), 43.

[136] See Gallina, *Società*, 43–44; Jacoby, "Migration," 124–25. According to a Cretan contract of 1352, the lessees of a fruit garden undertook to plant at least ten fruit trees each year, citrus included, the species being determined by the lessor: A. Lombardo, ed., *Zaccaria de Fredo, notaio in Candia (1352–1357)*, Fonti per la storia di Venezia, Sez. III, Archivi notarili (Venice, 1968), no. 82.

Constantinople in the second half of the twelfth century and around 1300 in Crete.[137] Citron, lemon, and bitter orange are mentioned in the Πωρικολόγος, a Byzantine satirical work that has been dated to the late thirteenth or the early fourteenth century.[138] Citrus growing appears to have been introduced in Latin Romania around that time, yet remained rather limited for a long period.[139] Significantly, in his commercial manual, completed between 1330 and 1340, Francesco Balducci Pegolotti includes *cetrine* and *cederni*, citron and cedrate fruit, among the *spezierie*, a term broadly applied in the Middle Ages to spices and other expensive luxury products traded in small amounts.[140] A Greek account book from Rhodes dated to the last two decades of the fourteenth century mentions two shipments including a total of 600 lemons, 40 oranges, and 6 thick-skinned citrons.[141] Venice was importing lemons from Alexandria in 1396 and 1404, a further proof that yields in Latin Romania were still small.[142] By 1450, however, citrons and oranges were being exported from Coron and Modon in larger amounts.[143]

As elsewhere, there were two basic patterns of maritime trade and transportation in Latin Romania. One of them was centered on bilateral exchanges between specific areas within that region or between them and other regions. The other was inserted within the broader trans-Mediterranean framework. Despite the collapse of the empire, subsequent warfare, and the establishment of new political entities, the maritime trade of western Romania displayed basic continuity with respect to the Byzantine period in its ranges and orientations. Nevertheless, new geopolitical conditions no less than economic factors both required and enabled several major adjustments. The thirteenth and fourteenth centuries witnessed changes in the relative importance of destinations, as well as a progressive growth in volume and an acceleration of exchanges, which called for a partial restructuring of commercial and shipping networks. Given the limitations of space, only the most important aspect of this evolution will be examined here.

The losses inflicted upon the infrastructure of Constantinople by widespread fires and warfare in 1203 and 1204 were compounded by a massive exodus of population from all

---

[137] Twelfth-century evidence in *Ptochoprodromos*, 4.328, ed. and trans. H. Eideneier (Cologne, 1991), 157: τὸ διακιτρίον, translated "Zitruskonfekt" (208), yet in fact the reference is to citron; the origin of the fruit is not stated. Alice-Mary Talbot has kindly drawn my attention to an epigram by Theodore Balsamon, Εἰς νέραντ-ζαν τῆς μονῆς τοῦ Ἀργυροπώλου: K. Horna, ed., "Die Epigramme des Theodoros Balsamon," *WSt* 25 (1903): 193–94, ep. 31; the correct name of the Constantinopolitan monastery is Ἀργύρων: see R. Janin, *La géographie ecclésiastique de l'Empire byzantin: Première partie. Le siège de Constantinople et le patriarcat oecuménique*, vol. 3, *Les églises et les monastères*, 2d. ed. (Paris, 1969), 51. For Crete, see below, note 139.

[138] In W. Wagner, ed., *Carmina graeca medii aevi* (Leipzig, 1874), 199; see M. Bartusis, "The Fruit Book: A Translation of the *Porikologos*. Translated from Byzantine Greek with an Introduction," *Modern Greek Studies Yearbook* 4 (1988): 205–12, esp. 206 for the dating and 208 for the relevant references.

[139] See Jacoby, "Migration," 124–25.

[140] Pegolotti, *Mercatura*, 294.

[141] P. Schreiner, ed., *Texte zur spätbyzantinischen Finanz- und Wirtschaftsgeschichte in Handschriften der Biblioteca Vaticana*, ST 344 (Vatican City, 1991), 70 and 73, lines 46–47 (text and trans.), 66–67 (dating), 78 (commentary).

[142] Noiret, *Documents*, 80, 150: freight charge for each casket of lemons. This was not lemon juice, as would seem at first glance. In maritime trade, caskets also served as containers for a variety of solid goods: see H. Zug Tucci, "Un aspetto trascurato del commercio medievale del vino," in *Studi in memoria di Federigo Melis* (Naples, 1978), 3:335–37.

[143] Giorgio di Lorenzo Chiarini, *El libro di mercantantie et usanze de' paesi*, ed. F. Borlandi (Turin, 1936), 55.

walks of life, including the Byzantine imperial court, the social elite, and craftsmen. As a result, Constantinople ceased to be the major consumption and industrial center of Romania it had been. The political and territorial fragmentation of Romania further undercut the city's economic centrality. After 1204 it was merely the capital of a reduced territorial entity, the size of which was continuously shrinking from the 1220s. This factor further contributed to a substantial reduction in the flow of cash and goods to Constantinople, whether in the form of fiscal revenue or in the framework of self-supply and trade. The Latin imperial court in Constantinople was chronically impoverished, the Latin nobility suffered from economic stress, and the rather meager Latin settlement in the city did not offset the consequences of large-scale depopulation. The economic contraction resulting from these events was only partly overcome in the last two decades of Latin rule.[144]

In these circumstances, surpluses exported from western Romania to Constantinople before 1204 had to be redirected toward other destinations. The need for a reorientation of trade networks occurred precisely in a period witnessing a rise in Western demand for specific commodities produced in Latin Romania, namely, foodstuffs, especially grain, cheese, wine, and salt, as well as industrial raw materials such as silk and colorants. This demand was linked to demographic expansion, a rise in living standards and purchasing power, as well as a growth in industrial production and an increase in the volume of goods available for exchange. These processes, already well under way in the twelfth century, gained momentum in the following period and had a decisive impact on the economy of Latin Romania. Soon after 1204 they contributed to a major shift in the orientation of this region's economy. Instead of being mainly geared toward Constantinople and the internal Byzantine market, as before 1204, it became rapidly inserted within the patterns of the Western supply system. This shift was decisively enhanced by Venetian presence and economic activity in the region, discussed below. By 1261 it had already become irreversible, despite the renewed expansion of Constantinople's economy after the Byzantine reconquest of 1261. This is not to say that Latin Romania failed to take advantage of the subsequent intensification of trade in Constantinople and the Black Sea.[145] The West, however, especially Italy, remained henceforth its main trade partner.

There was yet another powerful factor in Latin Romania itself that contributed to the shift in orientation of its economy, namely, the firm correlation existing between political factors, settlement, and economic activity in this region. This correlation, several instances of which we have already encountered, was particularly strong in Venetian

---

[144] L. B. Robbert, "Rialto Businessmen and Constantinople, 1204–61," *DOP* 49 (1995): 43–58, claims that Latin Constantinople experienced a continuous decline in economic activity, substantially enhanced since the 1230s. Yet see a different interpretation of the evidence by D. Jacoby, "Venetian Settlers in Latin Constantinople (1204–1261): Rich or Poor?" in Πλούσιοι και πτωχοί στην κοινωνία της ελληνολατινικῆς Ἀνατολῆς (= Ricchi e poveri nella società dell'Oriente grecolatino), ed. C. Maltezou, Biblioteca dell'Istituto ellenico di Studi bizantini e postbizantini di Venezia 19 (Venice, 1998), 181–204, partly based on unpublished documents.

[145] Venetian refugees from the imperial capital, mentioned below, presumably contributed their share in this respect. On some aspects of this trade, see Jacoby, "Creta," 80–87.

territories. Venetian rule over Crete, Coron, Modon, and Venice's quarter in Negroponte reinforced existing links or created new ones with Venice. The Venetian nuclei in Latin Romania were strengthened after the Byzantine reconquest of Constantinople in 1261, which triggered an exodus of some three thousand Latins, most of whom must have been Venetian citizens or subjects.[146] An unknown number among them, induced by earlier trade relations, the presence of relatives, Venetian rule, or the combination of these factors, settled in the city of Negroponte or in Crete.[147]

The partial reorientation of Latin Romania's maritime trade toward the West resulting from a spontaneous shift was significantly enhanced by Venice's policies. Protectionist measures as well as state intervention in and supervision over economic processes favored Venetian citizens in trade and shipping, yet also entailed for them some serious limitations. These citizens enjoyed preferential custom rates, and Venetian carriers benefited from a virtual monopoly on maritime transportation, since returning merchants were compelled to ship their goods to Venice exclusively on board their ships. The same rule applied to specific commodities that were to travel exclusively on board state galleys, in service since the early fourteenth century, unless the authorities issued other instructions.[148] In addition, the Commune strictly regulated the rhythm of navigation between Venice and other ports, especially with respect to returning ships, so as to prevent an overflow of merchandise and a slump in prices on the Venetian market.[149] Venice's restrictive and discriminatory policy toward foreigners in the field of seaborne trade did not deter fairly large numbers of them from settling in the Venetian colonies. While in Coron from 1289 to 1293 the notary Pasquale Longo recorded the names of settlers originating in areas of Italy extending from the Veneto and Lombardy in the north to Barletta in the south.[150] Similarly, there were numerous foreigners in Candia from the early stages of Latin settlement.[151] In business transactions with Venice, however, foreigners largely depended upon privileged Venetian citizens, with whom they sought joint ventures, at times in an attempt to defraud the Commune's treasury.[152] Not surprisingly, these foreigners were particularly eager to obtain Venetian citizenship, granted only to a small number of them, or at least Venetian nationality.[153]

State intervention also affected other aspects of trade and shipping. As early as 1211,

---

[146] For this figure, see Geanakoplos, *Michael Palaeologus*, 113–14.

[147] Ibid., 379–80, no. 2; Tsirpanles, Κατάστιχο, 182–84, nos. 99–100. No other territories of Latin Romania are known to have served as havens for these refugees, yet this is surely due to the paucity of evidence regarding them.

[148] On state galleys, see D. Stöckly, *Le système de l'incanto des galées du marché à Venise (fin XIIIe–milieu XVe siècle)* (Leiden, 1995).

[149] See D. Jacoby, "La Venezia d'oltremare nel secondo Duecento," in G. Cracco and G. Ortalli, eds., *Storia di Venezia*, vol. 2, *L'età del Comune* (Rome, 1995), 290.

[150] See Borsari, *Studi*, 113–14.

[151] See Jacoby, "Colonisation," 307.

[152] See Jacoby, "Venezia d'oltremare," 291.

[153] On the distinction between the two, see above, note 73. In his letters the Pisan Pignol Zucchello, a merchant who after residing in Crete settled in Venice, repeatedly requested intervention on his behalf to obtain Venetian citizenship, which he eventually was granted; his correspondents also deal with that subject: see R. Morozzo della Rocca, ed., *Lettere di mercanti a Pignol Zucchello (1336–1350)*, Fonti per la storia di Venezia, Sez. IV, Archivi privati (Venice, 1957), 23, 47–49, 54, 75, 97, 102, 113–15.

when the first military settlers were about to leave for Crete, Doge Pietro Ziani stipulated that exports of wheat from the island would be subject to state control, as noted earlier.[154] Later in the thirteenth century the Cretan authorities imposed on the Latin military settlers and Greek archontes quotas of wheat, which they undertook to buy at state regulated prices determined each year according to the anticipated yield. Although preventing bargaining by local producers, landlords, and wholesale merchants, this disposition was advantageous in various ways to those who delivered the wheat, since it ensured a convenient marketing, a rapid payment in cash, partly in advance of delivery, and a guaranteed price floor even in case of overflow due to good harvests. Prices appear to have been slightly on the rise in the second half of the thirteenth and again in the second half of the fourteenth century. There was also a free grain trade, though exports were controlled by the Commune and restricted to Venice, Venetian territories overseas, and other destinations when authorized.[155] Candia shared the export of wheat with Canea, a port serving as outlet for the large production of its own hinterland. Shipping from Crete to the ports of Latin Romania was often carried out by the Greeks of the region. Transportation to Venice was handled by both Venetian citizens and subjects, some residing in Crete and others in Venice.[156] In addition to its regulation of the wheat trade, the Venetian government established in 1279 a salt monopoly in Crete, and two years later imposed a new overall salt policy requiring all ships to carry salt on their return voyage to Venice and sell it to the Commune.[157]

The documentation regarding Latin Romania, which is largely Venetian, has created the wrong impression that Venice dominated the economy of that region beginning in the early thirteenth century. In fact, the strengthening of Venice's position was slow to come and its supremacy achieved only by the mid-fourteenth century. Several factors explain this rather lengthy process. In non-Venetian territories the absence of a strong, centralized government and of heavy-handed state intervention attracted settlers widely differing in origin and afforded more latitude for their activity, as well as more variety in the orientation of their operations. To be sure, Venetians also traded and resided in Thebes, Chiarenza, and Patras.[158] By early 1389 the Venetian Marco Morosini was settled in Nauplia, before Venice took hold of that city, and such was the case with Albano Contarini and other Venetians in Argos.[159] Yet in addition to Venetians, traveling

---

[154] See above, p. 207.

[155] See Gallina, "Finanza," 63–64, 127–32; D. Tsougarakes, "Ἡ σιτικὴ πολιτικὴ τῆς Βενετίας στὴν Κρήτη τὸν 13ο–14ο αἰώνα," Μεσαιωνικὰ καὶ νέα ἑλληνικά 3 (1990): 333–85, a full review of the policy.

[156] See C. Gaspares, "Ἡ ναυτιλιακὴ κίνηση ἀπὸ Κρήτη πρὸς τὴν Πελοπόννησο κατὰ τὸν 14ο αἰώνα," Τὰ Ἱστορικά 9 (1988): 287–318, passim, esp. 309–10, table 4. Two ships sailing in 1310 from Venice to load wheat in Crete: Theotokes, Ἀποφάσεις, 62–63, nos. 19–20. The measures used in Candia and Canea were identical, as revealed by their comparison with the one used in Rhodes: Pegolotti, Mercatura, 104 and 113. In the first case the ratio mentioned is 55:100, in the second 870:1560.

[157] See Jacoby, "Creta," 89, and for 1281, J.-C. Hocquet, Le sel et la fortune de Venise, vol. 2, Voiliers et commerce en Méditerranée (Lille, 1979), 199–208, 249–55.

[158] On 27 February 1275 Domenico Spadaro, a resident of Thebes, promises to maintain the local Venetian church of San Marco: Venice, Archivio di Stato, S. Nicolo di Lido, b. 2 perg. For Chiarenza, see Jacoby, "Venezia d'oltremare," 272–73, and E. Gerland, Neue Quellen zur Geschichte des lateinischen Erzbistums Patras (Leipzig, 1903), 30–66, 89–107, also relevant for Patras.

[159] Chrysostomides, Monumenta, 105, lines 163–66.

IX

and resident merchants from Modena, Parma, Cremona, Piacenza, and other cities of central Italy known for their commercial and banking activities are attested in Negroponte and Thebes from the 1220s.[160] Others from Milan and Ancona were active in Negroponte around 1270,[161] while Italians, French, and German immigrants, as well as an Englishman resided in Patras in the fourteenth century.[162]

The close political connections between the kingdom of Sicily and Frankish Morea beginning in the late 1260s resulted in a marked increase in exchanges between the two regions for about an entire century, a process surprisingly not reflected by commercial manuals. Grain was the main commodity shipped to the Peloponnesos from south Italian ports, which also served as transit stations for silk and kermes from the principality on their way to textile manufacturing centers.[163] The intensification of trade between the two regions was greatly enhanced by the operation and settlement in the Peloponnesos and neighboring areas of merchants, bankers, and officials hailing from central and southern Italy or involved in the operation of its economy. Prominent among them were Sienese and Florentine citizens, some of them operating with fairly large amounts of capital. They were originally attracted by the prospects of trade and credit operations in connection with the transfer of funds to or on behalf of the papal treasury, which they were already practicing in the West and in the Crusader Levant. Some of them acted on their own, like the Sienese merchants settled in Chiarenza who obtained fiefs between ca. 1260 and ca. 1325, and the Sienese banker based in Negroponte, who in 1310 supplied the duke of Athens, Walter V of Brienne, with the funds needed for the hiring of the Catalan Company. Others served as resident partners of the companies or as their resident agents in the branches they established beginning in the 1260s in Latin Romania.[164] Among these companies the Bardi, Peruzzi, and especially the Acciaiuoli of Florence were the most important ones until they collapsed in the 1340s.[165]

Sienese and Florentine merchants, whether acting on their own or on behalf of com-

---

[160] See Jacoby, "Migration," 107; P. Racine in P. Castignoli and M. A. Romanini, eds., *Storia di Piacenza,* vol. 2, *Dal vescovo conte alla signoria (996–1313)* (Piacenza, 1984), 200.

[161] TTh, 3:204, 209–10.

[162] Gerland, *Quellen,* 89.

[163] On Chiarenza and its trade with southern Italy, see Bon, *Morée,* 320–25; Jacoby, "Migration," 105–8, 112, and 120. On several occasions King Charles I ordered royal wheat and barley to be sold in Chiarenza in order to finance his military operations in the principality, for instance in 1273: R. Filangieri et al., eds., *I registri della cancelleria angioina* (Naples, 1950–), 10:42–43, reg. 40, no. 146. The relevant evidence on trade appearing in this series of documents, of which more than thirty volumes have been edited thus far, has yet to be exploited. On trade of Apulia and Naples with Chiarenza and Negroponte in 1274, see R. Cessi, "La tregua fra Venezia e Genova nella seconda metà del sec. XIII," *Archivio veneto-tridentino* 4 (1923): 35–38, and for the dating, 16–18; trade between Apulia and Nauplion in 1272: TTh, 3:274–76, with correct dating in G. Morgan, "The Venetian Claims Commission of 1278," *BZ* 69 (1976): 429, no. 60; Venetians in regular trade between Chiarenza and Apulia: R. Cessi, ed., *Deliberazioni del Maggior Consiglio di Venezia* (Bologna, 1931–50), 2:135 and 3:25–26 (1282 and 1283); Chrysostomides, *Monumenta,* 33, in 1381. On south Italian ceramics found in the Morea, see below, p. 232.

[164] See Jacoby, "Migration," 98–99, 107–18. On the Levant: D. Jacoby, "Migration, Trade and Banking in Crusader Acre," in Βαλκάνια και Ανατολική Μεσόγειος, 12ος–17ος αιωνες (= The Balkans and the Eastern Mediterranean, 12th–17th Centuries), The National Hellenic Research Foundation, Institute for Byzantine Research, Byzantium Today 2, ed. L. Mavromatis (Athens, 1998), 114–19.

[165] Ibid., 114–18.

panies, significantly contributed to economic growth in the non-Venetian territories of Latin Romania. Credit operations and transfers of money were partly achieved by investment in maritime trade. Sienese merchants conveyed wax from Romania to the fairs of Champagne, as attested in 1265 by Andrea Tolomei, member of an important company based in Siena, in a letter sent from Troyes.[166] An unidentified Sienese company apparently exported silk from Chiarenza in the 1270s, and kermes from Romania reached Siena, as attested by a Sienese custom list compiled between 1273 and 1313.[167] Continental Greece, especially the Peloponnesos, as well as some islands of the Aegean and the Ionian Sea, were major exporters of this expensive dyestuff used in textile manufacture.[168] The Florentine mercantile banking house of the Alberti shipped kermes from Corinth and Monemvasia, as well as from the islands of Cerigo and Cephalonia.[169] By the late thirteenth century, some Italian mercantile and banking companies had extended their operations to Corinth, a thriving and affluent economic center until the Catalan attack of 1312.[170] Their large-scale financing of warfare and of conspicuous consumption brought large infusions of liquid capital.

These activities, combined with the introduction of advanced business methods into Latin Greece from the second half of the thirteenth century, such as deposit accounts with payment on demand, transfer banking, double-entry bookkeeping and management, contributed to an intensification of trade and an acceleration of the monetary flow.[171] The banking practices introduced into the Frankish territories also spread to Venetian Coron and Modon, the economy of which was tightly linked to theirs.[172] I have already noted the integration of Italians within the knightly class of Frankish Morea beginning in the second half of the thirteenth century, among them merchants and bankers. In the following century we find Italian intendants administering large feudal estates, several of which belonged to absentee Italian landlords. Italian lords and intendants were familiar with sophisticated business techniques and had a clear impact on the exploitation of Moreot estates. They introduced structural changes in their management, a more rational organization of space and use of resources, whether land, water, beasts of labor

---

[166] C. Paoli and E. Piccolomini, eds., *Lettere volgari del secolo XIII scritte da Senesi* (Bologna, 1871), 57.

[167] See Jacoby, "Migration," 112–13; M. A. Ceppari and P. Turrini, eds., "Documenti: Il commercio delle stoffe; l'abbigliamento e le provvisioni di lusso; arredi sacri e profani," in *"Drappi, velluti, taffetà et altre cose."* *Antichi tessuti a Siena e nel suo territorio*, ed. M. Ciatti (Siena, 1994), 245.

[168] See Jacoby, "Silk Production," 45–47, 61.

[169] A. Sapori, *I libri degli Alberti del Giudice* (Milan, 1952), 71, 101, and 229.

[170] See Jacoby, "Migration," 103–4, 114. The assessment of destruction inflicted by the Catalans has recently been somewhat tempered by the suggestion that major destruction may have been caused by an earthquake that occurred ca. 1300: see C. K. Williams II, E. Barnes, and L. M. Snyder, "Frankish Corinth: 1996," *Hesp* 66 (1997): 41–42.

[171] See Jacoby, "Migration," 113, 121–27. Accounts are mentioned by Marino Sanudo Torsello in Hopf, *Chroniques*, 101–2: "Nel suo tempo fù nel principato tanta cortesia e amorevolezza, che non solamente li cavallieri mà anche li mercadanti andavano sù e giuso senza denari . . . e con il semplice loro scritto di mano se li dava denari." Since Sanudo refers to the reign of Prince William II, who ruled from 1248 to 1278, the introduction of deposit accounts into Greece should be placed in the latter's reign, thus earlier than in Venice, on which see R. C. Mueller, *The Venetian Money Market: Banks, Panics and the Public Debt, 1200–1500* (Baltimore, 1997), 9–18, esp. 15–16.

[172] See below, pp. 227–28, 231.

or the workforce, diversified crops, and achieved a rise in agricultural and pastoral productivity, a growth in output, and improvements in the marketing of products.[173]

In the thirteenth century, Genoese interests and trade were also important factors in the portion of Latin Romania not subject to Venetian rule, far more so than commonly assumed.[174] While importing silk fabrics from the eastern Mediterranean, Genoa also acted as the main supplier of raw materials to the expanding Lucchese silk industry from the beginning of its operation around the mid-twelfth century.[175] Not surprisingly, therefore, silk textiles, raw silk, and dyestuffs appear to have been the main commodities that Genoese merchants sought in Latin Romania, where their activity is documented as early as 1210. In that year two partners, one of them a Lucchese, bought in Genoa a certain amount of *grana de Romania,* kermes clearly originating in Latin Romania.[176] The silk called *seta de Romania,* documented in Genoa in 1269, also came from that region.[177] Sixteen contracts drafted in Genoa between 1274 and 1345 refer to trade with Chiarenza, some of 1287 explicitly mentioning the export of woolens, the sale of which was to finance purchases there.[178] Between 1330 and 1340 Pegolotti lists samite, by then a medium-grade silk textile, among the commodities in which merchants on business in Chiarenza reinvest proceeds from the sale of the goods they import.[179] Chiarenza was also a major exporter of silk cocoons, silk, and kermes collected from its own hinterland and neighboring areas.[180] Significantly, according to a Pisan trade manual of 1278, the units of Lucca were the standard used for the weighing of raw silk in Frankish Morea, which suggests that the Genoese, in view of their role as suppliers of Lucca, were then also the main exporters of silk from the principality.[181] Negroponte too shipped cocoons, silk, and silk fabrics on a fairly large scale to Italy.[182] A Genoese consul is attested in 1236 in the city of Negroponte, which implies Genoese trade and presumably also a resident community there. Genoese merchants are again documented in that city from 1245 to 1251.[183] By 1240 there was a well-established resident Genoese community headed by

---

[173] See Jacoby, "Migration," 121–27.

[174] E.g., by Balard, "Génois en Romanie," 467–89.

[175] See D. Jacoby, "Genoa, Silk Trade and Silk Manufacture in the Mediterranean Region (ca. 1100–1300)," in A. R. Calderoni Masetti et al., eds., *Tessuti, oreficerie, miniature in Liguria, XIII–XV secolo,* Istituto internazionale di Studi liguri, Atti dei Convegni, III (Bordighera, 1999), 16–29, 38.

[176] *Lanfranco,* no. 915. See also above, p. 225.

[177] Mentioned by E. Basso, "Le relazioni fra Genova e gli stati latini di Grecia nei secoli XIII–XIV," in *Studi balcanici: Pubblicati in occasione del VI Congresso internazionale dell'Association internationale d'Etudes Sud-Est Européennes, Sofia, 1989,* ed. F. Guida and L. Valmarin (Rome, 1989), 23, yet this was not silk textile as assumed by the author. Although Asia Minor was included in Romania, silk from that region had other names.

[178] See M. Balard, *La Romanie génoise (XIIe–début du XVe siècle),* vol. 1 (Rome, 1978), 163–64 and n. 211. A Pisan document drafted in Chiarenza in 1317 refers to three Genoese merchants who had apparently been on business there: ed. C. Otten-Froux in M. Balard, A. E. Laiou, and C. Otten-Froux, *Les Italiens à Byzance* (Paris, 1987), 175–77, no. 8.

[179] Pegolotti, *Mercatura,* 117. See also below, p. 228.

[180] See Jacoby, "Silk Production," 46–48, 55 n. 52, 60–61.

[181] R. Lopez and G. Airaldi, eds., "Il più antico manuale italiano di pratica della mercatura," in *Miscellanea di studi storici,* vol. 2 (Genoa, 1983), 127, fol. 360, lines 15–16. See Jacoby, "Migration," 120–21.

[182] Jacoby, "Silk Production," 61, and see also below, p. 228.

[183] See Balard, "Génois en Romanie," 480; Basso, "Relazioni," 24. A sailing contract of March 1254 mentions Negroponte among the ports at which the merchants may unload their goods: ed. E. H. Byrne, *Genoese Shipping in the Twelfth and Thirteenth Century* (Cambridge, Mass., 1930), 125–28, no. 37.

its consul in Thebes, the major center of silk manufacture in Latin Romania. Some time earlier Genoese entrepreneurs had begun to finance production in a number of this city's silk workshops, ordered textiles from others, and exported local fabrics. It follows that the infusion of cash into the economy of Latin Romania and the function of credit were not restricted to the rural sector or to trade, and also affected industrial production. However, by the late thirteenth century Genoese trade in Latin Romania appears to have been on the decline as a result of several developments. The continuous growth of high-grade silk manufacture in Lucca, as well as large-scale Genoese imports of eastern textiles and of high-grade silk from the countries around the Black Sea and the Caspian Sea offered advantageous alternatives to the products of Latin Romania.[184] In this region the Genoese also faced what appears to have been aggressive Venetian competition, backed by the Commune.

Pisans also traded in Latin Romania. They are attested in Frankish Morea from the 1270s, yet appear to have been active there earlier. In 1273 King Charles I of Sicily asked the Moreot prince William II to dispense justice to a Pisan citizen having a claim against one Scottus, apparently an Italian banker. The attention paid by the Pisan trade manual of 1278 to the silk standard of Lucca used in the Morea implies that Pisans too were involved in the export of this commodity to Lucca and other Italian manufacturers, though presumably on a much smaller scale than the Genoese. Pisans are mentioned in Chiarenza in 1303, 1307, and 1313, some of them being apparently settled in that city. The Pisan trade manual compares the measures for grain used in Negroponte and Pisa, which hints at Pisan trade in the island. No later evidence has surfaced until now, yet the continuation of Pisan trade in Byzantium in the Palaiologan period suggests that some activity must also have taken place in the ports of call of Latin Romania located along the maritime routes linking Pisa with Constantinople.[185]

The Venetians were familiar with the territories of Latin Romania ruled by feudal lords, in which they had traded before the Fourth Crusade. As early as 1209 Venice obtained full tax exemptions for its merchants, confirmed subsequently, from the lord of Frankish Morea and those of Euboea.[186] Coron, Modon, and the Venetian quarter of Negroponte depended heavily on the flow of products from their respective hinterlands, ruled by these lords. This explains why Venetian Coron and Frankish Chiarenza used the same light pound for the weighing of silk and kermes.[187] Around 1290 silk and kermes were arriving in Coron from both Venetian and Frankish territory, and this must have been customary for some time already.[188] It is not clear to what extent tax exemptions promoted Venetian penetration inland. Among the products handled, a few deserve particular attention. Since none of the Venetian colonies of Latin Romania pro-

[184] See Jacoby, "Migration," 118–20, and above, note 175. It is likely that Venetian merchants too acted as entrepreneurs in Thebes: see below, note 190.
[185] For Latin Romania: Filangieri et al., *I registri della cancelleria angioina* 10:93, no. 373, and Jacoby, "Migration," 112; above, note 181; R. Predelli, ed., *I libri commemoriali della repubblica di Venezia: Regesti (1293–1787)* (Venice, 1876–1914), 1:26, 80–81, lib. 1, nos. 108, 339, 344; above, note 178; Lopez and Airaldi, "Manuale," 127, fol. 360, line 10. For Byzantium: Otten-Froux in Balard, Laiou, and Otten-Froux, *Italiens* (as in note 178), 159 and n. 36, and documents in ibid., 168–91, nos. 3, 9, 11, 12, 16.
[186] TTh, 2:91, 94, 97, 176, 181, and 3:55.
[187] See Jacoby, "Silk Production," 55 n. 52.
[188] For this period and later, see Jacoby, "Silk Production," 41, 43–47, 55–56, 60–61. See also above, p. 216.

IX

228   *Changing Economic Patterns in Latin Romania*

duced quality silk textiles, Venetian merchants, like others, purchased them in the Peloponnesos, at Thebes, and at Negroponte.[189] Far more important in the long run was their quest for raw silk and dyestuffs. The development of the Venetian silk industry, apparently initiated after the Fourth Crusade, seems to have contributed significantly to the growth of Venetian activity and presence in Frankish Morea and Negroponte.[190] Yet for much of the thirteenth century the Venetian share in the handling of these commodities must have been fairly limited compared with that of the Genoese.

The intensification of long-distance Venetian shipping between Venice and Constantinople, especially from the 1270s, enhanced Venetian trade in the areas situated along the navigation routes. The convoys of state galleys, in service since the early fourteenth century, stopped at Chiarenza, or else some ships were sent there to pick up Venetian merchants and the goods they had bought in Frankish Morea.[191] Such was the case in 1338, in connection with the fair of St. Demetrius. The attendance of Venetians at that fair was by no means exceptional. It illustrates a pattern of penetration inland on quite an impressive scale. The six merchants from prominent families in Venice invested in that trade venture a total of 16,005 hyperpers in woolens and cash.[192] The Venetian silk trade in Patras around 1351 illustrates further expansion.[193] By the mid-fourteenth century the Venetians had consolidated their hold on trade and navigation in the portion of Latin Romania not ruled by the Commune. Genoese sources documenting trade with Chiarenza apparently cease after 1345. Genoa's failure to gain a foothold in the western Aegean, the Genoese occupation of Chios in 1346, and the Venetian-Genoese war of 1350–55 resulted in a shift of Genoese interest to the eastern Aegean.[194] These factors apparently also put a virtual end to Genoese involvement in the economy of continental Greece and neighboring islands.

The late eleventh century witnessed the establishment of a triangular transMediterranean trade network linking Italy with Egypt and Byzantium, as well as these states one to the other. The integration of western Romania within this network was enhanced after the First Crusade by the establishment of the Crusader states in the Levant and the intensification of maritime trade in the eastern Mediterranean. It was further promoted after the Fourth Crusade by the growing impact of Venice on the economy of Latin Romania. Ships engaging in free navigation as well as regular convoys of state galleys sailed from Venice via Modon, Coron, and Negroponte on their way to Constantinople and the Black Sea, and via Modon and Candia on the way to Cyprus, Lesser Armenia, Beirut, and Alexandria.[195] Thirteenth-century Byzantine, Muslim, and Crusader coins, as well as pharmaceutical containers from Egypt found at Corinth illustrate

[189] D. Jacoby, "The Production of Silk Textiles in Latin Greece," in *Technology in Latin-Occupied Greece*, ed. C. Maltezou and H. Kalligas (Athens, 1999), in press.
[190] See D. Jacoby, "Tra Bisanzio, il Levante e Venezia: Dalla materia prima ai drappi nel medioevo," in *Dal baco al drappo: La seta in Italia tra Medioevo e Seicento*, ed. R. Mueller (Venice, 1999), 265–304.
[191] See Stöckly, *Galées*, 101–8, esp. 103, 105.
[192] See above, pp. 215–16.
[193] Gerland, *Quellen*, 33 n.
[194] On the first two aspects, see M. Balard, "The Genoese in the Aegean (1204–1566)," *Mediterranean Historical Review* 4 (1989): 158–62, repr. in Arbel, Hamilton, and Jacoby, *Latins* (as in note 15).
[195] See Stöckly, *Galées*, 96–152, and Jacoby, "Creta," 94–102.

IX

the pivotal location of Latin Romania within the triangular trade network.[196] The sea-borne trade of Latin Romania became subordinated to the requirements, routes, and seasonal rhythm of long-distance maritime trade, increasingly dominated by Venetian merchants and carriers who took advantage of Venice's naval and diplomatic protection and of the infrastructure offered by its colonies and commercial outposts. Short-distance trade and shipping, carried out with small vessels often practicing cabotage, were partly redirected in order to convey goods collected in Latin Romania and neighboring regions to the main ports inserted within the trans-Mediterranean traffic. These same ships also took charge of the diffusion of imported goods.

While the functions of the major transit ports have drawn some attention, their contribution to the economy of Latin Romania itself has been largely overlooked and underestimated. These ports offered infrastructures and services assisting transiting merchants, ships, and goods.[197] Storage and transshipment, the supply of provisions, ship maintenance and repairs performed by qualified craftsmen, as well as money changing and banking provided substantial infusions of cash. The sailing of ships engaged in surveillance and the protection of convoys, naval warfare, piracy, and the recruitment of sailors, archers and crossbowmen, the latter especially in Crete, had similar effects.[198] To these we may add the building and enlargement of arsenals, as in Coron, Modon, Negroponte, and Candia, as well as repeated improvements in harbors that, although not always successful, ensured a flow of public money collected as taxes back into the local economy, instead of being siphoned off to Venice.[199] There is yet another function of transit ports that should be underlined. In addition to handling passing goods, resident merchants also served as middlemen in complex trade ventures between several regions. The function of intermediaries was particularly important in Crete.[200] All these activities generated profits, which were reinvested in Latin Romania's own economy, whether in the rural sector, in trade, or in transportation.

Greeks are clearly underrepresented in the extant, overwhelmingly Western documentation bearing on Latin Romania. The bias is less acute with respect to Venetian Crete beginning in the fourteenth century, in view of the large number of notarial deeds referring to Greeks. It is nevertheless impossible to arrive at a fair evaluation, let alone a quantitative assessment of the Greek share in the region's economy, dominated by the

[196] The coins are recorded in numerous annual reports of the excavations, published in the 1990s in *Hesp.* For the containers, see C. K. Williams II and O. H. Zervos, "Frankish Corinth: 1994," *Hesp* 64 (1995): 16–22.

[197] See F. Thiriet, "Candie, grande place marchande dans la première moitié du XVe siècle," Κρητικὰ Χρονικά 15–16 (1961–62): 343–47, repr. in idem, *Etudes*, no. IX.

[198] On Crete in the Venetian naval defense system, see Thiriet, *Romanie*, 243–51; D. Jacoby, "Les gens de mer dans la marine de guerre vénitienne de la mer Egée aux XIVe et XVe siècles," in *Le genti del Mare Mediterraneo (XVII Colloquio internazionale di storia marittima, Napoli, 1980)*, ed. R. Ragosta (Naples, 1981), 1:172–74, repr. in idem, *Studies*, no. XI; Jacoby, "Creta," 103–5.

[199] On work in harbors, see Hodgetts, "Colonies," 146–51; R. Gertwagen, "The Venetian Port of Candia, Crete (1299–1363): Construction and Maintenance," *Mediterranean Historical Review* 3 (1988): 141–58; eadem, "L'isola di Creta e i suoi porti (dalla fine del XII alla fine del XV secolo)," in Ortalli, *Venezia e Creta* (as above, note 68), 350–74; F. Thiriet, "Réthimo et son district au quinzième siècle," in Πεπραγμένα τοῦ Γ´ Διεθνοῦς Κρητολογικοῦ Συνεδρίου, vol. 2 (Athens, 1974), 305–6, repr. in idem, *Etudes*, no. XVI.

[200] See Jacoby, "Creta," 80–81, 83–84, 92–103, 105–6.

Latins. Fourteenth-century sources point to the growing integration of Greeks within the latter's patterns and networks. They appear as middlemen and wholesalers in local trade, invest in exports, participate in seaborne trade, sail on business to foreign countries, and enter into partnerships with Latins.[201]

It would seem that a decree issued in Crete in 1313 prohibited the exit of Greeks from the island or their sailing to other regions. Their participation in maritime trade would thus have been severely limited. In fact, the purpose of that decree was to prevent the flight of villeins belonging to the Commune, regardless of whether they were indigenous or of foreign origin.[202] It did not deal with villeins attached to landlords.[203] More extensive measures were introduced in 1349 to prevent both slaves and villeins belonging to individuals from leaving Crete and to ensure their arrest, should they reach other Venetian territories, as well as their return to the island.[204] It follows that there were no legal restrictions preventing free Greeks from engaging in maritime trade or in shipping, once the proper administrative formalities before departure had been completed.[205] Indeed, there is abundant evidence showing that Greek merchants, shipowners, skippers, and sailors from Crete participated in exchanges between their island and other areas. Greeks residing in other Venetian territories must have been equally active in this respect, yet the surviving evidence regarding them is fairly restricted. The bulk of Greek maritime activity took place within the Aegean,[206] yet it also extended further. In 1357 a Cretan nobleman, Marco Salamone, shipped more than 15 tons of cheese from Sitia to Cyprus on board the *griparia* of the Greek shipowner Costa Vlissima, who took along more than 5 tons of his own cheese.[207] In 1361 Dimitrius Siropulo from Candia sailed with his own *griparia* from Famagusta to Rhodes.[208] In the first half of the fifteenth century, Greek merchants and ships from Crete fairly regularly reached Alexandria with cargoes of cheese, wine, and other commodities and returned with spices among other goods. In the same period they also exported wine to Constantinople and reached Venice. Moreover, they expanded their activity beyond bilateral exchanges between Crete and the Byzantine capital, sailing from this city to Caffa in the Crimea, Cyprus, and Beirut, and via Crete also to Messina. In addition, Greek merchants and ships from Latin

---

[201] See A. E. Laiou, "Quelques observations sur l'économie et la société de Crète vénitienne (ca. 1270–ca. 1305)," in *Bisanzio e l'Italia: Raccolta di studi in memoria di Agostino Pertusi* (Milan, 1982), 177–98, esp. 193 ff, repr. in eadem, *Gender*, no. x; eadem, "Venetians and Byzantines: Investigation of Forms of Contact in the Fourteenth Century," Θησαυρίσματα 22 (1992): 33–35.

[202] *Bandi*, no. 8: "nullus villanus comunis tam terrigena quam forensis." The villein was allowed to reside in Candia or in the countryside, "sicut sibi placuerit," without fear of being considered the villein of a military settler, "et non timeat capi pro villano militum." Since state villeins enjoyed freedom of movement within Crete, it was more difficult to prevent their escape from the island.

[203] On the distinction between the two categories of villeins and on the legal limitations imposed upon them, see above, note 25.

[204] P. Ratti Vidulich, ed., *Duca di Candia: Quaternus consiliorum (1340–1350)*, Fonti per la storia di Venezia, Sez. I, Archivi pubblici (Venice, 1976), no. 233, esp. p. 131.

[205] Two sailing permits referring to this decree, issued by the Cretan authorities in 1356 and 1368, have been published by Gaspares, Ναυτιλιακὴ κίνησῃ, 289–90 nn. 9 and 8, respectively.

[206] Ibid., 287–318, on 14th-century Greek shipping from Candia and Canea; an earlier example of Greeks from Modon in TTh, 3:236–37.

[207] On this transaction and numerous others of Marco Salomone, see Gallina, *Società*, 99–100, 119.

[208] A. Lombardo, ed., *Nicola de Boateriis, notaio in Famagosta e Venezia (1355–1365)*, Fonti per la storia di Venezia, Sez. III, Archivi notarili (Venice, 1973), no. 125.

Romania reached Dubrovnik, and traders also traveled to Barcelona on their way to Saragossa in Spain, though it is unclear on which ships. In short, by the fourteenth century the Greeks were firmly inserted within the geographic pattern of Latin Romania's seaborne trade, with certain limitations.[209] The activity of these Greeks calls for a few remarks. It was generally based on relatively small amounts of capital and conducted with the help of small and medium-sized ships having a limited carrying capacity, manned by Greek or mixed crews.[210] Greeks only seldom participated directly in trans-Mediterranean traffic and, in any event, were totally excluded from commercial patterns sponsored by the Venetian government and directly subject to its control. The transportation of precious goods on board state galleys and the leasing of these ships were the exclusive preserve of Venetian citizens. It is therefore obvious that, despite their numbers, in terms of capital turnover and profits the Greeks of Latin Romania had a fairly limited share in medium and especially in long-distance maritime trade. Nevertheless, some of them based in the major transit ports greatly benefited from the general increase in economic and maritime activity and managed to accumulate considerable wealth in related activities, such as banking. Çan Cremolisi, a Greek resident of Coron, provided loans totaling 35,000 gold ducats to the lord of Corinth, Nerio Acciaiuoli, the reimbursement of which he sought for several years after the latter's death in 1394.[211] In the first half of the fifteenth century, high officials of Byzantine Morea were depositing valuables and cash in Coron and Modon in private banks operated by Greeks, who used the same sophisticated commercial techniques as their Latin counterparts.[212] In the same period a Greek family, the Filomati from Crete, settled in Venice and adopted a business strategy resting on the dispersal of its members, as commonly practiced by Venetian mercantile families, positioning some in Crete and one in Constantinople. Incidentally, some prominent Byzantine families appear to have acted in the same way both with respect to the Byzantine provinces and the cities of Latin Romania, namely, Venetian Coron and Modon.[213]

So far we have noted two important economic functions fulfilled by Latin Romania

[209] On this pattern, see Jacoby, "Venezia d'oltremare," 272–73; idem, "Cretan Cheese," 57–60; idem, "Creta," 83–84; S. Borsari, "Ricchi e poveri nelle comunità ebraiche di Candia e Negroponte," in Maltezou, Πλούσιοι (as above, note 144), 213–14, 216–18, on Cretan Jews providing maritime loans for trade with Cyprus, Alexandria, the Aegean islands, and Venice, partly on board Greek ships; B. Krekić, Dubrovnik (Raguse) et le Levant au moyen âge (Paris, 1961), 99–100, 103, 125–50; Gallina, Società, 123–27.
[210] See Gaspares, Ναυτιλιακή κίνηση, 293–305 (tables), and for a mixed crew with the sailors' names, ibid., 289–90 n. 9; mixed crew also on a small Venetian ship around 1270: TTh, 3:274–75. Further examples of small vessels appear above.
[211] See J. Chrysostomides, "Merchant versus Nobles: A Sensational Court Case in the Peloponnese (1391–1404)," in Πρακτικὰ τοῦ Δ' Διεθνοῦς Συνεδρίου Πελοποννησιακῶν Σπουδῶν (1992–93), 2:116–31, and for the documents, see now Chrysostomides, Monumenta, 626, General index, s.v. "Cremolisi, Court case."
[212] See K.-P. Matschke, "Geldgeschäfte, Handel und Gewerbe in spätbyzantinischen Rechenbüchern und in der spätbyzantinischen Wirklichkeit: Ein Beitrag zu den Produktions- und Austauschverhältnissen im byzantinischen Feudalismus," Jahrbuch für Geschichte des Feudalismus 3 (1979): 187–88; idem, "Griechische Kaufleute am Übergang von der byzantinischen Epoche zur Türkenzeit," in Lauer and Schreiner, Kultur Griechenlands (as in note 7), 78–79.
[213] Ibid., 77–78; Matschke, "Geldgeschäfte," 195–96; on the Filomati, see now D. Jacoby, "I Greci ed altre comunità fra Venezia ed oltremare," in I Greci a Venezia, nel V centenario della fondazione della comunità greca, ed. M. F. Tiepolo (Venice, 2000), in press; for the Latins, see D. Jacoby, "La dimensione demografica e sociale," in Cracco and Ortalli, Storia (as above, note 149), 2:703.

within the Mediterranean trade system: as a source of foodstuffs, raw materials, and semi-finished or finished products, and as a supplier of services to trade and shipping operations. In addition, the region was also a market for Western goods. Though concentrated in specific locations, the Latins remained a small minority in the midst of the Greek population. In particular within their upper ranks, this may have sharpened their awareness of the evolving attitudes, lifestyle, and consumption patterns of their peers in the West. Their approach in this respect stimulated the demand for Western manufactured goods, especially high-grade products serving as status symbols. This demand, also enhanced by a rise in the standard of living and a refinement in taste, was not confined to members of the knightly class in the feudalized territories of Latin Romania.[214] It also extended to the social elite in Venetian territories. In Crete, members of the Venetian elite granted their daughters dowries "according to the custom of the noblewomen of Venice."[215] Furthermore, conspicuous consumption was widespread among Latin commoners, Greeks and Jews alike. The display of luxury among prosperous Cretans prompted the Venetian authorities to publish in 1339 sumptuary laws regarding dress and jewelry, though with little effect.[216]

The rising volume of medium and high-grade consumption is evidenced by various imports, which partly enabled Western merchants to finance their purchases in Latin Romania. Fine ceramics manufactured in southern Italy, the Veneto, and Pisa, as well as Italian glassware found in recent excavations, reached Corinth from the 1260s.[217] They reflect the range of commercial exchanges of this city with Italy and the activity of south Italian, Venetian, and Florentine merchants, already encountered above. We have already noted in passing the woolens brought by Genoese and Venetian merchants to Chiarenza.[218] Among the luxury items imported to Crete in the 1370s, we find fine Flemish woolens and Italian silk textiles, most of which were presumably Venetian products.[219] In 1444 the eighteen-year-old Quirina, daughter of Alexios Kallergis, ordered from Venice a gold-interwoven silk garment costing between 90 and 100 ducats, as well as expensive pieces of velvet.[220]

These growing imports were not only related to the impact of Western consumption patterns and fashions on local demand. They were also connected with, and even enhanced by, the state of textile manufacture in Latin Romania itself. To be sure, the

[214] See D. Jacoby, "Knightly Values and Class Consciousness in the Crusader States of the Eastern Mediterranean," *Mediterranean Historical Review* 1 (1986): 158–86, repr. in idem, *Studies*, no. I.

[215] See S. McKee, "Households in Fourteenth-Century Venetian Crete," *Speculum* 70 (1995): 40–41.

[216] J. Jegerlehner, "Beiträge zur Verwaltungsgeschichte Kandias im XIV. Jahrhunderts," *BZ* 13 (1904): 464–65, para. 14–22. On sums above 500 hyperpers appearing in contracts regarding Latin, Greek, mixed Latin-Greek, and Jewish marriages, see McKee, "Households," 40–41, 46, 50–51; M. Gallina, "Diversi livelli di ricchezza e di penuria negli atti matrimoniali rogati a Candia nel corso del secolo XIV," in Maltezou, Πλούσιοι (as above, note 144), 268, 272, 280–91.

[217] See esp. Williams and Zervos, "Frankish Corinth: 1994," 16–24. See also A. Oikonomou-Laniado, "La céramique protomajolique d'Argos," in *La ceramica nel mondo bizantino tra XI e XV secolo e suoi rapporti con l'Italia*, ed. S. Gelichi (Siena, 1997), 307–16.

[218] See above, pp. 226, 228.

[219] See S. Borsari, "Il mercato dei tessuti a Candia (1373–1375)," *Archivio veneto*, 5th ser., 143 (1994): 5–30.

[220] See C. Maltezou, Βενετικὴ μόδα στὴν Κρήτη (Τα φορέματα μίας Καλλεργοπούλας), in *Byzantium: Tribute to Andreas N. Stratos* (Athens, 1986), 1:139–47, esp. document on pp. 145–46.

Theban silk industry was stimulated in the first half of the thirteenth century by Genoese and possibly also other Latin merchant-entrepreneurs, as noted above, yet it is not clear how long this support lasted. While silk textiles of Latin Romania continued to be exported to the West in the fifteenth century, they faced mounting competition from the high-grade products of the expanding Venetian and Luccan silk industries, which availed themselves of advanced technologies. The growing import of Italian silks into Romania reversed an age-old trend: instead of being exclusively the supplier of the West, Romania had also become its customer. Both foreign and local merchants increasingly viewed Latin Romania as a source of industrial raw materials for Western industries, rather than of finished products. The absence of new investments and technology transfers prevented the silk industries of Latin Romania from expanding and upgrading their production in a significant way, and Western imports further undermined their ability to compete.[221] The painted glassware manufactured in Venice for export to Romania from the late thirteenth century must have had a similar effect on some centers of glass production in Latin Romania.[222]

This survey has dealt with large portions of Latin Romania ruled by the Latins for more than two centuries after the Fourth Crusade. The evidence bearing on this region reveals that all the sectors of its economy underwent important structural changes in the period extending roughly to the mid-fifteenth century. The main factors contributing to this evolution were the constant interplay between micro- and macroeconomic factors, as well as between private initiative and political powers; geopolitical developments both within and outside Latin Romania; and, finally, the broader economic systems within which the provinces of the empire conquered by the Latins were integrated. After the conquest the economy of Latin Romania swiftly geared itself to Western demand, yet also took advantage of conjuncture to develop its bilateral exchanges with other regions.[223] Credit was a major factor stimulating a growth in export-oriented products, as well as in short- and medium-range trade and transportation.[224] In this respect, the economy of Venetian Crete appears to have been particularly dynamic, its landholders, peasants, and merchants being more responsive to market incentives than in the feudalized areas of Latin Romania. In addition to the factors just mentioned, the intensification of local, regional, and trans-Mediterranean trade and shipping and the supply of services in their framework generated substantial infusions of cash into Latin Romania, which from major ports trickled through the various sectors of its economy. As a result, the whole region experienced an ever stronger economic interaction between the countryside, the cities and maritime trade, as well as an acceleration of monetary circulation.

---

[221] See Jacoby, "The Production of Silk Textiles."

[222] On this production, see A. E. Laiou, "Venice as a Center of Trade and Artistic Production in the Thirteenth Century," in H. Belting, ed., *Il Medio Oriente e l'Occidente nell'arte del XIII secolo*, Atti del XXIV Congresso internazionale di storia dell'arte, Bologna, 1975 (Bologna, 1982), 2:14–15, 18–19.

[223] More evidence in this respect in Jacoby, "Creta," 80–106.

[224] On credit in seaborne trade, see Gallina, "Finanza," 13–21; idem, *Società*, 111–27.

DALLA MATERIA PRIMA AI DRAPPI TRA BISANZIO, IL LEVANTE E VENEZIA: LA PRIMA FASE DELL'INDUSTRIA SERICA VENEZIANA

Lo sviluppo dell'industria serica veneziana anteriore al 1314, quando la prima ondata di lavoratori e mercanti di seta lucchesi arrivò a Venezia, è stato esaminato sotto diversi aspetti a partire dal secolo scorso[1]. Alcuni studiosi hanno puntato le loro indagini sui drappi superstiti al fine di identificare e datare quelli che possono essere attribuiti a Venezia, basandosi sull'analisi dei materiali impiegati, della lavorazione e della decorazione, impiegando inoltre fonti scritte e figurative. Altri hanno trattato dell'industria serica veneziana e dei suoi prodotti in quest'epoca nel quadro di sintesi cronologiche più ampie[2]. Sinora questi argomenti sono stati dibattuti fra storici dei tessuti, dell'abbigliamento e dell'arte. Così è accaduto anche con l'esame di diversi tessuti e vestiti di seta scoperti negli ultimi anni, che hanno arricchito le nostre conoscenze sui drappi veneziani. Mi pare però che lo storico posto fuori dell'ambito di quegli studiosi possa contribuire ad allargare il campo dell'indagine, proporre un'interpretazione nuova e approfondita delle fonti, tanto scritte quanto materiali, e arrivare a una ricostruzione più completa dell'evoluzione dell'industria serica veneziana prima dell'arrivo dei fuoruscisti lucchesi[3].

A questo scopo è necessario procedere in tre tappe: sottoporre la documentazione scritta conosciuta e utilizzata già da molto tempo a una rilettura diretta, senza l'intermediazione di interpretazioni anteriori; arricchirla con l'aggiunta di fonti a stampa sfuggite alla nostra attenzione e soprattutto di documenti notarili inediti, totalmente ignorati sinora; infine, confrontare le testimonianze scritte con quelle materiali. Sebbene l'insieme delle fonti pertinenti rimanga sfortunatamente molto frammentario, dobbiamo resistere alla tentazione di colmare le lacune con anacronistiche proiezioni all'indietro. Tuttavia per sfruttare a fondo le informazioni e collegarle fra loro è soprattutto indispensabile adottare un approccio nuovo, cioè considerare i tessuti serici prodotti a Venezia e altrove non solo come opere artistiche ma come manufatti, soggetti come gli altri prodotti industriali al gioco delle forze economiche e alle fluttuazioni dei mercati. Inoltre è imperativo estendere il nostro esame all'intero ciclo produttivo, dalla bachicoltura alle materie prime tintorie e dalla tessitura delle stoffe alla loro commercializzazione, ricollocando l'industria serica veneziana sia nell'ambito dell'espansione commerciale e marittima di Venezia nel Mediterraneo, sia nel contesto della produzione italiana di seterie. Solamente così possiamo sperare di trovare risposte verisimili a una serie di domande fondamentali riguardanti le circostanze che favorirono l'avvio e l'espansione dell'industria serica veneziana, il suo finanziamento, la sua organizzazione, la diversificazione dei suoi prodotti e la loro diffusione fino al 1314.

I drappi serici sono attestati a Venezia a partire dal ix secolo. Il testamento del doge Giustiniano Particiaco, dell'829, menziona una pezza di zendado decorata con un ricamo d'oro e di perle. Quello di Orso Particiaco, vescovo di Olivolo, redatto nell'853, cita dei *pallia* o tessuti serici appartenenti alla basilica veneziana di San Lorenzo. È verisimile che già da quest'epoca diverse parti dell'abito cerimoniale dei dogi, ispirato ai modelli bizantini, fossero composte da drappi serici[4]. I Veneziani fornivano seterie bizantine e islamiche del Levante, tra le quali i famosi *tyria purpura*, alle fiere annuali di Pavia. Liutprando, vescovo di Cremona nella seconda metà del x secolo, le *Honorantie civitatis Papie* compilate nel secondo decennio dell'xi secolo, così come altre fonti confermano l'importazione di drappi tramite Venezia. Un decreto del doge Ottone Orseolo (1009-1026) impose lo smercio dei *pallia* solo a Pavia e nella fiera di Pasqua di Ferrara[5]. Per parecchi secoli Venezia fu la principale tappa occidentale di transito e di diffusione delle stoffe seriche originarie del Mediterraneo orientale, seguita al secondo posto da Amalfi[6]. La situazione cambiò nel xii secolo, nel corso del quale Genova estese sempre più il suo ruolo e divenne la principale rivale di Venezia in questo settore[7].

Al contrario di quanto si ritiene comunemente, a Bisanzio non esisteva un monopolio statale sulla fabbricazione o sul commercio dei drappi serici, tranne per certe categorie ristrette di stoffe pregiate. La diffusione degli altri drappi avveniva nel quadro di un mercato libero. Per questo motivo non sorprende che i mercanti veneziani fossero attivi nella città di Tebe già prima del 1071. Tebe era allora il più importante tra i nuovi centri di lavorazione serica dell'Impero Bizantino, in piena espansione per soddisfare una crescente domanda interna. Nel XII secolo, e forse anche prima, Tebe produceva drappi pregiati commissionati per la corte imperiale bizantina, tra i quali ve n'erano alcuni tinti con la porpora estratta dal mollusco *murex*, un colorante carissimo, il cui uso era riservato ai tessuti destinati all'imperatore e ad alcuni dei suoi parenti. Tutte queste stoffe rimanevano evidentemente fuori dal circuito commerciale. Inoltre Tebe era conosciuta per i suoi broccati d'oro, e in particolare per i suoi sciamiti tinti con la grana, un colorante rosso di alta qualità ottenuto dalle femmine gravide del parassita chiamato *kermes* (*coccum ilicis L.*). Fino alla quarta crociata e alla conquista latina di Tebe, avvenuta verso la fine del 1204, ci fu una presenza praticamente continua di Veneziani nella città, alcuni dei quali vi risiedettero per molti anni. Essi erano i soli stranieri autorizzati dal governo bizantino ad acquistare i manufatti tebani di alta qualità. Inoltre compravano drappi in un altro centro serico che stava sviluppandosi in quell'epoca, l'isola di Andro nell'Egeo, che produceva sciamiti, zendadi e altre stoffe. I Veneziani smerciavano una parte dei tessuti nell'Impero stesso ed esportavano gli altri a Venezia, assieme a oggetti serici di merceria[8]. Indicativa a questo proposito è la dote della figlia di Pietro Memmo di Ammiana, sposata nel 1145 a Giacomo Polani, figlio di Domenico e membro di una famiglia appartenente all'élite veneziana. La dote comprendeva diverse pezze di tessuto e passamaneria di seta di Tebe, un abito listato di drappo serico di Andro, due bende e quattro veli di seta di Modone (una città del sud-ovest del Peloponneso) e un abito di zendado di origine non specificata, ma senz'altro bizantino[9]. Notiamo che più tardi troveremo gli stessi tipi di stoffe prodotti a Tebe e ad Andro tra i drappi fabbricati a Venezia.

La creazione degli stati latini nel Vicino Oriente intorno al 1100, connessa alla prima crociata, e l'espansione posteriore del commercio veneziano in questa regione favorirono l'aumento degli acquisti veneziani di seterie. Nel 1153 Venezia otteneva una riduzione delle imposte pagate sulla loro esportazione dal principato di Antiochia[10]. È verisimile che tra queste stoffe fossero inclusi i famosi «diaspri antiocheni», altri tipi bizantini, oltre ai tipi islamici prodotti ad Antiochia e in altri centri serici sottoposti al dominio latino[11]. Sebbene manchino testimonianze dirette, è certo che i Veneziani compravano anche seterie originarie dei laboratori islamici del retroterra levantino, come facevano i Genovesi[12]. Eppure anche nel XII secolo sembra che le stoffe bizantine continuassero a predominare tra le importazioni di drappi a Venezia, come si può dedurre anche dalla produzione serica veneziana del Duecento, che sarà esaminata più avanti.

La preferenza veneziana per i tessuti bizantini era parzialmente legata al loro prestigio. A livello politico c'era a Venezia un'ispirazione diretta dai modelli imperiali. Le seterie avevano un ruolo importante nel cerimoniale dogale e nelle feste pubbliche della città. Come la nave imperiale a Bisanzio[13], anche quella del doge era adornata di seterie. Quando la galea di Enrico Dandolo lasciò Venezia nel 1202, all'inizio della quarta crociata, un padiglione di sciamito vermiglio era teso sopra la testa del doge[14]. L'inventario del tesoro della basilica di San Marco compilato nel 1283 elenca tessuti, cortine e gonfaloni di seta di origine bizantina, ostentati nella chiesa nelle feste maggiori e usati nelle processioni solenni, quando venivano fatti sfilare per la città. Alcune di quelle stoffe, pervenute a Venezia come doni o bottino, erano adorne di motivi imperiali o liturgici intessuti[15]. Altre furono convertite all'uso cerimoniale veneziano con ricami adeguati, come i vecchi vessilli di zendado commemoranti le vittorie veneziane di Tiro e di Chio nel 1124, di Zara nel 1202 e di Costantinopoli nel 1204[16]. Non possiamo determinare l'origine dei gonfaloni rossi inalberati sul Bucintoro, la nave dogale attestata per la prima volta nel 1253, uno dei quali con il simbolo di San Marco[17]. Considerato lo sviluppo cui era giunta a quell'epoca l'industria serica veneziana, di cui parleremo subito, è probabile che almeno alcuni dei gonfaloni fossero stati prodotti a Venezia, così come doveva essere per diversi drappi, vesti e gonfaloni di seta utilizzati nelle processioni[18].

Però il crescente flusso di seterie originarie del Mediterraneo orientale verso Venezia non era legato solamente alla loro funzione politica o religiosa. Esso era connesso a un processo economico e sociale più ampio, che cominciò nell'XI secolo in Italia e si estese progressivamente anche al di là delle Alpi. Attraverso testamenti, elenchi di corredi dotali e atti commerciali si può percepire una crescente domanda di prodotti di lusso importati da lontano, seterie incluse, che non era più ristretta all'élite sociale, ma alimentata da un alzamento del tenore di vita e da un maggiore potere d'acquisto dei ceti medi urbani. Questo fenomeno fu uno dei fattori che diedero l'avvio alla sofisticata industria serica di Lucca, probabilmente intorno al 1160. La manifattura lucchese fu sostenuta dai mercanti e trasportatori genovesi, che assicuravano il suo approvvigionamento di materie prime importandole per via marittima dall'Italia meridionale, dalla Sicilia e dai paesi del Mediterraneo orientale. Già nei primi del Duecento i manufatti lucchesi godevano di larga diffusione in Occidente[19]. È probabile che questo successo e i profitti che i Genovesi traevano dai loro servizi di intermediazione stimolassero i Veneziani a fondare e a sviluppare una loro industria serica.

Tuttavia prima di trattare della produzione dei tessuti dobbiamo considerare un'altra attività, anch'essa basata sulla seta, sebbene di peso minore. Dal 1018 l'isola di Arbe (oggi Rab), vicina alle coste della Croazia, pagava ogni anno a Natale un tributo di 10 libbre di seta di buona qualità al doge di Venezia[20]. Né il luogo di produzione della seta, né l'utilizzazione di questa esigua quantità di materia prima sono conosciute. Forse essa serviva in parte alla preparazione dei fili serici usati nella cancelleria dogale per appendere i sigilli ai documenti. Ma il tributo suggerisce anche l'importazione commerciale di seta su piccola scala. Considerando l'alto costo dei bozzoli di seta, non sorprende che ci fosse sempre stata una tendenza a sfruttare al massimo tutti i materiali prodotti dal baco da seta, comprese le fibre di bassa qualità chiamate «strosi» a Venezia. Queste fibre corte, irregolari e grossolane provengono sia dallo strato esterno dei bozzoli, sia dai bozzoli traforati o uniti[21]. Così come la seta di scarto devono essere filate col fuso o col filatoio, al pari della lana, del cotone e della canapa, prima della loro utilizzazione nella tessitura. A Venezia i merciai vendevano per usi domestici diverse varietà di seta in piccole quantità, oltre ai fili d'oro e d'argento, o affidavano queste materie prime a persone che eseguivano dei lavori su loro commissione[22]. È probabile che Oberto Ianasi o Zanassi fosse uno di questi merciai. Nel 1247 lasciava alla moglie seta di prima e seconda scelta destinata alla vendita, oltre a oggetti nuovi e vecchi fatti con quei due tipi di fibre[23].

Specialmente le donne praticavano a casa il ricamo, la produzione di cordoncini, passamani, bende, nastri e altri simili oggetti di merceria, oltre alla tessitura su telai a licci semplici e alla tessitura a cartoni di cinture, veli, fazzoletti e pezze di tessuto stretto usate per la fabbricazione di borse e guanciali, o applicate su altre stoffe come fregi e liste. A Venezia, così come altrove, molti di questi oggetti di merceria e di questi tessuti stretti erano probabilmente fatti di seta mista a filati di lino, cotone o canapa, al fine di abbassarne il costo, ed erano privi di valore artistico, sebbene ci fosse anche una produzione di pezze di migliore qualità, per esempio con l'impiego di filo d'oro[24]. È importante sottolineare che questi prodotti non attestano la manifattura di tessuti serici di alta qualità[25]. Essi continuarono ad essere fabbricati a Venezia anche quando l'industria serica vi si stava sviluppando nel Duecento, ma sempre in margine ad essa. Ciò è illustrato sia dal capitolare dei merciai sia dalla menzione di «fregi d'oro» veneziani in inventari compilati a Londra e a Roma nel 1245 e 1295[26]. Notiamo che questi lavori non erano organizzati nel quadro di una corporazione, né sottoposti a regolamenti.

La domanda per gli articoli veneziani di merceria non era limitata al mercato interno. Nel 1223 quattro dozzine di borse fatte di porpora, un tipo di drappo di alta qualità, furono rubate a un merciaio di Venezia fuori città, e una grande quantità di bende di seta furono sottratte a un altro merciaio[27]. Un fazzoletto veneziano listato con ricami di seta appare nel Mezzogiorno nel 1256[28]. A Venezia stessa troviamo una borsa di seta ricamata nel 1269[29], e un'altra ancora, assieme a una cintura di seta e argento, nel 1280[30]. Bon da Mosto, che era probabilmente un merciaio, importava seta dalla Grecia e produceva o faceva produrre borse di seta. Prima del 1313 due delle sue serve gli rubarono della materia prima e venti dozzine di borse[31]. È verisimile che tutte le stoffe citate in precedenza fossero di fattura veneziana, perché l'origine precisa di quelle importate è generalmente registrata[32]. Borse, fregi e bende appaiono in una legge suntuaria veneziana del 1299, ma senza indicazione di provenienza[33].

Al contrario del Mezzogiorno, l'Italia settentrionale e centrale esercitò la sericoltura solamente su piccola scala fino al Quattrocento. Come spiegazione di questo fenomeno sono sempre addotte le condizioni climatiche sfavorevoli[34]. Però dobbiamo anche tener conto che per un lungo periodo mancarono forti incentivi per promuovere l'allevamento dei bachi. Prima dello sviluppo delle industrie seriche in Italia l'utilizzazione della seta era ristretta alle produzioni domestiche descritte finora, per le quali erano sufficienti piccole quantità di materia prima locale o importata. Anche dopo l'avvio della manifattura serica su grande scala a Lucca nel XII secolo e più tardi in altre città, gli imprenditori e i tessitori preferirono appoggiarsi alle importazioni di seta per via marittima, che assicuravano un rifornimento più abbondante e costante. Al pari di altri centri serici italiani, Venezia dipendeva da queste importazioni, ma con il vantaggio di avere un accesso diretto alle fonti delle materie prime sfruttando a fondo l'attività dei suoi mercanti e delle sue navi. Le indicazioni generali fornite sinora a questo proposito sono parzialmente sbagliate, e ad ogni modo insufficienti. Una distinzione tra le fonti di approvvigionamento e una cronologia del loro rispettivo contributo sono essenziali per capire lo sviluppo dell'industria serica veneziana.

Soltanto dal Duecento abbiamo indizi diretti e indiretti su arrivi continui di seta a Venezia. Il testamento del 1215 di Pietro da Fano, un mercante veneziano attivo nell'Egeo, menziona seta valutata 270 bisanti saraceni di Gerusalemme. Ne consegue che era stata comprata nel Regno latino di Gerusalemme, dove si utilizzava questa moneta, ed era in transito nella città di Negroponte sulla via di Venezia. Sebbene in questo caso non conosciamo il prezzo per unità di peso, la quantità complessiva di seta nelle mani di quel singolo mercante pare fosse intorno alle 150 libbre sottili veneziane, o 45 chili circa, un ammontare molto più grande rispetto al tributo annuale dovuto da Arbe nel 1018[35]. Nel 1233 il volume di seta a bordo delle navi che tornavano dal Levante a Venezia si era molto accresciuto, al punto da giustificare l'inclusione di questo materiale fra le merci per le quali gli statuti marittimi del doge Giacomo Tiepolo fissavano il nolo di trasporto. La seta levantina appare nello stesso contesto negli statuti marittimi del 1255[36]. Il suo arrivo dalla Siria è menzionato anche nel 1303[37]. Inoltre i Veneziani acquistavano la seta a Laiazzo, divenuta intorno al 1260 il porto maggiore del Regno cristiano della Piccola Armenia, situato nel punto di congiunzione tra l'Anatolia e la Siria. Laiazzo era allora il principale sbocco mediterraneo della via transasiatica continentale[38]. Secondo un manuale di mercatura veneziano, il cosidetto *Zibaldone da Canal*, compilato al più tardi nel 1320, Venezia traeva da Laiazzo seta sottile prodotta nella regione, in parte tinta, così come seta in transito originaria di paesi asiatici più lontani[39]. Tuttavia a Venezia non ci sono tracce della seta cinese come ci sono a Genova[40]. Da Alessandria, Acri e Laiazzo arrivava anche l'indaco, il colorante con cui si copriva lo spettro cromatico dall'azzurro cilestrino al violetto. Una partita di indaco iracheno chiamato «di Bagdado», della migliore qualità e del

valore di 700 lire di denari piccoli, è attestata a Venezia nel 1247[41].
Dal primo Duecento il Levante forniva anche grossi volumi di cenere, a Venezia chiamata «lume gatina», usata nella produzione del sapone e come alcalinizzante in quella delle tinture[42]. L'allume importato dall'Egitto e da Laiazzo serviva da mordente per fissare i coloranti sulle fibre tessili[43].

Sebbene un flusso costante di seta raggiungesse Venezia dal Levante, questa regione non rimase la sua sola fonte di rifornimento. I Veneziani si appoggiavano alle loro estese reti di commerci e di navigazione per ampliare e diversificare progressivamente i rifornimenti della loro industria serica. Sembra che fino al Duecento Bisanzio abbia vietato l'esportazione di fibre di seta verso altri paesi, a meno che essa non fosse autorizzata eccezionalmente da parte degli ufficiali imperiali. Non c'è alcuna testimonianza sulla presenza di seta bizantina a Venezia in quest'epoca. Le condizioni cambiarono radicalmente con l'imposizione del dominio latino sulle provincie occidentali di Bisanzio nel decennio seguente la quarta crociata. I signori feudali latini, così come Venezia, abolirono la politica imperiale restrittiva in campo commerciale e aprirono i loro territori alla penetrazione dei mercanti occidentali. È molto probabile che prima del 1215 Pietro da Fano acquistasse seta anche nelle isole dell'Egeo dove si svolgeva la sua attività mercantile[44]. Nel 1240 Matteo de Manzolo inviò a Venezia da Negroponte, dove risiedeva, seta prodotta nei dintorni di Neopatras per un valore di 213 perperi, del peso di circa 75 libbre sottili. È chiaro che anche la sua attività nell'isola di Andro, grossa produttrice di seta e di drappi serici, era parzialmente legata al commercio della materia prima[45]. La continuità delle esportazioni da Negroponte è confermata da un manuale di mercatura inedito, compilato ad Acri intorno al 1270, che confronta l'unità di peso utilizzata per la seta a Negroponte con la libbra sottile di Venezia. Il manuale fa riferimento anche all'invio a Venezia di «valania» o «vallonea», la ghianda della quercia usata per la preparazione di tinture nere e grigie[46]. Dallo *Zibaldone da Canal* si deduce che nei primi decenni del Trecento l'isola forniva a Venezia bozzoli di seta, grana e vallania[47].

Nel Principato franco della Morea, nel Peloponneso, i Veneziani incontrarono un'aspra concorrenza da parte dei mercanti genovesi e senesi, che rifornivano l'industria serica di Lucca. Un manuale di mercatura pisano del 1278 documenta l'utilizzazione del sistema di pesatura di Lucca nel Principato tanto per la seta quanto per i drappi serici[48]. I piccoli territori veneziani di Corone e Modone, nel sud-ovest del Peloponneso, così come il loro retroterra franco, erano importanti produttori di seta e di grana, grossi volumi dei quali erano esportati a Venezia. Quando nel gennaio del 1263 Ermolao Zorzi morì a Corone, dove si era stabilito da molti anni, lasciò una balla di seta e due balle di grana[49]. L'esportazione di queste materie prime da Corone è bene attestata intorno al 1290[50]. Nel 1306 si parla del loro trasporto da Corone e da altri porti collocati più a ovest in direzione di Venezia[51]. Prima del 1313 il mercante Bon da Mosto importava seta da Corone, dove aveva un fattore[52]. Una partita di grana di Modone fu venduta a Venezia nel 1312[53]. Seta, grana e vallania partivano verso Venezia anche da Chiarenza, il principale porto del Principato della Morea[54]. Il manuale di mercatura di Francesco Balducci Pegolotti, portato a termine tra il 1330 e il 1340, che include anche informazioni sul periodo precedente, fornisce i noli pagati per il trasporto della seta da Negroponte, Corone, Modone e Chiarenza a Venezia a bordo delle galee armate dello stato[55]. Sembra che la Grecia sia divenuta la principale fonte veneziana di seta e di grana nel corso del secondo Duecento, anche se Venezia conquistò la preponderanza commerciale in questa regione solamente più tardi[56].

Venezia importava la seta anche dai territori rimasti sotto il dominio bizantino. Nel 1284 i capitani di due navi che trasportavano gli ambasciatori veneziani a Costantinopoli furono autorizzati a investire 500 lire veneziane ciascuno nell'acquisto di seta e di altre merci nella capitale bizantina[57]. Questa città era allora il principale centro di transito per le sete originarie dei paesi situati attorno al Mar Nero e al Mar Caspio[58]. I Veneziani avevano probabilmente già cominciato a comprare queste sete a Costantinopoli in precedenza. Lo *Zibaldone da Canal* conferma la continuazione di questo traffico nei primi decenni del Trecento, a fianco dell'importazione di seta da Tessalonica[59]. Anche il cosidetto Despotato greco dell'Epiro contribuiva all'approvvigionamento dell'industria serica veneziana. Quando Bartolomeo Cocco morì ad Arta nel 1284, aveva insieme a un altro Veneziano della seta per un valore di 225 lire veneziane[60]. Nel 1313 un sacco di 67 libbre di seta, stimato 167 1/2 soldi di grossi, e quattro sacchi di grana di 225 libbre, del valore di 258 soldi di grossi, furono rubati a Nicolò Moro quando era ad Arta[61].

È probabile che la maggior parte della seta che giungeva a Venezia fosse di prima scelta, anche se la sua qualità differiva secondo la regione di provenienza. Generalmente non sappiamo in quale stadio della lavorazione arrivava, se fosse greggia, cruda, cotta, torta o tinta[62]. Venezia importava anche seta di seconda scelta, che era venduta dai merciai[63]. Abbiamo già visto che queste fibre avevano il nome di «strosi» a Venezia, ma il fiorentino Pegolotti le chiama «filugello»[64]. Al più tardi dall'inizio del XIV secolo una parte di questo materiale trattato a Venezia era ricavata da bozzoli importati, il cui arrivo è attestato per la prima volta nel 1303[65]. La loro origine non è specificata, ma è probabile che provenissero dai territori ex-bizantini sotto dominio latino, poiché abbiamo già incontrato i bozzoli di Negroponte[66]. Ne consegue che a partire da quest'epoca la dipanatura dei bozzoli e la filatura della seta di seconda scelta si facevano nella stessa Venezia, quando ciò era necessario[67]. I dati quantitativi sui carichi di seta destinati a Venezia o arrivati in città sono rari, e perciò non c'è alcuna possibilità di stimare il loro volume complessivo in un determinato anno.

Torniamo adesso indietro al primo Duecento. Ci si può chiedere quale fosse la destinazione finale della seta i cui arrivi a Venezia sono attestati allora. Questo era un periodo di espansione per la manifattura dei drappi serici in Italia. Già prima del 1231 Milano e Modena producevano diversi tipi di tessuti lucchesi. Inoltre nel 1233 alcuni artigiani di queste due città si insediarono a Bologna[68]. È vero che Venezia esportava della seta, come attestato nel suo trattato del 1217 con il re Andrea II di Ungheria, ma probabilmente in piccole quantità[69]. Tuttavia pare escluso che essa approvvigionasse sia Lucca[70], ben rifornita tramite Genova, sia i nuovi centri serici italiani più vicini. Il crescente afflusso di materia prima a Venezia serviva senza dubbio ad alimentare la propria industria serica che, come vedremo subito, era in espansione. Nel secondo Duecento le grosse importazioni di seta determinarono talvolta una sovrabbondanza temporanea. Nel 1281, 1282 e 1283 i volumi di seta del Levante e di seta e grana della Romania, i territori bizantini ed ex-bizantini, accumulatisi a Venezia erano superiori alla capacità di assorbimento dell'industria serica locale. Per decongestionare il mercato e porre rimedio al forte calo dei prezzi di queste materie prime il governo permise eccezionalmente il loro trasporto verso la Provenza e il Maghreb e, nel 1283, per la sola seta, anche verso l'Egitto[71]. La riesportazione si orientava anche in altre direzioni. Nel 1316 un mercante tedesco fu multato per aver tentato di uscire da Venezia con 14 libbre di seta e una quantità di filati d'oro, superiori al volume delle merci che era stato autorizzato a esportare[72]. Una transazione del 1303 tra un lucchese e un altro toscano riguardante della seta di seconda scelta è stata interpretata come un indizio di esportazioni verso Lucca[73]. È più probabile che si trattasse di un'operazione locale, visto che era soprattutto Genova ad assicurare i rifornimenti di seta a Lucca[74]. La situazione in questa città cambiò dopo gli avvenimenti del 1314. Secondo Pegolotti, che scrive tra il 1330 e il 1340, Venezia esportava allora regolarmente della seta a Lucca, Firenze, Nîmes, Montpellier, Parigi, nelle Fiandre e a Londra, ma questo sembra essere uno sviluppo nuovo, avvenuto nel Trecento[75].

Abbiamo visto che le prime testimonianze che suggeriscono degli arrivi continui di seta a Venezia appaiono nel 1215 e nel 1233[76]. Nel periodo che intercorre tra questi anni, nel 1221, troviamo il primo riferimento a una produzione di drappi di alta qualità a Venezia. Già in precedenza Stefanino e Giovanni Bon, «ambo fratres laboratores de cendatis», avevano prodotto degli zendadi[77]. Poiché si tratta di due fratelli, è molto probabile che avessero imparato il mestiere dal padre nella bottega di famiglia, che di conseguenza esisteva già in precedenza. La convergenza cronologica fra le testimonianze sulle crescenti importazioni di seta e sui due tessitori di zendadi permette di datare l'avvio della produzione veneziana di drappi pregiati nel primo o al più tardi nel secondo decennio del Duecento. C'era allora una congiuntura economica e politica particolarmente favorevole a Venezia. La familiarità coi tessuti serici importati dal Mediterraneo orientale permetteva una buona conoscenza delle loro caratteristiche tecniche e artistiche. Il piccolo nucleo di lavoratori coinvolti nella manifattura domestica di oggetti di merceria e di piccole pezze di tessuti serici poteva fornire la manodopera di base per lo sviluppo dell'industria serica, a condizione di essere rinforzato da artigiani esperti nella produzione di stoffe più sofisticate con loro telai e tecnologie avanzate, compresa la tintura della seta. Inoltre si trovavano a Venezia tintori, così come battilori e filaori che concorrevano alla preparazione dei fili d'oro e d'argento utilizzati nella produzione di tessuti broccati. Alla possibilità di assicurare un approvvigionamento abbondante e continuo di materie prime, esaminata in precedenza, possiamo aggiungere l'espansione della domanda di drappi in città e all'estero, sulla quale torneremo subito. Tutti questi fattori erano precondizioni per l'investimento del grosso capitale indispensabile all'avvio e allo sviluppo dell'industria serica veneziana.

Gli avvenimenti della quarta crociata, conclusasi nel 1204 con la conquista latina di Costantinopoli, migliorarono ancora di più le prospettive di sviluppo. Essi provocarono il collasso della base economica sulla quale poggiava l'industria serica della capitale bizantina. La maggioranza dei finanziatori, lavoratori e clienti di questa industria furono rovinati e abbandonarono la città. Con la cessazione della produzione serica a Costantinopoli scompave dal mercato internazionale delle seterie un potente centro di produzione e di esportazione. D'altronde una parte del bottino fatto a Costantinopoli dopo la sua conquista nel 1204 fu trasferito a Venezia[78], dove stimolò la domanda per i drappi serici pregiati. Contribuirono a questo processo anche i mercanti veneziani che commerciavano a Costantinopoli e nella Romania. Alcuni tra loro si stabilirono di nuovo a Venezia dopo molti anni di residenza oltremare. Così fece per esempio Giovanni Martinacio del sestiere di Castello, un grosso mercante insediato a Costantinopoli nell'aprile 1207, che tornò a Venezia un po' prima del 1232. A quell'epoca possedeva zendadi del valore di 25 lire veneziane[79].

Abbiamo già sottolineato l'importanza di un apporto di manodopera esperta in processi di lavorazione sofisticata per avviare l'industria serica veneziana. Un problema da risolvere è la sua origine. L'affermazione spesso ripetuta che una bottega veneziana di drappi serici esisteva a Costantinopoli negli ultimi anni dell'XI secolo è senza fondamento. Essa è basata sull'errata interpretazione di un documento del 1090, col quale il doge Vitale Falier concesse al monastero veneziano di S. Giorgio Maggiore diversi beni dello stato collocati nella capitale imperiale, tra cui alcuni *ergasteria*[80]. Questa voce è la trascrizione del termine generico bizantino *ergasterion*, usato nel senso generale di bottega, senza alcun legame con la seta[81]. Anche un presunto apporto di artigiani dal Levante crociato è da scartare. Nel 1243 Marsilio Zorzi, il bailo veneziano in quella regione, menziona in una relazione i «texarini» o tessitori siriani che risiedevano da molto tempo nel quartiere veneziano di Tiro[82]. Però non esiste alcun indizio che questi artigiani lavorassero la seta, e inoltre se avessero prodotto drappi serici questi avrebbero dovuto essere conformi ai manufatti islamici. I primi tessuti serici attestati come prodotti veneziani, dei quali si parlerà subito, erano invece di tipo bizantino. Infine, prima del Trecento mancano totalmente testimonianze sull'impiego di schiavi nella produzione serica veneziana, e perciò è chiaro che essi non contribuirono alla prima fase del suo sviluppo[83].

Dobbiamo quindi tornare a considerare le conseguenze della conquista latina di Costantinopoli. Pare che molti tessitori di seta siano emigrati da quella città verso i centri serici dell'Asia Minore occidentale, una regione nella quale dopo il 1204 fu creato il cosidetto impero bizantino di Nicea[84]. Tuttavia non è escluso che alcuni tra loro o tessitori provenienti da altri centri serici sotto dominio latino, come Tebe, fossero attratti a Venezia da allettanti proposte di lavoro. Così accadde nell'industria vetraria veneziana del tardo Duecento, quando alcuni artigiani greci si stabilirono a Venezia e vi produssero articoli comuni nella Romania a scopo di esportazione[85]. I vetrai locali impararono le tecniche e i motivi bizantini e li trasmisero ai loro apprendisti. Per questo motivo non troviamo più tracce di greci nell'industria vetraria veneziana dell'epoca posteriore. Sebbene manchino testimonianze simili per la manifattura serica di Venezia, possiamo ipotizzare un processo analogo.

L'iniziativa di compiere un trasferimento di artigiani, attrezzi e tecnologia può essere attribuita senz'altro a mercanti che conoscevano i centri serici bizantini e che disponevano di abbondanti capitali liquidi. Tanto lo stabilimento delle infrastrutture industriali a Venezia quanto il funzionamento dell'industria richiedevano investimenti sostanziosi. L'alto costo delle materie prime, seta e coloranti pregiati importati da lontano (specialmente la grana e l'indaco), e l'uso di filati d'oro o d'argento per i broccati innalzavano notevolmente i costi di produzione. A questi fattori dobbiamo aggiungere il finanziamento della lavorazione, in particolare la tessitura, più complessa e più lunga che nella produzione di altri tessili e perciò più costosa.

Le testimonianze dirette sull'organizzazione economica dell'industria serica veneziana nei primi decenni del Duecento non sono numerose, ma nondimeno danno un'idea approssimativa a questo proposito. Nel 1248 il Maggior Consiglio di Venezia proibì agli ufficiali incaricati di percepire le tasse sullo smercio dei tessuti di seta di acquistarli o di farli acquistare per mezzo di altre persone[86]. In altre parole, gli vietò di approfittarsi delle loro funzioni per stabilire un monopolio di fatto sulla commercializzazione dei tessuti, facendo pressione sui produttori o esentandoli dal pagamento delle tasse al fine di acquistare i loro tessuti a basso prezzo. Inoltre il decreto del 1248 vietava agli ufficiali di produrre essi stessi le stoffe o di farle produrre[87]. È chiaro che questi agenti dello stato non si erano messi improvvisamente a fare gli artigiani. Essi avevano aperto o avevano intenzione di aprire delle botteghe con lavoratori salariati o, assumendo il ruolo di imprenditori, fornivano le materie prime e il capitale necessario al funzionamento di botteghe esistenti in cambio dei loro manufatti. Particolarmente i mercanti coinvolti nell'importazione della seta e dei coloranti, o quelli che avevano sbocchi sicuri per i prodotti finiti, erano in grado di fare gli imprenditori e di concentrare tutte le fasi della lavorazione, tessitura inclusa, in una singola impresa. Un testamento del 1287 nel quale Maria dalle Boccole lascia a tutti i suoi lavoranti 250 lire è stato invocato come illustrazione di una tale bottega. Però l'inclusione in esso di battitori ci fa concludere che non si trattava di lavorazione della seta, ma del cotone o piuttosto della lana[88].

L'attività degli imprenditori era solamente un aspetto del finanziamento della produzione dei drappi serici a Venezia. Il decreto del 1248 conferma l'attività di artigiani autonomi, proprietari di botteghe piccole o medie, alcune di esse familiari, una delle quali era documentata in precedenza. Questi artigiani compravano le materie prime dai mercanti e vendevano loro i propri prodotti. Nel 1221 i fratelli Stefanino e Giovanni Bon, produttori di zendadi in un'impresa familiare, erano debitori di 45 lire veneziane nei confronti del mercante Marco di Bernardo, probabilmente per materie prime ricevute da lui[89]. Nel novembre del 1243 Giovanni della Piçola, abitante nella contrada di S. Giacomo dell'Orio, promise di pagare 87 lire veneziane in sei rate annuali uguali, una somma dovuta per una grossa quantità di seta, che possiamo stimare a 696 libbre sottili, acquistata da Pietro Navager[90]. È chiaro che questa non era una vendita a credito del tipo comune. La transazione aveva avuto luogo poco tempo dopo l'arrivo a Venezia dei convogli marittimi autunnali con a bordo i carichi di seta proveniente dai paesi del Mediterraneo orientale. Il rimborso in denaro esteso su sei anni suggerisce che si tratta di un prestito in materie prime fatto da un mercante a un artigiano, benché quest'ultimo non sia identificato come tale. D'altronde, nel 1305 il mercante Marco Granello era debitore di più di 260 lire «a grossi», o circa 10 lire di grossi, nei confronti di due fratelli che esercitavano la tessitura della seta, ovviamente per drappi ricevuti da loro[91]. Dal secondo Duecento troviamo anche «samitari» o tessitori di seta che avevano accumulato capitali ed erano in grado di partecipare a imprese commerciali estranee alla loro attività artigianale. Nel 1273 Vidoto investì 100 lire veneziane in una commenda con Leonardo Foscarini[92]. Nel 1262 Ottobellino di

Cozzolano acquistò un terreno a Mogliano, una località tra Venezia e Treviso, città quest'ultima in cui prima del 1274 possedeva una grande casa. L'edificio, valutato 2.500 lire, comprendeva diverse botteghe e anche diritti sulle rive del Sile in un luogo di approdo per il traffico con Venezia[93]. Ne consegue che Ottobellino era in grado di finanziare da solo le operazioni della sua azienda e aveva investito una parte del suo capitale a Treviso allo scopo di promuovere la vendita dei suoi prodotti.

Il finanziamento della produzione di drappi poteva avvenire anche nel quadro di associazioni tra tessitori e altri individui. Prima del 1272 il tessitore di seta Salimbene e il sarto Giovanni possedevano un'impresa comune nella parrocchia di S. Marina. In quell'anno i due acquistarono insieme un terreno nella parrocchia di S. Felice che misurava 19,64 × 23,12 metri, con una casa costruita sopra, per 1.288 lire veneziane[94]. Non sappiamo come avessero raccolto questa somma e se si fossero basati solamente su capitale proprio o anche su prestiti, né possiamo determinare come avessero diviso le spese. È probabile che all'inizio della loro associazione il sarto fornisse il locale e i capitali necessari al funzionamento della bottega, mentre il tessitore contribuiva con gli attrezzi per la lavorazione, la sua perizia e la sua opera. Il sarto vendeva i manufatti prodotti dal suo socio sia sotto forma di stoffe sia di abiti cuciti, a richiesta dei clienti. Nel corso del tempo sembra che il tessitore fosse riuscito a mettere da parte un po' di denaro e che fosse diventato un socio investitore, sebbene di minoranza[95]. Ovviamente l'acquisto del terreno aveva come scopo l'allargamento della bottega con l'aggiunta di telai e di lavoratori, e forse anche la concentrazione di diverse fasi della lavorazione. L'esborso di una grossa somma in questa transazione è tanto più sorprendente in quanto i due soci sembrano essere di origine sociale piuttosto modesta. Non avevano cognomi, un tratto comune a molti tessitori di seta e, più generalmente, agli artigiani veneziani del Duecento, al contrario della maggioranza dei mercanti attestati nella documentazione notarile di quest'epoca. Nei primi del Trecento Giacomo di Raynerio e Gerardo Porpora o Porporario avevano stabilito un'associazione di tipo un po' differente. Essi non risiedevano insieme, abitando uno nella contrada di S. Maria Formosa e l'altro in quella di S. Giovanni Grisostomo. Il primo, che non era un artigiano, aveva investito una certa somma nell'impresa, inclusi anche alcuni attrezzi di lavoro. Nel dicembre del 1307 i due sciolsero il loro contratto, ma mantennero la proprietà comune di un grande

X

telaio e della sua attrezzatura anche dopo il 1315, quando il tessitore finì di rimborsare tutti i suoi debiti all'ex-socio[96].

Abbiamo già incontrato nel 1221 una coppia di fratelli che esercitavano insieme la tessitura di drappi di alta qualità, ai quali possiamo aggiungerne altri nel 1292 e nel 1305[97]. È molto probabile che in questi casi i fratelli fossero figli di artigiani, dai quali avevano imparato il mestiere in aziende familiari. Eppure non c'era sempre continuità in questo campo. Nel 1312 un figlio del samitario Lorenzo era zoccolaio[98], mentre il samitario Giacomo Albertino, attestato nel 1315, era figlio di un pellicciaio[99]. Anche la continuità della bottega familiare non significa che la sua localizzazione fosse stabile. La documentazione precedente all'insediamento degli esuli lucchesi a Venezia nel 1314 rivela sia la dispersione sia la mobilità dei samitari nello spazio urbano. Essi erano dispersi in tutti i sestieri della città; nel 1277 uno di loro risiedeva persino nell'isola di Torcello, nella contrada di S. Maria Assunta[100]. Nel 1243 Giovanni della Piçola abitava nella parrocchia di S. Giacomo dell'Orio (S. Croce)[101]. Nel 1262 Ottobellino di Cozzolano risiedeva in quella di S. Giovanni Grisostomo (Cannaregio)[102], e come visto in precedenza Salimbene e il suo socio, il sarto Giovanni, si spostarono nel 1272 dalla contrada di S. Marina (Castello) a quella di S. Felice (Cannaregio)[103]. Nel 1272 i tessitori Martino e Nascimbene lavorano drappi auroserici nella parrocchia di S. Bartolomeo (S. Marco)[104]. Prima del 1273 Angelo era insediato nella contrada di S. Gervasio (Dorsoduro)[105], Vidoto nello stesso anno viveva in quella di S. Lio (Castello)[106], e anche un altro stava lì, mentre nel 1280 un terzo abitava nella contrada di S. Sofia (Cannaregio)[107]. Due fratelli già menzionati risiedevano nella contrada di S. Marina (Castello) nel 1292[108], e due anni più tardi un altro tessitore in quella di S. Marcuola (Cannaregio)[109]. Nel 1301 troviamo samitari nelle contrade di S. Salvador (S. Marco) e S. Giacomo dall'Orio (S. Croce)[110], e nel 1305 in quella di S. Felice (Cannaregio)[111]. Negli anni 1312-1315 ce n'erano altri nelle contrade di S. Trinità (Castello), S. Samuele e S. Vidal (S. Marco), S. Ermagora e SS. Apostoli (Cannaregio), S. Agostin e S. Polo (S. Polo)[112].

Purtroppo i documenti veneziani si riferiscono all'origine dei drappi quasi solamente quando citano stoffe forestiere. Perciò non possiamo identificare con sicurezza i prodotti dell'industria serica veneziana, a meno che non siano menzionati esplicitamente. Considerando la produzione di zendadi a Venezia prima del 1221[113], non

280

è da escludere che già nel 1219 i sarti veneziani cucissero abiti con zendadi di produzione locale. Notiamo che questo tipo di tessuto serico è il solo citato allora nel loro capitolare[114]. Similmente, è possibile che almeno in parte le pezze e gli abiti di zendado rubati nel 1223 a parecchi mercanti di Venezia nel territorio di Ferrara o trovati nel 1225 in un negozio di Rialto fossero manufatti veneziani[115]. Nel 1224 tre sciamiti intessuti d'oro furono confiscati a un mercante veneziano in transito ad Ancona, e nel 1227 c'è un riferimento a un drappo auroserico e a uno zendado posseduti a Venezia[116]. Stranamente, la prima attestazione diretta di un drappo veneziano appare in una fonte straniera, un conto del 1247 della corte reale inglese. Esso stabilisce un pagamento di 23 scellini e 4 pence per una pezza di seta bianca, cioè monocroma, di Venezia, che era stata utilizzata per la confezione di una pianeta offerta alla chiesa di S. Pietro di Westminster[117]. È vero che questa menzione di un drappo veneziano è isolata, mentre troviamo parecchi riferimenti a drappi venduti da mercanti lucchesi, che possiamo considerare come manufatti della loro città a meno che non sia indicata un'altra provenienza. Forse la presenza più marcata dei drappi di Lucca nella capitale inglese era dovuta alla loro qualità superiore rispetto a quelli veneziani, ma essa può anche essere attribuita alla funzione dominante dei lucchesi sul mercato londinese delle seterie degli anni Quaranta del Duecento e alla loro preferenza per lo smercio di tessuti della loro città[118]. Infatti la pezza di drappo veneziano citata in precedenza fu venduta alla corte reale da Ranieri da Lucca, un mercante molto attivo nel commercio dei drappi nella capitale inglese. A questo proposito è utile notare che l'attività dei mercanti lucchesi a Venezia è documentata dagli anni Venti del Duecento, e che Luca da Lucca era insediato nel 1233 nella parrocchia veneziana di S. Cancian[119].

Ovviamente la corte reale inglese non era il solo acquirente di drappi a Londra nel 1247, e dunque è certo che la pezza veneziana non era l'unica disponibile allora su quel mercato. Ciò suggerisce che l'industria serica veneziana si fosse già sviluppata da molti anni, permettendo ad alcuni suoi manufatti di sostenere la concorrenza con le seterie prodotte altrove. Questo sviluppo è confermato nel 1248, l'anno seguente al documento inglese, dal decreto del Maggior Consiglio di Venezia citato in precedenza. Questo decreto menziona «pannos ad aurum, purpuras et cendatos»[120]. Possiamo identificare due di queste categorie di tessuti, i drappi auroserici e gli zendadi, mentre la natura delle *purpure* resta sconosciuta. A quest'epoca il termine non indicava più una stoffa di color porpora, ma un tipo di drappo dalla lavorazione particolare[121]. Sfortunatamente dai regolamenti di epoca posteriore, per esempio quelli lucchesi del 1376, non possiamo dedurre né la composizione né la lavorazione delle porpore verso il 1248, visto che in questi settori ci fu un'evoluzione costante nella fabbricazione dei tessuti serici italiani[122]. Notiamo che la delibera di quell'anno non cita gli sciamiti, un'omissione a prima vista sorprendente. Sebbene la prima testimonianza sulla produzione veneziana di drappi, del 1221, faccia riferimento agli zendadi[123], è verisimile che all'inizio del suo sviluppo l'industria serica veneziana producesse soprattutto sciamiti, al punto che a Venezia la parola *samito* divenne un termine generico per designare i drappi, come nel capitolare dei giubbettieri del 1219[124], e che i tessitori di drappi erano chiamati samitari, o samiteri nel linguaggio locale.

Il *Capitulare samitariorum* del 1265, una raccolta statutaria dell'arte dei tessitori di seta, è il più importante e dettagliato documento riguardante l'industria serica veneziana del Duecento, comprendendo regolamenti sulla natura, la qualità e l'uso delle fibre, il numero complessivo dei fili di ordito, le norme di lavorazione, oltre alla larghezza minima e alla lunghezza dei diversi tipi di tessuti[125]. Esso riflette uno stadio avanzato di organizzazione e di funzionamento dell'industria, capace di produrre una varietà di drappi sofisticati, e poiché era una versione emendata di regolamenti anteriori queste caratteristiche erano valide già prima del 1265. Il capitolare elenca sette categorie di tessuti, cioè *panni, catasamiti, sarantasimi, purpure, diaspri, meçanelli* e *samiti contrafacti*[126]. Come nel decreto del 1248, anche in questo documento mancano gli sciamiti, benché si faccia riferimento a due loro varietà, i *catasamiti* e i *samiti contrafacti*, dei quali parleremo subito[127]. Nel contesto di questo elenco la voce *panni* copriva probabilmente quella di sciamiti, sebbene sia utilizzata nel capitolare anche nel senso generale di drappi. Anche gli zendadi mancano nel capitolare del 1265. È improbabile che la loro produzione a Venezia, attestata già nel 1221, fosse stata sospesa, visto che nel capitolare dei merciai del 1278 la voce zendadi è usata quale termine generico per indicare i tessuti di seta, come a Lucca[128]. I *sarantasimi*, dal termine bizantino *exarentasmata*, sono citati in una lettera del 1189 riguardante i manufatti degli opifici stabiliti nel palazzo reale normanno di Palermo[129]. Al pari del termine *purpure*, anche quello di *diaspri* non riflette più come all'origine un colore, il bianco in questo caso, ma un tipo di lavorazione di tessuti monocromi tinti anche in altre tonalità[130]. Insomma, l'elenco dei tessuti del 1265 non concorda con quello del 1248, eccetto per le porpore.

Secondo il cronista Martino da Canal le arti veneziane ostentarono i loro migliori manufatti nella festa del 1268 in onore del neoeletto doge Lorenzo Tiepolo. I tessitori di seta si vestirono di drappi auroserici e i loro inservienti di porpore e di zendadi. Gli abiti dei maestri pellicciai, foderati di ricche pellicce, erano di sciamito e di zendado scarlatto, ovviamente anch'essi di produzione locale[131]. È significativo che nella prima di queste descrizioni il cronista si riferisce agli stessi tre tipi di tessuti menzionati nel decreto del 1248, nonostante scriva dopo la promulgazione del capitolare dei samitari del 1265. Ne consegue che la terminologia di questo capitolare non riflette un allargamento della gamma dei prodotti nello spazio di pochi anni, dal 1248 al 1265. Trattando di problemi tecnici, i redattori del capitolare e i tessitori non potevano accontentarsi dei nomi di grandi categorie di tessuti e preferirono utilizzare una terminologia più precisa. Anche questa, comunque, rimase fluttuante nei documenti ufficiali veneziani del Duecento e pone grossi ostacoli all'identificazione dei tessuti serici e alla datazione del loro inserimento nel ciclo di produzione a Venezia.

Tanto il termine generico di *samitarii* quanto i nomi di cinque categorie di stoffe citate nel capitolare del 1265, cioè *catasamiti, sarantasimi, purpure, diaspri* e *samiti*, sebbene modificati, sono di origine bizantina[132]. Queste stoffe sono conosciute come prodotti di alta qualità dell'industria serica bizantina. Gli artigiani bizantini deportati nel 1147 da Tebe e da Corinto a Palermo vi introdussero la fabbricazione di alcuni di questi tessuti[133]. D'altra parte l'impato bizantino sui manufatti serici veneziani, illustrato anche nel campo del linguaggio ornamentale[134], non esclude influenze posteriori da altre regioni, come vedremo più avanti. Tuttavia in due settori i drappi veneziani si staccarono dai prototipi bizantini. I *sarantasimi* si facevano in due versioni, una di tutta seta e un'altra di seta mista ad altri materiali. Quanto ai *samiti contrafacti* dei capitolari, essi erano imitazioni veneziane degli sciamiti bizantini, ovviamente con certe caratteristiche particolari[135]. Dunque è chiaro che già prima del 1265 i tessitori di seterie veneziani avevano introdotto nuovi tipi di drappi nel loro ciclo di produzione, uno sviluppo confermato anche dall'esame dei regolamenti riguardanti certe stoffe e dall'analisi di diversi drappi superstiti. Inoltre, notiamo che i tintori veneziani non

X

utilizzarono mai la porpora del *murex*, troppo cara per i tessuti destinati a una diffusione commerciale. Ad ogni modo sembra che la produzione di questo colorante fosse sospesa nella Romania dopo la caduta di Costantinopoli nel 1204[136]. Per ottenere il color porpora i Veneziani usavano miscele di coloranti alternativi, come si faceva a Bisanzio già prima di quella data[137]. In generale sembra che i tessitori veneziani utilizzassero dei filati colorati, ma stoffe monocrome non operate potevano anche essere tinte dopo la lavorazione. In certi casi i drappi erano venduti prima della tintura, ed era il cliente a portarli al tintore dove poi faceva la scelta dei colori[138].

L'introduzione dei nuovi tipi di drappi prodotti a Venezia impone alcune considerazioni generali. Anche se all'inizio del suo sviluppo l'industria serica veneziana lavorava soprattutto per soddisfare la domanda locale, presto estese il suo raggio d'azione verso i mercati esteri. Tuttavia la commercializzazione dei manufatti veneziani in Occidente si scontrava con due notevoli ostacoli. Il primo era costituito dall'aspra concorrenza dei manufatti di altri centri serici, il secondo dalla mancanza di una propria rete di distribuzione continentale, dal momento che in questo campo Venezia dipendeva largamente dall'attività dei mercanti stranieri che visitavano la città. Lucca era senz'altro la principale rivale di Venezia. Essa era entrata nel ciclo di produzione dei drappi di alta qualità con circa mezzo secolo d'anticipo, e nel primo Duecento produceva diversi tessuti che godevano di un'ampia diffusione, promossa dai suoi mercanti e da intermediari genovesi fino alle fiere della Champagne e ancora più in là fino a Londra, così come verso la Spagna e l'Asia Minore bizantina[139]. Anche i drappi prodotti in Spagna godevano di una larga diffusione nell'Occidente del Duecento[140]. D'altra parte, mentre Venezia produceva drappi continuava anche a importare dal Mediterraneo orientale diverse categorie di seterie bizantine e islamiche, destinate sia al mercato interno sia alla riesportazione. Nel 1223 tre veneziani compravano a Modone parecchie pezze di seterie, probabilmente manufatti del Peloponneso, per venderle a Venezia[141]. Alcuni dei mercanti veneziani attivi a Tebe erano probabilmente coinvolti come imprenditori nella produzione locale di drappi serici, al pari dei loro rivali genovesi, ed esportavano i prodotti dei laboratori che finanziavano. L'invio di seterie da Negroponte a Venezia è attestato negli anni Settanta del Duecento[142]. Inoltre Venezia importava molti drappi serici dal Levante. Tra quelli lasciati in eredità dal doge Raniero Zeno nel 1268 troviamo una pezza di zendado proveniente da Tripoli di Siria[143]. Nel secondo Duecento c'era in Occidente una crescente domanda per diversi tipi di seterie islamiche e orientali pregiate, i cosidetti *panni tartarici*[144]. Nel 1283 il mercato veneziano fu inondato di sciamiti e di altri drappi importati dagli stati crociati del Levante, al punto da indurre il governo a permetterne la riesportazione verso il Mediterraneo occidentale[145].

Queste circostanze spiegano un originale adattamento dell'industria serica veneziana alle esigenze del mercato. Invece di fare concorrenza ad altri centri serici nella produzione di seterie pregiate e carissime, indirizzate a un mercato ristretto, gli imprenditori, tessitori e mercanti veneziani decisero di competere sul versante della diffusione con il lancio di una nuova gamma di tessuti. A più riprese il capitolare dei samitari del 1265 vieta la mescolanza di altre fibre alla seta nella manifattura dei drappi e insiste sull'obbligo di utilizzare lo stesso genere di materiale per garantire la qualità costante della pezza[146]. A torto alcuni studiosi hanno interpretato questi regolamenti come una proibizione di produrre tessuti misti[147]. Eppure l'uso del termine *tutaseta* e la distinzione fra i tessuti di seta e quelli *de açis*, come per i *sarantasimi*, conduce alla conclusione opposta: già prima del 1265 Venezia fabbricava tessuti misti con ordito di lino o di canapa, la proibizione toccando solamente la mescolanza di materiali diversi nella trama dei tessuti[148].

Nel 1317 i tessuti misti veneziani *de açis* appaiono nei conti delle spese fatte per l'incoronazione del re di Francia Filippo V, detto il Lungo, sotto il nome di *draps d'ache*, termine sostituito con *draps de Venise* a proposito dell'incoronazione della regina. Il prezzo pagato nei due casi era di 55 *sous* la pezza, di molto inferiore a quello dei *draps de Luques* e *draps de Turquie*, che probabilmente erano di pura seta[149]. L'anno seguente un altro conto reale francese menziona lo stesso tipo di tessuto misto, ma con riferimento esplicito alla sua composizione: «ij draps à or sus chanvre, de Venise», o due drappi auroserici con ordito di canapa, originari di Venezia[150]. È molto probabile che tra le mezze sete dobbiamo anche includere il «drap d'or de Venise» citato in un elenco di tasse imposte sulla vendita di merci a Parigi, attribuito da uno studioso al 1296 e da un altro al 1324 o al 1337. Malgrado l'impiego di filo d'oro nella sua tessitura, la tassa pagata per questo tipo di drappo era uguale a quella imposta su una pezza di zendado forte di pura seta[151]. Come si può dedurre dal loro nome, anche i *meçanelli* o mezzanelli erano tessuti misti, probabilmente leggeri visto che potevano servire come fodere[152]. L'utilizzazione di fibre più semplici, più grosse e meno numerose di quelle di seta e la loro lavorazione più rapida nell'ordito abbassavano il prezzo dei tessuti e ne stimolavano la vendita. Sebbene non fossero di pura seta, le mezze sete erano di alta qualità. Esse allargavano la clientela dei prodotti serici veneziani e gli permettevano di conquistare nuovi mercati. L'approccio dinamico dei Veneziani in questo campo si rivelò giustificato, come vedremo più avanti.

Le mezze sete erano fabbricate da molto tempo a Bisanzio, nei paesi musulmani dell'Asia e in Spagna[153]. L'imitazione di questi tessuti a Venezia non urtava contro grossi ostacoli sul piano della lavorazione. Anche quando la diversificazione della produzione serica imponeva l'adozione di innovazioni tecniche, come il telaio al tiro utilizzato per la manifattura dei tessuti operati, non necessitava un apporto di manodopera straniera come per l'avvio dell'industria serica veneziana. La perizia acquisita sia dai mercanti sia dai tessitori veneziani nel corso del Duecento bastava. Molti mercanti veneziani coinvolti nel commercio marittimo avevano dimestichezza con i drappi stranieri, e specialmente quelli che visitavano le botteghe di tessitori di seta all'estero erano in grado di fornire informazioni utili per la costruzione dei telai e di altri attrezzi, così come per la lavorazione dei drappi. L'analisi dei tessuti forestieri da parte dei tessitori veneziani esperti poteva condurre agli stessi esiti o a risultati perfino migliori. Un tale processo è illustrato a Venezia nel secondo Trecento, quando alla richiesta di un mercante un tessitore preparò un modello di broccato d'oro a imitazione di un drappo orientale[154].

Donald King ha attribuito a Venezia e identificato come mezze sete del Duecento un gruppo di drappi operati, alcuni citati solo nelle fonti e altri ancora esistenti. King si basa su diversi criteri, cioè le materie impiegate nel caso dei tessuti superstiti e, per tutti, la loro lavorazione e misure, il loro linguaggio ornamentale di tipo bizantino con scene figurative o con motivi animali o vegetali, sia larghi sia contenuti in ruote tangenti a doppio contorno, la loro impaginazione, e inoltre lo stile e i colori utilizzati. L'origine veneziana è sicura per alcune di queste stoffe, descritte in inventari medievali in modo esplicito come provenienti da Venezia, mentre le altre dimostrano un'affinità con esse. La collocazione o la conservazione di diverse stoffe appartenenti a questo gruppo in Germania o in Scandinavia, regioni privilegiate per la diffusione delle merci provenienti da Venezia, esclude praticamente una provenienza italiana diversa da quella veneziana[155]. Le mezze sete attribuite a Venezia che fornisco-

X

no punti di riferimento cronologici precisi sono particolarmente preziose per il nostro proposito. Un *baudekyn* o drappo auroserico con una rappresentazione della Natività entrò nel tesoro della cattedrale inglese di Durham nel 1260[156]. Se la sua provenienza veneziana è corretta, ne consegue che Venezia produceva mezze sete con decorazione complessa già prima del 1260. Una tale datazione è corroborata dalla menzione di questo tipo di drappo nel capitolare del 1265 che, come notato sopra, era in parte una revisione di regolamenti anteriori. Forse anche lo sciamito bianco monocromo incontrato a Londra nel 1247 era una mezza seta, visto che il suo prezzo era piuttosto basso se paragonato a quello di altri drappi venduti a Londra intorno a quell'anno[157]. Però dobbiamo tener presente che i prezzi o le tasse sulla vendita non forniscono sempre indizi sicuri sulla qualità delle stoffe, perché generalmente non conosciamo le misure delle pezze. La continuazione della produzione delle mezze sete a Venezia è illustrata da due *baudekyns* raffiguranti S. Pietro, offerti alla cattedrale di St. Paul di Londra, uno nel 1271 e l'altro nel 1299[158]. Diversi tessuti con altri personaggi sono registrati nell'inventario del tesoro pontificio di Perugia compilato nel 1311[159], ai quali possiamo aggiungere le mezze sete attestate a Parigi nei primi decenni del Trecento, cui abbiamo accennato sopra.

È emblematico che il solo esempio concreto di drappo di manifattura indubbiamente veneziana sia una mezza seta. Si tratta di un grande telo ritrovato nel sarcofago del beato Giacomo Salomoni, un domenicano veneziano sepolto a Forlì nel maggio del 1314. Una bolla di piombo è attaccata al tessuto, con il leone alato di S. Marco raffigurato su una delle facce e, sull'altra, la testa di un animale non identificato circondata da una sigla composta da tre lettere, C I E[160]. Il drappo è uno sciamito operato, un tessuto in mezza seta con ordito di lino. Le materie impiegate, la lavorazione e le misure della pezza rimandano ai cinque tipi di setifici, e più precisamente ai *samiti contrafacti* del capitolare dei samitari del 1265[161]. La bolla indica chiaramente l'origine della pezza e illustra l'intervento degli ufficiali del Comune o dell'Arte dei samitari per certificare che essa era conforme alle norme di lavorazione prescritte dai regolamenti[162]. Considerando le circostanze del suo trasferimento a Forlì, il drappo è stato datato ai primi del Trecento. La bolla rimastagli attaccata suggerisce che esso arrivò direttamente da una bottega veneziana poco tempo prima di essere messo nel sarcofago nove mesi dopo la morte del Salomoni[163]. Anche il disegno con ruote tangenti a doppio con-

X

torno contenenti coppie di grifi mostra un'affinità con parecchie mezze sete del gruppo veneziano di King e rafforza l'attribuzione del drappo. Ci sono altri sciamiti in misto seta che avevano molteplici similitudini col drappo di Forlì in base alla loro esecuzione tecnica, decorazione e larghezza. L'ampio telo ritrovato con le reliquie di S. Procolo, nella chiesa che porta il suo nome a Bologna, è uno sciamito operato in mezza seta con filato di lino per l'ordito, adorno di un disegno a ruote contenente animali simmetrici come il precedente[164]. Stoffe simili sono il telo da parato appartenente al corredo funebre di S. Parisio nella chiesa di S. Pietro a Treviso, con filato di canapa per l'ordito di fondo e decorazione a ruote, una stoffa con pappagalli a Padova e due teli da parato con ordito di lino estratti dalla tomba di S. Antonio nella stessa città, l'uno con motivi di palmette stilizzate e l'altro con pappagalli[165]. La presenza su quest'ultimo tessuto di pollini di conifere tipiche di una zona submontana, lontana da Venezia, ha sollevato dubbi sulla sua provenienza veneziana[166], malgrado la sua affinità con le altre stoffe di questo gruppo. La presenza dei pollini potrebbe derivare dall'intervento diretto di individui venuti da quella zona alla traslazione del corpo del santo nel 1310, ma è possibile anche ipotizzare un'altra soluzione, sulla quale torneremo in seguito.

Venezia non era la sola produttrice italiana di mezze sete nell'epoca esaminata qui. Già negli anni Venti del Duecento Genova produceva piccole pezze quali veli, fazzoletti e guanciali di qualità discreta, tessuti con seta e filati di cotone o di lino. Nel corso del secolo si aggiunsero pezze di seterie più elaborate[167]. Uno statuto lucchese del 1308 rivela la tessitura a Lucca di imitazioni di broccati d'oro e di altri drappi fabbricati a Genova, a Venezia e ad Arezzo[168]. Il regolamento fu probabilmente promulgato su richiesta di mercanti e imprenditori che si lamentavano dei tessitori, perché prescrive a questi ultimi una stretta aderenza alle norme di lavorazione e alle misure dei modelli rispettivi delle tre città[169]. Visto che lo statuto aveva come scopo di assicurare una più ampia diffusione delle imitazioni lucchesi, è verisimile che non trattasse di drappi pregiati e carissimi, per i quali ad ogni modo la clientela era poco numerosa, ma di altri tessuti che nondimeno erano di alta qualità. Sinora i tessuti superstiti attribuiti a Lucca hanno indotto gli studiosi a credere che nel Duecento e nei primi del Trecento la città producesse solamente drappi di lusso. Non è mai stato tenuto conto della possibilità che in quest'epoca essa lavorasse anche mezze sete, benché questi

288

tessuti siano documentati più tardi nei regolamenti lucchesi del 1376[170]. Per affrontare i rivali forestieri su un mercato in piena espansione e allargare la sua clientela al di là dei più ricchi era indispensabile per Lucca diversificare la sua produzione, come Venezia aveva fatto in precedenza. Si è suggerito che diversi provvedimenti dello statuto lucchese del 1308 – citato sopra – che trattano delle imitazioni lucchesi fossero stati promulgati per la prima volta nel 1261[171], cioè quattro anni prima del capitolare dei samitari veneziani che tratta delle mezze sete. Questo non è da escludersi, visto che la tessitura di quelle stoffe è documentata per gli anni anteriori al 1265, come accennato in precedenza. In questo caso dovremmo ipotizzare che già intorno a quella data la loro produzione a Venezia fosse cresciuta a tal punto da conquistare una parte del mercato delle seterie, da colpire la diffusione dei manufatti più cari di Lucca e da costringere la rivale a trovare una risposta adeguata alla sfida veneziana.

L'inventario del tesoro pontificio compilato nel 1295 fornisce una conferma indiretta di una tale cronologia riguardante sia l'evoluzione della produzione veneziana di mezze sete sia quella delle imitazioni lucchesi[172]. Tuttavia prima di analizzare gli indizi a questo proposito dobbiamo scartare tutti gli equivoci sulla provenienza delle grandi e piccole pezze di drappi identificate nell'inventario come veneziane, cioè indumenti sacri, cuscini, coperte e sopraletti, sia semplici sia intessuti con fili d'oro, operati o ricamati[173]. Alcuni studiosi ritengono che queste pezze non fossero state prodotte a Venezia ma altrove, e che fossero chiamate «veneziane» perché erano pervenute a Roma tramite Venezia, in altre parole che fossero «veneziane» solamente dal punto di vista della loro provenienza commerciale[174]. Questa interpretazione è chiaramente sbagliata. Certo, è possibile che parecchi ricami «alla veneziana» fossero eseguiti fuori da Venezia[175]. Però nell'inventario la definizione delle pezze veneziane è in tutto simile a quella dei drappi attribuiti a Lucca, *sarantasimi* e *diaspri* inclusi, la cui manifattura in questa città non è mai stata negata[176]. Ne consegue che le indicazioni di origine dell'inventario sono affidabili anche per Venezia. Tuttavia va notata l'incertezza dei compilatori a proposito della fattura lucchese o veneziana di diversi drappi semplici o operati, in particolare perché essi non avevano simili dubbi riguardo ai tessuti di altre provenienze[177]. Ovviamente nel contesto delle imitazioni lucchesi menzionate sopra, la loro affinità con i modelli veneziani era tale da seminare confusione.

X

L'uso delle voci *antiquus* e *vetus* nella descrizione di diversi drappi appartenenti a questo gruppo fornisce un ulteriore indizio a nostro favore. Visto che queste voci contrastano con *novus* e *recentus*, parole utilizzate anche altrove nell'inventario pontificio[178], è escluso che avessero il senso di «fuori moda», come suggeriscono alcuni studiosi[179]. Ne consegue che la menzione di tessuti lucchesi o veneziani antichi nell'inventario del 1295 conferma che sia Venezia sia Lucca producevano mezze sete da molti anni.

Abbiamo visto che la gamma dei tessuti misti veneziani era molto ampia, dai più semplici, monocromi, passando per quelli operati con motivi a ripetizione, i broccati d'oro, sino a quelli decorati con scene figurative complesse. Le mezze sete veneziane erano utilizzate anche in ambiti prestigiosi. I più ricchi non disdegnavano di acquistarle, come illustrato dai conti reali francesi degli anni 1317 e 1318[180]. Alcuni di loro erano in grado di commissionare l'esecuzione di pezze particolari, come il vescovo Heinrich von Rotteneck, che tra 1277 e 1293 offrì alla sua cattedrale di Ratisbona un drappo, con il proprio nome inscritto, rappresentante la crocifissione, la Vergine e S. Giovanni[181]. Notiamo che nella stessa epoca anche Lucca produceva drappi su commissione, alcuni con stemmi stranieri, registrati negli inventari pontifici del 1295 e del 1311[182].

Anche un altro tipo di tessuto che sinora non ha attratto l'attenzione merita alcune considerazioni. Senza dubbio c'era sempre a Venezia, come altrove, una domanda a tutti i livelli sociali, eccetto i più alti, per tessuti di seta a basso prezzo che nondimeno avessero un po' dello splendore e del prestigio dei drappi più costosi. Sappiamo che nei territori della Romania l'utilizzazione della seta di qualità inferiore non era limitata al ricamo e alla fabbricazione di oggetti di merceria, ma si estendeva alla produzione di un tessuto chiamato *cocolario* o *cucolario*, una voce derivata dal greco bizantino *koukoulariko*[183]. Diverse fonti bizantine e italiane attestano il suo uso. Per esempio, quando il famoso viaggiatore Marco Polo morì a Venezia nel 1324 possedeva una pezza di *chocholario* verde e due coltri fatte con questo tessuto, una gialla e l'altra, nuova, di colore rosso-sangue[184]. È strano che non troviamo nessuna traccia del *cocolario* nei capitolari delle arti veneziane coinvolte nella produzione di tessuti, oggetti di merceria o abiti di seta. Questo silenzio suggerisce che nell'epoca esaminata qui l'importazione dei bozzoli a Venezia era ancora marginale, e che perciò il volume di seta di bassa qualità disponibile era assai ristretto[185]. Questa seta continuava a es-

sere utilizzata nei lavori domestici[186]. Tuttavia certi tessitori la usavano anche per i drappi, abbassandone la qualità. Il capitolare dei
samitari del 1265 vietava la mescolanza degli «strosi» sia nelle mezze sete sia nei drappi di alta qualità[187]. Tutto sommato, è possibile
che Venezia non producesse *cocolari* nel Duecento, ma che li impor-
tasse dalla Romania.

Nonostante l'importanza delle mezze sete nel quadro della produzione serica veneziana, non dobbiamo dimenticare i suoi tessuti
di pura seta, alcuni dei quali con scene e motivi simili[188]. Anche in
questa categoria di drappi c'era una grande diversità di tipi, di lavorazioni e di qualità[189]. Tornando all'inventario pontificio del 1295, è
verisimile che almeno in parte le stoffe seriche di provenienza veneziana certa fossero di pura seta. Agli inizi del Trecento comincia in
Italia la produzione di un nuovo tipo di drappo di lusso, il velluto.
Due pezze lucchesi appaiono nell'inventario pontificio compilato
nel 1311[190]. Secondo l'opinione comune gli esuli lucchesi introdussero a Venezia la produzione del velluto[191]. Eppure ci si può do-
mandare se essa non fosse già esercitata nella città prima del loro arrivo. Tra le merci confiscate in un negozio nel gennaio del 1309 troviamo forme per produrre «plumbatas et plumbinos a samitario»,
cioè piombi usati nella tessitura serica, probabilmente per mantene-
re la tensione dei fili, particolarmente importante nella manifattura
dei velluti[192].

È chiaro che dall'inizio del Duecento il consumo dei drappi serici a Venezia era in espansione. Due sarantasimi e uno sciamito rosso del valore di 150 lire veneziane sono registrati nel testamento del
1206 di Enrico Morosini[193]. In quel periodo i Veneziani non producevano ancora tali drappi di alta qualità. Tuttavia quelli attestati più
tardi a Venezia, almeno in parte, potrebbero essere di manifattura
veneziana. Non è sorprendente che quando morì nel 1268 il doge
Raniero Zeno avesse alcuni panni auroserici, uno dei quali valeva 22
lire veneziane a grossi[194]. Ma accanto ai tessuti pregiati, sia semplici
sia operati, troviamo anche una domanda e un consumo a livelli più
modesti di seterie destinate a usi diversi. Nel 1276 la vedova Alessandrina de Fruzerio aveva due coltri di zendado, nonostante la sua
posizione economica non molto elevata, dimostrata dalle piccole
somme che lasciava come legati[195]. Nel testamento del 1283 di Pietro Staniario di S. Severo appare una coltre di zendado rosso e verde[196]. Pietro Doro era più fortunato nel 1281, quando lasciava, tra
altri abiti, uno sciamito intessuto d'oro ornato con pellicce di zibel-

lino, una veste di zendado bianco e una tunica di seta verde[197]. Un contratto per la fabbricazione di un pallio d'altare broccato d'argento, del 1288, contiene istruzioni per l'acquisto del metallo e fissa il termine del lavoro alla prossima festa di S. Michele[198]. La legge suntuaria veneziana del 1299 vietava alle donne di possedere più di un singolo mantello di pelle foderato di zendado, eccetto in caso di lutto[199]. In un testamento del 1302 troviamo un mantello di sciamito foderato di zendado vermiglio, cioè due tipi di drappi sovrapposti[200]. L'uso frequente di tessuti serici come fodere di stoffe più semplici è illustrato in un elenco del 1311[201].

Anche all'estero ci sono testimonianze sull'utilizzazione dei drappi serici veneziani a vari livelli sociali, oltre a quelle già accennate sopra. Nel 1284 la tassa sulla vendita del «drap ab aur de Venecia o de Lucha» a Perpignano era uguale a quella pagata per gli zendadi semplici o rinforzati, ma superiore del 50% a quella sugli sciamiti rossi o intessuti con fili d'oro[202]. Due pianete di porpora veneziana sono incluse nell'inventario del 1313 della chiesa di Rodez, anch'essa nella Francia meridionale[203]. Cinque paia di «porporas de Veneçia», a 130 maravedis il paio, furono importate in Castiglia nel 1293 tramite il porto di San Sebastian[204]. Nei circoli della borghesia londinese troviamo la vedova del birraio Robert le Paumer, che nel 1305 lascia in eredità a sua nipote un copriletto di seta ornato da un pezzo di drappo veneziano, molto probabilmente di seta o di mezza seta[205]. Abbiamo già incontrato il «drap d'or de Venise» come merce comune sul mercato parigino all'incirca nello stesso periodo[206]. I drappi veneziani viaggiavano anche verso l'Oriente. Nell'agosto del 1277, prima della partenza del figlio oltremare per due anni, Simone della Fontana concluse venti contratti di commenda, uno dei quali comprendeva un investimento di 100 lire in sciamiti[207]. Nel 1283 il Maggior Consiglio permise l'esportazione di sciamiti ad Alessandria. In questi due ultimi casi si tratta senz'altro di manufatti veneziani, al contrario dei drappi provenienti dal Levante che erano esportati verso i paesi del Mediterraneo occidentale[208]. Queste informazioni casuali illustrano l'ampio ambito geografico in cui erano diffusi i drappi veneziani di diversi tipi e qualità nel secondo Duecento e nei primi del Trecento.

L'industria serica veneziana di quest'epoca è sempre stata considerata sottosviluppata e di peso minore rispetto a quella lucchese nella qualità dei suoi manufatti, nel volume della sua produzione e nella diffusione dei suoi prodotti. Perciò, secondo l'opinione comune, l'insediamento degli artigiani e dei mercanti di seta lucchesi a Venezia cominciato nel 1314 determinò una svolta fondamentale nell'evoluzione di quest'industria[209]. L'approccio economico adottato qui fornisce un quadro più ricco, diversificato ed equilibrato sull'avvio e sullo sviluppo della manifattura serica veneziana, così come sulle sue orientazioni e sulle sue scelte. La nostra ricostruzione impone una rivalutazione sia della produzione veneziana anteriore al 1314 sia dell'apporto lucchese dopo quella data. Abbiamo visto che le fonti scritte riguardanti i drappi veneziani prima dell'arrivo dei lucchesi sono piuttosto frammentarie, ma non così scarse come si crede. Certo, esse non permettono di rintracciare tutte le fasi del processo produttivo che conduceva dalle materie prime ai drappi, né l'articolazione dell'organizzazione finanziaria, industriale e commerciale connessa come si può fare per l'epoca posteriore, abbondantemente documentata. Tuttavia è chiaro che la concentrazione degli studiosi sui drappi di lusso, meglio attestati, non è giustificata, perché non fornisce una visione d'insieme sull'evoluzione della manifattura serica veneziana, né sul suo peso economico. La gamma dei manufatti serici veneziani era molto più ampia e si differenziò sempre più nel corso del Duecento e nei primi del Trecento. Un rifornimento sicuro e continuo di materie prime, appoggiato alle reti del commercio marittimo veneziano nel Mediterraneo orientale, e la ricerca di nuovi sbocchi per i prodotti finiti furono fattori determinanti in questo processo. Gli oggetti di merceria e le pezze prodotte con seta di bassa qualità godevano di una larga diffusione sul mercato interno, sebbene fossero anche esportate. D'altra parte, dalla seconda metà del Duecento Venezia fu in grado di competere con molto successo sui mercati esteri delle seterie grazie alla diffusione delle sue mezze sete, a scapito di Lucca. Per questo tipo di drappi misti c'era allora una domanda crescente, anche nei ceti superiori della società occidentale, accanto ai prodotti di lusso per i quali la clientela rimaneva sempre ristretta. Ne consegue che Venezia puntava a due livelli di clientela con possibilità finanziarie differenti.

La solida infrastruttura dell'industria veneziana, la sua flessibilità e la sua capacità tecnica, dimostrate dalla diversificazione dei suoi prodotti, così come l'ampio raggio geografico raggiunto nella loro distribuzione, testimoniano dell'alto livello di sviluppo del settore serico veneziano. Senza dubbio ai primi del Trecento tutti questi fattori influirono in modo determinante sulla destinazione di molti

X

esuli lucchesi. Mentre Genova, la principale fornitrice di materie prime per Lucca, produceva allora drappi su modesta scala[210], Venezia era senz'altro la sola in grado di assicurare la continuità delle loro attività artigianali, finanziarie o commerciali[211]. D'altra parte, è chiaro che la perizia dei lucchesi in questi campi, così come le loro reti di distribuzione, contribuirono allo sviluppo dell'industria serica veneziana nel corso del Trecento.

Un'ultima osservazione s'impone. Non è escluso che i risultati ottenuti qui promuovano l'identificazione di altri drappi come prodotti veneziani ma, paradossalmente, essi suggeriscono anche che diverse mezze sete tra quelle identificate da King e da altri come veneziane potrebbero essere lucchesi. Forse è questo il caso del telo trovato nella tomba di S. Antonio a Padova, sul quale furono rintracciati i pollini di conifere di una zona lontana da Venezia[212]. Ad ogni modo la mobilità della manodopera, dei telai e delle tecnologie, oltre alla produzione di imitazioni, dovrebbe incitare gli storici dei tessuti, dell'abbigliamento e dell'arte a una cautela estrema nell'attribuzione e nella datazione dei tessuti superstiti.

[1] Tutti i documenti dell'Archivio di Stato di Venezia citati sotto con la sigla ASV sono inediti.
[2] R. Broglio d'Ajano, *Die venetianische Seidenindustrie und ihre Organisation bis zum Ausgang des Mittelalters*, Münchener volkswirtschaftliche Studien, herausgegeben von L. Brentano und W. Lotz, II, Stuttgart 1893 (trad. it.: *L'industria della seta a Venezia*, in *Storia dell'economia italiana*, a cura di C.M. Cipolla, I, Torino 1959), ha molto influito sugli studi posteriori. Sfortunatamente, per l'epoca trattata qui questo saggio si basa su una documentazione insufficiente e contiene molti errori. I due recenti saggi di I. Chiappini di Sorio, *La tessitura serica a Venezia: dalle origini e di alcune influenze iconografiche*, in *Venezia e l'Oriente vicino. Arte veneziana e arte islamica. Atti del primo simposio internazionale sull'arte veneziana e l'arte islamica*, a cura di E.J. Grube, Venezia 1989, pp. 203-207, e Ead., *L'arte della tessitura serica a Venezia. Il tessuto d'arte*, in *Storia di Venezia. Temi. L'Arte*, II, Roma 1995, pp. 961-984, presentano pressappoco la stessa visione d'insieme, negando la produzione di drappi a Venezia nel periodo esaminato qui. D. Davanzi Poli adotta un approccio più positivo, sebbene con alcune riserve, in tre saggi molto simili: *L'arte e il mestiere della tessitura a Venezia nei secc. XIII-XVIII*, in *I mestieri della moda a Venezia dal XIII al XVIII secolo*, a cura di Ead., Venezia 1988, pp. 39-53; *La produzione serica a Venezia*, in *Tessuti nel Veneto. Venezia e la Terraferma*, a cura di G. Ericani e P. Frattaroli, Verona 1993, pp. 21-34; *Le origini*, in *Le stoffe dei Veneziani*, a cura di D. Davanzo Poli e S. Moronato, Venezia 1994, pp. 12-29, 161-162.
[3] L. Molà, *La comunità dei Lucchesi a Venezia. Immigrazione e industria della seta nel tardo Medioevo*, Istituto Veneto di Scienze, Lettere ed Arti. Memorie, Classe di Scienze morali, Lettere ed Arti, LIII, Venezia 1994, tratta dell'epoca posteriore.
[4] *Codice diplomatico padovano dal secolo sesto a tutto l'undecimo*, a cura di A. Gloria (Monumenti storici pubblicati dalla Deputazione veneta di storia patria, ser. I - Documenti, II), Venezia 1877, p. 14, n. 7; *S. Lorenzo*, a cura di F. Gaeta (Fonti per la storia di Venezia, Sez. II - Archivi ecclesiastici - Diocesi Castellana), Venezia 1959, p. 7, n. 1. Nei due testi, co-

294

DALLA MATERIA PRIMA AI DRAPPI TRA BISANZIO, IL LEVANTE E VENEZIA

me spesso altrove, *pallium* ha il senso di drappo serico. Per l'abito dei dogi, rappresentato su bolle, monete e mosaici, cfr. A. Pertusi, *Quedam regalia insignia. Ricerche sulle insegne del potere ducale a Venezia durante il Medioevo*, in «Studi Veneziani», 7, 1965, pp. 19-48, 88.

[5] Johannes Diaconus, *Chronicum venetum*, in *Cronache veneziane antichissime*, a cura di G. Monticolo, I (Fonti per la storia d'Italia, XXXVIII), Roma 1890, pp. 178-179. Per l'identificazione corretta dei luoghi, cfr. C. Brühl e C. Violante, *Die «Honorantie civitatis Papie». Transkription, Edition, Kommentar*, Köln-Wien 1983, pp. 43-44, e per gli strati di questo testo e la sua datazione, pp. 77-85.

[6] Per una visione d'insieme, cfr. D. Jacoby, *Silk crosses the Mediterranean*, in *Le vie del Mediterraneo. Idee, uomini, oggetti (secoli XI-XVI)*, a cura di G. Airaldi, Genova 1997, pp. 57-58. *****

[7] Cfr. D. Jacoby, *Genoa, Silk Trade and Silk Production in the Mediterranean region (ca. 1100-1300)*, in *Tessuti, oreficerie, miniature in Liguria, XIII-XV secolo*, a cura di M. Marcenaro, Genova-Bordighera 1999 (in corso di stampa). *****

[8] D. Jacoby, *Silk in Western Byzantium before the Fourth Crusade*, in «Byzantinische Zeitschrift», 84-85, 1991-92, pp. 452-500, e sui Veneziani in particolare pp. 464, 466-467, 479-480, 490-500; riprodotto in Id., *Trade, Commodities and Shipping in the Medieval Mediterranean*, Aldershot, Hampshire 1997, n. VII.

[9] Documento inserito in un altro del 1176, conservato in una copia sbagliata del Cinquecento nella Biblioteca Nazionale Marciana, Venezia, *Ms. Ital. Cl. VII*, Cod. 551 (7281), *Storia documentata del governo di Venezia dalle origini al 1253*, c. 66v, riprodotto con errori addizionali da S. Romanin, *Storia documentata di Venezia*, II, 1854, pp. 405-406. Domenico Polani appare tra i firmatari di un documento dogale del 1144, quando Pietro Polani era doge della città: *Gli atti originali della cancelleria veneziana, I (1090-1198)*, a cura di M. Pozza (Ricerche. Collana della Facoltà di Lettere e Filosofia dell'Università di Venezia), Venezia 1994, pp. 57-58, n. 9.

[10] *Urkunden zur älteren Handels- und Staatsgeschichte der Republik Venedig*, a cura di G.L.Fr. Tafel e G.M. Thomas, I, Wien 1856-1857, p. 133: «de sericis [...] pannis».

[11] Jacoby, *Silk crosses the Mediterranean* cit., pp. 63-64.

[12] Sui genovesi vedi Jacoby, *Genoa* cit., pp. 14-15.

[13] *Nicetae Choniatae historia*, a cura di I.A. Van Dieten (Corpus Fontium Historiae Byzantinae, XI/1), I, Berlin-New York 1975, p. 86.

[14] Robert de Clari, *La conquête de Constantinople*, a cura di Ph. Lauer, Paris 1956, p. 12, § XIII: «avoit un pavellon tendu par deseure lui d'un vermeil samit».

[15] R. Gallo, *Il tesoro di San Marco e la sua storia*, Venezia 1967, p. 275, nn. 25, 27, 28, 30-33, 35, 37, 38.

[16] *Ivi*, p. 275, nn. 40 e 36 rispettivamente.

[17] *Ivi*, p. 275, note 39, 41. Per la prima testimonianza sulla nave: L. Urban Padoan, *Il Bucintoro. La festa e la fiera della «Sensa» dalle origini alla caduta della Repubblica*, Venezia 1988, p. 58; prima descrizione della *desponsatio maris* in Martin da Canal, *Les estoires de Venise. Cronaca veneziana in lingua francese dalle origini al 1275*, a cura di A. Limentani, Firenze 1976, p. 250. Sull'uso dei vessilli e degli stendardi, cfr. anche Pertusi, *Quedam regalia insignia* cit., pp. 88-91, 115-117.

[18] Cfr. *infra*, p. 283.

[19] Jacoby, *Genoa* cit., pp. 19-20.

[20] *Documenta historiae Chroatiae periodum antiquam illustrantia*, a cura di F. Racki [*Monumenta spectantia historiae Slavorum meridionalium, VII*], Zagrabiae 1877, p. 32, n. 24: «omni anno libras de seta serica decem»; nuova ed. in *Codex diplomaticus regni Croatiae, Dalmatiae et Slavoniae, I. Diplomata annorum 743-1100*, a cura di M. Kostrencic, Zagreb 1967, p. 54, n. 37. L'espressione *seta serica* serviva probabilmente a precisare che si trattava di seta di prima e non di seconda scelta (sulla quale cfr. *infra*), o della cosidetta «seta di cavallo», i crini di cavallo utilizzati per la fabbricazione di setacci. Sul commercio di questa "seta": DCV, n. 149, del 1161; DMCV, I, p. 118, del 1223; altre fonti citate in D. Jacoby, *Silk Production in the Frankish Peloponnese: the Evidence of Fourteenth Century Surveys and Reports*, in *Travellers and Officials in the Peloponnese. Descriptions - Reports - Statistics, in Honour of Sir Steven Runciman*, a cura di H.A. Kalligas, Monemvasia 1994, p. 54, nota 46, riprodotto in Jacoby,

Trade cit., VIII; Molà, *op. cit.*, p. 243, nota 113. M. Bettelli Bergamaschi, *Seta e colori nell'alto Medioevo: il siricum del monastero bresciano di S. Salvatore* (Biblioteca dell'Archivio Storico Lombardo, Serie seconda, 5), Milano 1994, pp. 109-113, non tratta dell'espressione *seta serica* nel quadro della sua analisi linguistica di *sericus/siricus*, che in ogni modo non è esaustiva. Per un altro uso di *syricus*, cfr. *infra*, nota 23.

[21] Descrizione e rappresentazione grafica di una fibra nel manuale di Francesco Balducci Pegolotti, *La pratica della mercatura*, a cura di A. Evans, Cambridge (Mass.) 1936, p. 382.

[22] Capitolare dei merciai del 1271 in *I capitolari delle Arti veneziane sottoposte alla Giustizia e poi alla Giustizia Vecchia dalle origini al MCCCXXX*, a cura di G. Monticolo e E. Besta, II, Roma 1896-1914, pp. 308-309, § II, e pp. 318-319, § XXXVII, dove si parla di «merçarius vel alia persona tam homo quam femina», che «laborare vel facere laborari».

[23] ASV, *Procuratori di S. Marco de Citra*, busta 314, *Testamenti IV*, c. 226r: «dimitto eidem uxori mee omnem linum, setam et syricum et omnia que sunt de lino, seta et serico, tam nova quam vetera». È chiaro che in questo contesto *seta* e *syricum* sono fibre distinte. Da notare che il testamento non si riferisce a tessuti.

[24] Cfr. *supra*, p. 269. Esempi di pezze a Genova: Jacoby, *Genoa* cit., pp. 31-32; per Venezia, cfr. *infra*.

[25] Così era anche a Genova nei primi decenni del Duecento: Jacoby, *Genoa* cit., pp. 32-33. Considerazioni generali simili sulla produzione serica in Italia in B. Tietzel, *Italienische Seidengewebe des 13., 14. und 15. Jahrhunderts (Deutsches Textilmuseum, Krefeld)*, Köln 1984, p. 54 e note 373-374. Anche in paesi senza manifattura di stoffe seriche c'era una produzione di mercerie e di piccole pezze. Esempi in F. Pritchard, *Silk Braids and Textiles of the Viking Age from Dublin*, in *Archaeological Textiles, Report from the 2nd NESAT Symposium* (Arkaeologiske Skrifter, II), København 1988, pp. 149-161; L. von Wilckens, *Die Textilien Künste. Von der Spätantike bis um 1500*, München 1991, pp. 82-83, 97-103.

[26] Per Londra alle due date: O. Lehmann-Brockhaus, *Lateinische Schriftquellen zur Kunst in England, Wales und Schottland vom Jahre 901 bis zum Jahre 1307*, II, München, 1955-1960, §§ 2743, 2915. Per Roma nel 1295, cfr. *infra*, nota 177.

[27] DMCV, I, pp. 114 e 118, dove ci sono certamente errori nella trascrizione dei prezzi, troppo alti. Sulla porpora, cfr. *infra*, pp. 281-282.

[28] R. Bevere, *Vestimenti e gioielli in uso nelle provincie napoletane dal XII al XVI secolo*, in «Archivio Storico per le Province Napoletane», 22, 1897, p. 321: «faciolum de Venetiis listatum de serica».

[29] B. Cecchetti, *La vita dei Veneziani nel 1300. Le vesti*, Venezia 1886, p. 99, nota 6, riprodotto in Id., *La vita dei Veneziani nel 1300*, introd. di U. Stefanutti, Bologna 1980.

[30] S. Piasentini, *«Alla luce della luna». I furti a Venezia, 1270-1403*, Venezia 1992, appendice, p. 138, nn. 110, 114.

[31] *Testi veneziani del Duecento e dei primi del Trecento*, a cura di A. Stussi, Pisa 1965, p. 101, n. 66.

[32] Per esempio, nel 1223 sono menzionate delle borse di Siria accanto ad altre: DMCV, I, p. 118.

[33] *I capitolari delle Arti veneziane* cit., I, pp. 190-191, § 3; cfr. anche il capitolare dei sarti del 1219: *ivi*, I, pp. 14-15, § I. Il ricamo con fili di seta di diverse qualità si faceva anche su pelle: *ivi*, II, pp. 117-118, capitolare dei *blancarii* del 1271, § VI.

[34] La documentazione addotta da Bettelli Bergamaschi, *Seta e colori* cit., pp. 125-206, non è esaustiva. Perciò, cfr. H. Bresc, *Mûrier et ver à soie en Italie (Xe-XVe siècles)*, in *L'homme, l'animal domestique et l'environnement du Moyen Age au XVIIIe siècle*, a cura di R. Durand, Nantes 1993, pp. 329-342; Jacoby, *Genoa* cit., pp. 17-18.

[35] DCV, n. 559. Per mancanza di spazio posso dare soltanto alcuni degli indizi utilizzati, tutti approssimativi, per il calcolo della quantità. Nel 1215 circa il bisante saraceno valeva intorno a 36 soldi *parvi* veneziani o a 1 soldo e 8 denari di grossi; a quell'epoca il rapporto tra *parvo* e grosso era di 1: 26, e dal 1250 circa era di 1: 26 1/9; *ivi*, n. 529, e F.C. Lane e R.C. Mueller, *Money and Banking in Medieval and Renaissance Venice, I. Coins and Moneys of Account*, Baltimore and London 1985, pp. 113, 123-127. Perciò la somma di 270 bisanti equivaleva a 373 grossi. Nel 1303 il prezzo di una libbra sottile veneziana di seta, di 301 grammi, era

X

stimato a 2 soldi di grossi e 10 denari: cfr. *infra*, nota 61. Questo prezzo era più o meno costante, come attestato più tardi nel Peloponneso. Ne possiamo dedurre che il peso della seta era di 373 diviso 2½, o circa 150 libbre sottili, cioè un totale di 45 chili.

[36] *Gli statuti marittimi veneziani fino al 1255*, a cura di R. Predelli e A. Sacerdoti, Venezia 1903, p. 73, § 2; p. 161, § CV: «seta et opera sete».

[37] *Le deliberazioni del Consiglio dei Rogati (Senato), Serie mixtorum*, a cura di R. Cessi e P. Sambin, I, Venezia 1960, p. 93, § 318.

[38] Sul commercio veneziano a Laiazzo: D. Jacoby, *La Venezia d'oltremare nel secondo Duecento*, in *Storia di Venezia, II. L'età del Comune*, a cura di G. Cracco e G. Ortalli, Roma 1995, p. 274; Stussi, *Testi veneziani* cit., pp. 8-10, n. 3, testamento di un Veneziano che prima del 1282 commerciava tra Laiazzo e Montpellier, una città che importava seta da diverse regioni, Levante compreso: cfr. Jacoby, *A Venetian Manual of Commercial Practice from Crusader Acre*, in *I comuni italiani nel regno crociato di Gerusalemme*, a cura di G. Airaldi e B.Z. Kedar (Collana storica di fonti e studi, diretta da G. Pistarino, 48), Genova 1986, pp. 416-417, riprodotto in Id., *Studies on the Crusader States and on Venetian Expansion*, Northampton 1989, n. VII (questo manuale sarà edito prossimamente). Ne possiamo dedurre che altri mercanti veneziani esportavano la seta da Laiazzo verso Venezia.

[39] *Zibaldone da Canal. Manoscritto mercantile del sec. XIV*, a cura di A. Stussi (Fonti per la storia di Venezia, sez. V - Fondi vari), Venezia 1967, pp. 61, 109.

[40] Jacoby, *Genoa* cit., pp. 26-27.

[41] DCV, n. 778; il documento è datato gennaio 1246 *more veneto*; cfr. anche *Zibaldone da Canal* cit., p. 57.

[42] *Ivi*, pp. 66, 71. Sulle diverse qualità di ceneri, un materiale utilizzato anche per la fabbricazione del vetro, cfr. D. Jacoby, *Raw Materials for the Glass Industries of Venice and the Terraferma, about 1370 - about 1460*, in «Journal of Glass Studies», 35, 1993, pp. 67-68, riprodotto in Id., *Trade* cit., n. IX.

[43] *Gli statuti marittimi* cit., p. 73, § 2, e p. 160, § CIII; *Zibaldone da Canal* cit., pp. 71, 109. Soltanto la porpora del *murex* aderiva alle fibre senza mordente, usato per esempio con la grana: cfr. Jacoby, *Silk in Western Byzantium* cit., pp. 482-484.

[44] Su questo mercante, cfr. *supra*, p. 271.

[45] DCV, nn. 756, 774. Sull'attività di questo mercante nell'Egeo, cfr. D. Jacoby, *La dimensione demografica e sociale*, in *Storia di Venezia, II. L'età del Comune*, p. 700. La Patra è sicuramente Neopatras, vicina all'isola di Negroponte, e non Patrasso come suggerito da alcuni studiosi. L'iperpero utilizzato a Negroponte nel 1240 valeva probabilmente 23 soldi parvi o circa 88/100 di un soldo di grossi. Perciò 213 perperi erano equivalenti a 188 soldi di grossi, cioè circa 75 libbre sottili o 22,5 chili di seta. Per il rapporto tra le due monete e il prezzo della seta, cfr. *supra*, nota 23.

[46] Sul manuale, cfr. Jacoby, *A Venetian Manual* cit., pp. 403-428.

[47] *Zibaldone da Canal* cit., p. 59, che chiama i bozzoli *chuchulli*, dal greco *koukkouli* (singolare). La voce era utilizzata nel Peloponneso franco: cfr. Jacoby, *Silk Production* cit., p. 56, nota 53. Sui bozzoli, cfr. anche *infra*, p. 274. Altra testimonianza in Pegolotti, *op. cit.*, p. 149, dove invece di *grano* legge *grana*, poiché la merce era pesata come la seta con la libbra sottile di Venezia, mentre lo *stario* era usato per i grani menzionati più avanti nel testo.

[48] R. Lopez e G. Airaldi, *Il più antico manuale italiano di pratica della mercatura*, in *Miscellanea di studi storici*, II (Collana storica di fonti e studi, diretta da Geo Pistarino, XXXVIII), Genova 1983, p. 127, fol. 360, II 15-23; per l'interpretazione del testo e per il contesto generale, cfr. Jacoby, *Genoa* cit., pp. 22-23.

[49] Testamento in ASV, *Procuratori di S. Marco de Ultra*, busta 325.

[50] *Pasquale Longo notaio in Corone, 1289-1293*, a cura di A. Lombardo, Venezia 1951, nn. 1, 41, 47, 92, 109.

[51] *Le deliberazioni del Consiglio dei Rogati* cit., I, p. 116, n. 163; invece di *granum* leggi *granam*.

[52] Cfr. *supra*, p. 270 e nota 31. Sulla produzione di seta nel retroterra di Corone e per la funzione di questo porto nell'esportazione di seta e di grana verso Venezia, cfr. anche Jacoby, *Silk Production* cit., pp. 43-44, 46-47, 56; *Zibaldone da Canal* cit., p. 58.

⁵³ *Domenico prete di S. Maurizio, notaio in Venezia (1309-1316)*, a cura di M.F. Tiepolo (Fonti per la storia di Venezia, Sez. III - Archivi notarili), Venezia 1970, n. 212.

⁵⁴ *Zibaldone da Canal* cit., p. 58.

⁵⁵ Pegolotti, *op. cit.*, p. 145.

⁵⁶ Cfr. D. Jacoby, *Changing Economic Patterns in Latin Romania: The Impact of the West*, in *The Crusades from the Perspective of Byzantium and the Muslim World*, a cura di A.E. Laiou and R.P. Mottahedeh, Washington, D.C. 1999 (in corso di stampa).

⁵⁷ DMCV, III, p. 74, § 81.

⁵⁸ Cfr. Jacoby, *Genoa* cit., pp. 27-28.

⁵⁹ *Zibaldone da Canal* cit., rispettivamente pp. 70 e 69.

⁶⁰ ASV, *Procuratori di S. Marco, Misti, Miscellanea pergg.*, busta 7, sentenza del 13 dicembre 1284.

⁶¹ *Diplomatarium veneto-levantinum*, a cura di G.M. Thomas e R. Predelli, I, Venezia 1880-99, p. 135. Il prezzo della libbra sottile di seta era di 167 soldi di grossi: 67 = circa 2 soldi e 10 denari di grossi per unità di peso, quello della grana di 258 soldi di grossi: 225 = circa 1 grosso e 3 denari. Il mercante aveva con sé drappi e abiti di lana portati da Venezia per finanziare i suoi acquisti oltremare.

⁶² Questi tipi di seta sono citati per *Zibaldone da Canal* cit., pp. 57, 109. Per seta tinta da Laiazzo, cfr. *supra*, p. 271.

⁶³ Cfr. *supra*, p. 269.

⁶⁴ *Ibid.* e Pegolotti, *op. cit.*, p. 140. In Toscana la parola *folesellus* o filugello significa seta di seconda scelta, mentre al nord degli Appennini indica il bozzolo del baco da seta: S. Bongi, *Della mercatura dei Lucchesi nei secoli XIII e XIV*, Lucca 1858, p. 35 e nota 1. Quando il vocabolo appare al plurale è chiaro che ha il secondo significato: cfr. la nota seguente.

⁶⁵ *Le deliberazioni del Consiglio dei Rogati* cit., I, p. 91, § 315: «Quod folleselli possint venire Venecias cum navibus sicut alie mercationes»; cfr. anche p. 93, § 318.

⁶⁶ Cfr. *supra*, p. 272.

⁶⁷ L'importazione dei bozzoli e la loro dipanatura a Venezia sono spesso documentate nel Trecento e nel Quattrocento: Molà, *op. cit.*, pp. 182-183, 191-193, 211-214, 221-222, 306. Sulla filatura col fuso o col filatoio, cfr. *supra*, p. 269.

⁶⁸ M. Fennell Mazzaoui, *The Emigration of Veronese Textile Artisans to Bologna in the Thirteenth Century*, in «Atti e Memorie della Accademia di Agricoltura, Scienze e Lettere di Verona», s. VI, 19, 1967-68, pp. 2-6, 40, 43-45, nn. 60, 67-69, 123-124, 127-135.

⁶⁹ *Monumenta spectantia ad historiam slavorum meridionalium*, a cura di S. Ljubic, I, Zagreb 1868, p. 29, n. 38; cfr. G. Rösch, *Venedig und das Reich. Handels- und verkehrspolitische Beziehungen im der deutschen Kaiserzeit* (Bibliothek des Deutschen Historischen Instituts in Rom, LIII), Tübingen 1982, pp. 91-92.

⁷⁰ Così Molà, *op. cit.*, p. 208.

⁷¹ DMCV, II, p. 129, § X; II, pp. 137-138, § XLIII; III, pp. 32-33, § 76.

⁷² H. Simonsfeld, *Der Fondaco dei Tedeschi in Venedig und die deutsch-venezianischen Handelsbeziehungen*, I, Stuttgart 1887, p. 15, n. 43.

⁷³ *Cassiere della Bolla Ducale, Grazie, Novus Liber (1299-1305)*, a cura di E. Favaro (Fonti per la storia di Venezia, Sez. I, Archivi pubblici), Venezia 1962, n. 90; interpretazione di Molà, *op. cit.*, p. 23.

⁷⁴ Anche a Genova le transazioni tra Lucchesi non erano sempre legate all'approvvigionamento di Lucca: cfr. G. Petti Balbi, *La presenza lucchese a Genova in età medioevale*, in *Lucca e l'Europa degli affari, secoli XV-XVII*, a cura di R. Mazzei e T. Fanfani, Lucca 1990, pp. 29-35.

⁷⁵ Pegolotti, *op. cit.*, pp. 144, 147 (spese per il trasporto a Firenze), 148, 151.

⁷⁶ Cfr. *supra*, p. 271.

⁷⁷ DCV, n. 595.

⁷⁸ Cfr. *supra*, p. 268.

⁷⁹ DCV, nn. 485, 661. Su questo mercante, cfr. D. Jacoby, *Venetian Settlers in Latin Constantinople (1204-1261): Rich or Poor?*, in Πλούσιοι και φτωχοί στὴν κοινωνία τῆς ἑλληνολατινικῆς Ἀνατολῆς (= *Ricchi e poveri nella società dell'Oriente grecolatino*) (Biblio-

DALLA MATERIA PRIMA AI DRAPPI TRA BISANZIO, IL LEVANTE E VENEZIA

teca dell'Istituto ellenico di Studi bizantini e postbizantini di Venezia, n. 19), a cura di Ch.A. Maltezou, Venezia 1998, p. 183.
    [80] *Urkunden zur älteren Handels- und Staatsgeschichte* cit., i, pp. 53-63; nuova ed. a cura di Pozza, *op. cit.*, pp. 31-36, n. 1.
    [81] Già A. Schaube, *Handelsgeschichte der romanischen Völker des Mittelmeergebiets bis zum Ende der Kreuzzüge*, München 1906, p. 21, nota 4, aveva confutato l'interpretazione comune, ma senza spiegazione.
    [82] *Urkunden zur älteren Handels- und Staatsgeschichte* cit., ii, p. 359; nuova ed. O. Berggötz, *Der Bericht des Marsilio Zorzi. Codex Querini-Stampalia IV3 (1064)* (Kieler Werkstücke, Reihe C: Beiträge zur europäischen Geschichte des frühen und hohen Mittelalters, ii), Frankfurt am Main 1990, p. 140; *texarini* è una forma dialettale veneziana.
    [83] Su questi schiavi nel Trecento, cfr. Molà, *op. cit.*, pp. 75-76, 172-173.
    [84] Questo sviluppo sarà trattato in un mio libro sull'industria serica bizantina, in corso di preparazione.
    [85] A.E. Laiou, *Venice as a Center of Trade and Artistic Production in the Thirteenth Century*, in *Il Medio Oriente e l'Occidente nell'arte del XIII secolo*, a cura di H. Belting (Atti del xxiv Congresso internazionale di storia dell'arte, Bologna 1975), ii, Bologna 1982, pp. 14-15, 18-19.
    [86] DMCV, ii, p. 306, cap. xxi, § i: «quod illi qui preerunt ad recipiendum rectum seu dacium illorum hominum qui faciunt pannos ad aurum, purpuras et cendatos, non debeant emere nec emi facere de ipsis pannis, purpuris nec cendatis, nec etiam laborare nec facere laborari modo aliquo de ipsis».
    [87] Le stesse regole valevano per la produzione dei fustagni e dei panni di lana.
    [88] Cecchetti, *La vita dei Veneziani* cit., p. 31, e Chiappini di Sorio, *La tessitura serica* cit., p. 205. Per i battitori, cfr. il capitolare dei fabbricanti «de cordis budellorum ad batendum bambacium et lanam» in *I capitolari delle Arti veneziane* cit., iii, pp. 3-4; in rapporto al cotone, cfr. M. Fennell Mazzaoui, *The Italian Cotton Industry in the Later Middle Ages, 1100-1600*, Cambridge 1981, pp. 74-76.
    [89] DCV, n. 595.
    [90] ASV, *Procuratori di S. Marco de Ultra*, busta 211. La moneta di conto accennata era certamente la lira di grossi. Un totale di 1.740 soldi equivaleva a 696 libbre sottili di seta secondo il prezzo menzionato *supra*, nota 61. Nell'anno seguente la moglie di Pietro Navager investì denaro in una commenda: DCV, n. 767.
    [91] Stussi, *Testi veneziani* cit., p. 39, n. 29.
    [92] ASV, *Cancelleria Inferiore, Notai*, busta 154, notaio Giovanni di Raynerio. Sul termine *samitario*, cfr. *infra*, p. 282.
    [93] ASV, *S. Lorenzo*, busta 18, *Processo Moian 1*, per 1262; G. Cagnin, *Produzione e commercio dei panni a Treviso nel Medioevo*, in *Tessuti antichi. Tessuti - Abbigliamento - Merletti - Ricami. Secoli XIV-XIX*, a cura di D. Davanzo Poli, Treviso 1994, p. 294.
    [94] ASV, *Procuratori di S. Marco, Misti, Miscellanea pergg.*, busta 5, conferma del 10 settembre 1273 da parte del doge Lorenzo Tiepolo. Le misure del terreno erano di 56, 5 × 66, 5 piedi. Per alcuni prezzi di terreni a Venezia nel Duecento, cfr. I. Fees, *Reichtum und Macht im mittelalterlichen Venedig. Die Familie Ziani* (Bibliothek des Deutschen Historischen Instituts in Rom, Band 68), Tübingen 1988, pp. 140, 158, 164, 174-175.
    [95] Un'associazione di questo tipo è attestata a Genova nel 1231: S.E. Epstein, *Labour in Thirteenth Century Genoa*, in «Mediterranean Historical Review», 3, 1988, p. 130.
    [96] *Felice de Merlis, prete e notaio in Venezia ed Ayas (1315-1348)*, a cura di A. Bondi-Sebellico (Fonti per la storia di Venezia, Sez. iii - Archivi notarili), i, Venezia 1970, n. 28, del 18 settembre 1315: «excepto telario magno cum omnibus preparamentis et ornamentis ipsi telario pertinentibus quod remanet inter nos de suprascripta societate».
    [97] Cfr. *supra*, p. 275; *Notaio di Venezia del secolo XIII (1290-1292)*, a cura di M. Baroni (Fonti per la storia di Venezia, Sez. iii - Archivi notarili), Venezia 1977, n. 505; Stussi, *Testi veneziani* cit., p. 39, n. 29.
    [98] *Domenico prete di S. Maurizio* cit., n. 231.
    [99] *Felice de Merlis* cit., nn. 7-9.

[100] ASV, *Procuratori di San Marco, Misti,* busta 158, commissaria Vivarotto (di) Nicola.
[101] Cfr. *supra,* p. 278.
[102] Cfr. *supra,* pp. 278-279.
[103] Cfr. *supra,* p. 279.
[104] Piasentini, *op. cit.,* p. 133, n. 17. Prima, nel giugno del 1261, Nascimbene aveva ricevuto un terreno vicino a Mestre: ASV, *S. Salvatore,* vol. XXIV. La sua contrada di residenza a Venezia non è menzionata.
[105] ASV, *Procuratori di San Marco de Ultra,* busta 158: riferimento del 26 maggio 1273 alla sua vedova.
[106] Cfr. *supra,* p. 278.
[107] Piasentini, *op. cit.,* p. 134, n. 28 e p. 139, n. 124.
[108] Cfr. *supra,* p. 280.
[109] Piasentini, *op. cit.,* p. 149, n. 315.
[110] R. Predelli, *I libri Commemoriali della Republica di Venezia. Regesti,* I, Venezia 1876, pp. 19-20, n. 76 (Reg. I, c. 20v).
[111] Cfr. *supra,* p. 278.
[112] *Domenico prete di S. Maurizio* cit., nn. 220, 231, 330, 331, 356, 366, 367, 409-411, 519; *Felice de Merlis* cit., nn. 7-9, 1234. Per la residenza dei samitari nell'epoca posteriore, cfr. Molà, *op. cit.,* pp. 29-30, 44-45, 50 e note 83, 53-72.
[113] Cfr. *supra,* p. 275.
[114] *I capitolari delle Arti veneziane* cit., I, p. 11, § I.
[115] Per il 1223: DMCV, I, pp. 114, 122, 124, e per le circostanze, Rösch, *Venedig und das Reich* cit., p. 122; per il 1225: DMCV, p. 80, § 123.
[116] *Ivi,* I, p. 55, § 32; p. 184, § 53.
[117] *Calendar of Liberate Rolls Preserved in the Public Record Office, Henry III,* vol. III. A. D.1245-1251, London 1937, p. 123.
[118] Sulla loro attività a Londra, cfr. R.W. Kaeuper, *Bankers to the Crown: The Riccardi of Lucca and Edward I,* Princeton (N.J.) 1973, pp. 4-5, che tuttavia menziona la seta solo di sfuggita.
[119] Cfr. L.B. Robbert, *I Lucchesi ed i loro affari commerciali a Venezia al tempo di Castruccio Castrani,* in «Actum Luce» 13-14, 1984-85, pp. 187-191.
[120] Cfr. *supra,* nota 86.
[121] *I capitolari delle Arti veneziane* cit., II, p. 34, nota 3, e p. 591.
[122] Sull'interpretazione dei regolamenti lucchesi, cfr. D. King e M. King, *Silk Weaves of Lucca in 1376,* in *Opera Textilia Variorum Temporum, To honour Agnes Geijer on her ninetieth birthday 26th October 1988,* a cura di I. Estham e M. Nockert, Stockholm 1988, pp. 67-76, e per le *porpore,* p. 74. Queste ultime appaiono allora con gli sciamiti nella stessa categoria di stoffe seriche di discreta qualità. Il pericolo di una proiezione all'indietro è particolarmente ovvio nel caso dello sciamito, in origine molto pregiato ma divenuto un tessuto leggero fatto di seta di qualità inferiore e di filato di lino, come attestano i regolamenti lucchesi del 1376: *ivi,* p. 74. Anche altri tessuti serici subirono un'evoluzione "semantica" simile. Per tali sviluppi già nel Duecento, cfr. *infra,* pp. 283, 285-286.
[123] Cfr. *supra,* p. 275.
[124] *I capitolari delle Arti veneziane* cit., I, pp. 23-24, § I: «tam drapum quam bambacinum quam cendatos»; stesso uso della parola nel capitolare dei rivenditori di oggetti vecchi: *ivi,* I, p. 133, § 1: «drappos, telas seu cendatos». In questi due contesti la parola «drappi» aveva il senso di panni di lana, mentre «tele» indicava drappi di lino o di cotone, come nel decreto veneziano del 1265 sui dazi da pagare sui tessuti forestieri importati, «de draparia, telis et fustagnis»: DMCV, II, pp. 276-277, § V. Tra questi non c'erano tessuti serici, come ipotizza a torto Davanzo Poli, *Le origini* cit., p. 22.
[125] *I capitolari delle Arti veneziane* cit., II, pp. 27-38.
[126] *Ivi,* II, pp. 32-38; commenti sui tessuti nelle note, con aggiunte, *ivi,* pp. 589-595 e 678.
[127] Nei regolamenti lucchesi del 1376 gli sciamiti e le porpore sono inclusi nello stesso gruppo di tessuti (cfr. *supra,* nota 122), mentre i catasciamiti appaiono in un altro gruppo:

King, *Silk Weaves* cit., pp. 74-75. Però non sappiamo se ciò rifletta anche la composizione e la lavorazione dei manufatti serici veneziani di un secolo prima.

[128] *I capitolari delle Arti veneziane* cit., II, pp. 319-320, capitolare dei merciai, § XXXVIIII: «omnia laboreria pannorum, cendatorum et tellarum». Cf. *supra*, nota 124, le formule parallele in altri documenti veneziani. Per Lucca, cfr. *Statuto dell'Arte dei tintori di Lucca del MCCLV*, a cura di P. Guerra, Lucca 1864, pp. 13-15, 18-20: «tintores sendatorum sete»; la voce *sendatum* è menzionata nel prologo e nei §§ I-VI, XVI-XVII, XX, XXII (il solo che contiene anche un riferimento a *siamita*), XXV, XXVII. Tietzel (*Italianische Seideng Webe* cit., pp. 56-63) suggerisce che la differenza tra i drappi di Venezia e di Lucca fosse legata a lavorazioni diverse basate rispettivamente sugli sciamiti e sui diaspri, ma non fa riferimento agli zendadi che davano il loro nome ai tessitori di seta di Lucca.

[129] *La Historia o Liber de Regno Sicilie e la epistola ad Petrum Panormitane ecclesie thesaurarium di Ugo Falcando*, a cura di G.B. Siragusa (Fonti per la storia d'Italia, XXII), Roma 1897², pp. 178-180, e cfr. p. 179, nota 3, sulla decorazione di questi tessuti operati.

[130] *I capitolari delle Arti veneziane* cit., II, p. 35, nota 3, e pp. 591-593; Tietzel, *op. cit.*, pp. 27-33.

[131] Martin da Canal, *op. cit.*, pp. 282-304, in particolare pp. 286, 294, 296. Per la data di composizione della cronaca, tra 1267 e 1275, cfr. l'introduzione del Limentani, *ivi*, pp. XXVIII-XXXII.

[132] Sui mezzanelli, cfr. *infra*, pp. 285-286.

[133] Cfr. *supra*, nota 129, e Jacoby, *Silk in Western Byzantium* cit., pp. 463-468.

[134] See D. King, *Some Unrecognised Venetian Woven Fabrics*, in «Victoria and Albert Museum Yearbook», 1, 1969, pp. 59-62.

[135] *I capitolari delle Arti veneziane* cit., II, pp. 32-33, 36-37, §§ XIII, XXI, XXIII, XXVI, e sotto il nome *opus contrafactum*, *ivi*, p. 308, capitolare dei merciai, § II. Su questi due tipi di drappi, cfr. *infra*.

[136] D. Jacoby, *The Production of Silk Textiles in Latin Greece*, in *Technology in Latin- Occupied Greece*, a cura di Ch.A. Maltezou e H.A. Kalligas, Atene 1999, note 23-25, pp. 18, 20. ＊

[137] Cfr. Jacoby, *Silk in Western Byzantium* cit., pp. 482-483.

[138] *I capitolari delle Arti veneziane* cit., I, pp. 140, 142-143, capitolare dei tintori, §§ I e VIII: «quando homines petunt unum colorem»; III, p. 226, capitolare dei tintori, § X.

[139] Jacoby, *Genoa* cit.

[140] Cfr. von Wilckens, *Die Textilien Künste* cit., pp. 105-111.

[141] DMCV, I, pp. 50-51, § 15: «aliquante pecie de seta».

[142] Jacoby, *The Production of Silk Textiles* cit., note 21, 32, 76, 87. I principali signori feudali dell'isola di Negroponte avevano l'obbligo di consegnare ogni anno parecchi tessuti auroserici al doge di Venezia: cfr. Jacoby, *Silk in Western Byzantium* cit., pp. 469-470, e *Le promissioni del doge di Venezia dalle origini alla fine del Duecento*, a cura di G. Graziato (Fonti per la storia di Venezia, Sez. I - Archivi pubblici), Venezia 1986, pp. 34, 54, 74, 95, 120, 148: «De pannis vero ad aurum qui solent dari nostro predecessori et beato Marco a dominatoribus Nigropontis». Sui Genovesi a Tebe, cfr. Jacoby, *Silk crosses the Mediterraneo* cit., pp. 68-70, e Id., *Genoa* cit., pp. 29-31.

[143] ASV, *Procuratori di S. Marco de Citra*, busta 314, *Testamenti IV*, c. 138v.

[144] A.E. Wardwell, *Panni tartarici: Eastern Islamic Silks woven with Gold and Silver (13th and 14th Centuries)*, in «Islamic Art», 3, 1988-89, pp. 95-173, è il più ampio e sistematico saggio su questi tessuti.

[145] DMCV, III, pp. 32-33, § 76: «xamittos et drapos omnes sete ultramarinos [...] ad Garbum et in Proençam et [...] xamittos in Alexandriam». Su questi ultimi, cfr. *infra*.

[146] *I capitolari delle Arti veneziane* cit., II, pp. 34, 36, §§ XV-XVI, XXII, riguardanti cotone e canapa nei tessuti serici; *ivi*, pp. 33-35, §§ XIIII, XVIII, e pp. 318-319, capitolare dei merciai, § XXXVII, riguardante le qualità della seta e dei fili d'oro nei ricami e nella produzione di articoli di merceria. Anche gli *strosi*, filati di seta inferiore (sui quali cfr. *supra*, p. 269), erano utilizzati per questi lavori: *ivi*, e pp. 117-118, capitolare dei *blancarii*, §§ VI-VII.

[147] Cfr. Davanzo Poli, *Le origini* cit., p. 19; cfr. anche *infra*, nota 163.

[148] *I capitolari delle Arti veneziane* cit., II, p. 36, § 20, e p. 32, §§ XII-XIII. Per la spiegazione del termine *de açis, ivi*, p. 32, nota 1; inoltre, D. King, *Two Medieval Textile Terms:*
«draps d'ache», «draps de l'arrest», in «Bulletin du CIETA», 27, 1968, p. 26, e un più ampio
trattamento in Id., *Some Unrecognised Venetian Woven Fabrics* cit., pp. 55-56, che menziona
anche le fonti francesi citate sotto a questo proposito.
[149] *Comptes de l'argenterie des rois de France au XIVe siècle*, a cura di L. Douët d'Arcq,
Paris 1851, pp. 54, 65.
[150] *Nouveau recueil de l'argenterie des rois de France*, a cura di L. Douët d'Arcq, Paris
1874, p. 13.
[151] L. Douët d'Arcq, *Tarif des marchandises qui se vendaient à Paris à la fin du XIIIe*
siècle, in «Revue archéologique», 9, 1852, p. 224, e per la datazione nel 1296, pp. 213-214;
date posteriori in R.-H. Bautier, *La place de la draperie brabançone et plus particulièrement*
bruxelloise dans l'industrie textile du Moyen Age, in «Annales de la Société royale d'archéologie de Bruxelles», volume jubilaire, Bruxelles 1962, pp. 35-36, in particolare p. 36, nota 1, riprodotto in Id., *Sur l'histoire économique de la France médiévale. La route, le fleuve, la foire*,
London 1991, n. x.
[152] Per questo uso, cfr. *I capitolari delle Arti veneziane* cit., II, pp. 590-591.
[153] Cfr. Jacoby, *Silk in Western Byzantium* cit., pp. 474-475.
[154] Cfr. Molà, *op. cit.*, p. 228.
[155] King, *Some Unrecognised Venetian Woven Fabrics* cit., pp. 53-63, e sull'impatto bizantino in particolare pp. 59-62.
[156] Lehmann-Brockhaus, *op. cit.*, I, § 1464.
[157] Cfr. *supra*, p. 281.
[158] Lehmann-Brockhaus, *op. cit.*, II, §§ 2911, 2930, 2932.
[159] *Inventarium thesauri Ecclesiae Romanae... iussu Clementis Papae V factum*, in *Rege-*
stum Clementis Papae V, I. Appendices, Roma 1892, pp. 417, 427, 428, 431-432, 434, 441.
[160] Sul drappo, cfr. M. Cuoghi Costantini in *Il San Domenico di Forlì. La chiesa, il luogo,*
la città, a cura di M. Foschi e G. Viroli, Bologna 1991, pp. 123-124; Ead., *Le linceul du*
bienheureux Giacomo Salomoni, in «Bulletin du CIETA», 70, 1992, pp. 111-115.
[161] Misure attuali di 276 × 304 cm; il capitolare prescrive due braccia veneziane o 127
cm. di larghezza e cinque braccia o 317 cm. di lunghezza per cinque tipi di drappi, i sarantasimi essendo più larghi e i catasamiti più corti: cfr. *supra*, nota 135.
[162] Il capitolare dei samitari del 1265 si riferisce all'ispezione del tessuto dopo la lavorazione senza menzionare una bolla, al contrario dei regolamenti dei fustagnai: *I capitolari delle*
Arti veneziane cit., II, pp. 36-37, §§ XXV-XXVI, e p. 565, § 68. Eppure nel Trecento ci sono
molti riferimenti alla segnatura dei drappi con bolle: cfr. Molà, *op. cit.*, pp. 223-224, 228-229,
235. Cuoghi Costantini, *Le linceul* cit., pp. 111-113, ipotizza che le tre lettere rappresentino
la bottega di produzione, ma sembra più probabile che su una bolla ufficiale si tratti della sigla di un magistrato incaricato del controllo delle stoffe.
[163] La sicura origine veneziana di questa mezza seta induce Davanzo Poli, *Le origini* cit.,
p. 23, a proporre che la proibizione di fabbricare questo tipo di tessuto, promulgata secondo
la sua interpretazione nel capitolare del 1265, fosse stata abrogata nel frattempo. Una tale
ipotesi non è necessaria, visto che la produzione delle mezze sete a Venezia era cominciata
prima del 1265: cfr. *supra*, p. 285.
[164] M. Cuoghi Costantini, *Uno sciamito del XIII secolo*, in «Arte Tessile», 1, 1990, pp.
4-8; larghezza attuale di 120 cm.
[165] P. Frattaroli, *Tessuti medievali nell'entroterra veneto dalla metà del XIII alla metà del*
XIV secolo. Aspetti tecnici e desinenze ornamentali, in *Tessuti nel Veneto* cit., pp. 196-200, e
scheda di F. Luzi, *ivi*, pp. 310-311; D. Davanzo Poli, *Basilica del Santo. I tessuti*, a cura di Id.,
Padova 1995, pp. 19-21, schede alle pp. 59-61, e tavole a colori II e III; i teli padovani misura-
no rispettivamente 125 × 250 cm e 122 × 314 cm dopo il restauro. Queste ultime misure sono
pressappoco quelle prescritte dal capitolare dei samitari: cfr. *supra*, nota 161.
[166] Così conclude Davanzo Poli, *ivi*, p. 59.
[167] Jacoby, *Genoa* cit., pp. 35-36.
[168] *Statuto del Comune di Lucca dell'anno MCCCVIII*, a cura di S. Bongi e L. Del Prete

DALLA MATERIA PRIMA AI DRAPPI TRA BISANZIO, IL LEVANTE E VENEZIA

(Memorie e Documenti per servire alla Storia di Lucca, vol. III, parte III), Lucca 1867, p. 220, cap. CXXXVIIII: «intelligatur de illis qui [...] artem exercent de drappis aureis et sete, qui secundum artem Ianuensium facere debeant et in ipsa longitudine que Ianue consuetum fuerit fieri. Item intelligatur de illis qui faciunt et exercent artem drapporum ad similitudinem drapporum de Venetiis, qui illos ad dictam similitudinem facere teneantur». Si tratta nei due casi delle stesse categorie di stoffe, drappi auroserici e altri tessuti di seta.

[169] Un tale scenario è attesto a Firenze nel 1489: cfr. L. Monnas, *Loom Widths and Selvedges prescribed by Italian Silk Weaving Statutes 1265-1512: A Preliminary Investigation*, in «Bulletin du CIETA», 66, 1988, p. 35.

[170] Cfr. King, *Silk Weaves* cit., p. 74.

[171] Così Bongi nell'introduzione a *Statuto del Comune di Lucca* cit., p. XI, ma senza appoggio documentario; anche F.L. Mannucci, *Delle società genovesi d'arti e mestieri durante il secolo XIII*, in «Giornale Storico e Letterario della Liguria», 6, 1905, p. 274, senza riferimento al precedente.

[172] Introduzione di E. Molinier, *Inventaire du trésor du Saint Siège sous Boniface VIII (1295)*, in «Bibliothèque de l'Ecole des Chartes» (= «BEC»), 43, 1882, pp. 277-284. Le parti pertinenti alla nostra ricerca sono pubblicate in «BEC», 45, 1884, pp. 31-57; «BEC», 46, 1885, pp. 16-44; «BEC», 47, 1886, pp. 646-667; «BEC», 49, 1888, pp. 226-237. Di sotto cito soltanto i numeri delle pezze nell'inventario.

[173] Molinier, *op. cit.*, nn. 824, 826, 930, 934, 942, 961, 975, 990, 1122, 1127, 1437, 1440, 1447.

[174] Così Chiappini di Sorio, *La tessitura serica* cit., pp. 204-205; Davanzo Poli, *Le origini* cit., p. 23.

[175] Molinier, *op. cit.*, n. 1047, «de opere venetico», un'espressione utilizzata per i ricami. Cfr. anche *infra*, nota 177.

[176] Molinier, *op. cit.*, nn. 823, 1216-1221, 1223-1229, 1245, 1255, 1257.

[177] Molinier, *op. cit.*, n. 855: «unum copertorium [...] ornatum frisis lucanis vel veneticis ad aurum»; n. 1016: «duos camisos [...] de panno lucano vel venetico antiquo»; n. 1222: «centum xij. pannos lucanos et veneticos cum auro et sine auro ad diversa opera, computatis novis et veteribus»; n. 1438: «unam supralectum de panno venetico sive lucano rubeo ad leoncellos ad aurum». Per altri fregi di sicura provenienza veneziana: nn. 901, 921, 999 e 1072: «unum manipulum de frixio albo venetico ad aurum». *Frisium* appare nel senso di ornamento ricamato o di striscia di stoffa tessuta o ricamata spesso applicata ad altre pezze di tessuti o a vesti: cfr. «BEC», 46, 1885, p. 21, nota 1, e n. 830: «unum frixium [...] laboratum super xamito rubeo».

[178] Cfr. la nota precedente. Notiamo anche *ivi*, n. 854: «de panno lineo fracto antiquo»; n. 1144: «pannos [...] et sunt omnes quasi recentes»; n. 1196: «unam petiam de xamito rubeo recenti»; n. 1200: «xamitum bene antiquum»; n. 1441: «unam cultram [...] antiquam et fractam»; n. 1447: «unam cultram antiquam et vilem de panno venetico ad aurum». A Venezia c'era una corporazione di venditori di panni vecchi, *pannorum veterum*: capitolare in *I capitolari delle Arti veneziane* cit., II, pp. 457-486; pp. 319-320, capitolare dei merciai, § XXXVIIII: «de tella nova, cendato novo et de omni laborerio novo et non de veteri».

[179] Molinier, *op. cit.*, «BEC», 43, p. 278; *I capitolari delle Arti veneziane* cit., II, p. 595.

[180] Cfr. *supra*, p. 285.

[181] King, *Some Unrecognised Venetian Woven Fabrics* cit., pp. 56-58.

[182] Molinier, *op. cit.*, nn. 1216-1218, 1221; *Inventarium thesauri Ecclesiae Romanae* cit., pp. 429, 441.

[183] Jacoby, *Silk Production* cit., p. 54.

[184] Testo in Cecchetti, *op. cit.*, pp. 126, 127.

[185] Cfr. *supra*, p. 274.

[186] Cfr. *supra*, pp. 269-270.

[187] *I capitolari delle Arti veneziane* cit., II, pp. 33-35, §§ XIIII, XVIII.

[188] King, *Some Unrecognised Venetian Woven Fabrics* cit., pp. 56, 58-59.

[189] *Ivi*, p. 63, nota 11.

[190] *Inventarium thesauri Ecclesiae Romanae* cit., p. 431.

X

Cfr. Molà, *op. cit.*, p. 168.
Domenico prete di S. Maurizio cit., n. 7 (p. 18). Il riferimento al velluto è dovuto a Sophie Desrosiers, che ha l'intenzione di esplorare più a fondo questa ipotesi.
[193] ASV, *S. Salvatore*, t. LXXXIV, cc. 60v-61r.
[194] ASV, *Procuratori di S. Marco de Citra*, busta 314, *Testamenti IV*, c. 138v.
[195] *Ivi*, busta 319, *Miscellanea Testamenti*.
[196] *Ivi*, busta 314, *Testamenti IV*, c. 77v.
[197] G.M. Urbani de Gheltof, *Les arts industriels à Venise au Moyen Age et à la Renaissance. Notes*, Venise 1885, p. 146.
[198] Stussi, *Testi veneziani* cit., pp. 18-19, n. 8. Per l'uso ecclesiastico di seterie a Venezia nel Duecento, cfr. anche *I capitolari delle Arti veneziane* cit., II, pp. 308-309, capitolare dei merciai, § II.
[199] *Ivi*, I, p. 192.
[200] Cecchetti, *op. cit.*, p. 71, nota 10.
[201] *Ivi*, pp. 118-119.
[202] Ed. della tariffa in M. Gual Camarena, *Vocabolario del comercio medieval. Colección de aranceles aduaneros de la Corona de Aragón (Siglos XIII y XIV)*, Tarragona 1968, p. 144, nn. 58, 60, 65.
[203] Francisque-Michel, *Recherches sur le commerce, la fabrication et l'usage des étoffes de soie, d'or et d'argent et autres tissus précieux en Occident, principalement en France*, Paris 1854, II, p. 18, nota 3: «duas casulas purpurarum operis Venecie».
[204] *Cuentas y gastos del rey Sancho IV*, a cura di M. Gaibrois de Ballesteros, in *Historia del reinado de Sancho IV de Castilla*, I, Madrid 1928, p. x.
[205] *Calendar of Wills Proved Enrolled in the Court of Husting, London, I (1258-1358)*, a cura di R.R. Sharpe, I, London 1889, pp. 175-176.
[206] Cfr. *supra*, p. 285.
[207] ASV, *Procuratori di S. Marco de Ultra*, busta 129.
[208] Cfr. *supra*, p. 285.
[209] Questo approccio è anche stato condiviso recentemente da Molà, *op. cit.*, pp. 28, 49, 273-275.
[210] Cfr. Jacoby, *Genoa* cit., pp. 31-37.
[211] Molà, *op. cit.*, non ne tiene conto, perché sottovaluta l'industria serica veneziana prima del 1314; cfr. *supra*, nota 209.
[212] Cfr. *supra*, p. 288.

XI

GENOA, SILK TRADE AND SILK MANUFACTURE
IN THE MEDITERRANEAN REGION (CA. 1100-1300)

Genoa made a significant contribution to the growth of medieval silk economics in the Mediterranean region. Two developments in particular largely determined its function in this framework. One of these was its maritime expansion in the twelfth century, by the end of which its merchants and ships were operating within networks stretching from Provence, Spain and the Maghreb in the west, to Egypt, the Latin states of the Levant and Byzantium in the east. The other factor was the rise and growth of silk industries producing high-grade fabrics in Italy, a process that began in Lucca in the twelfth and spread to other cities in the thirteenth century. In these two centuries the Genoese were involved in four fields of silk related activities: trade in textiles, trade in raw materials, the manufacture of fabrics abroad and, finally, their production in Genoa itself (1).

Silk textiles must have been in liturgical use in Genoa by the early eleventh century. They were included among the booty collected by the Genoese and the Pisans in their joint expedition of 1087 against Mahdia, (2) a town located in present-day Tunisia, and Genoese merchants encountered them in Egypt, which they reached since the 1060s (3). Yet the Genoese apparently entered the silk trade only later, possibly at the time of the First Crusade. In 1097 their ships first sailed through the Byzantine region or Romania on their way to Syria, a navigation route that became customary for them since then (4). It is not excluded that some Genoese bought silk fabrics in the

---

(1) This study is purposely restricted to the Mediterranean region and does not cover Genoa's silk trade with northern countries. It is partly based on unpublished archival documents, for the location of which the following abbreviations are used: ASG: Archivio di Stato, Genova; ASL: Archivio di Stato, Lucca.

(2) *Gli Annales Pisani di Bernardo Maragone*, a cura di M. LUPO GENTILE, in *Rerum Italicarum Scriptores*, vol. VI/2, Bologna 1930, pp. 6-7.

(3) B.Z. KEDAR, *Mercanti genovesi in Alessandria d'Egitto negli anni sessanta dei secolo XI*, in *Miscellanea di studi storici*, II (*Collana storica di fonti e studi, diretta da Geo Pistarino, 38*), Genova 1983, pp. 21-30, repr. in ID., *The Franks in the Levant, 11th to 14th Centuries*, Aldershot 1993, no. I.

(4) Earlier they apparently reached Egypt by sailing along the African coast: D. JACOBY, *Byzantine Crete in the Navigation and Trade Networks of Venice and Genoa*, in L. BALLETTO (ed.), *Oriente e Occidente tra medioevo ed età moderna. Studi in onore di Geo Pistarino*, Genova 1997, pp. 530-532.

ports of the southern Aegean islands in which they anchored on the way, in order to sell them elsewhere. Until then only the merchants of Venice and, to a lesser extent, Amalfi, Bari and Gaeta had exported Byzantine silk textiles to the West (5). In any event, the involvement of the Genoese merchants in this activity was presumably furthered when they reached Constantinople, the main consumption center and luxury market of the Empire. By the 1130s they were apparently still travelling to the Byzantine capital on board foreign vessels, yet by the 1150s Genoese ships too were reaching this city (6). Genoa obtained its first privileges in Byzantium in 1155, as a result of which its trade and shipping in Romania intensified. However, the restriction of its fiscal exemptions from 1169 to 1192 limited the geographic range in which its merchants and vessels operated to Constantinople and some Aegean ports of call along the navigation routes leading to that city. The network and volume of their activity must have expanded after 1192, when Genoa obtained more extensive tax exemptions in the entire territory of the Empire (7).

The earliest direct evidence pointing to Genoese trade in Byzantine silk fabrics appears in a letter written around 1135, preserved in a stylized version, in which a Genoese woman asked her husband to send her two pieces of silk cloth manufactured in the Aegean island of Andros, one of sendal, a lightweight cloth in tabby weave, and another of samite, a rather heavy, strong and glossy silk cloth in twill weave (8). It is clear that by that time these two types of textiles were already known and marketed in Genoa and beyond in the West (9). In the twelfth century Byzantium and the West were experiencing similar economic and social processes. In both regions economic expansion, the rise in purchasing power, especially in cities, and a refinement in taste generated a growing demand for luxuries, including silk

(5) D. JACOBY, Silk in Western Byzantium before the Fourth Crusade, in Byzantinische Zeitschrift, LXXXIV-LXXXV,1991-1992, pp. 460, 476, note 131, 491, note 221, 494-495, repr. in ID., Trade, Commodities and Shipping in the Medieval Mediterranean, Aldershot 1997, no. VII; ID., Silk crosses the Mediterranean, in G. AIRALDI (ed.), Le vie del Mediterraneo. Idee, uomini, oggetti (secoli XI-XVI), Genova 1997, pp. 57-58.
(6) See JACOBY, Byzantine Crete, cited in note 4, pp. 532-533.
(7) D. JACOBY, Italian Privileges and Trade in Byzantium before the Fourth Crusade: A Reconsideration, in "Anuario de estudios medievales", XXIV, 1994, pp. 359-368, repr. in ID., Trade, Commodities and Shipping, no. II.
(8) W. WATTENBACH (ed.), Iter austriacum, 1853, in "Archiv für Kunde Österreichischer Geschichts-Quellen", XIV, 1855, p. 80, no. XIX: xamitum et duo xendata Andro insula. On the texture of the two silk fabrics and diversity in quality of each of them: D. KING, Types of Silk Cloth used in England 1200-1500, in S. CAVACIOCCHI (ed.), La seta in Europa, secc. XIII-XX (Istituto Internazionale di Storia Economica "F. Datini", Prato, Serie II - Atti delle "Settimane di Studi" e altri Convegni, 24), Firenze 1993, pp. 458-459.
(9) JACOBY, Silk in Western Byzantium, cited in note 5, pp. 460-462.

textiles. This demand was no more restricted to rulers and their courts nor to the social elite, but also extended to urban households of lower social and economic rank. In the West this development is illustrated by the letter of the Genoese woman mentioned earlier, dowry lists, and wills (10). In short, there was ample room for the marketing of silks both in the Empire and in the West.

It is generally believed that in Byzantium the state exercised a monopoly on silk trade until the Fourth Crusade. In fact, however, the bulk of this trade took place within a free market system. The imperial authorities maintained strict control exclusively over the marketing of specific types of high-quality silk fabrics and garments costing more than ten hyperpers or gold coins each, produced by private workshops. Among foreigners only the Venetians were allowed to purchase such pieces in Thebes, a city delivering a portion of its high-grade production to the imperial court for the latter's own ceremonial, political and diplomatic uses. In 1171 the Genoese failed in their attempt to gain access to these silks and, as before, their trade was restricted to medium and low-grade fabrics. Within these limits Genoese merchants gradually expanded their share in the silk trade of Romania in the second half of the twelfth century. They participated in the provisioning of Constantinople in silk textiles manufactured in provincial workshops, as in Andros, a maritime station along their way to the Byzantine capital, purchased silk fabrics in this city, and shipped Byzantine silks of various provenance to Genoa (11). In 1162 one of them lost silk pieces in the Pisan attack on the Genoese *embolos* or quarter of Santa Croce in Constantinople, the value of which is not stated. (12) A Genoese list of complaints drafted in 1174 and submitted shortly afterwards to Emperor Manuel I Comnenus reveals that several merchants had been robbed of silks by Byzantine pirates or officials, while others had lost them at sea (13).

Genoese purchases were sometimes substantial. Guglielmo Piccamiglio invested before 1174 no less than 900 hyperpers in samite, a variety of it, and sendal, all of which were loaded on a ship that sank off Chios. (14) Since he was restricted to the purchase of pieces costing up to ten hyperpers each, as noted earlier, he must have bought at least ninety of them. Before 1195 Bonifacio della Volta sold sendals, the origin of which is not stated, for somewhat less than 300 Genoese pounds to the wife of the future emperor

---

(10) IBID., pp. 472-473; JACOBY, *Silk crosses the Mediterranean*, cited in note 5, pp. 62-63.
(11) JACOBY, *Silk in Western Byzantium*, cited in note 5, pp. 466-467, 488-500.
(12) C. IMPERIALE DI SANT'ANGELO (ed.), *Codice diplomatico della repubblica di Genova*, Roma 1936-1942 [hereafter: *CDG*], vol. II, p. 208, note, col. 2.
(13) IBID., vol. II, pp. 212, note, col. 1; 215, note 1, col. 2; 217, note 1.
(14) IBID. vol. II, p. 217, note 1, col. 1.

Alexius III (15). Around the year 1200 a Genoese apparently imported expensive silks from Cyprus, then under Latin rule, as well as cheaper grades of silk textiles, including a rough fabric called *koukoulariko* in Greek, made of spinned waste and floss silk (16). It would seem that within the Empire itself Genoese merchants mostly handled medium and low grade silks. Their activity in this field came to an abrupt end in Constantinople in 1203 or 1204, as a result of the Fourth Crusade in which the Genoese did not participate. It was resumed only after the Byzantine recovery of the city in 1261 (17).

Twelfth century Genoese trade in silk fabrics was not limited to Byzantine products. Despite the absence of direct evidence, it also appears to have been pursued both by settled and visiting merchants in the Latin states of the Levant. The most renowned centers of silk manufacture in this region were Tripoli and Antioch, which apparently produced various types of Byzantine and Islamic silk textiles (18). The Genoese traded in both cities and had a quarter of their own in each of them (19). Their acquaintance with silks manufactured in the crusader Levant and their interest in them are illustrated, for instance, by the pledge of the Genoese Guglielmo Embriaco, who in 1154 obtained from Genoa the port city of Laodicea or Latakia, in the Principality of Antioch, for a period of twenty-nine years. His obligations included the yearly delivery of a silk cloth valued ten besants or gold pieces to the cathedral church of San Lorenzo in Genoa (20). Genoese merchants were also acquainted with silk fabrics manufactured in neighboring Muslim countries, which they acquired in the Latin states. Silk textiles originating in Baghdad known as *panni de Bagadello*, presumably in lampas weave, reached Genoa by 1160 (21). Somewhat later French and German literary works refer

---

(15) IBID., vol. II, p. 196: reference in instructions drafted in 1201. The 300 pounds also covered the sale of a horse, the price of which is unknown yet clearly represented a small fraction only of the total sum. The wife of Alexius III, who seized power in 1195, was Euphrosyne Doukaina Kamatera.

(16) IBID., vol. II, p. 197. See also JACOBY, *Silk in Western Byzantium*, cited in note 5, pp. 496-497.

(17) See below, pp. 22, 27.

(18) On Antioch: JACOBY, *Silk crosses the Mediterranean*, cited in note 5, pp. 62-63; later evidence on Tripoli, also relevant for the twelfth century, p. 65.

(19) M.-L. FAVREAU-LILIE, *Die Italiener im Heiligen Land vom ersten Kreuzzug bis zum Tode Heinrichs von Champagne (1098-1197)*, Amsterdam 1989, pp. 334-379, 418-424, 454-461.

(20) CDG, cited in note 12, vol. I, pp. 296-297; new ed. in A. ROVERE, *I Libri Iurium della Repubblica di Genova*, I/1, (*Fonti per la storia della Liguria*, II), Genova 1992, no. 164: *pallium unum valentem bisanciorum decem.*

(21) M. CHIAUDANO, M. MORESCO (eds.), *Il cartolare di Giovanni Scriba*, Torino 1935, vol. I, nos. 626, 771. However, not all silk pieces called *baldekinum* or *baudequin* in western sources necessarily came from Iraq; on their nature and imitations, see below, p. 15-16, 39. A consignment of 'Baghdadi' or Iraqi indigo (*de Bagadello*) was sent from Genoa to Palermo in 1161: IBID., vol. II, no. 1004.

to fabrics originating in Baghdad and Alexandria (22). Genoa re-exported some of these fabrics to the Muslim countries of the western Mediterranean.
Such was the case of Baghdadi silks shipped in 1160 from Genoa to Ceuta in
the Maghreb and to Valencia in Spain (23).

It is likely that Genoese imports of precious silk fabrics manufactured in
Muslim Spain began around the mid-twelfth century, parallel to that of silk,
(24) although they are not attested until later. These silks were highly valued
in Genoa. In 1149 the ruler of Valencia included silk fabrics, clearly local
products, in the payment he made to Guglielmo Lusio, the Genoese ambassador who concluded a ten-year treaty with him (25). In 1153 Genoa sold its
portion of the Spanish city of Tortosa to Count Raymond Berengar IV of
Barcelona, whose obligations included the yearly delivery of a silk cloth
worth 15 *morabetini* to the Genoese church of San Lorenzo (26). Judging by
this figure the cloth, surely produced by an Islamic workshop, would have
been a gold or silver-interwoven fabric. The production in Murcia of such types of sendals is attested by the list of maximum prices issued by King Alfonso VIII in 1207 at the Cortes of Toledo (27). Silk workshops in Muslim
Spain also imitated Baghdadi weaves and designs. A piece found in the cathedral of Burgo de Osma (Soria) in the tomb of bishop San Pedro, who died in
1009, carries a Kufic inscription ascribing it to Baghdad (28). In 1201 some

(22) JACOBY, *Silk crosses the Mediterranean*, cited in note 5, p. 65.
(23) See *ibid.*
(24) On which see below, p. 21.
(25) *CDG*, cited in note 12, vol. I, p. 248; new ed. ROVERE, cited in note 20, no. 118.
Around 1200 an Arabic source mentions Valencian brocade: O.R. CONSTABLE, *Trade and Traders in Muslim Spain. The Commercial Realignment of the Iberian Peninsula, 900-1500*, Cambridge 1994, p. 177.
(26) *CDG*, cited in note 12, vol. I, pp. 292, 294.
(27) F.J. HERNANDEZ (ed.), *Las Cortes de Toledo de 1207*, in *Las Cortes de Castilla y León
en la Edad Media. Congreso científico sobre la historia de las Cortes de Castilla y León*, Valladolid
1988, vol. I, p. 241. The maximum prices set for gold and silk-interwoven sendals are 18 and
17 *morabetini*, respectively, while that for plain ones is 9 *morabetini*. The fabrics are listed
without reference to origin, yet from the cheaper varieties that follow, «el otro cendal de Luca» and «los otros cendales murcis», i.e. from Murcia, we may gather that the previous, more
expensive types were also manufactured in these two cities. We may assume that prices changed over time, yet those of 1207 nevertheless provide useful indications about the nature of
the fabric mentioned in 1153.
(28) L. VON WILCKENS, *Die textilen Künste. Von der Spätantike bis um 1500*, München
1991, pp. 67-68, who also specifies the nature of that fabric. An Arabic author dealing with
the Almohad period mentions so-called Baghdadi cloth in connection with Almeria: CONSTA-
BLE, *Trade and Traders in Muslim Spain*, cited in note 25, pp. 145-146. For further Arabic sources on Spanish silks and imitations: R. B. SERJEANT, *Islamic Textiles. Material for a History up
to the Mongol Conquest*, Beirut 1972, pp. 89, 165-170. On *siglaton*: JACOBY, *Silk crosses the Mediterranean*, cited in note 5, pp. 61, 64.

bagadelli hispanici were shipped from Genoa to Ceuta. It would have been rather strange if they had made all the way from Spain to Genoa before being re-exported to Ceuta, located south of Spain across the Strait of Gibraltar. It is thus not excluded that these were imitations of Spanish *bagadelli*, yet even in that case one would have to assume that genuine ones had reached Genoa earlier (29). Mostly the origin of this type of cloth is not stated and can only be determined with the help of circumstantial evidence.

Genoese merchants also handled silk textiles in Sicily, as implied by the treaty of 1162 between Emperor Frederick I and Genoa (30). In 1194 some Pisans seized silk fabrics in a Genoese warehouse at Messina (31). The nature and provenance of these pieces is unknown. They may have been local, Levantine, Spanish or possibly also Lucchese products (32). The origin of some silk pieces found in Palermo in the tomb of King Henry VI of Hohenstaufen is still disputed (33). Whether Spanish or Levantine, there is good reason to believe that they reached Sicily by way of Genoa or with the help of Genoese merchants. In sum, in the second half of the twelfth century the Genoese had a major role in the marketing and diffusion of silk fabrics of various origin, acting to some extent as intermediaries in a two-way trans-Mediterranean traffic in silk textiles, like Amalfi's merchants in earlier centuries yet on a larger scale (34). A parallel Muslim and Jewish trade in silk fabrics and silk was being carried out between Muslim Spain and Egypt (35).

The rising demand for silks in the Latin West was not satisfied by fabrics imported from Byzantium, the Levant and Muslim Spain, whether in volume or variety or in view of their price. The Norman kingdom of Sicily was not an alternative source of supply. The prestigious products of the royal workshop at Palermo did not enter the trade circuit, while the private silk industry had a limited output, the kings did not encourage its growth, and its

---

(29) ASG, *Cartolari Notarili*, n. 102, fol. 209v. A previous shipment of *bagadelli* from Genoa to Ceuta is recorded in 1197: G. JEHEL, *Les Génois en Méditerranée occidentale (fin XIe - début XIVe siècle). Ebauche d'une stratégie pour un empire (Centre d'Histoire des Sociétés, Université de Picardie)*, Amiens-Paris 1993, p. 137. On the possible imitation of Spanish weaves in Lucca around that time, see below, pp. 39-40.

(30) *CDG*, cited in note 12, vol. I, p. 398; new ed. in D. PUNCUH, *I Libri Iurium della Repubblica di Genova*, I/2, *(Fonti per la storia della Liguria, IV)*, Genova 1996, no. 285.

(31) L.T. BELGRANO E C. IMPERIALE DI SANT'ANGELO (eds.), *Annali genovesi di Caffaro e de' suoi continuatori*, Roma 1890-1929, vol. II, p. 49.

(32) On silk manufacture in Sicily in that period, see JACOBY, *Silk crosses the Mediterranean*, cited in note 5, pp. 66-67; on Lucchese silks, see below.

(33) Latest reference by R. VAROLI PIAZZA in M. ANDALORO (ed.), *Federico e la Sicilia, dalla terra alla corona. Arti figurative e arti suntuarie*, catalogo della mostra, Palermo 1995, pp. 93-95.

(34) On the Amalfitans: JACOBY, *Silk crosses the Mediterranean*, cited in note 5, p. 58.

(35) CONSTABLE, *Trade and Traders in Muslim Spain*, cited in note 25, pp. 175-177.

fabrics were apparently inferior in quality to imported products. In any event, there is no western documentary evidence of twelfth or thirteenth century exports of Sicilian silk fabrics (36). As a result, there was room elsewhere in Italy for the establishment and expansion of a silk industry producing high-grade fabrics capable of competing with foreign textiles. Lucca was the first new silk center to emerge in the West and retained its leading role in this field until the early fourteenth century. This is all the more surprising, since it did not benefit from economic conditions favoring such a development. Small quantities of silk were being produced in several areas of central and northern Italy (37). Cocoons from the area of Lucca are attested in 1281. By 1284 Lombard silk was used in Lucca for embroidery (*seta de fregio, seta de fresio lumbarda*), and silk from the area of Modena is attested somewhat later (38). Yet Tuscan and Lombard silk yields were small and appa-

---

(36) See above, p. 16, note 32. It should be added that various silks formerly ascribed to Sicily are now considered as being of Spanish origin: VON WILCKENS, *Die textilen Künste*, cited in note 28, p. 111.

(37) On sericulture in Italy: M. BETTELLI BERGAMASCHI, *"Morarii" e "celsi": la gelsicoltura in Italia nell'alto medioevo*, in "Nuova Rivista Storica", LXXIII, 1989, pp. 13-22, repr. with some modifications in EAD., *Seta e colori nell'alto Medioevo: il "siricum" del monastero bresciano di S. Salvatore (Biblioteca dell'Archivio Storico Lombardo*, Serie seconda, 5), Milano 1994, pp. 366-389. Against the common belief that silk was produced in the area of Brescia around the mid-tenth century, see P. TOUBERT, *Un mythe historiographique: la sériciculture italienne du haut Moyen âge (IXe-Xe siècle)*, in H. DUBOIS, J.-CL. HOCQUET et A. VAUCHEZ, *Horizons marins. Itinéraires spirituels (Ve-XVIIIe siècles)*, vol. II, *Marins, navires et affaires*, Paris 1987, pp. 215-223. BETTELLI BERGAMASCHI, *"Morarii" e "celsi"*, has reopened the debate without solving the problem; for her latest overview of silk growing in Italy, not sufficiently based on primary sources, see EAD., *Seta e colori*, pp. 125-206. She has not taken into account H. BRESC, *Mûrier et ver à soie en Italie (X^e-XVe siècles)*, in R. DURAND (ed.), *L'homme, l'animal domestique et l'environnement du Moyen Age au XVIIIe siècle*, Nantes 1993, pp. 329-342, esp. 335-336.

(38) For Lucca: L.A. MURATORI, *Antiquitates italicae medii aevi*, vol. II, Mediolani 1739, coll. 901-902; T. BINI, *I Lucchesi a Venezia. Alcuni studi sopra i secoli XIII e XIV*, Lucca 1853, vol. I, p. 51; S. BONGI, *Della mercatura dei Lucchesi nei secoli XIII e XIV*, Lucca 1858, pp. 30-32, 35, 37. Yet see also below, note 44. For other areas: M.F. MAZZAOUI, *The Emigration of Veronese Textile Artisans to Bologna in the Thirteenth Century*, in *Atti e memorie della Accademia di agricoltura, scienze e lettere di Verona*, Serie VI, XIX, 1967-1968, p. 6, note 13; F. BATTISTINI, *La gelsibachicoltura e la trattura della seta in Toscana (secc. XIII-XVIII)*, in CAVACIOCCHI, *La seta in Europa*, cited in note 8, p. 294. Recent studies have overlooked the taxation of cocoons and silk in Modena in 1306-1307 (*redditus follisellorum, folexelli civitatis et districtus Mutinae, de soma sete laborate et non laborate*) and the extension of silk production in its contado by the mandatory planting of mulberry trees, imposed by the statutes of 1327: MURATORI, *Antiquitates italicae medii aevi*, vol. II, coll. 895-896; E.P. VICINI, *Respublica Mutinensis (1306-1307)* (*Corpus statutorum italicorum*, n. 11, 14), Milano 1929-1932, vol. I, p. 142, and vol. II, p. 138. In the 1330s Venice used low-grade silk from the areas of Bologna and Modena for the manufacture of light veils and permitted the import of Italian silk during the war of 1350-1355, when maritime traffic was disrupted: L. MOLÀ, *La comunità dei Lucchesi a Venezia. Immigrazione e industria della seta nel tardo medioevo* (in *Istituto Veneto di Scienze, Lettere a ed Arti. Memorie, Classe di Scienze morali, Lettere ed Arti*, vol. LIII), Venezia 1994, p. 213.

rently of poor quality. As a result, they could not ensure the steady supply indispensable for the continuous manufacture of high-quality fabrics by an expanding industry. The bulk of silk and dyestuffs, therefore, had to be imported by sea and, in view of Lucca's location inland, the provisioning of its silk manufacture in raw materials almost entirely depended on foreign maritime transportation. Incidentally, this was also the case of most Italian centers engaged in cotton weaving (39).

Despite these unfavourable conditions, several factors seem to have decisively furthered Lucca's initial development as a silk center in the second half of the twelfth century (40). The low-grade domestic production of woolens in the Lucchese countryside did not offer prospects for large profits and, therefore, did not attract investments. Moreover, the local woolen industry faced strong competition from foreign cloth brought in by Lucchese merchants, including from the fairs of Champagne, since the first half of the twelfth century (41). By that time cotton manufacture had already spread to numerous towns of northern Italy, the level of production exceeding by far the needs of home markets (42). Under these circumstances some Lucchese merchants and entrepreneurs opted for another textile branch, not developed in the cities of central or northern Italy, that would offer them a unique or at least a dominant position in the foreseeable future. The German romance *Ruodlieb*, composed in the second half of the eleventh century, mentions the purchase of silken ribbons in Lucca (43). This suggests the domestic production of small plain silk pieces woven on simple narrow looms, an activity that possibly relied on small-scale sericulture in the area (44). Moreover, the dyeing of

---

(39) A list of dyestuffs used in Italian textile manufacture, yet with too little information on their origin, in A.M. NADA PATRONE, *Per una storia del traffico commerciale in area Pedemontana nel Trecento. Fibre tessili, materiale tintorio e tessuti ai pedaggi di Vercelli e di Asti*, in *Studi in memoria di Mario Abrate*, Torino 1986, vol. II, pp. 655-660. Some of these dyestuffs were produced in Italy itself, the most expensive one being saffron. On cotton, see below, note 42.

(40) For this dating, see below pp. 19-20.

(41) A. SCHAUBE, *Handelsgeschichte der romanischen Völker des Mittelmeergebiets bis zum Ende der Kreuzzüge*, München 1906, p. 61; D. HERLIHY, *L'economia della città e del distretto di Lucca secondo le carte private nell'alto medioevo*, in *Atti del 5° Congresso internazionale di Studi sull'alto medioevo*, Spoleto 1973, pp. 362-388. The fairs of Champagne are mentioned in Lucca's treaty of 1153 with Genoa: see below, p. 20.

(42) M.F. MAZZAOUI, *The Italian Cotton Industry in the Later Middle Ages, 1100-1600*, Cambridge 1981, pp. 60-65.

(43) RUODLIEB, *The Earliest Court Novel (After 1050). Introduction, Text Translation, Commentary and Textual Notes*, by E.H. ZEYDEL (*Studies in Germanic Languages and Literature*, 23), Chapel Hill 1959, p. 108, verses 114-117.

(44) Note the names Sirico or Siricho and Sirichello in a Lucchese family of landowners, documented from 1019 to 1059: H. SCHWARZMEIER, *Lucca und das Reich bis zum Ende des 11. Jahrhunderts*, Tübingen 1972, pp. 110-111.

woolens and the production of gold thread were practiced at Lucca (45). The presence of workers in these three fields must have carried substantial weight with the merchants and entrepreneurs considering business ventures in new directions. In its initial phase of development, then, the Lucchese silk industry may have largely relied on the local work force. It is not excluded that, in addition, some workers engaged in the production of woolens switched over time to that of silks, although the skills and techniques required in this field were far more complex. Yet the growth of Lucca's silk industry and the rise in quality and variety of its silks would not have been possible without the addition of highly-skilled artisans from other silk centers bringing along sophisticated implements such as drawlooms enabling pattern weaving, as well as solid expertise in other advanced technologies. We do not know where nor how these artisans were recruited. None of the explanations offered until now, namely an influx of Arab, Byzantine Greek or Jewish workers from southern Italy or Sicily, is supported by documentary evidence (46). Significantly, a Jewish community existed in Lucca when the Jewish traveller Benjamin of Tudela visited the city around 1160, yet he did not link its members to local silk manufacture as when he referred to the Jews of Byzantine silk centers (47). In any event, heavy investments were indispensable for the building and expansion of the industrial infrastructure of the Lucchese silk industry and the initial recruitment of a highly-skilled work force, while the use of costly raw materials, silk, dyestuffs and gold thread, as well as the operation of the industry required a constant flow of liquid capital. These resources were clearly available in Lucca. Moreover, Lucchese merchants and entrepreneurs could take advantage of their existing trade networks to ensure the provisioning of the industry and the diffusion of locally made silks.

The emergence of Lucca's high-grade silk industry may be dated shortly after the mid-twelfth century, as implied by Genoese imports of silk documented since that period (48). Within the following decades this industry achie-

---

(45) See above, p. 18, note 41.

(46) F. EDLER DE ROOVER, *Lucchese Silks*, in "Ciba Review", LXXX, 1950, pp. 2902-2904, 2907-2909, offers a reconstruction of the development of Lucca's silk industry until 1314 marred by unwarranted assumptions and factual mistakes, unfortunately repeated by other authors.

(47) M.N. ADLER (ed.), *The Itinerary of Benjamin of Tudela. Critical Text, Translation and Commentary*, London 1912, pp. 7, 109 [Hebrew text]. On the Jews of Lucca in the twelfth century: A. MILANO, *Storia degli Ebrei in Italia*, Torino 1963, pp. 72-73. On Benjamin's references to Thebes, Thessalonica and Constantinople and their Jewish silk workers: JACOBY, *Silk in Western Byzantium*, pp. 466, 468, 473, 486-489, 497.

(48) JACOBY, *Silk crosses the Mediterranean*, cited in note 5, p. 71. There is no evidence that silks were exported from Lucca before 1153, as claimed by EDLER DE ROOVER, *Lucchese Silks*, cited in note 46, p. 2903. Benjamin of Tudela, who passed through Lucca around 1160, does not refer to silk manufacture: see above, p. 19.

ved a rapid and impressive expansion and a rise in the quality of its products. By the early thirteenth century its sendals and samites had already established their reputation abroad and were being sold at the fairs of Champagne, in Provence, Montpellier and Barcelona, as well as in Castile and Sicily. By the 1230s they had reached London as well as Byzantine Asia Minor (49). Lucchese silks were shipped to Mediterranean ports on board Genoese ships, and Genoese merchants were heavily involved in their marketing. Further proof of the high standard achieved by Lucca's silk industry around that time is provided by the attempts of Milan, Modena and Bologna to attract Lucca's skilled silk workers in order to develop their own silk industries. These attempts were partly successful, yet did not endanger Lucca's supremacy (50).

Lucca's strained and troubled relations with its neighbor Pisa, as well as its trade links with the fairs of Champagne through Genoese territory induced it to cooperate on a long-term basis with Genoa. An agreement between the two cities, which has not been preserved, already existed by 1143. A further treaty was concluded in 1153 and was followed by several others (51). As a result, Genoese merchants and ships became a decisive factor in the expansion of Lucca's silk industry since its initial phase. They took advantage of their extensive commercial and maritime networks throughout the Mediterranean and turned their city into a entrepôt and transit station ensuring Lucca's provisioning in raw silk and high-grade dyes and promoting the diffusion of its finished products. Many of the growing number of Lucchese settled in Genoa since the 1180s were closely connected with these developments (52).

Various general statements have been made in the past about Lucca's imports of silk yarn. It is important, however, to distinguish between sources of supply and the geographic range of the latter, which grew steadily, in order to establish a chronology of provenance, and to specify the nature of the imported silk, which could be raw, semi-processed or fully processed, such as cooked, dyed, double-twisted, or wound in skeins and ready for weaving (53).

(49) JACOBY, *Silk crosses the Mediterranean*, cited in note 5, p. 72; see also below, p. 24.

(50) See MAZZAOUI, *The Emigration of Veronese Textile Artisans*, cited in note 38, pp. 2-6, 40, 43-45, nos. 60, 67-69, 123-124, 127-135.

(51) *CDG*, cited in note 12, vol. I, p. 166, no. 128, *Breve* of the consuls of 1143, and pp. 287-288, the 1153 agreement; new ed. ROVERE, cited in note 20, no. 162. On this treaty, see SCHAUBE, *Handelsgeschichte*, cited in note 41, pp. 349-351, and on Lucca's relations with Pisa, IBID., pp. 645-654.

(52) G. PETTI BALBI, *La presenza lucchese a Genova in età medioevale*, in R. MAZZEI, T. FANFANI (eds.), *Lucca e l'Europa degli affari, secoli XV-XVII*, Lucca 1990, pp. 29-35.

(53) This last subject will not be treated here, since I am not dealing with the Lucchese manufacturing process. See examples in BINI, *I Lucchesi a Venezia*, cited in note 38, vol. I, pp. 46-53, with correct interpretations by BONGI, *Della mercatura dei Lucchesi*, cited in note 38, pp. 35-38.

Documentary evidence suggests the existence of a Genoese trans-Mediterranean two-way traffic in silk running parallel to that of silk fabrics. Silk from Muslim Spain is the earliest to be recorded in Genoa, namely in 1161 and 1163 (54). Yet at first the bulk of this material must have come from Sicily and Calabria, not too-distant regions practicing sericulture on a fairly large scale (55). Several factors prompted a search for additional sources of supply in the last decades of the twelfth century: Lucca's increasing demand for silk, the endeavor to refine and diversify products in order to reach an ever larger body of customers, and unstable political conditions in the Kingdom of Sicily from 1189 to 1220 (56).

It is not clear whether the Genoese traded in Byzantine raw silk within the Empire itself in the second half of the twelfth century (57). In any event, here is no evidence whatsoever that it was shipped to Genoa, nor to any other western city, possibly because its export was prohibited (58). However, there were other sources of supply in the eastern Mediterranean. In all likehood the Genoese imported high-grade silk and dyestuffs from the Levant, like the Venetians, as implied by the Iraqi indigo documented in Genoa in 1161 (59). They also purchased upper-grade silk from more distant regions, despite the higher cost involved in its transportation. Silk from Khorasan in eastern Iran crossing Asia Minor reached Attaleia or Satalia, a port on the southern coast of Asia Minor, in Byzantine hands until 1207, from where it was shipped to Genoa. This silk is first attested in Genoa in 1191, (60) yet may have already arrived there earlier, as suggested by Genoese trade in Satalia, documented since 1156, and the robbing of a Genoese ship in nearby waters sometime before 1174 (61).

The Fourth Crusade compelled the Genoese to restructure their trade and shipping patterns in the eastern Mediterranean, yet also offered them

(54) CHIAUDANO, MORESCO, *Il cartolare di Giovanni Scriba*, cited in note 21, vol. II, nos. 812, 882, 1132, silk re-exported to Bugia, Tunis and Alexandria, respectively. Convincing arguments for Spanish provenance in SCHAUBE, *Handelsgeschichte*, cited in note 41, pp. 160, 284 and 286. On Spanish exports of silk, see also CONSTABLE, *Trade and Traders in Muslim Spain*, cited in note 25, pp. 175-176.

(55) JACOBY, *Silk in Western Byzantium*, cited in note 5, pp. 464, note 60, 471-472, 475-476.

(56) JACOBY, *Silk crosses the Mediterranean*, cited in note 5, pp. 73-74.

(57) Some silk may have been imported from Cyprus around the year 1200, unless it was picked up on the way to Constantinople: see above, p. 14.

(58) I shall deal with this issue in a forthcoming study.

(59) See above, p. 14, note 21.

(60) M.W. HALL, H.C. KRUEGER, R.L. REYNOLDS (eds.), *Notai liguri del sec. XII, II. Guglielmo Cassinese (1190-1192)*, Torino 1938, vol. I, pp. 104-105, no. 256.

(61) JACOBY, *Silk crosses the Mediterranean*, cited in note 5, pp. 75-76, and CDG, cited in note 12, vol. II, p. 218, note, for 1174.

XI

new opportunities. The decisive political role of Venice in the Latin Empire of Constantinople excluded Genoa from the imperial city between 1204 to 1261, despite several treaties between the two rival powers in these years (62). Only few Genoese appear to have visited then Constantinople, (63) and there is no evidence that they were involved in silk trade. On the other hand, the political fragmentation of Romania opened the way to Genoese penetration on an unprecedented scale into territories other than those ruled by the Latin Empire or by Venice. The abolition of the imperial restrictions enforced before 1204 upon trade in silk textiles and especially in silk fibers enabled the Genoese to purchase these freely. While denied access to the high-grade silk fabrics of Thebes until 1204, as noted earlier, they exported them afterwards under particularly favorable conditions (64). A Genoese consul is attested in 1236 in Negroponte, the main city of the island of Euboea, and Genoese merchants conducted business there in the following decades (65). The island produced both silk and silk textiles (66).

Even more important was the activity of Genoese merchants in Chiarenza, the main port of the Frankish Principality of Morea since the mid-thirteenth century. This activity, documented from 1274 to around 1340, was at least partly related to the purchase of silk (67). There is good reason to believe that it began soon after the Latin conquest, as suggested by the Genoese involvement in silk ventures in Thebes, to which we shall soon return. Genoese purchases of silk in the Principality of Morea are further illustrated from the 1270s to the 1290s by the arrival of *seta de Chiarantana* and *seta de Romania de Patrasso*, respectively silk from Chiarenza and Patras, in Genoa

(62) On the treaties of 1218, 1228, 1232 and 1251: M. BALARD, *Les Génois en Romanie entre 1204 et 1261. Recherches sur les minutiers notariaux génois*, in "Mélanges d'archéologie et d'histoire, publiés par l'Ecole Française de Rome", LXXVIII, 1966, pp. 475-477, 479-480, 483. Yet all the clauses referring to a renewed official presence of Genoa in Constantinople were formulated in the future tense, and there is no evidence that they ever were implemented: S. ORIGONE, *Die Verträge der ersten Hälfte des 13. Jahrhunderts zwischen Genua und Venedig*, in "Mitteilungen des Bulgarischen Forschungsinstitutes in Österreich", VIII, 1986, pp. 89-95, esp. 92.
(63) In 1236 they participated in the city's defence against Byzantine and Bulgarian forces: BALARD, *Les Génois en Romanie*, cited in note 62, p. 480. A Genoese died there in 1250: IBID., pp. 483-484. In 1238 the barons in charge of the government of the Latin Empire acknowledged a large loan obtained from some Genoese: G.L. FR. TAFEL, G.M. THOMAS (eds.), *Urkunden zur älteren Handels- und Staatsgeschichte der Republik Venedig*, Wien 1856-1857, vol. II, pp. 346-349.
(64) See below, pp. 30-31.
(65) BALARD, *Les Génois en Romanie entre*, cited in note 62, p. 480.
(66) JACOBY, *Silk in Western Byzantium*, cited in note 5, p. 469.
(67) BALARD, *La Romanie génoise (XIIe - début du XVe siècle) (Bibliothèque des Ecoles françaises d'Athènes et de Rome*, 235), Rome 1978, vol. I, pp. 163-164.

and Lucca (68). More significantly, a Pisan commercial manual composed in 1278 records that «in della Morea si pesa libra lucchese», a clear reference to the exclusive use of a Lucchese weight unit for silk by western merchants operating in the Principality (69). It follows that Lucca was then the main destination of raw silk exported from this region, and Genoese merchants and carriers the main intermediaries in this traffic. This was apparently also the case of kermes (*coccum ilicis L.*), a high-quality and costly vermilion colorant exclusively used for high-grade textiles. Kermes from Romania, in all likelihood from the Peloponnese, was sold in Genoa in 1210 (70). A consignment from Corinth is documented in Lucca in 1273, (71) and in 1292 two Genoese bought in Monemvasia, a city of the south-eastern Peloponnese under Byzantine rule since 1262, a large quantity of this dyestuff for 1,648 hyperpers, yet the merchandise was not delivered to them (72). Incidentally, Lucchese imports of kermes from Spain are attested since the late twelfth century and from Provence in the thirteenth, clearly via Genoa (73). A regulation of the Lucchese corporation of dyers dated 1255 refers to kermes as the highest-grade colorant used for the production of red sendal (74).

The steady expansion of silk manufacture in Italy and elsewhere in the West resulted in a growing shift in Genoese silk priorities since the first half of the thirteenth century. While purchasing silk fabrics, as in Thebes (75), Ge-

---

(68) BINI, *I Lucchesi a Venezia*, cited in note 38, vol. I, pp. 49, 51-52, with correct identification by Bongi, *Della mercatura dei Lucchesi*, cited in note 38, pp. 36-37.

(69) R. LOPEZ, G. AIRALDI (eds.), *Il più antico manuale italiano di pratica della mercatura*, in "Miscellanea di studi storici", II , cited in note 3, p. 127, fol. 360, lines 15-23.

(70) H.C. KRUEGER, R.L. REYNOLDS (eds.), *Notai liguri del sec. XII e del sec. XIII*, VI. *Lanfranco (1202-1226)*, Genova 1953, vol. I, no. 915.

(71) ASL, *Cartolari Notarili*, n. 12, Paganello di Fiandrada, fol. 54r.

(72) G. BERTOLOTTO, *Nuova serie di documenti sulle relazioni di Genova con l'impero bizantino*, in "Atti della Società Ligure di Storia Patria", XXVIII, 1896, p. 516. Further evidence on kermes in the Peloponnese: D. JACOBY, *Silk Production in the Frankish Peloponnese: the Evidence of Fourteenth Century Surveys and Reports*, in H.A. KALLIGAS (ed.), *Travellers and Officials in the Peloponnese. Descriptions - Reports - Statistics, in Honour of Sir Steven Runciman*, Monemvasia 1994, pp. 45-47, 55, 61, repr. in ID., *Trade, Commodities and Shipping*, no. VIII.

(73) From Spain: *grana de Ispania* for Lucca in 1192 in CONSTABLE, *Trade and Traders in Muslim Spain*, cited in note 25, p. 172; in 1284: ASL, *Cartolari Notarili*, n. 15, Bartolomeo Fulceri, fol. 406r, 77 pounds, and 484r, 250 pounds; from Spain and Provence in 1294: BINI, *I Lucchesi a Venezia*, cited in note 38, vol. I, p. 29. According to a contemporary customs tariff, these two varieties were imported to Siena, in all likelihood also via Genoa: M.A. CEPPARI [e] P. TURRINI (eds.), *Documenti: il commercio delle stoffe; l'abbigliamento e le provvisioni di lusso; arredi sacri e profani*, in *"Drappi, velluti, taffetà et altre cose". Antichi tessuti a Siena e nel suo territorio*, a cura di M. CIATTI, Siena 1994, p. 245.

(74) P. GUERRA (ed.), *Statuto dell'Arte dei tintori di Lucca del MCCLV*, Lucca 1864, pp. 18-19, par. XVII; see also pars. XVI, XXII.

(75) On Thebes, see below, pp. 30-31.

noese merchants realized that the handling of raw materials was profitable to the same extent, if not more. This new attitude was not limited to the Peloponnese and was also reflected in another region of Romania. The Greek state of Nicaea was established in western Asia Minor soon after the Fourth Crusade. Since the 1230s at the latest this region became another source of raw silk for Lucca. Genoese and Lucchese purchases there were partly financed by the sale of Lucca's own silk fabrics, which successfully competed with local silks thanks to their high quality, attractive price, a change in taste within the ranks of the social elite of the Greek state, or as a result of all these factors. In any event, around 1243 Emperor John III Vatatzes imposed in his territories a ban on the use of Italian silk textiles for clothing (76). These were clearly Lucchese products, the only silks to be widely exported from Italy at that time. Genoese purchases of raw silk from Byzantine and Turkish Asia Minor substantially increased in the second half of the thirteenth century (77). On the other hand, the Genoese were not attracted by silks manufactured in the state of Nicaea, the quality of which appears to have gradually diminished. The famous *pallio* of San Lorenzo, preserved at the Palazzo Bianco in Genoa, may offer an illustration in this respect. It is noteworthy that instead of being woven into the cloth, its decoration was embroidered with gold and silk threads on plain samite, a device that substantially reduced manufacturing costs. The work was performed shortly before the *pallio* reached Genoa in 1261 (78). At that time Lucca was producing far more sophisticated and luxurious pieces.

Genoa continued in the thirteenth century to import Levantine silk fabrics manufactured in cities under Latin rule as well as in others under Muslim domination (79). In contrast to the twelfth century, however, Genoese merchants occasionally travelled inland to Aleppo and Damascus, as atte-

---

(76) L. SCHOPEN, I. BEKKER (eds.), *Nicephori Gregorae Historiae Byzantinae (Corpus Scriptorum Historiae Byzantinae)*, Bonn 1829-1854 , vol. I, pp. 43-44 (1.II.6).

(77) For instance, *seta de Smirro* or Smyrna in 1284 and 1286, *seta turchia* in 1295: BINI, *I Lucchesi a Venezia*, cited in note 38, vol. I, p. 48; P. RACINE, *Le marché génois de la soie en 1288*, in "Revue des études sud-est européennes", VIII, 1970, p. 416. I will examine silk growing and the manufacture of silk fabrics in the Empire of Nicaea in a forthcoming study.

* (78) P. JOHNSTONE, *The Byzantine 'Pallio' in the Palazzo Bianco at Genoa*, in "Gazette des Beaux Arts", LXXXVII, 1976, pp. 99-109; E. PARMA ARMANI, *Nuove indagini sul 'Pallio' bizantino duecentesco di San Lorenzo in Palazzo Bianco a Genova*, in "Studi di Storia delle Arti" (Università di Genova, Istituto di storia dell'arte), V, 1983, 1984, 1985, pp. 31-47; especially for the dating, see P. SCHREINER, *Zwei Denkmäler aus der frühen Paläologenzeit: ein Bildnis Michael VIII und der genueser Pallio*, in M. RESTLE (ed.), *Festschrift für Klaus Wessel zum 70. Geburtstag in memoriam*, München 1988, pp. 249-258; lately, C. FALCONE, *Il Pallio bizantino di San Lorenzo a Genova*, in "Arte Cristiana", LXXXIV, 1996, pp. 337-352.

(79) See above, p. 14.

sted in 1203 and 1227 (80). Many of them operated in Acre until Genoa's eviction from this city in 1258 (81). Acre was the main Levantine port visited by merchants from Mosul, a renowned manufacturer of silk and gold-interwoven fabrics. A number of these merchants settled in Acre after the Mongol sack of their city in 1261 (82). The flow of silk textiles from the Levant to the West substantially increased after the consolidation of Mongol rule over western Asia in the 1250s, which resulted in a shift in trade routes in favor of Laiazzo in Lesser Armenia. This port became the main Mediterranean outlet for commodities crossing the vast expanses of the continent and the focus of Genoese trade in the Levant after Genoa's ouster from Acre (83). Sendal of unknown origin was shipped from Laiazzo to Genoa in 1274 (84). The treaty of 1288 between Genoa and King Leo III of Lesser Armenia specifies the customs rate for a camel load of silk cloth and for a similar load of raw silk (85). It is thus obvious that by then the Genoese were handling large quantities of both these commodities in Laiazzo and were decisively

------

(80) S. ORIGONE, *Genova, Costantinopoli e il Regno di Gerusalemme (prima metà sec. XIII)*, in G. AIRALDI, B. Z. KEDAR (eds.), *I comuni italiani nel regno crociato di Gerusalemme (Collana storica di fonti e studi diretta da G. Pistarino)*, 48, Genova 1986, p. 300, note 43.

(81) On which see D. JACOBY, *L'expansion occidentale dans le Levant: les Vénitiens à Acre dans la seconde moitié du treizième siècle*, in "Journal of Medieval History", III 1977, pp. 227-228, repr. in ID., *Recherches sur la Méditerranée orientale du XIIe au XVe siècle. Peuples, sociétés, économies*, London 1979, no. VII.

(82) On Acre's trade with Muslim inland cities, not directly documented for the Genoe- * se: D. JACOBY, *The Venetian Privileges in the Latin Kingdom of Jerusalem: Twelfth and Thirteenth-Century Interpretations and Implementation*, in B.Z. KEDAR, J. RILEY-SMITH, R. HIESTAND (eds.), *Montjoie. Studies in Crusade History in Honour of Hans Eberhard Mayer*, Aldershot 1997, pp. 168-169; D. JACOBY, *The Trade of Crusader Acre: the Levantine Context*, in *Economia e Territorio nel Medioevo*, Barcelona 1999 [in press]. On the merchants of Mosul: J. RICHARD, *La confrérie des Mosserins d'Acre et les marchands de Mossoul au XIIIe siècle*, in "L'Orient syrien", XI, 1966, pp. 451-460, repr. in ID., *Orient et Occident au Moyen Age: contacts et relations (XIIe-XVe s.)*, London 1976, no. XI. On their settlement in Acre after 1261: D. JACOBY, *The Kingdom of Jerusalem and the Collapse of Hohenstaufen Power in the Levant*, in "Dumbarton Oaks Papers", XL, 1986, p. 99, note 112, repr. in ID., *Studies on the Crusader States and on Venetian Expansion*, Northampton 1989, no. III.

(83) W. HEYD, *Histoire du commerce du Levant au moyen âge*, Leipzig, 1885-1886, vol. II, pp. 73-92; R.-H. BAUTIER, *Les relations économiques des Occidentaux avec les pays d'Orient au moyen âge. Points de vue et documents*, in M. MOLLAT (ed.), *Sociétés et compagnies de commerce en Orient et dans l'Océan indien (Actes du 8e Congrès international d'histoire maritime, Beyrouth, 1966)*, Paris 1970, pp. 281, 284, repr. in R.-H. BAUTIER, *Commerce méditerranéen et banquiers italiens au Moyen Age*, Aldershot 1992, no. IV.

(84) L. BALLETTO (ed.), *Notai genovesi in Oltremare. Atti rogati a Laiazzo da Federico di Piazzalunga (1274) e Pietro di Bargone (1277, 1279) (Collana storica di fonti e studi diretta da G. Pistarino, 53)*, Genova 1989, Federico di Piazzalunga, no. 40.

(85) *Liber Jurium Reipublicae Genuensis*, vol. II *(Historiae Patriae Monumenta*, vol. IX), Augustae Taurinorum 1857, col. 184.

contributing to the westward flow of Asian silks. These appear in fairly large numbers in western inventories of the late thirteenth and the fourteenth century, many under the generic name of *panni tartarici* (86). Genoese imports of Spanish silks, namely *cendates* or sendals and *bagadelli*, also continued in the thirteenth century. Some of these pieces remained in Genoa, while most of them were re-exported (87). Thus, for instance, in 1236 the widow of a furrier living in Bonifacio owned a *bagadello* bedcover and two and a half pieces of striped sendal *de Ispania* which had obviously reached Corsica by way of Genoa (88).

Genoa's thirteenth century imports of silk appear to have substantially grown since around 1250 (89). Silk from Antioch is recorded in Genoa in 1252 and 1254 and silk from *Ultramare* in 1263 (90). Several Lucchese documents of 1287 mention *seta soriana* or Syrian silk (91). High-grade silk from Mamistra in Lesser Armenia is attested in Genoa since 1259, yet must have arrived there earlier (92). The high-quality varieties from the regions of Gandja, Lahidjan and Djurdjan, respectively to the southwest, south and south-east of the Caspian Sea, which had crossed Asia Minor in the first half of the thirteenth century, apparently travelled to Genoa via Laiazzo since the 1250s (93). Silk from Georgia in the Caucasus (*seta iurea*), attested in Genoa

---

(86) A.E. WARDWELL, *"Panni Tartarici": Eastern Islamic Silks Woven with Gold and Silver (13th and 14th Centuries)*, in "Islamic Art", III, 1988-1989, pp. 95-173, esp. pp. 134-144, Appendix II, Descriptions of Asian Textiles in European Inventories. Note, however, that *cinericeus* (no. 5) means ash grey, not Chinese. Wardwell has not included in her list plain *panni tartarici*, numerous pieces of which appear in inventories.

(87) R. LOPEZ, *Nota sulla composizione dei patrimoni privati nella prima metà del Duecento*, in ID., *Studi sull'economia genovese nel Medio Evo*, Torino 1936, p. 235: *pecias quatuor cendatorum Yspanie* in 1238; pp. 246-247: *bagadello* without origin in 1240, yet presumably Spanish; CONSTABLE, *Trade and Traders in Muslim Spain*, cited in note 25, p. 180.

(88) V. VITALE (ed.), *Documenti sul Castello di Bonifacio nel secolo XIII*, in "Atti della Società Ligure di Storia Patria", N. S., I, 1936-1944, p. 40, Tealdo de Sigestro, no. 107.

(89) JACOBY, *Silk crosses the Mediterranean*, cited in note 5, pp. 65, 76-79.

(90) JEHEL, *Les Génois en Méditerranée occidentale*, cited in note 29, pp. 326, 467; R. DOEHAERD (ed.), *Les relations commerciales entre Gênes, la Belgique et l'Outremont d'après les archives notariales génoises aux XIIIe et XIVe siècles*, Bruxelles-Rome 1941, vol. II, pp. 662-663, nos. 1202-1203.

(91) BINI, *I Lucchesi a Venezia*, cited in note 38, vol. I, pp. 49-50; reading and interpretation corrected by Bongi, *Della mercatura dei Lucchesi*, cited in note 38, p. 34.

(92) R.S. LOPEZ, *Nuove luci sugli Italiani in Estremo Oriente prima di Colombo*, repr. in ID., *Su e giù per la storia di Genova (Collana storica di fonti e studi diretta da G. Pistarino*, 20), Genova 1975, p. 101, note 59. Also in 1273: ASL, *Cartolari Notarili*, n. 12, Paganello di Fiandrada, fol. 61v; in 1288: RACINE, *Le marché génois de la soie en 1288*, cited in note 77, p. 415. A Florentine commercial manual of the 1320s refers to the *molto finissima seta* of Lesser Armenia, *quaxi della migliore che sia in ongni parte*: BAUTIER, *Les relations économiques des Occidentaux*, cited in note 83, p. 318.

(93) JACOBY, *Silk crosses the Mediterranean*, cited in note 5, pp. 76, 78-79.

since 1256, presumably also travelled via Laiazzo until 1261 (94). Chinese silk (*seta catuia*), first attested in Genoa in January 1257, came by way of Laiazzo (95). Genoese merchants seem to have handled most of the silk shipped westwards from this city (96), which apparently also served as transit station for Iraqi indigo (97). Yet some merchants may have travelled inland as far as Tabriz in northern Iran to buy these commodities (98).

The Byzantine recovery of Constantinople in 1261 added another route of silk supply. It enabled Genoese merchants and ships to return to Constantinople and to extend their activity into the Black Sea (99). As a result, a growing volume of the silk previously flowing toward Laiazzo was diverted to the Genoese commercial outposts established in several Black Sea ports. Especially Caffa and Trebizond served as transit stations for high-quality silk originating in the Crimea, the Caucasus, territories around the Caspian Sea and Merv Chadijan, the oasis of Sogdiana in central Asia. Genoese and Lucchese documents of the 1280s and 1290s point to the arrival of large quantities of these varieties (100). Some Genoese even went one step further. The famous Marco Polo reports in his travel account that shortly before his return to the West in 1296 the Genoese had transferred ships to the Caspian Sea, presumably from the Black Sea upstream on the river Don, then by land and, finally, downstream on the Volga. Polo himself links this arduous enterprise to the silk of Ghilan. It was obviously aimed at reaching the silk producing regions around the Caspian Sea, in order to bypass intermediaries stationed

---

(94) BINI, *I Lucchesi a Venezia*, cited in note 38, vol. I, p. 50, mistakenly reads *diuria*. See also JACOBY, *Silk crosses the Mediterranean*, cited in note 5, p. 79. On the change of route after 1261, see below.

(95) DOEHAERD, *Les relations commerciales*, cited in note 90, vol. II, no. 986; see also LOPEZ, *Nuove luci sugli Italiani*, cited in note 92, pp. 100-101, and documents on pp. 129-131. See also BAUTIER, *Les relations économiques des Occidentaux*, cited in note 83, pp. 288-291; BALARD, *La Romanie génoise*, cited in note 67, vol. II, pp. 727-728.

(96) Silk of unknown origin from Laiazzo to Genoa in 1279: BALLETTO, *Notai genovesi in Oltremare*, cited in note 84, Pietro di Bargone, no. 83.

(97) BINI, *I Lucchesi a Venezia*, cited in note 38, vol. I, p. 29, in 1284 and 1294.

(98) BAUTIER, *Les relations économiques des Occidentaux*, cited in note 83, pp. 282-286, 290-291.

(99) BALARD, *La Romanie génoise*, cited in note 67, vol. I, pp. 45-55, 105-118, 127-162, 179-215.

(100) G.I. BRATIANU (ed.), *Actes des notaires génois de Péra et de Caffa de la fin du treizième siècle (1281-1289)*, Bucarest 1927, nos. CC, CCIX, CCXI, CCXIII, and p. 337, no. 263, all of 1289; S.P. KARPOV, *L'impero di Trebisonda, Venezia, Genova e Roma, 1204-1461. Rapporti politici, diplomatici e commerciali*, Roma 1986, pp. 41, 61-62, notes 109-110; RACINE, *Le marché génois de la soie en 1288*, cited in note 77, pp. 415-417; BINI, *I Lucchesi a Venezia*, cited in note 38, vol. I, pp. 46-47. In 1276 a Lucchese buys silk from Tana: A. FERRETTO, *Codice diplomatico delle relazioni fra la Liguria, la Toscana e la Lunigiana ai tempi di Dante (1265-1321)*, parte II: *Dal 1275 al 1281*, in "Atti della Società Ligure di Storia Patria", XXXI/2, 1903, p. 99.

XI

between them and the Black Sea coast, enlarge the volume of purchases, and lower the latter's cost (101). Silk varieties brought in from the eastern Mediterranean appear to have become dominant on the Genoese market in the last decades of the thirteenth century. Yet Lucca continued to draw supplies via Genoa from other regions as well. Based on evidence from 1240 and from the reign of Charles I of Anjou (1265-1285), Calabria had a fairly large silk yield, estimated at some 20,000 pounds annually (102). A portion of this yield presumably passed through Genoa on its way to Lucca, workshops located elsewhere absorbing the rest. Semi-processed silk from Cosenza is documented in Lucca in 1248 and silk from Calabria in 1266, 1288 and 1295. The last variety must have been of good quality, since in 1266 it fetched the same price as silk from the Caspian region and Georgia in 1288, despite smaller transportation costs (103). Sicilian silk was shipped from Messina to Genoa in 1271 (104). Spanish silk is documented there in 1225 and 1280 (105).

Genoa's increasing silk related imports warrant a few remarks. First, we have already noted that Genoa re-exported silk and dyestuffs to destinations other than Lucca since the 1160s (106). This traffic continued in the thirteenth century (107). The development of additional centers of silk manufacture in Italy and other western countries in this period generated a growing demand for raw materials and more complex networks of supply, in which the Genoese were joined by competitors (108). In 1248 a Lucchese shipped semi-processed silk and gold thread on behalf of another Lucchese via Genoa and Marseilles to Montpellier (109). Dyed silk was sent from Genoa to Sicily

(101) MARCO POLO, *Il libro di Messer Marco Polo Cittadino di Venezia detto Milione, dove si raccontano le Meraviglie del mondo*, a cura di L.F. BENEDETTO, Milano-Roma 1932, p. 17, chap. 23. See HEYD, *Histoire du commerce du Levant*, cited in note 83, vol. II, pp. 111-112.

(102) Assessment by G. PETRALIA, *Calabria medievale e operatori mercantili toscani: un problema di fonti?*, in *Mestieri, lavoro e professioni nella Calabria medievale: tecniche, organizzazioni, linguaggi* (Atti dell'VIII Congresso storico calabrese, Palmi (RC), 1987), Soveria Manelli (CZ), 1993, pp. 303-304.

(103) FERRETTO, *Codice diplomatico*, cited in note 100, parte I: *Dal 1265 al 1274*, in "Atti della Società ligure di storia patria", XXXI/1, 1901, p. 28; BINI, *I Lucchesi a Venezia*, cited in note 38, vol. I, pp. 49-50; BONGI, *Della mercatura dei Lucchesi*, cited in note 38, pp. 33-34; PETRALIA, *Calabria medievale*, cited in note 102, p. 302.

(104) S.R. EPSTEIN, *An Island for itself. Economic Development and Social Change in Late Medieval Sicily*, Cambridge 1992, p. 202.

(105) CONSTABLE, *Trade and Traders in Muslim Spain*, cited in note 25, p. 176; JEHEL, *Les Génois en Méditerranée occidentale*, cited in note 29, p. 350.

(106) See above, p. 14, note 21, and p. 21.

(107) JEHEL, *Les Génois en Méditerranée occidentale*, cited in note 29, pp. 350, 416, 466-467.

(108) On new centers, see above, p. 20.

(109) L. BLANCARD (ed.), *Documents inédits sur le commerce de Marseille au Moyen Age*, Marseille 1885, vol. II, p. 232, no. 871: *in seta cocta et in auro filato de Luca*.

and 50 pounds of silk from Lahidjan to an unspecified destination in 1257 (110). Florentine, Sienese and Lucchese merchants and bankers bought silk and kermes in various regions and shipped them to ports other than Genoa. In 1269 Bononione de Luca sent silk and kermes from Durazzo to Brindisi and from there by land to Naples, presumably in order to forward them to Lucca (111). Around that time a Florentine merchant sold in Bologna 716 pounds of silk from Romania, in all likelihood from the Peloponnese, and silk belonging to Lucchese traders was confiscated by that city's authorities (112). An unidentified Sienese company having a branch at Chiarenza in the years 1277-1282 exported silk from this port to Italy, yet since its *livro de la ragione di Romania* has not survived, it is impossible to assess the volume of this activity (113). Silk, floss silk, gold-interwoven cloth and samites listed together with kermes from Romania appear in a Sienese customs tariff compiled between 1273 and 1313, and were thus all from that region (114). A commercial manual compiled in Pisa in 1278 suggests Pisan purchases of silk in Alexandria, Acre, Laiazzo, Ania in Asia Minor, the Frankish Peloponnese as well as other territories of Romania (115). Some of that silk may have reached Lucca, as implied by the author's knowledge of this city's silk weight (116). Despite the rise of rival Italian silk centers and networks, Genoa remained in the last decades of the thirteenth century the main Mediterranean importer of silk related raw materials from the eastern Mediterranean, and the Lucchese retained an overwhelming share in silk transactions concluded in Genoa (117).

The Genoese function in the Mediterranean silk economy of the thirteenth century was not limited to trade in textiles and raw materials. It also extended to the manufacturing of silk fabrics. Genoese involvement in this

---

(110) ASG, *Cartolari Notarili*, n. 60, ANGELINO DE SIGESTRO, fol. 83v, 94 r: 50 pounds of *sete legie*.

(111) A. DUCELLIER, *La façade maritime de l'Albanie au Moyen Age. Durazzo et Valona du XIᵉ au XVᵉ siècle*, Thessaloniki 1981, p. 289.

(112) References in MAZZAOUI, *The Emigration of Veronese Textile Artisans*, cited in note 38, p. 7, note 13, sales by Lucchese in 1269 and 1270.

(113) D. JACOBY, *Italian Migration and Settlement in Latin Greece: the Impact on the Economy*, in H.E. MAYER (ed.), *Die Kreuzfahrerstaaten als Multikulturelle Gesellschaft. Einwanderer und Minderheiten im 12. und 13. Jahrhundert* (Schriften des Historischen Kollegs, Kolloquien, 37), München 1997, pp. 112-113.

(114) CEPPARI [e] TURRINI, *Documenti*, cited in note 73, p. 245.

(115) See above, p. 23, note 69.

(116) See above, p. 23.

(117) D. GIOFFRÈ, *L'attività economica dei lucchesi a Genova tra il 1190 e il 1280*, in "Lucca archivistica, storica e economica" (Fonti e Testi del *Corpus Membranarum Italicarum*, X), Roma 1973, pp. 99, 106-107; RACINE, *Le marché génois de la soie en 1288*, cited in note 77, pp. 410-413; PETTI BALBI, *La presenza lucchese a Genova*, cited in note 52, pp. 34-35.

process in Thebes, the most important and successful silk center of Latin Greece, began sometime between 1204, the year in which the Latins captured the city, and 1240, when Genoa renewed its treaty with the lord of Athens, Guy I of La Roche, whose territory included Thebes. This treaty mentions «silk fabrics woven or composed by the Genoese themselves or woven» by others «for them» (118).

At first glance it would seem that Genoese silk workers had settled in Thebes and were directly participating in the production of its high-grade silks. If this indeed had been the case, it would have resulted in a substantial contemporary improvement in the quality and sophistication of silk fabrics manufactured in Genoa itself which, as we shall soon note, did not occur. Therefore, in all likelihood the Genoese merchants active in Thebes, some of whom resided there, fulfilled another role. On the one hand, they acted as entrepreneurs who ensured the operation of a number of local silk workshops by supplying them with raw materials, liquid capital, or both, in return for the exclusive right to sell their finished products. In addition, they purchased silk fabrics from other Theban workshops, whose activity they did not finance. In both cases, though, the Genoese must have specified the weaves, designs, colors and measurements of the fabrics they commissioned. Therefore, one could consider these fabrics either as being woven or 'composed' by them. The Genoese involvement in production created particularly favourable conditions for the export of the silks they acquired and for their marketing in the West. It should be noted, though, that the diffusion of Theban textiles was not exclusively in Genoese hands, which explains why the Genoese requested a reduction of the export taxes imposed upon their fabrics in order to make them more competitive. This attempt failed, and while the Genoese still appear to have been present in Thebes after 1240, there is no more evidence of any silk related activity on their part (119). In any event, it would seem that the Genoese ceased to act as silk entrepreneurs in Thebes sometime in the second half of the thirteenth century. Two closely related factors may explain this development. First, on the Genoese market the Theban silks could apparently not withstand in the long run the competition of the high-grade fabrics manufactured in Lucca, whether in quality, price, or both, especially since Genoa's failure to obtain

---

(118) *Liber Jurium Reipublicae Genuensis*, vol. I (*Historiae Patriae Monumenta*, vol. VII), Augustae Taurinorum 1854, coll. 992-993, no. 757: *«de pannis sericis ab eisdem Ianuensibus vel pro eis in terra nostra textis seu compositis, ipsi Ianuenses nobis solvere teneantur id quod ab aliis exigi solitum est et haberi»*.

(119) This may also be due to the paucity of Genoese documentation regarding Greece in that period. Only few notarial charters attest Genoese activity in Chiarenza, although circumstantial evidence points to a much wider involvement in silk trade and shipping there: see above, pp. 22-23, 29.

a tax reduction in 1240 (120). The Theban silks may have lost further ground with the influx of *panni tartarici* from the Levant since the last decades of the thirteenth century, a development linked to a change in western taste and fashion. Secondly, the combination of these factors appears to have accelerated the Genoese shift in silk related activities in Latin Greece. It was increasingly more profitable to purchase raw materials and ship them to western silk manufacturing centers than to deal in finished products. Added weight to this explanation is suggested by a possible transfer of silk technology from Thebes to Lucca, to which we shall soon return.

Until now none of the extant silk pieces has been identified as a product of thirteenth century Genoa. As a result, the reconstruction of the city's silk manufacture in that period must entirely rely on written evidence. A recent study contends that this activity enjoyed a major growth, especially since around the mid-thirteenth century. Unfortunately, this study is marred by numerous misreadings of the sources and uses only part of the available evidence (121). A reconsideration of the issue is therefore imperative. It faces two major problems: how to identify Genoese silks beyond those clearly labelled as such and, more generally, how to determine the nature of Genoese products.

An apprenticeship contract of 1222 offers some important clues with respect to these issues. It deals with a young girl who during six years would learn the weaving of veils with a woman from Asti, «de arte sua oralibus texendis» (122).In addition to these veils, attested in Genoa since 1190, Genoese wills, dowries, household inventories and commercial contracts refer to headscarfs (*facioles*) and to pillow cases or covers (*oregerii*) (123). Some of these pieces were made of silk only, while others were half-silks combining silk

---

(120) See also JACOBY, *Italian Migration and Settlement in Latin Greece*, cited in note 113, pp. 118-120.

(121) P. SPAGIARI, *Cartulari notarili e produzione serica a Genova nel XIII secolo*, in catalogue *Seta a Genova, 1491-1991*, Genova 1991, pp. 13-17. Several of her citations and references are mistaken. Contrary to her view, neither the supposed absence of light sendals from Genoese imports, nor Genoese sales of sendals to Lucchese merchants warrant the assumption that this type of silk textile was produced in Genoa. Moreover, *drappus* and *tela* are generic terms for all textiles, regardless of their fibers, yet stand for silk only if specifically stated, as in *pannus sericus*, *pannus deauratus*, silk being then the only fiber interwoven with gold thread, or *pannus de Bagadello*, clearly made of silk. Moreover, when *drappus* appears next to sendal in mixed consignments, it denotes woolens and not silks. Finally, the production of gold thread in Genoa does not offer any indication about local silk manufacture, since it began earlier than the latter and was largely geared toward export.

(122) A. FERRETTO, *Liber magistri Salmonis, Sacri Palatii notarii (1222-1226)*, in "Atti della Società Ligure di Storia Patria", XXXVI, 1906, no. 468.

(123) M. CHIAUDANO e R. MOROZZO DELLA ROCCA (eds.), *Oberto Scriba de Mercato (1190)*, Torino 1938, no. 586: *duos orales sete*; DOEHAERD, *Les relations commerciales*, cited in note 90, vol. II, no. 305: silk *orales* in 1213; ASG, *Cartolari Notarili*, n. 60, ANGELINO DE SIGESTRO, fol. 85r: *in (...) oregeriis sete* in 1257. See also below, notes 124-125.

with cotton or linen (124). Most of them did apparently not require high-quality fibers, did not absorb much silk, and were of little or no artistic value. They demanded only modest investments in raw materials and work and were relatively cheap. Gold-interwoven or gold-embroidered small pieces of the same types were obviously more expensive (125). Veils, headscarfs and pillow cases or covers were woven on simple narrow looms operated by a single person and could easily be manufactured by women working at home. This is suggested by the apprenticeship contract mentioned earlier, the direct involvement of several Genoese women in the sale of these pieces, as well as by the latter's nature. The domestic production of these pieces appears to have largely depended upon specific orders from local merchants or private customers, or else upon their direct marketing by producers who entrusted single pieces or a number of them to merchants sailing as far as Romania and the Levant (126). In sum, there is good reason to believe that when they appear in Genoese documents these small pieces were local products.

Genoa also manufactured two types of silks, gold-interwoven fabrics and *purpure*, both larger in size and of higher quality (127). The *purpurerii* who produced them, as explicitly stated in 1255, (128) are attested in Genoa since

---

(124) *Liber magistri Salmonis*, cited in note 122, no. 1050: *duo oralia de septa et unum de septa et bombecini* in 1226; LOPEZ, *Nota sulla composizione dei patrimoni privati*, cited in note 87, p. 234: *tria oralia de syrico et lino* in 1238.

(125) A. FERRETTO, *Documenti intorno alle relazioni fra Alba e Genova (1141-1270) (Corpus chartarum Italiae*, XIV e XXXIII, 1), Pinerolo 1906-1910, vol. I, no. 164: Simone Celebrino de Alba buys *tantum opus auri et sete* in 1248; M.W. HALL-COLE, H. C. KRUEGER, R.G. RENERT, R. L. REYNOLDS (eds.), *Notai liguri del sec. XII, V. Giovanni de Guiberto (1200-1211)*, Torino 1939, no. 1216: *in oralibus de sea cum auro et sine auro* in 1205, to be carried to ports located along the Levantine coast, *Ultramare (...) per riveiram Solie* [sic for *Sorie*], and see also nos. 1223, 1370; G. ROSSO (ed.), *Documenti sulle relazioni commercali fra Asti e Genova (1182-1310) con appendice documentaria sulle relazioni commercali fra Asti e l'Occidente (1181-1312)*, Pinerolo 1913, no. 522: a *commenda* of 25 Genoese pounds *in faciolis deauratis* in 1281. It is not always possible to distinguish between cloth interwoven with gold thread and gold embroidery, the term *opus* being used for both types of work: G. MONTICOLO e E. BESTA (eds.), *I capitolari delle arti veneziane sottoposte alla Giustizia Vecchia dalle origini al MCCCXXX*, Roma 1896-1914, vol. II, pp. 594-595. Examples of embroidery in E. MOLINIER, *Inventaire du trésor du Saint Siège sous Boniface VIII (1295)*, in "Bibliothèque de l'Ecole des Chartes", XLVII, 1886, p. 659, no. 1390: *tobaleam de opere racamato laboratam per totum ad aurum et sericum rubeum*; IBID., XLIX, 1888, p. 22, no. 1544: *operatum ad acum de auro et serico*.

(126) See above, notes 123-125.

(127) By the thirteenth century *purpura* had ceased to stand for a purple fabric and had become a generic term for a specific category of silk cloth, distinct from both gold-interwoven fabric and samite, regardless of colour; see a testimony of 1248: R. CESSI (ed.), *Deliberazioni del Maggior Consiglio di Venezia*, Bologna 1931-1950, vol. II, p. 306, XXI/I. Indeed, *purpure* appear in a wide range of colours: MONTICOLO, BESTA, *I capitolari delle arti veneziane*, cited in note 125, vol. II, p. 34, note 3, and p. 591.

(128) F.L. MANNUCCI, *Delle società genovesi d'arti e mestieri durante il secolo XIII*, in "Giornale storico e letterario della Liguria", VI, 1905, p. 292, no. IV.

XI

the early thirteenth century (129). Both types of silks were included in the consignment which one of them, Iohannes de Castello, sent to Lyon in 1248 (130). In 1255 thirteen *purpurerii* producing these silks agreed to comply for two years with existing regulations regarding their measurements and quality standards and to refrain from mixing cotton or wool fibers in their fabrics. These regulations, which could have only been drafted by the purpurerii themselves, imply that some time earlier the latter had established a body to protect their common interests. However, this body had failed to ensure fair competition among its members and to uphold the quality and credibility of their products. The agreement of 1255 was to put an end to these evils and ensure a wider diffusion of their silks. In 1257, at the expiration of their agreement, the purpurerii strengthened their organization, which included then seventeen members, by electing among themselves two consuls and three counselors who would assist them in legislation and in the imposition of sanctions on offenders (131). Their solemn promise to submit to the consuls' authority was not limited in time, as the obligations of 1255, since it also extended to future consuls. Moreover, the presence of two city officials at the ceremony provided an additional sanction to the whole arrangement. In sum, while the document of 1255 points to a voluntary association, the one of 1257 clearly reflects the foundation of an authoritative institution, in fact a guild, under the aegis of the Commune.

There were no prospects that the restrictions imposed upon the *purpurerii's* activity both in 1255 and 1257 would be effectively implemented, unless all the producers of *purpure* and gold-interwoven silks active in Genoa at that time subscribed to them. No *purpurerii* other than those participating in the two ceremonies just mentioned have been found in notarial charters of these same years. We may safely assume, therefore, that their total numbers were indeed limited to thirteen in 1255 and to seventeen in 1257 (132).

---

(129) In 1202-1203: see below, note 131; in 1226: *Liber magistri Salmonis*, cited in note 122, no. 1050.

(130) DOEHAERD, *Les relations commerciales*, cited in note 90, vol. II, no. 571. He appears both in 1255 and 1257 as Iohannes de Castro: see next note.

(131) MANNUCCI, *Delle società genovesi d'arti e mestieri*, cited in note 128, pp. 292-293, nos. IV-V. Newly listed in 1257 were Iohanninus son of Iohannes de Castro, still active as *purpurerius*, two sons of the deceased Isenbardus, previously recorded, and two other individuals. Iohanninus' own son Jacobinus is attested as *purpurerius* in 1281: ROSSO, *Documenti sulle relazioni commercali fra Asti e Genova*, cited in note 125, no. 522.

(132) Four participants also appear in commercial documents drafted in 1257: Enrico de Sancto Ambrosio: ASG, Cartolari Notarili, n. 60, ANGELINO DE SIGESTRO, fol. 83v and 130r; Oberto de Sancto Ambrosio: IBID., fol. 107r; Iohannes de Castro: IBID., fol. 85r; Gullielmus de Sancto Matheo: IBID., fol. 94r. The latter sold two bales of cloth, the nature of which is not specified, in 1265: ed. by L. BALLETTO, *Studi e documenti su Genova e la Sardegna nel secolo XIII*, in "Saggi e documenti" (Civico Istituto Colombiano, Studi e testi, Serie storica a cura di Geo Pistarino, II/2), Genova 1981, pp. 132-133, nos. 10-11.

XI

34

However, the actual number of workers engaged in the manufacturing of the two types of silks was undoubtedly larger. While all the *purpurerii* presumably operated their own looms, some of them also employed weavers in their ateliers or acted as entrepreneurs financing the operation of other workshops (133). These workers were not included in the *purpurerii's* guild, nor were those engaged in the domestic weaving of small silk pieces mentioned earlier. It is noteworthy that no Genoese apprenticeship contracts for the weaving of sendals similar to those of Lucca have been found until now (134). As for the *samitarii* or weavers of samites, they are only seldom attested as residents of Genoa in the period considered here. Of the six known documents in which they appear, three drafted between 1186 and 1203 seem to refer to the same individual (135). It is not clear how the samitarii related to the *purpurerii* (136). In any event, it is obvious that the latter had an overwhelming share in local silk manufacturing, yet the range of their products appears to have been limited to purpure and gold-interwoven silks and was thus smaller than in contemporary Lucca or Venice. The prescribed sizes of these two types of fabrics, restated in 1255, were 12 palms length and 6 width, respectively 2.976 and 1.488 meters. These pieces were thus smaller than contemporary Venetian *purpure* (137). Genoese *purpure* and gold-interwoven silks, the most prestigious local textiles, may have also been

(133) MANNUCCI, *Delle società genovesi d'arti e mestieri*, cited in note 128, p. 292, no. IV: manufacturing *per se vel per aliquem laboratorem suum* [...] *seu aliquam personam pro eis vel habentem causam ab eis*. A salaried weaver working for a *purpurerius* is already attested in 1202-1203: *Lanfranco (1202-1226)*, cited in note 70, vol. I, nos. 201, 230, 414.

(134) Examples for Lucca in BINI, *I Lucchesi a Venezia*, cited in note 38, vol. I, pp. 59-60.

(135) M. CHIAUDANO (ed.), *Oberto Scriba de Mercato (1186)*, Torino 1940, no. 22, Fredericus Xamirarius (*sic!*); *Oberto Scriba de Mercato (1190)*, cited in note 123, no. 222: Fredacius Xamitarius; *Giovanni de Guiberto*, cited in note 125, no. 1013, in 1203: Fredançonus Samitarius. Note the similarity of the first names in these three cases. See also *Lanfranco*, cited in note 70, vol. I, nos. 154, 274, 316.

(136) MANNUCCI, *Delle società genovesi d'arti e mestieri*, cited in note 128, pp. 274-275, argues that the *samitarii* formed a branch of the guild of *purpurerii*, yet without any supporting evidence.

(137) IBID., p. 292, no. IV. The Venetian regulations of 1265 prescribe a length of 5 brachia and a width of 2, respectively 3.415 and 1.366 meters, for *purpure* and several other types of silk cloth; there were also larger as well as smaller sizes for other categories: MONTICOLO, BESTA, *I capitolari delle arti veneziane*, cited in note 125, vol. II, p. 36, par. XXI, and see pp. 34-35, pars. XVIII-XVIIII. Later evidence on dimensions and standards of Lucchese silks have been analyzed by D. and M. KING, *Silk Weaves of Lucca in 1376*, in I. ESTHAM and M. NOCKERT (eds.), *Opera Textilia Variorum Temporum, To honour Agnes Geijer on her Ninetieth Birthday 26th October 1988*, Stockholm 1988, pp. 67-76. However, these data should not be adduced in our context, in view of the significant changes that occured in Italian silk manufacture in the preceding century.

often inferior in quality to those manufactured in other silk centers. We have noted earlier that in 1255 their producers agreed to abstain for two years from weaving them in half-silks (138). Such Genoese fabrics are indirectly attested both earlier and later, in 1246 and 1257, which explains why some Genoese merchants stressed that the *purpure* they sold were made of silk only (139).

It is with the preceding considerations in mind that we should examine a Lucchese statute of 1308. It enjoined Lucchese weavers imitating gold-interwoven cloth and silk fabrics produced in Genoa, Venice and Arezzo, to adhere to the standards and dimensions common in these cities (140). The statute was most likely issued at the request of merchants complaining about the weavers producing these imitation silks. The strict adherence to the standards and measurements common in the three cities was to ensure their broader diffusion in a highly competitive market (141). This suggests that the Lucchese statute did not refer to high-quality silks, affordable only to a select and restricted clientele, but to medium-grade products, essentially half-silks, the production of which is attested both in Genoa, as noted above, as well as in Venice (142). In short, the Lucchese statute of 1308 cannot be adduced as proof of high-quality silk production in Genoa, as argued sometimes. On the contrary, it provides indirect confirmation about the inferiority of Genoese products compared with the high-grade silks of Lucca. Incidentally, it may be fitting to stress in this context that silk manufacture in thirteenth century Lucca was not restricted to elaborate and costly silks, the almost exclusive focus of scholarly attention, but also included lower grades of plain fabrics. This is already obvious by the distinction between light and heavy sendals

---

(138) See above, p. 33.

(139) DOEHARD, *Les relations commerciales*, cited in note 90, vol. II, no. 562, *in (...) peciis tribus purpuretis sete* in 1246; also ASG, Cartolari Notarili, n. 60, ANGELINO DE SIGESTRO, fol. 94r, 107r, 130r (the latter shipped to Maiorca) in 1257. Venice also produced half-silk and even fustian *purpure*: MONTICOLO, BESTA, *I capitolari delle arti veneziane*, cited in note 125, vol. II, p. 34, note 3. For 1255, see above, p. 33.

(140) S. BONGI, L. DEL PRETE (eds.), *Statuto del Comune di Lucca dell'anno MCCCVIII (Memorie e Documenti per servire alla Storia di Lucca*, vol. III , parte III), Lucca 1867, p. 220, cap. CXXXVIIII: *intelligatur de illis qui (...) artem exercent de drappis aureis et sete, qui secundum artem Ianuensium facere debeant et in ipsa longitudine que Ianue consuetum fuerit fieri*. According to Bongi, IBID., p. XI, some of the regulations of 1308 had already been issued in 1261, yet it is impossible to determine whether such was the case of this chapter.

(141) A similar scenario is attested for Florence in 1489: L. MONNAS, *Loom Widths and Selvedges prescribed by Italian Silk Weaving Statutes 1265-1512: a Preliminary Investigation*, in "Centre International d'Etude des Textiles Anciens (CIETA) - Bulletin", LXVI, 1988, p. 35. *

(142) See D. JACOBY, *Tra Bisanzio, il Levante e Venezia: dalle materie prime ai drappi nel Duecento e nei primi Trecento*, in R. MUELLER (ed.), *Dal baco al drappo. La seta in Italia tra medioevo e seicento*, Venezia 1999 [in press]. There is no evidence about silks woven in Arezzo.

found in some Genoese documents of that period, (143) which recalls the later one between light and heavy satins in Lucca (144).

Not surprisingly, the medium-grade silks presumably produced and marketed by the Genoese *purpurerii* appear only seldom among the pieces acquired or collected by the foreign lay and ecclesiastical elite. An overlooked reference to such fabrics, in fact the earliest one, warrants particular attention. In 1242 the English royal court paid a total of 9 marks for two pieces of Genoese silk and a Milanese fabric (145). The nature of the Genoese pieces is not specified, yet we may safely assume that they were not high-quality silks such as the sendals, samites, baudekins and gold-interwoven textiles registered in other entries of the royal registers. They must have been rather relatively small-sized, medium-grade and plain fabrics, as suggested by their price. At an average of 3 marks or 2 pounds 5 shillings each, they were inexpensive compared with high-grade Lucchese samites costing more than 4 pounds apiece in London around that time (146). It may be safely assumed that the two Genoese pieces were not the only ones available there, yet so far no further evidence of Genoese silks of that type has been found in the English royal registers of the thirteenth and early fourteenth century. Various documents of that period, in particular inventories of ecclesiastical institutions, yield much information about the diffusion in the West of high-grade silks produced in Spain, Romania, the Levant, Lucca and Venice, as well as about the influx of *panni tartarici* manufactured in the Muslim Near East and beyond. Genoese textiles are only seldom mentioned in these sources. In 1292 the church of St. Paul in London owned two Genoese fabrics bearing designs often found on silk textiles (147). It has been taken for granted, therefore, that they were silks (148). However, it is not clear whether their de-

---

(143) *Giovanni de Guiberto*, cited in note 125, nos. 1439, 1686, 1796: *de cendatis grossis* in 1205-1206; *Lanfranco*, cited in note 70, vol. I, no. 574: *postam unam cendati grossi et duas subtiles*.

(144) D. and M. KING, *Silk Weaves of Lucca in 1376*, cited in note 137, pp. 74-75.

(145) *Calendar of Liberate Rolls Preserved in the Public Record Office, Henry III*, vol. II, A.D. 1240-1245, London 1930, p. 121; see IBID., another payment of 9 marks for three baudekins.

(146) The mark was equivalent to 3/4 of the English pound, hence 3 marks were 2 and 1/4 pounds. In 1244 the English court paid far less for two pieces of Genoese cloth without gold, not registered as being silks, which were included in a large consignment of several types of cloth, the total sum being 66 shillings or 3 and 1/3 pounds: IBID., p. 248. In 1245 it paid 40 pounds 13 shillings for 9 pieces of Lucchese samite, or somewhat more than 4 pounds each: IBID., p. 307. However, the comparison is not entirely conclusive since we do not know the measurements of these pieces.

(147) Sir W.E. DUGDALE, *The History of Saint Paul's Cathedral in London from its Foundation until this Time*, London 1658, pp. 208, 224; *capa de panno januensi (sic), cum circulis et avibus croceis et leopardis; item unus pannus de Janue (sic) rotellatus cum avibus bicapitibus.*

(148) L.T. BELGRANO, *Della vita privata dei Genovesi*, seconda edizione, Genova 1875,

coration was woven into the cloth or embroidered on a plain fabric. This appears to have precisely been the case of two other pieces having the appearance of diasper, registered in 1315 in the treasury of Canterbury cathedral (149). Finally, two pieces of Genoese cloth appear in 1295 in the papal treasury next to two pieces of woolens and coupons of samites, diaspers and *panni tartarici*. It is likely that in this context too the Genoese fabrics were silks, although no indication about their nature is provided (150).

We have noted that Genoese merchants had an intimate knowledge of Spanish, Byzantine, Islamic and oriental silk textiles, which they imported in large numbers. They dominated the Mediterranean market of raw silk, Venetians being their only serious competitors, and assumed an important role in entrepreneurship at Thebes in the first half of the thirteenth century. Why, then, did they not take advantage of these assets to develop a sophisticated silk industry in Genoa? The absence of such a process is all the more surprising since it took place in Venice precisely in the same period. Both cities faced similar problems of supply in raw materials and technology, while enjoying at the same time extensive trade and shipping networks capable of a significant contribution to the development of high-grade silk manufacture. Until some time after 1240, the absence of any initiative in this direction in Genoa may have been partly linked to the Genoese involvement in Thebes and to the import of Theban textiles to Genoa. More generally, though, it was in line with Genoese economic priorities in the twelfth and thirteenth century. Large investments went into trade and naval construction, yet not into the promotion of other industries such as textiles. The local Genoese consumption of silks was still modest, even in fairly affluent households, judging by extant inventories and wills listing pieces of clothing and bedcovers made of silk and others lined with silk fabrics (151). Moreover, most of these silks were foreign, although this is usually not stated (152).

---

p. 202, followed by F. PODREIDER, *Storia dei tessuti d'arte in Italia (secoli XII-XVIII)*, Bergamo 1928, p. 53.

(149) J. DART, *The History and Antiquities of the Cathedral Church of Canterbury and the once-adjoining Monastery*, London 1726, Appendix, p. VII: *par unum de rubeo panno de Genne (sic) diasperatum, cum stragulis et stellis aureis*. On the meaning of *diasperatus* as embroidery giving the cloth the look of diasper, see MONTICOLO, BESTA, *I capitolari delle arti veneziane*, cited in note 125, vol. II, pp. 592-593; see also IBID., p. 34, note 3.

(150) Specifications are also missing for several other pieces included in the same list: MOLINIER, *Inventaire du trésor du Saint Siège*, cited in note 125, pp. 650-652, nos. 1230-1262; no.1259: *duos pannos januenses albos*.

(151) LOPEZ, *Nota sulla composizione dei patrimoni privati*, cited in note 87, pp. 224, 225, 227, 232, 233, 241, 243, 246, 247, 259, 262; among the pieces, *cultram cendati, mantellum stanfortis cum cendato ialno*, and in one case two types of silk fabrics are joined, *supracotum xamiti vermilii cum cendato ialno* (p. 243).

(152) Some exceptions, as above, p. 26, note 87.

XI

38

These factors explain the Genoese attitude toward local silk manufacture, which bears a strong resemblance to the one displayed toward the local production of woolens (153). In Thebes Genoese merchants and entrepreneurs sustained experienced workshops producing high-standard fabrics. On the other hand, in Genoa they were reluctant to invest in the development and upgrading of a fairly modest industrial infrastructure and in the financing of a local silk industry, which they considered a rather risky venture. This also accounts for the absence of governmental incentives aimed at attracting skilled silk workers, as found in other cities (154). On the whole the number of artisans involved in Genoese silk manufacture appears to have remained small and increased only as a result of local professional training, attested for the sons of some *purpurerii* and the son of a *draperius* or cloth dealer (155) or of spontaneous individual immigration. Conditions changed somewhat in the early fourteenth century, when political upheaval in Lucca since 1314 induced many of this city's silk-workers to emigrate. Yet even then only a small number of them spontaneously settled in Genoa (156). The full development of the Genoese silk industry occurred much later, which accounts for the inferior standard of Genoese silks, compared with those of Lucca and Venice in the thirteenth century. In sum, while some Genoese merchants were importing silks, many others had a vested interest in the smooth operation and enhancement of Lucca's solid and sophisticated silk industry. Its supply in raw materials and the diffusion of its textiles, which largely depended upon them, yielded substantial profits. It is not excluded, therefore, that Genoese merchants and entrepreneurs were involved in a transfer of silk designs, looms and technology from Thebes to Lucca (157). Unfortunately, only seldom can such a process be securely documented.

It has been argued in recent years that Lucca's location in the western Mediterranean and the broad diffusion of Spanish silks in the twelfth century West provided the initial impetus to the development of the Lucchese silk industry (158). It would be mistaken, however, to underestimate the im-

(153) On the latter attitude, see R. LOPEZ, Le origini dell'arte della lana, in ID., Studi sull'economia genovese, cited in note 87, pp. 69-95, 124-130.
(154) See above, p. 20.
(155) For the former, see above, p. 33, note 131; for the latter, MANNUCCI, Delle società genovesi d'arti e mestieri, cited in note 128, p. 293, no. V.
(156) MOLÀ, La comunità dei Lucchesi a Venezia, cited in note 38, pp. 25-27.
(157) M.F. MAZZAOUI, Artisan Migration and Technology in the Italian Textile Industry in the Late Middle ages (1100-1500), in R. COMBA, G. PICCINI, G. PINTO (eds.), Stutture familiari, epidemie, migrazioni nel Italia medievale, Napoli 1984, p. 524, rightly insists on the role of merchants and entrepreneurs in technology transfers.
(158) B. TIETZEL, Italienische Seidengewebe des 13., 14. und 15. Jarhunderts, Köln 1984, p. 58; VON WILCKENS, Die textilen Künste, cited in note 28, pp. 105-106, 111.

portance of Byzantine fabrics in this respect. Genoa imported them even before the rise of Lucca as silk manufacturer around the mid-twelfth century and was deeply involved in their marketing in the Latin West in the following period. These silks could not have failed to leave their imprint on early Lucchese silk products, none of which has been identified so far. The Byzantine imprint on some categories of Lucchese silks was presumably strengthened in the first half of the thirteenth century by Genoese imports from Thebes, known for its samites and gold-interwoven cloth, (159) by Genoese silk entrepreneurship in that city, and by the possible transfer of silk weaves, implements and technical expertise from Thebes to Lucca. It is noteworthy that the Lucchese silk fabrics of the thirteenth century, namely sendals, samites, *sarantasimi* and *catasamita*, all bore Byzantine names (160). This is yet another argument for a Byzantine, rather than a Spanish origin of the skilled workers and the advanced technologies enabling the initial rise and development of the high-grade Lucchese silk industry. Such a process does not necessarily contradict the possible adoption of Spanish weaves and designs under the influence of silk fabrics imported by the Genoese from Muslim Spain. The gold and silver-interwoven, as well as the plain sendals of Lucca sold in Castile in 1207 may well have been similar to the Islamic textiles of Spain with which they had to compete, and the *bagadelli hispanici* shipped to Ceuta may well have been Lucchese imitations (161). Genoa also had a major share in the influx into Italy of Spanish silks with Moorish geometrical or arabesque-like patterns and that of *panni tartarici* since the second half of the thirteenth century. The great favour enjoyed by these silks is reflected by their depiction in Italian paintings of the following period and by a fairly large number of datable pieces that have survived. Moreover, in the third decade of the fourteenth century Italian designers began to create patterns either imitating Chinese or Islamic textiles or closely based on their designs (162).

Genoa was located at the crossroad of these multiple currents and decisively contributed to their imprint. Its involvement in silk trade and in the

---

(159) JACOBY, *Silk in Western Byzantium*, cited in note 5, pp. 462-463, 466-467.

(160) Sendals and samites are mentioned in the *Statuto dell'Arte dei tintori di Lucca*, cited in note 74, pp. 13-15, 18-20, and other sources. Lucchese diaspers appear in the papal inventory of 1295: MOLINIER, *Inventaire du trésor du Saint Siège*, cited in note 125, pp. 650-651, nos. 1229, 1245; *sarantasimi* are cited IBID., no. 1226, and a *catasamitum* in 1311: MONTICOLO, BESTA, *I capitolari delle arti veneziane*, cited in note 125, vol. II, p. 33, note 1.

(161) See above, pp. 15-16.

(162) See above, p. 26, note 86; B. KLESSE, *Seidenstoffe in der italienischen Malerei des 14. Jahrhunderts*, Bern 1967; A.E. WARDWELL, *Flight of the Phoenix: Crosscurrents in Late Thirteenth- to Fourteenth-Century Silk Patterns and Motifs*, in *The Bulletin of the Cleveland Museum of Art*, LXXIV, January 1987, pp. 23-29; VON WILCKENS, *Die textilen Künste*, cited in note 28, pp. 113-120.

production of silk fabrics in the Mediterranean region in the twelfth and thirteenth century clearly illustrates the interrelation and interaction existing between silk economics and the artistic aspects of silk manufacture. It points to the possible impact of economic factors upon the choice and transfer of raw materials, weaves, designs, iconography, silk related technologies, and skilled workers. It is obvious that the mobility and chronology of all these factors must be taken into account in the dating and attribution of extant silk fabrics. In this respect it may render the task of textile historians even more difficult than hitherto.

The Production of Silk Textiles in Latin Greece

Silk fabrics were already known and produced around the Mediterranean before sericulture, the growing of the domesticated silkworm, was introduced into Byzantium in the sixth century, during the reign of Emperor Justinian I. By that time they had already acquired great importance in the ritual and decoration of the imperial court, the liturgy of the Church and as symbols of social status. Their role in these contexts grew further in the following centuries. Our knowledge about silk production and consumption in Byzantium and elsewhere in the Middle Ages mainly derives from a highly selective body of evidence. Written sources mostly refer to sumptuous, costly, and prestige-linked textiles offered to ruler, lay and church dignitaries and ecclesiastical institutions, or else acquired by them. Moreover, silk textiles preserved over the centuries mostly belong to these same categories of high-grade products. Yet the Empire also produced silk fabrics of lower quality. Some types of silk cloth will be examined below.

Since the eleventh century the growing internal demand for a large variety of silk textiles generated an expansion of the Byzantine silk industry, in particular in the western provinces of the Empire[1]. The silk centres of this region, some of which produced high-quality fabrics in fairly large quantities, were all conquered by the Latins shortly after the Fourth Crusade, which ended in 1204, and remained under their rule for more than two centuries. Their activity might have been temporarily hampered or halted by turmoil and warfare in the last years of Byzantine rule, the time of the Latin conquest, or the early years of Latin domination. Yet, once conditions were stabilized, the supply of these centres in raw materials, their manufacturing of textiles, and the diffusion of their finished products could be resumed. The purpose of this paper is to evaluate the short and long-term impact of the Latin conquest and rule upon the activity of these centres and upon the nature of their products. Until recently textile historians have been unaware of the latter's importance and, as a result, have not identified any of them among extant pieces. As a result, the reconstruction of silk manufacture in Latin Greece will have to rely entirely on written sources.

By the time of the Latin conquest silk industries had developed in Thebes, Corinth, the Peloponnese, Euboea, known as Negroponte in the Latin period, and the island of Andros. All these industries produced samite, a rather heavy, strong and glossy silk cloth in twill weave, the name of which was derived from the Greek ἑξάμιτον (examiton) or "six-threaded", since the weave units used were composed of six threads[2]. There were many varieties of this textile, yet the exact nature of most of them is unknown[3]. A few of the industrial centres mentioned above also manufactured gold-interwoven samite, a textile combining silk with flattened and spinned gold wire, which required a particularly sophisticated weaving technique and was extremely costly because of the use of precious metal and a substantial labor input[4]. In the twelfth century the island of Andros was also known for the production of another high-quality silk fabric, sendal, a lightweight cloth in tabby weave imitating an Islamic textile. Its Greek name, σενδές (*sendes*), was derived from the Arabic *sundus*[5]. At that time Byzantine samite and sendal were in high demand within the Empire itself, not only in Muslim countries but in the West as well[6]. We have no information about the nature of other high-quality fabrics manufactured by the silk industries of Byzantine Greece. On the other hand, two types of lower-grade silk textiles produced in the Empire are documented. A rough fabric, known as κουκουλάριχο (*koukoulariko*) cloth, was manufactured from waste and floss silk spun into yarn, while other fabrics were in fact half-silks combining silk with linen, cotton or wool[7].

In the twelfth century Thebes was the main producer of silk textiles in western Byzantium, some of its products surpassing in quality those of all other silk centres of that region. Thebes was apparently the only one to utilize silk dyed with murex purple, the highest grade of purple colorant, derived from various marine mollusk genera. A considerable number of mollusks was needed for the production of a small amount of dye, a process that accounted for the high cost of this colorant, the production and use of which was entirely subsidized by the imperial court[8]. Purple fishers from Athens, together with those from Euripos and Karystos in Euboea operated off the island of Gyaros, located between Andros and Kea[9]. The extraction of purple from the mollusks, the preparation of the colorant in Athens, and the dyeing of silk in Thebes were highly sophisticated activities requiring particular expertise and were practiced by few skilled workers[10]. Silk dyed with murex purple was woven into fabrics exclusively intended for the emperors and some members of their close entourage. These fabrics, therefore, were not marketed[11]. On the other hand, the dyeing of silk with kermes, a high-quality, solid red colorant, appears to have been common to all silk centres of western Byzantium captured by the Latins. This dyestuff was obtained from the dried and crushed female kermes parasite living mainly on the holly oak, an arborescent bush common in Boeotia, Euboea and practically the entire Peloponnese[12]. All production centres of Latin Greece thus enjoyed an abundant and readily available supply of this colorant. However, because of its high cost kermes-dyed silk was only used for high-grade textiles[13]. The silk centres of western Byzantium which came under Latin rule in the early thirteenth century also utilized other colorants, as implied by the evidence adduced below, yet their nature is not documented except in one case.

In the eleventh and twelfth century some Greek *archontes,* members of the local elite living in cities, were the driving force behind the expansion of the silk industries of that region. They acted as employers, entrepreneurs or associates of independent silk artisans, providing workshops with silk, cocoons and dyes, or else advancing liquid capital to purchase these raw materials and pay the workers' wages. In return, they received finished products, the marketing of which was primarily geared toward the supply of the internal Byzantine market and Constantinople in particular[14]. The Latin conquest proved to be a decisive turning point in silk economics by generating three important developments, which disrupted the existing production and trading patterns. First, the financial capacity of the *archontes* was seriously weakened by the partial or total expropriation of their resources by the Latin conquerors[15]. In addition, imperial control over the production of specific types of silk textiles and their trade collapsed in

23

the wake of the Fourth Crusade. The political fragmentation of Latin Greece prevented any single lord from limiting access to raw silk or silk fabrics manufactured on his territory, or from supervising their distribution. It also stimulated fierce competition between silk centres located in different lordships. Latin lords, therefore, considered it in their best interest to further sericulture and the production of silk fabrics, attract investments, enhance foreign purchases, and thereby ensure themselves of increased revenues from trade and from custom dues. As a result the *archontes* lost their dominant role in silk manufacture and marketing. They were replaced in these fields, whether partially or entirely, by western merchants who had the double advantage of handling liquid capital on a larger scale and of being familiar with western trade, shipping and marketing networks. These merchants decisively contributed to a marked change in the orientation of Greece's trade pattern. Silk exports became increasingly geared toward the western market and integrated within the Mediterranean trade system dominated by Venice and Genoa[16].

This whole evolution is well illustrated in Thebes, the best documented silk centre among those of western Byzantium that came under Latin rule. The city was captured by Boniface of Montferrat without any resistance late in 1204 and did not suffer any demographic loss[17]. In 1209 its whole population headed by the local clergy and the *archontes* solemnly welcomed the Latin emperor of Constantinople, Henry of Hainaut, when he entered Thebes[18]. However, because of the particular function of this city as supplier of the imperial court in the twelfth century, the production and marketing of its silk fabrics were more affected by the Latin conquest than those of other centers. In the Byzantine period Venetian merchants, some of whom resided in the city, were restricted to the purchase of specific types of textiles[19]. The successful operation of the Theban silk industry prompted western investors to promote its activity after 1204. Both resident and visiting Venetian merchants are attested in the city in the thirteenth century[20]. In this period they apparently expanded their involvement in silk, previously limited to trade, to the field of entrepreneurship. This is hinted by the role assumed by rival Genoese merchants, whose activity in Thebes began only after the Latin conquest[21].

In 1240 Genoa concluded a treaty with the lord of Athens, Guy I of La Roche, whose territory included Thebes. This treaty, which renewed a previous one, the date of which is unknown, points to the free export of Theban silk textiles. More specifically, it reveals that some Genoese merchants financed the activity of a number of local silk workshops producing cloth exclusively for them and, in addition, ordered silk fabrics from other manufacturers. In both cases, though, they must have specified the weaves, colors and designs of the fabrics they commissioned in order to ensure that they would be easily marketable in the West, their main destination[22]. Significantly, in spite of the cooperation of the Greek *archontes* of Thebes with the Latin conquerors, noted above, there is no evidence implying that they or their successors were involved in either silk entrepreneurship or marketing after 1204. This may be due to the fragmentary nature of the extant sources. More likely, though, it appears that they were ousted from these activities by Genoese and Venetian merchants.

Most products of the Theban silk industry exported by these and other western

XII

merchants must have been similar to those marketed prior to the Fourth Crusade. They included samites dyed with the prized kermes and with other colorants, as well as gold-interwoven fabrics[23]. On the other hand, there is good reason to believe that Thebes ceased to produce silk fabrics dyed with murex purple, or at best used this dyestuff for small pieces only[24]. Neither the Latin emperors of Constantinople, nor the Latin lords of Greece or the Greek rulers of Nicaea and Epiros were capable of, or willing to sustain the high cost of production and extensive use of this colorant, as done by the Byzantine emperors before 1204. Instead, cheaper dyes must have been utilized to obtain substitute purple, a practice already attested in the Empire before that date[25].

Thebes and its countryside suffered from military incursions in the 1230s and the 1250s. Letters written by Pope Gregory IX in 1235 and 1236 mention frequent Greek attacks against the city and its rural territory, although it is not clear where they came from[26]. In 1258 the prince of Frankish Morea, William II of Villehardouin, besieged Thebes and devastated its surroundings in order to compel Guy I of La Roche, lord of Athens, to recognize him as overlord[27]. The following year the brother of Emperor Michael VIII, John Palaeologus, defeated the prince and his vassals at the battle of Pelagonia and advanced from Thessaly into Frankish Greece, where he plundered Thebes[28]. However, the industrial capacity of the city does not seem to have been seriously affected by these events. Indeed, a few years later, in 1262, Pope Urban IV ordered the prior of the Dominicans in Andreville or Andravida, the capital of the Principality of Frankish Morea, and a canon of the episcopal church of Corinth to purchase for him forty or more pieces of high-quality samite produced in Greece, green, purple, red or white, for a total of 2,000 hyperpers[29]. The average price of these pieces, some 50 hyperpers each, confirms that they would indeed be high-grade products, yet excludes the use of genuine murex dye for the purple silks. In addition, the Pope wrote to the archbishops of Thebes, Athens and Patras and to the bishops of Argos, Coron, Modon, Sparta and Negroponte, requesting each of them to send him four high-grade, well-woven and well-dyed pieces of samite, each of a different color, namely green, purple, red and white, in fact similar to those mentioned in the previous letter[30]. The archbishops of Thebes and Athens must have purchased Theban silks, and this may have also been the case of some pieces bought by the other prelates. Since we do not know whether the samites bought for the pope were plain, as it would seem at first glance, or figured, it is impossible to identify them among the silks listed in 1295 in the inventory of the papal treasury as coming from Romania, the region of Byzantine and former Byzantine territories[31]. Somewhat later, in 1300, the Duke of Athens, Guy II of La Roche, sent to the papal court at Rome twenty pieces of samite, obviously Theban products. At his request Venice exempted him from the custom dues amounting to some forty-five Venetian pounds, to which he would have been liable[32]. Theban and other Greek silks were thus well-known and appreciated in Italy.

There was apparently also a fairly important demand for Theban silks in Latin Greece itself. The lifestyle of the knightly class and the individual social status of its members were expressed in conspicuous consumption, and there was ample room for the display of precious clothes at numerous occasions, such as court gatherings and festivities. In addition, largesse or generous giving ranked high in the social ethos of the nobility and

25

was one of the virtues expected from feudal lords[33]. Two instances provide vivid illustrations of these features. For the knighting ceremony of the young Duke of Athens, Guy II of La Roche, which took place at Thebes in 1294, all the high clergy, barons and knights invited six months ahead prepared precious garments, in all likelihood mostly of silk, for themselves as well as for their retinue[34]. The Duke of Athens must have bought at Thebes some, if not all the cloth required for his own needs and those of the members of his court, like the samites he sent to Rome a few years later, in 1300[35]. It is unclear whether his guests acted similarly or acquired textiles from other Greek manufacturing centres. At the invitation of the Prince of Morea, Philip of Savoy, the knights of Latin Greece convened in 1304 in Corinth for a parliament and festivities that were to last twenty days and include jousts with seven western knights. The prince ordered garments of green sendal strewn with golden shells, presumably embroidered, to be prepared for the seven knights of Greece who would oppose them in single combats[36]. Thebes seem to have been the most likely place at which the sendal was purchased, since Corinth apparently did not produce any silks at that time[37]. We may thus add one more type of silk cloth to those already mentioned above as products of Theban workshops.

The manufacture of silk fabrics in Thebes and their export continued after the Catalan conquest of 1311. According to an unpublished commercial manual completed at Florence around 1320, kermes-dyed samites were exported from Thebes, Negroponte and other localities of Romania to Egypt[38]. The Syrian scholar and prince Abū al-Fidā' author of a geographic treatise composed in 1321, mentions a silk cloth for which Thebes was famous, yet it is not clear whether it was gold-interwoven or a type of satin. For information about Romania he apparently relied on eyewitnesses[39]. Francesco Balducci Pegolotti, an agent of the Florentine commercial and banking company of the Bardi, composed between 1330 and 1340 a trade manual in which he mentions the *braccia* or "arm-length" of Thebes, a measure obviously used for silk fabrics[40]. In 1322 Theban kermes-dyed and other samites, the colors of which are not stated, appear among the precious fabrics belonging to King Philip V of France[41]. The inventory of the papal treasury compiled at Avignon in 1353 records a total of eight pieces and coupons of red and one piece of white Theban samite[42]. These were clearly not among the samites sent by Guy II of La Roche to Rome in 1300, mentioned above. Only relatively few objects transferred from Rome reached Avignon after Pope Clemens V settled in that city in 1309, and no Theban samites appear in the earliest lists established there in 1314[43]. We may thus safely assume that Theban silks reached Avignon between 1309 at the earliest and some time before 1353, since some of the pieces listed in that year were coupons, which implies that the missing sections had already been used earlier. A later inventory of 1369 records four pieces of red and two pieces of white Theban samite[44], which implies that at least one of the latter had reached Avignon after 1353.

As political centre of the Catalan state in Greece Thebes was the scene of a power-struggle and much turmoil in the late 1350s and in the 1360s[45]. One may wonder to what extent the events of these troubled years affected its silk manufacture. In August 1362 the Venetian Nicoletto Bassadona incurred in Thebes losses amounting to 522 hyperpers[46], which suggests that he was engaged in the export of either silk or local silk fabrics. The Florentine Nerio I Acciaiuoli became lord of Thebes in the spring of 1378 or rather 1379[47]. It is likely that he purchased in that city some of the silk pieces which were in his possession at the time of his death in 1394. These included *catasamiti*, a variety of samite that has not been identified[48]. A red samite from Thebes is listed in an inventory of objects belonging to King Charles V of France, who reigned from 1364 to 1380[49]. Thebes also produced red satin, apparently a half-silk with silk warp and cotton weft. According to an inventory compiled in 1387, this cloth was used for upholstery and hangings in the chambers of King Charles VI of France[50]. No later evidence regarding Theban silk textiles has been found so far. One may wonder, therefore, until when their production continued.

Corinth also manufactured high-grade silk textiles in the twelfth century, although its products competed neither in quality nor in sophistication with those of Thebes[51]. Corinth appears to have been the second most important silk centre of western Byzantium at that time. The total absence of evidence regarding silk manufacture in the city after the Latin conquest is therefore puzzling. Corinth's occupation by Leo Sgouros since 1201 or 1202 and the Latin siege of Acrocorinth from 1205 to 1209 or 1210 clearly inflicted economic and demographic losses on the city[52]. "Where are the prosperous citizens of Corinth? Are they not all gone, unseen, unheard of?", bemoaned Michael Choniates in 1208 at the latest[53]. According to a synodical act of unknown date referred to in 1396 many of the city's inhabitants allegedly resettled in Monemvasia[54], yet no silk industry was established in this city by refugees. Under these circumstances, one would have expected silk manufacture to be continued or be resumed in Corinth, as after the deportation of this city's silk workers by Roger II of Sicily in 1147[55]. Such was apparently not the case, despite the practice of sericulture and the collection of kermes in its rural hinterland[56]. It would seem, therefore, that the events of the early thirteenth century and especially the departure of rich entrepreneurs, who had previously financed the activity of the local silk industry, caused the collapse of this branch of urban economy[57].

Such a course of events appears to be supported by the fact that in 1262 the bishop of Corinth was not among the prelates of Latin Greece whom Gregory IX asked to send silk textiles to the papal court[58]. If nevertheless Corinth's silk industry survived until the early fourteenth century, its collapse surely came in 1312, when the Catalans of the Duchy of Athens attacked and looted the city. Recent excavations carried out at Corinth by the American School of Classical Studies at Athens confirm that the city suffered then severe damage[59]. Shortly afterwards the bishop of Corinth obtained from Pope Clement V a dispensation of three years for the payment of papal taxes[60]. The pope's grant implies that Corinth and its rural area had not been totally devastated and were expected to yield again a sizeable revenue within a few years. Indeed, imports of Veneto and Pisan ceramics, among them high-grade tableware, between 1312 and the mid-fourteenth century suggest a process of recovery[61]. Economic activity in Corinth was apparently conducted on a larger scale since the 1360s, as suggested by some finds of Venetian coins[62], yet apparently without reaching the early-thirteenth century level, as we may gather from the seigniorial revenues yielded by the city[63]. The expansion of Corinth's economy may be partly credited to Nerio I Acciaiuoli, the city's lord from *c.* 1365 to 1394[64]. However, this development was not accompanied by a revival of silk manufacture, despite the abundance of silk and kermes available in Corinth's countryside[65]. It is noteworthy that the list of seigniorial dues levied in the city in 1365 does not include taxes on the sale of silk textiles[66].

The manufacture of silk fabrics in the Peloponnese under Latin rule is duly documented. By the treaty of Sapientsa, concluded in June 1209, the lord of Frankish Morea, Geoffrey I of Villehardouin, pledged that each year he and his successors would deliver two high-grade pieces of gold-interwoven silk fabrics to the church of San Marco in Venice and another, similar piece, to the doge of that city[67]. The following year the archbishop of Patras, Antelmus, promised to send each year a high-grade piece of samite to the abbey of Cluny in Burgundy[68]. The two Frankish lords might have intended to purchase some or all of these textiles in Thebes or in Corinth, if this city's industry still pursued its activity. More likely, though, they obtained them from silk centres located within their respective domains[69]. Silk weaving was presumably practiced in the region of Patras since the late ninth and apparently expanded in the eleventh and twelfth century[70]. In 1223 three Venetian merchants on business in Modon bought from four other Venetians several pieces of silk cloth which most likely had been manufactured in that region, though not necessarily in Modon itself[71]. Messenia produced then large quantities of silk and kermes[72]. It is unclear whether the bishops of Modon, Coron, Sparta and Argos obtained from local producers or purchased elsewhere the pieces which Pope Urban IV requested from them in 1262[73]. In any event, small production centres manufacturing low-grade silk textiles clearly existed in the Peloponnese. Some *koukoulariko* silk fabric was exported from Nauplia in 1273, a port that served exclusively as an outlet for its own products and those of its hinterland. At his death in 1281 the chancellor of the Principality of Morea, Leonardo da Veroli, owned a bed cover of that same type of rough cloth, in all likelihood a product of the Peloponnese[74].

Interesting evidence regarding silk textiles in Patras in the late Latin period appears in the will of Bartolomeo Zane de Visdanelis, drafted in April 1430, about a year after the city's reconquest by the Empire. This rich merchant, a local resident, did not engage in entrepreneurship, nor in the manufacture of silk textiles, as we may gather from the fact that the will does not refer to such activities. On the other hand, he had clearly been active in silk trade for many years, dealing on a large scale in satin and in *cataxamita*, a variety of samite already encountered above. We may safely assume that both these types of silk cloth were produced in Patras or in its vicinity, since some pieces of *cataxamita* were sold as half-finished products. They were afterwards dyed in the dyeshop of the merchant's brother-in-law, Nicolò de Leonessa, at the request of customers. A *papas* or Greek priest appears among the three mentioned by name who had chosen kermes red dye, yet had still to pay for the work. In all likelihood the dyeshop also used indigo, a cargo of which was sent by the merchant and a partner of his to Venice. In addition, Bartolomeo Zane de Visdanelis had given his uncle no less than hundred and twenty pieces of satin and six garments made of *cataxamita*, which had not yet been sold. There is no indication about their destination, yet some, if not all of them must have been intended for export[75].

The manufacture of silk textiles in the island of Euboea or Negroponte, including

XII

gold-interwoven cloth, had begun in the Byzantine period and is attested since the early years of Latin rule. In 1209 the lord of the island, Ravano dalle Carceri, promised the annual delivery of a gold-interwoven samite to the doge of Venice and another silk piece of lesser quality to the church of San Marco in that city. Since 1216 this obligation was carried out by the three major lords of the island, as we also learn from the formal declarations made by the newly elected Venetian doges upon taking office[76]. In 1256 one of these lords, Narzotto dalle Carceri, renewed this commitment, similarly emphasizing the superior quality of the cloth intended for the doge[77]. In addition, it would seem that every year since 1209 each of the three major lords of Negroponte delivered a gold-interwoven samite to the Latin emperor of Constantinople, whose vassals they were, and since 1248 to the prince of Frankish Morea, William II of Villehardouin, after the latter had replaced the emperor as their overlord[78]. The refusal of two of the major lords of Negroponte to acknowledge the suzerainty of the prince in 1256 led to war, which ended with the renewal of their subordination in 1262. The treaty between the two sides implies that the prince obtained the resumption of the annual delivery of the silk textiles[79]. It may be taken for granted that these silks, as well as those sent by the bishop of Negroponte to Rome in 1262 were local products[80].

Venetian and other western merchants in fairly large numbers traded in the port of Negroponte in the thirteenth and fourteenth century[81]. Some of them presumably engaged in entrepreneurship and promoted the development of the local silk industry, like their Latin counterparts in Thebes[82]. In all likelihood most, if not all the pieces of samite shipped to Venice from Negroponte in the 1270s were produced in that city[83]. As noted earlier, such was the case of kermes-dyed samite exported to Egypt around 1320[84]. The neighboring island of Andros was renowned in the twelfth century for its high-grade silk textiles, yet its silk industry may have suffered a contraction resulting from the emigration of some of its skilled artisans to Thebes in the second half of that period[85]. No silk fabrics of Andros are attested after 1204. The island was then exclusively known for its skeins of high-grade twisted silk fibers, called *cappelletti d'Andria*[86]. One may wonder, therefore, whether a further contraction of Andros' industry occurred in the thirteenth century, this time following a drain of its skilled manpower to Negroponte. One of the merchants residing in this city and involved in the shipping of silk textiles to Venice in the 1270s held land in Andros[87]. It is impossible to know, however, whether any of the fabrics he handled originated in that island.

Some additional sources refer directly or indirectly to the manufacture of silk fabrics in Latin Greece, yet without offering clues about the latter's precise origin. After leaving Chiarenza, the main port along the western coast of the Peloponnese, a ship sailing to Crete in 1271 was robbed of her cargo, which included gold-interwoven silk textiles[88]. In 1294 King Charles II of Sicily enfeoffed Philip of Taranto with the Principality of Morea, the Duchy of Athens, the Kingdom of Albania and the province of Thessaly, as well as with other territories on the mainland and some islands of Romania. Philip undertook to deliver each year a total of six pieces of samite in three different colors as feudal due. A similar obligation was set down for Corfu and for the castle of Buthrinto, located on the mainland opposite the island[89]. Pegolotti's work, completed between 1330 and 1340, offers further evidence about the production of silk

29

textiles and their trade in the Peloponnese and neighboring territories. It specifically mentions samite among the commodities in which merchants on business in Chiarenza reinvest proceeds from the sale of imported goods. Pegolotti also records the freight rates for the shipment of silk fabrics from Chiarenza, Coron, Modon and Negroponte to Venice[90]. The papal inventory of 1369 mentions two chasubles made of gold-interwoven cloth *de Grecia*[91]. A commercial manual composed in the 1380s, ascribed to a member or an employee of the Datini firm of Prato, refers in the same terms as Pegolotti to the reinvestment of money in samite[92]. Gold-interwoven and other silk textiles "from Chiarenza" or "from Morea" reached Ragusa or Dubrovnik on the Dalmatic coast and Ancona in Italy, as revealed by the treaties concluded between these two cities in 1340 and 1372, the latter confirmed in 1378 and 1397[93]. In neither of these cases is it possible to determine where these fabrics were produced, since several silk centres of Latin Greece manufactured them, as noted above. Moreover, the main ports of Latin Greece served as outlets for their respective hinterland as well as for neighboring territories and islands. The silk textiles they shipped, therefore, were not necessarily local products and may have often included fabrics manufactured elsewhere[94].

Our survey reveals that several silk centers of western Byzantium pursued their activity after the Fourth Crusade. Thebes maintained a clear lead and a distinctive status among them, as illustrated by the fact that after 1204 its products, especially its samites, were the only ones manufactured in Romania to be identified by their place of origin. The silk workshops of Latin Greece apparently upheld Byzantine tradition both in the nature and quality of their textiles. This continuity ensured them a share of domestic and foreign markets in the thirteenth and, to a lesser degree, in the fourteenth century. In the long run, however, continuity contributed to their decline. Lack of adaptation to new fashions and innovative technologies developed in Italy in the fourteenth century weakened their ability to withstand the fierce competition of the silk industries of Venice and Lucca. Yet, this is a topic that will be treated elsewhere.

Notes

1. See D. Jacoby, "Silk in Western Byzantium before the Fourth Crusade", *Byzantinische Zeitschrift* 84/85 (1991-1992), pp. 452-500, repr. with corrections in Idem, *Trade, Commodities and Shipping in the Medieval Mediterranean*, Aldershot, Hampshire 1997, no. VII.

2. On the texture of samite and that of sendal, mentioned below, and the diversity in quality of both, see D. King, "Types of Silk Cloth used in England 1200-1500", in S. Cavaciocchi (ed.), *La seta in Europa secc. XIII-XX* (Istituto Internazionale di Storia Economica "F. Datini", Prato, Pubblicazioni - Serie II, Atti delle "Settimane di Studio" e altri Convegni 24), Firenze 1993, pp. 458-459.

3. On various types of samite, see Jacoby, "Silk in Western Byzantium", pp. 460, 461, n. 42, and 496. In a letter written in 1190 Hugo Falcandus mentions *amita, dimita, triamita*, Byzantine varieties produced in Sicily: G.B. Siragusa (ed.), *La Historia o Liber de Regno Sicilie e la epistola ad Petrum Panormitane ecclesie thesaurarium di Ugo Falcando*[2] (Fonti per la Storia d'Italia, 22), Roma 1897, pp. 178-180.

4. See Jacoby, "Silk in Western Byzantium", pp. 462-463, 465.

5. On *sendes*, see ibid., pp. 458-460, and above, n. 2. Andros also manufactured other, unidentified types of silk fabrics. On these and its silk industry, see Jacoby, "Silk in Western Byzantium", pp. 460-462, 486-488, 496, 500.

6. Ibid., pp. 467-468, 493-500.

7. Ibid., pp. 474-475, 496 and n. 254.

8. Ibid., pp. 455-458.

9. According to a letter written sometime after 1208 by the self-exiled metropolitan of Athens, Michael Choniates: Sp. P. Lampros (ed.), Μιχαὴλ Ἀχομινάτου τοῦ Χωνιάτου τὰ σωζόμενα, Athens 1879-1880, II, p. 275, II. 9-14, no. 135; for the dating, see G. Stadtmüller, "Michael Choniates, Metropolit von Athen (ca. 1138-ca. 1222), *Orientalia Christiana* 33/2=91 (1934), p. 260, and for the identification of Gyaros, K.M. Setton, "Athens in the Later Twelfth Century", *Speculum* 19 (1944), p. 196, repr. in Idem, *Athens in the Middle Ages*, London 1975, no. III.

10. See Jacoby, "Silk in Western Byzantium", pp. 481-482, 485-486, 488, 498.

11. Ibid., pp. 466, 468, 488-490, 492.

12. See A. Dunn, "The Exploitation and Control of the Woodland and Scrubland in the Byzantine World", *Byzantine and Modern Greek Strudies* 16 (1992), pp. 274-275, 285-286, 290-291.

13. See Jacoby, "Silk in Western Byzantium", pp. 464, 483-484, 485, n. 186.

14. Ibid., pp. 470-471, 476-480, 492.

15. On the social aspects of Frankish policy toward the *archontes*, see D. Jacoby, "The Encounter of Two Societies: Western Conquerors and Byzantines in the Peloponnesus after the Fourth Crusade", *American Historical Review* 78 (1973), pp. 889-903, repr. in Idem, *Recherches sur la Méditerranée orientale du XIIe au XVe siècle. Peuples, sociétés, économies*, London 1979, no. II.

16. On these developments, see D. Jacoby, "Silk crosses the Mediterranean", in G. Airaldi (ed.), *Le vie del Mediterraneo. Idee uomini oggetti (secoli XI-XVI)* (Università degli studi di Genova, Collana dell' Istituto di Storia del medioevo e della espansione europea, n. 1), Genova 1997, pp. 67-68, and D. Jacoby, "Italian Migration and Settlement in Latin Greece: the Impact on the Economy", in H.E. Mayer (ed.), *Die Kreuzfahrerstaaten als Multikulturelle Gesellschaft. Einwanderer und Minderheiten* (Schriften des Historischen Kollegs, Kolloquien Band 37), München 1997, pp. 99-103.

17. According to a letter written by Michael Choniates in 1208 at the latest: Lampros, Μιχαὴλ Ἀχομινάτου [...] τὰ σωζόμενα, II, p. 170, ep. 100, par. 31; English translation in K.M. Setton, *The Papacy and the Levant (1204-1571)*, I, *The Thirteenth and Fourteenth Centuries*, Philadelphia 1976, p. 23: "The Thebans [...] remain at home and have not yet fled". For the dating, see Stadtmüller, "Michael Choniates", pp. 254-256.

18. Henri de Valenciennes, *Histoire de l'empereur Henri de Constantinople*, ed. J. Longnon, Paris 1948, p. 111, par. 672.

19. See Jacoby, "Silk in Western Byzantium", pp. 464, 466-469, 479, 490-497.

20. According to some unpublished notarial documents preserved at the Archivio di Stato in Venice, to be discussed elsewhere.

21. On their absence from Thebes in the twelfth century, see Jacoby, "Silk in Western Byzantium", pp. 466-467, 491.

22. See Jacoby, "Silk crosses the Mediterranean", nn. 97-105, and Idem, "Italian Migration and Settlement in Latin Greece", pp. 118-120.

23. On other merchants active in Thebes, see ibid., p. 107.

24. See above, n. 9, on purple fishers seemingly operating also sometime after 1208, yet it is not clear to what extent. On the activity of purple fishers along the Levantine coast around that time and some limited use of murex purple in Egypt, see Jacoby, "Silk in Western Byzantium", p. 493.

25. References ibid., pp. 482-483, 489, 491.

26. L. Auvray (ed.), *Les registres de Grégoire IX: recueil des bulles de ce pape*, Paris, 1896-1955, II, cols. 108 et 421, nos. 2671 et 3214; see also Setton, *The Papacy and the Levant*, I, pp. 65, 420.

27. J. Longnon (ed.), *Livre de la conqueste de la princée de l'Amorée. Chronique de Morée (1204-1305)*, Paris 1911, pars. 232-235; J. Schmitt (ed.), *The Chronicle of Morea. Τὸ χρονικὸν τοῦ Μορέως*, London 1904, vv. 3282-3331; A. Morel-Fatio (ed.), *Libro de los fechos et conquistas del principado de la Morea*, Genève 1885, pars. 222-225. On this episode, see D. Jacoby, *La féodalité en Grèce médiévale. Les "Assises de Romanie": sources, application et diffusion*, Paris - La Haye 1971, p. 24.

28. George Acropolites, *Opera*, cap. 82, ed. A. Heisenberg, Leipzig 1903, I, pp. 171-172.

29. J. Guiraud (ed.), *Les registres d'Urbain IV (1261-1264): recueil des bulles de ce pape*. Paris 1901-1958, I, pp. 16-17, no. 66: *De dictis vero duo millibus yperperorum quadraginta exameta vel plura, de melioribus et electoribus que in ipsis partibus poterunt inveniri, diversorum colorum et bene tincta viridis, violacei, rubei et albi.*

30. Ibid., p. 17, no. 67, which for red has *rubei, bene coccati*, thus made of kermes-dyed silk. To the evidence about the production of silk fabrics in Negroponte adduced in Jacoby, "Silk in Western Byzantium", p. 469, add a reference of 1224 to *opus sete* in a decision of the Maggior Consiglio of Venice: R. Cessi (ed.), *Deliberazioni del Maggior Consiglio di Venezia*, Bologna 1931-1950, I, p. 55, par. 34.

31. See E. Molinier, "Inventaire du trésor du Saint Siège sous Boniface VIII (1295)", *Bibliothèque de l' École des Chartes* 46 (1885), pp. 17-41, and ibid., 47 (1886), pp. 647-662, passim.

32. E. Favaro (ed.), *Cassiere della Bolla Ducale, Grazie, Novus Liber (1299-1305)* (Fonti per la storia di Venezia, Sez. I, Archivi pubblici), Venezia 1962, p. 32, no. 136; according to the doge of Venice, the pieces should have been taxed since they travelled *per aquas nostras.*

33. D. Jacoby, "Knightly Values and Class Consciousness in the Crusader States of the Eastern Mediterranean", *Mediterranean Historical Review* 1 (1986), pp. 158-186, repr. in Idem, *Studies on the Crusader States and on Venetian Expansion*, Northampton 1989, no. I.

34. Ramon Muntaner, *Crònica*, chap. 244, ed. E.B., Barcelona 1951, VI, 115: *cascun s'esforca de fer vestits a si e a sa companya; per honor de la cort.*

35. On which see above.

36. *Chronique de Morée* (as in n. 27), par. 1013-1017: *chendal vert a coquilles d'or semées.* Embroidered designs are more likely than woven ones, in view of the short time left before the festivities. The choice of shells suggests that the western knights, called *pelerins* or pilgrims, had been in Santiago de Compostella, which viewed from the Morea was *outre mer.* Since they arrived with horses and full armour, a visit to Jerusalem was anyhow excluded, the Holy land being then under the rule of Mamluk Egypt. For the correct date, see A. Kiesewetter, "Das Ende des *Livre de la conqueste de l'Amorée* (1301-1304). Ein Beitrag zur Geschichte des fränkischen Griechenland zu Beginn des 14. Jahrhunderts", *Byzantiaka* 16 (1996), p.p. 166, 178-179, 184-186.

37. See below.

38. Firenze, Biblioteca Marucelliana, ms. C 226, fol. 52r: *scamiti di Stivo e di Negroponte e di Romania in cholori vermigli.*

39. Abū al-Fidā' *Kitāb Taqwin al-Buldān*, Dresden 1846, p. 294: *al-atlas al-ma'dani*: the twelfth century Nizāmī ' Arūdī also refers to this type of silk cloth: R.B. Serjeant, *Islamic textiles. Material for a History up to the Mongol Conquest*, Beirut 1972, p. 18. J.T. Reinaud, *Géographie d'Aboulféda*, Paris 1848, II/1, p. 310, translates "de la soie minérale", suggesting that this was a gold or silver-interwoven cloth; see also E.W. Lane, *Arabic-English Lexicon*, London 1863-1893, V, p. 1977a, yet according to R. Dozy, *Supplément aux dictionnaires arabes*, Leiden 1881, II, p. 104, this was "une sorte de satin". On the nature of Theban satin, documented later, see below. See also *The Oxford Dictionary of Byzantium*, Oxford 1991, I, p. 7, s. v. Abū al-Fidā.

40. Francesco Balducci Pegolotti, *La pratica della mercatura*, ed. A. Evans, Cambridge (Mass.) 1936, pp. 118-119.

41. L. Douët d'Arcq (ed.), *Nouveau recueil de l'argenterie des rois de France*, Paris 1874, p. 7: *samit d' Estive vermeil*; also ibid., p. 2. "Estives" was the medieval French name of Thebes.

42. H. Hoberg (ed.), *Die Inventare des päpstlichen Schatzes in Avignon, 1314-1376* (Studi e Testi, 111), Città del Vaticano 1944, pp. 206-207, under the heading *Secuntur panni de samito de stina.* The last word does not make sense and should read *Stiva*, and the same in the following item. It is clear that the editor was not aware that this was the name of a city (see the French version in the previous note), and mistook the letter *u*, which stands for *v* in medieval script, for an *n.*

43. Ibid., pp. XI-XIV.

44. Ibid., pp. 456-457; instead *destina*, read *d'Estiva.*

45. See K.M. Setton, *Catalan Domination of Athens, 1311-1388*, revised edition, London 1975, pp. 52-62, and Idem, *The Papacy and the Levant*, I, pp. 456-459; R.-J. Loenertz, "Athènes et Néopatras, I. Regestes et notices pour servir à l'histoire des duchés catalans (1311-1394)", *Archivum Fratrum Praedicatorum* 25 (1955),

XII

revised version in Idem, *Byzantina et Franco-Graeca*, Roma 1970-1978, II, pp. 262-269, 285-289, 291-303.

46. A. Rubió i Lluch (ed.), *Diplomatari de l'Orient català (1301-1409)*, Barcelona 1947, p. 344, no. 240, and p. 400, no. 313. See also Setton, *The Papacy and the Levant*, I, pp. 457-458.

47. Dating by Loenertz, "Athènes et Néopatras, I", pp. 229-230, no. 144, and pp. 289-290; Idem, "Hospitaliers et Navarrais en Grèce. Regestes et documents", *Archivum Fratrum Praedicatorum* 26 (1956), revised version in Idem, *Byzantina et Franco-Graeca*, I, pp. 341-342, no. 12; see also J. Chrysostomides, "An Unpublished Letter of Neri Acciaiuoli (30 October [1384])", *Byzantina* 7 (1975), pp. 116-118.

48. J. Chrysostomides (ed.), *Monumenta Peloponnesiaca. Documents for the History of the Peloponnese in the 14th and 15th centuries*, Camberley, Surrey 1995, p. 430, no. 221, 1.39: *coltre de seta, de catasamiti*; p. 445, no. 225, 1.187: *panni de siricho.*

49. J. Labarte (ed.), *Inventaire du mobilier de Charles V, roi de France*, Paris 1879, p. 348, no. 3383: *Une autre pièce de samyt d'Estive vermeil, doublé de toille vert, semée de paons d'or en brodeure, qui font la roe, et deux larges lites de brodeure comme dessus.*

50. Douët d'Arcq, *Nouveau recueil*, pp. 176-177. On the nature of this cloth, see references in Jacoby, "Silk in Western Byzantium", p. 474, n. 123.

51. Ibid., pp. 462-466, 468-470, 480-481, 487, 496, 498.

52. The precise dating of these events is disputed: see A. Ilieva, *Frankish Morea (1205-1262). Socio-Cultural Interaction between the Franks and the Local Population*, Athens 1991, pp. 120-121, 133-134.

53. For this text, see above, n. 17.

54. Latest discussion of this testimony by H.A. Kalligas, *Byzantine Monemvasia. The Sources*, Monemvasia 1990, pp. 67-68, 208-211, who ascribes the event to the mid-twelfth century, contrary to the common view that it was related to the Frankish conquest: see Setton, *The Papacy and the Levant*, I, p. 36 and n. 43.

55. See Jacoby, "Silk in Western Byzantium", pp. 462-466, 468-470.

56. See D. Jacoby, "Silk Production in the Frankish Peloponnese: the Evidence of Fourteenth Century Surveys and Reports", in H.A. Kalligas (ed.), *Travellers and Officials in the Peloponnese. Descriptions - Reports - Statistics, in Honour of Sir Steven Runciman*, Monemvasia 1994, p. 46, repr. in Jacoby, *Trade, Commodities and Shipping in the Medieval Mediterranean*, no. VIII.

57. On the evolution of Corinth and its countryside in the thirteenth and fourteenth century, see Jacoby, "Silk Production in the Frankish Peloponnese", pp. 48-49, 58; Idem, "Italian Migration and Settlement in Latin Greece", pp. 103-105, 114, 121, 124, 126.

58. On this request, see above, n. 29.

59. It has recently been suggested that major destruction was caused by an earthquake c.1300, prior to the Catalan attack: see Ch.K. Williams II, E. Barnes, and L.M. Snyder, "Frankish Corinth: 1996", *Hesperia* 66 (1997), pp. 41-42.

60. Rubió i Lluch, *Diplomatari de l'Orient català*, p. 73, no. 57 (23 June 1312).

61. On the most recent archeological evidence and especially ceramic imports ascribed to that period, see Ch.K. Williams and O.H. Zervos, "Frankish Corinth: 1994", *Hesperia* 64 (1995), pp. 8-10, 22-28, 33-37; Williams, Barnes, and Snyder, "Frankish Corinth: 1996", p. 42.

62. See Ch.K. Williams II and O.H. Zervos, "Corinth, 1990: Southeast Corner of Temenos E", *Hesperia* 60 (1991), p. 51; "Frankish Corinth: 1991", *Hesperia* 61 (1992), p. 185; "Frankish Corinth: 1992", *Hesperia* 62 (1993), p. 46; "Frankish Corinth: 1993", *Hesperia* 63 (1994), p. 51. The only earlier Venetian coin that was found antedates the Catalan attack: *Hesperia* 64 (1995), p. 53.

63. In 1365 the total seignorial revenue from Corinth amounted to 615 hyperpers only: J. Longnon (et) P. Topping (eds), *Documents sur le régime des terres dans la principauté de Morée au XIVe siècle*, Paris - La Haye 1969, p. 162. In 1210 it appears to have been substantially larger, yet this was not necessarily due to local silk manufacture which, as noted above, is not attested for this period: see D. Jacoby, "From Byzantium to Latin Romania: Continuity and Change", *Mediterranean Historical Review* 4 (1989), pp. 14-15, repr. with identical pagination in B. Arbel, B. Hamilton and D. Jacoby (eds), *Latins and Greeks in the Eastern Mediterranean after 1204*, London 1989.

64. On Nerio Acciaiuoli, see Setton, *Catalan Domination of Athens*, pp. 67-68, 189-200. On his wealth in

33

1394, the year of his death, and testimonies about the prosperity of Corinth and its countryside at that time, see J. Chrysostomides, "Merchant versus Nobles: A Sensational Court Case in the Peloponnese (1391-1404), *Πρακτικά του Δ΄ Διεθνούς Συνεδρίου Πελοποννησιακών Σπουδών*, II, Athens 1993, pp. 116-131, and for relevant documents, Chrysostomides, *Monumenta Peloponnesiaca*, p. 626, General index, s.v. Cremolisi, Giovanni.

65. See above, n. 57, and Chrysostomides, *Monumenta Peloponnesiaca*, p. 452, I. 429.

66. See above, n. 63.

67. G.L.Fr. Tafel und G.M. Thomas (eds), *Urkunden zur älteren Handels- und Staatsgeschichte der Republik Venedig*, Wien 1856-1857 [hereafter: TTh], II, p. 97: *duos pannos sericos optimos auratos*. For the correct dating, see J. Longnon, *Recherches sur la vie de Geoffroy de Villehardouin, suivies du catalogue des actes des Villehardouin*, Paris 1939, p. 31, n. 6.

68. L. de Mas Latrie (ed.), "Donation à l'abbaye de Cluny du monastère de Hiero Komio près de Patras, en 1210", *Bibliothèque de l'École des Chartes*, 2e série, 5 (1848-1849), p. 312: *optimum exsamitum*.

69. As was the case of the lords of Negroponte: see below.

70. See Jacoby, "Silk in Western Byzantium", pp. 458-460, 469-470, 487, 498.

71. Cessi, *Deliberazioni del Maggior Consiglio di Venezia*, I, pp. 50-51, par. 15: *aliquante pecie de seta*.

72. See Jacoby, "Silk Production in the Frankish Peloponnese", pp. 44, 46-47, 55-57, 59-61.

73. On these pieces, see above, n. 29.

74. See Jacoby, "Silk Production in the Frankish Peloponnese", pp. 45-46, 53-54.

75. The will has been edited by E. Gerland, *Neue Quellen zur Geschichte des lateinischen Erzbistums Patras*, Leipzig 1903, pp. 211-216, no. 17; see especially from p. 213, l.26, to p. 214, l.29. On family connections, see ibid., p. 112, and on the family's fortune, pp. 113-126.

76. TTh, II, pp. 90, 93: in 1209 *unum examitum pro vobis honorabilem, auro textum, et unum pallium alium ad ornatum altaris ecclesie*; the same formulation appears in 1216: ibid., pp. 176, 181. *Seta et sete opera* in these same documents clearly refer to products of the island: ibid., pp. 92 (where *seta* was accidentally omitted), 95, 179, 183; this is confirmed by other sources. See also Jacoby, "Silk in Western Byzantium", pp. 469-470.

77. TTh, II, p. 14. On the circumstances of that renewal, see Jacoby, *La féodalité en Grèce médiévale*, pp. 190-191.

78. On these overlords, see ibid., pp. 186-187, 21-26, respectively.

79. TTh, III, p. 48: *De vero facto xammitorum auri remanet sicut dixerit dominus princeps*. On the political background, see Jacoby, *La féodalité en Grèce médiévale*, pp. 190-193.

80. On these fabrics, see above, n. 29.

81. See Jacoby, "Italian Migration and Settlement in Latin Greece", pp. 106-110, 114-115, 119-120.

82. On whom see above.

83. See above, n. 20.

84. See above, n. 38.

85. See above, n. 5.

86. Pegolotti, *La pratica della mercatura*, p. 298. *Cappelletti, cappelle* and *cappelli* were terms used for such skeins: S. Bongi, *Della mercatura dei Lucchesi nei secoli XIII e XIV*, Lucca 1858, p. 37. These were not varieties of silk, as mistakenly stated in Jacoby, "Silk in Western Byzantium", p. 462, and idem, "Silk Production in the Frankish Peloponnese", p. 47.

87. See above, n. 20.

88. TTh, III, pp. 242-243: *drapos de auro*. For the dating, see G. Morgan, "The Venetian Claims Commission of 1278", *Byzantinische Zeitschrift* 69 (1976), p. 428, no. 30.

89. Ch. Perrat et J. Longnon (eds), *Actes relatifs à la principauté de Morée. 1289-1300* (Collection de documents inédits sur l'histoire de France, série in 8°, vol. 6), Paris 1967, pp. 113-115, nos 116-117, without indication of colors.

90. Pegolotti, *La pratica della mercatura*, pp. 117, 145.

91. Hoberg, *Die Inventare des päpstlichen Schatzes*, p. 454.

92. C. Ciano (ed.), *La "pratica di mercatura" datiniana (secolo XIV)*, Milano 1964, p. 53, and for the dating, pp. 7-13 and 30-39. The commercial manual of Giovanni Uzzano, compiled in Florence in 1440, repeats the same piece of information: G.F. Pagnini della Ventura (ed.), *Della decima e di varie altre gravezze*

imposte della commune di Firenze, Lisbonna - Lucca 1765-1766, II, tomo quarto, p. 89. However, since political and economic conditions had changed by that time, it is unclear whether on this point this manual reflects contemporary conditions or merely reproduces outdated information: see U. Tucci, "Per un'edizione moderna della pratica di mercatura dell'Uzzano", in *Studi di storia economica toscana nel medioevo e nel Rinascimento in memoria di Federico Melis*, Ospedaletto (Pisa) 1987, pp. 365-389.

93. B. Krekic, *Dubrovnik (Raguse) et le Levant au Moyen Age*, Paris - La Haye 1961, pp. 78-79, 101; treaty of 1372 in C. Ciavarini (ed.), *Statuti anconitani del mare, del terzenale e dalla dogana, e patti con diverse nazioni*, Ancona 1896, pp. 238-246, esp. 240: *drappi de seta da Moree de le dicte parti overo contrate*; confirmation of 1397 in Italian, without specific reference to silk textiles: ibid., pp. 246-250; Latin version of the same: J.-F. Leonhard, *Die Seestadt Ancona im Spätmittelalter. Handel und Politik* (Bibliothek des deutschen historischen Instituts in Rom, Band 55), Tübingen 1983, pp. 431-434.

94. See Jacoby, "Silk Production in the Frankish Peloponnese", pp. 46-48, 59-60, and Idem, "Italian Migration and Settlement in Latin Greece", pp. 103-105.

ADDENDA ET CORRIGENDA

Only mistakes impairing the understanding or accuracy of text or notes are corrected below. For that reason the faulty division of words into syllables, maintained by editors and printers despite proper corrections of the proofs, has not been revised. Such mistakes as well as others are numerous in article IV, for which no proofs were available. The bibliographical information has been updated wherever possible. The following studies of mine are mentioned below: those cited as being in press that have appeared; studies reproduced in two previous volumes of mine in the *Variorum* series, *Trade, Commodities and Shipping in the Medieval Mediterranean*, Aldershot, 1997 (cited as Jacoby, *Trade*), and *Byzantium, Latin Romania and the Mediterranean*, Aldershot, 2001 (cited as Jacoby, *Byzantium*); finally, others reproduced in this volume.

I. Byzantine trade with Egypt from the mid-tenth century to the Fourth Crusade

p. 33, n. 24, lines 6–8: the study is reproduced as article II in Jacoby, *Byzantium*.

p. 36, n. 40, line 3: *instead of* (in press) *read* pp. 102–32. The study is reproduced as article II in this volume.

p. 42, n. 72: the study is reproduced as article X in Jacoby, *Byzantium*.

p. 46, n. 94: the study is reproduced as article I in Jacoby, *Byzantium*.

p. 47, text, lines 3–4 from bottom, *replace* by the following: presumably originating in Italy although possibly also from the wooded provinces of southern Asia Minor. The Genoese sailed along that region on their way to Egypt.

p. 48, n. 100: the second study is reproduced as article V in Jacoby, *Byzantium*.

p. 50, n. 113: the first study by D. Jacoby is reproduced as article V in this volume. The last study mentioned as being 'in press' has not been published so far.

p. 50, n. 116: the study is reproduced as article IV in this volume.

p. 65, n. 206: the study is reproduced as article III in this volume.

p. 76, n. 254: the study is reproduced as article VII in this volume.

II. The supply of war materials to Egypt in the crusader period

p. 108, text, line 4–5 from bottom: *instead of* Saladin's brother al-ʿĀdil *read* elder brother Turanshah

p. 108, n. 41, add: Saladin's letter of November 1173 deals with his elder brother Turanshah: see J.-M. Mouton, "Saladin et les Pisans", in *Tous azimuts. Mélanges de recherches en l'honneur du Professeur Georges Jehel = Histoire médiévale et archéologie, C.A.H.M.E.R, Laboratoire d'Archéologie de l'Université de Picardie*, 13 (2002), pp. 350–51.

p. 116, n. 86, replace by: Document edited with commentary by D. Jacoby, "Le consultat vénitien d'Alexandrie d'après un document inédit de 1284", in D. Coulon, C. Otten-Froux, P. Pagès et D. Valérian, eds., *Chemins d'outre-mer. Études sur la Méditerranée médiévale offertes à Michel Balard (Byzantina Sorbonensia*, 20), Paris, 2004, II, pp. 461–74.

III. The Venetian quarter of Constantinople from 1082 to 1261: topographical considerations

p. 159, n. 38, lines 7–8, *after* Century *replace* text by the following: in C. Scholz und G. Makris, eds., ΠΟΛΥΠΛΕΥΡΟΣ ΝΟΥΣ. *Miscellanea für Peter Schreiner zu seinem 60. Geburtstag (Byzantinisch Archiv*, Band 19), München-Leipzig, 2000, pp. 96–7.

p. 169: Jacoby, "Settlers", is reproduced as article VII in Jacoby, *Byzantium*.

IV. The trade of crusader Acre in the Levantine context: an overview

p. 107, n. 5, *add*: See now D. Jacoby, "The *fonde* of Crusader Acre and its Tariff. Some New Considerations", in M. Balard, B.Z. Kedar, J. Riley-Smith, eds., *Dei Gesta per Francos. Études sur les croisades dédiées à Jean Richard*. Aldershot, 2001, pp. 277–93; for the location of the fonde, see *ibid.*, pp. 281–3.

p. 110, n. 14: the study is reproduced as article III in this volume.

p. 114, n. 30, *add*: See now D. Jacoby, "Migrations familiales et stratégies commerciales vénitiennes aux XIIᵉ et XIIIᵉ siècles," in M. Balard et A. Ducellier, eds., *Migrations et diasporas méditerranéennes (Xᵉ–XVIᵉ siècles) (Byzantina Sorbonensia*, 19), Paris, 2002, pp. 363–4.

V. The Venetian privileges in the Latin Kingdom of Jerusalem: twelfth and thirteenth-century interpretations and implementation

p. 156, text, lines 1–2 after n. 3, *erase*: After the conquest of Haifa,

p. 159, n. 18: the two studies by D. Jacoby are reproduced respectively as articles VII and II in Jacoby, *Trade*.

p. 161, text, line 6 from bottom, *instead of* foreigners *read* non-Venetians

p. 163, n. 39: the study is reproduced as article IV in Jacoby, *Trade*.

p. 166, n. 46, add: In order to strengthen its standing Venice had presented Baldwin's charter to Pope Alexander III (1159–1181), who confirmed it at an unknown date, and in 1226 both documents were shown by the Venetian ambassador Marino Storlato to Pope Honorius III (1216–1227): Roberto Cessi, ed., *Deliberazioni del Maggior Consiglio di Venezia*, 3 vols. (Bologna, 1931–1950), 1: 97.

p. 172, text, lines 5–6 from bottom, read: his city, apparently in the autumn of 1257 before the War of St. Sabas resumed.

p. 172, n. 84, add: Yet see now D. Jacoby, "New Venetian Evidence on Crusader Acre", in Peter Edbury and Jonathan Phillips, eds., *The Experience of Crusading, II, Defining the Crusader Kingdom*, Cambridge, 2003, pp. 241, 245–6.

VI. Migration, trade and banking in crusader Acre

p. 110, n. 17: the study is reproduced as article VII in Jacoby, *Trade*.

VII. Creta e Venezia nel contesto economico del Mediterraneo orientale sino alla metà del Quattrocento

p. 74, n. 2: the study by Jacoby is reproduced as article II in Jacoby, *Byzantium*.

p. 76, n. 11: the study is reproduced as article IX in this volume.

p. 77, n. 14, three last lines: *after Le partage du monde read* M. Balard –A. Ducellier, eds., *Échanges et colonisation dans la Méditerranée médiévale* (*Byzantina Sorbonensia*, 17), Paris 1998, p. 298.

p. 79, n. 21, lines 11–14: the two studies by Jacoby are reproduced respectively as articles VIII and IX in this volume. To "Cretan Cheese" add pp. 51–6; to "Changing Economic Patterns" add pp. 218–20.

VIII. Cretan cheese: a neglected aspect of Venetian medieval trade

p. 61, n. 6: the study is reproduced as article VII in Jacoby, *Byzantium*.

IX. Changing economic patterns in Latin Romania: the impact of the West

p. 200, n. 15: the study by Jacoby, "From Byzantium to Latin Romania" is reproduced as article VII in Jacoby, *Byzantium*.

p. 203, n. 41: the study by Jacoby is reproduced as article IX in Jacoby, *Byzantium*.

p. 208, n. 68: the study is reproduced as article VII in this volume.

p. 208, n. 69: the study is reproduced as article VI in Jacoby, *Byzantium*.

p. 216, n. 111: the study by Jacoby is reproduced as article VIII in this volume.

p. 221, n. 144: the study by Jacoby is reproduced as article VII in Jacoby, *Byzantium*.

p. 224, n. 164: the second study is reproduced as article VI in this volume.

p. 226, n. 175: the study is reproduced as article XI in this volume.

p. 228, n. 189: the study is reproduced as article XII in this volume.

p. 228, n. 190: the study is reproduced as article X in this volume.

p. 231, n. 213, *between* Filomati *and* for the Latins, *read* see now: D. Jacoby, "I Greci ed altre comunità tra Venezia e oltremare," in M.F. Tiepolo and E. Tonetti, eds., *I Greci a Venezia* (Atti del Convegno Internazionale di Studio, Venezia, 5–7 novembre 1998) (Istituto Veneto di Scienze, Lettere ed Arti), Venice 2002, 57–9;

X. Dalla materia prima ai drappi tra Bisanzio, il Levante e Venezia: la prima fase dell'industria serica veneziana

p. 295, n. 6: the study is reproduced as article X in Jacoby, *Byzantium*.

p. 295, n. 7: the study is reproduced as article XI in this volume.

p. 298, n. 56: the study is reproduced as article IX in this volume.

p. 298, n. 79: the study is reproduced as article VII in Jacoby, *Byzantium*.

p. 301, n. 136: the study is reproduced as article XII in this volume.

XI. Genoa, silk trade and silk manufacture in the Mediterranean region (ca. 1100–1300)

p. 11, n. 4: the study is reproduced as article II in Jacoby, *Byzantium*.

p. 24, n. 78 add: A. Paribeni, "Il Pallio di San Lorenzo a Genova", in *L'Arte di Bisanzio e l'Italia al tempo dei Paleologi, 1261–1453*, Roma 1999, pp. 229–52.

p. 25, n. 82: the two studies by D. Jacoby are reproduced respectively as articles V and IV in this volume.

p. 29, n. 113: the study is reproduced as article IX in Jacoby, *Byzantium*.

p. 35, n. 142: the study by D. Jacoby is reproduced as article X in this volume; add pp. 286–9.

XII. The production of silk textiles in Latin Greece

p. 31, n. 16: the two studies by D. Jacoby are reproduced respectively as articles X and IX in Jacoby, *Byzantium*.

p. 33, n. 63: the study by D. Jacoby is reproduced as article VIII in Jacoby, *Byzantium*.

INDEX OF NAMES

Individuals and *families* are listed either under their name, surname (dynastic, topographical, or other), or the name of their lordship. Names having both a French and an English version appear under the latter (e.g. Marie under Mary), yet the names of Italian individuals are italianized (e.g. Pietro instead of Peter). The following have been omitted: Arabs, Franks, Greeks, Latins and Muslims, mentioned throughout all studies; the numerous silk workers cited only once in study XI, pp. 33–4; the names of ecclesiastical institutions, except for religious orders; the names of modern scholars appearing in the text.

All *geographic names* are included, except often recurring ones such as Aegean, Greece, Italy, Levant, Mediterranean, Romania, the West. Location is not mentioned for well-known sites and cited according to present state boundaries, except for Asia Minor, Cilician Armenia, Crete and the Peloponnese. Sites or areas within cities are not listed separately. The names of cities and regions also refer to the latter's citizens and inhabitants (e.g. 'Venice' to 'Venetians').

Abbreviations: A. M. = Asia Minor; Byz. = Byzantine; CP = Constantinople; co. = company; emp. = emperor; Eg. = Egyptian; fam. = family; Flor. = Florentine; Gen. = Genoese; Jew. = Jewish; k./K. = king/Kingdom of; Pelop. = Peloponnese; res. = resident of; Sien. = Sienese; Ven. = Venetian.

Abbasids: II 108
Abu 'l-Fidā, Arab geographer:
    VII 98; VIII 58
Acciaiuoli, Flor. banking co.: IX 224
    Nerio I, lord Athens, Thebes and Corinth:
    IX 231; XII 26–7
Acotanto, Matteo, Ven. res. CP: III 166
Acre (Israel): I 49, 55–6, 59, 63, 69, 75;
    II 114–16, 118, 122–7; IV *passim*;
    V *passim*; VI *passim*; VII 75, 95, 97;
    X 271–2; XI 25, 29
Acrocorinth: XII 27; *see also* Corinth
Aden: II 102
Adige, river (Italy): II 110
al-ʿĀdil, Eg. sultan: II 107
Adrianople (Turkey): V 159
Adriatic Sea: II 107, 111–13; VII 78
Aegean Sea, islands: I 51, 67; VII 80, 92, 94,
    103; IX 197, 202–4, 219, 225, 228,
    230–31; X 267, 271–2, 297; XI 12
al-Afḍal, Eg. sultan: I 56
Alanya (A. M.): II 121–2
Albania: XII 29
Albanians: IX 203
Alberti, Flor. banking co.: IX 225
Albertini, Boscolo, Sien. banker: VI 117
Albertino, Giacomo, res. Venice: X 280

Aleppo (Syria): I 38–9, 50; IV 118; VI 108;
    XI 24
Alessandrina de Fruzerio, res. Venice: X 291
Alexander III, pope: II 109; V 166
Alexandretta (Iskenderun, Turkey):
    city: II 120
    Gulf of: I 35
Alexandria (Egypt): I 26, 28, 30, 33, 39,
    42–9, 51–6, 59, 61–6, 68–72, 74–6;
    II 103–8, 110–18, 120–21, 123, 127;
    IV 104, 112–14, 116, 118–19; V 163;
    VI 106, 111; VII 74–5, 78, 84, 87, 95,
    97–100; VIII 51, 58–9, 68; IX 206,
    220, 228, 230–31; X 271, 292; XI 15,
    21, 29
Alfonso III, k. Aragon: II 118
Alfonso VIII, k. Castile: XI 15
Almeria (Spain): XI 15
Almohads: XI 15
Alps: II 107; X 268
Amalfi (Italy): I 28, 34, 36–7, 42, 47–50, 57–61;
    II 105–6; X 266; XI 12, 16
Amalric, k. Jerusalem: I 61, 64;
    II 126; V 170
al-Amīr, Eg. caliph: II 105
Ammannati, banking co., Pistoia:
    VI 118

Ranieri, doge: IX 207; X 284, 290
Ziani, Ven. fam.:
    Maria, wife of Pietro, doge: VII 77–8;
        IX 206
    Pietro, doge: III 161, 164; VII 77;
        VIII 50; IX 200, 206–7,
        223
    Pietro, res. Acre: V 161; VI 113
    Pietro, res. Halmyros: VI 113
    Sebastiano, doge: II 107

Zorzi, Ven. fam.:
    Ermolao, res. Coron: X 273
    Marsilio, bailo Acre: IV 110, 114, 116;
        V 155, 166–75; X 276
Zucchello, Pignol:
    Pisan res. Candia, then Venice: IX 222
al-Zuhrī, Arab geographer: II 106
Zusto, Ven. fam.:
    Enrico: I 72
    Pietro: I 72

INDEX OF SUBJECTS

Only important subjects are listed in this index. Trade and shipping have been omitted since they appear frequently in all the articles.

For Product Safety Concerns and Information please contact our EU representative GPSR@taylorandfrancis.com Taylor & Francis Verlag GmbH, Kaufingerstraße 24, 80331 München, Germany

T - #0083 - 160425 - C0 - 224/150/20 - PB - 9781138375727 - Gloss Lamination